CONCEPTS

# Strategic Management

## COMPETITIVENESS & GLOBALIZATION

11e

Michael A. Hitt
Texas A&M University

R. Duane Ireland
Texas A&M University

Robert E. Hoskisson
Rice University

Australia • Brazil • Japan • Korea • Mexico • Singapore • Spain • United Kingdom • United States

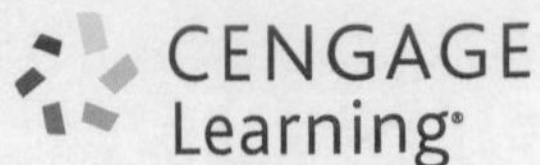

*Strategic Management: Competitiveness & Globalization: Concepts*, **Eleventh Edition**

**Michael A. Hitt, R. Duane Ireland, and Robert E. Hoskisson**

Senior Vice President, Global Product Manager, Higher Education:
Jack W. Calhoun

Vice President, General Manager, Social Science & Qualitative Business:
Erin Joyner

Product Director:
Mike Schenk

Sr. Product Manager:
Scott Person

Sr. Content Developer:
Julia Chase

Product Assistant:
Tamara Grega

Sr. Content Project Manager:
Holly Henjum

Media Developer:
Courtney Bavaro

Manufacturing Planner:
Ron Montgomery

Production Service:
Cenveo Publisher Services

Sr. Art Director:
Stacy Jenkins Shirley

Rights Acquisitions Specialist:
Amber Hosea

Cover and Internal Designer:
Lou Ann Thesing

Cover Images:
© leonello calvetti/Shutterstock.com



Library of Congress Control Number: 2013952676

ISBN-13: 978-1-285-42518-4
ISBN-10: 1-285-42518-9

**Cengage Learning**
200 First Stamford Place, 4th Floor
Stamford, CT 06902
USA

Cengage Learning is a leading provider of customized learning solutions with office locations around the globe, including Singapore, the United Kingdom, Australia, Mexico, Brazil, and Japan. Locate your local office at: **www.cengage.com/global**

Cengage Learning products are represented in Canada by **Nelson Education, Ltd.**

To learn more about Cengage Learning Solutions, visit **www.cengage.com**

Purchase any of our products at your local college store or at our preferred online store **www.cengagebrain.com**

Printed in Canada
1 2 3 4 5 6 7 17 16 15 14 13

*With each edition of this book, our goal has been to develop an effective learning tool for students and an effective teaching tool for instructors. Accordingly, we dedicate this 11th edition to all students and instructors past and present who have used or currently use this book. We sincerely hope that it proves to be of value as you learn about and successfully use the strategic management process.*

—**MICHAEL A. HITT, R. DUANE IRELAND, ROBERT E. HOSKISSON**

# Brief Contents

# Contents

©Bikeworldtravel/Shutterstock.com

©Vividfour / Shutterstock.com

Photo ITAR-TASS Itar-Tass Photos/Newscom

Yanice Idir/Alamy

## 6: Corporate-level Strategy 164

Alessia Pierdomenico/Bloomberg/Getty Images



## 7: Merger and Acquisition Strategies 192

VINCENZO PINTO/AFP/Getty Images

© Torsten Lorenz/Shutterstock.com

WOLFGANG RATTAY/Reuters/Landov

## Part 3: Strategic Actions: Strategy Implementation

Tom Williams/CQ Roll Call/Getty Images

Justin Sullivan/Getty Images

AP Photo/Al Behrman

AP Photo/Procter & Gamble Co.

# Preface

Our goal in writing each edition of this book is to present a new, up-to-date standard for explaining the strategic management process. To reach this goal with the 11th edition of our market-leading text, we again present you with an intellectually rich yet thoroughly practical analysis of strategic management.

With each new edition, we are challenged and invigorated by the goal of maintaining the standard that we established for presenting strategic management knowledge in a readable style. To prepare for each new edition, we carefully study the most recent academic research to ensure that the strategic management content we present to you is highly current and relevant. In addition, we continuously read articles appearing in many different and widely read business publications (e.g., *Wall Street Journal, Bloomberg Businessweek, Fortune, Financial Times, Fast Company*, and *Forbes*, to name a few). We also study postings through social media (such as blogs), given their increasing use as channels of information distribution. By studying a wide array of sources, we are able to identify valuable examples of how companies are using (or not using) the strategic management process. Though many of the hundreds of companies we discuss in the book will be quite familiar, some will likely be new to you. One reason for this is that we use examples of companies from around the world to demonstrate how globalized business has become. To maximize your opportunities to learn as you read and think about how actual companies use strategic management tools, techniques, and concepts (based on the most current research), we emphasize a lively and user-friendly writing style.

Several *characteristics* of this 11th edition of our book will enhance your learning opportunities:

- This book presents you with the most comprehensive and thorough coverage of strategic management that is available on the market.
- The research used in this book is drawn from the "classics" as well as the most recent contributions to the strategic management literature. The historically significant "classic" research provides the foundation for much of what is known about strategic management, while the most recent contributions reveal insights about how to effectively use strategic management in the complex, global business environment in which firms now compete. Our book also presents you with many up-to-date examples of how firms use the strategic management tools, techniques, and concepts developed by leading researchers. Indeed, although this book is grounded in relevant theory and current research, it also is strongly application-oriented and presents you, our readers, with a vast number of examples and applications of strategic management concepts, techniques, and tools. In this edition, for example, we examine more than 500 companies to describe the use of strategic management. Collectively, no other strategic management book presents you with the *combination* of useful and insightful *research* and *applications* in a wide variety of organizations as does this text.

  Company examples range from the large U.S.-based firms such as Apple, Amazon.com, Boeing, Starbucks, Walmart, Walt Disney, General Electric, Dell, Campbell Soup, Coca-Cola, Hewlett-Packard, Ford, United Parcel Service, JPMorgan Chase, and Merck, to major foreign-based firms such as Carrefour, Nestlé, Ericsson, Nokia, Virgin Group,

Tokyo Electric Power, Rio Tinto, CEMEX, Cadbury, IKEA, FEMSA, Takeda, Publicis, Sany Heavy Equipment, Hutchison Whampoa, and Zara. As this list suggests, the firms examined in this book compete in a wide range of industries and produce a diverse set of goods and services.

- We use the ideas of prominent scholars (e.g., Ron Adner, Rajshree Agarwal, Gautam Ahuja, Raffi Amit, Africa Arino, Jay Barney, Paul Beamish, Peter Buckley, Ming-Jer Chen, Russ Coff, Rich D'Aveni, Kathy Eisenhardt, Gerry George, Javier Gimeno, Luis Gomez-Mejia, Melissa Graebner, Ranjay Gulati, Don Hambrick, Connie Helfat, Amy Hillman, Tomas Hult, Dave Ketchen, Dovev Lavie, Michael Lennox, , Yadong Luo, Shige Makino, Costas Markides, Danny Miller, Will Mitchell, Margie Peteraf, Michael Porter, Nandini Rajagopalan, Jeff Reuer, Joan Ricart, Alan Rugman, Richard Rumelt, David Sirmon, Ken Smith, Steve Tallman, David Teece, Michael Tushman, Margarethe Wiersema, Oliver Williamson, Mike Wright, Anthea Zhang, and Ed Zajac) to shape the discussion of *what* strategic management is. We describe the practices of prominent executives and practitioners (e.g., Michael Corbat, Jamie Dimon, Carlos Ghosn, Heinrich Hiesinger, Marilyn Hewson, Jeff Immelt, Elon Musk, Paul Pullman, and many others) to help us describe *how* strategic management is used in many types of organizations.

The authors of this book are also active scholars. We conduct research on different strategic management topics. Our interest in doing so is to contribute to the strategic management literature and to better understand how to effectively apply strategic management tools, techniques, and concepts to increase organizational performance. Thus, our own research is integrated in the appropriate chapters along with the research of numerous other scholars, some of whom are noted above.

In addition to our book's *characteristics*, there are some specific *features* and *revisions* that we have made in this 11th edition that we are pleased to highlight for you:

- **New Opening Cases and Strategic Focus Segments.** We continue our tradition of providing all-new Opening Cases and Strategic Focus segments (a few are on the same company[ies] but are substantially updated). Many of these deal with companies located outside North America. In addition, virtually all of the company-specific examples included in each chapter are new or substantially updated. Through all of these venues, we present you with a wealth of examples of how actual organizations, most of which compete internationally as well as in their home markets, use the strategic management process for the purpose of outperforming rivals and increasing their performance.
- **New Strategy Right Now Callouts.** Each chapter contains four Strategy Right Now icons (up from three in the last edition) that direct the student to the CourseMate site. There students can find out how to access the Gale Business Insights: Essentials content. This material includes recent articles covering most of the concepts and companies highlighted in each of the Opening Cases, Strategic Focus segments, and other important areas in the chapter. In addition, online quizzes are associated with all of the BIE content in CengageNow.
- **Thirty All-New Cases** with an effective mix of organizations headquartered or based in the United States and a number of other countries. Many of the cases have full financial data (the analyses of which are in the Case Notes that are available to instructors). These timely cases present active learners with opportunities to apply the strategic management process and understand organizational conditions and contexts and to make appropriate recommendations to deal with critical concerns. These cases can also be found in CengageNow.
- **More than 1000 New References** (2012, 2013) are included in the chapters' endnotes to support new material added or current strategic management concepts used in the

book. In addition to demonstrating the classic and recent research from which we draw our material, these data support the fact that this book references the current cutting-edge research and thinking in the field.

- **New Concepts** were added in several chapters. Examples include executive ambidexterity and ambicultural executives (Chapter 1), the informal economy (Chapter 2), private-public partnerships in strategic alliances such as those found in industrial clusters (Chapter 9), and strategic change (Chapter 12).
- **New Content** was added to several chapters. Examples include the Analysis-Strategy-Performance framework (Chapter 1 and referenced in several other chapters), the importance of emerging economies and influence of emerging economy multinationals (Chapters 1 and 8), the size and scope of the informal economy (Chapter 2), innovators' dilemma (Chapter 4), the use of TQM in cost leadership and differentiation strategies (Chapter 4), and intra-industry diversification (Chapter 6).
- **New Information** was provided in several chapters. Examples include the stakeholder host communities (Chapter 1), all-new and current demographic data (e.g., ethnic mix, geographic distribution) and on the economic environment (Chapter 2), the general partner strategies of private equity firms (Chapter 7), information from the *World Economic Forum Competitiveness Report* regarding political risks of international investments (Chapter 8), examples of industrial clusters or districts of geographic concentrations of a set of interconnected companies and public organizations (Chapter 9), new and updated information on corporate governance in different countries (Chapter 10), discussion of how online retailers are changing the structures of big box retailers (Chapter 11), and updated data about the number of internal and external CEO selections occurring in companies today (Chapter 12).
- **New and Revised Experiential Exercises** are at the end of each chapter to support individuals' efforts to understand the use of the strategic management process. These exercises place active learners in a variety of situations requiring application of some part of the strategic management process.
- **An Exceptional Balance** between current research and up-to-date applications of it in actual organizations. The content has not only the best research documentation but also the largest number of effective real-world examples to help active learners understand the different types of strategies that organizations use to achieve their vision and mission.
- **Access to Harvard Business School (HBS) Cases.** We have developed a set of assignment sheets and AACSB International assessment rubrics to accompany 10 of the best-selling HBS cases. Instructors can customize the text to include these cases (www.cengage.com/custom/makeityours/hitt11e) and utilize the accompanying set of teaching notes and assessment rubrics to formalize assurance of learning efforts in the capstone Strategic Management/Business Policy course. Contact your Cengage Learning representative for more information.

# Supplements to Accompany This Text

**Instructor Web site.** Access important teaching resources on this companion Web site. For your convenience, you can download electronic versions of the instructor supplements from the password-protected section of the site, including Instructor's Resource Manual, Comprehensive Case Notes, Cognero Testing, Word Test Bank files, PowerPoint® slides, and Video Segments and Guide. To access these additional course materials and companion resources, please visit www.cengagebrain.com. On the Cengagebrain.com homepage, use the search box at the top of the page to search for the ISBN of your title (from the back cover of your book). This will take you to the product page where free companion resources can be found.

- **Instructor's Resource Manual.** The Instructor's Resource Manual, organized around each chapter's knowledge objectives, includes teaching ideas for each chapter and how to reinforce essential principles with extra examples. This support product includes lecture outlines, detailed answers to end-of-chapter review questions, instructions for using each chapter's experiential exercises and video cases, and additional assignments.
- **Case Notes.** These notes include directed assignments, financial analyses, and thorough discussion and exposition of issues in the case. Select cases also have assessment rubrics tied to National Standards (AACSB outcomes) that can be used for grading each case. The Case Notes provide consistent and thorough support for instructors, following the method espoused by the author team for preparing an effective case analysis.
- **Cengage Learning Testing Powered by Cognero.** This is a flexible, online system that allows you to author, edit, and manage test bank content from multiple Cengage Learning solutions; create multiple test versions in an instant; and deliver tests from your LMS, your classroom, or wherever you want. Cengage Learning Testing Powered by Cognero works on any operating system or browser, no special installs or downloads needed. You can create tests from school, home, the coffee shop—anywhere with Internet access and enhanced, test bank questions are linked to each chapter's knowledge objectives and are ranked by difficulty and question type. We provide an ample number of application questions throughout, and we have also retained scenario-based questions as a means of adding in-depth problem-solving questions. The questions are also tagged to National Standards (AACSB outcomes), Bloom's Taxonomy, and the Dierdorff/Rubin metrics.
- **PowerPoints®.** An all-new PowerPoint presentation, created for the 11th edition, provides support for lectures, emphasizing key concepts, key terms, and instructive graphics.
- **Video Segments.** A collection of 13 BBC videos have been included in the end-of-chapter material. These new videos are short, compelling, and timely illustrations of today's management world. Topics include Brazil's growing global economy, the aftermath of BP's oil spill, Zappos.com, the Southwest merger with AirTrans, and more. Available on the DVD and Instructor Web site. Detailed case write-ups including questions and suggested answers appear in the Instructor's Resource Manual and Video Guide.

**CengageNow.** This robust online course management system gives you more control in less time and delivers better student outcomes—NOW. CengageNow includes teaching and learning resources organized around lecturing, creating assignments, casework, quizzing, and gradework to track student progress and performance. The 30 comprehensive cases appear in CengageNow. There are 13 Guided Cases that bring students to a higher level of understanding in preparation for in-class activities. Multiple types of quizzes, including BBC video quizzes and YouTube video quizzes, are assignable and gradable. We also include assignable and gradable Business Insights: Essentials (BIE) quizzes that direct students to Gale articles to find expansive, current event coverage for companies, including a wealth of daily updated articles and company financials. Flexible assignments, automatic grading, and a gradebook option provide more control while saving you valuable time. A Personalized Study diagnostic tool empowers students to master concepts, prepare for exams, and become more involved in class.

**Cengage Learning Write Experience 2.0.** This new technology is the first in higher education to offer students the opportunity to improve their writing and analytical skills without adding to your workload. Offered through an exclusive agreement with Vantage Learning, creator of the software used for GMAT essay grading, Write Experience evaluates students' answers to a select set of writing assignments for voice, style, format, and originality. We have trained new prompts for this edition!

**The Business Insights: Essentials Resource Center (BIE).** Put a complete business library at your students' fingertips! This premier online business research tool allows you and your students to search thousands of periodicals, journals, references, financial data, industry reports, and more. This powerful research tool saves time for students—whether they are preparing for a presentation or writing a reaction paper. You can use the BIE to quickly and easily assign readings or research projects.

**Micromatic Strategic Management Simulation (for bundles only).** The Micromatic Business Simulation Game allows students to decide their company's mission, goals, policies, and strategies. Student teams make their decisions on a quarter-by-quarter basis, determining price, sales and promotion budgets, operations decisions, and financing requirements. Each decision round requires students to make approximately 100 decisions. Students can play in teams or play alone, compete against other players or the computer, or use Micromatic for practice, tournaments, or assessment. You can control any business simulation element you wish, leaving the rest alone if you desire. Because of the number and type of decisions the student users must make, Micromatic is classified as a medium to complex business simulation game. This helps students understand how the functional areas of a business fit together without being bogged down in needless detail and provides students with an excellent capstone experience in decision making.

**Smartsims (for bundles only).** MikesBikes Advanced is a premier strategy simulation, providing students with the unique opportunity to evaluate, plan, and implement strategy as they manage their own company while competing online against other students within their course. Students from the management team of a bicycle manufacturing company make all the key functional decisions involving price, marketing, distribution, finance, operations, HR, and R&D. They formulate a comprehensive strategy, starting with their existing product, and then adapt the strategy as they develop new products for emerging markets. Through the Smartsims easy-to-use interface, students are taught the cross-functional disciplines of business and how the development and implementation of strategy involves these disciplines. The competitive nature of MikesBikes encourages involvement and learning in a way that no other teaching methodology can, and your students will have fun in the process!

**MindTap.** MindTap is a fully online digital learning platform of authoritative Cengage Learning content, assignments, and services that engages your students with interactivity while also offering you choice in the configuration of coursework and enhancement of the curriculum via complimentary Web apps known as MindApps. MindApps range from ReadSpeaker (which reads the text out loud to students), to Kaltura (allowing you to insert inline video and audio into your curriculum), to ConnectYard (allowing you to create digital "yards" through social media—all without "friending" your students). This is well beyond an eBook, a homework solution or digital supplement, a resource center website, a course delivery platform or a Learning Management System. It is the first in a new category—the Personal Learning Experience.

### Make It Yours—Custom Case Selection

Cengage Learning is dedicated to making the educational experience unique for all learners by creating custom materials that best suit your course needs. With our Make It Yours program, you can easily select a unique set of cases for your course from providers such as Harvard Business School Publishing, Darden, and Ivey. See http://www.custom.cengage.com/makeityours/hitt11e for more details.

## Acknowledgments

We express our appreciation for the excellent support received from our editorial and production team at Cengage Learning. We especially wish to thank Scott Person, our Senior Product Manager; and Julia Chase, our Senior Content Developer. We are grateful for their dedication, commitment, and outstanding contributions to the development and publication of this book and its package of support materials.

We are highly indebted to all of the reviewers of past editions. Their comments have provided much insight in the preparation of this current edition:

Jay Azriel
*York College of Pennsylvania*

Lana Belousova
*Suffolk University*

Ruben Boling
*North Georgia University*

Matthias Bollmus
*Carroll University*

Erich Brockmann
*University of New Orleans*

David Cadden
*Quinnipiac University*

Ken Chadwick
*Nicholls State University*

Bruce H. Charnov
*Hofstra University*

Jay Chok
*USC Marshall*

Peter Clement
*State University of New York – Delhi*

Terry Coalter
*Northwest Missouri University*

James Cordeiro
*SUNY Brockport*

Deborah de Lange
*Suffolk University*

Irem Demirkan
*Northeastern University*

Dev Dutta
*University of New Hampshire*

Scott Elston
*Iowa State University*

Harold Fraser
*California State University, Fullerton*

Robert Goldberg
*Northeastern University*

Monica Gordillo
*Iowa State University*

George Griffin
*Spring Arbor University*

Susan Hansen
*University of Wisconsin-Platteville*

Glenn Hoetker
*Arizona State University*

James Hoyt
*Troy University*

Miriam Huddleston
*Harford Community College*

Carol Jacobson
*Purdue University*

James Katzenstein
*California State University, Dominguez Hills*

Robert Keidel
*Drexel University*

Nancy E. Landrum
*University of Arkansas at Little Rock*

Mina Lee
*Xavier University*

Patrice Luoma
*Quinnipiac University*

Mzamo Mangaliso
*University of Massachusetts – Amherst*

Michele K. Masterfano
*Drexel University*

James McClain
*California State University, Fullerton*

Jean McGuire
*Louisiana State University*

John McIntyre
*Georgia Tech*

Rick McPherson
*University of Washington*

Karen Middleton
*Texas A&M–Corpus Christi*

Raza Mir
*William Paterson University*

Martina Musteen
*San Diego State University*

Louise Nemanich
*Arizona State University*

Frank Novakowski
*Davenport University*

Consuelo M. Ramirez
*University of Texas at San Antonio*

Barbara Ribbens
*Western Illinois University*

Jason Ridge
*Clemson University*

William Roering
*Michigan State University*

Manjula S. Salimath
*University of North Texas*

Deepak Sethi
*Old Dominion University*

Manisha Singal
*Virginia Tech*

Warren Stone
*University of Arkansas at Little Rock*

Elisabeth Teal
*University of North Georgia*

Jill Thomas Jorgensen
*Lewis and Clark State College*

Len J. Trevino
*Washington State University*

Edward Ward
*Saint Cloud State University*

Marta Szabo White
*Georgia State University*

Michael L. Williams
*Michigan State University*

Diana J. Wong-MingJi
*Eastern Michigan University*

Patricia A. Worsham
*California State Polytechnic University, Pomona*

William J. Worthington
*Baylor University*

Wilson Zehr
*Concordia University*

Finally, we are very appreciative of the following people for the time and care that went into preparing the supplements to accompany this edition:

Charlie Cook

Richard H. Lester
*Texas A&M University*

Susan Leshnower
*Midland College*

Paul Mallette
*University of West Alabama*

Kristi L. Marshall

Patricia A. Worsham
*California State Polytechnic University, Pomona*

*Michael A. Hitt*
*R. Duane Ireland*
*Robert E. Hoskisson*

# About the Authors

## Michael A. Hitt

Michael A. Hitt is a University Distinguished Professor and holds the Joe B. Foster Chair in Business Leadership at Texas A&M University. He received his Ph.D. from the University of Colorado. He has more than 260 publications including 26 co-authored or co-edited books and was cited as one of the 10 most-cited scholars in management over a 25-year period in an article published in the 2008 volume of the *Journal of Management*. In 2010, *Times Higher Education* listed him as one of the top scholars in economics, finance, and management.

Some of his books are *Downscoping: How to Tame the Diversified Firm* (Oxford University Press, 1994); *Mergers and Acquisitions: A Guide to Creating Value for Stakeholders* (Oxford University Press, 2001); *Competing for Advantage*, 3rd edition (South-Western, 2013); and *Understanding Business Strategy*, 3rd edition (South-Western Cengage Learning, 2012). He is co-editor of several books including the following: *Managing Strategically in an Interconnected World* (1998); *New Managerial Mindsets: Organizational Transformation and Strategy Implementation* (1998); *Dynamic Strategic Resources: Development, Diffusion, and Integration* (1999); *Winning Strategies in a Deconstructing World* (John Wiley & Sons, 2000); *Handbook of Strategic Management* (2001); *Strategic Entrepreneurship: Creating a New Integrated Mindset* (2002); *Creating Value: Winners in the New Business Environment* (Blackwell Publishers, 2002); *Managing Knowledge for Sustained Competitive Advantage* (Jossey-Bass, 2003); *Great Minds in Management: The Process of Theory Development* (Oxford University Press, 2005); and *The Global Mindset* (Elsevier, 2007). He has served on the editorial review boards of multiple journals, including the *Academy of Management Journal, Academy of Management Executive, Journal of Applied Psychology, Journal of Management, Journal of World Business*, and *Journal of Applied Behavioral Sciences*. Furthermore, he has served as consulting editor and editor of the *Academy of Management Journal*. He was a founding co-editor and currently a consulting editor for the *Strategic Entrepreneurship Journal*. He is a past president of the Strategic Management Society and of the Academy of Management.

He is a Fellow in the Academy of Management and in the Strategic Management Society. He received an honorary doctorate from the Universidad Carlos III de Madrid and is an Honorary Professor and Honorary Dean at Xi'an Jiao Tong University. He has been acknowledged with several awards for his scholarly research and he received the Irwin Outstanding Educator Award and the Distinguished Service Award from the Academy of Management. He has received best paper awards for articles published in the *Academy of Management Journal, Academy of Management Executive, Journal of Management, and Family Business Review*.

# R. Duane Ireland

R. Duane Ireland is a University Distinguished Professor and holds the Conn Chair in New Ventures Leadership in the Mays Business School, Texas A&M University where he previously served as head of the management department. He teaches strategic management courses at all levels (undergraduate, masters, doctoral, and executive). He has over 200 publications including more than a dozen books. His research, which focuses on diversification, innovation, corporate entrepreneurship, and strategic entrepreneurship, has been published in a number of journals, including *Academy of Management Journal, Academy of Management Review, Academy of Management Executive, Administrative Science Quarterly, Strategic Management Journal, Journal of Management, Strategic Entrepreneurship Journal, Human Relations, Entrepreneurship Theory and Practice, Journal of Business Venturing*, and *Journal of Management Studies*, among others. His recently published books include *Understanding Business Strategy*, 3rd edition (SouthWestern Cengage Learning, 2012), *Entrepreneurship: Successfully Launching New Ventures*, 4th edition (Prentice-Hall, 2012), and *Competing for Advantage*, 3rd edition (South-Western, 2013). He is serving or has served as a member of the editorial review boards for a number of journals, including *Academy of Management Journal, Academy of Management Review, Academy of Management Executive, Journal of Management, Strategic Entrepreneurship Journal, Journal of Business Venturing, Entrepreneurship Theory and Practice, Journal of Business Strategy, Academy of Management Perspectives*, and *European Management Journal*. He recently completed a term as editor of the *Academy of Management Journal*. He has completed terms as an associate editor for *Academy of Management Journal*, as an associate editor for *Academy of Management Executive*, and as a consulting editor for *Entrepreneurship Theory and Practice*. He has co-edited special issues of *Academy of Management Review, Academy of Management Executive, Journal of Business Venturing, Strategic Management Journal, Journal of High Technology and Engineering Management*, and *Organizational Research Methods*. He received awards for the best article published in *Academy of Management Executive* (1999) and *Academy of Management Journal* (2000). In 2001, his co-authored article published in *Academy of Management Executive* won the Best Journal Article in Corporate Entrepreneurship Award from the U.S. Association for Small Business & Entrepreneurship (USASBE).

He is a Fellow of the Academy of Management, a Fellow of the Strategic Management Society, and a 21st Century Entrepreneurship Research Scholar. He is the current President of the Academy of Management. He received the 1999 Award for Outstanding Intellectual Contributions to Competitiveness Research from the American Society for Competitiveness and the USASBE Scholar in Corporate Entrepreneurship Award (2004).

# Robert E. Hoskisson

Robert E. Hoskisson is the George R. Brown Chair of Strategic Management at the Jesse H. Jones Graduate School of Business, Rice University. He received his Ph.D. from the University of California-Irvine. Professor Hoskisson's research topics focus on corporate governance, acquisitions and divestitures, corporate and international diversification, corporate entrepreneurship, privatization, and cooperative strategy. He teaches courses in corporate and international strategic management, cooperative strategy, and strategy consulting, among others. Professor Hoskisson's research has appeared in over 120 publications, including articles in the *Academy of Management Journal, Academy of Management Review, Strategic Management Journal, Organization Science, Journal of Management, Journal of International Business Studies, Journal of Management Studies, Organization Research Methods, Journal of Business Venturing, Entrepreneurship Theory and Practice, Academy of Management*

*Perspectives, Academy of Management Executive, Journal of World Business, California Management Review*, and 26 co-authored books. In 2010, *Times Higher Education* listed him as one of the most highly cited scholars in economics, finance, and management. He is currently an associate editor of the *Strategic Management Journal* and serves on the Editorial Review board of the *Academy of Management Journal.* Professor Hoskisson has served on several editorial boards for such publications as the *Academy of Management Journal* (including consulting editor and guest editor of a special issue), *Journal of Management* (including associate editor), *Organization Science, Journal of International Business Studies* (including consulting editor), *Journal of Management Studies* (guest editor of a special issue), and *Entrepreneurship Theory and Practice.* He has co-authored several books including *Understanding Business Strategy*, 3rd Edition (South-Western Cengage Learning, 2012), *Competing for Advantage*, 3rd edition (South-Western, 2013), and *Downscoping: How to Tame the Diversified Firm* (Oxford University Press, 1994).

He has an appointment as a Special Professor at the University of Nottingham and as an Honorary Professor at Xi'an Jiao Tong University. He is a Fellow of the Academy of Management and a charter member of the Academy of Management Journals Hall of Fame. He is also a Fellow of the Strategic Management Society. In 1998, he received an award for Outstanding Academic Contributions to Competitiveness, American Society for Competitiveness. He also received the William G. Dyer Distinguished Alumni Award given at the Marriott School of Management, Brigham Young University. He completed three years of service as a representative at large on the Board of Governors of the Academy of Management and currently is President of the Strategic Management Society.

# 1

# Strategic Management and Strategic Competitiveness

***Studying this chapter should provide you with the strategic management knowledge needed to:***

1. Define strategic competitiveness, strategy, competitive advantage, above-average returns, and the strategic management process.
2. Describe the competitive landscape and explain how globalization and technological changes shape it.
3. Use the industrial organization (I/O) model to explain how firms can earn above-average returns.
4. Use the resource-based model to explain how firms can earn above-average returns.
5. Describe vision and mission and discuss their value.
6. Define stakeholders and describe their ability to influence organizations.
7. Describe the work of strategic leaders.
8. Explain the strategic management process.

## THE GLOBAL IMPACT OF THE GOLDEN ARCHES

McDonald's has achieved substantial success over the years, which is exemplified by its impact throughout the world. Many people know about and are customers of McDonald's. For example, a recent survey found that 88 percent of people recognize the golden arches and associate them with McDonald's. This is likely because McDonald's touches a lot of people in a year. Each day, about 68 million people eat at a McDonald's, which equates to almost one percent of the world's population. In the United States alone, McDonald's hires approximately one million employees per year. Approximately 12 to 13 percent of all U.S. workers have been employed at McDonald's at one time (including such famous people as actress Sharon Stone, singer, Shania Twain and comedian Jay Leno). Given that McDonald's includes a toy in about 20 percent of its sales, it is the world's largest distributor of toys. Finally, McDonald's serves about one billion pounds of beef annually in the United States, which requires approximately 5.5 million head of cattle.

McDonald's is larger and has been more successful in the market than its close competitors, Burger King and Wendy's, as well as other large competitors for the fast food customer, such as Subway and Starbucks. It has been estimated that McDonald's has about 17 percent of the limited service restaurants in the United States. Its success against competitors is demonstrated by the results of a recent review of the specialty coffees offered by fast food outlets. McDonald's McCafé was rated higher than the "gourmet" coffees sold by Burger King (a new entrant in this product category), Wendy's, Subway, and 7-Eleven. In fact, McCafé even stole some customers from Starbucks when it was first offered by McDonald's.

McDonald's made a decision early to move into international markets and now one can find the golden arches in many countries across the world. However, its success has created a company of such size and reach that it is also easy to criticize. For example, in 2012 it created an advertisement that received acclaim because it included farmers and ranchers who supplied the food to McDonald's. The evaluations showed that it was perceived to be authentic. Early responses from the public were positive but over time the tweets became more negative with people voicing criticisms of the company and its food. It especially has been criticized because of its supposed contribution to the obesity problems in the United States.

McDonald's has tried to respond to this criticism and the public's concerns about obesity by offering more healthy food alternatives such as salads, chicken, and fish and by providing the amount of calories in its foods on their packaging. McDonald's now serves more Happy Meals with Chicken McNuggets than with hamburgers.

It also offers apple slices in place of French fries. It recently has introduced Fish McBites following its popular entry of Chicken McBites. In addition to providing new food products for customers, McDonald's now offers Wi-Fi, which has been particularly popular with students.

Even with all of its success and rapid responses to criticism, McDonald's must always be prepared to react to negative outcomes. For example, while its global sales revenue in 2012 increased by 6.7 percent over 2011 sales, early sales in 2013 have been discouraging. Sales in January dropped significantly in Asia, the Middle East, and Africa. It also has experienced recent sales declines in Europe, especially Germany and France. Some of these reductions in sales reflect general economic conditions with which McDonald's must regularly cope with intensifying competition from regional and global rivals. These results suggest that its global reach has helped the firm in many ways (massive economies of scope, recognition in the market) but also means that it must deal with geographic economic differences and varying competitive forces across the globe.

Sources: K. Mayo & V. Wong, 2013, Who serves the best fast-food coffee? *Bloomberg Businessweek*, March 4, 76–77; C. Choi, 2013, McDonald's sales fall with tough year ahead, *Bloomberg Businessweek*, www.businessweek.com, February 8; C. Choi, McDonald's to put "Fish McBites" in happy meals, *Bloomberg Businessweek*, www.businessweek.com, February 4; A. Troianovovski, 2013, The web-deprived study at McDonald's, *Wall Street Journal*, www.wsj.com, January, 28; G. Lubin & M. Badkar, 2012, 17 facts about McDonald's that will blow your mind, *Yahoo! Finance*, http://finance.yahoo.com, December 7; K. O'Brien, 2012, How McDonald's came back bigger than ever, *New York Times*, www.nytimes.com, May 4.

**Learn more about Burger King, a large competitor of McDonald's.**
**www.cengagebrain.com**

As we see from the Opening Case, McDonald's is highly successful because of its strategy to grow globally and gain massive economies of scale (keeping costs low) that provide widespread name/brand recognition. These attributes along with other critical strategic decisions (e.g., adding new food and drink products such as salads, Chicken and Fish McBites, and McCafé) have enhanced its ability to compete against other major fast food restaurants. Therefore, we can conclude that McDonald's has achieved *strategic competitiveness*. It clearly has been able to earn *above-average returns*. Yet McDonald's has received its share of criticism because of its perceived contribution to the childhood obesity problem in the United States. In addition, it continues to cope with global economic problems and fierce competition. For example, Burger King and Wendy's now serve gourmet coffee in response to the success of McDonald's McCafé. The top management of McDonald's has used the strategic management process (see Figure 1.1) as the foundation for the commitments, decisions, and actions they took to pursue strategic competitiveness and above-average terms. The strategic management process is fully explained in this book. We introduce you to this process in the next few paragraphs.

**Strategic competitiveness** is achieved when a firm successfully formulates and implements a value-creating strategy. A **strategy** is an integrated and coordinated set of commitments and actions designed to exploit core competencies and gain a competitive advantage. When choosing a strategy, firms make choices among competing alternatives as the pathway for deciding how they will pursue strategic competitiveness.[1] In this sense, the chosen strategy indicates what the firm *will do* as well as what the firm *will not do*.

As explained in the Opening Case, McDonald's has been a leader in its industry as one of the first fast food companies to enter global markets and is now a highly global business. However, it continues to change its product line in response to a changing environment. In fact, to adapt to local environments, it sometimes makes major changes. For example, it has changed its name to Macca in Australia because people there often abbreviate names to avoid pronouncing multiple syllables. So, McDonald's shortened its name to two syllables (from three) and used its highly recognizable golden arches as the symbol of the firm.[2]

**Strategic competitiveness** is achieved when a firm successfully formulates and implements a value-creating strategy.

A **strategy** is an integrated and coordinated set of commitments and actions designed to exploit core competencies and gain a competitive advantage.

A recent study conducted to identify the factors that contribute to the success of top corporate performers showed why McDonald's has been successful. This study found that the top performers were entrepreneurial, market oriented (effective knowledge of the customers' needs), used valuable competencies, and offered innovative products and services.[3] McDonald's displays several of these attributes. It clearly understands its market and

M. Stasy

customers and is innovative. Therefore, its success is not surprising. A firm's strategy also demonstrates how it differs from its competitors. Recently, Ford Motor Company devoted efforts to explain to stakeholders how the company differs from its competitors. The main idea is that Ford claims that it is "greener" and more technically advanced than its competitors, such as General Motors and Chrysler Group LLC (with majority ownership held by Fiat SpA).[4]

A firm has a **competitive advantage** when it implements a strategy that creates superior value for customers and that its competitors are unable to duplicate or find too costly to imitate.[5] An organization can be confident that its strategy has resulted in one or more useful competitive advantages only after competitors' efforts to duplicate its strategy have ceased or failed. In addition, firms must understand that no competitive advantage is permanent.[6] The speed with which competitors are able to acquire the skills needed to duplicate the benefits of a firm's value-creating strategy determines how long the competitive advantage will last.[7]

**Above-average returns** are returns in excess of what an investor expects to earn from other investments with a similar amount of risk. **Risk** is an investor's uncertainty about the economic gains or losses that will result from a particular investment.[8] The most successful companies learn how to effectively manage risk. Effectively managing risks reduces investors' uncertainty about the results of their investment.[9] Returns are often measured in terms of accounting figures, such as return on assets, return on equity, or return on sales. Alternatively, returns can be measured on the basis of stock market returns, such as monthly returns (the end-of-the-period stock price minus the beginning stock price, divided by the beginning stock price, yielding a percentage return). In smaller, new venture firms, returns are sometimes measured in terms of the amount and speed of growth (e.g., in annual sales) rather than more traditional profitability measures[10] because new ventures require time to earn acceptable returns (in the form of return on assets and so forth) on investors' investments.[11]

Understanding how to exploit a competitive advantage is important for firms seeking to earn above-average returns.[12] Firms without a competitive advantage or that are not competing in an attractive industry earn, at best, average returns. **Average returns** are returns equal to those an investor expects to earn from other investments with a similar amount of risk. In the long run, an inability to earn at least average returns results first in decline and, eventually, failure.[13] Failure occurs because investors withdraw their investments from those firms earning less-than-average returns.

As previously noted, there are no guarantees of permanent success. For example, American Airlines was very successful at one time earning above average returns. But in recent years, it has performed very poorly and had to declare bankruptcy. As a result it is being acquired by US Airways. Companies that are prospering must not become overconfident. For example, even considering Apple's excellent current performance, it still must be careful not to become overconfident and continue its quest to be the leader for its markets.

The **strategic management process** (see Figure 1.1) is the full set of commitments, decisions, and actions required for a firm to achieve strategic competitiveness and earn above-average returns.[14] The process involves analysis, strategy and performance (the A-S-P model—see Figure 1.1). The firm's first step in the process is to *analyze* its external environment and internal organization to determine its resources, capabilities, and core competencies—on which its strategy likely will be based. McDonald's has excelled in using this process over the years. The *strategy* portion of the model entails strategy formulation and strategy implementation.

With the information gained from external and internal analyses, the firm develops its vision and mission and formulates one or more *strategies*. To implement its strategies, the firm takes actions to enact each strategy with the intent of achieving strategic

A firm has a **competitive advantage** when it implements a strategy that creates superior value for customers and competitors are unable to duplicate or find too costly to try to imitate.

**Above-average returns** are returns in excess of what an investor expects to earn from other investments with a similar amount of risk.

**Risk** is an investor's uncertainty about the economic gains or losses that will result from a particular investment.

**Average returns** are returns equal to those an investor expects to earn from other investments with a similar amount of risk.

The **strategic management process** is the full set of commitment, decisions, and actions required for a firm to achieve strategic competitiveness and earn above-average returns.

**Figure 1.1** The Strategic Management Process

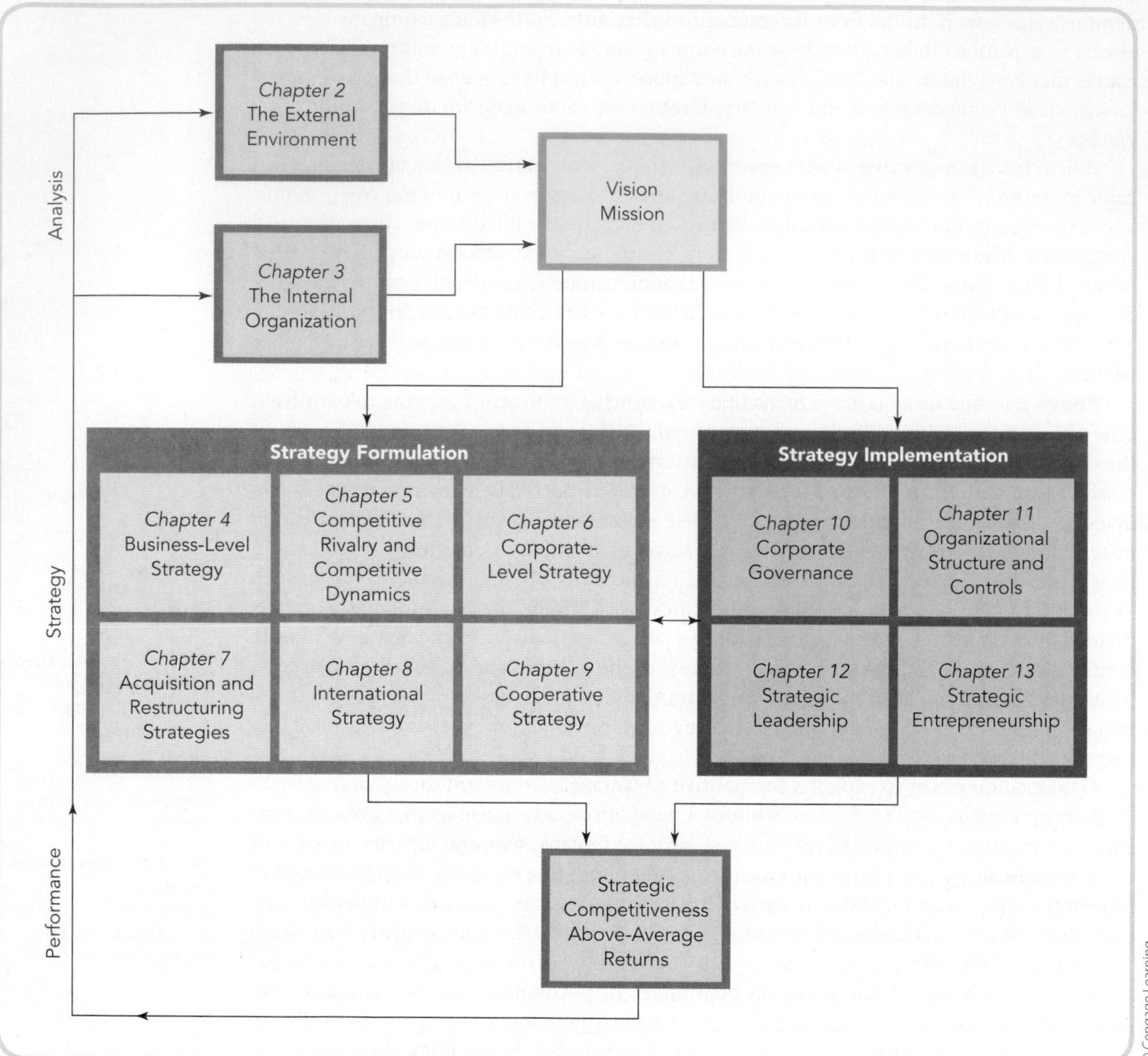


competitiveness and above-average returns (*performance*). Effective strategic actions that take place in the context of carefully integrated strategy formulation and implementation efforts result in positive performance. This dynamic strategic management process must be maintained as ever-changing markets and competitive structures are coordinated with a firm's continuously evolving strategic inputs.[15]

In the remaining chapters of this book, we use the strategic management process to explain what firms do to achieve strategic competitiveness and earn above-average returns. We demonstrate why some firms consistently achieve competitive success while others fail to do so.[16] As you will see, the reality of global competition is a critical part of the strategic management process and significantly influences firms' performances.[17] Indeed, learning how to successfully compete in the globalized world is one of the most significant challenges for firms competing in the current century.[18]

Several topics will be discussed in this chapter. First, we describe the current competitive landscape. This challenging landscape is being created primarily by the emergence of a global economy, globalization resulting from that economy, and rapid technological changes. Next, we examine two models that firms use to gather the information and knowledge required to choose and then effectively implement their strategies. The insights gained from these models also serve as the foundation for forming the firm's vision and mission. The first model (the industrial organization or I/O model) suggests that the external environment is the primary determinant of a firm's strategic actions. According to this model, identifying and then operating effectively in an attractive (i.e., profitable) industry or segment of an industry are the keys to competitive success.[19] The second model (resource-based) suggests that a firm's unique resources and capabilities are the critical link to strategic competitiveness.[20] Thus, the first model is concerned primarily with the firm's external environment while the second model is concerned primarily with the firm's internal organization. After discussing vision and mission, direction-setting statements that influence the choice and use of strategies, we describe the stakeholders that organizations serve. The degree to which stakeholders' needs can be met increases when firms achieve strategic competitiveness and earn above-average returns. Closing the chapter are introductions to strategic leaders and the elements of the strategic management process.

## 1-1 The Competitive Landscape

The fundamental nature of competition in many of the world's industries is changing. The reality is that financial capital continues to be scarce and markets are increasingly volatile.[21] Because of this, the pace of change is relentless and ever-increasing. Even determining the boundaries of an industry has become challenging. Consider, for example, how advances in interactive computer networks and telecommunications have blurred the boundaries of the entertainment industry. Today, not only do cable companies and satellite networks compete for entertainment revenue from television, but telecommunication companies are moving into the entertainment business through significant improvements in fiber-optic lines.[22] Partnerships among firms in different segments of the entertainment industry further blur industry boundaries. For example, MSNBC is co-owned by NBC Universal and Microsoft. At one time, General Electric owned 49 percent of NBC Universal while Comcast owned the remaining 51 percent. In March 2013, Comcast acquired the remaining shares in the firm.[23]

Other characteristics of the current competitive landscape are noteworthy. Conventional sources of competitive advantage such as economies of scale and huge advertising budgets are not as effective as they once were in terms of helping firms earn above-average returns. Moreover, the traditional managerial mind-set is unlikely to lead a firm to strategic competitiveness. Managers must adopt a new mind-set that values flexibility, speed, innovation, integration, and the challenges that evolve from constantly changing conditions.[24] The conditions of the competitive landscape result in a perilous business world, one in which the investments that are required to compete on a global scale are enormous and the consequences of failure are severe.[25] Effective use of the strategic management process reduces the likelihood of failure for firms as they encounter the conditions of today's competitive landscape.

*Hypercompetition* is a term often used to capture the realities of the competitive landscape. Under conditions of hypercompetition, assumptions of market stability are replaced by notions of inherent instability and change.[26] Hypercompetition results from the dynamics of strategic maneuvering among global and innovative combatants.[27] It is a condition of rapidly escalating competition based on price-quality positioning, competition to create new know-how and establish first-mover advantage, and competition to protect or invade established product or geographic markets.[28] In a hypercompetitive market, firms often aggressively challenge their competitors in the hopes of improving their competitive position and ultimately their performance.[29]

Several factors create hypercompetitive environments and influence the nature of the current competitive landscape. The emergence of a global economy and technology, specifically rapid technological change, are the two primary drivers of hypercompetitive environments and the nature of today's competitive landscape.

## 1-1a The Global Economy

A **global economy** is one in which goods, services, people, skills, and ideas move freely across geographic borders. Relatively unfettered by artificial constraints, such as tariffs, the global economy significantly expands and complicates a firm's competitive environment.[30]

Interesting opportunities and challenges are associated with the emergence of the global economy.[31] For example, the European Union (composed of several countries) has become one of the world's largest markets, with 700 million potential customers. "In the past, China was generally seen as a low-competition market and a low-cost producer. Today, China is an extremely competitive market in which local market-seeking MNCs [multinational corporations] must fiercely compete against other MNCs and against those local companies that are more cost effective and faster in product development. While China has been viewed as a country from which to source low-cost goods, lately, many MNCs, such as P&G [Procter and Gamble], are actually net exporters of local management talent; they have been dispatching more Chinese abroad than bringing foreign expatriates to China."[32] China has become the second-largest economy in the world, surpassing Japan. India, the world's largest democracy, has an economy that also is growing rapidly and now ranks as the fourth largest in the world.[33] Simultaneously, many firms in these emerging economies are moving into international markets and are now regarded as multinational firms. This fact is demonstrated by the case of Huawei, a Chinese company that has entered the U.S. market. Barriers to entering foreign markets still exist and Huawei has encountered several, such as the inability to gain the U.S. government's approval for acquisition of U.S. firms. Essentially, Huawei must build credibility in the U.S. market, and especially build a positive relationship with stakeholders such as the U.S. government.

Find out more about Evolution Fresh, a Starbucks acquisition.
www.cengagebrain.com

The nature of the global economy reflects the realities of a hypercompetitive business environment and challenges individual firms to seriously evaluate the markets in which they will compete. This is reflected in Starbucks' actions and outcomes. While Starbucks has enjoyed substantial success in North America and Asia, it is struggling in Europe. It has substantial competition there. Alternatively, the fact that a company that sells cups of coffee is a multinational firm suggests the reach and influence of the global economy.

Consider the case of General Electric (GE). Although headquartered in the United States, GE expects that as much as 60 percent of its revenue growth through 2015 will be generated by competing in rapidly developing economies (e.g., China and India). The decision to count on revenue growth in emerging economies instead of in developed countries such as the United States and in Europe seems quite reasonable in the global economy. GE achieved significant growth in 2010 partly because of signing contracts for large infrastructure projects in China and Russia. GE's CEO, Jeffrey Immelt, argues that we have entered a new economic era in which the global economy will be more volatile and that most of the growth will come from emerging economies such as Brazil, China, and India.[34] Therefore, GE is investing significantly in these emerging economies, in order to improve its competitive position in vital geographic sources of revenue and profitability.

A **global economy** is one in which goods, services, people, skills, and ideas move freely across geographic borders.

M. Stasy

# Strategic Focus — GLOBALIZATION

## Starbucks is a New Economy Multinational

Starbucks is not an ordinary purveyor of a cup of coffee. It is a large and innovative multinational firm that engages in major strategic actions to enter new international and product markets (e.g., acquisitions). It is a multibillion-dollar company with many stores operating in multiple countries. By 2015, Starbucks plans to have more than 12,500 stores in the United States, up from 11,128 in 2012. For example, Starbucks has become a major player in Asian markets, which is interesting because it took on a largely tea-drinking culture. By 2015, Starbucks expects to have 1,500 stores operating in China, a major increase over its 700 stores there in 2012. Starbucks adapts to local market tastes by developing larger stores where, for example, the Chinese can lounge and meet with friends. It also has introduced flavors specifically for the Chinese market, such as red-bean frappuccinos. It also has products that cater to tea drinkers as well. Starbucks' success in China is reflected by the fact that China is expected to become the company's second largest market by 2014. The average annual single store sales in China have increased by almost 75 percent since 2008 to $886,000 at the end of 2012.

Starbucks has also entered Vietnam and India with high expectations. In 2013 it opened its first store in Vietnam. Interestingly, Vietnam is the second largest producer of coffee beans in the world behind only Brazil. Starbucks hopes to work with local Vietnamese farmers to grow a high-quality Arabica coffee bean. In partnership with the Tata Group, Starbucks also recently opened its first stores (three) in India with plans to have 50 stores there within a year.

Although Starbucks has experienced significant success in Asia, its experience in Europe has been mixed. It has had some success but has also encountered a different coffee culture. At first, it tried to have Europeans adapt to the Starbucks approach. Now, because of the importance Starbucks places on its future in Europe, the company is adapting to the European café culture. This means that Starbucks is building larger stores with additional seating to allow people to meet and spend time in their stores, as they have done in Asia. It has implemented other practices and products that adapt even more to local (country) cultures and tastes (e.g., France, England).

*Customers line up to purchase drinks on the opening day of the first Starbucks outlet in Ho Chi Minh City on February 1, 2013. Starbucks opened its first store in coffee-loving Vietnam, seeking to compete with local rivals in a country known for its strong café culture.*

In addition to Starbucks' international thrust, it also engages in significant innovation and strategic actions to add to its product line. In recent years, it has introduced Via, an instant coffee, and a single-cup coffee maker (named the Verismo) that allows customers to make their own lattes at home. Another attempt to add to its product line is evidenced in its recent acquisition of the tea chain, Teavana. In fact, it paid $620 million to acquire the Atlanta-based company. In recent times it also acquired a juice maker, Evolution Fresh, and Bay Bread, the operator of La Boulange bakeries.

Starbucks' strategic actions have enjoyed much success. In fact, Starbucks announced major increases in stores' sales open at least 13 months (7 percent in the Americas and 11 percent in China) and in profits (13 percent overall) in the last quarter of 2012.

Sources: J. Gertner, 2013, For infusing a steady stream of new ideas to revive its business, *Fast Company*, www.fastcompany.com, accessed on January 30; A. Gasparro, 2013, Starbucks enjoys sales jolt from its U.S., China stores, *Wall Street Journal*, www.wsj.com, January 24; J. Noble, 2013, Starbucks takes on Vietnam coffee culture, *Financial Times*, www.ft.com, January 3; A. Gasparro, 2012, Starbucks: China to become no. 2 market, *Wall Street Journal*, www.wsj.com, December 6; 2012, A look at Starbucks' U.S. presence over the years, *Bloomberg Businessweek*, www.businessweek.com, December 5; L. Burkitt, 2012, Starbucks plays to local Chinese tastes, *Wall Street Journal*, www.wsj.com, November 26; J. Jargon, 2012, Starbucks CEO: 'We will do for tea what we did for coffee,' *Wall Street Journal*, www.wsj.com, November 14; V. Bajaj, 2012, Starbucks opens in India with pomp and tempered ambition, *New York Times*, www.nytimes.com, October 19; S. Strom, 2012, Starbucks to introduce single-serve coffee maker, *New York Times*, www.nytimes.com, September 20; L. Alderman, 2012, In Europe, Starbucks adjusts to a café culture, *New York Times*, www.nytimes.com, March 30.

## The March of Globalization

*Globalization* is the increasing economic interdependence among countries and their organizations as reflected in the flow of goods and services, financial capital, and knowledge across country borders.[35] Globalization is a product of a large number of firms competing against one another in an increasing number of global economies.

In globalized markets and industries, financial capital might be obtained in one national market and used to buy raw materials in another. Manufacturing equipment bought from a third national market can then be used to produce products that are sold in yet a fourth market. Thus, globalization increases the range of opportunities for companies competing in the current competitive landscape.[36]

Firms engaging in globalization of their operations must make culturally sensitive decisions when using the strategic management process, as is the case in Starbucks' operations in European countries. Additionally, highly globalized firms must anticipate ever-increasing complexity in their operations as goods, services, people, and so forth move freely across geographic borders and throughout different economic markets.

Overall, it is important to note that globalization has led to higher performance standards in many competitive dimensions, including those of quality, cost, productivity, product introduction time, and operational efficiency. In addition to firms competing in the global economy, these standards affect firms competing on a domestic-only basis. The reason is that customers will purchase from a global competitor rather than a domestic firm is that the global company's good or service is superior. Workers now flow rather freely among global economies, and employees are a key source of competitive advantage.[37] Thus, managers have to learn how to operate effectively in a "multi-polar" world with many important countries having unique interests and environments.[38] Firms must learn how to deal with the reality that in the competitive landscape of the twenty-first century, only companies capable of meeting, if not exceeding, global standards typically have the capability to earn above-average returns.

Although globalization offers potential benefits to firms, it is not without risks. Collectively, the risks of participating outside of a firm's domestic markets in the global economy are labeled a "liability of foreignness."[39]

Learn more about the emerging economies of the BRIC countries (Brazil, Russia, India, & China).
www.cengagebrain.com

One risk of entering the global market is the amount of time typically required for firms to learn how to compete in markets that are new to them. A firm's performance can suffer until this knowledge is either developed locally or transferred from the home market to the newly established global location.[40] Additionally, a firm's performance may suffer with substantial amounts of globalization. In this instance, firms may overdiversify internationally beyond their ability to manage these extended operations.[41] Overdiversification can have strong negative effects on a firm's overall performance.

A major factor in the global economy in recent years has been the growth in the influence of emerging economies. The important emerging economies include not only the BRIC countries (Brazil, Russia, India and China) but also the VISTA countries (Vietnam, Indonesia, South Africa, Turkey, and Argentina). Mexico and Thailand also have become increasingly important markets.[42] Obviously, as these economies have grown, their markets have become targets for entry by large multinational firms. Emerging economy firms have also began to compete in global markets, some with increasing success.[43] For example, there are now more than 1,000 multinational firms home-based in emerging economies with more than $1 billion in annual sales.[44] In fact, the emergence of emerging-market multinational firms in international markets has forced large multinational firms based in developed markets to enrich their own capabilities to compete effectively in global markets.[45]

Thus, entry into international markets, even for firms with substantial experience in the global economy, requires effective use of the strategic management process. It is also

M. Stasy

important to note that even though global markets are an attractive strategic option for some companies, they are not the only source of strategic competitiveness. In fact, for most companies, even for those capable of competing successfully in global markets, it is critical to remain committed to and strategically competitive in both domestic and international markets by staying attuned to technological opportunities and potential competitive disruptions that innovations create.[46]

## 1-1b Technology and Technological Changes

Technology-related trends and conditions can be placed into three categories: technology diffusion and disruptive technologies, the information age, and increasing knowledge intensity. Through these categories, technology is significantly altering the nature of competition and contributing to highly dynamic competitive environments as a result of doing so.

### Technology Diffusion and Disruptive Technologies

The rate of technology diffusion, which is the speed at which new technologies become available and are used, has increased substantially over the past 15 to 20 years. Consider the following rates of technology diffusion:

*It took the telephone 35 years to get into 25 percent of all homes in the United States. It took TV 26 years. It took radio 22 years. It took PCs 16 years. It took the Internet 7 years.*[47]

The impact of technological changes on individual firms and industries has been broad and significant. For example, in the not-too-distant-past, people rented movies on videotapes at retail stores. Now, movie rentals are almost entirely electronic. The publishing industry (books, journals, magazines, newspapers) is moving rapidly from hard copy to electronic form. Many firms in these industries operating with a more traditional business model are suffering. These changes are also affecting other industries, from trucking to mail services (public and private).

*Perpetual innovation* is a term used to describe how rapidly and consistently new, information-intensive technologies replace older ones. The shorter product life cycles resulting from these rapid diffusions of new technologies place a competitive premium on being able to quickly introduce new, innovative goods and services into the marketplace.[48]

In fact, when products become somewhat indistinguishable because of the widespread and rapid diffusion of technologies, speed to market with innovative products may be the primary source of competitive advantage (see Chapter 5).[49] Indeed, some argue that the global economy is increasingly driven by constant innovations. Not surprisingly, such innovations must be derived from an understanding of global standards and expectations of product functionality.[50] Although some argue that large established firms may have trouble innovating, evidence suggests that today these firms are developing radically new technologies that transform old industries or create new ones.[51] Apple is an excellent example of a large established firm capable of radical innovation. Also, in order to diffuse the technology and enhance the value of an innovation, additional firms need to be innovative in their use of the new technology, building it into their products.[52]

Another indicator of rapid technology diffusion is that it now may take only 12 to 18 months for firms to gather information about their competitors' research and development and product decisions.[53] In the global economy, competitors can sometimes imitate a firm's successful competitive actions within a few days. In this sense, the rate of technological diffusion has reduced the competitive benefits of patents. Today, patents may be an effective way of protecting proprietary technology in a small number of industries such as pharmaceuticals. Indeed, many firms competing in the electronics industry often do not apply for

Iain Masterton / Alamy

*Reading a book on an iPad. In recent years Apple has brought to market several disruptive technologies that create new markets and change existing industries.*

patents to prevent competitors from gaining access to the technological knowledge included in the patent application.

Disruptive technologies—technologies that destroy the value of an existing technology and create new markets[54]—surface frequently in today's competitive markets. Think of the new markets created by the technologies underlying the development of products such as iPods, iPads, Wi-Fi, and the browser. These types of products are thought by some to represent radical or breakthrough innovations.[55] (We discuss more about radical innovations in Chapter 13.) A disruptive or radical technology can create what is essentially a new industry or can harm industry incumbents. However, some incumbents are able to adapt based on their superior resources, experience, and ability to gain access to the new technology through multiple sources (e.g., alliances, acquisitions, and ongoing internal research).[56]

Clearly, Apple has developed and introduced "disruptive technologies" such as the iPod, and in so doing changed several industries. For example, the iPod and its complementary iTunes revolutionized how music is sold to and used by consumers. In conjunction with other complementary and competitive products (e.g., Amazon's Kindle), Apple's iPad is contributing to and speeding major changes in the publishing industry, moving from hard copies to electronic books. Apple's new technologies and products are also contributing to the new "information age." Thus, Apple provides an example of entrepreneurship through technology emergence across multiple industries.[57]

## The Information Age

Dramatic changes in information technology have occurred in recent years. Personal computers, cellular phones, artificial intelligence, virtual reality, massive databases, and multiple social networking sites are only a few examples of how information is used differently as a result of technological developments. An important outcome of these changes is that the ability to effectively and efficiently access and use information has become an important source of competitive advantage in virtually all industries. Information technology advances have given small firms more flexibility in competing with large firms, if that technology can be efficiently used.[58]

Both the pace of change in information technology and its diffusion will continue to increase. For instance, the number of personal computers in use globally is expected to surpass 2.3 billion by 2015. More than 372 million were sold globally in 2011. This number is expected to increase to about 518 million in 2015.[59] The declining costs of information technologies and the increased accessibility to them are also evident in the current competitive landscape. The global proliferation of relatively inexpensive computing power and its linkage on a global scale via computer networks combine to increase the speed and diffusion of information technologies. Thus, the competitive potential of information technologies is now available to companies of all sizes throughout the world, including those in emerging economies.[60]

The Internet is another technological innovation contributing to hypercompetition. Available to an increasing number of people throughout the world, the Internet provides an infrastructure that allows the delivery of information to computers in any location. Access to the Internet on smaller devices such as cell phones is having an ever-growing impact on competition in a number of industries. However, possible changes to Internet Service Providers' (ISPs) pricing structures could affect the rate of growth of Internet-based applications. Users downloading or streaming high-definition movies, playing video games online, and so forth would be affected the most if ISPs were to base their pricing structure around total usage.

### Increasing Knowledge Intensity

Knowledge (information, intelligence, and expertise) is the basis of technology and its application. In the competitive landscape of the twenty-first century, knowledge is a critical organizational resource and an increasingly valuable source of competitive advantage.[61]

Indeed, starting in the 1980s, the basis of competition shifted from hard assets to intangible resources. For example, "Wal-Mart transformed retailing through its proprietary approach to supply chain management and its information-rich relationships with customers and suppliers."[62] Relationships with customers and suppliers are an example of an intangible resource.

Knowledge is gained through experience, observation, and inference and is an intangible resource (tangible and intangible resources are fully described in Chapter 3). The value of intangible resources, including knowledge, is growing as a proportion of total shareholder value in today's competitive landscape.[63] In fact, the Brookings Institution estimates that intangible resources contribute approximately 85 percent of that value.[64] The probability of achieving strategic competitiveness is enhanced for the firm that develops the ability to capture intelligence, transform it into usable knowledge, and diffuse it rapidly throughout the company.[65] Therefore, firms must develop (e.g., through training programs) and acquire (e.g., by hiring educated and experienced employees) knowledge, integrate it into the organization to create capabilities, and then apply it to gain a competitive advantage.[66]

A strong knowledge base is necessary to create innovations. In fact, firms lacking the appropriate internal knowledge resources are less likely to invest money in research and development.[67] Firms must continue to learn (building their knowledge stock) because knowledge spillovers to competitors are common. There are several ways in which knowledge spillovers occur, including the hiring of professional staff and managers by competitors.[68] Because of the potential for spillovers, firms must move quickly to use their knowledge in productive ways. In addition, firms must build routines that facilitate the diffusion of local knowledge throughout the organization for use everywhere that it has value.[69] Firms are better able to do these things when they have strategic flexibility.

**Strategic flexibility** is a set of capabilities used to respond to various demands and opportunities existing in a dynamic and uncertain competitive environment. Thus, strategic flexibility involves coping with uncertainty and its accompanying risks.[70] Firms should try to develop strategic flexibility in all areas of their operations. However, those working within firms to develop strategic flexibility should understand that the task is not easy, largely because of inertia that can build up over time. A firm's focus and past core competencies may actually slow change and strategic flexibility.[71]

To be strategically flexible on a continuing basis and to gain the competitive benefits of such flexibility, a firm has to develop the capacity to learn. Continuous learning provides the firm with new and up-to-date skill sets, which allow it to adapt to its environment as it encounters changes.[72] Firms capable of rapidly and broadly applying what they have learned exhibit the strategic flexibility and the capacity to change in ways that will increase the probability of successfully dealing with uncertain, hypercompetitive environments.

**Strategic flexibility** is a set of capabilities used to respond to various demands and opportunities existing in a dynamic and uncertain competitive environment.

# 1-2 The I/O Model of Above-Average Returns

From the 1960s through the 1980s, the external environment was thought to be the primary determinant of strategies that firms selected to be successful.[73] The industrial organization model of above-average returns explains the external environment's dominant influence on a firm's strategic actions. The model specifies that the industry or segment of an industry in which a company chooses to compete has a stronger influence on performance than do the choices managers make inside their organizations.[74] The firm's performance is believed to be determined primarily by a range of industry properties, including economies of scale, barriers to market entry, diversification, product differentiation, the degree of concentration of firms in the industry, and market frictions.[75] We examine these industry characteristics in Chapter 2.

Grounded in economics, the I/O model has four underlying assumptions. First, the external environment is assumed to impose pressures and constraints that determine the strategies that would result in above-average returns. Second, most firms competing within an industry or within a segment of that industry are assumed to control similar strategically relevant resources and to pursue similar strategies in light of those resources. Third, resources used to implement strategies are assumed to be highly mobile across firms, so any resource differences that might develop between firms will be short-lived. Fourth, organizational decision makers are assumed to be rational and committed to acting in the firm's best interests, as shown by their profit-maximizing behaviors.[76] The I/O model challenges firms to find the most attractive industry in which to compete. Because most firms are assumed to have similar valuable resources that are mobile across companies, their performance generally can be increased only when they operate in the industry with the highest profit potential and learn how to use their resources to implement the strategy required by the industry's structural characteristics. To do so, they must imitate each other.[77]

The five forces model of competition is an analytical tool used to help firms find the industry that is the most attractive for them. The model (explained in Chapter 2) encompasses several variables and tries to capture the complexity of competition. The five forces model suggests that an industry's profitability (i.e., its rate of return on invested capital relative to its cost of capital) is a function of interactions among five forces: suppliers, buyers, competitive rivalry among firms currently in the industry, product substitutes, and potential entrants to the industry.[78]

Firms use the five forces model to identify the attractiveness of an industry (as measured by its profitability potential) as well as the most advantageous position for the firm to take in that industry, given the industry's structural characteristics.[79] Typically, the model suggests that firms can earn above-average returns by producing either standardized goods or services at costs below those of competitors (a cost leadership strategy) or by producing differentiated goods or services for which customers are willing to pay a price premium (a differentiation strategy). (The cost leadership and product differentiation strategies are discussed in Chapter 4.) The fact that "… the fast food industry is becoming a 'zero-sum industry' as companies battle for the same pool of customers"[80] suggests that fast food giant McDonald's is competing in a relatively unattractive industry. And, its problems in dealing with competitors as described in the Opening Case exemplify these facts. However, by focusing on product innovations and enhancing existing facilities while increasing its presence in international markets, McDonald's has earned above-average returns over time.

As shown in Figure 1.2, the I/O model suggests that above-average returns are earned when firms are able to effectively study the external environment as the foundation for identifying an attractive industry and implementing the appropriate strategy. For example,

**Figure 1.2** The I/O Model of Above-Average Returns

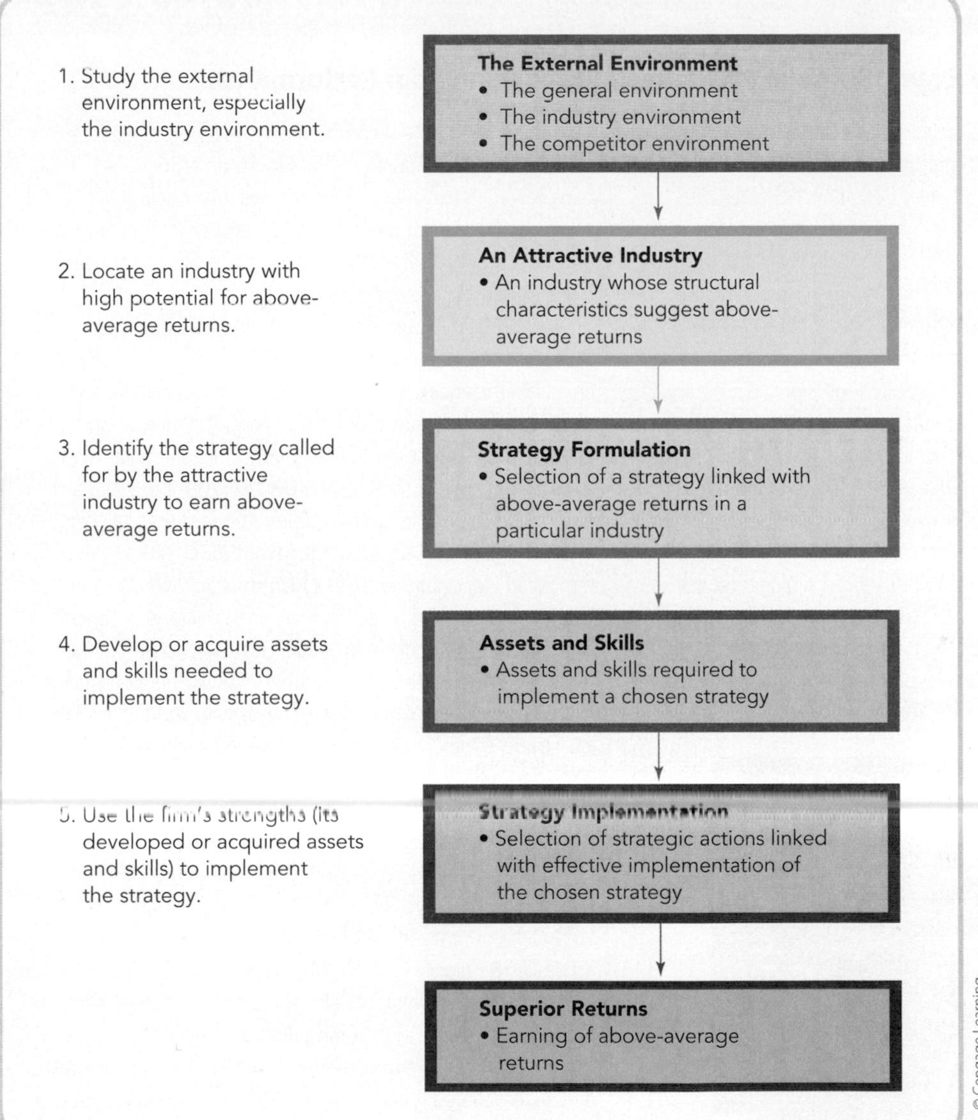


in some industries, firms can reduce competitive rivalry and erect barriers to entry by forming joint ventures. Because of these outcomes, the joint ventures increase profitability in the industry.[81] Companies that develop or acquire the internal skills needed to implement strategies required by the external environment are likely to succeed, while those that do not are likely to fail.[82] Hence, this model suggests that returns are determined primarily by external characteristics rather than by the firm's unique internal resources and capabilities.

Research findings support the I/O model in that approximately 20 percent of a firm's profitability is explained by the industry in which it chooses to compete. However, this research also shows that 36 percent of the variance in firm profitability can be attributed to the firm's characteristics and actions.[83] Thus, managers' strategic actions affect the firm's performance in addition to or in conjunction with external environmental influences.[84]

Strategic Focus TECHNOLOGY

## The Airlines Industry Exemplifies the I/O Model Imitation and Poor Performance

The airline industry is a living example of the I/O model. For many years, the airline industry was highly regulated, which resulted in most airlines acting like each other by definition. However, the similarities among the large airline companies remained after the industry was partially deregulated more than 30 years ago. These similarities in services, routes and performance have persisted even to the present time. For example, airlines often offer a new service (e.g., Wi-Fi availability on flights) but these services are easily imitated; therefore, any differentiation in offerings is only temporary.

In recent times, consolidation has occurred in both the European and U.S. airline industries. In particular, poor performance led US Airways and America West to merge. Additionally, much for the same reasons, Northwest Airlines and Delta merged. More recently, United and Continental merged to create the largest airline in the industry. Finally, American Airlines and US Air have announced that they plan to merge. All of these mergers have not created highly differentiated services (or prices). All of them largely provide the same type of services and prices do not differ greatly among the large "full-service" carriers. In fact, it seems that the primary competition is in trying to make fewer mistakes. Positive industry reports focus on reductions in lost bags, fewer cancellations of flights, and fewer delays. What this suggests is that all of these areas still represent a major problem. It looks pretty bad when the most positive statement one can make is that lately fewer bags have been lost.

*A passenger using WiFi on a plane. Innovations in the airline industry that create differentiation are often easily copied by rivals.*

Obviously, there are differences between airlines across time. United, the largest airline, which was created to provide more financial efficiencies and to offer greater travel options to customers, has had significant problems making the merger of the two systems work effectively. In fact, it announced a major net loss for 2012 because of these problems. In November 2012, a computer malfunction (software problem) caused the delay of 250 of United's flights globally for almost two hours. Its reservation system failed twice during 2012, which shut down its Web site and stranded passengers as flights were then delayed or cancelled. United's on-time performance suffered and was one of the worst in the industry for 2012. The number of customer complaints for United was much higher than in the past. In short, it is relatively easy to determine why the airline suffered a serious net loss in 2012. Yet Delta, which performed very poorly a few years earlier, performed better in 2012. It made a net profit for the third year in a row. Its on-time performance was about 10 percentage points higher than United's. While United is eliminating flights and furloughing employees to cuts costs (trying to make a profit), in 2012 Delta purchased a 49 percent share of Virgin Atlantic to gain access to the highly valuable New York–London routes and gates in both locations. Delta was also one of the first airlines to introduce Wi-Fi to passengers during flights.

Certainly, some reduced-service airlines, such as Southwest Airlines, have fared much better in most of these categories (e.g., profits, on-time flights, customer complaints). Interestingly, while it started as a low-price airline (and maintained that feature over time), it also has generally offered superior service compared to the full-service airlines. The large airlines tried but were unable to imitate Southwest Airlines. In effect, Southwest developed its resources and capabilities over time, allowing it to provide service much more effectively and at a lower price than its full-service rivals.

Sources: 2013, Anatomy of 99.5%, Delta Airlines Web site, http://blog.delta.com, February 15; S. McCartney, 2013, Believe it or not, flying is improving, *Wall Street Journal*, www.wsj.com, January 9; J. Freed, 2012, Delta grabs bigger share of key NY-London route, *Bloomberg Businessweek*, www.businessweek.com, December 11; D. Benoit, 2012, Delta lands London space with Virgin joint venture, *Wall Street Journal*, http://blogs.wsj.com/deals, December 11; J. Mouawad, 2012, For United, big problems at biggest airline, *New York Times*, www.nytimes.com, November 28; C. Negroni, 2012, Good airlines news: Losing fewer bags, *New York Times*, www.nytimes.com, August 6.

These findings suggest that the external environment and a firm's resources, capabilities, core competencies, and competitive advantages (see Chapter 3) influence the company's ability to achieve strategic competitiveness and earn above-average returns.

The Strategic Focus explains how most of the firms in the airline industry are similar in services offered and in performance. They largely imitate each other and have performed poorly over the years. The few airlines which have not followed in the mode of trying to imitate others, such as Southwest Airlines, have developed unique and valuable resources and capabilities on which they have relied to provide a superior product (better service at a lower price) than major rivals.

As shown in Figure 1.2, the I/O model assumes that a firm's strategy is a set of commitments and actions flowing from the characteristics of the industry in which the firm has decided to compete. The resource-based model, discussed next, takes a different view of the major influences on a firm's choice of strategy.

Strategy Right NOW

Learn about the merger of American Airlines and US Airways.
www.cengagebrain .com

## 1-3 The Resource-Based Model of Above-Average Returns

The resource-based model assumes that each organization is a collection of unique resources and capabilities. The *uniqueness* of its resources and capabilities is the basis of a firm's strategy and its ability to earn above-average returns.[85]

**Resources** are inputs into a firm's production process, such as capital equipment, the skills of individual employees, patents, finances, and talented managers. In general, a firm's resources are classified into three categories: physical, human, and organizational capital. Described fully in Chapter 3, resources are either tangible or intangible in nature.

Individual resources alone may not yield a competitive advantage.[86] In fact, resources have a greater likelihood of being a source of competitive advantage when they are formed into a capability. A **capability** is the capacity for a set of resources to perform a task or an activity in an integrative manner. Capabilities evolve over time and must be managed dynamically in pursuit of above-average returns.[87] **Core competencies** are resources and capabilities that serve as a source of competitive advantage for a firm over its rivals. Core competencies are often visible in the form of organizational functions. For example, Apple's R&D function is one of its core competencies, as its ability to produce innovative new products that are perceived as valuable in the marketplace is a critical reason for Apple's success.

According to the resource-based model, differences in firms' performances across time are due primarily to their unique resources and capabilities rather than the industry's structural characteristics. This model also assumes that firms acquire different resources and develop unique capabilities based on how they combine and use the resources; that resources and certainly capabilities are not highly mobile across firms; and that the differences in resources and capabilities are the basis of competitive advantage.[88] Through continued use, capabilities become stronger and more difficult for competitors to understand and imitate. As a source of competitive advantage, a capability must not be easily imitated but also not too complex to understand and manage.[89]

The resource-based model of superior returns is shown in Figure 1.3. This model suggests that the strategy the firm chooses should allow it to use its competitive advantages in an attractive industry (the I/O model is used to identify an attractive industry).

Not all of a firm's resources and capabilities have the potential to be the foundation for a competitive advantage. This potential is realized when resources and capabilities are valuable, rare, costly to imitate, and nonsubstitutable.[90] Resources are *valuable* when they allow a firm to take advantage of opportunities or neutralize threats in its external environment. They are *rare* when possessed by few, if any, current and potential competitors.

**Resources** are inputs into a firm's production process, such as capital equipment, the skills of individual employees, patents, finances, and talented managers.

A **Capability** is the capacity for a set of resources to perform a task or an activity in an integrative manner.

**Core competencies** are capabilities that serve as a source of competitive advantage for a firm over its rivals.

**Figure 1.3** The Resource-Based Model of Above-Average Returns

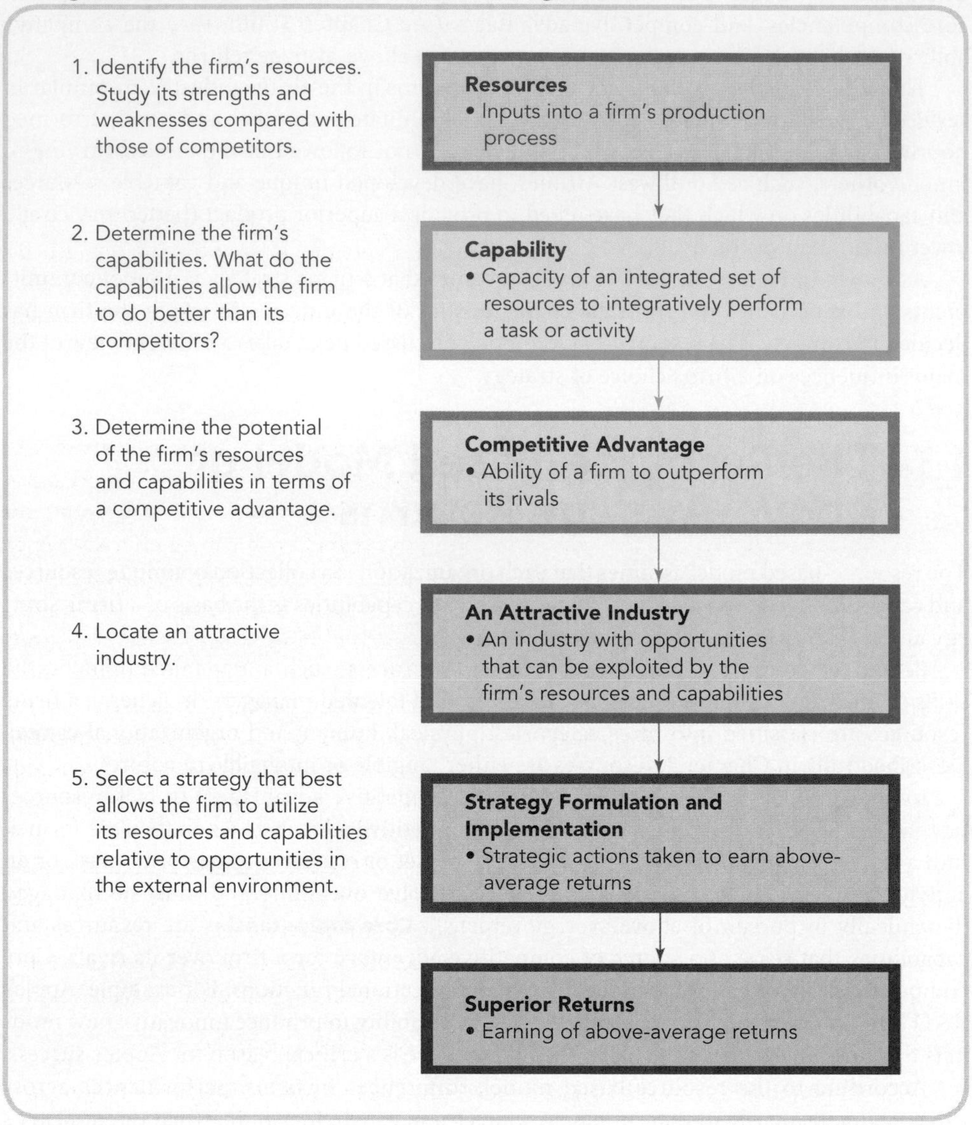

| | |
|---|---|
| 1. Identify the firm's resources. Study its strengths and weaknesses compared with those of competitors. | **Resources** • Inputs into a firm's production process |
| 2. Determine the firm's capabilities. What do the capabilities allow the firm to do better than its competitors? | **Capability** • Capacity of an integrated set of resources to integratively perform a task or activity |
| 3. Determine the potential of the firm's resources and capabilities in terms of a competitive advantage. | **Competitive Advantage** • Ability of a firm to outperform its rivals |
| 4. Locate an attractive industry. | **An Attractive Industry** • An industry with opportunities that can be exploited by the firm's resources and capabilities |
| 5. Select a strategy that best allows the firm to utilize its resources and capabilities relative to opportunities in the external environment. | **Strategy Formulation and Implementation** • Strategic actions taken to earn above-average returns |
| | **Superior Returns** • Earning of above-average returns |



Resources are *costly to imitate* when other firms either cannot obtain them or are at a cost disadvantage in obtaining them compared with the firm that already possesses them. And they are *nonsubstitutable* when they have no structural equivalents. Many resources can either be imitated or substituted over time. Therefore, it is difficult to achieve and sustain a competitive advantage based on resources alone.[91] Individual resources are often integrated to produce configurations in order to build capabilities. These capabilities are more likely to have these four attributes.[92] When these four criteria are met, however, resources and capabilities become core competencies.

As noted previously, research shows that both the industry environment and a firm's internal assets affect that firm's performance over time.[93] Thus, to form a vision and mission, and subsequently to select one or more strategies and determine how to implement them, firms use both the I/O and resource-based models.[94] In fact, these models complement each other in that one (I/O) focuses outside the firm while the other (resource-based) focuses inside the firm. Next, we discuss the formation of a firm's vision and mission—actions taken after the firm understands the realities of its external environment (Chapter 2) and internal organization (Chapter 3).

# 1-4 Vision and Mission

After studying the external environment and the internal organization, the firm has the information it needs to form its vision and a mission (see Figure 1.1). Stakeholders (those who affect or are affected by a firm's performance, as explained later in the chapter) learn a great deal about a firm by studying its vision and mission. Indeed, a key purpose of vision and mission statements is to inform stakeholders of what the firm is, what it seeks to accomplish, and who it seeks to serve.

## 1-4a Vision

**Vision** is a picture of what the firm wants to be and, in broad terms, what it wants to ultimately achieve.[95] Thus, a vision statement articulates the ideal description of an organization and gives shape to its intended future. In other words, a vision statement points the firm in the direction of where it would like to be in the years to come.[96] An effective vision stretches and challenges people as well. In her book about Steve Jobs, Apple's phenomenally successful CEO, Carmine Gallo argues that one of the reasons that Apple is so innovative was Jobs' vision for the company. She suggests that he thought bigger and differently than most people. To be innovative, she explains that one has to think differently about the firm's products and customers—"sell dreams not products"—and differently about the story to "create great expectations."[97] With Steve Jobs' death, Apple will be challenged to remain highly innovative. Interestingly, similar to Jobs, many new entrepreneurs are highly optimistic when they develop their ventures.[98] However, very few are able to develop and successfully implement a vision in the manner that Jobs did.

It is also important to recognize that vision statements reflect a firm's values and aspirations and are intended to capture the heart and mind of each employee and, hopefully, many of its other stakeholders. A firm's vision tends to be enduring while its mission can change with new environmental conditions. A vision statement tends to be relatively short and concise, making it easily remembered. Examples of vision statements include the following:

*Our vision is to be the world's best quick service restaurant. (McDonald's)*

*To make the automobile accessible to every American. (Ford Motor Company's vision when established by Henry Ford)*

As a firm's most important and prominent strategic leader, the CEO is responsible for working with others to form the firm's vision. Experience shows that the most effective vision statement results when the chief executive officer (CEO) involves a host of stakeholders (e.g., other top-level managers, employees working in different parts of the organization, suppliers, and customers) to develop it. In short, they need to develop a shared vision for it to be successful.[99] In addition, to help the firm reach its desired future state, a vision statement should be clearly tied to the conditions in the firm's external environment and internal organization. Moreover, the decisions and actions of those involved with developing the vision, especially the CEO and the other top-level managers, must be consistent with that vision.

## 1-4b Mission

The vision is the foundation for the firm's mission. A **mission** specifies the business or businesses in which the firm intends to compete and the customers it intends to serve.[100] The firm's mission is more concrete than its vision. However, similar to the vision,

**Vision** is a picture of what the firm wants to be and, in broad terms, what it wants to ultimately achieve.

A **mission** specifies the businesses in which the film intends to compete and the customers it intends to serve.

a mission should establish a firm's individuality and should be inspiring and relevant to all stakeholders.[101] Together, the vision and mission provide the foundation that the firm needs to choose and implement one or more strategies. The probability of forming an effective mission increases when employees have a strong sense of the ethical standards that guide their behaviors as they work to help the firm reach its vision.[102] Thus, business ethics are a vital part of the firm's discussions to decide what it wants to become (its vision) as well as who it intends to serve and how it desires to serve those individuals and groups (its mission).[103]

Even though the final responsibility for forming the firm's mission rests with the CEO, the CEO and other top-level managers often involve more people in developing the mission. The main reason is that the mission deals more directly with product markets and customers, and middle- and first-level managers and other employees have more direct contact with customers and the markets in which they are served. Examples of mission statements include the following:

*Be the best employer for our people in each community around the world and deliver operational excellence to our customers in each of our restaurants. (McDonald's)*

*Our mission is to be recognized by our customers as the leader in applications engineering. We always focus on the activities customers desire; we are highly motivated and strive to advance our technical knowledge in the areas of material, part design and fabrication technology. (LNP, a GE Plastics Company)*

McDonald's mission statement flows from its vision of being the world's best quick-service restaurant. LNP's mission statement describes the business areas (material, part design, and fabrication technology) in which the firm intends to compete.

Clearly, vision and mission statements that are poorly developed do not provide the direction a firm needs to take appropriate strategic actions. Still, as shown in Figure 1.1, a firm's vision and mission are critical aspects of the *analysis* and the base required to engage in *strategic actions* that help to achieve strategic competitiveness and earn above-average returns. Therefore, firms must accept the challenge of forming effective vision and mission statements.

## 1-5 Stakeholders

Every organization involves a system of primary stakeholder groups with whom it establishes and manages relationships.[104] **Stakeholders** are the individuals, groups, and organizations who can affect the firm's vision and mission, are affected by the strategic outcomes achieved, and have enforceable claims on the firm's performance.[105] Claims on a firm's performance are enforced through the stakeholders' ability to withhold participation essential to the organization's survival, competitiveness, and profitability.[106] Stakeholders continue to support an organization when its performance meets or exceeds their expectations.[107] Also, research suggests that firms that effectively manage stakeholder relationships outperform those that do not. Stakeholder relationships can therefore be managed to be a source of competitive advantage.[108]

**Stakeholders** are the individuals, groups, and organizations that can affect the firm's vision and mission, are affected by the strategic outcomes achieved, and have enforceable claims on the firm's performance.

Although organizations have dependency relationships with their stakeholders, they are not equally dependent on all stakeholders at all times; as a consequence, not every stakeholder has the same level of influence.[109] The more critical and valued a stakeholder's participation, the greater a firm's dependency on it. Greater dependence, in turn, gives the stakeholder more potential influence over a firm's commitments, decisions, and actions. Managers must find ways to either accommodate or insulate the organization from the demands of stakeholders controlling critical resources.[110]

## 1-5a Classifications of Stakeholders

The parties involved with a firm's operations can be separated into at least three groups.[111] As shown in Figure 1.4, these groups are the capital market stakeholders (shareholders and the major suppliers of a firm's capital), the product market stakeholders (the firm's primary customers, suppliers, host communities, and unions representing the workforce), and the organizational stakeholders (all of a firm's employees, including both nonmanagerial and managerial personnel).

Each stakeholder group expects those making strategic decisions in a firm to provide the leadership through which its valued objectives will be reached.[112] The objectives of the various stakeholder groups often differ from one another, sometimes placing those involved with a firm's strategic management process in situations where trade-offs have to be made. The most obvious stakeholders, at least in U.S. organizations, are *shareholders*—individuals and groups who have invested capital in a firm in the expectation of earning a positive return on their investments. These stakeholders' rights are grounded in laws governing private property and private enterprise.

In contrast to shareholders, another group of stakeholders—the firm's customers—prefers that investors receive a minimum return on their investments. Customers could have their interests maximized when the quality and reliability of a firm's products are improved, but without high prices. High returns to customers, therefore, might come at the expense of lower returns for capital market stakeholders.

Because of potential conflicts, each firm must carefully manage its stakeholders. First, a firm must thoroughly identify and understand all important stakeholders. Second, it must prioritize them in case it cannot satisfy all of them. Power is the most critical criterion in

**Figure 1.4** The Three Stakeholder Groups

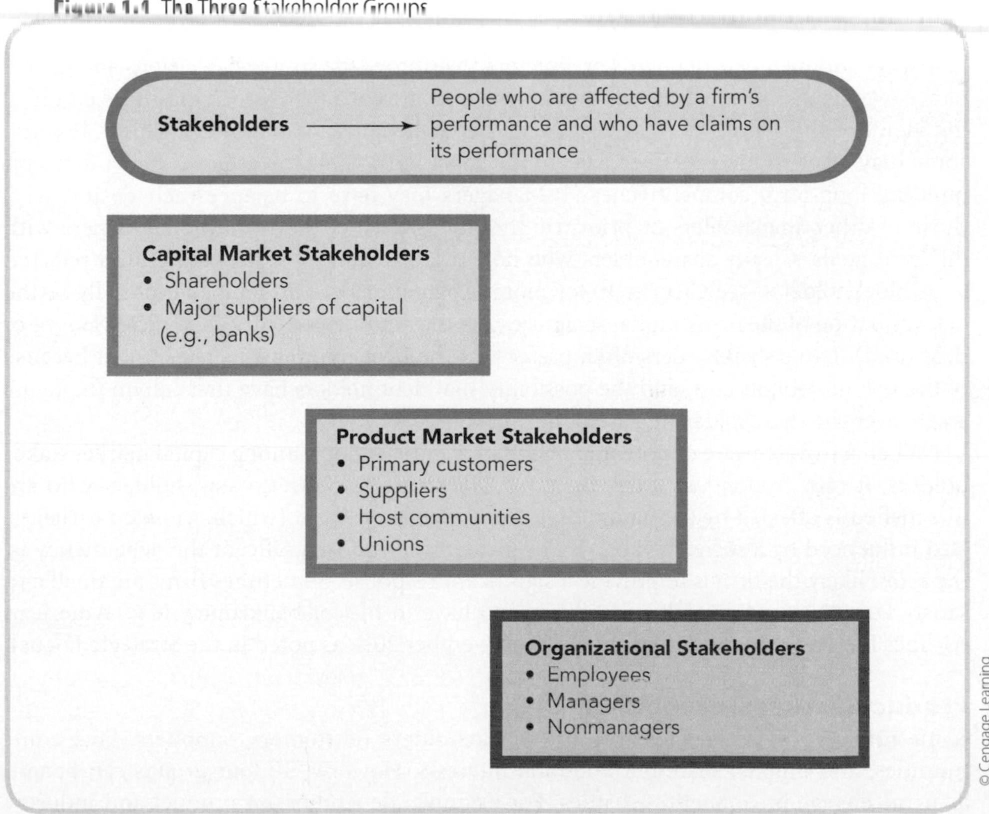

prioritizing stakeholders. Other criteria might include the urgency of satisfying each particular stakeholder group and the degree of importance of each to the firm.[113]

When the firm earns above-average returns, the challenge of effectively managing stakeholder relationships is lessened substantially. With the capability and flexibility provided by above-average returns, a firm can more easily satisfy multiple stakeholders simultaneously. When the firm earns only average returns, it is unable to maximize the interests of all stakeholders. The objective then becomes one of at least minimally satisfying each stakeholder.

Trade-off decisions are made in light of how important the support of each stakeholder group is to the firm. For example, environmental groups may be very important to firms in the energy industry but less important to professional service firms.[114] A firm earning below-average returns does not have the capacity to minimally satisfy all stakeholders. The managerial challenge in this case is to make trade-offs that minimize the amount of support lost from stakeholders. Societal values also influence the general weightings allocated among the three stakeholder groups shown in Figure 1.4. Although all three groups are served by and, in turn, influence firms in the major industrialized nations, the priorities in their service and influence vary because of cultural and institutional differences. Next, we present additional details about each of the three major stakeholder groups.

## Capital Market Stakeholders

Shareholders and lenders both expect a firm to preserve and enhance the wealth they have entrusted to it. The returns they expect are commensurate with the degree of risk they accept with those investments (i.e., lower returns are expected with low-risk investments while higher returns are expected with high-risk investments). Dissatisfied lenders may impose stricter covenants on subsequent borrowing of capital. Dissatisfied shareholders may reflect their concerns through several means, including selling their stock. Institutional investors (e.g., pension funds, mutual funds) often are willing to sell their stock if the returns are not what they desire, or take actions to improve the firm's performance such as pressuring top managers and members of boards of directors to improve the strategic decisions and governance oversight. Some institutions owning major shares of a firm's stock may have conflicting views of the actions needed, which can be challenging for managers. This is because some may want an increase in returns in the short term while the others desire a focus on building long-term competitiveness.[115] Managers may have to balance their desires with those of other shareholders or prioritize the importance of the institutional owners with different goals. Clearly shareholders who hold a large share of stock (sometimes referred to as blockholders—see Chapter 10 for more explanation) are influential, especially in the determination of the firm's capital structure (i.e., the amount of equity versus the amount of debt used). Large shareholders often prefer that the firm minimize its use of debt because of the risk of debt, its cost, and the possibility that debt holders have first call on the firm's assets over the shareholders in case of default.[116]

When a firm is aware of potential or actual dissatisfactions among capital market stakeholders, it may respond to their concerns. The firm's response to stakeholders who are dissatisfied is affected by the nature of its dependence on them (which, as noted earlier, is also influenced by a society's values). The greater and more significant the dependency is, the more likely the firm is to provide a significant response. Sometimes firms are unable to satisfy key stakeholders such as creditors and have to file for bankruptcy (e.g., American Airlines filed for Chapter 11 bankruptcy in November 2011, as noted in the Strategic Focus).

## Product Market Stakeholders

Some might think that product market stakeholders (customers, suppliers, host communities, and unions) share few common interests. However, all four groups can benefit as firms engage in competitive battles. For example, depending on product and industry characteristics, marketplace competition may result in lower product prices being charged to a firm's customers and higher prices being paid to its suppliers (the firm might be willing to pay higher supplier prices to ensure delivery of the types of goods and services that are linked with its competitive success).[117]

Customers, as stakeholders, demand reliable products at the lowest possible prices. Suppliers seek loyal customers who are willing to pay the highest sustainable prices for the goods and services they receive. Although all product market stakeholders are important, without customers, the other product market stakeholders are of little value. Therefore, the firm must try to learn about and understand current and potential customers.[118]

Host communities are represented by national (home and abroad), state/province, and local government entities with which the firm must deal. Governments want companies willing to be long-term employers and providers of tax revenue without placing excessive demands on public support services. These stakeholders also influence the firm through laws and regulations. In fact, firms must deal with laws and regulations developed and enforced at the national, state, and local levels (the influence is polycentric—multiple levels of power and influence).[119]

Union officials are interested in secure jobs, under highly desirable working conditions, for employees they represent. Thus, product market stakeholders are generally satisfied when a firm's profit margin reflects at least a balance between the returns to capital market stakeholders (i.e., the returns lenders and shareholders will accept and still retain their interests in the firm) and the returns in which they share.

### Organizational Stakeholders

Employees—the firm's organizational stakeholders—expect the firm to provide a dynamic, stimulating, and rewarding work environment. Employees generally prefer to work for a company that is growing and actively developing their skills, especially those skills required to be effective team members and to meet or exceed global work standards. Workers who learn how to use new knowledge productively are critical to organizational success. In a collective sense, the education and skills of a firm's workforce are competitive weapons affecting strategy implementation and firm performance.[120] Strategic leaders are ultimately responsible for serving the needs of organizational stakeholders on a day-to-day basis. In fact, to be successful, strategic leaders must effectively use the firm's human capital.[121] The importance of human capital to their success is likely why outside directors are more likely to propose layoffs compared to inside strategic leaders, while such insiders are likely to use preventative cost-cutting measures and seek to protect incumbent employees.[122] A highly important means of building employee skills for the global competitive landscape is through international assignments. The process of managing expatriate employees and helping them build knowledge can have significant effects over time on the firm's ability to compete in global markets.[123]

## 1-6 Strategic Leaders

**Strategic leaders** are people located in different areas and levels of the firm using the strategic management process to select strategic actions that help the firm achieve its vision and fulfill its mission. Regardless of their location in the firm, successful strategic leaders are decisive, committed to nurturing those around them, and committed to helping the firm create value for all stakeholder groups.[124] In this vein, research evidence suggests that employees who perceive that their CEO is a visionary leader also believe that the CEO leads the firm to operate in ways that are consistent with the values of all stakeholder groups rather than emphasizing only maximizing profits for shareholders. In turn, visionary leadership motivates employees to expend extra effort, thereby helping to increase firm performance.

**Strategic leaders** are people located in different areas and levels of the firm using the strategic management process to select strategic actions that help the firm achieve its vision and fulfill its mission.

*Strategic leaders shape the organization's culture. Culture affects how work gets done and people interact with each other.*

When identifying strategic leaders, most of us tend to think of CEOs and other top-level managers. Clearly, these people are strategic leaders. In the final analysis, CEOs are responsible for making certain their firm effectively uses the strategic management process. Indeed, the pressure on CEOs to manage strategically is stronger than ever.[125] However, many other people help choose a firm's strategy and then determine the actions for successfully implementing it.[126] The main reason is that the realities of twenty-first-century competition that we discussed earlier in this chapter (e.g., the global economy, globalization, rapid technological change, and the increasing importance of knowledge and people as sources of competitive advantage) are creating a need for those "closest to the action" to be making decisions and determining the actions to be taken. In fact, all managers (as strategic leaders) must think globally and act locally.[127] Thus, the most effective CEOs and top-level managers understand how to delegate strategic responsibilities to people throughout the firm who influence the use of organizational resources. Delegation also helps to avoid too much managerial hubris at the top and the problems it causes, especially in situations allowing significant managerial discretion.[128]

Organizational culture also affects strategic leaders and their work. In turn, strategic leaders' decisions and actions shape a firm's culture. **Organizational culture** refers to the complex set of ideologies, symbols, and core values that are shared throughout the firm and that influence how the firm conducts business. It is the social energy that drives—or fails to drive—the organization.[129] For example, Southwest Airlines is known for having a unique and valuable culture. Its culture encourages employees to work hard but also to have fun while doing so. Moreover, its culture entails respect for others—employees and customers alike. The firm also places a premium on service, as suggested by its commitment to provide POS (Positively Outrageous Service) to each customer.

## 1-6a The Work of Effective Strategic Leaders

Perhaps not surprisingly, hard work, thorough analyses, a willingness to be brutally honest, a penchant for wanting the firm and its people to accomplish more, and tenacity are prerequisites to an individual's success as a strategic leader. The top strategic leaders are chosen on the basis of their capabilities (their accumulation of human capital over time). Potent top management teams (human capital, management skills, and cognitive abilities) make better strategic decisions.[130] In addition, strategic leaders must have a strong strategic orientation while simultaneously embracing change in the dynamic competitive landscape we have discussed.[131] In order to deal with this change effectively, strategic leaders must be innovative thinkers and promote innovation in their organization.[132] Promoting innovation is facilitated by a diverse top management team representing different types of expertise and leveraging relationships with external parties.[133] Strategic leaders can best leverage partnerships with external parties and organizations when their organizations are ambidextrous. That is, the organizations simultaneously promote exploratory learning of new and unique forms of knowledge and exploitative learning that adds incremental knowledge to existing knowledge bases, allowing them to better understand and use their existing products.[134] In addition, strategic leaders need to have a global mind-set, or what some refer to as an ambicultural approach to management.[135]

**Organizational culture** refers to the complex set of ideologies, symbols, and core values that are shared throughout the firm and that influence how the firm conducts business.

Strategic leaders, regardless of their location in the organization, often work long hours, and their work is filled with ambiguous decision situations. However, the opportunities afforded by this work are appealing and offer exciting chances to dream and to act. The following words, given as advice to the late Time Warner chair and co-CEO Steven J. Ross by his father, describe the opportunities in a strategic leader's work:

*There are three categories of people—the person who goes into the office, puts his feet up on his desk, and dreams for 12 hours; the person who arrives at 5 A.M. and works for 16 hours, never once stopping to dream; and the person who puts his feet up, dreams for one hour, then does something about those dreams.*[136]

The operational term used for a dream that challenges and energizes a company is vision. The most effective strategic leaders provide a vision as the foundation for the firm's mission and subsequent choice and use of one or more strategies.

## 1-6b Predicting Outcomes of Strategic Decisions: Profit Pools

Strategic leaders attempt to predict the outcomes of their decisions before taking efforts to implement them, which is difficult to do. Many decisions that are a part of the strategic management process are concerned with an uncertain future and the firm's place in that future. As such, managers try to predict the effects on the firm's profits of strategic decisions that they are considering.[137]

Mapping an industry's profit pool is something strategic leaders can do to anticipate the possible outcomes of different decisions and to focus on growth in profits rather than strictly growth in revenues. A **profit pool** entails the total profits earned in an industry at all points along the value chain.[138] (We explain the value chain in Chapter 3 and discuss it further in Chapter 4.) Analyzing the profit pool in the industry may help a firm see something others are unable to see and to understand the primary sources of profits in an industry. There are four steps to identifying profit pools: (1) define the pool's boundaries, (2) estimate the pool's overall size, (3) estimate the size of the value-chain activity in the pool, and (4) reconcile the calculations.[139]

A **profit pool** entails the total profits earned in an industry at all points along the value chain.

For example, McDonald's might desire to map the quick-service restaurant industry's profit pools. First, McDonald's would need to define the industry's boundaries and, second, estimate its size (which is large because McDonald's operates in markets across the globe, as noted in the Opening Case). The net result of this is that McDonald's tries to take market share away from competitors such as Burger King and Wendy's, and growth is more likely in international markets. Armed with information about its industry, McDonald's could then estimate the amount of profit potential in each part of the value chain (step 3). In the quick-service restaurant industry, marketing campaigns and customer service are likely more important sources of potential profits than are inbound logistics' activities (see Chapter 3). With an understanding of where the greatest amount of profits are likely to be earned, McDonald's would then be ready to select the strategy to use to be successful where the largest profit pools are located in the value chain.[140] As this brief discussion shows, profit pools are a

McDonald's customer service gives it an advantage over its rivals.

Justin Sullivan/Getty Images

potentially useful tool to help strategic leaders recognize the actions to take to increase the likelihood of increasing profits. Of course, profits made by a firm and in an industry can be partially interdependent on the profits earned in adjacent industries.[141] For example, profits earned in the energy industry can affect profits in other industries (e.g., airlines). When oil prices are high, it can reduce the profits earned in industries that must use a lot of energy to provide their goods or services.

## 1-7 The Strategic Management Process

As suggested by Figure 1.1, the strategic management process is a rational approach firms use to achieve strategic competitiveness and earn above-average returns. Figure 1.1 also features the topics we examine in this book to present the strategic management process to you.

This book is divided into three parts aligned with the A-S-P process explained in the beginning of the chapter. In Part 1, we describe the *analyses* (A) necessary for developing strategies. Specifically, we explain what firms do to analyze their external environment (Chapter 2) and internal organization (Chapter 3). These analyses are completed to identify marketplace opportunities and threats in the external environment (Chapter 2) and to decide how to use the resources, capabilities, core competencies, and competitive advantages in the firm's internal organization to pursue opportunities and overcome threats (Chapter 3). The analyses explained in Chapters 2 and 3 are the well-known SWOT analyses (strengths, weaknesses, opportunities, threats).[142] With knowledge about its external environment and internal organization, the firm formulates its strategy taking into account the firm's vision and mission.

The firm's analyses (see Figure 1.1) provide the foundation for choosing one or more *strategies* (S) and deciding how to implement them. As suggested in Figure 1.1 by the horizontal arrow linking the two types of strategic actions, formulation and implementation must be simultaneously integrated for a successful strategic management process. Integration occurs as decision makers think about implementation issues when choosing strategies and as they think about possible changes to the firm's strategies while implementing a current strategy.

In Part 2 of this book, we discuss the different strategies firms may choose to use. First, we examine business-level strategies (Chapter 4). A business-level strategy describes the actions a firm takes to exploit its competitive advantage over rivals. A company competing in a single product market (e.g., a locally owned grocery store operating in only one location) has but one business-level strategy while a diversified firm competing in multiple product markets (e.g., General Electric) forms a business-level strategy for each of its businesses. In Chapter 5, we describe the actions and reactions that occur among firms in marketplace competition. Competitors typically respond to and try to anticipate each other's actions. The dynamics of competition affect the strategies firms choose as well as how they try to implement the chosen strategies.[143]

For the diversified firm, corporate-level strategy (Chapter 6) is concerned with determining the businesses in which the company intends to compete as well as how to manage its different businesses. Other topics vital to strategy formulation, particularly in the diversified company, include acquiring other businesses and, as appropriate, restructuring the firm's portfolio of businesses (Chapter 7) and selecting an international strategy (Chapter 8). With cooperative strategies (Chapter 9), firms form a partnership to share their resources and capabilities in order to develop a competitive advantage. Cooperative strategies are becoming increasingly important as firms seek ways to compete in the global economy's array of different markets.[144]

To examine actions taken to implement strategies, we consider several topics in Part 3 of the book. First, we examine the different mechanisms used to govern firms (Chapter 10).

With demands for improved corporate governance being voiced by many stakeholders in the current business environment, organizations are challenged to learn how to simultaneously satisfy their stakeholders' different interests.[145] Finally, the organizational structure and actions needed to control a firm's operations (Chapter 11), the patterns of strategic leadership appropriate for today's firms and competitive environments (Chapter 12), and strategic entrepreneurship (Chapter 13) as a path to continuous innovation are addressed.

It is important to emphasize that primarily because they are related to how a firm interacts with its stakeholders, almost all strategic management process decisions have ethical dimensions.[146] Organizational ethics are revealed by an organization's culture; that is to say, a firm's decisions are a product of the core values that are shared by most or all of a company's managers and employees. Especially in the turbulent and often ambiguous competitive landscape in the global economy, those making decisions as a part of the strategic management process must understand how their decisions affect capital market, product market, and organizational stakeholders differently and regularly evaluate the ethical implications of their decisions.[147] Decision makers failing to recognize these realities accept the risk of placing their firm at a competitive disadvantage.[148]

As you will discover, the strategic management process examined in this book calls for disciplined approaches to serve as the foundation for developing a competitive advantage. Therefore, it has a major effect on the *performance* (P) of the firm.[149] Performance is reflected in the firm's ability to achieve strategic competitiveness and earn above-average returns. Mastery of this strategic management process will effectively serve you, our readers, and the organizations for which you will choose to work.

## SUMMARY

- Firms use the strategic management process to achieve strategic competitiveness and earn above-average returns. Firms *analyze* the external environment and their internal organization, then formulate and implement a *strategy* to achieve a desired level of *performance* (A-S-P). Performance is reflected by the firm's level of strategic competitiveness and the extent to which it earns above-average returns. Strategic competitiveness is achieved when a firm develops and implements a value-creating strategy. Above-average returns (in excess of what investors expect to earn from other investments with similar levels of risk) provide the foundation needed to simultaneously satisfy all of a firm's stakeholders.

- The fundamental nature of competition is different in the current competitive landscape. As a result, those making strategic decisions must adopt a different mind-set, one that allows them to learn how to compete in highly turbulent and chaotic environments that produce a great deal of uncertainty. The globalization of industries and their markets and rapid and significant technological changes are the two primary factors contributing to the turbulence of the competitive landscape.

- Firms use two major models to help develop their vision and mission and then choose one or more strategies in pursuit of strategic competitiveness and above-average returns. The core assumption of the I/O model is that the firm's external environment has a large influence on the choice of strategies more than do the firm's internal resources, capabilities, and core competencies. Thus, the I/O model is used to understand the effects an industry's characteristics can have on a firm when deciding what strategy or strategies to use in competing against rivals. The logic supporting the I/O model suggests that above-average returns are earned when the firm locates an attractive industry or part of an industry and successfully implements the strategy dictated by that industry's characteristics. The core assumption of the resource-based model is that the firm's unique resources, capabilities, and core competencies have more of an influence on selecting and using strategies than does the firm's external environment. Above-average returns are earned when the firm uses its valuable, rare, costly-to-imitate, and nonsubstitutable resources and capabilities to compete against its rivals in one or more industries. Evidence indicates that both models yield insights that are linked to successfully selecting and using strategies. Thus, firms want to use their unique resources, capabilities, and core competencies as the foundation to engage in one or more strategies that allow them to effectively compete against rivals in their industry.

- Vision and mission are formed to guide the selection of strategies based on the information from the analyses of the firm's internal organization and external environment. Vision is a picture of what the firm wants to be and, in broad terms, what it wants to ultimately achieve. Flowing from the vision, the mission specifies the business or businesses in which the firm intends to compete and the customers it intends to serve. Vision and mission provide direction to the firm and signal important descriptive information to stakeholders.

- Stakeholders are those who can affect, and are affected by, a firm's performance. Because a firm is dependent on the continuing support of stakeholders (shareholders, customers, suppliers, employees, host communities, etc.), they have enforceable claims on the company's performance. When earning above-average returns, a firm generally has the resources it needs to satisfy the interests of all stakeholders. However, when earning only average returns, the firm must carefully manage its stakeholders in order to retain their support. A firm earning below-average returns must minimize the amount of support it loses from unsatisfied stakeholders.
- Strategic leaders are people located in different areas and levels of the firm using the strategic management process to help the firm achieve its vision and fulfill its mission. In general, CEOs are responsible for making certain that their firms properly use the strategic management process. The effectiveness of the strategic management process is increased when it is grounded in ethical intentions and behaviors. The strategic leader's work demands decision trade-offs, often among attractive alternatives. It is important for all strategic leaders and especially the CEO and other members of the top-management team to conduct thorough analyses of conditions facing the firm, be brutally and consistently honest, and work jointly to select and implement the correct strategies.
- Strategic leaders predict the potential outcomes of their strategic decisions. To do this, they must first calculate profit pools in their industry (and adjacent industries as appropriate) that are linked to value chain activities. Predicting the potential outcomes of their strategic decisions reduces the likelihood of the firm formulating and implementing ineffective strategies.

## REVIEW QUESTIONS

1. What are strategic competitiveness, strategy, competitive advantage, above-average returns, and the strategic management process?
2. What are the characteristics of the current competitive landscape? What two factors are the primary drivers of this landscape?
3. According to the I/O model, what should a firm do to earn above-average returns?
4. What does the resource-based model suggest a firm should do to earn above-average returns?
5. What are vision and mission? What is their value for the strategic management process?
6. What are stakeholders? How do the three primary stakeholder groups influence organizations?
7. How would you describe the work of strategic leaders?
8. What are the elements of the strategic management process? How are they interrelated?

## EXPERIENTIAL EXERCISES

### EXERCISE 1: STAKEHOLDER ANALYSIS, STRATEGIC PLANNING, AND STRATEGIC LEADERSHIP

Every organization relies on its own unique bundle of organizational stakeholders. Each one of the relationships between the organization and its stakeholders is influential in its ability to serve its mission and achieve above-average profits in the for-profit sector, or to create value in the not-for-profit sector. However, there are many ways that stakeholder management differs between the for-profit and not-for-profit worlds. It is easy to think of a for-profit firm that has product market stakeholders, such as customers, who can add or subtract their support by their decision of whether or not to purchase the firm's products or services. But who is the customer for a not-for-profit, and are the categories of product, market, organization, and capital market stakeholders very different from the for-profit arena? This exercise challenges you to uncover some of the more influential ways in which this is so.

#### Part One

In this exercise, you will be working in teams of approximately four students per team.

1. Decide which not-for-profit organization you wish to analyze. If you would like assistance in identifying a not-for-profit organization, a good Web source is the IRS. You may search for charities at http://www.irs.gov/app/pub-78/.

2. Determine two or three key strategic initiatives of this not-for-profit organization. Most not-for-profits, particularly well-known ones, are good about posting their strategic plans on their Web sites.
3. Now perform a macro environmental analysis, and list all known or expected stakeholders for the organization. You should place them in the context of product, market, and organizational stakeholders.

### Part Two

Now you are ready to start thinking critically about the organization and the challenges it faces among its stakeholders as it attempts to roll out its strategic initiatives.

1. For each strategic initiative that the organization has announced, analyze each stakeholder for the organization, and list areas in which the proposed strategy is likely to be supported, or not, by that particular stakeholder.
2. For the purpose of presenting to the class, organize your list so as to be able to present those strategies upon which expected support is likely to be gained and those strategies upon which support is likely to be discouraged.
3. Present to the class your recommendation for how the organization should proceed. For instance, if perceived support is critical to the successful strategic initiative but the strategy is likely to be viewed negatively by the stakeholder, provide some potential actions that the organization might take to mitigate the negative reaction or, alternatively, that might gain the stakeholders' support.

Conflicts are normal among organizational stakeholders, and deciding which must be attended to and at which time for which strategic action is a critical strategic leadership activity for every firm.

## EXERCISE 2: PUTTING ABOVE AVERAGE RETURNS TO THE I/O MODEL TEST

For some time, the Industrial Organization (I/O) model of above-average returns has adopted as principal that the primary source of above average returns rested with the industry in which a firm competed. However, the strength of this model has been brought into question with the rise of rapid technological and business model innovation. Additionally the link between leadership effectiveness and the I/O model seems incomplete.

Working in teams, pick one firm from the *Fortune* 500 "Top Companies: Most Profitable Firm" annually published in CNNMoney (http://money.cnn.com/). Pick a firm you find of interest that represents as close as possible a single industry (i.e., automobiles, oil and gas, telecommunications) and avoid conglomerates (i.e., General Electric).

Following your text descriptions of the I/O model, identify:

1. Identify the external environment pressures and constraints.
2. List the similar strategically and relevant resources available to other firms competing in the industry.
3. What resources are highly mobile across firms and think through those that you believe will be short-lived.
4. Identify the strategies of your most profitable firm in the industry and decide if each of these are signals that management is committed to acting in the firm's best interests as shown by their profit-maximizing behavior.

Be prepared to present in class your findings. Pay particular attention to performance of closely related competitors. Does the I/O model explain well the firm's above average returns?

# VIDEO CASE

## BRAZIL: AN EMERGING ECONOMY WITH STRATEGIC COMPETITIVENESS

Brazil had the lowest GDP growth rate among BRICS countries (Brazil, Russia, India, China and South Africa) in 2012, according to by the Organization for Economic Cooperation and Development (OECD). The OECD said Brazil's economy grew by only 1.3 percent. A country rich in natural resources and sophisticated in hydropower and biofuels, Brazil has emerged with strategic competitiveness. Being one of the greenest economies, Brazil is one of the largest producers of iron ore and one of the leading exporters of many popular commodities. After surviving historic financial collapse, Brazil has risen to have a strong manufacturing base, and the country's poor now have more purchasing power. (Please note that Brazil's current president is Dilma Rousseff.)

Be prepared to discuss the following concepts and questions in class:

### Concepts

- Strategic competitiveness
- Strategy
- Hypercompetition
- Global economy
- Resources
- Capabilities
- Core competencies
- Stakeholders
- Strategic leaders

## Questions

1. How is Brazil a strategic competitor?
2. What is Brazil's strategy?
3. Is Brazil a hypercompetitor?
4. What impact does Brazil have on the global economy?
5. What resources, capabilities, and core competencies does Brazil have?
6. What are the stakeholders associated with Brazil's thriving economy? Explain their significance.

# NOTES


1. J. McGregor, 2009, Smart management for tough times, *Businessweek*, www.businessweek.com, March 12.
2. M. Wembridge, 2013, McDonald's goes native down under, *Financial Times*, www.ft.com, January 21.
3. K. Matzler, F. Bailom, M. Anschober, & S. Richardson, 2010, Sustaining corporate success: What drives the top performers? *Journal of Business Strategy*, 31(5): 4–13.
4. Chrysler, 2013, Wikipedia, http://en.wikipedia.org, accessed on March 8; D. Kiley, 2009, Ford heats out on a road of its own, *Businessweek*, January 19, 47–49.
5. C. Sialas & V. P. Economou, 2013, Revisiting the concept of competitive advantage, *Journal of Strategy and Management*, 6: 61–80; D. G. Sirmon, M. A. Hitt, R. D. Ireland, & B. A. Gilbert, 2011. Resource orchestration to create competitive advantage: Breadth, depth and life cycle effects, *Journal of Management*, 37: 1390–1412; D. G. Sirmon, M. A. Hitt, & R. D. Ireland, 2007, Managing firm resources in dynamic environments to create value: Looking inside the black box, *Academy of Management Review*, 32: 273–292.
6. R. D'Aveni, G. B. Dagnino, & K. G. Smith, 2010, The age of temporary advantage, *Strategic Management Journal*, 31: 1371–1385; R. D. Ireland & J. W. Webb, 2009, Crossing the great divide of strategic entrepreneurship: Transitioning between exploration and exploitation, *Business Horizons*, 52(5): 469–479.
7. J. A. Lamberg, H. Tikkanen, T. Nokelainen, & H. Suur-Inkeroinen, 2009, Competitive dynamics, strategic consistency, and organizational survival, *Strategic Management Journal*, 30: 45–60; G. Pacheco-de-Almeida & P. Zemsky, 2007, The timing of resource development and sustainable competitive advantage, *Management Science*, 53: 651–666.
8. K. D. Miller, 2007, Risk and rationality in entrepreneurial processes, *Strategic Entrepreneurship Journal*, 1: 57–74.
9. R. M. Stulz, 2009, 6 ways companies mismanage risk, *Harvard Business Review*, 87(3): 86–94.
10. P. Steffens, P. Davidsson, & J. Fitzsimmons, 2009, Performance configurations over time: Implications for growth- and profit-oriented strategies, *Entrepreneurship Theory and Practice*, 33: 125–148.
11. E. Karniouchina, S. J. Carson, J. C. Short, & D. J. Ketchen, 2013, Extending the firm vs. industry debate: Does industry life cycle stage matter? *Strategic Management Journal*, in press; J. C. Short, A. McKelvie, D. J. Ketchen, Jr., & G. N. Chandler, 2009, Firm and industry effects on firm performance: A generalization and extension for new ventures, *Strategic Entrepreneurship Journal*, 3: 47–65.
12. D. G. Sirmon, M. A. Hitt, J.-L. Arregle, & J. T. Campbell, 2010, The dynamic interplay of capability strengths and weaknesses: Investigating the bases of temporary competitive advantage, *Strategic Management Journal*, 31: 1386–1409; A. M. McGahan & M. E. Porter, 2003, The emergence and sustainability of abnormal profits, *Strategic Organization*, 1: 79–108.
13. D. Ucbasaran, D. A. Shepherd, A. Lockett, & S. J. Lyon, 2013, Life after business failure: The process and consequences of business failure for entrepreneurs, *Journal of Management*, 39: 163–202.
14. Y. Zhang & J. Gimeno, 2010, Earnings pressure and competitive behavior: Evidence from the U.S. electronics industry, *Academy of Management Journal*, 53: 743–768; T. R. Crook, D. J. Ketchen, Jr., J. G. Combs, & S. Y. Todd, 2008, Strategic resources and performance: A meta-analysis, *Strategic Management Journal*, 29: 1141–1154.
15. A. J. Bock, T. Opsahl, G. George, & D. M. Gann, 2012, The effects of culture and structure on strategic flexibility during business model innovation, *Journal of Management Studies,* 49: 275–305; J. Barthelemy, 2008, Opportunism, knowledge, and the performance of franchise chains, *Strategic Management Journal*, 29: 1451–1463.
16. Bock, Opsahl, George, & Gann, The effects of culture and structure on strategic flexibility; J. Li, 2008, Asymmetric interactions between foreign and domestic banks: Effects on market entry, *Strategic Management Journal*, 29: 873–893.
17. R. G. Bell, I. Filatotchev, & A. A. Rasheed, 2012, The liability of foreignness in capital markets: Sources and remedies, *Journal of International Business Studies*, 43: 107–122; L. Nachum, 2010, When is foreignness an asset or a liability? Explaining the performance differential between foreign and local firms, *Journal of Management*, 36: 714–739.
18. J. H. Fisch, 2012, Information costs and internationalization performance, *Global Strategy Journal*, 2: 296–312.
19. Karniouchina, Carson, Short, & Ketchen, Extending the firm vs. industry debate; M. A. Delmas & M. W. Toffel, 2008, Organizational responses to environmental demands: Opening the black box, *Strategic Management Journal*, 29: 1027–1055.
20. J. Barney, D. J. Ketchen, & M. Wright, 2011, The future of resource-based theory: Revitalization or decline? *Journal of Management*, 37: 37: 1299–1315; T. R. Holcomb, R. M. Holmes, Jr., & B. L. Connelly, 2009, Making the most of what you have: Managerial ability as a source of resource value creation, *Strategic Management Journal*, 30: 457–485.
21. M. Statman, 2011, Calm investment behavior in turbulent investment times, in *What's Next 2011*, New York: McGraw-Hill Professional, E-Book; E. Thornton, 2009, The new rules, *Businessweek*, January 19, 30–34; T. Friedman, 2005, *The World is Flat: A Brief History of the 21st Century*, New York: Farrar, Strauss and Giroux.
22. D. Searcey, 2006, Beyond cable. Beyond DSL. *Wall Street Journal*, July 24, R9.
23. 2013, NBC Universal, Wikipedia, http://en.wikipedia.org/wiki/NBC Universal, accessed March 8.
24. B. Agypt & B. A. Rubin, 2012, Time in the new economy: The impact of the interaction of individual and structural temporalities and job satisfaction, *Journal of Management*, 49: 403–428; D. F. Kuratko & D. B. Audretsch, 2009, Strategic entrepreneurship: Exploring different perspectives of an emerging concept, *Entrepreneurship Theory and Practice*, 33: 1–17.

25. J. Hagel, III, J. S. Brown, & L. Davison, 2008, Shaping strategy in a world of constant disruption, *Harvard Business Review*, 86(10): 81–89; G. Probst & S. Raisch, 2005, Organizational crisis: The logic of failure, *Academy of Management Executive*, 19(1): 90–105.
26. D'Aveni, Dagnino, & Smith, The age of temporary advantage; A. V. Izosimov, 2008, Managing hypergrowth, *Harvard Business Review*, 86(4): 121–127; J. W. Selsky, J. Goes, & O. N. Babüroglu, 2007, Contrasting perspectives of strategy making: Applications in "Hyper" environments, *Organization Studies*, 28(1): 71–94.
27. D'Aveni, Dagnino, & Smith, The age of temporary advantage; R. A. D'Aveni, 1995, Coping with hyper-competition: Utilizing the new 7S's framework, *Academy of Management Executive*, 9(3): 46.
28. D'Aveni, Dagnino, & Smith, The age of temporary advantage.
29. D. J. Bryce & J. H. Dyer, 2007, Strategies to crack well-guarded markets, *Harvard Business Review* 85(5): 84–92.
30. S. H. Lee & M. Makhija, 2009, Flexibility in internationalization: Is it valuable during an economic crisis? *Strategic Management Journal*, 30: 537–555; S. J. Chang & S. Park, 2005, Types of firms generating network externalities and MNCs' co-location decisions, *Strategic Management Journal*, 26: 595–615.
31. Y. Luo & S. L. Wang, 2012, foreign direct investment strategies by developing country multinationals: A diagnostic model for home country effects, *Global Strategy Journal*, 2: 244–261; S. E. Feinberg & A. K. Gupta, 2009, MNC subsidiaries and country risk: Internalization as a safeguard against weak external institutions, *Academy of Management Journal*, 52: 381–399.
32. Y. Luo, 2007, From foreign investors to strategic insiders: Shifting parameters, prescriptions and paradigms for MNCs in China, *Journal of World Business*, 42(1): 14–34.
33. M. A. Hitt & X. He, 2008, Firm strategies in a changing global competitive landscape, *Business Horizons*, 51: 363–369; A. Ratanpal, 2008, Indian economy and Indian private equity, *Thunderbird International Business Review*, 50: 353–358.
34. J.-F. Hennart, 2012, Emerging market multinationals and the theory of the multinational enterprise, *Global Strategy Journal*, 2: 168–187; S. Malone, 2011, GE's Immelt sees new economic era for globe, *Financial Post*, www.financialpost.com, March 13.
35. R. M. Holmes, T. Miller, M. A. Hitt, & M. P. Salmador, 2013, The interrelationships among informal institutions, formal institutions, and inward foreign direct investment, *Journal of Management*, 39: 531–566; K. D. Brouthers, 2013, A retrospective on: Institutions, cultural and transaction cost influences on entry mode choice and performance, *Journal of International Business Studies*, 44: 14–22.
36. A. H. Kirca, G. T. Hult, S. Deligonul, M. Z. Perry, & S. T. Cavusgil, 2012, A multilevel examination of the drivers of firm multinationality: A meta-analysis, *Journal of Management*, 38: 502–530; A. Ciarione, P. Piselli, & G. Trebeschi, 2009, Emerging markets' spreads and global financial conditions, *Journal of International Financial Markets, Institutions and Money*, 19: 222–239.
37. Y.-Y. Chang, Y. Gong, & M. W. Peng, 2012, Expatriate knowledge transfer, subsidiary absorptive capacity, and subsidiary performance, *Academy of Management Journal*, 55: 927–948.
38. J. P. Quinlan, 2011, Speeding towards a messy, multi-polar world, in *What's Next 2011*, New York: McGraw-Hill Professional, E-Book.
39. B. Elango, 2009, Minimizing effects of "liability of foreignness": Response strategies of foreign firms in the United States, *Journal of World Business*, 44: 51–62; D. B. Fuller, 2010, How law, politics and transnational networks affect technology entrepreneurship: Explaining divergent venture capital investing strategies in China, *Asia Pacific Journal of Management*, 27: 445–459.
40. J. Mata & E. Freitas, 2012, Foreignness and exit over the life cycle of firms, *Journal of International Business Studies*, 43: 615–630.
41. M. A. Hitt, R. E. Hoskisson, & H. Kim, 1997, International diversification: Effects on innovation and firm performance in product-diversified firms, *Academy of Management Journal*, 40: 767–798.
42. Hennart, Emerging market multinationals.
43. R. Ramamurti, 2012, What is really different about emerging market multinationals? *Global Strategy Journal*, 2: 41–47.
44. M. Naim, 2013, Power outage, *Bloomberg Businessweek*, March 3: 4–5.
45. G. McDermott, R. Mudambi, & R. Parente, 2013, Strategic modularity and the architecture of the multinational firm, *Global Strategy Journal*, 3: 1–7.
46. R. D. Ireland & J. W. Webb, 2007, Strategic entrepreneurship: Creating competitive advantage through streams of innovation, *Business Horizons*, 50(1): 49–59; G. Hamel, 2001, Revolution vs. evolution: You need both, *Harvard Business Review*, 79(5): 150–156.
47. K. H. Hammonds, 2001, What is the state of the new economy? *Fast Company*, September, 101–104.
48. S. W. Bradley, J. S. McMullen, K. W. Artz, & E. M. Simiyu, 2012, Capital is not enough: Innovation in developing economies, *Journal of Management Studies*, 49: 684–717; D. Dunlap-Hinkler, M. Kotabe, & R. Mudambi, 2010, A story of breakthrough versus incremental innovation: Corporate entrepreneurship in the global pharmaceutical industry, *Strategic Entrepreneurship Journal*, 4: 106–127.
49. C. Beckman, K. Eisenhardt, S. Kotha, A. Meyer, & N. Rajagopalan, 2012, Technology entrepreneurship, *Strategic Entrepreneurship Journal*, 6: 89–93; K. Z. Zhou & F. Wu, 2010, Technological capability, strategic flexibility and product innovation, *Strategic Management Journal*, 31: 547–561.
50. J. Kao, 2009, Tapping the world's innovation hot spots, *Harvard Business Review*, 87(3): 109–117.
51. N. Furr, F. Cavarretta, & S. Garg, 2012, Who changes course? The role of domain knowledge and novel framing in making technological changes, *Strategic Entrepreneurship Journal*, 6: 236–256; L. Jiang, J. Tan, & M. Thursby, 2011, Incumbent firm invention in emerging fields: Evidence from the semiconductor industry, *Strategic Management Journal*, 32: 55–75.
52. R. Adner & R. Kapoor, 2010, Value creation in innovation ecosystems: How the structure of technological interdependence affects firm performance in new technology generations, *Strategic Management Journal*, 31: 306–333.
53. J. L. Funk, 2008, Components, systems and technological discontinuities: Lessons from the IT sector, *Long Range Planning*, 41: 555–573; C. M. Christensen, 1997, *The Innovator's Dilemma*, Boston: Harvard Business School Press.
54. A. Kaul, 2012, Technology and corporate scope: Firm and rival innovation as antecedents of corporate transactions, *Strategic Management Journal*, 33: 347–367; Dunlap-Hinkler, Kotabe, & Mudambi, A story of breakthrough versus incremental innovation.
55. C. M. Christensen, 2006, The ongoing process of building a theory of disruption, *Journal of Product Innovation Management*, 23(1): 39–55.
56. H. K. Steensma, M. Howard, M. Lyles, & C Dhanaraj, 2012, The compensatory relationship between technological relatedness, social interaction, and knowledge flow between firms, *Strategic Entrepreneurship Journal*, 6: 291–306; A. Phene, S. Tallman, & P. Almeida, 2012, When do acquisitions facilitate technological exploration and exploitation? *Journal of Management*, 38: 753–783; M. Makri, M. A. Hitt, & P. J. Lane, 2010, Complementary technologies, knowledge relatedness and invention outcomes in high technology mergers and acquisitions, *Strategic Management Journal*, 31: 602–628.
57. R. Kapoor & J. M. Lee, 2013, Coordinating and competing in ecosystems: How organizational forms shape new technology investments, *Strategic Management Journal*, 34: 274–296; J. Woolley, 2010, Technology emergence through entrepreneurship across multiple industries, *Strategic Entrepreneurship Journal*, 4: 1–21.

58. K. Celuch, G. B. Murphy, & S. K. Callaway, 2007, More bang for your buck: Small firms and the importance of aligned information technology capabilities and strategic flexibility, *Journal of High Technology Management Research*, 17: 187–197.
59. 2013, Worldwide PC Market, eTForecasts, www.etforecasts.com, accessed on March 10, 2013.
60. M. S. Giarratana & S. Torrisi, 2010, Foreign entry and survival in a knowledge-intensive market: Emerging economy countries' international linkages, technology competences and firm experience, *Strategic Entrepreneurship Journal*, 4: 85–104.
61. C. Phelps, R. Heidl, & A., Wadhwa, 2012, Knowledge, networks, and knowledge networks: A review and research agenda, *Journal of Management*, 38: 1115–1166; R. Agarwal, D. Audretsch, & M. B. Sarkar, 2010, Knowledge spillovers and strategic entrepreneurship, *Strategic Entrepreneurship Journal*, 4: 271–283.
62. M. Gottfredson, R. Puryear, & S. Phillips, 2005, Strategic sourcing: From periphery to the core, *Harvard Business Review*, 83(2): 132–139.
63. J. T. Macher & C. Boerner, 2012, Technological development at the boundary of the firm: A knowledge-based examination in drug development, *Strategic Managment Journal*, 33: 1016–1036; K. G. Smith, C. J. Collins, & K. D. Clark, 2005, Existing knowledge, knowledge creation capability, and the rate of new product introduction in high-technology firms, *Academy of Management Journal*, 48: 346–357.
64. E. Sherman, 2010, Climbing the corporate ladder, *Continental Magazine*, November, 54–56.
65. K. Z. Zhou & C. B. Li, 2012, How knowledge affects radical innovation: Knowledge base, market knowledge acquisition, and internal knowledge sharing, *Strategic Management Journal*, 33: 1090–1102; A. Capaldo, 2007, Network structure and innovation: The leveraging of a dual network as a distinctive relational capability, *Strategic Management Journal*, 28: 585–608.
66. C. A. Siren, M. Kohtamaki, & A. Kuckertz, 2012, Exploration and exploitation strategies, profit performance and the mediating role of strategic learning: Escaping the exploitation trap, *Strategic Entrepreneurship Journal*, 6: 18–41; Sirmon, Hitt, & Ireland, Managing firm resources.
67. A. Cuervo-Cazurra & C. A. Un, 2010, Why some firms never invest in formal R&D, *Strategic Management Journal*, 31: 759–779.
68. H. Yang, C. Phelps, & H. K. Steensma, 2010, Learning from what others have learned from you: The effects of knowledge spillovers on originating firms, *Academy of Management Journal*, 53: 371–389.
69. A. C. Inkpen, 2008, Knowledge transfer and international joint ventures: The case of NUMMI and General Motors, *Strategic Management Journal*, 29: 447–453; P. L. Robertson & P. R. Patel, 2007, New wine in old bottles: Technological diffusion in developed economies, *Research Policy*, 36: 708–721.
70. R. E. Hoskisson, M. A. Hitt, R. D. Ireland, & J. S. Harrison, 2013, *Competing for Advantage*, 3rd ed., Mason, OH: South-Western Cengage Learning; K. R. Harrigan, 2001, Strategic flexibility in old and new economies, in M. A. Hitt, R. E. Freeman, & J. S. Harrison (eds.), *Handbook of Strategic Management*, Oxford, UK: Blackwell Publishers, 97–123.
71. S. Nadkarni & P. Herrmann, 2010, CEO personality, strategic flexibility, and firm performance: The case of the Indian business process outsourcing industry, *Academy of Management Journal*, 53: 1050–1073; S. Nadkarni & V. K. Narayanan, 2007, Strategic schemas, strategic flexibility, and firm performance: The moderating role of industry clockspeed, *Strategic Management Journal*, 28: 243–270.
72. M. L. Santos-Vijande, J. A. Lopez-Sanchez, & J. A. Trespalacios, 2011, How organizational learning affects a firm's flexibility, competitive strategy and performance, *Journal of Business Research*, 65: 1079–1089; A. C. Edmondson, 2008, The competitive imperative of learning, *Harvard Business Review*, 86(7/8): 60–67; K. Shimizu & M. A. Hitt, 2004, Strategic flexibility: Organizational preparedness to reverse ineffective strategic decisions, *Academy of Management Executive*, 18(4): 44–59.
73. R. E. Hoskisson, M. A. Hitt, W. P. Wan, & D. Yiu, 1999, Swings of a pendulum: Theory and research in strategic management, *Journal of Management*, 25: 417–456.
74. E. H. Bowman & C. E. Helfat, 2001, Does corporate strategy matter? *Strategic Management Journal*, 22: 1–23.
75. J. T. Mahoney & L. Qian, 2013, Market frictions as building blocks of an organizational economics approach to strategic management, *Strategic Management Journal*, in press; M. A. Delmas & M. W. Toffel, 2008, Organizational responses to environmental demands: Opening the black box, *Strategic Management Journal*, 29: 1027–1055.
76. J. Galbreath & P. Galvin, 2008, Firm factors, industry structure and performance variation: New empirical evidence to a classic debate, *Journal of Business Research*, 61: 109–117.
77. H. E. Posen, J. Lee, & S. Yi, 2013, The power of imperfect imitation, *Strategic Management Journal*, 34: 149–164; M. F. Brauer & M. F. Wiersema, 2012, Industry divestiture waves: How a firm's position influences investor returns, *Academy of Management Journal*, 55: 1472–1492; M. B. Lieberman & S. Asaba, 2006, Why do firms imitate each other? *Academy of Management Journal*, 31: 366–385.
78. M. E. Porter, 1985, *Competitive Advantage*, New York: Free Press; M. E. Porter, 1980, *Competitive Strategy*, New York: Free Press.
79. J. C. Short, D. J. Ketchen, Jr., T. B. Palmer, & G. T. M. Hult, 2007, Firm, strategic group, and industry influences on performance, *Strategic Management Journal*, 28: 147–167.
80. P. Ziobro, 2009, McDonald's pounds out good quarter, *Wall Street Journal*, www.wsj.com, April 23.
81. T. W. Tong and J. J. Reuer, 2010, Competitive consequences of interfirm collaboration: How joint ventures shape industry profitability, *Journal of International Business Studies*, 41: 1056–1073.
82. C. Moschieri, 2011, The implementation and structuring of divestitures: The unit's perspective, *Strategic Management Journal*, 32: 368–401.
83. A. M. McGahan, 1999, Competition, strategy and business performance, *California Management Review*, 41(3): 74–101; McGahan & Porter, How much does industry matter, really?
84. M. Schijven & M. A. Hitt, 2012, The vicarious wisdom of crowds: Toward a behavioral perspective of investor reactions to acquisition announcements, *Strategic Management Journal*, 33: 1247–1268; J. W. Upson, D. J. Ketchen, B. L. Connelly, & A. L. Ranft, 2012, Competitor analysis and foothold moves, *Academy of Management Journal*, 55: 93–110; A. Zavyalova, M. D. Pfarrer, R. K. Reger, & D. K. Shapiro, 2012, Managing the message: The effects of firm actions and industry spillovers on media coverage following wrongdoing, *Academy of Management Journal*, 55: 1079–1101.
85. M. G. Jacobides, S. G. Winter, & S. M. Kassberger, 2012, The dynamics of wealth, profit and sustainable advantage, *Strategic Management Journal*, 33: 1384–1410; J. Kraaijenbrink, J.-C. Spender, & A. J. Groen, 2010, The resource-based view: A review and assessment of its critiques, *Journal of Management*, 38: 349–372.
86. A. Arora & A. Nandkumar, 2012, Insecure advantage? Markets for technology and the value of resources for entrepreneurial ventures, *Strategic Management Journal*, 33: 231–251; S. L. Newbert, 2008, Value, rareness, competitive advantage, and performance: A conceptual-level empirical investigation of the resource-based view of the firm, *Strategic Management Journal*, 29: 745–768.
87. Kraaijenbrink, Spender, & Groen, The resource-based view; E. Verwall, H. Commandeur, & W. Verbeke, 2009, Value creation and value claiming in strategic outsourcing decisions: A resource contingency perspective, *Journal of Management*, 35: 420–444.
88. H. Wang & K. F. E. Wong, 2012, The effect of managerial bias on employees' specific human capital investments, *Journal of Management Studies*, 49: 1435–1458; P. L. Drnevich & A. P. Kriauciunas, 2011, Clarifying the conditions and limits of the contributions of ordinary and dynamic capabilities to relative firm performance, *Strategic Management Journal*, 32: 254–279.

89. C. Weigelt, 2013, Leveraging supplier capabilities: The role of locus of capability development, *Strategic Management Journal*, 34: 1–21; S. L. Newbert, 2007, Empirical research on the resource-based view of the firm: An assessment and suggestions for future research, *Strategic Management Journal*, 28: 121–146.
90. R. Nag & D. A. Gioia, 2012, From common to uncommon knowledge: Foundations of firm-specific use of knowledge as a resource, *Academy of Management Journal*, 55: 421–455; D. M. DeCarolis, 2003, Competencies and imitability in the pharmaceutical industry: An analysis of their relationship with firm performance, *Journal of Management*, 29: 27–50.
91. C. Zott, 2003, Dynamic capabilities and the emergence of intraindustry differential firm performance: Insights from a simulation study, *Strategic Management Journal*, 24: 97–125.
92. M. Gruber, F. Heinemann, & M. Brettel, 2010, Configurations of resources and capabilities and their performance implications: An exploratory study on technology ventures, *Strategic Management Journal*, 31: 1337–1356.
93. E. Levitas & H. A. Ndofor, 2006, What to do with the resource-based view: A few suggestions for what ails the RBV that supporters and opponents might accept, *Journal of Management Inquiry*, 15(2): 135–144; G. Hawawini, V. Subramanian, & P. Verdin, 2003, Is performance driven by industry or firm specific factors? A new look at the evidence, *Strategic Management Journal*, 24: 1–16.
94. M. Makhija, 2003, Comparing the source-based and market-based views of the firm: Empirical evidence from Czech privatization, *Strategic Management Journal*, 24: 433–451; T. J. Douglas & J. A. Ryman, 2003, Understanding competitive advantage in the general hospital industry: Evaluating strategic competencies, *Strategic Management Journal*, 24: 333–347.
95. R. D. Ireland, R. E. Hoskisson, & M. A. Hitt. 2012, *Understanding Business Strategy*, 3rd ed., Mason, OH: South-Western Cengage Learning.
96. S. Ward, 2009, Vision statement, *About.com*, www.sbinfocanada.about.com, April 22; R. Zolli, 2006, Recognizing tomorrow's hot ideas today, *Businessweek*, September 25: 12.
97. C. Gallo, 2010, *The Innovation Secrets of Steve Jobs*, NY: McGraw-Hill.
98. G. Cassar, 2010, Are individuals entering self-employment overly optimistic? An empirical test of plans and projections on nascent entrepreneur expectations, *Strategic Management Journal*, 31: 822–840.
99. O. R. Mihalache, J. J. J. P. Jansen, F. A. J. Van Den Bosch, & H. W. Volberda, 2012, Offshoring and firm innovation: The role of top management team attributes, *Strategic Management Journal*, 33: 1480–1498.
100. S. Kemp & L. Dwyer, 2003, Mission statements of international airlines: A content analysis, *Tourism Management*, 24: 635–653; R. D. Ireland & M. A. Hitt, 1992, Mission statements: Importance, challenge, and recommendations for development, *Business Horizons*, 35(3): 34–42.
101. A. S. Khalifa, 2012, Mission, purpose, and ambition: Redefining the mission statement, *Journal of Business and Strategy*, 5: 236–251; J. I. Siciliano, 2008, A comparison of CEO and director perceptions of board involvement in strategy, *Nonprofit and Voluntary Sector Quarterly*, 27: 152–162.
102. J. H. Davis, J. A. Ruhe, M. Lee, & U. Rajadhyaksha, 2007, Mission possible: Do school mission statements work? *Journal of Business Ethics*, 70: 99–110.
103. L. W. Fry & J. W. Slocum, Jr., 2008, Maximizing the triple bottom line through spiritual leadership, *Organizational Dynamics*, 37: 86–96; A. J. Ward, M. J. Lankau, A. C. Amason, J. A. Sonnenfeld, & B. A. Agle, 2007, Improving the performance of top management teams, *MIT Sloan Management Review*, 48(3): 85–90.
104. K. Basu & G. Palazzo, 2008, Corporate social responsibility: A process model of sensemaking, *Academy of Management Review*, 33: 122–136.
105. G. Kenny, 2012, From a stakeholder viewpoint: Designing measurable objectives, *Journal of Business Strategy*, 33(6): 40–46; D. A. Bosse, R. A. Phillips, & J. S. Harrison, 2009, Stakeholders, reciprocity, and firm performance, *Strategic Management Journal*, 30: 447–456.
106. N. Darnell, I. Henrique, & P. Sadorsky, 2010, Adopting proactive environmental strategy: The influence of stakeholders and firm size, *Journal of Management Studies*, 47: 1072–1122; G. Donaldson & J. W. Lorsch, 1983, *Decision Making at the Top: The Shaping of Strategic Direction*, New York: Basic Books, 37–40.
107. S. Sharma & I. Henriques, 2005, Stakeholder influences on sustainability practices in the Canadian forest products industry, *Strategic Management Journal*, 26: 159–180.
108. D. Crilly & P. Sloan, 2012, Enterprise logic: Explaining corporate attention to stakeholders from the 'inside-out', *Strategic Management Journal*, 33: 1174–1193.
109. G. Van der Laan, H. Van Ees, & A. Van Witteloostuijn, 2008, Corporate social and financial performance: An extended stakeholder theory, and empirical test with accounting measures, *Journal of Business Ethics*, 79: 299–310; M. L. Barnett & R. M. Salomon, 2006, Beyond dichotomy: The curvilinear relationship between social responsibility and financial performance, *Strategic Management Journal*, 27: 1101–1122.
110. G. Pandher & R. Currie, 2013, CEO compensation: A resource advantage and stakeholder-bargaining perspective, *Strategic Management Journal*, 34: 22–41; T. Kuhn, 2008, A communicative theory of the firm: Developing an alternative perspective on intra-organizational power and stakeholder relationships, *Organization Studies*, 29: 1227–1254.
111. D. Bush & B. D. Gelb, 2012, Antitrust enforcement: An inflection point? *Journal of Business Strategy*, 33(6): 15–21; J. P. Doh, T. C. Lawton, & T. Rajwani, 2012, *Academy of Management Perspectives*, 26(3): 22–39; J. L. Murrillo-Luna, C. Garces-Ayerbe, & P. Rivera-Torres, 2008, Why do patterns of environmental response differ? A stakeholders' pressure approach, Strategic *Management Journal*, 29: 1225–1240.
112. R. Boutilier, 2009, *Stakeholder Politics: Social Capital, Sustainable Development, and the Corporation*, Sheffield, UK: Greenleaf Publishing; C. Caldwell & R. Karri, 2005, Organizational governance and ethical systems: A conventional approach to building trust, *Journal of Business Ethics*, 58: 249–267.
113. F. G. A. de Bakker & F. den Hond, 2008, Introducing the politics of stakeholder influence, *Business & Society*, 47: 8–20.
114. Darnell, Henrique, & Sadorsky, Adopting proactive environmental strategy; P. Berrone & L. R. Gomez-Meija, 2009, Environmental performance and executive compensation: An integrated agency-institutional perspective, *Academy of Management Journal*, 52: 103–126.
115. B. L. Connelly, L. Tihanyi, S. T. Certo, & M. A. Hitt, 2010, Marching to the beat of different drummers: The influence of institutional owners on competitive actions, *Academy of Management Journal*, 53: 723–742.
116. X. Zuoping, 2010, Large shareholders, legal institution and capital structure decision, *Nankai Business Review International*, 1: 59–86.
117. L. Pierce, 2009, Big losses in ecosystems niches: How core firm decisions drive complementary product shakeouts, *Strategic Management Journal*, 30: 323–347; B. A. Neville & B. Menguc, 2006, Stakeholder multiplicity: Toward an understanding of the interactions between stakeholders, *Journal of Business Ethics*, 66: 377–391.
118. O. D. Fjeldstad & A. Sasson, 2010, Membership matters: On the value of being embedded in customer networks, *Journal of Management Studies*, 47: 944–966.
119. B. Batjargal, M. A. Hitt, A. S. Tsui, J.-L. Arregle, J. Webb, & T. Miller, 2013, Institutional polycentrism, entrepreneurs' social networks and new venture growth, *Academy of Management Journal*, in press.
120. D. A. Ready, L. A. Hill, & J. A. Conger, 2008, Winning the race for talent in emerging markets, *Harvard Business* Review, 86(11): 62–70; A. M. Grant, J. E. Dutton, & B. D. Rosso, 2008, Giving commitment: Employee support programs and the prosocial sensemaking process, *Academy of Management Journal*, 51: 898–918.
121. T. R. Crook, S.Y. Todd, J. G. Combs, D. J. Woehr & D. J. Ketchen, 2011, Does human capital matter? A meta-analysis of the relationship between human capital

and firm performance, *Journal of Applied Psychology*, 96: 443–456; M. A. Hitt, K. T. Haynes, & R. Serpa, 2010, Strategic leadership for the 21st century, *Business Horizons*, 53: 437–444.

122. J. I. Hancock, D. G. Allen, F. A. Bosco, K. R. McDaniel, & C. A. Pierce, 2013, Meta-analytic review of employee turnover as a predictor of firm performance, *Journal of Management*, 39: 573–603; N. Abe & S. Shimizutani, 2007, Employment policy and corporate governance—An empirical comparison of the stakeholder and the profit-maximization model, *Journal of Comparative Economics*, 35: 346–368.

123. R. Takeuchi, 2010, A critical review of expatriate adjustment research through a multiple stakeholder view: Progress, emerging trends and prospects, *Journal of Management*, 36: 1040–1064.

124. Hitt, Haynes, & Serpa, Strategic leadership for the 21st century; J. P. Jansen, D. Vera, & M. Crossan, 2008, Strategic leadership for exploration and exploitation: The moderating role of environmental dynamism, *The Leadership Quarterly*, 20: 5–18.

125. E. F. Goldman, 2012, Leadership practices that encourage strategic thinking, *Journal of Strategy and Management*, 5: 25–40; D. C. Hambrick, 2007, Upper echelons theory: An update, *Academy of Management Review*, 32: 334–339.

126. J. C. Camillus, 2008, Strategy as a wicked problem, *Harvard Business Review* 86(5): 99–106; A. Priestland & T. R. Hanig, 2005, Developing first-level managers, *Harvard Business Review*, 83(6): 113–120.

127. B. Gutierrez, S. M. Spencer, & G. Zhu, 2012, Thinking globally, leading locally: Chinese, Indian, and Western leadership, *Cross Cultural Management*, 19: 67–89; R. J. Harrington & A. K. Tjan, 2008, Transforming strategy one customer at a time, *Harvard Business Review*, 86(3): 62–72.

128. J. Li & Y. Tang, 2010, CEO hubris and firm risk taking in China: The moderating role of managerial discretion, *Academy of Management Journal*, 53: 45–68; Y. L. Doz & M. Kosonen, 2007, The new deal at the top, *Harvard Business Review*, 85(6): 98–104.

129. B. Stevens, 2008, Corporate ethical codes: Effective instruments for influencing behavior, *Journal of Business Ethics*, 78: 601–609; D. Lavie, 2006, The competitive advantage of interconnected firms: An extension of the resource-based view, *Academy of Management Review*, 31: 638–658.

130. K. D. Clark & P. G. Maggitti, 2012, TMT potency and strategic decision making in high technology firms, *Journal of Management Studies*, 49: 1168–1193; C. Salvato, A. Minichilli, & R. Piccarreta, 2012, *Family Business Review*, 25: 206–224; H. Ibarra & O. Obodru, 2009, Women and the vision thing, *Harvard Business Review*, 87(1): 62–70.

131. R. Shambaugh, 2011, Leading in today's economy: The transformational leadership model, in *What's Next 2011*, NY: McGraw-Hill.

132. S. Khavul & G. D. Bruton, 2013, Harnessing innovation for change: Sustainability and poverty in developing countries, *Journal of Management Studies*, 50: 285–306; A. Leiponen & C. E. Helfat, 2010, Innovation objectives, knowledge sources and the benefits of breadth, *Strategic Management Journal*, 31: 224–236.

133. T. Buyl, C. Boone, W. Hendriks, & P. Matthyssens, 2011, Top management team functional diversity and firm performance: The moderating role of CEO characteristics, *Journal of Management Studies*, 48: 151–177; S. Nadkarni & P. Hermann, 2010, CEO personality, strategic flexibility and firm performance: The case of Indian business process outsourcing industry, *Academy of Management Journal*, 53: 1050–1073.

134. Q. Cao, Z. Simsek, & H. Zhang, 2010, Modelling the joint impact of the CEO and the TMT on organizational ambidexterity, *Journal of Management Studies*, 47: 1272–1296.

135. M.-J. Chen & D. Miller, 2010, West meets east: Toward an ambicultural approach to management, *Academy of Management Perspectives*, 24(4): 17–37.

136. M. Loeb, 1993, Steven J. Ross, 1927–1992, *Fortune*, January 25, 4.

137. Y.-C. Tang & F.-M. Liou, 2010, Does firm performance reveal its own causes? The role of Bayesian inference, *Strategic Management Journal*, 31: 39–57.

138. O. Gadiesh & J. L. Gilbert, 1998, Profit pools: A fresh look at strategy, *Harvard Business Review*, 76(3): 139–147.

139. O. Gadiesh & J. L. Gilbert, 1998, How to map your industry's profit pool, *Harvard Business Review*, 76(3): 149–162.

140. C. Zook, 2007, Finding your next CORE business, *Harvard Business Review*, 85(4): 66–75; M. J. Epstein & R. A. Westbrook, 2001, Linking actions to profits in strategic decision making, *Sloan Management Review*, 42(3): 39–49.

141. M. J. Lenox, S. F. Rockart, & A. Y. Lewin, 2010, Does interdependency affect firm and industry profitability? An empirical test, *Strategic Management Journal*, 31: 121–139.

142. M. M. Helms & J. Nixon, 2010, Exploring SWOT analysis—where are we now? A review of the academic research from the last decade, *Journal of Strategy and Management*, 3: 215–251.

143. T. Yu, M. Subramaniam, & A. A. Cannella, Jr., 2009, Rivalry deterrence in international markets: Contingencies governing the mutual forbearance hypothesis, *Academy of Management Journal*, 52: 127–147; D. J. Ketchen, C. C. Snow, & V. L. Street, 2004, Improving firm performance by matching strategic decision-making processes to competitive dynamics, *Academy of Management Executive*, 18(4): 29–43.

144. D. Li, L. Eden, M. A. Hitt, R. D. Ireland, & R. P. Garrett, 2012, Governance in multilateral R&D alliances, *Organization Science*, 23: 1191–1210; D. Li, S. R. Miller, L. Eden, & M. A. Hitt, 2012, The impact of rule of law on market value creation for local alliance partners in BRIC countries, *Journal of International Management*, 18: 305–321.

145. S. D. Julian, J. C. Ofori-Dankwa, & R. T. Justis, 2008, Understanding strategic responses to interest group pressures, *Strategic Management Journal*, 29: 963–984; C. Eesley & M. J. Lenox, 2006, Firm responses to secondary stakeholder action, *Strategic Management Journal*, 27: 765–781.

146. Y. Luo, 2008, Procedural fairness and interfirm cooperation in strategic alliances, *Strategic Management Journal*, 29: 27–46; S. J. Reynolds, F. C. Schultz, & D. R. Hekman, 2006, Stakeholder theory and managerial decision-making: Constraints and implications of balancing stakeholder interests, *Journal of Business Ethics*, 64: 285–301; L. K. Trevino & G. R. Weaver, 2003, *Managing Ethics in Business Organizations*, Stanford, CA: Stanford University Press.

147. D. Pastoriza, M. A. Arino, & J. E. Ricart, 2008, Ethical managerial behavior as an antecedent of organizational social capital, *Journal of Business Ethics*, 78: 329–341.

148. B. W. Heineman Jr., 2007, Avoiding integrity land mines, *Harvard Business Review*, 85(4): 100–108.

149. P. Klarner & S. Raisch, 2013, Move to the beat—Rhythms of change and firm performance, *Academy of Management Journal*, 56: 160–184.

# 2

# The External Environment: Opportunities, Threats, Industry Competition, and Competitor Analysis

***Studying this chapter should provide you with the strategic management knowledge needed to:***

1 Explain the importance of analyzing and understanding the firm's external environment.

2 Define and describe the general environment and the industry environment.

3 Discuss the four parts of the external environmental analysis process.

4 Name and describe the general environment's seven segments.

5 Identify the five competitive forces and explain how they determine an industry's profitability potential.

6 Define strategic groups and describe their influence on firms.

7 Describe what firms need to know about their competitors and different methods (including ethical standards) used to collect intelligence about them.

## THE COCA-COLA CO. AND PEPSICO: RIVALS COMPETING IN A CHALLENGING ENVIRONMENT

Recognized throughout the world, Coca-Cola and PepsiCo are both successful companies. At least historically, these firms are best known for their soft drinks or sodas. Interestingly, some believe that the United States "has been defined by soda in the same way France defined its empire on wine, Germany on beer, and Britain on tea."

Even though they differ in the total set of products they offer, the rivalry between these companies remains intense, particularly in terms of both carbonated and noncarbonated beverages. These competitions play out in many nations and regions of the world.

Of the two companies, PepsiCo is more diversified in that, through its Frito-Lay business unit, it is a leader in the global snack industry. The importance of this unit to PepsiCo is shown by the fact that it recently accounted for 21 percent of the firm's sales revenue but 35 percent of its operating profits. In contrast, Coca-Cola is the world's largest producer of soft drink concentrates and syrups and is also the world's largest producer of juice and juice-related products; however, it does not have a snack business unit.

Changing conditions in the external environment are affecting these firms' competitive choices. Overall declining sales in the soda category in the United States in particular but in other parts of the world as well are one reason for this. Soda sales appear to be declining partly as a result of changes in societies' attitudes toward the "value" associated with consuming soda products, particularly full-calorie versions of them. In response, Coca-Cola is finding ways to generate more returns through its juice products. To ensure access to the supply of oranges it needs, the firm recently established long-term leases with two large Florida growers. This deal gives Coca-Cola access to the production of 5 million orange trees for a period of 20 years. PepsiCo's recent competitive actions include paying $4.2 billion for Russian yogurt giant Wimm-Bill-Dann Foods. This is PepsiCo's largest-ever foreign acquisition and is seen as a path to reach consumers in neighboring countries such as Ukraine, Turkmenistan, and Kyrgyzstan for the purpose of successfully distributing its Frito-Lay products.

In addition, these firms continue competing aggressively against each other in sodas. Each firm has developed fountain machines that allow customers to create a variety of flavor combinations, such as strawberry Mountain Dew (a Pepsi-Cola product). To better attract younger consumers, PepsiCo completed an endorsement deal with pop star Beyoncé. And both firms are competing against each other to gain market share in noncarbonated beverage products such as waters, juices, and sports drinks.

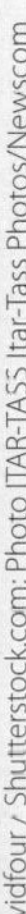

Suggested links between obesity and some of these firms' products is another condition in the external environment that is affecting these firms, causing them to compete against each other to find ways to most effectively respond to this threat. Coca-Cola has announced that it is committed to contributing to individuals' health on a global basis. Supporting physical activities programs in every country where the firm competes is one action it is taking to demonstrate this commitment. In addition to committing to sell healthier products through its Quaker Oats, Gatorade, and Tropicana divisions, PepsiCo has established the "Global Nutrition Group" for the purpose of developing breakthrough products that will satisfy customers' needs for enjoyable but healthy products.

Sources: 2013, Coca-Cola Co, *Standard & Poor's Stock Report*, www.standardandpoors.com, May 17; 2013, PepsiCo Inc., *Standard & Poor's Stock Report*, www.standardandpoors.com, May 17; A. Cardenal, 2013, The battle of the soda giants: Coke vs. Pepsi, www.beta.fool.com, April 10; C. Passy, 2013, Why soda is the great American beverage, *Wall Street Journal*, www.wsj.com, March 12; D. Stanford, 2013, Cola-Cola expands calorie labels and emphasizes no-cals, *Bloomberg Businessweek*, www.businessweek.com, May 9; D. Stanford, 2013, PepsiCo's East European snack attack, *Bloomberg Businessweek*, www.businessweek.com, February 28; K. Stock, 2013, Coke's sweet $2 billion orange juice deal, *Bloomberg Businessweek*, www.businessweek.com, May 8.

Learn more about Tropicana, a company acquired by Coca-Cola.
www.cengagebrain.com

As described in the Opening Case and suggested by research, the external environment (which includes the industry in which a firm competes as well as those against whom it competes) affects the competition actions and responses firms take to outperform competitors and earn above-average returns.[1] For example, Coca-Cola and PepsiCo are trying to effectively address the allegation that some and perhaps many of their products contribute to obesity. The sociocultural segment of the general environment (discussed in this chapter) is the source of this allegation and the threat it represents to the two firms. The Opening Case also describes some of the ways these two firms compete against each other in markets throughout the world.

As noted in Chapter 1, the characteristics of today's external environment differ from historical conditions. For example, technological changes and the continuing growth of information gathering and processing capabilities increase the need for firms to develop effective competitive actions and responses on a timely basis.[2] (We fully discuss competitive actions and responses in Chapter 5.) Additionally, the rapid sociological changes occurring in many countries affect labor practices and the nature of products that increasingly diverse consumers demand. Governmental policies and laws also affect where and how firms choose to compete.[3] And, changes to a number of nations' financial regulatory systems that have been enacted since 2010 are expected to increase the complexity of organizations' financial transactions.[4]

Firms understand the external environment by acquiring information about competitors, customers, and other stakeholders to build their own base of knowledge and capabilities.[5] On the basis of the new information, firms take actions, such as building new capabilities and core competencies, in hopes of buffering themselves from any negative environmental effects and to pursue opportunities as the basis for better serving their stakeholders' needs.[6]

In summary, a firm's competitive actions and responses are influenced by the conditions in the three parts (the general, industry, and competitor) of its external environment (see Figure 2.1) and its understanding of those conditions. Next, we fully describe each part of the firm's external environment.

## 2-1 The General, Industry, and Competitor Environments

The **general environment** is composed of dimensions in the broader society that influence an industry and the firms within it.

The **general environment** is composed of dimensions in the broader society that influence an industry and the firms within it.[7] We group these dimensions into seven environmental *segments:* demographic, economic, political/legal, sociocultural, technological, global, and physical. Examples of *elements* analyzed in each of these segments are shown in Table 2.1.

M. Stasy

**Figure 2.1** The External Environment

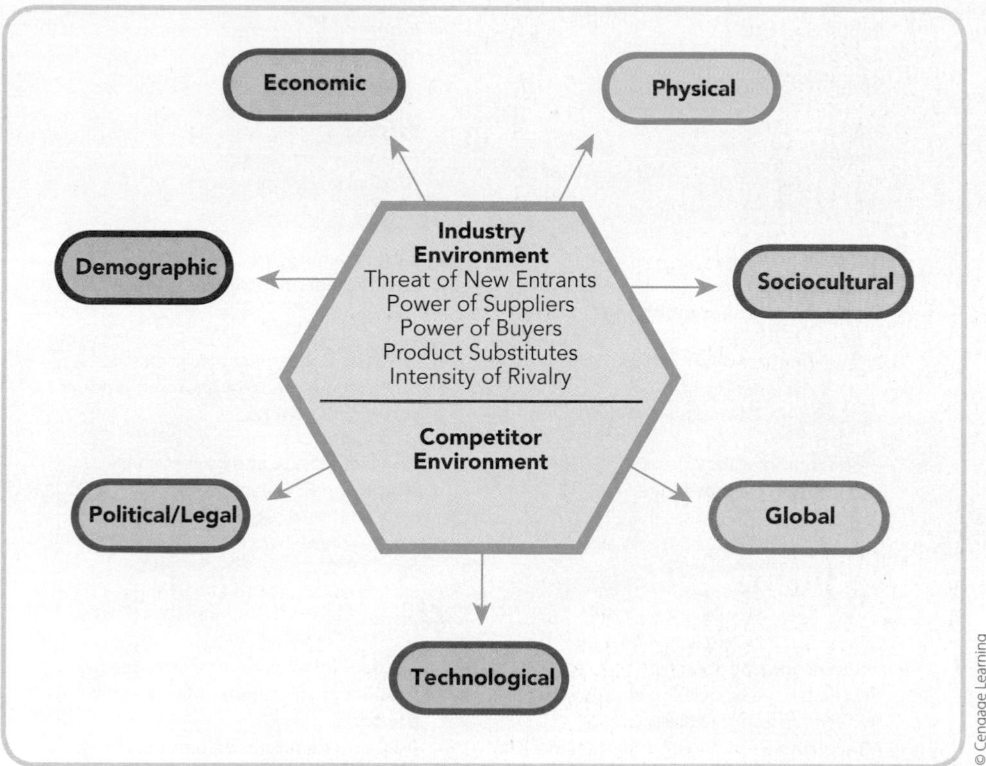


Firms cannot directly control the general environment's segments. Accordingly, what a company seeks to do is recognize trends in each segment of the general environment and then *predict* each trend's effect on it. For example, some believe that over the next 10 to 20 years, millions of people living in emerging market countries will join the middle class. Of course no firm, including large multinationals, is able to control where growth in potential customers may take place in the next decade or two. Nonetheless, firms must study this anticipated trend as a foundation for predicting its effects on their ability to identify strategies to use that will allow them to remain successful as market conditions change.[8]

The **industry environment** is the set of factors that directly influences a firm and its competitive actions and responses:[9] the threat of new entrants, the power of suppliers, the power of buyers, the threat of product substitutes, and the intensity of rivalry among competing firms. In total, the interactions among these five factors determine an industry's profitability potential; in turn, the industry's profitability potential influences the choices each firm makes about its competitive actions and responses. The challenge for a firm is to locate a position within an industry where it can favorably influence the five factors or where it can successfully defend itself against their influence. The greater a firm's capacity to favorably influence its industry environment, the greater the likelihood it will earn above-average returns.

How companies gather and interpret information about their competitors is called **competitor analysis**. Understanding the firm's competitor environment complements the insights provided by studying the general and industry environments.[10] This means, for example, that Coca-Cola and PepsiCo want to learn as much about each other as they can while each company simultaneously seeks to understand its general and industry environments.

The **industry environment** is the set of factors that directly influences a firm and its competitive actions and responses: the threat of new entrants, the power of suppliers, the power of buyers, the threat of product substitutes, and the intensity of rivalry among competing firms.

How companies gather and interpret information about their competitors is called **competitor analysis**.

**Table 2.1** The General Environment: Segments and Elements

| Segment | Elements | Elements |
|---|---|---|
| Demographic segment | • Population size<br>• Age structure<br>• Geographic distribution | • Ethnic mix<br>• Income distribution |
| Economic segment | • Inflation rates<br>• Interest rates<br>• Trade deficits or surpluses<br>• Budget deficits or surpluses | • Personal savings rate<br>• Business savings rates<br>• Gross domestic product |
| Political/Legal segment | • Antitrust laws<br>• Taxation laws<br>• Deregulation philosophies | • Labor training laws<br>• Educational philosophies and policies |
| Sociocultural segment | • Women in the workforce<br>• Workforce diversity<br>• Attitudes about the quality of work life | • Shifts in work and career preferences<br>• Shifts in preferences regarding product and service characteristics |
| Technological segment | • Product innovations<br>• Applications of knowledge | • Focus of private and government-supported R&D expenditures<br>• New communication technologies |
| Global segment | • Important political events<br>• Critical global markets | • Newly industrialized countries<br>• Different cultural and institutional attributes |
| Physical environment segment | • Energy consumption<br>• Practices used to develop energy sources<br>• Renewable energy efforts<br>• Minimizing a firm's environmental footprint | • Availability of water as a resource<br>• Producing environmentally friendly products<br>• Reacting to natural or man-made disasters |



An analysis of the general environment focuses on environmental trends and their implications, an analysis of the industry environment focuses on the factors and conditions influencing an industry's profitability potential, and an analysis of competitors is focused on predicting competitors' actions, responses, and intentions. In combination, the results of these three analyses influence the firm's vision, mission, its choice of strategies, and the competitive actions and responses it will take to implement those strategies. Although we discuss each analysis separately, performance improves when the firm effectively integrates the insights provided by analyses of the general environment, the industry environment, and the competitor environment.

## 2-2 External Environmental Analysis

Most firms face external environments that are turbulent, complex, and global—conditions that make interpreting those environments difficult.[11] To cope with often ambiguous and incomplete environmental data and to increase understanding of the general environment, firms complete an *external environmental analysis*. This analysis has four parts: scanning, monitoring, forecasting, and assessing (see Table 2.2).

An **opportunity** is a condition in the general environment that, if exploited effectively, helps a company reach strategic competitiveness.

Identifying opportunities and threats is an important objective of studying the general environment. An **opportunity** is a condition in the general environment that, if exploited effectively, helps a company reach strategic competitiveness. Most companies—and certainly large ones—continuously encounter multiple opportunities as well as threats.

**Table 2.2** Parts of the External Environment Analysis

| | |
|---|---|
| Scanning | • Identifying early signals of environmental changes and trends |
| Monitoring | • Detecting meaning through ongoing observations of environmental changes and trends |
| Forecasting | • Developing projections of anticipated outcomes based on monitored changes and trends |
| Assessing | • Determining the timing and importance of environmental changes and trends for firms' strategies and their management |



In terms of possible opportunities, we can note that a combination of cultural, political, and economic factors is resulting in rapid retail growth in Africa and the Middle East as well as in Latin America. Accordingly Walmart, the world's largest retailer, and the next three largest global giants (France's Carrefour, U.K.–based Tesco, and Germany's Metro) are planning to expand in these regions. "Walmart is expanding its horizon to Chile, India and South Africa; Carrefour will open stores in Bulgaria, India and Iran. Tesco is also opening stores in India, and Metro will open in Egypt and Kazakhstan."[12] Similarly, Google intends to partner with local telecommunications firms and equipment providers to help build and operate wireless networks in emerging markets such as sub-Saharan Africa and Southeast Asia. Pursuing these opportunities is part of Google's goal of connecting a billion or more new users to the Internet.[13]

A **threat** is a condition in the general environment that may hinder a company's efforts to achieve strategic competitiveness.[14] Finnish-based Nokia Corp. is dealing with threats including one regarding its intellectual property rights. In roughly mid-2013, the company filed two additional complaints against competitor HTC Corp. alleging that the Taiwanese smartphone manufacturer had infringed on nine of Nokia's patents.[15] This threat obviously deals with the political/legal segment. From the technological segment, Nokia is facing a potential threat from a new device called Jolla. Created by former Nokia executives and developers who founded their own firm in Helsinki in 2011, its manufacturer believes that the Jolla operating system is "a truly independent and open alternative in mobile."[16] While its competitive success is yet to be determined, this product does appear to represent a technological threat for Nokia and others smartphone manufacturers as well.

Firms use multiple sources to analyze the general environment through scanning, monitoring, forecasting, and assessing. Examples of these sources include a wide variety of printed materials (such as trade publications, newspapers, business publications, and the results of academic research and public polls), trade shows and suppliers, customers, and employees of public-sector organizations. Of course, the information available from Internet sources is of increasing importance to a firm's efforts to study the general environment.

## 2-2a Scanning

*Scanning* entails the study of all segments in the general environment. Although challenging, scanning is critically important to firms' efforts to understand trends in the general environment and predict their implications. This is particularly the case for companies competing in highly volatile environments.[17]

Through scanning, firms identify early signals of potential changes in the general environment and detect changes that are already under way.[18] Scanning activities must be aligned with the organizational context; a scanning system designed for a volatile environment is inappropriate for a firm in a stable environment.[19] Scanning often reveals ambiguous, incomplete, or unconnected data and information that require careful analysis.

A **threat** is a condition in the general environment that may hinder a company's efforts to achieve strategic competitiveness.

Many firms use special software to help them identify events that are taking place in the environment and that are announced in public sources. For example, news event detection uses information-based systems to categorize text and reduce the trade-off between an important missed event and false alarm rates. Increasingly, these systems are used to study social media outlets as sources of information.[20]

Broadly speaking, the Internet provides a wealth of opportunities for scanning. Amazon.com, for example, records information about individuals visiting its Web site, particularly if a purchase is made. Amazon then welcomes these customers by name when they visit the Web site again. The firm sends messages to customers about specials and new products similar to those they purchased in previous visits. A number of other companies, such as Netflix, also collect demographic data about their customers in an attempt to identify their unique preferences (demographics is one of the segments in the general environment).

## 2-2b Monitoring

When *monitoring*, analysts observe environmental changes to see if an important trend is emerging from among those spotted through scanning.[21] Critical to successful monitoring is the firm's ability to detect meaning in environmental events and trends. For example, those monitoring retirement trends in the United States learned in 2013 that 57 percent of U.S. workers surveyed reported that excluding the value of their home, they have only $25,000 or less in savings and investments set aside for their retirement. This particular survey also discovered "that 28% of Americans have no confidence they will have enough money to retire comfortably—the highest level in the (survey's) 23-year history."[22] Historically, U.S. workers saved larger percentages of their earned income as a foundation for retirement. Firms seeking to serve retirees' financial needs will continue monitoring this change in workers' savings and investment patterns to see if a trend is developing. Once convinced that saving less for retirement is indeed a trend, these firms will seek to understand its competitive implications.

Effective monitoring requires the firm to identify important stakeholders and understand its reputation among these stakeholders as the foundation for serving their unique needs.[23] (Stakeholders' unique needs are described in Chapter 1.) Scanning and monitoring are particularly important when a firm competes in an industry with high technological uncertainty.[24] Scanning and monitoring can provide the firm with information; these activities also serve as a means of importing knowledge about markets and about how to successfully commercialize the new technologies the firm has developed.[25]

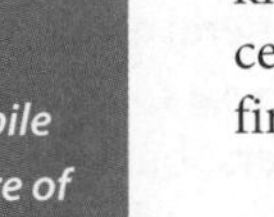

*A variety of microprocessors are displayed at the Mobile World Congress in Barcelona, Spain. The global showcase for the mobile technology industry draws 1,500 exhibitors to discuss the future of wireless communication.*

Bloomberg/Getty Images

## 2-2c Forecasting

Scanning and monitoring are concerned with events and trends in the general environment at a point in time. When *forecasting*, analysts develop feasible projections of what might happen, and how quickly, as a result of the events and trends detected through scanning and monitoring.[26] For example, analysts might forecast the time that will be required for a new technology to reach the marketplace, the length of time before different corporate training procedures are required to deal with anticipated changes in the composition of the workforce, or how much time will elapse before changes in governmental taxation policies affect consumers' purchasing patterns.

Forecasting events and outcomes accurately is challenging. Forecasting demand for new technological products is difficult because technology trends are continually driving product life cycles shorter. This is particularly difficult for a firm such as Intel, whose products go into many customers' technological products, which are consistently updated. Increasing the difficulty, each new wafer fabrication or silicon chip technology production plant in which Intel invests becomes significantly more expensive for each generation of chip products. In this instance, having access to tools that allow better forecasting of electronic product demand is of value to Intel as the firm studies conditions in its external environment.[27]

### 2-2d Assessing

When *assessing*, the objective is to determine the timing and significance of the effects of environmental changes and trends that have been identified.[28] Through scanning, monitoring, and forecasting, analysts are able to understand the general environment. Going a step further, the intent of assessment is to specify the implications of that understanding. Without assessment, the firm is left with data that may be interesting but of unknown competitive relevance. Even if formal assessment is inadequate, the appropriate interpretation of that information is important.

Accurately assessing the trends expected to take place in the segments of a firm's general environment is important. However, accurately interpreting the meaning of those trends is even more important. In slightly different words, although gathering and organizing information is important, appropriately interpreting the intelligence the collected information provides to determine if an identified trend in the general environment is an opportunity or threat is critical.[29]

## 2-3 Segments of the General Environment

The general environment is composed of segments that are external to the firm (see Table 2.1). Although the degree of impact varies, these environmental segments affect all industries and the firms competing in them. The challenge to each firm is to scan, monitor, forecast, and assess the elements in each segment to predict their effects on it. Effective scanning, monitoring, forecasting, and assessing are vital to the firm's efforts to recognize and evaluate opportunities and threats.

### 2-3a The Demographic Segment

The **demographic segment** is concerned with a population's size, age structure, geographic distribution, ethnic mix, and income distribution.[30] Demographic segments are commonly analyzed on a global basis because of their potential effects across countries' borders and because many firms compete in global markets.

#### Population Size

The world's population doubled (from 3 billion to 6 billion) between 1959 and 1999. Current projections suggest that population growth will continue in the twenty-first century, but at a slower pace. The U.S. Census Bureau projects that the world's population will be 9 billion by 2042 and roughly 9.25 billion by 2050.[31] In 2012, China was the world's largest country by population with over 1.3 billion people. By 2050, however, India is expected to be the most populous nation in the world (approximately 1.69 billion). China (1.3 billion), the United States (439 million), Indonesia (313 million), and Pakistan (276 million) are expected to be the next four most populous countries in 2050.[32] Firms seeking to find growing markets in which to sell their goods and services want to recognize the market potential that may exist for them in these five nations.

The **demographic segment** is concerned with a population's size, age structure, geographic distribution, ethnic mix, and income distribution.

While observing the population of nations and regions of the world, firms also want to study changes occurring within different populations to assess their strategic implications. For example, in 2011, 23 percent of Japan's citizens were 65 or older, while the United States and China will not reach this level until 2036.[33] Aging populations are a significant problem for countries because of the need for workers and the burden of supporting retirement programs. In Japan and some other countries, employees are urged to work longer to overcome these problems.

## Age Structure

The most noteworthy aspect of this element of the demographic segment is that the world's population is rapidly aging. For example, predictions are that, "By 2050, over one-fifth of the U.S. population will be 65 or older up from the current figure (in 2012) of one-seventh. The number of centenarians worldwide will double by 2023 and double again by 2035. Projections suggest life expectancy will surpass 100 in some industrialized countries by the second half of this century—roughly triple the lifespan that prevailed worldwide throughout most of human history."[34] In China, the 65 and over population is expected to reach roughly 330 million by 2050, which will be close to one-fourth of the nation's total population.[35] In the 1950s, Japan's population was one of the youngest in the world. However, 45 is now the median age in Japan, with the projection that it will be 55 by 2040. With a fertility rate that is below replacement value, another prediction is that by 2040, there will be almost as many Japanese people 100 years old or older as there are newborns.[36]

These predictions lead to different possibilities. In Japan, an expectation that the working age population will shrink from 81 million in 2012 to about 57 million in 2040 seems to threaten companies' ability to operate. On the other hand, is there an opportunity for Japanese firms to find ways to increase the productivity of their workers and/or to establish additional operations in other nations? From an opportunity perspective, delayed retirements of baby boomers (those born between 1947 and 1965) that are expected in the United States (and perhaps other countries as well) create the possibility of helping companies "avoid or defer the baby-boomer brain drain that has been looming for so long." In this sense, "organizations now have a fresh opportunity to address the talent gap created by a shortage of critical skills in the marketplace as well as the experience gap created by multiple waves of downsizing over the past decade."[37] Having those delaying their retirement use their knowledge to help younger employees quickly gain valuable skills is another opportunity that the age structure element suggests firms should consider.

## Geographic Distribution

How a population is distributed within countries and regions is subject to change over time. For example, the last few decades have seen the U.S. population shifting from states in the Northeast and Great Lakes region to states in the west (California), south (Florida), and southwest (Texas). These changes can be seen as moving from the "Frost Belt" to the "Sun Belt." Outcomes from these shifts include the facts that the gross domestic product (GDP) of California in 2011 was just under $2 trillion, an amount that makes California the ninth-largest economy in the world. In this same year, at a value of $1.3 trillion, Texas' GDP was second to that of California.[38]

Recent shifts show that New Jersey had the highest ratio of people moving out compared to the number of people moving into the state in 2012. Illinois, New York, Michigan, Maine, Connecticut, and Wisconsin are additional states for which a large net migration occurred in 2012. In a shift in the pattern witnessed for the first decade-plus of the twenty-first century, Washington, D.C., was the most popular destination for relocation in 2012 with Oregon being the second most popular. Washington, D.C., seemed to be popular because of its somewhat recession-proof economic opportunities that are generated by a maturing high-tech sector and federal government jobs. In particular, the city of Portland appears to capture the allure of Oregon in terms of its mix of economic growth, cutting edge urban planning, and scenic landscapes.[39]

Firms want to carefully study the patterns of population distributions in countries and regions to identify opportunities and threats. Thus in the United States, current patterns suggest the possibility of opportunities in Washington, D.C., as well as in states on the West Coast including Oregon and those in the South and Southwest. In contrast, firms competing in the Northeast and Great Lakes areas may concentrate on identifying threats to their ability to operate profitably in those areas.

Of course, geographic distribution patterns differ throughout the world. For example, in China, the majority of the population still lives in rural areas; however, today's growth patterns are toward urban communities such as Shanghai and Beijing.[40] Shifts that occurred between 2011 and 2012 in Europe show net (but small) population gains for countries such as France, Germany, and the United Kingdom while Greece experienced a net (again, small) population decline. Overall, the geographic distribution patterns at least for this year in Europe were quite stable.[41] This fact too has relevance for firms studying this segment of their general environment.

## Ethnic Mix

The ethnic mix of countries' populations continues to change, creating opportunities and threats for many companies as a result. For example, Hispanics are now the largest ethnic minority in the United States.[42] In fact, the U.S. Hispanic market is the third largest "Latin American" economy behind Brazil and Mexico. Spanish is now the dominant language in parts of U.S. states such as Texas, California, Florida, and New Mexico. Given these facts, some firms might want to assess the degree to which their goods or services could be adapted to serve the unique needs of Hispanic consumers.

Additional evidence is of interest to firms when examining this segment. For example, African countries are the most ethnically diverse in the world, with Uganda having the highest ethnic diversity rating with Liberia second. In contrast, Japan and the Koreas are the least diversified from the perspective of a mix of ethnicities in their populations. European countries are ethnically homogeneous while the Americas are often diverse. "From the United States through Central America down to Brazil, the 'new world' countries, maybe in part because of their histories of relatively open immigration (and, in some cases, intermingling between natives and new arrivals) tend to be pretty diverse."[43]

## Income Distribution

Understanding how income is distributed within and across populations informs firms of different groups' purchasing power and discretionary income. Of particular interest to firms are the average incomes of households and individuals. For instance, the increase in dual-career couples has had a notable effect on average incomes. Although real income has been declining in general in some nations, the household income of dual-career couples has increased, especially in the United States. These figures yield strategically relevant information for firms. For instance, research indicates that whether an employee is part of a dual-career couple can strongly influence the willingness of the employee to accept an international assignment. However, because of recent global

Patterns of population distribution present both opportunities and threats to companies.

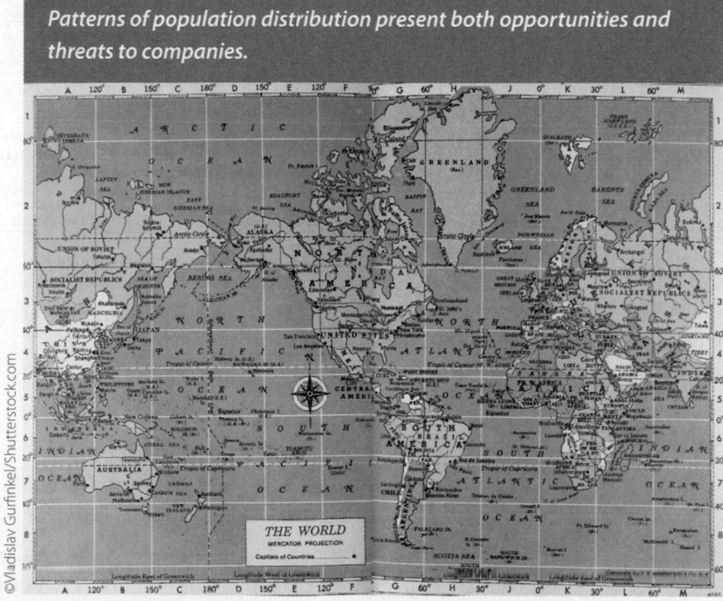


©Vladislav Gurfinkel/Shutterstock.com

economic conditions, many companies were still pursuing international assignments but changing them to avoid some of the additional costs of funding expatriates abroad.[44]

The growth of the economy in China has drawn many firms, not only for the low-cost production, but also because of the large potential demand for products, given its large population base. However, in recent times, the amount of China's gross domestic product that makes up domestic consumption is the lowest of any major economy at less than one-third. In comparison, India's domestic consumption of consumer goods accounts for two-thirds of its economy, or twice China's level. As such, many western multinationals are considering entering India as a consumption market as its middle class grows extensively. Although India as a nation has poor infrastructure, its consumers are in a better position to spend. Furthermore, the urban-rural income difference has been declining in India more rapidly than in China. Because of situations such as this, paying attention to the differences between markets based on income distribution can be very important.[45]

## 2-3b The Economic Segment

The **economic environment** refers to the nature and direction of the economy in which a firm competes or may compete.[46] In general, firms seek to compete in relatively stable economies with strong growth potential. Because nations are interconnected as a result of the global economy, firms must scan, monitor, forecast, and assess the health of their host nation as well as the health of the economies outside it.

For firms studying the economic environment today for purposes of being able to predict trends that may occur in this segment of the general environment and their effects on them, the picture remains unclear and challenging. There are at least two reasons for this. First, the global recession of 2008 and 2009 created numerous problems for companies throughout the world, including those of reduced consumer demand, increases in firms' inventory levels, development of additional governmental regulations, and a tightening of access to financial resources. The second reason to consider is that the global recovery from the 2008 and 2009 recession remains persistently slow and relatively weak compared to previous recoveries. Some argue that enhanced *economic uncertainty* (which refers to an environment in which relatively little and perhaps nothing at all is known about the future state of an economy) is a major cause of the "less-than-robust-recovery" that was experienced at least through mid-2013. Of likely concern to firms studying the economic segment today is the fact that historically, high degrees of economic uncertainty coincide with periods of lower growth. And again, according to some research, "it is clear that (economic) uncertainty has increased in recent times."[47] This increase suggests the possibility of slower growth in the foreseeable future.

When facing economic uncertainty, firms want to be certain to study the economic environment in multiple regions and countries throughout the world. Although economic growth remains relatively weak and economic uncertainty has been strong in Europe and the United States in recent times, this was not the case in other settings. In 2013, for example, growth was projected to increase by 8.2 percent in China, by 4 percent in Brazil, and by 3.5 percent in Mexico. From a regional perspective, 2013 projections were for growth of 5.8 percent in Southeast Asia and 5.7 percent in sub-Saharan Africa, estimates that highlight the anticipation of the continuing development of emerging economies.[48] Ideally, firms will be able to pursue growth opportunities in regions and nations where they exist while avoiding the threats of slow growth periods in other settings.

The **economic environment** refers to the nature and direction of the economy in which a firm competes or may compete.

The **political/legal segment** is the arena in which organizations and interest groups compete for attention, resources, and a voice in overseeing the body of laws and regulations guiding interactions among nations as well as between firms and various local governmental agencies.

## 2-3c The Political/Legal Segment

The **political/legal segment** is the arena in which organizations and interest groups compete for attention, resources, and a voice in overseeing the body of laws and regulations guiding interactions among nations as well as between firms and various local governmental agencies.[49] Essentially, this segment is concerned with how organizations try to influence governments and how they try to understand the influences (current and projected) of those governments on their competitive actions and responses. Commonly, firms develop a political strategy to specify how they will study the political/legal segment as well as approaches they might take (such as lobbying efforts) in order to successfully deal with opportunities and threats that surface within this segment at different points in time.[50]

Regulations formed in response to new national, regional, state, and/or local laws that are legislated often influence a firm's competitive actions and responses. For example, the state of Nevada in the United States recently legalized the business of online poker/gambling. New Jersey and Delaware quickly took the same action. In response to Nevada's regulatory change, firms such as MGM Resorts International were trying to decide the degree to which these decisions represented a viable opportunity. According to a MGM official, the immediate concern with respect to Nevada is that "the state may be too small to provide a lucrative online market on a standalone basis."[51]

At a regional level, changes in the laws regarding the appropriate regulation of European banks are still being actively debated.[52] For interactive, technology-based firms such as Facebook, Google, and Amazon, among others, "the effort in Europe to adopt the world's strongest data protection law has drawn the attention of dozens of lobbyists from U.S. technology and advertising companies."[53] Highly restrictive laws about consumer privacy could threaten how these firms conduct business in the European Union. Finally, in a comprehensive sense, recent transformations from state-owned to private firms occurring in multiple nations have substantial implications for the competitive landscapes in a number of countries and across multiple industries.[54]

## 2-3d The Sociocultural Segment

The **sociocultural segment** is concerned with a society's attitudes and cultural values. Because attitudes and values form the cornerstone of a society, they often drive demographic, economic, political/legal, and technological conditions and changes.

Individual societies' attitudes and cultural orientations are anything other than stable, meaning that firms must carefully scan, monitor, forecast, and assess them to recognize and study associated opportunities and threats. Another way of thinking about this is to note that companies do not exist in an isolated state. Because of this, even successful firms must have an awareness of changes taking place in the societies and their associated cultures in which they are competing. Indeed, societal and culture changes challenge firms to find ways to "adapt to stay ahead of their competitors and stay relevant in the minds of their consumers."[55]

Attitudes about and approaches to health care are issues being considered in nations and regions throughout the world. For Europe, the European Commission has developed a health care strategy for all of Europe that is oriented to preventing diseases while tackling lifestyle factors influencing health such as nutrition, working conditions, and physical activity. This Commission argues that promoting attitudes to take care of one's health is especially important in the context of an aging Europe as shown by the projection that the proportion of people over 65 living in Europe will increase from 17 percent in 2010 to almost 30 percent by 2060.[56]

In the United States, costs remain at the forefront of discussions about health care. Recent surveys show that consumers are dissatisfied with the cost of health care and do not understand why these costs continue to increase. Simultaneously though, most patients (as many as 80 percent of women and 85 percent of men) fail to compare the costs of doctors and recommended procedures.[57] At issue for business firms is that attitudes and values about health care can affect them; accordingly, they must carefully examine trends regarding health care in order to anticipate the effects on their operations.

As the U.S. labor force has increased, it has become more diverse, as significantly more women and minorities from a variety of cultures enter the workplace. In 1993, the total U.S. workforce was slightly less than 130 million; in 2005, it was slightly greater than 148 million. It is predicted to grow to more than 192 million by 2050.

The **sociocultural segment** is concerned with a society's attitudes and cultural values.

Chris Sattlberger/Photographer's Choice RF/Getty Images

*Greater workforce diversity has become the norm in many industries. These changes have forced many companies to challenge the notion of traditional organizational roles for men and women.*

However, the rate of growth in the U.S. labor force has declined over the past two decades largely as a result of slower growth of the nation's population and because of a downward trend in the labor force participation rate. More specifically, data show that "after nearly five decades of steady growth, the overall participation rate—defined as the proportion of the civilian noninstitutional population in the labor force—peaked at an annual average of 67.1 percent for each year from 1997 to 2000… By September 2012, the rate had dropped to 63.6 percent"[58] and is expected to fall to 58.5 percent by 2050. Other changes in the U.S. labor force between 2010 and 2050 are expected. During this time period, the Asian labor force is projected to more than double in size while the growth in the white labor force is predicted to be much slower compared to other racial groups. In contrast, people of Hispanic origin are expected to account for roughly 80 percent of the total growth in the labor force. Finally, "it is projected that the higher growth rate of the female labor force relative to that of men will end by 2020 and the growth rates for men and women will be similar for the 2020–2050 period."[59]

Greater diversity in the workforce creates challenges and opportunities, including combining the best of both men's and women's traditional leadership styles. Although diversity in the workforce has the potential to improve performance, research indicates that diversity initiatives must be successfully managed in order to reap these organizational benefits. Human resource practitioners are trained to successfully manage diversity issues to enhance positive outcomes.[60] In an overall sense though, learning how to effectively manage a firm's workforce is increasingly important in that "many companies recognize today, more than ever, their people have become their most critical competitive asset."[61]

Although the lifestyle and workforce changes referenced previously reflect the attitudes and values of the U.S. population, each country is unique with respect to these sociocultural indicators. National cultural values affect behavior in organizations and thus also influence organizational outcomes such as differences in CEO compensation.[62] Likewise, the national culture influences to a large extent the internationalization strategy that firms pursue relative to one's home country.[63] Knowledge sharing is important for dispersing new knowledge in organizations and increasing the speed in implementing innovations. Personal relationships are especially important in China as *guanxi* (personal relationships or good connections) has become a way of doing business within the country and for individuals to advance their careers in what is becoming a more open market society. Understanding the importance of guanxi is critical for foreign firms doing business in China.[64]

## 2-3e The Technological Segment

The **technological segment** includes the institutions and activities involved in creating new knowledge and translating that knowledge into new outputs, products, processes, and materials.

Pervasive and diversified in scope, technological changes affect many parts of societies. These effects occur primarily through new products, processes, and materials. The **technological segment** includes the institutions and activities involved in creating new knowledge and translating that knowledge into new outputs, products, processes, and materials.

Given the rapid pace of technological change and risk of disruption, it is vital for firms to thoroughly study the technological segment.[65] The importance of these efforts is suggested by the finding that early adopters of new technology often achieve higher market shares and earn higher returns. Thus, both large and small firms should continuously scan the general environment to identify potential substitutes for technologies that are in current use, as well as to identify newly emerging technologies from which their firm could derive competitive advantage.[66]

As a significant technological development, the Internet offers firms a remarkable capability in terms of their efforts to scan, monitor, forecast, and assess conditions in their general environment. Companies continue to study the Internet's capabilities to anticipate how it may allow them to create more value for customers in the future and to anticipate future trends.

Additionally, the Internet generates a significant number of opportunities and threats for firms across the world. Predictions about Internet usage in the years to come are one reason for this. By 2016, the estimate is that there will be 3 billion Internet users globally. This is almost one-half of the world's population. Moreover, "the Internet economy will reach $4.2 trillion in the G-20 economies. If it were a national economy, the Internet economy would rank in the world's top five, behind only the U.S., China, Japan, and India, and ahead of Germany."[67] Overall, firms can expect that the future is a time period in which the Internet "will have more users (especially in developing markets), more mobile users, more users using various devices throughout the day, and many more people engaged in an increasingly participatory medium."[68]

In spite of the Internet's far-reaching effects and the opportunities and threats associated with its potential, wireless communication technology is becoming a significant technological opportunity for companies to pursue. Handheld devices and other wireless communications equipment are used to access a variety of network-based services. The use of handheld computers with wireless network connectivity, Web-enabled mobile phone handsets, and other emerging platforms (e.g., consumer Internet-access devices such as the iPhone, iPad, and Kindle) has increased substantially and may soon become the dominant form of communication and commerce. In fact, with each new version of these products, additional functionalities and software applications are generating multiple opportunities—and potential threats—for companies of all types.

## 2-3f The Global Segment

The **global segment** includes relevant new global markets, existing markets that are changing, important international political events, and critical cultural and institutional characteristics of global markets.[69] For example, firms competing in the automobile industry must study the global segment. The fact that consumers in multiple nations are willing to buy cars and trucks "from whatever area of the world"[70] supports this position.

When studying the global segment, firms (including automobile manufacturers) should recognize that globalization of business markets may create opportunities to enter new markets as well as threats that new competitors from other economies may also enter their market. In terms of an opportunity for automobile manufacturers, the possibility for these firms to sell their products outside of their home market would seem attractive. But what markets might firms choose to enter? Currently, Brazil, Russia, India, China, and to a lesser extent Indonesia and Malaysia are nations in which automobile and truck sales are expected to increase. In contract, sales are expected to decline, at least in the near term, in Europe and Japan. These expectations suggest the most and least attractive markets for automobile manufacturers desiring to sell outside their domestic market. At the same time, from the perspective of a threat, Japan, Germany, Korea, Spain, France, and the United States are nations in which there appears to be excess production capacity in the automobile manufacturing industry. In turn, overcapacity signals the possibility that companies based in markets where this is the case will simultaneously attempt to increase their exports as well

The **global segment** includes relevant new global markets, existing markets that are changing, important international political events, and critical cultural and institutional characteristics of global markets.

as sales in their domestic market.[71] Thus, global automobile manufacturers should carefully examine the global segment in order to precisely identify all opportunities and threats.

In light of threats associated with participating in international markets, some firms choose to take a more cautious approach to globalization. These firms participate in what some refer to as *globalfocusing*. Globalfocusing often is used by firms with moderate levels of international operations who increase their internationalization by focusing on global niche markets.[72] This approach allows firms to build on and use their core competencies while limiting their risks within the niche market. Another way in which firms limit their risks in international markets is to focus their operations and sales in one region of the world.[73] Success with these efforts finds a firm building relationships in and knowledge of its markets. As the firm builds these strengths, rivals find it more difficult to enter its markets and compete successfully.

Firms competing in global markets should recognize each market's sociocultural and institutional attributes. For example, Korean ideology emphasizes communitarianism, a characteristic of many Asian countries. Alternatively, the ideology in China calls for an emphasis on *guanxi*—personal connections—while in Japan, the focus is on *wa*, or group harmony and social cohesion.[74] The institutional context of China suggests a major emphasis on centralized planning by the government. The Chinese government provides incentives to firms to develop alliances with foreign firms having sophisticated technology in hopes of building knowledge and introducing new technologies to the Chinese markets over time.[75] As such, it is important to analyze the strategic intent of foreign firms when pursuing alliances and joint ventures abroad, especially where the local partners are receiving technology which may in the long run reduce the foreign firms' advantages.[76]

Learn more about Spain's Informal Economy.
www.cengagebrain.com

Increasingly, the *informal economy* as it exits throughout the world is another aspect of the global segment requiring analysis. Growing in size, this economy has implications for firms' competitive actions and responses in that increasingly firms competing in the formal economy (defined in the Strategic Focus) will find that they are competing against informal economy companies as well. We provide additional insights about the informal economy in the Strategic Focus.

## 2-3g The Physical Environment Segment

The **physical environment segment** refers to potential and actual changes in the physical environment and business practices that are intended to positively respond to and deal with those changes.[77] Concerned with trends oriented to sustaining the world's physical environment, firms recognize that ecological, social, and economic systems interactively influence what happens in this particular segment and that they are part of an interconnected global society.[78]

Companies across the globe are concerned about the physical environment and many record the actions they are taking in reports with names such as "Sustainability" and "Corporate Social Responsibility." Moreover and in a comprehensive sense, an increasing number of companies are interested in sustainable development, which is "the development that meets the needs of the present without compromising the ability of future generations to meet their own needs."[79]

The **physical environment segment** refers to potential and actual changes in the physical environment and business practices that are intended to positively respond to and deal with those changes.

There are many parts or attributes of the physical environment that firms consider as they try to identify trends in the physical environment segment.[80] For example, McDonald's seeks to become a sustainable influence on the global food industry. Receiving certification from the Marine Stewardship Council (MCS) for its U.S. supply signals that the company is sourcing fish from "suppliers that follow strict MSC standards for ecosystem impact, management, and health of fish stock."[81] As the world's largest retailer, Walmart's environmental footprint is huge, meaning that trends in the physical environment can significantly affect this firm and how it chooses to operate. Perhaps in light of trends occurring in the physical environment, Walmart has announced that its goal is to produce zero waste and to use 100 percent renewable energy to power its operations.[82]

M. Stasy

## Strategic Focus GLOBALIZATION

### The Informal Economy: What It Is and Why It Is Important

The informal economy refers to commercial activities that occur at least partly outside a governing body's observation, taxation, and regulation. In slightly different words, sociologists Manuel Castells and Alejandro Portes suggest that the "informal economy is characterized by one central feature: it is unregulated by the institutions of society in a legal and social environment in which similar activities are regulated." Firms located in the informal economy are typically thought of as businesses that are unregistered but that are producing and selling legal products. In contrast to the informal economy, the formal economy is comprised of commercial activities that a governing body taxes and monitors for society's benefit and whose outputs are included in a country's gross domestic product.

For some, working in the informal economy is a choice, such as is the case when individuals decide to supplement the income they are earning through employment in the formal economy with a second job in the informal economy. However, for most people working in the informal economy is a necessity rather than a choice—a reality that contributes to the informal economy's size and significance. Although generalizing about the quality of informal employment is difficult, evidence suggests that it typically means poor employment conditions and greater poverty for workers.

Estimates of the informal economy's size across countries and regions vary. In developing countries, the informal economy accounts for as much as three-quarters of all nonagricultural employment, and perhaps as much as 90 percent in some countries in South Asia and sub-Saharan Africa. But the informal economy is also prominent in developed countries such as Finland, Germany, and France (where this economy is estimated to account for 18.3 percent, 16.3 percent, and 15.3 percent, respectively, of these nations' total economic activity). In the United States, recent estimates are that the informal economy is now generating as much as $2 trillion in economic activity on an annual basis. This is double the size of the U.S. informal economy in 2009. In terms of the number of people working in an informal economy, we can consider the suggestion that "India's informal economy...(includes) hundreds of millions of shopkeepers, farmers, construction workers, taxi drivers, street vendors, rag pickers, tailors, repairmen, middlemen, black marketers and more."

There are various causes of the informal economy's growth, including an inability of a nation's economic environment to create a significant number of jobs relative to available workers. This has been a particularly acute problem during the recent global recession. In the words of a person living in Spain: "Without the underground (informal) economy, we would be in a situation of probably violent social unrest." Governments' inability to facilitate growth efforts in their nation's economic environment is another issue. In this regard, another Spanish citizen suggests that "What the government should focus on is reforming the formal economy to make it more efficient and competitive."

In a general sense, the informal economy yields threats and opportunities for formal economy firms. One threat is that informal businesses may have a cost advantage when competing against formal economy firms in that they do not pay taxes or incur the costs of regulations. But the informal economy surfaces opportunities as well. For example, formal economy firms can try to understand the needs of customers that informal economy firms are satisfying and then find ways to better meet their needs. Another valuable opportunity is to attract some of the informal economy's talented human capital to accept positions of employment in formal economy firms.

Sources: A. Picchi, 2013, A shadow economy may be keeping the US afloat, *MSN Money*, www.msn.com, May 3; 2013, Meeting on informal economy statistics: Country experience, international recommendations, and application, *United Nations Economic Commission for Africa*, www.uneca.org, April; 2013, About the informal economy, *Women in informal employment: Globalizing and organizing*, www.wiego.org, May; G. Bruton, R. D. Ireland, & D. J. Ketchen, Jr., 2012, Toward a research agenda on the informal economy, *Academy of Management Perspectives*, 26(3): 1–11; R. D. Ireland, 2012, 2012 program theme: The informal economy, *Academy of Management*, www.meeting.aomonline.org, March; R. Minder, 2012, In Spain, jobless find a refuge off the books, *New York Times*, www.nytimes.com, May 18.



As our discussion of the general environment shows, identifying anticipated changes and trends among segments and their elements is a key objective of analyzing this environment. With a focus on the future, the analysis of the general environment allows firms to identify opportunities and threats. It is necessary to have a top management team with the experience, knowledge, and sensitivity required to effectively analyze a firm's general environment.[83] Also critical to a firm's choices of strategies and their associated competitive actions and responses is an understanding of its industry environment and its competitors; next, we discuss the analyses firms complete to gain such an understanding.

## 2-4 Industry Environment Analysis

An **industry** is a group of firms producing products that are close substitutes. In the course of competition, these firms influence one another. Typically, companies use a rich mix of different competitive strategies to pursue above-average returns when competing in a particular industry. An industry's structural characteristics influence a firm's choice of strategies.[84]

Compared with the general environment, the industry environment (measured primarily in the form of its characteristics) has a more direct effect on the competitive actions and responses a firm takes to succeed.[85] To study an industry, the firm examines five forces that affect the ability of all firms to operate profitably within a given industry. Shown in Figure 2.2, the five forces are: the threats posed by new entrants, the power of suppliers, the power of buyers, product substitutes, and the intensity of rivalry among competitors.

The five forces of competition model depicted in Figure 2.2 expands the scope of a firm's competitive analysis. Historically, when studying the competitive environment, firms concentrated on companies with which they directly competed. However, firms must search more broadly to recognize current and potential competitors by identifying potential customers as well as the firms serving them. For example, the communications industry is now broadly defined as encompassing media companies, telecoms, entertainment companies, and companies producing devices such as smartphones.[86] In such an environment, firms must study many other industries to identify companies with capabilities (especially technology-based capabilities) that might be the foundation for producing a good or a service that can compete against what they are producing.

When studying the industry environment, firms must also recognize that suppliers can become a firm's competitors (by integrating forward) as can buyers (by integrating

**Figure 2.2** The Five Forces of Competition Model

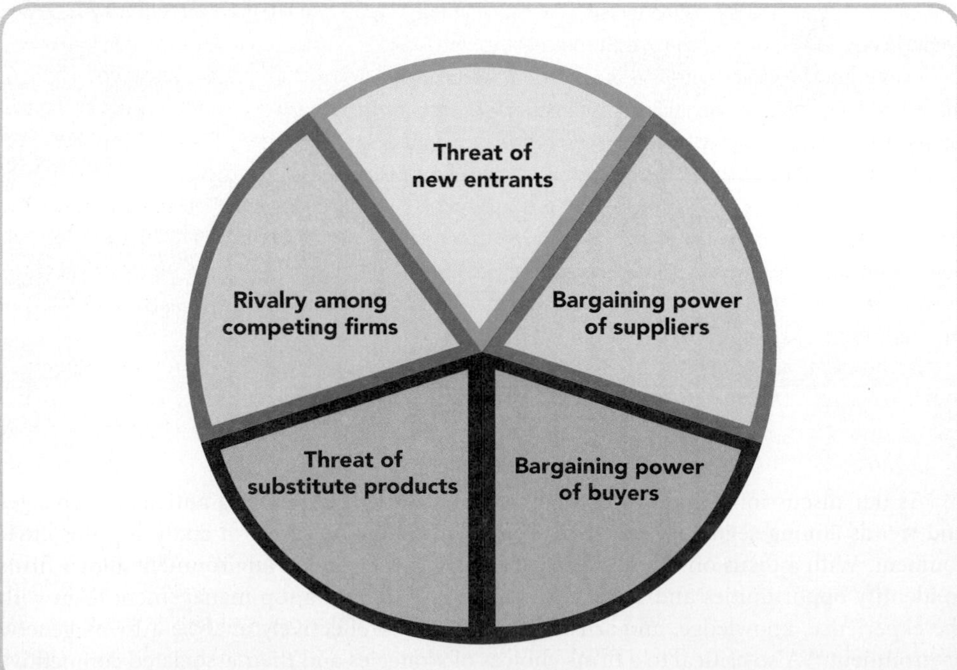


An **industry** is a group of firms producing products that are close substitutes.

backward). For example, several firms have integrated forward in the pharmaceutical industry by acquiring distributors or wholesalers. In addition, firms choosing to enter a new market and those producing products that are adequate substitutes for existing products can become a company's competitors.

Next, we examine the five forces the firm analyzes to understand the profitability potential within an industry (or a segment of an industry) in which it competes or may choose to compete.

## 2-4a Threat of New Entrants

Identifying new entrants is important because they can threaten the market share of existing competitors.[87] One reason new entrants pose such a threat is that they bring additional production capacity. Unless the demand for a good or service is increasing, additional capacity holds consumers' costs down, resulting in less revenue and lower returns for competing firms. Often, new entrants have a keen interest in gaining a large market share. As a result, new competitors may force existing firms to be more efficient and to learn how to compete in new dimensions (e.g., using an Internet-based distribution channel).

The likelihood that firms will enter an industry is a function of two factors: barriers to entry and the retaliation expected from current industry participants. Entry barriers make it difficult for new firms to enter an industry and often place them at a competitive disadvantage even when they are able to enter. As such, high entry barriers tend to increase the returns for existing firms in the industry and may allow some firms to dominate the industry.[88] Thus, firms competing successfully in an industry want to maintain high entry barriers in order to discourage potential competitors from deciding to enter the industry.

### Barriers to Entry

Firms competing in an industry (and especially those earning above-average returns) try to develop entry barriers to thwart potential competitors. In general, more is known about entry barriers (with respect to how they are developed as well as paths firms can pursue to overcome them) in industrialized countries such as those in North America and Western Europe. In contrast, relatively little is known about barriers to entry in the rapidly emerging markets such as those in China. However, recent research suggests that Chinese executives perceive that advertising effects are the most significant of seven barriers to China while capital requirements are viewed as the least important.[89]

There are different kinds of barriers to entering a market that firms study when examining an industry environment. Companies competing within a particular industry study these barriers to determine the degree to which their competitive position reduces the likelihood of new competitors being able to enter the industry for the purpose of competing against them. Firms considering entering an industry study entry barriers to determine the likelihood of being able to identify an attractive competitive position within the industry being analyzed. Next, we discuss several significant entry barriers that may discourage competitors from entering a market and that may facilitate a firm's ability to remain competitive in a market in which it currently competes.

**Economies of Scale** *Economies of scale* are derived from incremental efficiency improvements through experience as a firm grows larger. Therefore, the cost of producing each unit declines as the quantity of a product produced during a given period increases. A new entrant is unlikely to quickly generate the level of demand for its product that in turn would allow it to develop economies of scale.

Economies of scale can be developed in most business functions, such as marketing, manufacturing, research and development, and purchasing.[90] Firms sometimes form strategic alliances or joint ventures to gain scale economies. This is the case for Mitsubishi Heavy Industries Ltd. and Hitachi Ltd., as these companies "merged their operations for fossil-fuel-based power systems into a joint venture aimed at gaining scale to compete against global rivals."[91]

Becoming more flexible in terms of being able to meet shifts in customer demand is another benefit for an industry incumbent and another possible entry barrier for the firm thinking of entering an industry. For example, a firm may choose to reduce its price with the intention of capturing a larger share of the market. Alternatively, it may keep its price constant to increase profits. In so doing, it likely will increase its free cash flow, which is very helpful during financially challenging times.

Some competitive conditions reduce the ability of economies of scale to create an entry barrier. Many companies now customize their products for large numbers of small customer groups. In these cases, customized products are not manufactured in the volumes necessary to achieve economies of scale. Customization is made possible by several factors including flexible manufacturing systems (this point is discussed further in Chapter 4). In fact, the new manufacturing technology facilitated by advanced information systems has allowed the development of mass customization in an increasing number of industries. Although it is not appropriate for all products and implementing it can be challenging, mass customization has become increasingly common in manufacturing products.[92] Online ordering has enhanced customers' ability to buy customized products. Companies manufacturing customized products learn how to respond quickly to customers' needs in lieu of developing scale economies.

**Product Differentiation** Over time, customers may come to believe that a firm's product is unique. This belief can result from the firm's service to the customer, effective advertising campaigns, or being the first to market a good or service. Greater levels of perceived product uniqueness create customers who consistently purchase a firm's products. To combat the perception of uniqueness, new entrants frequently offer products at lower prices. This decision, however, may result in lower profits or even losses.

As noted in the Opening Case, Coca-Cola Company and PepsiCo have established strong brands in the markets in which they compete, and these companies compete against each other in countries throughout the world. Because each of these competitors has allocated a significant amount of resources over many decades to build its brands, customer loyalty is strong for each firm. When considering entry into the soft drink market, a potential entrant would be well advised to pause to determine actions it would take for the purpose of trying to overcome the brand image and consumer loyalty each of these giants possess.

**Capital Requirements** Competing in a new industry requires a firm to have resources to invest. In addition to physical facilities, capital is needed for inventories, marketing activities, and other critical business functions. Even when a new industry is attractive, the capital required for successful market entry may not be available to pursue the market opportunity.[93] For example, defense industries are difficult to enter because of the substantial resource investments required to be competitive. In addition, because of the high knowledge requirements of the defense industry, a firm might acquire an existing company as a means of entering this industry, but it must have access to the capital necessary to do this.

**Switching Costs** Switching costs are the one-time costs customers incur when they buy from a different supplier. The costs of buying new ancillary equipment and of retraining employees, and even the psychic costs of ending a relationship, may be incurred in switching to a new supplier. In some cases, switching costs are low, such as when the consumer switches to a different brand of soft drink. Switching costs can vary as a function of time as shown by the fact that in terms of credit hours toward graduation, the cost to a student to transfer from one university to another as a freshman is much lower than it is when the student is entering the senior year.

Occasionally, a decision made by manufacturers to produce a new, innovative product creates high switching costs for customers. Customer loyalty programs, such as airlines' frequent flyer miles, are intended to increase the customer's switching costs. If switching costs are high, a new entrant must offer either a substantially lower price or a much better product to attract buyers. Usually, the more established the relationships between parties, the greater the switching costs.

**Access to Distribution Channels** Over time, industry participants commonly learn how to effectively distribute their products. Once a relationship with its distributors has been built a firm will nurture it, thus creating switching costs for the distributors. Access to distribution channels can be a strong entry barrier for new entrants, particularly in consumer nondurable goods industries (e.g., in grocery stores where shelf space is limited) and in international markets. New entrants have to persuade distributors to carry their products, either in addition to or in place of those currently distributed. Price breaks and cooperative advertising allowances may be used for this purpose; however, those practices reduce the new entrant's profit potential. Interestingly, access to distribution is less of a barrier for products that can be sold on the Internet.

Trish Gant/Alamy

*The Naked Grocer provides boxes of assorted, locally sourced vegetables to order. By offering locally-sourced produce the company is trying to reduce the strategic relevance of advantages possessed by established firms.*

**Cost Disadvantages Independent of Scale** Sometimes, established competitors have cost advantages that new entrants cannot duplicate. Proprietary product technology, favorable access to raw materials, desirable locations, and government subsidies are examples. Successful competition requires new entrants to reduce the strategic relevance of these factors. For example, delivering purchases directly to the buyer can counter the advantage of a desirable location; new food establishments in an undesirable location often follow this practice. Zara is owned by Inditex, the largest fashion clothing retailer in the world.[94] From the time of its launching, Spanish clothing company Zara relied on classy, well-tailored, and relatively inexpensive items that were produced and sold by adhering to ethical practices to successfully enter the highly competitive global clothing market and overcome that market's entry barriers.[95]

**Government Policy** Through their decisions about issues such as the granting of licenses and permits, governments can also control entry into an industry. Liquor retailing, radio and TV broadcasting, banking, and trucking are examples of industries in which government decisions and actions affect entry possibilities. Also, governments often restrict entry into some industries because of the need to provide quality service or the desire to protect jobs. Alternatively, deregulating industries such as the airline and utilities industries in the United States, generally results in additional firms choosing to enter and compete within an industry.[96] Governmental decisions and policies regarding antitrust issues also affect entry barriers. For example, in the United States, the Antitrust Division of the Justice Department or the Federal Trade Commission will sometimes disallow a proposed merger because officials conclude that approving it would create a firm that is too dominant in an industry and would thus create unfair competition.[97] Such a negative ruling would obviously be an entry barrier for an acquiring firm.

## Expected Retaliation

Companies seeking to enter an industry also anticipate the reactions of firms in the industry. An expectation of swift and vigorous competitive responses reduces the likelihood of entry. Vigorous retaliation can be expected when the existing firm has a major stake in the industry (e.g., it has fixed assets with few, if any, alternative uses), when it has substantial resources, and when industry growth is slow or constrained. For example, any firm attempting to enter the airline industry can expect significant retaliation from existing competitors due to overcapacity.

Locating market niches not being served by incumbents allows the new entrant to avoid entry barriers. Small entrepreneurial firms are generally best suited for identifying and serving neglected market segments. When Honda first entered the U.S. motorcycle market, it concentrated on small-engine motorcycles, a market that firms such as Harley-Davidson ignored. By targeting this neglected niche, Honda initially avoided a significant amount of head-to-head competition with well-established competitors. After consolidating its position, Honda used its strength to attack rivals by introducing larger motorcycles and competing in the broader market.

## 2-4b Bargaining Power of Suppliers

Increasing prices and reducing the quality of their products are potential means suppliers use to exert power over firms competing within an industry. If a firm is unable to recover cost increases by its suppliers through its own pricing structure, its profitability is reduced by its suppliers' actions. A supplier group is powerful when

- It is dominated by a few large companies and is more concentrated than the industry to which it sells.
- Satisfactory substitute products are not available to industry firms.
- Industry firms are not a significant customer for the supplier group.
- Suppliers' goods are critical to buyers' marketplace success.
- The effectiveness of suppliers' products has created high switching costs for industry firms.
- It poses a credible threat to integrate forward into the buyers' industry. Credibility is enhanced when suppliers have substantial resources and provide a highly differentiated product.

The airline industry is one in which suppliers' bargaining power is changing. Though the number of suppliers is low, the demand for major aircraft is also relatively low. Boeing and Airbus aggressively compete for orders of major aircraft, creating more power for buyers in the process. When a large airline signals that it might place a "significant" order for wide-body airliners that either Airbus or Boeing might produce, both companies are likely to battle for the business and include a financing arrangement, highlighting the buyer's power in the potential transaction.

## 2-4c Bargaining Power of Buyers

Firms seek to maximize the return on their invested capital. Alternatively, buyers (customers of an industry or a firm) want to buy products at the lowest possible price—the point at which the industry earns the lowest acceptable rate of return on its invested capital. To reduce their costs, buyers bargain for higher quality, greater levels of service, and lower prices.[98] These outcomes are achieved by encouraging competitive battles among the industry's firms. Customers (buyer groups) are powerful when

- They purchase a large portion of an industry's total output.
- The sales of the product being purchased account for a significant portion of the seller's annual revenues.
- They could switch to another product at little, if any, cost.
- The industry's products are undifferentiated or standardized, and the buyers pose a credible threat if they were to integrate backward into the sellers' industry.

Consumers armed with greater amounts of information about the manufacturer's costs and the power of the Internet as a shopping and distribution alternative have increased bargaining power in many industries.

## 2-4d Threat of Substitute Products

Substitute products are goods or services from outside a given industry that perform similar or the same functions as a product that the industry produces. For example, as a sugar substitute, NutraSweet (and other sugar substitutes) places an upper limit on sugar manufacturers' prices—NutraSweet and sugar perform the same function, though with different characteristics. Other product substitutes include e-mail and fax machines instead of overnight deliveries, plastic containers rather than glass jars, and tea instead of coffee.

Learn more about Substitute Products.
www.cengagebrain.com

Newspaper firms have experienced significant circulation declines over the past decade or more. The declines are a result of the ready availability of substitute outlets for news including Internet sources, cable television news channels, and e-mail and cell phone alerts. Likewise, satellite TV and cable and telecommunication companies provide substitute services for basic media services such as television, Internet, and phone. Tablets such as the iPad are reducing the number of PCs sold as suggested by the fact that worldwide shipments of PCs declined 14 percent during the first quarter of 2013 compared to the same quarter a year earlier. At the same time, "tablets like Apple's iPad flew off the shelves."[99]

In general, product substitutes present a strong threat to a firm when customers face few if any switching costs and when the substitute product's price is lower or its quality and performance capabilities are equal to or greater than those of the competing product. Differentiating a product along dimensions that are valuable to customers (such as quality, service after the sale, and location) reduces a substitute's attractiveness.

## 2-4e Intensity of Rivalry among Competitors

Because an industry's firms are mutually dependent, actions taken by one company usually invite responses. In many industries, firms actively compete against one another. Competitive rivalry intensifies when a firm is challenged by a competitor's actions or when a company recognizes an opportunity to improve its market position.

Firms within industries are rarely homogeneous; they differ in resources and capabilities and seek to differentiate themselves from competitors. Typically, firms seek to differentiate their products from competitors' offerings in ways that customers value and in which the firms have a competitive advantage. Common dimensions on which rivalry is based include price, service after the sale, and innovation.

Next, we discuss the most prominent factors that experience shows affect the intensity of rivalries among firms.

### Numerous or Equally Balanced Competitors

Intense rivalries are common in industries with many companies. With multiple competitors, it is common for a few firms to believe they can act without eliciting a response. However, evidence suggests that other firms generally are aware of competitors' actions, often choosing to respond to them. At the other extreme, industries with only a few firms of equivalent size and power also tend to have strong rivalries. The large and often similar-sized resource bases of these firms permit vigorous actions and responses. The competitive battles between Airbus and Boeing exemplify intense rivalry between relatively equal competitors, especially as airlines place bids for the new wide-body planes they are producing. As discussed in the Opening Case, Coca-Cola Company and PepsiCo have a strong rivalry in an array of liquid drinks as consumers demand great taste and real health benefits.[100]

M. Stasy

## Slow Industry Growth

When a market is growing, firms try to effectively use resources to serve an expanding customer base. Markets increasing in size reduce the pressure to take customers from competitors. However, rivalry in no-growth or slow-growth markets becomes more intense as firms battle to increase their market shares by attracting competitors' customers. Certainly, this has been the case in the fast-food industry as McDonald's, Wendy's, and Burger King use their resources, capabilities, and core competencies to try to win each other's customers.[101] The instability in the market that results from these competitive engagements may reduce the profitability for all firms engaging in such battles.

## High Fixed Costs or High Storage Costs

When fixed costs account for a large part of total costs, companies try to maximize the use of their productive capacity. Doing so allows the firm to spread costs across a larger volume of output. However, when many firms attempt to maximize their productive capacity, excess capacity is created on an industry-wide basis. To then reduce inventories, individual companies typically cut the price of their product and offer rebates and other special discounts to customers. However, doing this often intensifies competition. The pattern of excess capacity at the industry level followed by intense rivalry at the firm level is frequently observed in industries with high storage costs. Perishable products, for example, lose their value rapidly with the passage of time. As their inventories grow, producers of perishable goods often use pricing strategies to sell products quickly.

## Lack of Differentiation or Low Switching Costs

When buyers find a differentiated product that satisfies their needs, they frequently purchase the product loyally over time. Industries with many companies that have successfully differentiated their products have less rivalry, resulting in lower competition for individual firms. Firms that develop and sustain a differentiated product that cannot be easily imitated by competitors often earn higher returns. However, when buyers view products as commodities (i.e., as products with few differentiated features or capabilities), rivalry intensifies. In these instances, buyers' purchasing decisions are based primarily on price and, to a lesser degree, service. Personal computers are a commodity product and the cost to switch from a computer manufactured by one firm to another is low. Thus, the rivalry among Dell, Hewlett-Packard, Lenovo, and other computer manufacturers is strong as these companies consistently seek to find ways to differentiate their offerings.

## High Strategic Stakes

Competitive rivalry is likely to be high when it is important for several of the competitors to perform well in the market. Competing in diverse businesses (such as semiconductors, petrochemicals, fashion, medicine, and skyscraper and plant construction, among others), Samsung has now become a formidable foe for Apple in the global smartphone market. Samsung has committed a significant amount of resources to develop innovative products as the foundation for its efforts to try to outperform Apple in selling this particular product. The fact that the end of the first quarter of 2013 found Samsung holding 33 percent of the global smartphone market compared to an 18 percent share for Apple seemed to suggest that the firm's commitment was yielding desirable outcomes.[102] However, this market is extremely important to Apple as well, suggesting that the smartphone rivalry between these two firms (along with others) will remain quite intense.

High strategic stakes can also exist in terms of geographic locations. For example, a number of automobile manufacturers have committed or are committing to establishing manufacturing facilities in China, which has been the world's largest car market since 2009.[103] General Motors recently announced that it received permission from Chinese authorities to build an 8 billion yuan ($1.3 billion) factory to manufacture its Cadillac brand. The Shanghai GM joint venture is to build this facility.[104] Because of the high stakes involved in China for both General Motors and other firms producing luxury cars (including Audi, BMW, and Mercedes-Benz), rivalry among these firms in this market is quite intense.

### High Exit Barriers

Sometimes companies continue competing in an industry even though the returns on their invested capital are low or negative. Firms making this choice likely face high exit barriers, which include economic, strategic, and emotional factors causing them to remain in an industry when the profitability of doing so is questionable.

Exit barriers are especially high in the airline industry. Profitability in this industry has been very difficult to achieve since the start of the latest global financial crisis (beginning in roughly late 2007 or early 2008). However, profits in the airline industry were expected to increase by approximately 40 percent in 2013 compared to 2012. Industry consolidation and efficiency enhancements to how airline alliances integrate their activities helped reduce airline companies' costs while improving economic conditions in a number of countries. This resulted in a greater demand for travel. These are positive signs, at least in the short run, for these firms given that they do indeed face very high barriers if they were to contemplate leaving the airline travel industry.[105] Common exit barriers that firms face include the following:

- Specialized assets (assets with values linked to a particular business or location)
- Fixed costs of exit (such as labor agreements)
- Strategic interrelationships (relationships of mutual dependence, such as those between one business and other parts of a company's operations, including shared facilities and access to financial markets)
- Emotional barriers (aversion to economically justified business decisions because of fear for one's own career, loyalty to employees, and so forth)
- Government and social restrictions (often based on government concerns for job losses and regional economic effects; more common outside the United States).

## 2-5 Interpreting Industry Analyses

Effective industry analyses are products of careful study and interpretation of data and information from multiple sources. A wealth of industry-specific data is available for firms to analyze for the purpose of better understanding an industry's competitive realities. Because of globalization, international markets and rivalries must be included in the firm's analyses. And, because of the development of global markets, a country's borders no longer restrict industry structures. In fact, in general, entering international markets enhances the chances of success for new ventures as well as more established firms.[106]

Analysis of the five forces within a given industry allows the firm to determine the industry's attractiveness in terms of the potential to earn average or above-average returns. In general, the stronger the competitive forces, the lower the potential for firms to generate profits by implementing their strategies. An unattractive industry has low entry barriers, suppliers and buyers with strong bargaining positions, strong competitive threats from product substitutes, and intense rivalry among competitors. These industry characteristics make it difficult for firms to achieve strategic competitiveness and earn above-average returns. Alternatively, an attractive industry has high entry barriers, suppliers and buyers with little bargaining power, few competitive threats from product substitutes, and relatively moderate rivalry.[107] Next, we explain strategic groups as an aspect of industry competition.

Find out more about Mercedes.
www.cengagebrain.com

## 2-6 Strategic Groups

A set of firms emphasizing similar strategic dimensions and using a similar strategy is called a **strategic group.**[108] The competition between firms within a strategic group is greater than the competition between a member of a strategic group and companies outside that strategic group. Therefore, intra-strategic group competition is more intense than is inter-strategic group competition. In fact, more heterogeneity is evident in the performance of firms within strategic groups than across the groups. The performance leaders within groups are able to follow strategies similar to those of other firms in the group and yet maintain strategic distinctiveness as a foundation for earning above-average returns.[109]

The extent of technological leadership, product quality, pricing policies, distribution channels, and customer service are examples of strategic dimensions that firms in a strategic group may treat similarly. Thus, membership in a particular strategic group defines the essential characteristics of the firm's strategy.[110]

The notion of strategic groups can be useful for analyzing an industry's competitive structure. Such analyses can be helpful in diagnosing competition, positioning, and the profitability of firms competing within an industry.[111] High mobility barriers, high rivalry, and low resources among the firms within an industry limit the formation of strategic groups.[112] However, after strategic groups are formed, their membership remains relatively stable over time.[113] Using strategic groups to understand an industry's competitive structure requires the firm to plot companies' competitive actions and responses along strategic dimensions such as pricing decisions, product quality, distribution channels, and so forth. This type of analysis shows the firm how certain companies are competing similarly in terms of how they use similar strategic dimensions.

Strategic groups have several implications. First, because firms within a group offer similar products to the same customers, the competitive rivalry among them can be intense. The more intense the rivalry, the greater the threat to each firm's profitability. Second, the strengths of the five forces differ across strategic groups. Third, the closer the strategic groups are in terms of their strategies, the greater is the likelihood of rivalry between the groups.

German-based car manufacturers Audi (a part of the Volkswagen group), Bayerische Motoren Werke AG (BMW), and Daimler-Benz (Mercedes-Benz) implement similar strategies (based on the differentiation business-level strategy), emphasize similar strategic dimensions, and compete aggressively against each other. These three firms constitute a strategic group (in the performance/luxury segment) as do Maruti-Suzuki, Tata Motors, and Skoda (these three firms form a passenger car strategic group with the distinctive feature that they sell their products primarily in their domestic markets and very little internationally). We describe the strategic group featuring the three German companies in the Strategic Focus.

## 2-7 Competitor Analysis

The competitor environment is the final part of the external environment requiring study. Competitor analysis focuses on each company against which a firm competes directly. Coca-Cola Company and PepsiCo, Home Depot and Lowe's, Carrefour SA and Tesco PLC, and Boeing and Airbus are examples of competitors who are keenly interested in understanding each other's objectives, strategies, assumptions, and capabilities. Indeed, intense rivalry creates a strong need to understand competitors.[114] In a competitor analysis, the firm seeks to understand the following:

A set of firms emphasizing similar strategic dimensions and using a similar strategy is called a **strategic group**.

- What drives the competitor, as shown by its *future objectives*
- What the competitor is doing and can do, as revealed by its *current strategy*

M. Stasy

## Strategic Focus — GLOBALIZATION

### German Performance/Luxury Cars: If You Have Seen One, Have You Seen Them All?

Audi, BMW, and Mercedes-Benz (Mercedes) have long competed against each other in the performance/luxury segment of the automobile industry. Given that they implement similar strategies in many of the same markets throughout the world and emphasize similar dimensions to do so, these firms form a strategic group. This means that the rivalry within this group is more intense than is the rivalry between members of this group and companies offering products that are intended to functionally serve and satisfy a mass-market appeal among large customer groups. One could even argue that three sub-strategic groups exist for these firms in that each offers products in the large, mid-size, and small parts of the performance/luxury segment. (Think of the Audi S8 versus the BMW 7 series versus the S Mercedes series as products through which these firms compete against each other in terms of large performance/luxury cars.)

The similarities among these firms as they compete are extensive. For example, the Chinese and U.S. markets are critical to their success. With respect to China, an analyst recently noted that "BMW, Audi and Daimler's Mercedes-Benz units have benefited as China's fast growing wealthy population has flocked to high-end cars in recent years." In response to this growth in demand for their products, all three firms are investing billions of dollars to expand production and their sales operations in China.

For the U.S. market, the firms are introducing new models that are intended to significantly expand their sales. One way these competitors are doing this is to offer "lower priced models that would draw younger, less affluent U.S. customers away from mass market brands such as Ford Motor Co., Honda Motor Co., and Toyota Motor Corp." A lower-cost version of the A3 sedan is Audi's initial offering to reach this objective. BMW has developed a new version of its top-selling 3 series sedan (the 320) that will have a base price roughly $4,000 below the currently least expensive car in this series. Similarly, Mercedes intends to offer the CLA, which is a 4-cyclinder car with a base price just below $30,000. Essentially, introducing these products is a strong attempt by the three firms to lower price as an entry barrier to their products among consumers in their 20s, 30s, and early 40s.

These firms are emphasizing similar dimensions or product features to produce these new models as well as some existing ones. For example, diesel engines are important to the companies and their efforts to sell more cars in China, the United States, and other countries as well. Because of this, the three of them recently joined a few other companies to develop a Web site (www.clearlybetterdiesel.org) that touts diesel's benefits of superior fuel economy and a reduced environmental impact. To better serve the needs of younger consumers, all three companies are "re-thinking everything from dashboard entertainment systems to the relative importance of mileage over horsepower to fundamental marketing strategies." An initial outcome from these evaluation processes is a decision to include smartly presented, smartphone-driven multimedia systems in models being developed for the U.S. market.

*The 2014 CLA 45 AMG Mercedes-Benz is presented at the New York International Auto Show in New York's Javits Center in March 2013. The new addition to Mercedes-Benz' product mix is aimed at customers typically targeted by mass market brands.*

As is often the case with strategic groups, the one among Audi, BMW, and Mercedes has remained stable over the years. As such, we can anticipate that the rivalry among them will remain intense as they rely on similar strategic dimensions to implement similar strategies.

Sources: C. Carroll, 2013, Audi plans to attract more U.S. buyers with diesels, *Wall Street Journal*, www.wsj.com, February 8; V. Fuhrmans, 2013, Europe bets U.S. auto demand to stay high, *Wall Street Journal*, www.wsj.com, January 16; V. Fuhrmans, 2013, German auto makers to shake up luxury market, *Wall Street Journal*, www.wsj.com, January 14; V. Fuhrmans & F. Geiger, 2013, VW to bolster its output in China, *Wall Street Journal*, www.wsj.com, March 14; F. Geiger, 2013, Daimler boosts investment in China, *Wall Street Journal*, www.wsj.com, February 1; J. W. White, 2013, Beyond boomer buyers: Car makers seek younger crop of customers, *Wall Street Journal*, www.wsj.com, January 16.

- What the competitor believes about the industry, as shown by its *assumptions*
- What the competitor's capabilities are, as shown by its *strengths* and *weaknesses*.[115]

Knowledge about these four dimensions helps the firm prepare an anticipated response profile for each competitor (see Figure 2.3). The results of an effective competitor analysis help a firm understand, interpret, and predict its competitors' actions and responses. Understanding competitors' actions and responses clearly contributes to the firm's ability to compete successfully within the industry.[116] Interestingly, research suggests that executives often fail to analyze competitors' possible reactions to competitive actions their firm takes,[117] placing their firm at a potential competitive disadvantage as a result.

Critical to an effective competitor analysis is gathering data and information that can help the firm understand its competitors' intentions and the strategic implications resulting from them.[118] Useful data and information combine to form **competitor intelligence**, the set of data and information the firm gathers to better understand and anticipate competitors' objectives, strategies, assumptions, and capabilities. In competitor analysis, the firm gathers intelligence not only about its competitors, but also regarding public policies in countries around the world. Such intelligence facilitates an understanding of the strategic posture of foreign competitors. Through effective competitive and public policy intelligence, the firm gains the insights needed to make effective strategic decisions regarding how to compete against rivals.

**Competitor intelligence** is the set of data and information the firm gathers to better understand and anticipate competitors' objectives, strategies, assumptions, and capabilities.

When asked to describe competitive intelligence, phrases such as "competitive spying" and "corporate espionage" come to my mind for some. These phrases denote the fact that

**Figure 2.3** Competitor Analysis Components

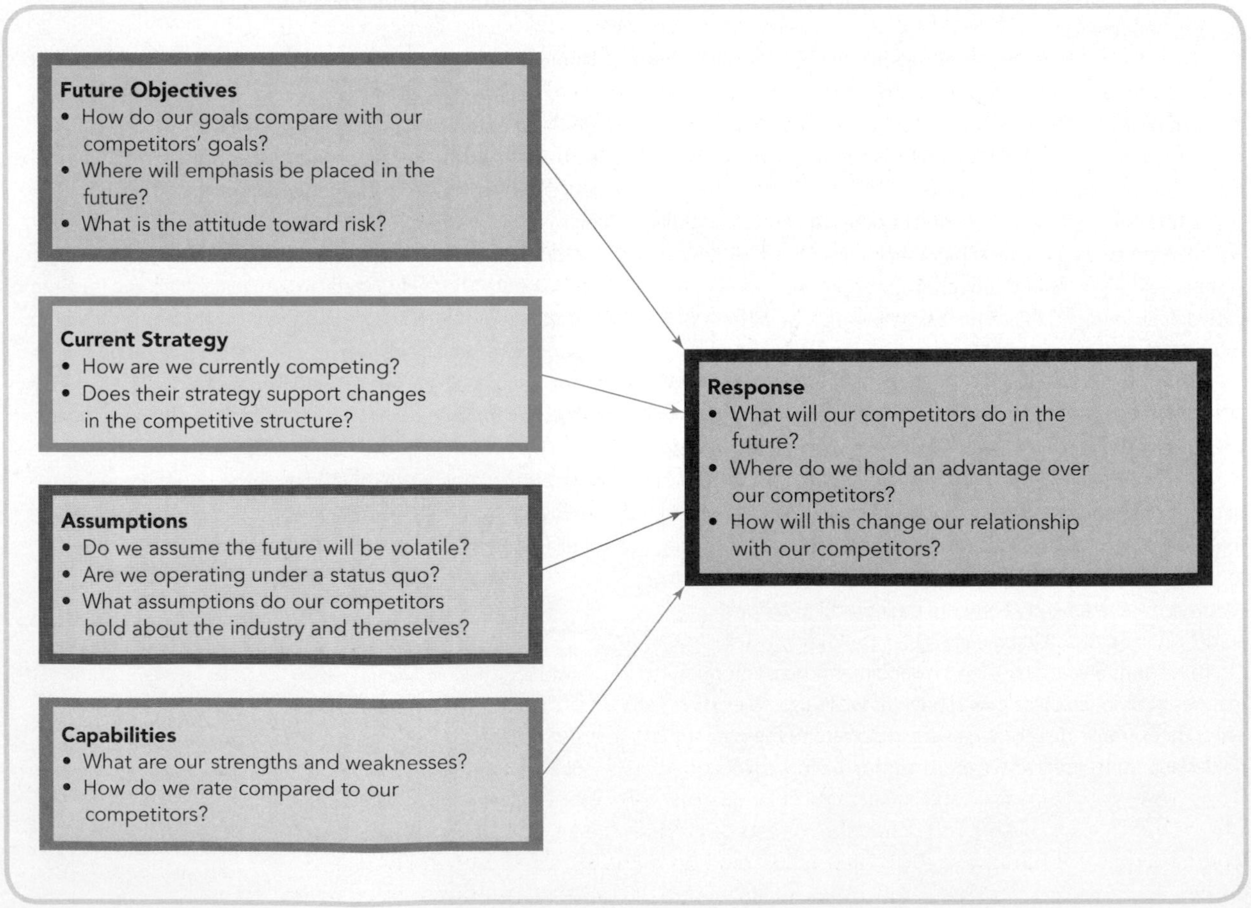

competitive intelligence is an activity that appears to involve trade-offs.[119] The reason for this is that "what is ethical in one country is different from what is ethical in other countries." This position implies that the rules of engagement to follow when gathering competitive intelligence change in different contexts.[120] However, firms avoid the possibility of legal entanglements and ethical quandaries only when their competitive intelligence gathering methods are governed by a strict set of legal and ethical guidelines.[121] This means that ethical behavior and actions as well as the mandates of relevant laws and regulations should be the foundation on which a firm's competitive intelligence-gathering process is formed.

When gathering competitive intelligence, firms must also pay attention to the complementors of its products and strategy.[122] **Complementors** are companies or networks of companies that sell goods or services that are compatible with the focal firm's good or service. When a complementor's good or service contributes to the functionality of a focal firm's good or service, it in turn creates additional value for that firm.

There are many examples of firms whose good or service complements other companies' offerings. For example, firms manufacturing affordable home photo printers complement other companies' efforts to sell digital cameras. Intel and Microsoft are perhaps the most widely recognized complementors. The Microsoft slogan "Intel Inside" demonstrates the relationship between two firms who do not directly buy from or sell to each other but whose products have a strong complementary relationship. Gasoline and automobiles are obvious complementors in that gasoline-powered cars are useless without gas while the price of gasoline would decline significantly without cars.

Alliances among airline companies such as Oneworld and Star find member companies sharing their route structures and customer loyalty programs as a means of complementing each other's operations. (Alliances and other cooperative strategies are described in Chapter 9.) In the example we are considering here, each of the two alliances is a network of complementors. American Airlines, British Airways, Finnair, Japan Airlines, and Royal Jordanian are among the airlines forming the Oneworld alliance. Air Canada, Brussels Airlines, Croatia Airlines, Lufthansa, and United Airlines are five of the total of 27 members forming the Star alliance. Both of these alliances constantly adjust their members and services offered to better meet customers' needs. For example, SriLankan Airlines is scheduled to join Oneworld in 2014 while Qatar Airways is to join the alliance in late 2013 or early 2014. In terms of services, the Star alliance announced in May of 2013 that it was expanding its mobile device capabilities by introducing a customized Navigator application for iPads.

As our discussion shows, complementors expand the set of competitors firms must evaluate when completing a competitor analysis. In this sense, American Airlines and United Airlines examine each other both as direct competitors on multiple routes but also as complementors who are part of different alliances (Oneworld for American and Star for United). In all cases though, ethical commitments and actions should be the foundation on which competitor analyses are developed.

## 2-8 Ethical Considerations

Firms must follow relevant laws and regulations as well as carefully articulated ethical guidelines when gathering competitor intelligence. Industry associations often develop lists of these practices that firms can adopt. Practices considered both legal and ethical include (1) obtaining publicly available information (e.g., court records, competitors' help-wanted advertisements, annual reports, financial reports of publicly held corporations, and Uniform Commercial Code filings) and (2) attending trade fairs and shows to obtain competitors' brochures, view their exhibits, and listen to discussions about their products. In contrast,

**Complementors** are companies or networks of companies that sell complementary goods or services that are compatible with the focal firm's good or service.

certain practices (including blackmail, trespassing, eavesdropping, and stealing drawings, samples, or documents) are widely viewed as unethical and often are illegal as well.

Some competitor intelligence practices may be legal, but a firm must decide whether they are also ethical, given the image it desires as a corporate citizen. Especially with electronic transmissions, the line between legal and ethical practices can be difficult to determine. For example, a firm may develop Web site addresses that are similar to those of its competitors and thus occasionally receive e-mail transmissions that were intended for those competitors. The practice is an example of the challenges companies face in deciding how to gather intelligence about competitors while simultaneously determining how to prevent competitors from learning too much about them. To deal with these challenges, firms should establish principles and take actions that are consistent with them.

Professional associations are available to firms as sources of information regarding competitive intelligence practices. For example, while pursuing its mission to help firms make "better decisions through competitive intelligence," the association known as the Strategy and Competitive Intelligence Professionals offers codes of professional practice and ethics to firms for their possible use when deciding how to gather competitive intelligence.[123]

Open discussions of intelligence-gathering techniques can help a firm ensure that employees, customers, suppliers, and even potential competitors understand its convictions to follow ethical practices when gathering intelligence about its competitors. An appropriate guideline for competitor intelligence practices is to respect the principles of common morality and the right of competitors not to reveal certain information about their products, operations, and intentions.[124]

## SUMMARY

- The firm's external environment is challenging and complex. Because of its effect on performance, the firm must develop the skills required to identify opportunities and threats that are a part of its external environment.
- The external environment has three major parts: (1) the general environment (segments and elements in the broader society that affect industries and the firms competing in them), (2) the industry environment (factors that influence a firm, its competitive actions and responses, and the industry's profitability potential), and (3) the competitor environment (in which the firm analyzes each major competitor's future objectives, current strategies, assumptions, and capabilities).
- Scanning, monitoring, forecasting, and assessing are the four parts of the external environmental analysis process. Effectively using this process helps the firm in its efforts to identify opportunities and threats.
- The general environment has seven segments: demographic, economic, political/legal, sociocultural, technological, global, and physical. For each segment, the firm has to determine the strategic relevance of environmental changes and trends.
- Compared with the general environment, the industry environment has a more direct effect on the firm's competitive actions and responses. The five forces model of competition includes the threat of entry, the power of suppliers, the power of buyers, product substitutes, and the intensity of rivalry among competitors. By studying these forces, the firm finds a position in an industry where it can influence the forces in its favor or where it can buffer itself from the power of the forces to achieve strategic competitiveness and earn above-average returns.
- Industries are populated with different strategic groups. A strategic group is a collection of firms following similar strategies along similar dimensions. Competitive rivalry is greater within a strategic group than between strategic groups.
- Competitor analysis informs the firm about the future objectives, current strategies, assumptions, and capabilities of the companies with which it competes directly. A thorough competitor analysis examines complementors that support forming and implementing rivals' strategies.
- Different techniques are used to create competitor intelligence: the set of data, information, and knowledge that allows the firm to better understand its competitors and thereby predict their likely competitive actions and responses. Firms absolutely should use only legal and ethical practices to gather intelligence. The Internet enhances firms' ability to gather insights about competitors and their strategic intentions.

# REVIEW QUESTIONS

1. Why is it important for a firm to study and understand the external environment?
2. What are the differences between the general environment and the industry environment? Why are these differences important?
3. What is the external environmental analysis process (four parts)? What does the firm want to learn when using this process?
4. What are the seven segments of the general environment? Explain the differences among them.
5. How do the five forces of competition in an industry affect its profitability potential? Explain.
6. What is a strategic group? Of what value is knowledge of the firm's strategic group in formulating that firm's strategy?
7. What is the importance of collecting and interpreting data and information about competitors? What practices should a firm use to gather competitor intelligence and why?

# EXPERIENTIAL EXERCISES

## EXERCISE 1: CREATING A FIVE FORCES INDUSTRY MODEL

The five forces model is designed to better understand the competitive forces in an industry in which a firm competes. For example, if the combination of forces in an industry serves to restrict or reduce profitability, the industry is said to be unattractive. Naturally the inverse is true—if the combined forces serve to improve or increase the firm's chances for profitability, this is said to be an attractive industry in which to compete.

Michael Porter's analysis explores the three horizontal forces (threat of new entrants, threat of substitutes, and threat from rivals) and two vertical forces (bargaining power of buyers and bargaining power of suppliers).

The following exercise asks you to work in teams to evaluate the U.S. automotive industry. Bear in mind you are evaluating an industry and not a particular firm, and your analysis should be positioned to evaluate the industry in which rivals compete in manufacturing and selling cars and trucks. This exercise will be all the more compelling since the industry has undergone some relatively significant economic shifts in the past few years as well as the potential for disruption due to new technology.

Each team will be required to present a summary of its analysis using the following table. As you will note after completing the exercise, a five forces model requires some solid research but also requires judgment and intuition as to how the forces interact. There are relatively few concrete answers to any of the forces. Your team should fill out and hand in the accompanying table along with your supporting analysis.

Once your team has identified and supported its rating for each force, summarize the results and indicate your assessment that the industry is either attractive or unattractive with respect to its profitability potential. Also, be prepared to examine the impact of your analysis on an individual firm in the industry.

| Overall Rating | Favorable | Team Rating | Unfavorable |
|---|---|---|---|
| Threat of New Entrants | 10 | | 1 |
| Intensity of Rivalry | 10 | | 1 |
| Threat of Substitutes | 10 | | 1 |
| Bargaining Power of Buyers | 10 | | 1 |
| Bargaining Power of Suppliers | 10 | | 1 |

## EXERCISE 2: WHAT DOES THE FUTURE LOOK LIKE?

A critical ingredient to studying the general environment is identifying opportunities and threats. An opportunity is a condition in the environment that, if exploited, helps a company achieve strategic competitiveness. In order to identify opportunities, you must be aware of trends that affect the world around us now or that are projected to do so in the future.

Thomas Fry, executive director and senior futurist at the DaVinci Institute, believes that the chaotic nature of interconnecting trends and the vast array of possibilities that arise from them are somewhat akin to watching a spinning compass needle. From the way we use phones or e-mail, or how we recruit new workers to organizations, the climate for business is changing and shifting dramatically, and at rapidly increasing rates. Sorting these trends out and making sense of them provides the basis for opportunity decision making. Which ones will dominate and which ones will fade? Understanding this is crucial for business success.

Your challenge (either individually or as a group) is to identify a trend, technology, entertainment mode, or design that is likely to alter the way in which business is conducted in the future. Once you have identified this, be prepared to discuss:

- Which of the seven dimensions of the general environment will this affect (may be more than one)?
  - Describe the effect.
  - List some business opportunities that will come from this.
  - Identify some existing organizations that stand to benefit.
  - What, if any, are the ethical implications?

You should consult a wide variety of sources. For example, the Gartner Group and McKinsey & Company both produce market research and forecasts for business. There are also many Web forecasting tools and addresses such as TED (technology, entertainment, design, where you can find videos of their discussions; see www.ted.com), that host an annual conference for path-breaking new ideas. Similarly, the DaVinci Institute and the Institute for Global Futures as well as many others have their own unique vision for tomorrow's environment.

## VIDEO CASE

### THE NEED TO EXAMINE THE EXTERNAL ENVIRONMENT: DISASTER IN THE GULF THREE-PLUS YEARS LATER

The Gulf Coast oil spill disaster not only resulted in oil and tar balls washing up on local beaches but contributed to the evaporation of the wedding business on the beach. In one family business, 85 percent of the business and $90,000 were lost while the firm received only $20,000 in emergency payments. The first year after the spill, resentful wedding business owners were still living day to day. They contended that British Petroleum (BP), which owned the Deepwater Horizon oil rig where the explosion and subsequent leak occurred, had not fulfilled its obligations to them and their true losses would never be recovered. With government intervention, the $20 billion fund established by BP had paid out only $3.8 billion at the end of the first year. Government attorney Kenneth Feinberg emphasized at that time that 200,000 claimants had been compensated in nine months.

Be prepared to discuss the following concepts and questions in class:

### Concepts

- The external environment
- External environmental analysis
- Five forces of competition
- Strategic groups
- Competitor analysis

### Questions

1. What parts of the external environment (general, industry, and competitive) do you believe BP considered or didn't consider prior to drilling off the Gulf Coast? What should the wedding business owners now consider in their external environment?
2. How should BP have handled an external environmental analysis and what environmental changes and trends (opportunities and threats) might the firm have discovered?
3. Analyze BP using the five forces of competition model to determine the industry's current attractiveness in terms of profitability potential.
4. Who might be in BP's strategic group and why?
5. What would a competitor of BP now discover about the firm by completing a competitor analysis?

## NOTES

1. R. Krause, M. Semadeni, & A. A. Cannella, 2013, External COO/presidents as expert directors: A new look at the service of role of boards, *Strategic Management Journal*, 34: in press; Y. Y. Kor & A. Mesko, 2013, Dynamic managerial capabilities: Configuration and orchestration of top executives' capabilities and the firm's dominant logic, *Strategic Management Journal*, 34: 233–234.

2. R. Kapoor & J. M. Lee, 2013, Coordinating and competing in ecosystems: How organizational forms shape new technology investments, *Strategic Management Journal*, 34: 274–296; M. J. Benner & R. Ranganathan, 2012, Offsetting illegitimacy? How pressures from securities analysts influence incumbents in the face of new technologies, *Academy of Management Journal*, 55: 213–233.

3. A. R. Fremeth & J. M. Shaver, 2013, Strategic rationale for responding to extra-jurisdictional regulation: Evidence from firm adoption of renewable power in the US, *Strategic Management Journal*, 34: in press; E.-H. Kim, 2013, Deregulation and differentiation: Incumbent investment in green technologies, *Strategic Management Journal*, 34: in press.

4. R. J. Sawant, 2012, Asset specificity and corporate political activity in regulated industries, *Academy of Management Review*, 37: 194–210; S. Hanson, A. Kashyap, & J. Stein, 2011, A macroprudential approach to financial regulation. *Journal of Economic Perspectives*, 25(1): 3–28.
5. S. Garg, 2013, Venture boards: Distinctive monitoring and implications for firm performance, *Academy of Management Review*, 38: 90–108; J. Harrison, D. Bosse, & R. Phillips, 2010, Managing for stakeholders, stakeholder utility functions, and competitive advantage, *Strategic Management Journal*, 31(1): 58–74.
6. S. C. Schleimer & T. Pedersen, 2013, The driving forces of subsidiary absorptive capacity, *Journal of Management Studies*, 50: 646–672; M. T. Lucas & O. M. Kirillova, 2011, Reconciling the resource-based and competitive positioning perspectives on manufacturing flexibility, *Journal of Manufacturing Technology Management*, 22(2): 189–203.
7. C. Qian, Q. Cao, & R. Takeuchi, 2013, Top management team functional diversity and organizational innovation in China: The moderating effects of environment, *Strategic Management Journal*, 34: 110–120; L. Fahey, 1999, *Competitors*, New York: John Wiley & Sons.
8. Z. Lindgardt, C. Nettesheim, & T. Chen, 2012, Unlocking growth in the middle, *bcg. perspectives*, www.bcgperspectives.com, May 9.
9. E. V. Karniouchina, S. J. Carson, J. C. Short, & D. J. Ketchen, 2013, Extending the firm vs. industry debate: Does industry life cycle stage matter? *Strategic Management Journal*, 34: in press; B. Larraneta, S. A. Zahra, & J. L. Gonzalez, 2013, Strategic repertoire variety and new venture growth: The moderating effects of origin and industry dynamism, *Strategic Management Journal*, 34: in press.
10. R. B. MacKay & R. Chia, 2013, Choice, chance, and unintended consequences in strategic change: A process understanding of the rise and fall of NorthCo Automotive, *Academy of Management Journal*, 56: 208–230; J. P. Murmann, 2013, The coevolution of industries and important features of their environments, *Organization Science*, 24: 58–78; G. J. Kilduff, H. A. Elfenbein, & B. M. Staw, 2010, The psychology of rivalry: A relationally dependent analysis of competition, *Academy of Management Journal*, 53: 943–969.
11. A. Hecker & A. Ganter, 2013, The influence of product market competition on technological and management innovation: Firm-level evidence from a large-scale survey, *European Management Review*, 10: 17–33; W. K. Smith & M. W. Lewis, 2011, Toward a theory of paradox: A dynamic equilibrium model of organizing, *Academy of Management Review*, 36(2): 381–403.
12. W. Loeb, 2013, Successful global growers: What we can learn from Walmart, Carrefour, Tesco, Metro, *Forbes*, www.forbes.com, March 7.
13. A. Efrati, 2013, Google to fund, develop wireless in networks in emerging markets, *Wall Street Journal*, www.wsj.com, May 24.
14. F. Bridoux & J. W. Stoelhorst, 2013, Microfoundations for stakeholder theory: Managing stakeholders with heterogeneous motives, *Strategic Management Journal*, in press; B. Gilad, 2011, The power of blindspots. What companies don't know, surprises them. What they don't want to know, kills them, *Strategic Direction*, 27(4): 3–4.
15. A. Poon & J. Rossi, 2013, Patent battle between Nokia, HTC heats up, *Wall Street Journal*, www.wsj.com, May 24.
16. J. Rossi, 2013, Jolla set to join global smartphone market, *Wall Street Journal*, www.wsj.com, May 21.
17. D. Li, 2013, Multilateral R&D alliances by new ventures, *Journal of Business Venturing*, 28: 241–260; A. Graefe, S. Luckner, & C. Weinhardt, 2010, Prediction markets for foresight, *Futures*, 42(4): 394–404.
18. J. Tang, K. M. Kacmar, & L. Busenitz, 2012, Entrepreneurial alertness in the pursuit of new opportunities, *Journal of Business Venturing*, 27: 77–94; D. Chrusciel, 2011, Environmental scan: Influence on strategic direction, *Journal of Facilities Management*, 9(1): 7–15.
19. D. E. Hughes, J. Le Bon, & A. Rapp, 2013, Gaining and leveraging customer-based competitive intelligence: The pivotal role of social capital and salesperson adaptive selling skills, *Journal of the Academy of Marketing Science*, 41: 91–110; J. R. Hough & M. A. White, 2004, Scanning actions and environmental dynamism: Gathering information for strategic decision making, *Management Decision*, 42: 781–793; V. K. Garg, B. A. Walters, & R. L. Priem, 2003, Chief executive scanning emphases, environmental dynamism, and manufacturing firm performance, *Strategic Management Journal*, 24: 725–744.
20. C.-H. Lee & T.-F. Chien, 2013, Leveraging microblogging big data with a modified density-based clustering approach for event awareness and topic ranking, *Journal of Information Science*, in press.
21. S. Garg, 2013, Venture boards: Distinctive monitoring and implications for firm performance, *Academy of Management Review*, 38: 90–108; Fahey, *Competitors*, 71–73.
22. K. Greene & V. Monga, 2013, Workers saving too little to retire, *Wall Street Journal*, www.wsj.com, March 19.
23. B. L. Connelly & E. J. Van Slyke, 2012, The power and peril of board interlocks, *Business Horizons*, 55: 403–408; C. Dellarocas, 2010, Online reputation systems: How to design one that does what you need, *MIT Sloan Management Review*, 51(3): 33–37.
24. K. L. Turner & M. V. Makhija, 2012, The role of individuals in the information processing perspective, *Strategic Management Journal*, 33: 661–680; X. Zhang, S. Majid, & S. Foo, 2010, Environmental scanning: An application of information literacy skills at the workplace, *Journal of Information Science*, 36(6): 719–732; M. J. Leiblein & T. L. Madsen, 2009, Unbundling competitive heterogeneity: Incentive structures and capability influences on technological innovation, *Strategic Management Journal*, 30: 711–735.
25. L. Sleuwaegen, 2013, Scanning for profitable (international) growth, *Journal of Strategy and Management*, 6: 96–110; J. Calof & J. Smith, 2010, The integrative domain of foresight and competitive intelligence and its impact on R&D management, *R & D Management*, 40(1): 31–39.
26. A. Chwolka & M. G. Raith, 2012, The value of business planning before start-up—A decision-theoretical perspective, *Journal of Business Venturing*, 27: 385–399; Fahey, *Competitors*.
27. S. D. Wu, K. G. Kempf, M. O. Atan, B. Aytac, S. A. Shirodkar, & A. Mishra, 2010, Improving new-product forecasting at Intel Corporation, *Interfaces*, 40: 385–396.
28. R. Klingebiel, 2012, Options in the implementation plan of entrepreneurial initiatives: Examining firms' attainment of flexibility benefit, *Strategic Entrepreneurship Journal*, 6: 307–334; T. Sueyoshi & M. Goto, 2011, Methodological comparison between two unified (operational and environmental) efficiency measurements for environmental assessment, *European Journal of Operational Research*, 210(3): 684–693; Fahey, *Competitors*, 75–77.
29. N. J. Foss, J. Lyngsie, & S. A. Zahra, 2013, The role of external knowledge sources and organizational design in the process of opportunity exploitation, *Strategic Management Journal*, 34: in press; M. Exu, V. Ong, Y. Duan, & B. Mathews, 2011, Intelligent agent systems for executive information scanning, filtering and interpretation: Perceptions and challenges, *Information Processing & Management*, 47(2): 186–201.
30. D. Grewal, A. Roggeveen, & R. C. Runyan, 2013, Retailing in a connected world, *Journal of Marketing Management*, 29: 263–270; R. King, 2010, Consumer demographics: Use demographic resources to target specific audiences, *Journal of Financial Planning*, 23(12): S4–S6.
31. 2013, U.S. Census Bureau, International Programs World Population, www.census.gov/population/international/data/worldpop/, May 21.
32. 2013, The world population and the top ten countries with the highest population, *Internet World Stats*, www.internetworldstats.com, May 21.
33. T. Kambayashi, 2011, Brief: Aging Japan sees slowest population growth yet, *McClatchy-Tribune Business News*, www.mcclatchy.com,

February 25; S. Moffett, 2005, Fast-aging Japan keeps its elders on the job longer, *Wall Street Journal*, June 15, A1, A8.

34. D. Bloom & D. Canning, 2012, How companies must adapt for an aging workforce, *HBR Blog Network*, www.hbr.org, December 3.
35. 2012, Humanity's aging, *National Institute on Aging*, www.nia.nih.gov, March 27.
36. M. B. Dougherty, 2012, Stunning facts about Japan's demographic implosion, *Business Insider*, www.businessinsider.com, April 24.
37. 2013, The aging workforce: Finding the silver lining in the talent gap, *Deloitte*, www.deloitte.com, February.
38. 2013, 2013 Cal Facts, Legislative Analysts' Office, www.lao.ca.gov, January 2.
39. J. Goudreau, 2013, The states people are fleeing in 2013, *Forbes*, www.forbes.com, February 7.
40. R. Dobbs, S. Smit, J. Remes, J. Manyika, C. Roxburgh, & A. Restrepo, 2011, Urban world: Mapping the economic power of cities, Chicago: McKinsey Global Institute, March.
41. 2012, Population and population change statistics, *European Commission*, www.epp.eurostat.ec.europa.eu, October.
42. S. Reddy, 2011, U.S. News: Latinos fuel growth in decade, *Wall Street Journal*, March 25, A2.
43. M. Fisher, 2013, A revealing map of the world's most and least ethnically diverse countries, *The Washington Post*, www.washingtonpost.com, May 16.
44. A. Hain-Cole, 2010, Companies juggle cost cutting with competitive benefits for international assignments, *Benefits & Compensation International: A Magazine for Global Companies*, 40(5): 26.
45. J. Lee, 2010, Don't underestimate India's consumers, *Bloomberg Businessweek*, www.businessweek.com, January 21.
46. G. A. Shinkle & B. T. McCann, 2013, New product deployment: The moderating influence of economic institutional context, *Strategic Management Journal*, in press; L. Fahey & V. K. Narayanan, 1986, *Macroenvironmental Analysis for Strategic Management (The West Series in Strategic Management)*, St. Paul, Minnesota: West Publishing Company, 105.
47. N. Bloom, M. A. Kose, & M. E. Terrones, 2013, Held back by uncertainty, *Finance & Development*, 50: 38–41, March.
48. 2013, Global economy in 2013: Uncertainty weighing on growth, *Grant Thornton International Business Report*, www.internationalbusinessreport.com, March.
49. R. J. Sawant, 2012, Asset specificity and corporate political activity in regulated industries, *Academy of Management Review*, 37: 194–210; G. F. Holburne & B. A. Zelner, 2010, Political capabilities, policy risk, and international investment strategy: Evidence from the global electric power generation industry, *Strategic Management Journal*, 31(12): 1290–1315; C. Oliver & I. Holzinger, 2008, The effectiveness of strategic political management: A dynamic capabilities framework, *Academy of Management Review*, 33: 496–520.
50. N. Jia, 2013, Are collective political actions and private political actions substitutes or complements? Empirical evidence from China's private sector, *Strategic Management Journal*, in press; R. K. Kozhikode & J. Li, 2012, Political pluralism, public schools, and organizational choices: Banking branch expansion in India, 1948–2003, *Academy of Management Journal*, 55: 339–359.
51. S. Zeidler, 2013, MGM assessing costs of operating online poker in Nevada, *Reuters*, www.mobile,reuters.com, May 2.
52. R. Ayadi, E. Arbak, W. P. de Goren, & D. T. Llewellyn, 2013, *Regulation of European Banks and Business Models: Towards a New Paradigm?* Brookings Institution Press, Washington, D.C.
53. K. J. O'Brien, 2013, Firms brace for new European data privacy law, *New York Times*, www.nytimes.com, May 13.
54. C. Jiang, S. Yao, & G. Feng, 2013, Bank ownership, privatization, and performance: Evidence from a transition country, *Journal of Banking & Finance*, 37: 3364–3372; N. Boubakri & L. Bouslimi, 2010, Analysts following of privatized firms around the world: The role of institutions and ownership structure, *International Journal of Accounting*, 45(4): 413–442.
55. L. Richards, 2013, The effects of socio-culture on business, *The Houston Chronicle*, www.chron.com, May 26.
56. 2013, Health strategy, *European Commission Public Health*, www.europa.eu, May 23.
57. C. Conover, 2013, Needed: A health system for adults, *Forbes*, www.forbes.com, April 30.
58. M. Toosi, 2012, Projections of the labor force to 2050: A visual essay, *Monthly Labor Review*, October.
59. Ibid., 13.
60. A. N. Smith, W. B. Morgan, E. B. King, M. R. Hebl, & C. I. Peddie, 2012, The ins and outs of diversity management: The effect of authenticity on outsider perceptions and insider behaviors, *Journal of Applied Psychology*, 42: E21–E55; M. DelCarmen Triana, M. F. Garcia, & A. Colella, 2010, Managing diversity: How organizational efforts to support diversity moderate the effects of perceived racial discrimination on affective commitment, *Personnel Psychology*, 63(4): 817–843.
61. R. Strack, J.-M. Caye, V. Bhalla, P. Tollman, C. von der Linden, P. Haen, & H. Quiros, 2012, Creating people advantage 2012, *bcg. perspectives*, www.bcgperspectives.com, October 18.
62. T. Grenness, 2011, The impact of national culture on CEO compensation and salary gaps between CEOs and manufacturing workers, *Compensation & Benefits Review*, 43(2): 100–108.
63. Y. Zeng, O. Shenkar, S.-H. Lee, & S. Song, 2013, Cultural differences, MNE learning abilities, and the effect of experience on subsidiary mortality in a dissimilar culture: Evidence from Korean MNEs, *Journal of International Business Studies*, 44: 42–65; P. Dimitratos, A. Petrou, F. Plakoyiannaki, & J. E. Johnson, 2011, Strategic decision-making processes in internationalization: Does national culture of the focal firm matter?, *Journal of World Business*, 46(2): 194–204.
64. J. Liu, C. Hui, C. Lee, & Z. X. Chen, 2013, Why do I feel valued and why do I contribute? A relational approach to employee's organization-based self-esteem and job performance, *Journal of Management Studies*, in press; C. M. Chan, S. Makino, & T. Isobe, 2010, Does subnational region matter? Foreign affiliate performance in the United States and China, *Strategic Management Journal*, 31: 1226–1243; P. J. Buckley, J. Clegg, & H. Tan, 2006, Cultural awareness in knowledge transfer to China—The role of guanxi and mianzi, *Journal of World Business*, 41: 275–288.
65. N. Gil, M. Miozzo, & S. Massini, 2012, The innovation potential of new infrastructure development: An empirical study of Heathrow Airport's T5 project, *Research Policy*, 41: 452–466; J. Euchner, 2011, Managing disruption: An interview with Clayton Christensen, *Research Technology Management*, 54(1): 11–17; R. K. Sinha & C. H. Noble, 2008, The adoption of radical manufacturing technologies and firm survival, *Strategic Management Journal*, 29: 943–962.
66. B. I. Park & P. N. Ghauri, 2011, Key factors affecting acquisition of technological capabilities from foreign acquiring firms by small and medium-sized local firms, *Journal of World Business*, 46(1): 116–125; K. H. Tsai & J.-C. Wang, 2008, External technology acquisition and firm performance: A longitudinal study, *Journal of Business Venturing*, 23: 91–112.
67. D. Dean, S. DiGrande, D. Field, A. Lundmark, J. O'Day, J. Pineda, & P. Zwillenberg, 2012, The Internet economy in the G-20. *bcg. perspectives*, www.bcgperspectives.com, March 19.
68. 2013, Consumers (everywhere) know a good deal when they see it, *bcg. perspectives*, www.bcgperspectives.com, January 11.
69. E. R. Banalieva & C. Dhanaraj, 2013, Home-region orientation in international expansion strategies, *Journal of International Business Studies*, 44: 89–116.
70. K. Kyung-Tae, R. Seung-Kyu, & O. Joongsan, 2011, The strategic role evolution of foreign automotive parts subsidiaries in China, *International Journal of Operations & Production Management*, 31(1): 31–55.
71. 2013, Growth and globalization: Keeping a lid on capacity, KPMG, Automotive executive survey, www.kpmb.com, January 15.
72. K. E. Meyer, 2009, Uncommon commonsense, *Business Strategy Review*, 20: 38–43; K. E. Meyer, 2006, Globalfocusing: From

domestic conglomerates to global specialists, *Journal of Management Studies*, 43: 1110–1144.

73. R. G. Flores, R. V. Aguilera, A. Mahdian, & P. M. Vaaler, 2013, How well do supra-national regional grouping schemes fit international business research models? *Journal of International Business Studies*, 44: 451–474; R. E. Hoskisson, M. Wright, I. Filatotchev, & M. W. Peng, 2013, Emerging multinationals form mid-range economies: The influence of institutions and factor markets, *Journal of Management Studies*, in press.
74. F. J. Froese, 2013, Work values of the next generation of business leaders in Shanghai, Tokyo, and Seoul, *Asia Pacific Journal of Management*, 30: 297–315; M. Muethel & M. H. Bond, 2013, National context and individual employees' trust of the out-group: The role of societal trust, *Journal of International Business Studies*, 4: 312–333; M. A. Hitt, M. T. Dacin, B. B. Tyler, & D. Park, 1997, Understanding the differences in Korean and U.S. executives' strategic orientations, *Strategic Management Journal*, 18: 159–167.
75. X. Li, 2012, Behind the recent surge of Chinese patenting: An institutional view, *Research Policy*, 41: 236–249; M. A. Hitt, D. Ahlstrom, M. T. Dacin, E. Levitas, & L. Svobodina, 2004, The institutional effects on strategic alliance partner selection: China versus Russia, *Organization Science*, 15: 173–185.
76. T. Yu, M. Subramaniam, & A. A. Cannella, Jr., 2013, Competing globally, allying locally: Alliances between global rivals and host-country factors, *Journal of International Business Studies*, 44: 117–137; T. K. Das & R. Kumar, 2011, Regulatory focus and opportunism in the alliance development process, *Journal of Management*, 37(3): 682–708.
77. A. G. Scherer, G. Palazzo, & D. Seidl, 2013, Managing legitimacy in complex and heterogeneous environments: Sustainable development in a globalized world, *Journal of Management Studies*, 50: 259–284; J. Harris, 2011, Going green to stay in the black: Transnational capitalism and renewable energy, *Perspectives on Global Development & Technology*, 10(1): 41–59; L. Berchicci & A. King, 2008, Postcards from the edge: A review of the business and environment literature, in J. P. Walsh & A. P. Brief (eds.), *Academy of Management Annals*, New York: Lawrence Erlbaum Associates, 513–547.
78. P. Berrone, A. Fosfuri, L. Gelabert, & L. R. Gomez-Mejia, 2013, Necessity as the mother of 'green' inventions: Institutional pressures and environmental innovations, *Strategic Management Journal*, 34: 891–909; M. Delmas, V. H. Hoffmann, & M. Kuss, 2011, Under the tip of the iceberg: Absorptive capacity, environmental strategy, and competitive advantage, *Business & Society*, 50(1): 116–154.
79. 2013, What is sustainable development? International institute for sustainable development, www.iisd.org, May 5.
80. J. K. Hall, G. A. Daneke, & M. J. Lenox, 2010, Sustainable development and entrepreneurship: Past contributions and future directions, *Journal of Business Venturing*, 25(5): 439–448.
81. A. Schwartz, 2013, McDonald's now serves certifiably sustainable fish, but does it matter? *Fast Company*, www.fastcompany.com, January 25.
82. D. Ferris, 2012, Will economic growth destroy the environment—or save it? *Forbes*, www.forbes.com, October 17.
83. S. M. Ben-Menahern, Z. Kwee, H. W. Volberda, & F. A. J. Van Den Bosch, 2013, Strategic renewal over time: The enabling role of potential absorptive capacity in aligning internal and external rates of change, *Long Range Planning*, 46: 216–235; V. Souitaris & B. Maestro, 2010, Polychronicity in top management teams: The impact on strategic decision processes and performance of new technology ventures, *Strategic Management Journal*, 31(6): 652–678.
84. M. Schimmer & M. Brauer, 2012, Firm performance and aspiration levels as determinants of a firm's strategic repositioning within strategic group structures, *Strategic Organization*, 10: 406–435; J. Galbreath & P. Galvin, 2008, Firm factors, industry structure and performance variation: New empirical evidence to a classic debate, *Journal of Business Research*, 61: 109–117.
85. J. J. Tarzijan & C. C. Ramirez, 2011, Firm, industry and corporation effects revisited: A mixed multilevel analysis for Chilean companies, *Applied Economics Letters*, 18(1): 95–100; V. F. Misangyl, H. Elms, T. Greckhamer, & J. A. Lepine, 2006, A new perspective on a fundamental debate: A multilevel approach to industry, corporate, and business unit effects, *Strategic Management Journal*, 27: 571–590.
86. E. T. Fukui, A. B. Hammer, & L. Z. Jones, 2013, Are U.S. exports influenced by stronger IPR protection measures in recipient markets? *Business Horizons*, 56: 179-188; D. Sullivan & J. Yuening, 2010, Media convergence and the impact of the internet on the M&A activity of large media companies, *Journal of Media Business Studies*, 7(4): 21–40.
87. K. Muller, K. Huschelrath, & V. Bilotkach, 2012, The construction of a low-cost airline network—facing competition and exploring new markets, *Managerial and Decision Economics*, 33: 485–499; C. Lutz, R. Kemp, & S. Gerhard Dijkstra, 2010, Perceptions regarding strategic and structural entry barriers, *Small Business Economics*, 35(1): 19–33.
88. F. Karakaya & S. Parayitam, 2013, Barriers to entry and firm performance: A proposed model and curvilinear relationships, *Journal of Strategic Marketing*, 21: 25–47; B. F. Schivardi & E. Viviano, 2011, Entry barriers in retail trade, *Economic Journal*, 121(551): 145–170; A. V. Mainkar, M. Lubatkin, & W. S. Schulze, 2006, Toward a product-proliferation theory of entry barriers, *Academy of Management Review*, 31: 1062–1075.
89. V. Niu, L. C. Dong, & R. Chen, 2012, Market entry barriers in China, *Journal of Business Research*, 65: 68–76.
90. V. K. Garg, R. L. Priem, & A. A. Rasheed, 2013, A theoretical explanation of the cost advantages of multi-unit franchising, *Journal of Marketing Channels*, 20(1–2): 52–72; S. S. Kien, C. Soh, & P. Weil, 2010, Global IT management: Structuring for scale, responsiveness, and innovation, *Communications of the ACM*, 53(3): 59–64; S. K. Ethiraj & D. H. Zhu, 2008, Performance effects of imitative entry, *Strategic Management Journal*, 29: 797–817.
91. P. Jackson & M. Iwata, 2012, Global deal: Mitsubishi Heavy, Hitachi to merge businesses, *Wall Street Journal*, www.wsj.com, November 30.
92. G. Yeung & V. Mok, 2013, Manufacturing and distribution strategies, distribution channels, and transaction costs: The case of parallel imported automobiles, *Managerial and Decision Economics*, 34: 44–58; X. Huang, M. Kristal, & R. G. Schroeder, 2010, The impact of organizational structure on mass customization capability: A contingency view, *Production & Operations Management*, 19(5): 515–530; M. J. Rungtusanatham & F. Salvador, 2008, From mass production to mass customization: Hindrance factors, structural inertia, and transition hazard, *Production and Operations Management*, 17: 385–396.
93. J. J. Ebbers & N. M. Wijnberg, 2013, Nascent ventures competing for start-up capital: Matching reputations and investors, *Journal of Business Venturing*, 27: 372–384; T. Rice & P. E. Strahan, 2010, Does credit competition affect small-firm finance? *Journal of Finance*, 65(3): 861–889.
94. 2013, Zara-owned Inditex's profits rise by 22%, *BBC News Business*, www.bbc.co.uk, March 13.
95. M. Hume, 2011, The secrets of Zara's success, *Telegraph.co.uk*, www.telegraph.co.uk, June 22.
96. S. Ansari & P. Krop, 2012, Incumbent performance in the face of radical innovation: Towards a framework for incumbent challenger dynamics, *Research Policy*, 41: 1357–1374; 2011, Airline deregulation, revisited, *Bloomberg Businessweek*, www.businessweek.com, January 21.
97. J. Jaeger, 2010, Anti-trust reviews: Suddenly, they're a worry, *Compliance Week*, 7(80): 48–59.
98. S. Bhattacharyya & A. Nain, 2011, Horizontal acquisitions and buying power: A product market analysis, *Journal of Financial Economics*, 99(1): 97–115.

99. I. Sherr & S. Ovide, 2013, Computer sales in free fall, *Wall Street Journal*, www.wsj.com, April 11.
100. S. Cernivec, 2013, Refreshing the carbonated soft drink category, *Beverage Industry*, www.bevindustry.com, April 11; C. Dieroff, 2011, Beverage trends: Consumers want it all, *Prepared Foods*, February: 49–55.
101. J. Cahill, 2012, How McDonald's is losing the burger brawl, *Chicago Business*, www.chicagobusiness.com, December 1.
102. P. Cohan, 2013, Samsung trouncing Apple, *Forbes*, http://www.forbes.com, April 26.
103. K. Bradsher, 2013, Chinese auto buyers grow hungry for larger cars, *New York Times*, www.nytimes.com, April 21.
104. C. Murphy, 2013, GM to build Cadillac plant in China, *Wall Street Journal*, www.wsj.com, May 7.
105. R. Wall, 2013, Airline profits to top $10 billion on improving sales outlook, *Bloomberg*, www.bloomberg.com, March 20; R. García-Castro & M. A. Ariño, 2011, The multidimensional nature of sustained competitive advantage: Test at a United States airline, *International Journal of Management*, 28(1): 230–248.
106. A. Goerzen, C. G. Asmussen & B. B. Nielsen, 2013, Global cities and multinational enterprise location strategy, *Journal of International Business Studies*, 44: 427–450; S. Nadkarni, P. Herrmann, & P. Perez, 2011, Domestic mindsets and early international performance: The moderating effect of global industry conditions, *Strategic Management Journal*, 32(5): 510–531.
107. M. E. Porter, 1980, *Competitive Strategy*, New York: Free Press.
108. F. J. Mas-Ruiz, F. Ruiz-Moreno, & A. L. de Guevara Martinez, 2013, Asymmetric rivalry within and between strategic groups, *Strategic Management Journal*, in press; M. S. Hunt, 1972, Competition in the major home appliance industry, 1960–1970 (doctoral dissertation, Harvard University); Porter, *Competitive Strategy*, 129.
109. D. Miller, I. Le Breton-Miller, & R. H. Lester, 2013, Family firm governance, strategic conformity, and performance: Institutional vs. strategic perspectives, *Organization Science*, 24: 189–209; S. Cheng & H. Chang, 2009, Performance implications of cognitive complexity: An empirical study of cognitive strategic groups in semiconductor industry, *Journal of Business Research*, 62(12): 1311–1320; G. McNamara, D. L. Deephouse, & R. A. Luce, 2003, Competitive positioning within and across a strategic group structure: The performance of core, secondary, and solitary firms, *Strategic Management Journal*, 24: 161–181.
110. N. Phillips, P. Tracey, & N. Karra, 2013, Building entrepreneurial tie portfolios through strategic homophily: The role of narrative identity work in venture creation and early growth, *Journal of Business Venturing*, 28: 134–150; D. Williams, C. Young, R. Shewchuk, & H. Qu, 2010, Strategic groupings of U.S. biotechnology initial public offerings and a measure of their market influence, *Technology Analysis & Strategic Management*, 22(4): 399–415.
111. M. Sytch & A. Tatarynowicz, 2013, Exploring the locus of invention: The dynamics of network communities and firms' invention productivity, *Academy of Management Journal*, in press; W. S. DeSarbo & R. Grewal, 2008, Hybrid strategic groups, *Strategic Management Journal*, 29: 293–317; M. Peteraf & M. Shanley, 1997, Getting to know you: A theory of strategic group identity, *Strategic Management Journal*, 18 (Special Issue): 165–186.
112. B. P. S. Murthi, A. A. Rasheed, & I. Goll, 2013, An empirical analysis of strategic groups in the airline industry using latent class regressions, *Managerial and Decision Economics*, 34(2): 59–73; J. Lee, K. Lee, & S. Rho, 2002, An evolutionary perspective on strategic group emergence: A genetic algorithm-based model, *Strategic Management Journal*, 23: 727–746.
113. T. Staake, F. Thiesse, & E. Fleisch, 2012, Business strategies in the counterfeit market, *Journal of Business Research*, 65: 658–665; P. Ebbes, R. Grewal, & W. S. DeSarbo, 2010, Modeling strategic group dynamics: A hidden Markov approach, *Quantitative Marketing and Economics*, 8: 241–274.
114. T. Keil, T. Laarmanen, & R. G. McGrath, 2013, Is a counterattack the best defense? Competitive dynamics through acquisitions, *Long Range Planning*, 46: 195–215; T. Yu, M. Subramaniam, & A. A. Cannella, Jr., 2009, Rivalry deterrence in international markets: Contingencies governing the mutual forbearance hypothesis, *Academy of Management Journal*, 52: 127–147.
115. Porter, *Competitive Strategy*, 49.
116. R. L. Priem, S. Li, & J. C. Carr, 2012, Insights and new directions from demand-side approaches to technology innovation, entrepreneurship, and strategic management research, *Journal of Management*, 38: 346–374; J. E. Prescott & R. Herko, 2010, TOWS: The role of competitive intelligence, *Competitive Intelligence Magazine*, 13(3): 8–17.
117. D. E. Hughes, J. Le Bon, & A. Rapp, 2013. Gaining and leveraging customer-based competitive intelligence: The pivotal role of social capital and salesperson adaptive selling skills, *Journal of the Academy of Marketing Science*, 41: 91–110; D. B. Montgomery, M. C. Moore, & J. E. Urbany, 2005, Reasoning about competitive reactions: Evidence from executives, *Marketing Science*, 24: 138–149.
118. H. Akbar & N. Tzokas, 2012, An exploration of new product development's front-end knowledge conceptualization process in discontinuous innovations, *British Journal of Management*, 24: 245–263; K. Xu, S. Liao, J. Li, & Y. Song, 2011, Mining comparative opinions from customer reviews for competitive intelligence, *Decision Support Systems*, 50(4): 743–754; S. Jain, 2008, Digital piracy: A competitive analysis, *Marketing Science*, 27: 610–626.
119. S. Wright, 2013, Converting input to insight: Organising for intelligence-based competitive advantage. In S. Wright (ed.), *Competitive Intelligence, Analysis and Strategy: Creating Organisational Agility*. Abingdon: Routledge, 1–35; J. G. York, 2009, Pragmatic sustainability: Translating environmental ethics into competitive advantage, *Journal of Business Ethics*, 85: 97–109.
120. X. Luo, J. Wieseke, & C. Homburg, 2012, Incentivizing CEOs to build customer- and employee-firm relations for higher customer satisfaction and firm value, *Journal of the Academy of Marketing Science*, 40: 745–758; R. Huggins, 2010, Regional competitive intelligence: Benchmarking and policy-making. *Regional Studies*, 44(5): 639–658.
121. L. T. Tuan, 2013, Leading to learning and competitive intelligence, *The Learning Organization*, 20: 216–239; K. A. Sawka, 2008, The ethics of competitive intelligence, *Kiplinger Business Resource Center Online*, www.kiplinger.com, March.
122. R. B. Bouncken & S. Kraus, 2013, Innovation in knowledge-intensive industries: The double-edged sword of coopetition, *Journal of Business Research*, 66: 2060–2070; T. Mazzarol & S. Reboud, 2008, The role of complementary actors in the development of innovation in small firms, *International Journal of Innovation Management*, 12: 223–253; A. Brandenburger & B. Nalebuff, 1996, *Co-opetition*, New York: Currency Doubleday.
123. 2013, SCIP Code of ethics for CI professionals, www.scip.org, May 22.
124. J. S. Harrison & D. A. Bosse, 2013, How much is too much? The limits to generous treatment of stakeholders, *Business Horizons*, 56: 313–322; L. T. Tuan, 2013, Corporate social responsibility, upward influence behavior, team processes and competitive intelligence, *Team Performance Management*, 19(1/2): 6–33; C. S. Fleisher & S. Wright, 2009, Examining differences in competitive intelligence practice: China, Japan, and the West, *Thunderbird International Business Review*, 51: 249–261.

# 3

# The Internal Organization: Resources, Capabilities, Core Competencies, and Competitive Advantages

***Studying this chapter should provide you with the strategic management knowledge needed to:***

**1** Explain why firms need to study and understand their internal organization.

**2** Define value and discuss its importance.

**3** Describe the differences between tangible and intangible resources.

**4** Define capabilities and discuss their development.

**5** Describe four criteria used to determine whether resources and capabilities are core competencies.

**6** Explain how firms analyze their value chain for the purpose of determining where they are able to create value when using their resources, capabilities, and core competencies.

**7** Define outsourcing and discuss reasons for its use.

**8** Discuss the importance of identifying internal strengths and weaknesses.

**9** Discuss the importance of avoiding core rigidities.

## ZARA: THE CAPABILITIES BEHIND THE SPANISH "FAST FASHION" RETAIL GIANT

Amancio Ortega built the world's largest fashion empire through his Zara branded products and company-owned stores. Through his management approach, Ortega has become the third richest man in the world behind Microsoft's Bill Gates and Mexico's Carlos Slim Helú.

Headquartered in La Coruña in Spain's Galicia region, Ortega founded the Inditex Group with Zara as its flagship brand. Despite Spain's 24 percent unemployment rate and crippling debt, in 2012 Zara increased its revenue 17 percent. Also, in 2012 Zara averaged a new store opening every day, including its six thousandth store launched on London's Oxford Street. Although the influence of the economic environment (an influence from the external environment that we examined in Chapter 2) affects Zara's success, the way Zara uses its resources and capabilities as the foundation for core competencies (defined in Chapter 1, core competencies are capabilities that serve as a potential source of competitive advantage for a firm over its rivals) demonstrates the value of understanding a firm's internal organization (this chapter's subject).

Ortega built this successful business based on two critical goals: Give customers what they want, and get it to them faster than anyone else. To do "fast fashion" as it is called, there are several critical capabilities that must be in place. The first critical capability is the ability to design quickly; the design pace at Zara has been described as "frantic". The designers create about three items of new clothing a day, and pattern makers cut one sample for each. Second are the commercial sales specialists from each region where Zara has stores. They provide input on customer tastes and buying habits which are reported through store managers. Each specialist is trained to keep an eye on what people are wearing, which Ortega does personally as well since founding Zara. As such, Zara has a team approach to match quick and creative design to information coming in from the sales staff through regional specialists and sector specialists to operationalize new fashion ideas.

The supply chain is also managed much more efficiently than those of other companies. The logistics department is the essence of the company; rather than waiting for cloth to come in after designing, it already has much basic cloth and owns its own dyeing operation to maintain control and speed. Zara's objective is to deliver customized orders to every store in its empire with a 24-hour turnaround deadline for Europe, the Mideast, and much of the United States, and 48 hours for Asia and Latin America. The frequent shipments keep product inventories fresh but also scarce since they send out very few items in each shipment. This approach compels customers to visit stores frequently in search of what they want and, because of the scarcity, creates an incentive for them to buy on the spot because it will likely not be in stock tomorrow. Accordingly, Zara's global store average of 17 visits per customer per year is considerably higher than the average of three visits per year for its competitors.

Until 2010 Zara did not have an online strategy. Unlike most retailers it has used very little advertising because it has focused on a rather cheap but fashionable approach. The fashion draws the interest of customers, and thereby created a huge following on Facebook, with approximately 10 million followers. This compares favorably to other competitors such as Gap. The rarity of the individual pieces of clothing gives customers a sense of individuality. This gives Zara a stronger potential to pursue an online strategy relative to its competitors.

Most Zara stores are owned by the parent company, and many of its suppliers, although not owned by the company, are considered long-time, relationship-oriented partners. As such, these partners identify with the company and thereby are also loyal. This approach also sets it apart and makes its strategy difficult to duplicate because all of the various facets and capabilities of the company fit together through a unified culture. As noted above, Zara also operates its own dyeing plant for cloth, giving it significant control over its products. Likewise, it sews many of these garments in its own factories, and thus maintains a high level of quality control and an ability to make quick changes. Overall, the company has a unique set of capabilities which fit together well as it manages their activities to produce "fast fashion," which creates demand from their customers and loyalty from their partner suppliers.

Sources: E. Carlyle, 2013, The year's biggest winner: Zara billionaire Amancio Ortega, *Forbes*, www.forbes.com, March 4; R. Dudley, A. Devnath, & M. Townsend, 2013, The hidden cost of fast fashion, *Bloomberg Businessweek*, February 11, 15–17; V. Walt, 2013, Meet the third-richest man in the world, *Fortune*, January 14, 74–79; 2012, Inditex, Asos post double-digit sales gains, *Women's Wear Daily*, September 20, 6; B. Borzykowski, 2012, Zara eludes the pain in Spain, *Canadian Business*, September 17, 67; K. Willems, W. Janssens, G. Swinnen, M. Brengman, S. Streukens, & N. Vancauteren, 2012, From Armani to Zara: Impression formation based on fashion store patronage, *Journal of Business Research*, (65)10: 1487–1494.

**Find out how fashion draws the interest of customers on Facebook.**
**www.cengagebrain.com**

As discussed in the first two chapters, several factors in the global economy, including the rapid development of the Internet's capabilities[1] and globalization in general have made it increasingly difficult for firms to find ways to develop sustainable competitive advantages.[2] Increasingly, innovation appears to be a vital path to efforts to develop such advantages.[3] As the Opening Case indicates, Zara's ability to produce new clothing designs quickly is definitely an advantage for them; the continual appearance of fresh designs has led to 17 visits per customer per year in its stores compared to the average of three visits per year in competitor stores.

Innovation is key at most organizations, like Zara, to maintain their competitive advantage. For example, at General Motors, efforts are underway to reduce the "drag" the firm's bureaucracy creates on innovation. According to a company official, "GM still wastes millions of dollars developing engines and vehicle variants that interest few customers." To remedy this problem, GM is making changes with the intention of having the "right people and the right engineers on the right priorities and products, not just do the most vehicles possible."[4]

People are an especially critical resource for helping organizations learn how to continuously innovate as a means of achieving successful growth.[5] This is the case at 3M, where harnessing the innovative powers of the firm's employees is the means for rekindling growth; in 2012 3M was ranked third on Booz & Company's list of most innovative behind Apple and Google but did not spend the same proportion on R&D relative to its sales as many other companies.[6] At 3M and other companies, people who are able to facilitate their firm's efforts to innovate are themselves a valuable resource with the potential to be a competitive advantage.[7] A sign of the times is the fact that a global labor market now exists as firms seek talented individuals to add to their fold. As Richard Florida argues, "[W]herever talent goes, innovation, creativity, and economic growth are sure to follow."[8]

To identify and successfully use resources over time, those leading firms need to constantly think about how to manage resources for the purpose of increasing the value their

M. Stasy

goods or services create for customers as compared to the value rivals' products create. As this chapter shows, firms achieve strategic competitiveness and earn above-average returns by acquiring, bundling, and leveraging their resources for the purpose of taking advantage of opportunities in the external environment in ways that create value for customers.[9]

Even if the firm develops and manages resources in ways that create core competencies and competitive advantages, competitors will eventually learn how to duplicate the benefits of any firm's value-creating strategy; thus all competitive advantages have a limited life.[10] Because of this, the question of duplication of a competitive advantage is not if it will happen, but when. In general, a competitive advantage's sustainability is a function of three factors: (1) the rate of core competence obsolescence because of environmental changes, (2) the availability of substitutes for the core competence, and (3) the imitability of the core competence.[11] For all firms, the challenge is to effectively manage current core competencies while simultaneously developing new ones.[12] Only when firms are able to do this can they expect to achieve strategic competitiveness, earn above-average returns, and remain ahead of competitors (see Chapter 5).

We studied the general, industry, and competitor environments in Chapter 2. Armed with knowledge about the realities and conditions of their external environment, firms have a better understanding of marketplace opportunities and the characteristics of the competitive environment in which those opportunities exist. In this chapter, we focus on the firm itself. By analyzing its internal organization, a firm determines what it can do. Matching what a firm *can do* (a function of its resources, capabilities, and core competencies in the internal organization) with what it *might do* (a function of opportunities and threats in the external environment) is a process that yields insights the firm requires to select its strategies.

We begin this chapter by briefly describing conditions associated with analyzing the firm's internal organization. We then discuss the roles of resources and capabilities in developing core competencies, which are the sources of the firm's competitive advantages. Included in this discussion are the techniques firms use to identify and evaluate resources and capabilities and the criteria for identifying core competencies from among them. Resources by themselves typically are not competitive advantages; in fact, resources create value when the firm uses them to form capabilities, some of which become core competencies, and hopefully competitive advantages. Because of the relationship among resources, capabilities, and core competencies, we also discuss the value chain and examine four criteria firms use to determine if their capabilities are core competencies and, as such, sources of competitive advantage.[13] The chapter closes with cautionary comments about outsourcing and the need for firms to prevent their core competencies from becoming core rigidities. The existence of core rigidities indicates that the firm is too anchored to its past, which prevents it from continuously developing new capabilities and core competencies.

# 3-1 Analyzing the Internal Organization

## 3-1a The Context of Internal Analysis

One of the conditions associated with analyzing a firm's internal organization is the reality that in today's global economy, some of the resources that were traditionally critical to firms' efforts to produce, sell, and distribute their goods or services such as labor costs, access to financial resources and raw materials, and protected or regulated markets, although still important, are now less likely to become competitive advantages.[14] An important reason for this is that an increasing number of firms are using their resources to form core competencies through which they successfully implement an international strategy (discussed in Chapter 8) as a means of overcoming the advantages created by these more traditional resources.

The Volkswagen Group has established "Strategy 2018" as its international strategy. The firm, which sells its products in over 150 countries, employs 550,000 people to operate more than 100 production plants around the world. By using its resources to form technological and innovation capabilities, Volkswagen intends to create superior customer service and product quality as core competencies on which it will rely to implement its international strategy.[15]

Increasingly, those analyzing their firm's internal organization should use a global mind-set to do so. A **global mind-set** is the ability to analyze, understand, and manage an internal organization in ways that are not dependent on the assumptions of a single country, culture, or context.[16] Because they are able to span artificial boundaries, those with a global mind-set recognize that their firms must possess resources and capabilities that allow understanding of and appropriate responses to competitive situations that are influenced by country-specific factors and unique cultures. Using a global mind-set to analyze the internal organization has the potential to significantly help the firm in its efforts to outperform rivals.[17] A global mind-set was used to develop Volkswagen Group's "Strategy 2018."

A **global mind-set** is the ability to analyze, understand, and manage an internal organization in ways that are not dependent on the assumptions of a single country, culture, or context.

Finally, analyzing the firm's internal organization requires that evaluators examine the firm's entire portfolio of resources and capabilities. This perspective suggests that individual firms possess at least some resources and capabilities that other companies do not—at least not in the same combination. Resources are the source of capabilities, some of which lead to the development of core competencies; in turn, some core competencies may lead to a competitive advantage for the firm.[18] Understanding how to leverage the firm's unique bundle of resources and capabilities is a key outcome decision makers seek when analyzing the internal organization.[19] Figure 3.1 illustrates the relationships among resources, capabilities, core competencies, and competitive advantages and shows how their integrated use can lead to strategic competitiveness. As we discuss next, firms use the assets in their internal organization to create value for customers.

**Figure 3.1** Components of an Internal Analysis

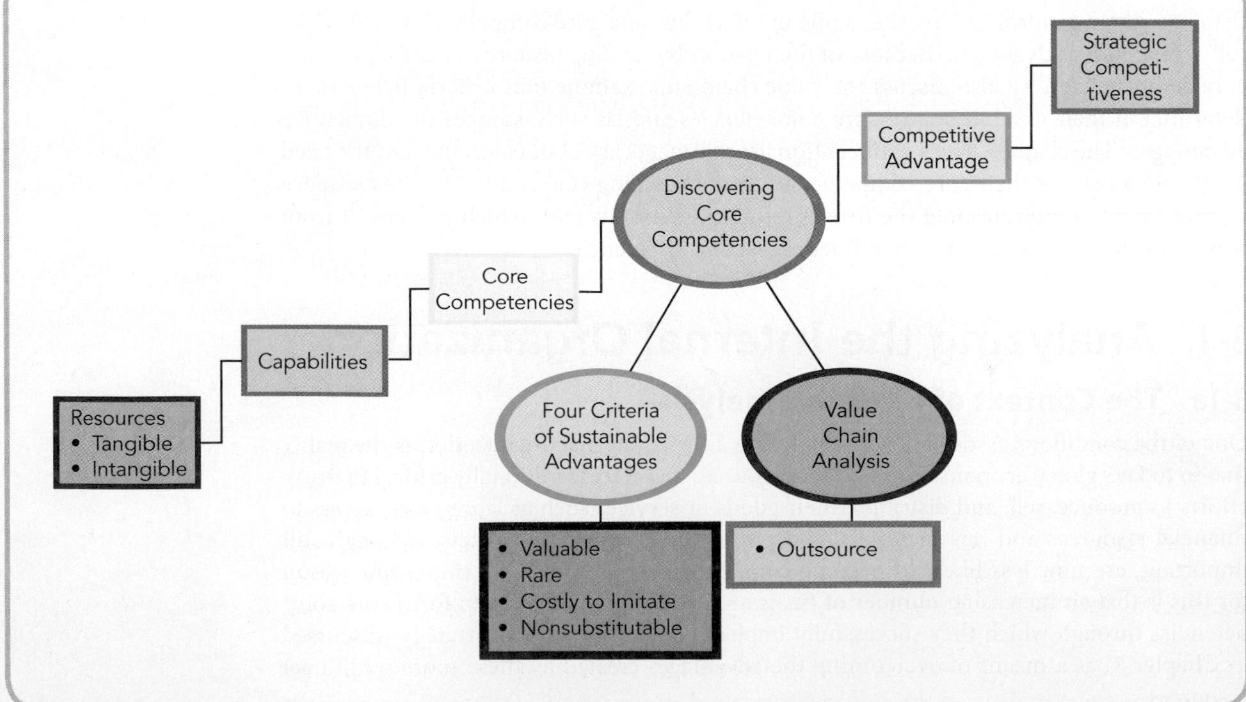

## 3-1b Creating Value

Firms use their resources as the foundation for producing goods or services that will create value for customers.[20] **Value** is measured by a product's performance characteristics and by its attributes for which customers are willing to pay. Firms create value by innovatively bundling and leveraging their resources to form capabilities and core competencies.[21] Firms with a competitive advantage create more value for customers than do competitors.[22] Walmart uses its "every day low price" approach to doing business (an approach that is grounded in the firm's core competencies, such as information technology and distribution channels) to create value for those seeking to buy products at a low price compared to competitors' prices for those products.[23] The stronger these firms' core competencies, the greater the amount of value they're able to create for their customers.[24]

Ultimately, creating value for customers is the source of above-average returns for a firm. What the firm intends regarding value creation affects its choice of business-level strategy (see Chapter 4) and its organizational structure (see Chapter 11).[25] In Chapter 4's discussion of business-level strategies, we note that value is created by a product's low cost, by its highly differentiated features, or by a combination of low cost and high differentiation, compared with competitors' offerings. A business-level strategy is effective only when it is grounded in exploiting the firm's capabilities and core competencies. Thus, the successful firm continuously examines the effectiveness of current capabilities and core competencies while thinking about the capabilities and competencies it will require for future success.[26]

At one time, the firm's efforts to create value were largely oriented to understanding the characteristics of the industry in which it competed and, in light of those characteristics, determining how it should be positioned relative to competitors. This emphasis on industry characteristics and competitive strategy underestimated the role of the firm's resources and capabilities in developing core competencies as the source of competitive advantages. In fact, core competencies, in combination with product market positions, are the firm's most important sources of competitive advantage.[27] A firm's core competencies, integrated with an understanding of the results of studying the conditions in the external environment, should drive the selection of strategies.[28] As Clayton Christensen noted, "Successful strategists need to cultivate a deep understanding of the processes of competition and progress and of the factors that undergird each advantage. Only thus will they be able to see when old advantages are poised to disappear and how new advantages can be built in their stead."[29] By emphasizing core competencies when selecting and implementing strategies, companies learn to compete primarily on the basis of firm-specific differences. However, while doing so they must be simultaneously aware of how things are changing in the external environment.[30]

## 3-1c The Challenge of Analyzing the Internal Organization

The strategic decisions managers make about their firm's internal organization are nonroutine,[31] have ethical implications,[32] and significantly influence the firm's ability to earn above-average returns.[33] These decisions involve choices about the resources the firm needs to collect and how to best manage them.

Making decisions involving the firm's assets—identifying, developing, deploying, and protecting resources, capabilities, and core competencies—may appear to be relatively easy. However, this task is as challenging and difficult as any other with which managers are involved; moreover, the task is increasingly internationalized.[34] Some believe that the pressure on managers to pursue only decisions that help the firm meet the quarterly earnings expected by market analysts makes it difficult to accurately examine the firm's internal organization.[35]

**Value** is measured by a product's performance characteristics and by its attributes for which customers are willing to pay.

The challenge and difficulty of making effective decisions are implied by preliminary evidence suggesting that one-half of organizational decisions fail.[36] Sometimes, mistakes are made as the firm analyzes conditions in its internal organization.[37] Managers might, for example, think a capability is a core competence when it is not. This may have been the case at Polaroid Corporation as decision makers continued to believe that the capabilities it used to build its instant film cameras were highly relevant at the time its competitors were developing and using the capabilities required to introduce digital cameras. In this instance, Polaroid's decision makers may have concluded that superior manufacturing was a core competence, as was the firm's ability to innovate in terms of creating value-adding features for its instant cameras. If a mistake is made when analyzing and managing a firm's resources, such as appears to have been the case some years ago at Polaroid, decision makers must have the confidence to admit it and take corrective actions.[38]

A firm can improve by studying its mistakes; in fact, the learning generated by making and correcting mistakes can be important to efforts to create new capabilities and core competencies.[39] One capability that can be learned from failure is when to quit. Polaroid should have obviously changed its strategy earlier than it did, and by doing so it may have been able to avoid more serious failure. Another example is News Corp.'s acquisition of MySpace in 2006. It poured over $580 million of investment for several years as it lost market share to FaceBook, and the acquisition was eventually sold for only $34 million.[40]

As we discuss next, three conditions—uncertainty, complexity, and intraorganizational conflict—affect managers as they analyze the internal organization and make decisions about resources (see Figure 3.2).

Managers face uncertainty because of a number of issues, including those of new proprietary technologies, rapidly changing economic and political trends, transformations in societal values, and shifts in customers' demands.[41] Environmental uncertainty increases the complexity and range of issues to examine when studying the internal environment.[42] Consider how uncertainty affects how to use resources at coal companies such as Peabody Energy Corp and Arch Coal Corp.

Peabody is the world's largest private-sector coal company. The firm's coal products fuel approximately 11 percent of all U.S. electricity generation and 2 percent of worldwide electricity. But the firm faces a great deal of uncertainty with respect to how it might best use its resources today to prepare for its future. One reason for this is that at least for some, coal is thought of as a "dirty fuel." Partly to reduce the uncertainty the firm faces because of this, Peabody is using some of its resources to build a "clean" coal-fired plant and has signed agreements to develop clean coal in China. As a proponent of strong emissions standards, Peabody's leaders argue for more use of "clean coal." Besides having to deal with increasingly advanced technological improvements such as clean coal, demand situations around the world are also creating uncertainty. China, for instance, one of the U.S.'s largest coal

**Figure 3.2** Conditions Affecting Managerial Decisions about Resources, Capabilities, and Core Competencies

| | | |
|---|---|---|
| Conditions | Uncertainty | Uncertainty exists about the characteristics of the firm's general and industry environments and customers' needs. |
| | Complexity | Complexity results from the interrelationships among conditions shaping a firm. |
| | Intraorganizational Conflicts | Intraorganizational conflicts may exist among managers making decisions as well as among those affected by the decisions. |

export markets, is increasing its own capacity in clean coal. Although India has continuingly increasing demand as it builds more coal-fired generating plants, pressure is growing to reduce their plants' $CO_2$ emissions. Tougher environmental regulations in Europe and a sluggish economy there have crippled coal demand in that region. Likewise, cheaper natural gas is continuing to displace coal in power generation in the United States.[43]

Also, biases about how to cope with uncertainty affect decisions made about how to manage the firm's resources and capabilities to form core competencies.[44] Additionally, intraorganizational conflict may surface when decisions are made about the core competencies a firm should develop and nurture. Conflict might surface in Peabody or Arch Coal about the degree to which resources and capabilities should be used to form new core competencies to support newer "clean technologies."

In making decisions affected by these three conditions, judgment is required. *Judgment* is the capability of making successful decisions when no obviously correct model or rule is available or when relevant data are unreliable or incomplete. In such situations, decision makers must be aware of possible cognitive biases, such as overconfidence. Individuals who are too confident in the decisions they make about how to use the firm's resources may fail to fully evaluate contingencies that could affect those decisions.[45]

When exercising judgment, decision makers often take intelligent risks. In the current competitive landscape, executive judgment can become a valuable capability. One reason is that, over time, effective judgment that decision makers demonstrate allows a firm to build a strong reputation and retain the loyalty of stakeholders whose support is linked to above-average returns.[46]

Finding individuals who can make the most successful decisions about using the organization's resources is challenging. Being able to do this is important because the quality of leaders' decisions regarding resources and their management affect a firm's ability to achieve strategic competitiveness. Individuals holding these key decision making positions are called *strategic leaders*. Discussed fully in Chapter 12, for our purposes in this chapter we can think of strategic leaders as individuals with an ability to make effective decisions when examining the firm's resources, capabilities, and core competencies for the purpose of making choices about their use.

Next, we consider the relationships among a firm's resources, capabilities, and core competencies. While reading these sections, keep in mind that organizations have more resources than capabilities and more capabilities than core competencies.

## 3-2 Resources, Capabilities, and Core Competencies

Resources, capabilities, and core competencies are the foundation of competitive advantage. Resources are bundled to create organizational capabilities. In turn, capabilities are the source of a firm's core competencies, which are the basis of establishing competitive advantages.[47] We show these relationships in Figure 3.1. Here, we define and provide examples of these building blocks of competitive advantage.

### 3-2a Resources

Broad in scope, resources cover a spectrum of individual, social, and organizational phenomena. By themselves, resources do not allow firms to create value for customers as the foundation for earning above-average returns. Indeed, resources are combined to form capabilities.[48] Subway links its fresh ingredients with several other resources including the continuous training it provides to those running the firm's fast food restaurants as the foundation for customer service as a capability; customer service is also a core competence for Subway. As its sole distribution channel, the Internet is a resource for Amazon.com. The firm uses the Internet to sell goods at prices that typically are lower than those offered by competitors selling the same goods through what are more costly brick-and-mortar storefronts. By combining other resources (such as access to a wide product inventory), Amazon has developed a reputation for excellent customer service. Amazon's capability in terms of customer service is a core competence as well in that the firm creates unique value for customers through the services it provides to them. Amazon also uses its technological core competence to offer AWS (Amazon Web Services), services through which businesses can rent computing power from Amazon at a cost of pennies per hour. In the words of the leader of this effort, "AWS makes it possible for anyone with an Internet connection and a credit card to access the same kind of world-class computing systems that Amazon uses to run its $34 billion-a-year retail operation."[49]

Some of a firm's resources (defined in Chapter 1 as inputs to the firm's production process) are tangible while others are intangible. **Tangible resources** are assets that can be observed and quantified. Production equipment, manufacturing facilities, distribution centers, and formal reporting structures are examples of tangible resources. As indicated in the Strategic Focus, Kinder Morgan's pipelines are a tangible resource. **Intangible resources** are assets that are rooted deeply in the firm's history and have accumulated over time. Because they are embedded in unique patterns of routines, intangible resources are difficult for competitors to analyze and imitate. Knowledge, trust between managers and employees, managerial capabilities, organizational routines (the unique ways people work together), scientific capabilities, the capacity for innovation, brand name, the firm's reputation for its goods or services and how it interacts with people (such as employees, customers, and suppliers), and organizational culture are intangible resources.[50] As illustrated in the Strategic Focus, the marketing routines and brand Coca-Cola uses to facilitate consumer demand for its products are examples of intangible resources.

The four primary categories of tangible resources are financial, organizational, physical, and technological (see Table 3.1). The three primary categories of intangible resources are human, innovation, and reputational (see Table 3.2).

**Tangible resources** are assets that can be observed and quantified.

**Intangible resources** include assets that are rooted deeply in the firm's history, accumulate over time, and are relatively difficult for competitors to analyze and imitate.

## Tangible Resources

As tangible resources, a firm's borrowing capacity and the status of its physical facilities are visible. The value of many tangible resources can be established through financial statements, but these statements do not account for the value of all the firm's assets, because they disregard some intangible resources.[51] The value of tangible resources is also constrained

**Table 3.1** Tangible Resources

| | |
|---|---|
| Financial Resources | • The firm's capacity to borrow<br>• The firm's ability to generate funds through internal operations |
| Organizational Resources | • Formal reporting structures |
| Physical Resources | • The sophistication of a firm's plant and equipment and the attractiveness of its location<br>• Distribution facilities<br>• Product inventory |
| Technological Resources | • Availability of technology-related resources such as copyrights, patents, trademarks, and trade secrets |

Sources: Adapted from J. B. Barney, 1991, Firm resources and sustained competitive advantage, *Journal of Management*, 17: 101; R. M. Grant, 1991, *Contemporary Strategy Analysis*, Cambridge: U.K.: Blackwell Business, 100-102.

**Table 3.2** Intangible Resources

| | |
|---|---|
| **Human Resources** | • **Knowledge**<br>• **Trust**<br>• **Skills**<br>• **Abilities to collaborate with others** |
| **Innovation Resources** | • **Ideas**<br>• **Scientific capabilities**<br>• **Capacity to innovate** |
| **Reputational Resources** | • **Brand name**<br>• **Perceptions of product quality, durability, and reliability**<br>• **Positive reputation with stakeholders such as suppliers and customers** |

Sources: Adapted from R. Hall, 1992, The strategic analysis of intangible resources, *Strategic Management Journal*, 13: 136-139: R. M. Grant, 1991, *Contemporary Strategy Analysis*, Cambridge: U.K.: Blackwell Business, 101-104.

# Strategic Focus SUCCESS

## Emphasis on Value Creation through Tangible (Kinder Morgan) and Intangible (Coca-Cola Inc.) Resources

Some firms have valuable resources which allow them to ultimately create value as they manage these resources through their capabilities. As outlined in the chapter, tangible resources can be categorized into financial, organizational, physical, and technological, whereas intangible resources are human, innovation, and reputational.

Kinder Morgan is a company that has vast tangible resources through its system of oil and gas pipelines throughout the United States and into Canada. Richard Kinder, CEO of Kinder Morgan, manages the Kinder Morgan Corporation, which is the third largest energy firm headquartered in the United States in terms of overall valuation. In regard to specific physical tangible resources, Kinder Morgan has 75,000 miles of pipe and 180 storage terminals capable of handling 2.5 million barrels of oil and 55 billion cubic feet of gas per day. It has a number of publicly traded entities which total $100 billion in enterprise value (equity plus debt). Kinder Morgan also has assets in Canada to facilitate transporting gas liquids to Alberta to dilute thick tar sands, which are then carried to tankers on the Pacific Coast. Much of this natural gas comes from as far south as Texas. Furthermore, additional physical assets were picked up in an acquisition of El Paso, another pipeline company, which allows natural gas to be liquefied and transported to energy-starved markets such as Japan and Korea. The liquid natural gas is a nice play because gas prices in Japan and Korea can be $12 per thousand cubic feet, where the same gas in the United States may cost less than $4 per thousand cubic feet, creating a nice profit potential.

Interestingly, Kinder Morgan also has financial assets, as many firms do, but some of these assets come through creative tax

*Bulk terminals in Tampa, Florida are some of Kinder Morgan's above-ground tangible resources.*

approaches to earnings distribution. Most pipelines in the United States have the availability of a corporate structure known as a master limited partnership (MLP). MLPs have income-producing assets which are handled by the general partner and distributed to the limited partners. As such, all profits and tax liabilities are passed on to the unit holders such that the corporations involved pay no income tax. This has created an incentive to acquire assets where a corporate tax is paid and incorporating them into the MLP framework such that corporate taxes are no longer paid, although the unit limited partners do pay taxes. Although the resources noted above create the potential for value, the capabilities to choose the right resources and pipelines to buy as well as strong management capabilities and the foresight needed to manage the whole system is, of course, relevant to the ultimate profits that will be garnered. In this case, the U.S. shale drilling boom has created a significant increase in gas, propane, and oil liquid volumes on the market and has created a huge opportunity for MLPs such as Kinder Morgan because they can charge for every cubic foot of gas or barrel of oil passing through their pipelines, gas terminals, or storage tanks.

Coca-Cola Inc. likewise has many assets; however, many of the resources associated with Coca-Cola are of the intangible variety. In particular, Coca-Cola has its brand name and the ability to manage this brand in a way that creates continual value for its family of products. Coca-Cola has many ad agencies to help it manage its reputational message to its consumers. Although in the past TV spots were at the center of Coca-Cola's marketing strategy, more recently Coca-Cola's team has been able to create online viral approaches to support its image. It also created a musical single entitled "Anywhere in the World", which was heard throughout the 2012 Olympics. Furthermore, its online videos associated with the Super Bowl featuring its polar bears, which have been part of Coca-Cola advertising dating back to 1922, got 9.09 million live stream views. This shareable, online content was estimated to give soft drink earnings a 5 percent bump in global sales in 2012. Of course, a firm must be able to manage its reputational resources and brand through distinctive marketing capabilities as exampled here by Coca-Cola.

Coca-Cola also has resources that are focused on tangible financial abilities. Coke accounts for 17 percent of juice-related volume sold in the world's top 22 markets, compared with 9 percent for PepsiCo. It has massive storage tanks in Florida insulated and full of fresh-squeezed juice chilling at 30 °F to 34 °F. Coke and Cutrale (Coca-Cola's Brazilian juice partner) buy almost one-third of the 145 million boxes of oranges grown by more than 400 Florida growers. Coca-Cola markets its juice in the United States through the Minute Maid brand, which it bought in 1960. The "secret" formula in juices is the complex algorithm of business analytics to manage the flow from the farm to the distribution center, including the large tanks of frozen juice concentrate which is the base material used in the beverage. The financial analytics to manage this process are a distinct tangible resource that Coca-Cola uses to manage the flow of these products. Again, it takes distinct capabilities to manage both the intangible, reputational resources, as well as the tangible financial analytics that manage the flow of juices in Coke's worldwide operations.

Sources: 2013, Super Bowl: Classic vs. fresh, *Fast Company*, February, 22; J. Kirby, 2013, Creative that cracks the code, *Harvard Business Review*, (91)3: 86–89; Z. R. Mider, 2013, It pays to own a pipeline, *Bloomberg Businessweek*, January 28, 26–28; D. Stanford, 2013, Coke has a secret formula for orange juice, too, *Bloomberg Businessweek*, February 4, 19–21; N. Zmuda, 2013, Behind the scenes of Coca-Cola's Super Bowl in 2013 ad plans, *Advertising Age*, February 4, 24; C. Helman, 2012, Richard Kinder's energy kingdom, *Forbes*, December 10, 76–84; T. Shufelt, 2012, Why Kinder is winning the pipeline race, *Canadian Business*, October 1, 21; T. Stynes & A. Sider, 2012, Kinder Morgan sells assets as part of El Paso deal, *Wall Street Journal*, August 21, B3.

**Find out more about Cutrale, Coca-Cola's Brazilian juice partner.**
**www.cengagebrain.com**

because they are hard to leverage—it is difficult to derive additional business or value from a tangible resource. For example, an airplane is a tangible resource, but "You can't use the same airplane on five different routes at the same time. You can't put the same crew on five different routes at the same time. And the same goes for the financial investment you've made in the airplane."[52]

Although production assets are tangible, many of the processes necessary to use these assets are intangible. Thus, the learning and potential proprietary processes associated with a tangible resource, such as manufacturing facilities, can have unique intangible attributes, such as quality control processes, unique manufacturing processes, and technologies that develop over time.[53]

## Intangible Resources

Compared to tangible resources, intangible resources are a superior source of capabilities and subsequently, core competencies.[54] In fact, in the global economy, "the success of a corporation lies more in its intellectual and systems capabilities than in its physical assets. [Moreover], the capacity to manage human intellect—and to convert it into useful products and services—is fast becoming the critical executive skill of the age."[55]

Because intangible resources are less visible and more difficult for competitors to understand, purchase, imitate, or substitute for, firms prefer to rely on them rather than on tangible

M. Stasy

resources as the foundation for their capabilities. In fact, the more unobservable (i.e., intangible) a resource is, the more valuable that resource is to create capabilities.[56] Another benefit of intangible resources is that, unlike most tangible resources, their use can be leveraged. For instance, sharing knowledge among employees does not diminish its value for any one person. To the contrary, two people sharing their individualized knowledge sets often can be leveraged to create additional knowledge that, although new to each individual, contributes potentially to performance improvements for the firm.

Reputational resources (see Table 3.2) are important sources of a firm's capabilities and core competencies. Indeed, some argue that a positive reputation can even be a source of competitive advantage.[57] Earned through the firm's actions as well as its words, a value-creating reputation is a product of years of superior marketplace competence as perceived by stakeholders.[58] A reputation indicates the level of awareness a firm has been able to develop among stakeholders and the degree to which they hold the firm in high esteem.[59]

©iStockPhoto.com/Courtney Keating

*Developing capabilities in specific functional areas can give companies a competitive edge. The effective use of social media to direct advertising to specific market segments has given some firms an advantage over their rivals.*

A well-known and highly valued brand name is a specific reputational resource.[60] A continuing commitment to innovation and aggressive advertising facilitates firms' efforts to take advantage of the reputation associated with their brands.[61] Harley-Davidson has a reputation for producing and servicing high-quality motorcycles with unique designs. Because of the desirability of its reputation, the company also produces a wide range of accessory items that it sells on the basis of its reputation for offering unique products with high quality. Sunglasses, jewelry, belts, wallets, shirts, slacks, belts, and hats are just a few of the large variety of accessories customers can purchase from a Harley-Davidson dealer or from its online store.[62] However, reputation is also being facilitated more quickly now through social media. As one analyst wrote, "your brand is nothing more than the sum of conversations being had about it. That is why social media is so powerful."[63] One study showed that Hokey Pokey, a popular "super premium" ice cream retailer with a dozen outlets in India, improved its brand equity "by using social media platforms to connect with its target consumers and create an engaging brand experience."[64] As noted in the Strategic Focus, Coca-Cola is using social media effectively to build its reputational resources.

## 3-2b **Capabilities**

The firm combines individual tangible and intangible resources to create capabilities. In turn, capabilities are used to complete the organizational tasks required to produce, distribute, and service the goods or services the firm provides to customers for the purpose of creating value for them.[65] As a foundation for building core competencies and hopefully competitive advantages, capabilities are often based on developing, carrying, and exchanging information and knowledge through the firm's human capital.[66] Hence, the value of human capital in developing and using capabilities and, ultimately, core competencies cannot be overstated.[67] At IBM, for example, human capital is critical to forming and using the firm's capabilities for long-term customer relationships and deep scientific and research skills, and the breadth of the firm's technical skills in hardware, software, and services.[68]

As illustrated in Table 3.3, capabilities are often developed in specific functional areas (such as manufacturing, R&D, and marketing) or in a part of a functional area (e.g., advertising). Table 3.3 shows a grouping of organizational functions and the capabilities that some companies are thought to possess in terms of all or parts of those functions.

### 3-2c Core Competencies

Defined in Chapter 1, core competencies are capabilities that serve as a source of competitive advantage for a firm over its rivals. Core competencies distinguish a company competitively and reflect its personality. Core competencies emerge over time through an organizational process of accumulating and learning how to deploy different resources and capabilities.[69] As the capacity to take action, core competencies are "crown jewels of a company," the activities the company performs especially well compared to competitors and through which the firm adds unique value to the goods or services it sells to customers.[70]

Innovation is thought to be a core competence at Apple. As a capability, R&D activities are the source of this core competence. More specifically, the way Apple has combined some of its tangible (e.g., financial resources and research laboratories) and intangible (e.g., scientists and engineers and organizational routines) resources to complete research and development tasks creates a capability in R&D. By emphasizing its R&D capability, Apple is able to innovate in ways that create unique value for customers in the form of the products it sells, suggesting that innovation is a core competence for Apple.

Excellent customer service in its retail stores is another of Apple's core competencies. In this instance, unique and contemporary store designs (a tangible resource) are combined with knowledgeable and skilled employees (an intangible resource) to provide superior service to customers. A number of carefully developed training and development procedures are capabilities on which Apple's core competence of excellent customer service is based. The procedures that are capabilities include "… intensive control of how employees interact

**Table 3.3** Example of Firms' Capabilities

| Functional Areas | Capabilities | Examples of Firms |
|---|---|---|
| Distribution | • Effective use of logistics management techniques | • Walmart |
| Human Resources | • Motivating, empowering, and retaining employees | • Microsoft |
| Management Information Systems | • Effective and efficient control of inventories through point-of-purchase data collection methods | • Walmart |
| Marketing | • Effective promotion of brand-name products<br>• Effective customer service<br>• Innovative merchandising | • Procter & Gamble<br>• Ralph Lauren Corp.<br>• McKinsey & Co.<br>• Nordstrom Inc.<br>• Crate & Barrel |
| Management | • Ability to envision the future of clothing | • Hugo Boss<br>• Zara |
| Manufacturing | • Design and production skills yielding reliable products<br>• Product and design quality<br>• Miniaturization of components and products | • Komatsu<br>• Witt Gas Technology<br>• Sony |
| Research & Development | • Innovative technology<br>• Development of sophisticated elevator control solutions<br>• Rapid transformation of technology into new products and processes<br>• Digital technology | • Caterpillar<br>• Otis Elevator Co.<br>• Chaparral Steel<br>• Thomson Consumer Electronics |

## Strategic Focus TECHNOLOGY

### Samsung Bests Apple in Smartphone Sales by Its Imitation Capability

Samsung is a large, diversified business group located in South Korea and accounts for 17 percent of South Korea's gross domestic product (GDP). The overall business group employs 370,000 people in more than 80 countries. Samsung's largest separate business is Samsung Electronics, which has grown to over $141 billion in sales in 2012. In particular, it has had strong strategic success in smartphones; in 2012 it overtook Apple, with 29 percent market share versus Apple's 22 percent. It realized a 7 percent gain in smartphone market share relative to other competitors compared to its position in 2011. Samsung got into the electronics business like other Korean conglomerates such as LG and Hyundai by starting small, making components for other firms in the industry.

*Samsung has pursued a competitive strategy based on both innovation and imitation.*

Getting into the semiconductor industry requires a semiconductor fab (i.e., a silicon wafer fabrication plant) which costs $2 to $3 billion. Once you have the infrastructure in place, you can begin selling semiconductor components to other companies. The knowledge that comes from developing key components allows strong insight into how the industry works. "Indeed, part of Samsung's secret sauce is that it controls and manufactures many of the building blocks of its phones." The firm leverages this foothold to develop an advantage that other companies have little chance of matching. In 2012, Samsung Electronics devoted $21.5 billion to capital expenditures, more than twice the investment spent by Apple.

To get into smartphones, Samsung built upon an existing innovation, the iPhone. Over time, it built a more advanced product that sold better than the iPhone. Samsung has pursued a "copycat" strategy by innovating where it has an advantage and imitating every place else. The proof of the imitation strategy is found in a recent court ruling that went against Samsung in a case where Apple claimed patent infringement. Although Samsung has copied some design aspects of the iPhone, it has been in high technology screens for quite a long time, having been a maker of televisions and other LED screen technology applications. Product improvements in the smartphone came through Samsung's core competence, "producing big, beautiful screens." Furthermore, Samsung has cultivated an ability to quickly understand the functions and imitate—and where possible given its strengths, improve on—competitors' products. Because it has the ability to manufacture products quickly as a contract manufacturer, it has the skill to produce incremental product improvements quickly.

Interestingly, Samsung has risen with this strategic approach, which is focused on manufacturing its own components as well as other competitors' components, while others have failed in the smartphone market. Motorola split up its handset business and sold part of it to Google. Nokia's longstanding number one position in cell phones was eroded. Not only was it blindsided by smartphones earlier, but it was overtaken by Samsung on cell phones. Sony Ericsson's partnership dissolved, and Palm disappeared into Hewlett-Packard. BlackBerry is on the edge of failure as well. Samsung Electronics strives for manufacturing efficiency and excellence and stellar new product development across a range or product lines. It also has established a new institute in Silicon Valley to develop its own software, one area where it is behind. Samsung's Galaxy line of smartphones uses the Android operating system created by Google.

Although Samsung produces key components for other producers, including Apple, it suggests that it has a walled-off business where one side does not talk to the other to know what the other is doing. However, because they manufacture components for many other firms, "they can see three years ahead," one analyst commented. Of course, there are upstart Chinese firms that might become the next Samsung, just as Samsung has displaced Sony in consumer electronics. As such, Samsung's chairman, D. J. Lee, continues to suggest that, "We are in danger. We are in jeopardy." However, this perpetual crisis mentality has helped them to maintain their lead.

Source: M. Chafkin, 2013, Samsung: For elevating imitation to an art form, *Fast Company*, March, 108; S. Grobart, 2013, Think colossal: How Samsung became the world's no. 1 smartphone maker – and its plans to stay on top, *Bloomberg Businessweek*, April 1–April 7, 58–64; R. Hof, 2013, Report: Samsung gains in grab for Google's mobile ad revenues, *Forbes*, www.forbes.com, April 3; Y. Kim, F. Bellman, & S. Grundberg, 2013, Samsung covets low-end of smartphone market, too, *Wall Street Journal*, March 22, B5; M. Lev-Ram, 2013, Samsung's road to mobile domination, *Fortune*, February 4, 98–102; J. Osawa, M. Lee, & D. Wakabayashi, 2013, Samsung in talks to invest in Sharp, in deal that could lead to purchase of LCD panels, *Wall Street Journal*, March 6, B3; O. Shenkar, 2010, *Copycats: How Smart Companies Use Imitation to Gain a Strategic Edge*, Cambridge: Harvard Business School Press.

with customers, scripted training for on-site tech support and consideration of every store detail down to the pre-loaded photos and music on demo devices."[71]

Interestingly, even though Apple has excellent innovation capabilities, Samsung has overtaken Apple in smartphone sales, as illustrated in the Strategic Focus. It has done so largely through imitating Apple's products and by adding additional features such as larger screens, one of Samsung Electronics' core competencies. Samsung also has core competencies in manufacturing its own components and components for other competitors, which give it insight into future innovations and allow it to produce new products quickly. It also seems to retain these capabilities by continually maintaining a crisis mentality.[72]

Learn about Samsung, a competitor of Apple.
www.cengagebrain.com

## 3-3 Building Core Competencies

Two tools help firms identify their core competencies. The first consists of four specific criteria of sustainable competitive advantage that can be used to determine which capabilities are core competencies. Because the capabilities shown in Table 3.3 have satisfied these four criteria, they are core competencies. The second tool is the value chain analysis. Firms use this tool to select the value-creating competencies that should be maintained, upgraded, or developed and those that should be outsourced.

### 3-3a The Four Criteria of Sustainable Competitive Advantage

Capabilities that are valuable, rare, costly to imitate, and nonsubstitutable are core competencies (see Table 3.4). In turn, core competencies can lead to competitive advantages for the firm over its rivals. Capabilities failing to satisfy the four criteria are not core competencies, meaning that although every core competence is a capability, not every capability is a core competence. In slightly different words, for a capability to be a core competence, it must be valuable and unique from a customer's point of view. For a core competence to be a potential source of competitive advantage, it must be inimitable and nonsubstitutable by competitors.[73]

A sustainable competitive advantage exists only when competitors cannot duplicate the benefits of a firm's strategy or when they lack the resources to attempt imitation. For some period of time, the firm may have a core competence by using capabilities that are valuable and rare, but imitable. For example, some firms are trying to develop a core competence and potentially a competitive advantage by out-greening their competitors. (Interestingly, developing a "green" core competence can contribute to the firm's efforts to earn above-average returns while benefitting the broader society.) Since 2005, Walmart has used its

**Table 3.4** The Four Criteria of Sustainable Competitive Advantage

| | |
|---|---|
| Valuable Capabilities | • Help a firm neutralize threats or exploit opportunities |
| Rare Capabilities | • Are not possessed by many others |
| Costly-to-Imitate Capabilities | • Historical: A unique and a valuable organizational culture or brand name<br>• Ambiguous cause: The causes and uses of a competence are unclear<br>• Social complexity: Interpersonal relationships, trust, and friendship among managers, suppliers, and customers |
| Nonsubstitutable Capabilities | • No strategic equivalent |

resources in ways that have allowed it to reduce its stores' carbon footprint by more than 10 percent and the carbon footprint of its trucking fleet by several times this percentage. It is also influencing its supply chain vendors to foster this same goal. For example, it has aligned with Patagonia, an outdoor apparel firm with a strong record in sustainability, "to launch the Sustainable Apparel Coalition, whose members now produce more than 30% of all clothing sold globally. The goal is to develop the tools to measure, monitor, and reduce the impact the apparel industry has on the environment."[74]

The length of time a firm can expect to create value by using its core competencies is a function of how quickly competitors can successfully imitate a good, service, or process. Value-creating core competencies may last for a relatively long period of time only when all four of the criteria we discuss next are satisfied. Thus, either Walmart or Patagonia would know that it has a core competence and possibly a competitive advantage in terms of green practices if the way the firm uses its resources to complete these practices satisfies the four criteria.

## Valuable

**Valuable capabilities** allow the firm to exploit opportunities or neutralize threats in its external environment. By effectively using capabilities to exploit opportunities or neutralize threats, a firm creates value for customers.[75] For example, Groupon created the "daily deal" marketing space and reached $1 billion in revenue faster than any other company in history. However, many imitators appeared very quickly and often with lower fixed costs, which allowed them to survive in the space even though they were not the first mover. Groupon may succeed but shorter development cycles, especially for such online firms, makes it harder for successful startups to create enduring competitive advantage. "In other words, they are increasingly vulnerable to the same capital-market pressures that plague big companies—but before they've developed lasting corporate assets."[76]

## Rare

**Rare capabilities** are capabilities that few, if any, competitors possess. A key question to be answered when evaluating this criterion is, "How many rival firms possess these valuable capabilities?" Capabilities possessed by many rivals are unlikely to become core competencies for any of the involved firms. Instead, valuable but common (i.e., not rare) capabilities are sources of competitive parity.[77] Competitive advantage results only when firms develop and exploit valuable capabilities that become core competencies and that differ from those shared with competitors. The central problem for Groupon is that its capabilities to produce the "daily deal" reached competitive parity quickly. Similarly, Walmart has developed capabilities to foster their sustainability/green initiatives which are valuable, but Target, another big-box retailer, may duplicate them and as such they may not be rare.

## Costly to Imitate

**Costly-to-imitate capabilities** are capabilities that other firms cannot easily develop. Capabilities that are costly to imitate are created because of one reason or a combination of three reasons (see Table 3.4). First, a firm sometimes is able to develop capabilities because of *unique historical conditions*. As firms evolve, they often acquire or develop capabilities that are unique to them.[78]

A firm with a unique and valuable *organizational culture* that emerged in the early stages of the company's history "may have an imperfectly imitable advantage over firms founded in another historical period;"[79] one in which less valuable or less competitively useful values and beliefs strongly influenced the development of the firm's culture. Briefly discussed in Chapter 1, organizational culture is a set of values that are shared by members in the organization. We explain this in greater detail in Chapter 12. An organizational culture is a source of advantage when employees are held together tightly by their belief in it and the leaders

**Valuable capabilities** allow the firm to exploit opportunities or neutralize threats in its external environment.

**Rare capabilities** are capabilities that few, if any, competitors possess.

**Costly-to-imitate capabilities** are capabilities that other firms cannot easily develop.

ZUMA Press, Inc./Alamy

*Even though it has well over 100 stores and 18,000 employees, CarMax has developed a small-company culture that is difficult for competitors to imitate.*

who helped to create it.[80] With its emphasis on cleanliness, consistency, and service and the training that reinforces the value of these characteristics, McDonald's culture is thought by some to be a core competence and a competitive advantage. The same appears to be the case for CarMax, one of *Fortune* magazine's 100 Best Companies to Work For. CEO Tom Folliard visited 70 stores in 2012 and hosted grand openings, employee town hall meetings, and steak cookouts. CarMax epitomizes "the small-company culture" even as it "has grown to 119 stores and 18,000 employees."[81] Folliard states that "I've always believed the saying, 'if you take care of your associates, they'll take care of your customers, and the rest will take care of itself'."[82]

A second condition of being costly to imitate occurs when the link between the firm's core competencies and its competitive advantage is *causally ambiguous*.[83] In these instances, competitors can't clearly understand how a firm uses its capabilities that are core competencies as the foundation for competitive advantage. As a result, firms are uncertain about the capabilities they should develop to duplicate the benefits of a competitor's value-creating strategy. For years, firms tried to imitate Southwest Airlines' low-cost strategy but most have been unable to do so, primarily because they can't duplicate this firm's unique culture.

*Social complexity* is the third reason that capabilities can be costly to imitate. Social complexity means that at least some, and frequently many, of the firm's capabilities are the product of complex social phenomena. Interpersonal relationships, trust, friendships among managers and between managers and employees, and a firm's reputation with suppliers and customers are examples of socially complex capabilities. Southwest Airlines is careful to hire people who fit with its culture. This complex interrelationship between the culture and human capital adds value in ways that other airlines cannot, such as jokes on flights by the flight attendants or the cooperation between gate personnel and pilots.

## Nonsubstitutable

**Nonsubstitutable capabilities** are capabilities that do not have strategic equivalents. This final criterion "is that there must be no strategically equivalent valuable resources that are themselves either not rare or imitable. Two valuable firm resources (or two bundles of firm resources) are strategically equivalent when they each can be separately exploited to implement the same strategies."[84] In general, the strategic value of capabilities increases as they become more difficult to substitute. The more intangible and hence invisible capabilities are, the more difficult it is for firms to find substitutes and the greater the challenge is to competitors trying to imitate a firm's value-creating strategy. Firm-specific knowledge and trust-based working relationships between managers and nonmanagerial personnel, such as existed for years at Southwest Airlines, are examples of capabilities that are difficult to identify and for which finding a substitute is challenging. However, causal ambiguity may make it difficult for the firm to learn as well and may stifle progress, because the firm may not know how to improve processes that are not easily codified and thus are ambiguous.[85]

In summary, only using valuable, rare, costly-to-imitate, and nonsubstitutable capabilities has the potential for the firm to create sustainable competitive advantages. Table 3.5 shows the competitive consequences and performance implications resulting from combinations of the four criteria of sustainability. The analysis suggested by the table helps managers determine the strategic value of a firm's capabilities. The firm should not emphasize

**Nonsubstitutable capabilities** are capabilities that do not have strategic equivalents.

**Table 3.5** Outcomes from Combinations of the Criteria for Sustainable Competitive Advantage

| Is the Capability Valuable? | Is the Capability Rare? | Is the Capability Costly to Imitate? | Is the Capability Nonsubstitutable? | Competitive Consequences | Performance Implications |
|---|---|---|---|---|---|
| No | No | No | No | • Competitive disadvantage | • Below-average returns |
| Yes | No | No | Yes/no | • Competitive parity | • Average returns |
| Yes | Yes | No | Yes/no | • Temporary competitive advantage | • Average returns to above-average returns |
| Yes | Yes | Yes | Yes/no | • Sustainable competitive advantage | • Above-average returns |



capabilities that fit the criteria described in the first row in the table (i.e., resources and capabilities that are neither valuable nor rare and that are imitable and for which strategic substitutes exist). Capabilities yielding competitive parity and either temporary or sustainable competitive advantage, however, will be supported. Some competitors such as Coca-Cola and PepsiCo and Boeing and Airbus may have capabilities that result in competitive parity. In such cases, the firms will nurture these capabilities while simultaneously trying to develop capabilities that can yield either a temporary or sustainable competitive advantage.

## 3-3b Value Chain Analysis

Value chain analysis allows the firm to understand the parts of its operations that create value and those that do not.[86] Understanding these issues is important because the firm earns above-average returns only when the value it creates is greater than the costs incurred to create that value.[87]

The value chain is a template that firms use to analyze their cost position and to identify the multiple means that can be used to facilitate implementation of a chosen strategy.[88] Today's competitive landscape demands that firms examine their value chains in a global rather than a domestic-only context.[89] In particular, activities associated with supply chains should be studied within a global context.[90]

We show a model of the value chain in Figure 3.3. As depicted in the model, a firm's value chain is segmented into value chain activities and support functions. **Value chain activities** are activities or tasks the firm completes in order to produce products and then sell, distribute, and service those products in ways that create value for customers. **Support functions** include the activities or tasks the firm completes in order to support the work being done to produce, sell, distribute, and service the products the firm is producing. A firm can develop a capability and/or a core competence in any of the value chain activities and in any of the support functions. When it does so, it has established an ability to create value for customers. In fact, as shown in Figure 3.3, customers are the ones firms seek to serve when using value chain analysis to identify their capabilities and core competencies. When using their unique core competencies to create unique value for customers that competitors cannot duplicate, firms have established one or more competitive advantages. This appears to be the case for Samsung as it relies on several core competencies, described earlier in a Strategic Focus, to quickly produce high-quality electronic products that are sold at lower prices than those of their competitors to customers throughout the world.

**Value chain activities** are activities or tasks the firm completes in order to produce products and then sell, distribute, and service those products in ways that create value for customers.

**Support functions** include the activities or tasks the firm completes in order to support the work being done to produce, sell, distribute, and service the products the firm is producing.

**Figure 3.3** A Model of the Value Chain

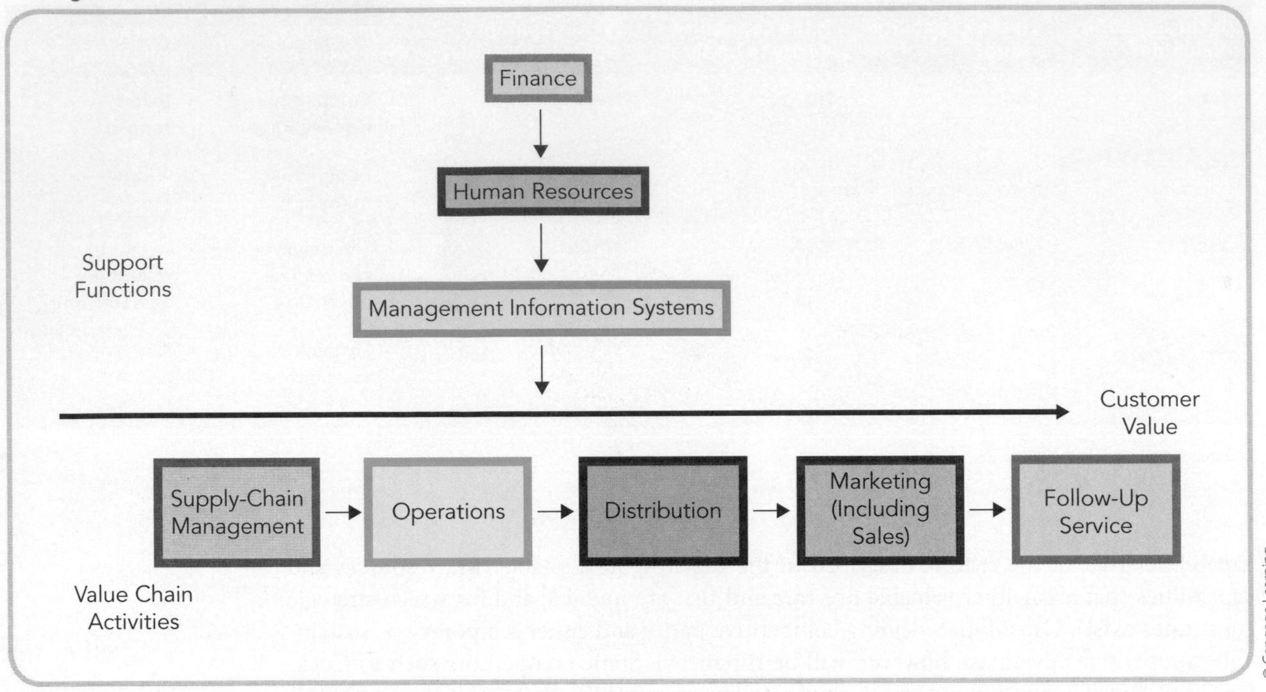


The activities associated with each part of the value chain are shown in Figure 3.4, while the activities that are part of the tasks firms complete when dealing with support functions appear in Figure 3.5. All items in both figures should be evaluated relative to competitors' capabilities and core competencies. To become a core competence and a source of competitive advantage, a capability must allow the firm (1) to perform an activity in a manner that provides value superior to that provided by competitors, or (2) to perform a value-creating activity that competitors cannot perform. Only under these conditions does a firm create value for customers and have opportunities to capture that value.

Creating value for customers by completing activities that are part of the value chain often requires building effective alliances with suppliers (and sometimes others to which the firm outsources activities, as discussed in the next section) and developing strong positive relationships with customers. When firms have such strong positive relationships with suppliers and customers, they are said to have "social capital."[91] The relationships themselves have value because they produce knowledge transfer and access to resources that a firm may not hold internally.[92] To build social capital whereby resources such as knowledge are transferred across organizations requires trust between the parties. The partners must trust each other in order to allow their resources to be used in such a way that both parties will benefit over time and neither party will take advantage of the other.[93] Trust and social capital usually evolve over time with repeated interactions, but firms can also establish special means to jointly manage alliances that promote greater trust with the outcome of enhanced benefits for both partners.[94]

Evaluating a firm's capability to execute its value chain activities and support functions is challenging. Earlier in the chapter, we noted that identifying and assessing the value of a firm's resources and capabilities requires judgment. Judgment is equally necessary when using value chain analysis because no obviously correct model or rule is universally available to help in the process.

**Figure 3.4** Creating Value through Value Chain Activities

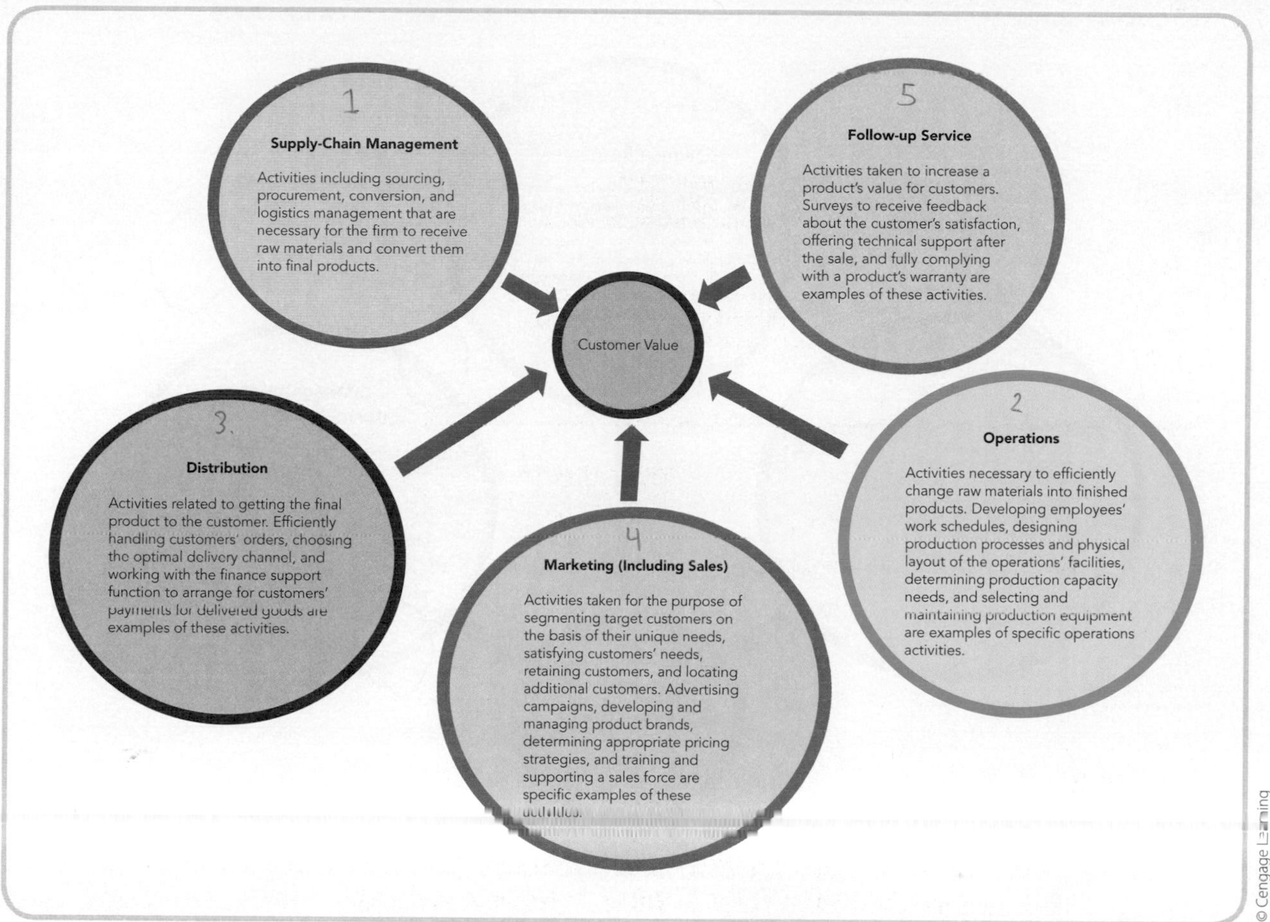




What should a firm do about value chain activities and support functions in which its resources and capabilities are not a source of core competence? Outsourcing is one solution to consider.

## 3-4 Outsourcing

Concerned with how components, finished goods, or services will be obtained, **outsourcing** is the purchase of a value-creating activity or a support function activity from an external supplier. Not-for-profit agencies as well as for-profit organizations actively engage in outsourcing. Firms engaging in effective outsourcing increase their flexibility, mitigate risks, and reduce their capital investments.[95] In multiple global industries, the trend toward outsourcing continues at a rapid pace.[96] Moreover, in some industries virtually all firms seek the value that can be captured through effective outsourcing. As with other strategic management process decisions, careful analysis is required before the firm decides to outsource.[97] And if outsourcing is to be used, firms must recognize that only activities where they cannot create value or where they are at a substantial disadvantage compared to competitors should be outsourced.[98]

**outsourcing** is the purchase of a value-creating activity or a support function activity from an external supplier.

**Figure 3.5** Creating Value through Support Functions

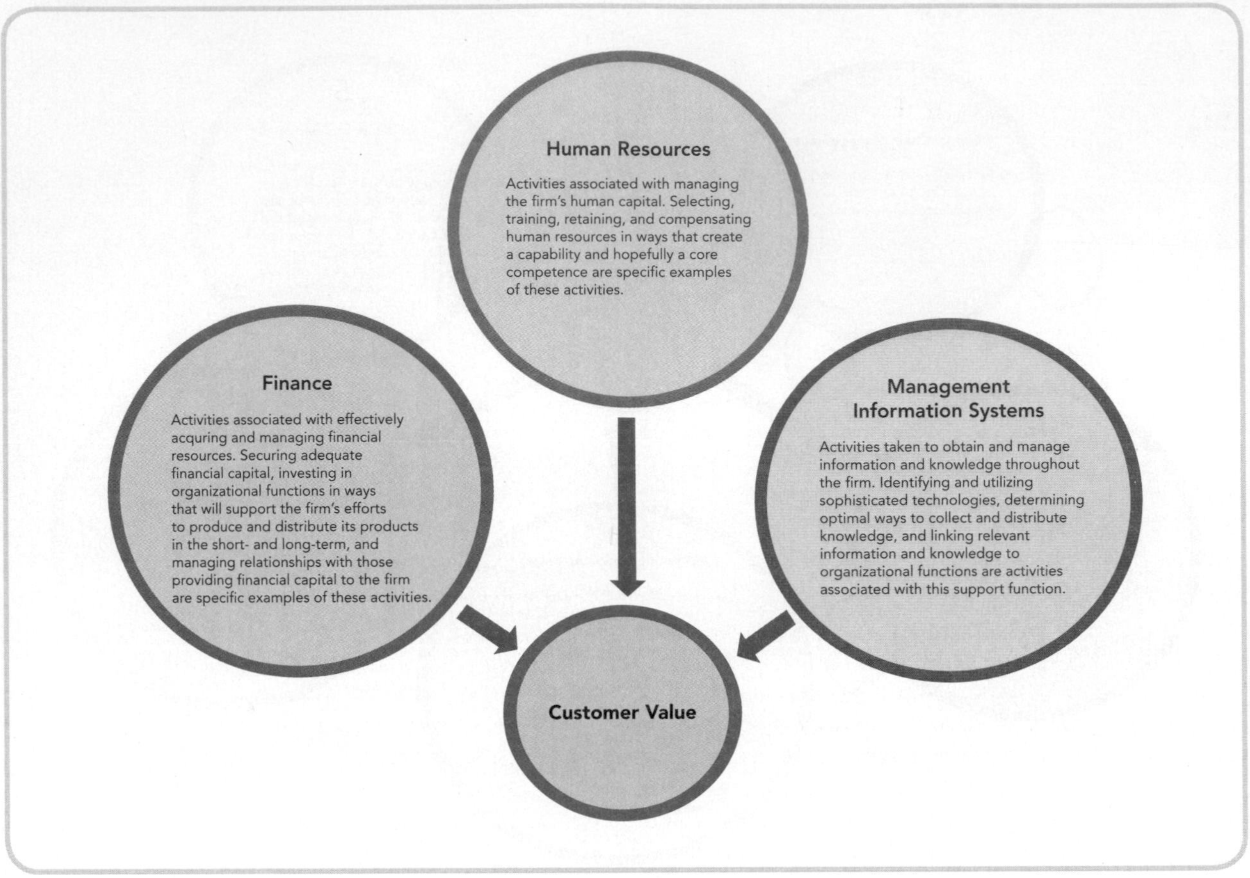

**Human Resources**

Activities associated with managing the firm's human capital. Selecting, training, retaining, and compensating human resources in ways that create a capability and hopefully a core competence are specific examples of these activities.

**Finance**

Activities associated with effectively acquring and managing financial resources. Securing adequate financial capital, investing in organizational functions in ways that will support the firm's efforts to produce and distribute its products in the short- and long-term, and managing relationships with those providing financial capital to the firm are specific examples of these activities.

**Management Information Systems**

Activities taken to obtain and manage information and knowledge throughout the firm. Identifying and utilizing sophisticated technologies, determining optimal ways to collect and distribute knowledge, and linking relevant information and knowledge to organizational functions are activities associated with this support function.

**Customer Value**

Learn more about new dimensions in outsourcing.
www.cengagebrain.com



Outsourcing can be effective because few, if any, organizations possess the resources and capabilities required to achieve competitive superiority in all value chain activities and support functions. For example, research suggests that few companies can afford to develop internally all the technologies that might lead to competitive advantage.[99] By nurturing a smaller number of capabilities, a firm increases the probability of developing core competencies and achieving a competitive advantage because it does not become overextended. In addition, by outsourcing activities in which it lacks competence, the firm can fully concentrate on those areas in which it can create value. Many times firms establish cooperative relationships with outsourcing partners as illustrated in Chapter 9 on cooperative strategy.

The consequences of outsourcing cause additional concerns.[100] For the most part, these concerns revolve around the potential loss in firms' innovative ability and the loss of jobs within companies that decide to outsource some of their work activities to others. Thus, innovation and technological uncertainty are two important issues to consider when making outsourcing decisions. However, firms can also learn from outsource suppliers how to increase their own innovation capabilities.[101] Companies must be aware of these issues and be prepared to fully consider the concerns about opportunities from outsourcing suggested by different stakeholders (e.g., employees). The opportunities and concerns may be especially significant when firms outsource activities or functions to a foreign supply source (often referred to as offshoring).[102] Bangalore and Belfast are hotspots for technology outsourcing, competing with major operations in other nations such as China. Yet many firms, including Apple and General Electric, are moving activities back to the United States or keeping them home instead of moving them to a foreign location.[103] This is due in part to increasing wages in countries like China, but also because of abundant energy with low natural gas prices in the United States.

David Silverman/Getty Images

This Belfast outsourcing center provides support for a U.S.-based telecom firm. Outsourcing can help firms lower costs and focus on those areas in which they can create value.

## 3-5 Competencies, Strengths, Weaknesses, and Strategic Decisions

By analyzing the internal organization, firms are able to identify their strengths and weaknesses in resources, capabilities, and core competencies. For example, if a firm has weak capabilities or does not have core competencies in areas required to achieve a competitive advantage, it must acquire those resources and build the capabilities and competencies needed. Alternatively, the firm could decide to outsource a function or activity where it is weak in order to improve its ability to use its remaining resources to create value.[104]

In considering the results of examining the firm's internal organization, managers should understand that having a significant quantity of resources is not the same as having the "right" resources. The "right" resources are those with the potential to be formed into core competencies as the foundation for creating value for customers and developing competitive advantages as a result of doing so. Interestingly, decision makers sometimes become more focused and productive when seeking to find the right resources when the firm's total set of resources is constrained.[105]

Tools such as outsourcing help the firm focus on its core competencies as the source of its competitive advantages. However, evidence shows that the value-creating ability of core competencies should never be taken for granted. Moreover, the ability of a core competence to be a permanent competitive advantage can't be assumed. The reason for these cautions is that all core competencies have the potential to become *core rigidities*.[106] Typically, events occurring in the firm's external environment create conditions through which core competencies can become core rigidities, generate inertia, and stifle innovation. "Often the flip side, the dark side, of core capabilities is revealed due to external events when new competitors figure out a better way to serve the firm's customers, when new technologies emerge, or when political or social events shift the ground underneath."[107]

Historically, Borders Group Inc. relied on its large storefronts that were conveniently located for customers to visit and browse through books and magazines in a pleasant atmosphere as sources of its competitive success. Over the past decade or so, though, digital technologies (part of the firm's external environment) rapidly changed customers' shopping patterns for reading materials. Amazon.com's use of the Internet significantly changed the competitive landscape for Borders and similar competitors such as Barnes & Noble. It is possible that Borders' core competencies of store locations and a desirable physical environment for customers became core rigidities for this firm, eventually leading to its filing of bankruptcy in early 2011 and subsequent liquidation.[108] Managers studying the firm's internal organization are responsible for making certain that core competencies do not become core rigidities.

After studying its external environment to determine what it might choose to do (as explained in Chapter 2) and its internal organization to understand what it can do (as explained in this chapter), the firm has the information required to select a business-level strategy that it will use to compete against rivals. We describe different business-level strategies in the next chapter.

## SUMMARY

- In the current competitive landscape, the most effective organizations recognize that strategic competitiveness and above-average returns result only when core competencies (identified by studying the firm's internal organization) are matched with opportunities (determined by studying the firm's external environment).
- No competitive advantage lasts forever. Over time, rivals use their own unique resources, capabilities, and core competencies to form different value-creating propositions that duplicate the focal firm's ability to create value for customers. Because competitive advantages are not permanently sustainable, firms must exploit their current advantages while simultaneously using their resources and capabilities to form new advantages that can lead to future competitive success.
- Effectively managing core competencies requires careful analysis of the firm's resources (inputs to the production process) and capabilities (resources that have been purposely integrated to achieve a specific task or set of tasks). The knowledge the firm's human capital possesses is among the most significant of an organization's capabilities and ultimately provides the base for most competitive advantages. The firm must create an organizational culture that allows people to integrate their individual knowledge with that held by others so that, collectively, the firm has a significant amount of value-creating organizational knowledge.
- Capabilities are a more likely source of core competence and subsequently of competitive advantages than are individual resources. How a firm nurtures and supports its capabilities so they can become core competencies is less visible to rivals, making efforts to understand and imitate the focal firm's capabilities difficult.
- Only when a capability is valuable, rare, costly to imitate, and nonsubstitutable is it a core competence and a source of competitive advantage. Over time, core competencies must be supported, but they cannot be allowed to become core rigidities. Core competencies are a source of competitive advantage only when they allow the firm to create value by exploiting opportunities in its external environment. When this is no longer possible, the company shifts its attention to forming other capabilities that satisfy the four criteria of a sustainable competitive advantage.
- Value chain analysis is used to identify and evaluate the competitive potential of resources and capabilities. By studying their skills relative to those associated with value chain activities and support functions, firms can understand their cost structure and identify the activities through which they can create value.
- When the firm cannot create value in either a value chain activity or a support function, outsourcing is considered. Used commonly in the global economy, outsourcing is the purchase of a value-creating activity from an external supplier. The firm should outsource only to companies possessing a competitive advantage in terms of the particular primary or support activity under consideration. In addition, the firm must continuously verify that it is not outsourcing activities from which it could create value.

## REVIEW QUESTIONS

1. Why is it important for a firm to study and understand its internal organization?
2. What is value? Why is it critical for the firm to create value? How does it do so?
3. What are the differences between tangible and intangible resources? Why is it important for decision makers to understand these differences? Are tangible resources more valuable for creating capabilities than are intangible resources, or is the reverse true? Why?

4. What are capabilities? How do firms create capabilities?
5. What four criteria must capabilities satisfy for them to become core competencies? Why is it important for firms to use these criteria to evaluate their capabilities' value-creating potential?
6. What is value chain analysis? What does the firm gain by successfully using this tool?
7. What is outsourcing? Why do firms outsource? Will outsourcing's importance grow in the future? If so, why?
8. How do firms identify internal strengths and weaknesses? Why is it vital that managers have a clear understanding of their firm's strengths and weaknesses?
9. What are core rigidities? What does it mean to say that each core competence could become a core rigidity?

# EXPERIENTIAL EXERCISES

## EXERCISE 1: WHAT MAKES A GREAT OUTSOURCING FIRM?

The focus of this chapter is on understanding how firm resources and capabilities serve as the cornerstone for competencies and, ultimately, a competitive advantage. However, when firms cannot create value in either a value chain or support activity, outsourcing becomes a potential strategy. According to the International Association of Outsourcing Professionals (IAOP) (http://www.iaop.org/) at their latest longitudinal survey the results suggested some interesting trends:

1. Outsourcing service providers are taking increased steps to diversify their services as offerings are becoming more globally commoditized.
2. Firms are offering more low end and high end services in search of improving margins.
3. There is a resurgent trend toward nearshoring, where service providers are relocating around the globe to be closer to their clients.
4. This is changing dramatically both the scale and scope of operations for outsourcing firms.

The IAOP annually announces its Global Outsourcing 100, which represents the world's best outsourcing service providers. The evaluation process mirrors that employed by many top customers and considers four key criteria: (1) size and growth in revenue, employees, centers, and countries served; (2) customer experience as demonstrated through the value being created at the company's top customers; (3) depth and breadth of competencies as demonstrated through industry recognition, relevant certifications, and investment in the development of people, processes, and technologies; and (4) management capabilities as reflected in the experience and accomplishments of the organization's top leaders and investment in management systems that ensure outsourcing success.

With a team, pick one of the Top 100 Global best outsourcing firms to analyze from the list on the IAOP Web site at (http://www.iaop.org/). Prepare a brief presentation formed around the contents of the chapter that addresses at a minimum the following questions:

- Why was this company chosen to be in the top 100? What has been the company's history as regards outsourcing as a source of revenue?
- How does the firm describe, or imply, its value proposition?
- What unique competitive advantage does the firm exhibit?
- Do you consider this to be a sustainable competitive advantage? Utilize the four criteria of sustainable competitive advantage as your guide.

## EXERCISE 2: WHAT IS YOUR CORE COMPETENCY?

In this chapter, the concepts of resources, capabilities, and core competencies were introduced as the foundation for establishing a competitive advantage. Resources (tangible and intangible) alone do not create value for customers but are bundled to create organizational capabilities, which are the basis for a firm's core competencies.

According to Prahalad and Hamel (Harvard Business Review, May-June 1990) there are four guidelines to identifying core competencies:

1. They support the delivery and production of a variety of services and products (thereby giving access to a variety of markets).
2. They always make a significant contribution to perceptions of services and products (i.e., they impact something that your client cares about).
3. They are often difficult for competition to imitate (because they are generally developed with a significant investment of time and resources).
4. They tend to be relatively stable over time.

However, while we normally think of core competency as a concept to be applied to existing organizations, it can equally be effective in application to one personally. If done well the result can be a strategic advantage as you enter the hiring process in that you will be able to define your core competency on your resume and at interviews.

Some interesting research in this area is being done at the University of Victoria Co-Operative Education Program and Career Services. Their work highlights some areas that are the key to developing personal core competencies, as follows:

- Personal management
- Communication
- Managing information
- Research and analysis

- Project and task management
- Teamwork
- Commitment to quality
- Professional behavior
- Social responsibility
- Continuous learning

More information on this as well as worksheets to guide you through each area may be found at http://www.uvic.ca/coopandcareer/studentsalumni/resources/competencykit/core.php. However numerous other avenues can provide you with a criteria map or create your own that best describes you.

This is an individual assignment. You are to create a personal core competency profile that assesses your individual assets (both tangible and intangible) as well as how those have or are developing into specific capabilities. Lastly identify 3-5 core competencies you currently possess. Your analysis will be due in a written report to your professor.

# VIDEO CASE

## ORGANIZATIONAL CULTURE CREATES STRATEGIC COMPETITIVENESS

Zappos.com, an online shoe retailer, has been listed in *Fortune* magazine's 100 best companies to work for over the past two years because employees feel empowered and respected. Recognized as a thriving company due to its unique organizational culture, from its untimed and unscripted call centers to "bald and blue" days, Zappos gives its employees the opportunity to shine in the workplace. Tony Shay, CEO, believes that Zappos is making the world a better place by allowing employees to be happy and to look at their job as a place to be for life. By receiving job security and benefits on par with competitors, Zappos employees remain dedicated to promoting branding opportunities with every customer. As a result, Amazon.com willingly purchased Zappos for $1.2 billion, and with both companies sharing such a strong passion for customer service, Zappos was excited to begin growing together. In 2010, Zappos experienced so much growth that it restructured the company into ten separate companies. The goal is to position Zappos as the online service leader.

Be prepared to discuss the following concepts and questions in class:

### Concepts

- Value
- Resources, capabilities, and core competencies
- Sustainable competitive advantage
- Value chain
- Outsourcing

### Questions

1. How is Zappos' organizational culture creating value?
2. What resources and resulting capabilities and core competencies do you see within the Zappos organization that gives it strategic competitiveness?
3. Will Zappos' competitive advantage be sustainable?
4. What value chain activities performed by Zappos help to create value for its customers?
5. Why do you think Zappos is not outsourcing its call centers?

# NOTES

1. E. Rueda-Sabater & D. Derosby, 2011, The evolving Internet in 2025: Four scenarios, *Strategy & Leadership*, 39(1): 32–38.
2. C. Gilbert, M. Eyring, & R. N. Foster, 2012, Two routes to resilience. *Harvard Business Review*, 90(12): 65–73; H. A. Ndofor, D. G. Sirmon, & X. He, 2011, Firm resources, competitive actions and performance: Investigating a mediated model with evidence from the in-vitro diagnostics industry, *Strategic Management Journal*, 32: 640–657.
3. K. Wilson & Y. L. Doz, 2012, 10 rules for managing global innovation, *Harvard Business Review*, 90(10): 84–90; D. Dunlap-Hinkler, M. Kotabe, & R. Mudambi, 2010, A story of breakthrough versus incremental innovation: Corporate entrepreneurship in the global pharmaceutical industry, *Strategic Entrepreneurship Journal*, 4: 106–127.
4. S. Terlep, 2011, GM's latest change agent tackles designs, red tape, *Wall Street Journal*, www.wsj.com, June 15.
5. R. Bapna, N. Langer, A. Mehra, R. Gopal, & A. Gupta, 2013, Human capital investments and employee performance: An analysis of IT services industry, *Management Science*, 59(3): 641–658; R. E. Ployhart & T. P. Moliterno, 2011, Emergence of the human capital resource: A multilevel model, *Academy of Management Review*, 36: 127–150; A. Leiponen, 2008, Control of intellectual assets in client relationships: Implications for innovation, *Strategic Management Journal*, 29: 1371–1394.
6. 2012, 3M ranks as one of the top innovators on Booz & Company list for third straight year, www.3m.com, press release, November 1.
7. M. A. Hitt, R. D. Ireland, D. G. Sirmon, & C. A. Trahms, 2011, Strategic entrepreneurship: Creating value for individuals, organizations, and society, *Academy of Management Perspective*, 25: 57–75;

C. D. Zatzick & R. D. Iverson, 2007, High-involvement management and work force reduction: Competitive advantage or disadvantage? *Academy of Management Journal*, 49: 999–1015.

8. R. Florida, 2005, *The Flight of the Creative Class*, New York: HarperBusiness.

9. L. Ngo & A. O'Cass, 2012, In search of innovation and customer-related performance superiority: The role of market orientation, marketing capability, and innovation capability interactions, *Journal of Product Innovation Management*, 29(5): 861–877; M. Gruber, F. Heinemann, M. Brettel, & S. Hunbeling, 2010, Configurations of resources and capabilities and their performance implications: An exploratory study on technology ventures, *Strategic Management Journal*, 31: 1337–1356; D. G. Sirmon, M. A. Hitt, & R. D. Ireland, 2007, Managing firm resources in dynamic markets to create value: Looking inside the black box, *Academy of Management Review*, 32: 273–292.

10. F. Polidoro, Jr. & P. K. Toh, 2011, Letting rivals come close or warding them off? The effects of substitution threat on imitation deterrence, *Academy of Management Journal*, 54: 369–392; A. W. King, 2007, Disentangling interfirm and intrafirm causal ambiguity: A conceptual model of causal ambiguity and sustainable competitive advantage, *Academy of Management Review*, 32: 156–178.

11. M. Semadeni & B. S. Anderson, 2010, The follower's dilemma: Innovation and imitation in the professional services industry, *Academy of Management Journal*, 53: 1175–1193; U. Ljungquist, 2007, Core competency beyond identification: Presentation of a model, *Management Decision*, 45: 393–402.

12. M. G. Jacobides, S. G. Winter, & S. M. Kassberger, 2012, The dynamics of wealth, profit, and sustainable advantage, *Strategic Management Journal*, 33(12): 1384–1410.

13. L. A. Costa, K. Cool, & I. Dierickx, 2013, The competitive implications of the deployment of unique resources, *Strategic Management Journal*, 34(4): 445–463; M. A. Peteraf & J. B. Barney, 2003, Unraveling the resource-based tangle, *Managerial and Decision Economics*, 24: 309–323; J. B. Barney, 2001, Is the resource-based "view" a useful perspective for strategic management research? Yes, *Academy of Management Review*, 26: 41–56.

14. T. N. Garavan, 2012, Global talent management in science-based firms: An exploratory investigation of the pharmaceutical industry during the global downturn, *International Journal of Human Resource Management*, 23(12): 2428–2449; P. Clements & J. McGregor, 2012, Better, faster, cheaper: Pick any three, *Business Horizons*, 55(2): 201–208; G. Zied & J. McGuire, 2011, Multimarket competition, mobility barriers, and firm performance, *Journal of Management Studies*, 48: 857–890.

15. Facebook, 2013, Volkswagen home page, www.volkswagen.com, March 20.

16. A. Arino, 2011, Building the global enterprise: Strategic assembly, *Global Strategy Journal*, 1: 47–49; M. Javidan, R. M. Steers, & M. A. Hitt (eds.), 2007, *The Global Mindset*: Amsterdam: Elsevier Ltd; T. M. Begley & D. P. Boyd, 2003, The need for a corporate global mindset, *MIT Sloan Management Review*, 44(2): 25–32.

17. A. Diaz, M. Magni, & F. Poh, 2012, From oxcart to Wal-Mart: Four keys to reaching emerging-market consumers, *McKinsey Quarterly*, October, 58–67; O. Levy, S. Taylor, & N. A. Boyacigiller, 2010, On the rocky road to strong global culture, *MIT Sloan Management Review*, 51: 20–22; O. Levy, S. Beechler, S. Taylor, & N. A. Boyacigiller, 2007, What we talk about when we talk about "global mindset": Managerial cognition in multinational corporations, *Journal of International Business Studies*, 38: 231–258.

18. R. A. D'Aveni, G. B. Dagnino, & K. G. Smith, 2010, The age of temporary advantage, *Strategic Management Journal*, 31: 1371–1385; E. Danneels, 2008, Organizational antecedents of second-order competences, *Strategic Management Journal*, 29: 519–543.

19. S. A. Zahra & S. Nambisan, 2012, Entrepreneurship and strategic thinking in business ecosystems, *Business Horizons*, 55(3): 219–229; H. Hoang & F. T. Rothaermel, 2010, Leveraging internal and external experience: Exploration, exploitation, and R&D project performance, *Strategic Management Journal*, 31: 734–758.

20. D. G. Sirmon, M A. Hitt, R. D. Ireland, & B. A. Gilbert, 2011, Resource orchestration to create competitive advantage: Breadth, depth, and life cycle effects, *Journal of Management*, 37(5): 1390–1412; P. L. Drnevich & A. P. Kriauciunas, 2011, Clarifying the conditions and limits of the contributions of ordinary and dynamic capabilities to relative firm performance, *Strategic Management Journal*, 32: 254–279; R. Adner & R. Kapoor, 2010, Value creation in innovation ecosystems: How the structure of technological interdependence affects firm performance in new technology generations, *Strategic Management Journal*, 31: 306–333.

21. M. A. Hitt, R. D. Ireland, D. G. Sirmon, & C. A. Trahms, 2011, Strategic entrepreneurship: Creating value for individuals, organizations, and society, *Academy of Management Perspectives*, 25(2): 57–75; D. G. Sirmon, S. Gove, & M. A. Hitt, 2008, Resource management in dyadic competitive rivalry: The effects of resource bundling and deployment, *Academy of Management Journal*, 51: 919–935.

22. J. S. Harrison, D. A. Bosse, & R. A. Phillips, 2010, Managing for stakeholders, stakeholder utility functions, and competitive advantage, *Strategic Management Journal*, 31: 58–74; J. L. Morrow, Jr., D. G. Sirmon, M. A. Hitt, & T. R. Holcomb, 2007, Creating value in the face of declining performance: Firm strategies and organizational recovery, *Strategic Management Journal*, 28: 271–283.

23. 2012, Why Walmart can pull off "everyday low prices" but everyone else keeps failing, www.businessinsider.com, September 3; K. Talley, 2011, Wal-Mart results to grab investor interest, *Wall Street Journal*, www.wsj.com, May 13.

24. V. Rindova, W. J. Ferrier, & R. Wiltbank, 2010, Value from gestalt: How sequences of competitive actions create advantage for firms in nascent markets, *Strategic Management Journal*, 31: 1474–1497.

25. A. O'Cass & P. Sok, 2012, Examining the role of within functional area resource–capability complementarity in achieving customer and product-based performance outcomes, *Journal of Strategic Marketing*, 20(4): 345–363; D. G. Sirmon, M. A. Hitt, J.-L. Arregle, & J. T. Campbell, 2010, The dynamic interplay of capability strengths and weaknesses: Investigating the bases of temporary competitive advantage, *Strategic Management Journal*, 31: 1386–1409.

26. F. Aime, S. Johnson, J. W. Ridge, & A. D. Hill, 2010, The routine may be stable but the advantage is not: Competitive implications of key employee mobility, *Strategic Management Journal*, 31: 75–87.

27. D. J. Teece, 2012, Dynamic capabilities: Routines versus entrepreneurial action, *Journal of Management Studies*, 49(8): 1395–1401; K. Z. Zhou & F. Wu, 2010, Technological capability, strategic flexibility, and product innovation, *Strategic Management Journal*, 31: 547–561.

28. M. H. Kunc & J. D. W. Morecroft, 2010, Managerial decision making and firm performance under a resource-based paradigm, *Strategic Management Journal*, 31: 1164–1182; J. Woiceshyn & L. Falkenberg, 2008, Value creation in knowledge-based firms: Aligning problems and resources, *Academy of Management Perspectives*, 22(2): 85–99; M. R. Haas & M. T. Hansen, 2005, When using knowledge can hurt performance: The value of organizational capabilities in a management consulting company, *Strategic Management Journal*, 26: 1–24.

29. C. M. Christensen, 2001, The past and future of competitive advantage, *Sloan Management Review*, 42(2): 105–109.

30. S. K. Parker & C. G. Collins, 2010, Taking stock: Integrating and differentiating multiple proactive behaviors, *Journal of Management*, 36: 633–662; O. Gottschalg & M. Zollo, 2007, Interest alignment and competitive advantage, *Academy of Management Review*, 32: 418–437.

31. Y. Y. Kor & A. Mesko, 2013, Dynamic managerial capabilities: Configuration and orchestration of top executives' capabilities and the firm's dominant logic, *Strategic Management Journal*, 34(2): 233–244; D. P. Forbes, 2007, Reconsidering

the strategic implications of decision comprehensiveness, *Academy of Management Review*, 32: 361–376.
32. J. Surroca, J. A. Tribo, & S. Waddock, 2010, Corporate responsibility and financial performance: The role of intangible resources, *Strategic Management Journal*, 31: 463–490; T. M. Jones, W. Felps, & G. A. Bigley, 2007, Ethical theory and stakeholder-related decisions: The role of stakeholder culture, *Academy of Management Review*, 32: 137–155.
33. M. S. Gary & R. E. Wood, 2011, Mental models, decision rules, and performance heterogeneity, *Strategic Management Journal*, 32: 569–594; Y. Deutsch, T. Keil, & T. Laamanen, 2007, Decision making in acquisitions: The effect of outside directors' compensation on acquisition patterns, *Journal of Management*, 33: 30–56.
34. C. B. Bingham & K. M. Eisenhardt, 2011, Rational heuristics: The 'simple rules' that strategists learn from process experience, *Strategic Management Journal*, 32(13): 1437–1464; S. W. Bradley, H. Aldrich, D. A. Shepherd, & J. Wiklund, 2011, Resources, environmental change and survival: Asymmetric paths of young independent and subsidiary organizations, *Strategic Management Journal*, 32: 486–509; A. Phene & P. Almieda, 2008, Innovation in multinational subsidiaries: The role of knowledge assimilation and subsidiary capabilities, *Journal of International Business Studies*, 39: 901–919.
35. Y. Zhang & J. Gimeno, 2010, Earnings pressure and competitive behavior: Evidence from the U.S. electricity industry, *Academy of Management Journal*, 53: 743–768; L. M. Lodish & C. F. Mela, 2007, If brands are built over years, why are they managed over quarters? *Harvard Business Review*, 85(7/8): 104–112.
36. P. M. Madsen & V. Desai, 2010, Failing to learn? The effects of failure and success on organizational learning in the global orbital launch vehicle industry, *Academy of Management Journal*, 53: 451–476; P. C. Nutt, 2002, *Why Decisions Fail*, San Francisco: Berrett-Koehler Publishers.
37. J. P. Eggers, 2012, All experience is not created equal: Learning, adapting and focusing in product portfolio management, *Strategic Management Journal*, 33(3): 315–335.
38. J. D. Ford & L. W. Ford, 2010, Stop blaming resistance to change and start using it, *Organizational Dynamics*, 39: 24–36.
39. K. Muehlfeld, P. Rao Sahib, & A. Van Witteloostuijn, 2012, A contextual theory of organizational learning from failures and successes: A study of acquisition completion in the global newspaper industry, 1981–2008, *Strategic Management Journal*, 33(8): 938–964; Y. Zhang, H. Li, Y. Li, & L.-A. Zhou, 2010, FDI spillovers in an emerging market: The role of foreign firms' country origin diversity and domestic firms' absorptive capacity, *Strategic Management Journal*, 31: 969–989.
40. M. Nisen, 2012, You can learn more from failure than success, *Business Insider*, www.businessinsider.com, December 17.
41. 2013, Strategy in a world of "biblical change": Our era of uncertainty calls for business leaders with vision, foresight and a global perspective, *Strategic Direction*, 29(3): 19–22; G. S. Dowell, M. B. Shackell, & N. V. Stuart, 2011, Boards, CEOs, and surviving a financial crisis: Evidence from the internet shakeout, *Strategic Management Journal*, 32(10): 1025–1045; R. E. Hoskisson & L. W. Busenitz, 2001, Market uncertainty and learning distance in corporate entrepreneurship entry mode choice, in M. A. Hitt, R. D. Ireland, S. M. Camp, & D. L. Sexton (eds.), *Strategic Entrepreneurship: Creating a New Integrated Mindset*, Oxford, UK: Blackwell Publishers, 151–172.
42. A. Arora & A. Nandkumar, 2012, Insecure advantage? Markets for technology and the value of resources for entrepreneurial ventures, *Strategic Management Journal*, 33(3): 231–251; S. S. K. Lam & J. C. K. Young, 2010, Staff localization and environmental uncertainty on firm performance in China, *Asia Pacific Journal of Management*, 27: 677–695.
43. K. Harlin, 2012, Arch, Peabody down on slowing China coal imports, *Investor's Business Daily*, www.ibd.com, December 21.
44. A. Leiponen & C. E. Helfat, 2010, Innovation objectives, knowledge sources, and the benefits of breadth, *Strategic Management Journal*, 31: 224–236; G. P. West, III, 2007, Collective cognition: When entrepreneurial teams, not individuals, make decisions, *Entrepreneurship Theory and Practice*, 31: 77–102.
45. M. Gary, R. E. Wood, & T. Pillinger, 2012, Enhancing mental models, analogical transfer, and performance in strategic decision making, *Strategic Management Journal*, 33(11): 1229–1246; J. R. Mitchell, D. A. Shepherd, & M. P. Sharfman, 2011, Erratic strategic decisions: When and why managers are inconsistent in strategic decision making, *Strategic Management Journal*, 32(7): 683–704.
46. P. D. Windschitl, A. M. Scherer, A. R. Smith, & J. P. Rose, 2013, Why so confident? The influence of outcome desirability on selective exposure and likelihood judgment, *Organizational Behavior & Human Decision Processes*, 120(1): 73–86; G. Davies, R. Chum, & M. A. Kamins, 2010, Reputation gaps and the performance of service organizations, *Strategic Management Journal*, 31: 530–546.
47. C. Weigelt, 2013, Leveraging supplier capabilities: The role of locus of capability deployment, *Strategic Management Journal*, 34(1): 1–21; Ndofor, Sirmon, & He, Firm resources, competitive actions and performance; P. A. Geroski, J. Mata, & P. Portugal, 2010, Founding conditions and the survival of new firms, *Strategic Management Journal*, 31: 510–529.
48. J. M. Shaver, 2011, The benefits of geographic sales diversification: How exporting facilitates capital investment, *Strategic Management Journal*, 32(10): 1046–1060; Sirmon, Hitt, Ireland, & Gilbert, Resource orchestration to create competitive advantage; K. Meyer, S. Estrin, S. K. Bhaumik, & M. W. Peng, 2009, Institutions, resources, and entry strategies in emerging economies, *Strategic Management Journal*, 30: 61–80.
49. A. Vance, 2011, The cloud: Battle of the tech titans, *Bloomberg Businessweek*, www.businessweek.com, March 3.
50. B. S. Anderson & Y. Eshima, 2013, The influence of firm age and intangible resources on the relationship between entrepreneurial orientation and firm growth among Japanese SMEs, *Journal of Business Venturing*, 28(3): 413–429; D. Somaya, Y. Kim, & N. S. Vonortas, 2011, Exclusivity in licensing alliances: Using hostages to support technology commercialization, *Strategic Management Journal*, 32: 159–186.
51. J. Choi, G. W. Hecht, & W. B. Tayler, 2012, Lost in translation: The effects of incentive compensation on strategy surrogation, *Accounting Review*, 87(4): 1135–1163; A. M. Arikan & L. Capon, 2010, Do newly public acquirers benefit or suffer from their pre-IPO affiliations with underwriters and VCs? *Strategic Management Journal*, 31: 1257–1298; J. A. Dubin, 2007, Valuing intangible assets with a nested logit market share model, *Journal of Econometrics*, 139: 285–302.
52. A. M. Webber, 2000, New math for a new economy, *Fast Company*, January/February, 214–224.
53. F. Neffke & M. Henning, 2013, Skill relatedness and firm diversification, *Strategic Management Journal*, 34(3): 297–316; E. Danneels, 2011, Trying to become a different type of company: Dynamic capability at Smith Corona, *Strategic Management Journal*, 32: 1–31; M. Song, C. Droge, S. Hanvanich, & R. Calantone, 2005, Marketing and technology resource complementarity: An analysis of their interaction effect in two environmental contexts, *Strategic Management Journal*, 26: 259–276.
54. J. Gómez & P. Vargas, 2012, Intangible resources and technology adoption in manufacturing firms, *Research Policy*, 41(9): 1607–1619; K. E. Meyer, R. Mudambi, & R. Narula, 2011, Multinational enterprises and local contexts: The opportunities and challenges of multiple embeddedness, *Journal of Management Studies*, 48: 235–252.
55. J. B. Quinn, P. Anderson, & S. Finkelstein, 1996, Making the most of the best, *Harvard Business Review*, 74(2): 71–80.
56. R. E. Ployhart, C. H. Van Iddekinge, & W. I. MacKenzie, Jr., 2011, Acquiring and developing human capital in service

contexts: The interconnectedness of human capital resources, *Academy of Management Journal*, 54: 353–368; N. Stieglitz & K. Heine, 2007, Innovations and the role of complementarities in a strategic theory of the firm, *Strategic Management Journal*, 28: 1–15.

57. K. Kim, B. Jeon, H. Jung, W. Lu, & J. Jones, 2012, Effective employment brand equity through sustainable competitive advantage, marketing strategy, and corporate image, *Journal of Business Research*, 65(11): 1612–1617; L. Diestre & N. Rajagopalan, 2011, An environmental perspective on diversification: The effects of chemical relatedness and regulatory sanctions, *Academy of Management Journal*, 54: 97–115.

58. G. Dowling & P. Moran, 2012, Corporate reputations: Built in or bolted on? *California Management Review*, 54(2): 25–42; M. D. Pfarrer, T. G. Pollock, & V. P. Rindova, 2010, A tale of two assets: The effects of firm reputation and celebrity on earnings surprises and investors' reactions, *Academy of Management Journal*, 53: 1131–1152; T. G. Pollock, G. Chen, & E. M. Jackson, 2010, How much prestige is enough? Assessing the value of multiple types of high-status affiliates for young firms, *Journal of Business Venturing*, 25: 6–23.

59. Y. Wang, G. Berens, & C. van Riel, 2012, Competing in the capital market with a good reputation, *Corporate Reputation Review*, 15(3): 198–221; J. J. Ebbers & N. M. Wijnberg, 2012, Nascent ventures competing for start-up capital: Matching reputations and investors, *Journal of Business Venturing*, 27(3): 372–384; P. M. Lee, T. G. Pollock, & K. Jin, 2011, The contingent value of venture capitalist reputation, *Strategic Organization*, 9: 33–69.

60. J. D. Townsend, S. Cavusgil, & R. J. Calantone, 2012, Building market-based assets in a globally competitive market: A longitudinal study of automotive brands, *Advances in International Marketing*, 11(23): 3–37; K. T. Smith, M. Smith, & K. Wang, 2010, Does brand management of corporate reputation translate into higher market value? *Journal of Strategic Marketing*, 18: 201–221.

61. N. Rosenbusch & J. Brinckmann, 2011, Is innovation always beneficial? A meta-analysis of the relationship between innovation and performance in SMEs, *Journal of Business Venturing*, 26: 441–457; J. Blasberg & V. Vishwanath, 2003, Making cool brands hot, *Harvard Business Review*, 81(6): 20–22.

62. 2013, Harley-Davidson Motor Apparel, www.harley-davidson.com, April 5.

63. D. Sacks, 2013, Can you hear me now? *Fast Company*, February, 40.

64. V. V. Kumar, V. Bhaskaran, R. Mirchandani, & M. Shah, 2013, Creating a measurable social media marketing strategy: Increasing the value and ROI of intangibles and tangibles for Hokey Pokey, *Marketing Science*, 32(2): 194–212.

65. D. Lessard, R. Lucea, & L. Vives, 2013, Building your company's capabilities through global expansion, *MIT Sloan Management Review*, 54(2): 61–67; T. Isobe, S. Makino, & D. B. Montgomery, 2008, Technological capabilities and firm performance: The case of small manufacturing firms in Japan, *Asia Pacific Journal of Management*, 25: 413–425; S. Dutta, O. Narasimhan, & S. Rajiv, 2005, Conceptualizing and measuring capabilities: Methodology and empirical application, *Strategic Management Journal*, 26: 277–285.

66. R. W. Coff, 2010, The coevolution of rent appropriation and capability development, *Strategic Management Journal*, 31: 711–733; M. Kroll, B. A. Walters, & P. Wright, 2008, Board vigilance, director experience and corporate outcomes, *Strategic Management Journal*, 29(4): 363–382; J. Bitar & T. Hafsi, 2007, Strategizing through the capability lens: Sources and outcomes of integration, *Management Decision*, 45: 403–419.

67. A. M. Subramanian, 2012, A longitudinal study of the influence of intellectual human capital on firm exploratory innovation, *IEEE Transactions on Engineering Management*, 59(4): 540–550; T. Dalziel, R. J. Gentry, & M. Bowerman, 2011, An integrated agency-resource dependence view of the influence of directors' human and relational capital on firms' R&D spending, *Journal of Management Studies*, 48(6): 1217–1242; T. A. Stewart & A. P. Raman, 2007, Lessons from Toyota's long drive, *Harvard Business Review*, 85(7/8): 74–83.

68. G. Colvin, 2012, The economy is scary, but smart companies can still dominate, *Fortune*, September 24, 77; S. Lohr, 2011, Lessons in longevity, from IBM, *New York Times*, www.nytimes.com, June 18.

69. K. M. Heimeriks, M. Schijven, & S. Gates, 2012, Manifestations of higher-order routines: The underlying mechanisms of deliberate learning in the context of postacquisition integration, *Academy of Management Journal*, 55(3): 703–726; N. P. Tuan & T. Yoshi, 2010, Organisational capabilities, competitive advantage and performance in supporting industries in Vietnam, *Asian Academy of Management Journal*, 15: 1–21; C. Zott, 2003, Dynamic capabilities and the emergence of intraindustry differential firm performance: Insights from a simulation study, *Strategic Management Journal*, 24: 97–125.

70. H. R. Greve, 2009, Bigger and safer: The diffusion of competitive advantage, *Strategic Management Journal*, 30: 1–23; C. K. Prahalad & G. Hamel, 1990, The core competence of the corporation, *Harvard Business Review*, 68(3): 79–93.

71. Y. I. Kane & I. Sherr, 2011, Secrets from Apple's genius bar: Full loyalty, no negativity, *Wall Street Journal*, www.wsj.com, June 15.

72. S. Grobart, 2013, Think colossal: How Samsung became the world's no. 1 smartphone maker – and its plans to stay on top, *Bloomberg Businessweek*, April 1–April 7, 58–64.

73. C. Welter, D. A. Bosse, & S. A. Alvarez, 2013, The interaction between managerial and technological capabilities as a determinant of company performance: An empirical study of biotech firms, *International Journal of Management*, 30(2): 272–284; M. Makri, M. A. Hitt, & P. J. Lane, 2010, Complementary technologies, knowledge relatedness, and invention outcomes in high technology mergers and acquisitions, *Strategic Management Journal*, 31: 602–628; S. Newbert, 2008, Value, rareness, competitive advantage, and performance: A conceptual-level empirical investigation of the resource-based view of the firm, *Strategic Management Journal*, 29: 745–768.

74. B. Dumaine, 2012, Built to last, *Fortune*, August 13, 16; 2011, Wal-Mart's green initiatives shouldn't be ignored, *Los Angeles Times*, www.latimes.com, May 30.

75. D. S. K. Lim, N. Celly, E. A. Morse, & W. G. Rowe, 2013, Rethinking the effectiveness of asset and cost retrenchment: The contingency effects of a firm's rent creation mechanism, *Strategic Management Journal*, 34(1): 42–61.

76. S. D. Anthony, 2012, The new corporate garage, *Harvard Business Review*, 90(9): 44–53.

77. Q. Gu & J. W. Lu, 2011, Effects of inward investment on outward investment: The venture capital industry worldwide—1985–2007, *Journal of International Business Studies*, 42: 263–284; S. A. Zahra, 2008, The virtuous cycle of discovery and creation of entrepreneurial opportunities, *Strategic Entrepreneurship Journal*, 2: 243–257.

78. H. Rahmandad, 2012, Impact of growth opportunities and competition on firm-level capability development trade-offs, *Organization Science*, 23(1): 138–154; C. A. Coen & C. A. Maritan, 2011, Investing in capabilities: The dynamics of resource allocation, *Organization Science*, 22: 199–217.

79. J. B. Barney, 1991, Firm resources and sustained competitive advantage, *Journal of Management*, 17: 99–120.

80. C. M. Wilderom, P. T. van den Berg, & U. J. Wiersma, 2012, A longitudinal study of the effects of charismatic leadership and organizational culture on objective and perceived corporate performance, *Leadership Quarterly*, 23(5): 835–848; C. C. Maurer, P. Bansal, & M. M. Crossan, 2011, Creating economic value through social values: Introducing a culturally informed resource-based view, *Organization Science*, 22: 432–448.

81. E. Fry, 2013, How CarMax cares, *Fortune*, April 8, 21.

82. Ibid., 21.

83. L. Mulotte, P. Dussauge, & W. Mitchell, 2013, Does pre-entry licensing undermine the

performance of subsequent independent activities? Evidence from the global aerospace industry, 1944–2000, *Strategic Management Journal*, 34(3): 358–372; M. H. Kunc & J. D. W. Morecroft, 2010, Managerial decision making and firm performance under a resource-based paradigm, *Strategic Management Journal*, 31: 1164–1182; A. W. King & C. P. Zeithaml, 2001, Competencies and firm performance: Examining the causal ambiguity paradox, *Strategic Management Journal*, 22: 75–99.

84. Barney, Firm resources, 111.

85. E. Beleska-Spasova & K. W. Glaister, 2013, Intrafirm causal ambiguity in an international context, *International Business Review*, 22(1): 32–46; K. Srikanth & P. Puranam, 2011, Integrating distributed work: Comparing task design, communication, and tacit coordination mechanisms, *Strategic Management Journal*, 32: 849–875; A. K. Chatterji, 2009, Spawned with a silver spoon? Entrepreneurial performance and innovation in the medical device industry, *Strategic Management Journal*, 30: 185–206.

86. G. K. Acharyulu & B. Shekhar, 2012, Role of value chain strategy in healthcare supply chain management: An empirical study in India, *International Journal of Management*, 29(1): 91–97; R. Belderbos, W. van Olffen, & J. Zou, 2011, Generic and specific social learning mechanisms in foreign entry location choice, *Strategic Management Journal*, 32(12): 1309–1330; A. Leiponen & C. E. Helfat, 2010, Innovation objectives, knowledge sources, and the benefits of breadth, *Strategic Management Journal*, 31: 224–236.

87. M. E. Porter, 1985, *Competitive Advantage*, New York: Free Press, 33–61.

88. R. Amit & C. Zott, 2012, Creating value through business model innovation, *MIT Sloan Management Review*, 53(3): 41–49; Z. G. Zacharia, N. W. Nix, & R. F. Lusch, 2011, Capabilities that enhance outcomes of an episodic supply chain collaboration, *Journal of Operations Management*, 29: 591–603; J. Alcacer, 2006, Location choices across the value chain: How activity and capability influence co-location, *Management Science*, 52: 1457–1471.

89. N. Haworth, 2013, Compressed development: Global value chains, multinational enterprises and human resource development in 21st century Asia, *Journal of World Business*, 48(2): 251–259; A. Rugman, A. Verbeke, & W. Yuan, 2011, Re-conceptualizing Bartlett and Ghoshal's classification of national subsidiary roles in the multinational enterprise, *Journal of Management Studies*, 48: 253–277.

90. A. Jara & H. Escaith, 2012, Global value chains, international trade statistics and policymaking in a flattening world, *World Economics*, 13(4): 5–18; S. M. Mudambi & S. Tallman, 2010, Make, buy or ally? Theoretical perspectives on knowledge process outsourcing through alliances, *Journal of Management Studies*, 47: 1434–1456; R. Locke & M. Romis, 2007, Improving world conditions in a global supply chain, *MIT Sloan Management Review*, 48(2): 54–62.

91. C. Galunic, G. Ertug, & M. Gargiulo, 2012, The positive externalities of social capital: Benefiting from senior brokers, *Academy of Management Journal*, 55(5): 1213–1231; U. Zander & L. Zander, 2010, Opening the grey box: Social communities, knowledge and culture in acquisitions, *Journal of International Business Studies*, 41: 27–37.

92. R. M. Wiseman, G. Cuevas-Rodriguez, & L. R. Gomez-Mejia, 2012, Towards a social theory of agency, *Journal of Management Studies*, 49(1): 202–222; L. F. Mesquita, J. An, & T. H. Brush, 2008, Comparing the resource-based and relational views: Knowledge transfer and spillover in vertical alliances, *Strategic Management Journal*, 29: 913–941.

93. S. E. Fawcett, S. L. Jones, & A. M. Fawcett, 2012, Supply chain trust: The catalyst for collaborative innovation, *Business Horizons*, 55(2): 163–178; A. A. Lado, R. R. Dant, & A. G. Tekleab, 2008, Trust-opportunism paradox, relationalism, and performance in interfirm relationships: Evidence from the retail industry, *Strategic Management Journal*, 29: 401–423; S. N. Wasti & S. A. Wasti, 2008, Trust in buyer-supplier relations: The case of the Turkish automotive industry, *Journal of International Business Studies*, 39: 118–131.

94. D. Lavie, P. R. Haunschild, & P. Khanna, 2012, Organizational differences, relational mechanisms, and alliance performance, *Strategic Management Journal*, 33(13): 1453–1479; D. Faems, M. Janssens, A. Madhok, & B. Van Looy, 2008, Toward an integrative perspective on alliance governance: Connecting contract design, trust dynamics and contract application, *Academy of Management Journal*, 51: 1053–1078.

95. S. Nadkami & P. Hermann, 2010, CEO personality, strategic flexibility, and firm performance: The case of the Indian business process outsourcing industry, *Academy of Management Journal*, 53: 1050–1073.

96. A. J. Mauri & J. Neiva de Figueiredo, 2012, Strategic patterns of internationalization and performance variability: Effects of US-based MNC cross-border dispersion, integration, and outsourcing, *Journal of International Management*, 18(1): 38–51; R. Liu, D. J. Feils, & B. Scholnick, 2011, Why are different services outsourced to different countries? *Journal of International Business Studies*, 42: 558–571.

97. C. Weigelt & M. B. Sarkar, 2012, Performance implications of outsourcing for technological innovations: Managing the efficiency and adaptability trade-off, *Strategic Management Journal*, 33(2): 189–216; F. Castellucci & G. Ertug, 2010, What's in it for them? Advantages of higher-status partners in exchange relationships, *Academy of Management Journal*, 53: 149–166; C. C. De Fontenay & J. S. Gans, 2008, A bargaining perspective on strategic outsourcing and supply competition, *Strategic Management Journal*, 29: 819–839.

98. J. Li, 2012, The alignment between organizational control mechanisms and outsourcing strategies: A commentary essay, *Journal of Business Research*, 65(9): 1384–1386; M. H. Zack & S. Singh, 2010, A knowledge-based view of outsourcing, *International Journal of Strategic Change Management*, 2: 32–53.

99. N. Raassens, S. Wuyts, & I. Geyskens, 2012, The market valuation of outsourcing new product development, *Journal of Marketing Research*, 49(5): 682–695; M. Reitzig & S. Wagner, 2010, The hidden costs of outsourcing: Evidence from patent data, *Strategic Management Journal*, 31: 1183–1201; A. Tiwana, 2008, Does interfirm modularity complement ignorance? A field study of software outsourcing alliances, *Strategic Management Journal*, 29: 1241–1252.

100. A. Martinez-Noya, E. Garcia-Canal, & M. F. Guillen, 2013, R&D outsourcing and the effectiveness of intangible investments: Is proprietary core knowledge walking out of the door? *Journal of Management Studies*, 50(1): 67–91; C. S. Katsikeas, D. Skarmeas, & D. C. Bello, 2009, Developing successful trust-based international exchange relationships, *Journal of International Business Studies*, 40: 132–155.

101. S. Sonenshein, 2013, How organizations foster the creative use of resources, *Academy of Management Journal*, in press; C. Grimpe & U. Kaiser, 2010, Balancing internal and external knowledge acquisition: The gains and pains from R&D outsourcing, *Journal of Management Studies*, 47: 1483–1509; C. Weigelt & M. B. Sarkar, 2009, Learning from supply-side agents: The impact of technology solution providers' experiential diversity on clients' innovation adoption, *Academy of Management Journal*, 52: 37–60.

102. S. M. Handley, 2012, The perilous effects of capability loss on outsourcing management and performance, *Journal of Operations Management*, 30(1/2): 152–165; P. D. O. Jensen & T. Pederson, 2011, The economic geography of offshoring: The fit between activities and local context, *Journal of Management Studies*, 48: 352–372; F. J. Contractor, V. Kumar, S. K. Kundu, & T. Pedersen, 2010, Reconceptualizing the firm in a world of outsourcing and offshoring: The organizational and geographical relocation of high-value company functions, *Journal of Management Studies*, 47: 1417–1433.

103. A. Smith, 2013, Foreign factories come back home, *Kiplinger's Personal Finance*, March, 11–12.

104. M. Kang, X. Wu, P. Hong, & Y. Park, 2012, Aligning organizational control practices with competitive outsourcing performance, *Journal of Business Research*, 65(8): 1195–1201; Y. Li, Z. Wei, & Y. Liu, 2010, Strategic orientations, knowledge acquisition, and firm performance: The perspective of the

vendor in cross-border outsourcing, *Journal of Management Studies*, 47: 1457–1482.

105. D. M. Sullivan & M. R. Marvel, 2011, Knowledge acquisition, network reliance, and early-stage technology venture outcomes, *Journal of Management Studies*, 48(6): 1169–1193; M. Gibbert, M. Hoegl, & L. Valikangas, 2007, In praise of resource constraints, *MIT Sloan Management Review*, 48(3): 15–17.

106. E. Rawley, 2010, Diversification, coordination costs, and organizational rigidity: Evidence from microdata, *Strategic Management Journal*, 31: 873–891.

107. D. L. Barton, 1995, *Wellsprings of Knowledge: Building and Sustaining the Sources of Innovation*, Boston: Harvard Business School Press, 30–31.

108. J. Milliot, 2013, As E-books grow, so does Amazon, *Publishers Weekly*, February 11, 4.

# 4

# Business-Level Strategy

***Studying this chapter should provide you with the strategic management knowledge needed to:***

**1** Define business-level strategy.

**2** Discuss the relationship between customers and business-level strategies in terms of *who, what,* and *how*.

**3** Explain the differences among business-level strategies.

**4** Use the five forces of competition model to explain how above-average returns can be earned through each business-level strategy.

**5** Describe the risks of using each of the business-level strategies.

## IS J.C. PENNEY KILLING ITSELF WITH A FAILED STRATEGY?

A few years ago, J.C. Penney (JCP) was a traditional low-end department store chain that appeared to be in a slow decline. Bill Ackman of Pershing Square Capital Management, a hedge fund investor, bought a large stake in the company and pushed to hire a new CEO, Ron Johnson. Johnson, who had successfully created the Apple retail store concept, was tasked with turning around the company's fortunes.

In January 2012, Johnson announced a new strategy for the company and the rebranding of JCP. This strategy entailed a remake of the JCP retail stores to create shops focused on specific brands, such as Levi's, IZOD, and Liz Claiborne, and types of goods, such as home goods featuring Martha Stewart products within each store. Simultaneously, Johnson announced a new pricing system. The old approach of offering special discounts throughout the year was eliminated in favor of a new customer-value pricing approach that reduced prices on goods across the board by as much as 40 percent. The price listed was the price to be paid without further discounts. The intent was to offer customers a "better deal" on all products as opposed to providing special high discounts on selected products.

The intent of these changes was to build J.C. Penney into a higher-end (a little more upscale) retailer that provided good prices on branded merchandise (mostly clothes and home goods). However, these changes overlooked the firm's current customers; JCP began competing for customers who normally shopped at Target, Macy's, Nordstrom, and other similar stores. Unfortunately, the first year of this new strategy appeared to be a failure. Total sales in 2012 were $4.28 billion less than in 2011 and the firm's stock price declined by 55 percent. Interestingly, its Internet sales declined by 34 percent compared to an increase of 48 percent for its new rival, Macy's. All of this translated into a net loss for the year of slightly less than $1 billion for JCP.

It seems that the new executive team at Penney's thought that they could retain their current customer base (perhaps with the value pricing across the board) while attracting new customers with the "store-within-a-store" concept. According to Roger Martin, a former executive, strategy expert, and current dean at the University of Toronto, "...the new J.C. Penney is competing against and absolutely slaughtering an important competitor, and it's called the old J.C. Penney." Only about one-third of the stores had been converted to the new approach when the company began to heavily promote the concept. Its new store sales produced increases in sales per square foot, but the old stores' sales per square foot markedly declined. It appears that Penney was not attracting customers from its rivals but rather cannibalizing customers from its old stores.

According to Martin, the new CEO likely understands a lot about capital markets but does not know how to satisfy customers and gain a competitive advantage. Additionally, the former CEO of J.C. Penney, Allen Questrom, described Johnson as having several capabilities (e.g., intelligent, strong communicator) but believes that he and his executive team made a major strategic error and were especially insensitive to the JCP customer base.

The question now is whether the company can survive such a major decline in sales and stock price. It recently announced the layoff of approximately 2,200 employees to reduce costs. CEO Johnson announced he was reinstituting selected discounts in pricing and offering comparative pricing on products (relative prices with rivals). The good news is that the transformed stores are obtaining sales of $269 per square foot whereas the older stores are producing $134 per square foot. Will Ron Johnson's strategy survive long enough for all of the stores to be converted and save the company? The answer is probably not, as Johnson was fired by the Penney board of directors on April 8, 2013, about a year and a half after he assumed the CEO position.

Sources: J. Reingold, A. Sloan, & D. Burke, 2013, When Wall Street wears the pants, *Fortune,* April 8, 74–81; Ron Johnson out as J.C. Penney chief, 2013, *New York Times,* www.nytimes.com, April 8; M. Nisen, 2013, Former JC Penney CEO says Ron Johnson is 'a very nice man' who will probably fail, *Yahoo! Finance,* http://finance.yahoo.com, accessed April 6; B. Byrnes, 2013, How J.C. Penney is killing itself, *The Motley Fool,* www.fool.com, March 31; B. Jopson, 2013, JC Penney cuts 2,200 jobs as retailer struggles, *Financial Times,* www.ft.com, March 8; J. Macke, 2013, J.C. Penney's last shot at survival, *Yahoo! Finance,* http://finance.yahoo.com, accessed March 1; S. Clifford, 2013, Chief talks of mistakes and big loss at J.C. Penney, *New York Times,* www.nytimes.com, February 27; M. Halkias, 2013, J.C. Penney CEO Ron Johnson says changes will return retailer to growth, *Dallas Morning news,* www.dallasnews.com, February 9; They're back: J.C. Penney adds sales, 2013, *USA Today,* www.usatoday.com, January 28; A. R. Sorkin, 2012, A dose of realism for the chief of J.C. Penney, *New York Times DealBook,* http://dealbook.nytimes.com, November 12.

**Find out more about Martha Stewart products and which retailers feature them.**
**www.cengagebrain.com**

Increasingly important to firm success,[1] strategy is concerned with making choices among two or more alternatives.[2] As we noted in Chapter 1, when choosing a strategy, the firm decides to pursue one course of action instead of others. The choices are influenced by opportunities and threats in the firm's external environment[3] (see Chapter 2) as well as the nature and quality of the resources, capabilities, and core competencies in its internal organization[4] (see Chapter 3). As we see in the Opening Case, J.C. Penney, which was once a formidable retailer, has recently suffered a significant decline in sales (25 percent in 2012 alone) due to a poor strategy. It tried to develop more upscale stores and enrich its product offerings. However, doing so placed it in direct competition with other major retailers such as Macy's and Target. Thus, it lost most of its perceived differentiation and advantage. It also changed its pricing strategy. As a result, it appears that the "new" J.C. Penney has developed a competitive advantage—but only over the "old" J.C. Penney. So, it cannibalized its own sales and in the process suffered a severe decline. It lost many of its old customers and was unable to attract new ones. Therefore, it satisfied very few customers' needs.

In previous chapters, analysis of the external environment and of internal firm resources and capabilities, which is the first step in the strategic management process, was discussed. This chapter is the first on strategy, which is the second part of the strategic management process explained in Chapter 1. The fundamental objective of using any type of strategy (see Figure 1.1) is to gain strategic competitiveness and earn above-average returns.[5] Strategies are purposeful, precede the taking of actions to which they apply, and demonstrate a shared understanding of the firm's vision and mission.[6] An effectively formulated strategy marshals, integrates, and allocates the firm's resources, capabilities, and competencies so that it will be properly aligned with its external environment.[7] A properly developed strategy also rationalizes the firm's vision and mission along with the actions taken to achieve them.[8] Information about a host of variables including markets, customers, technology, worldwide finance, and the changing world economy must be collected and analyzed to properly form and use strategies. In the final analysis, sound strategic choices that reduce uncertainty regarding outcomes are the foundation for building successful strategies.[9]

A **business-level strategy** is an integrated and coordinated set of commitments and actions the firm uses to gain a competitive advantage by exploiting core competencies in specific product markets.

**Business-level strategy**, this chapter's focus, is an integrated and coordinated set of commitments and actions the firm uses to gain a competitive advantage by exploiting core

M. Stasy

competencies in specific product markets.[10] Business-level strategy indicates the choices the firm has made about how it intends to compete in individual product markets. The choices are important because long-term performance is linked to a firm's strategies. Given the complexity of successfully competing in the global economy, the choices about how the firm will compete can be difficult.[11] For example, in 2006 Myspace, a social networking site, was the largest such site, with approximately 50 million users. But, within two years, it lost the lead to a fast-developing social networking site, Facebook. Facebook quickly enlarged its market share with more than 600 million users in 2011, while Myspace had only about 34 million users. Facebook has made several major competitive moves in recent years, challenging Myspace to further adjust its strategy as it engaged in various competitive battles. As a result, Myspace has steadily declined from 1600 employees in 2008 to around 200 in 2013. The company is now ranked 220th in amount of total traffic on the Internet.[12] Thus, it is now only a minor competitor trying to survive.

Every firm must develop and implement a business-level strategy. However, some firms may not use all the strategies—corporate-level, merger and acquisition, international, and cooperative—that we examine in Chapters 6 through 9. A firm competing in a single-product market in a single geographic location does not need a corporate-level strategy regarding product diversity or an international strategy to deal with geographic diversity. In contrast, a diversified firm will use one of the corporate-level strategies as well as a separate business-level strategy for each product market in which it competes. Every firm—ranging from the local dry cleaner to the multinational corporation—must develop and use at least one business-level strategy. Thus business-level strategy is the *core* strategy—the strategy that the firm forms to describe how it intends to compete in a product market.[13]

We discuss several topics to examine business-level strategies. Because customers are the foundation of successful business-level strategies and should never be taken for granted,[14] we present information about customers that is relevant to business-level strategies. In terms of customers, when selecting a business-level strategy the firm determines (1) *who* will be served, (2) *what* needs those target customers have that it will satisfy, and (3) *how* those needs will be satisfied. Selecting customers and deciding which of their needs the firm will try to satisfy, as well as how it will do so, are challenging tasks. Global competition has created many attractive options for customers, thus making it difficult to determine the strategy to best serve them.[15] Effective global competitors have become adept at identifying the needs of customers in different cultures and geographic regions as well as learning how to quickly and successfully adapt the functionality of a firm's good or service to meet those needs.

Descriptions of the purpose of business-level strategies—and of the five business-level strategies—follow the discussion of customers. The five strategies we examine are called *generic* because they can be used in any organization competing in any industry.[16] Our analysis describes how effective use of each strategy allows the firm to favorably position itself relative to the five competitive forces in the industry (see Chapter 2). In addition, we use the value chain (see Chapter 3) to show examples of the primary and support activities necessary to implement specific business-level strategies. Because no strategy is risk-free,[17] we also describe the different risks the firm may encounter when using these strategies. In Chapter 11, we explain the organizational structures and controls linked with the successful use of each business-level strategy.

## 4-1 Customers: Their Relationship with Business-Level Strategies

Strategic competitiveness results only when the firm satisfies a group of customers by using its competitive advantages as the basis for competing in individual product markets.[18] A key

Rubberball/Mike Kemp/Getty Images

*Customers standing in a grocery store checkout line. Successful business strategies satisfy customers' needs.*

reason firms must satisfy customers with their business-level strategy is that returns earned from relationships with customers are the lifeblood of all organizations.[19]

The most successful companies try to find new ways to satisfy current customers and/or to meet the needs of new customers. Being able to do this can be even more difficult when firms and consumers face challenging economic conditions. During such times, firms may decide to reduce their workforce to control costs. This can lead to problems, however, because having fewer employees makes it more difficult for companies to meet individual customers' needs and expectations. In these instances, firms can follow several possible courses of action, including paying extra attention to their best customers and developing a flexible workforce by cross-training employees so they can undertake a variety of responsibilities on their jobs.

## 4-1a Effectively Managing Relationships with Customers

The firm's relationships with its customers are strengthened when it delivers superior value to them. Strong interactive relationships with customers often provide the foundation for the firm's efforts to profitably serve customers' unique needs.

As the following statement shows, Caesars Entertainment (the world's largest provider of branded casino entertainment) is committed to providing superior value to customers: "At Caesars we believe that every guest should be treated as a Caesar...Caesars sets the standard of excellence...with employees who are devoted to delivering truly great service."[20] Importantly, as Caesars appears to anticipate, delivering superior value often results in increased customer satisfaction. In turn, customer satisfaction has a positive relationship with profitability because satisfied customers are most likely to be repeat customers. However, more choices and easily accessible information about the functionality of firms' products are creating increasingly sophisticated and knowledgeable customers, making it difficult to earn their loyalty.[21]

A number of companies have become skilled at the art of *managing* all aspects of their relationship with their customers.[22] For example, Amazon.com is widely recognized for the quality of information it maintains about its customers, the services it renders, and its ability to anticipate customers' needs. Using the information it has, Amazon tries to serve what it believes are the unique needs of each customer; and it has a strong reputation for being able to successfully do this.[23]

As we discuss next, firms' relationships with customers are characterized by three dimensions. Companies such as Acer and Amazon.com understand these dimensions and manage their relationships with customers in light of them.

## 4-1b Reach, Richness, and Affiliation

The *reach* dimension of relationships with customers is concerned with the firm's access and connection to customers. In general, firms seek to extend their reach, adding customers in the process of doing so.

Reach is an especially critical dimension for social networking sites such as Facebook and Myspace in that the value these firms create for users is to connect them with others.

As noted earlier, traffic to Myspace has been declining in recent years; at the same time, the number of Facebook users has been dramatically increasing in the United States and abroad. As a result, Facebook had more than 1 billion users in 2013—more than 1500 percent greater than the number of Myspace users.[24] Reach is also important to Netflix. Fortunately for this firm, recent results indicate that its reach continues to expand: Netflix ended 2012 with approximately 33 million total subscribers, representing a 43.5 percent increase from 2011.[25]

*Richness,* the second dimension of firms' relationships with customers, is concerned with the depth and detail of the two-way flow of information between the firm and the customer. The potential of the richness dimension to help the firm establish a competitive advantage in its relationship with customers leads many firms to offer online services in order to better manage information exchanges with their customers. Broader and deeper information-based exchanges allow firms to better understand their customers and their needs. Such exchanges also enable customers to become more knowledgeable about how the firm can satisfy them. Internet technology and e-commerce transactions have substantially reduced the costs of meaningful information exchanges with current and potential customers. As we have noted, Amazon is a leader in using the Internet to build relationships with customers. In fact, it bills itself as the most "customer-centric company" on earth. Amazon and other firms use rich information from customers to help them develop innovative new products that better satisfy customers' needs.[26]

*Affiliation,* the third dimension, is concerned with facilitating useful interactions with customers. Viewing the world through the customer's eyes and constantly seeking ways to create more value for the customer have positive effects in terms of affiliation. This approach enhances customer satisfaction and produces fewer customer complaints. In fact, for services, customers often do not complain when dissatisfied; instead they simply go to competitors for their service needs.[27] Internet navigators such as Microsoft's MSN Autos help online clients find and sort information. MSN Autos provides data and software to prospective car buyers that enable them to compare car models along multiple objective specifications. A prospective buyer who has selected a specific car based on comparisons of different models can then be linked to dealers that meet the customer's needs and purchasing requirements. Because its revenues come not from the final customer or end user but from other sources (such as advertisements on its Web site, hyperlinks, and associated products and services), MSN Autos represents the customer's interests, a service that fosters affiliation.[28]

As we discuss next, effectively managing customer relationships (along the dimensions of reach, richness, and affiliation) helps the firm answer questions related to the issues of *who, what,* and *how.*

## 4-1c Who: Determining the Customers to Serve

Deciding *who* the target customer is that the firm intends to serve with its business-level strategy is an important decision.[29] Companies divide customers into groups based on differences in the customers' needs (needs are discussed further in the next section) to make this decision. Dividing customers into groups based on their needs is called **market segmentation**, which is a process that clusters people with similar needs into individual and identifiable groups.[30] In the animal food products business, for example, the food-product needs of owners of companion pets (e.g., dogs and cats) differ from the needs for food and health-related products of those owning production animals (e.g., livestock). A subsidiary of Colgate-Palmolive, Hill's Pet Nutrition sells food products for pets. In fact, the company's mission is "to help enrich and lengthen the special relationship between people and their pets."[31] Thus, Hill's Pet Nutrition targets the needs of different segments of customers with the food products it sells for animals.

**Market segmentation** is a process used to cluster people with similar needs into individual and identifiable groups.

**Table 4.1** Basis for Customer Segmentation

| Basis for Customer Segmentation |
|---|
| **Consumer Markets** |
| 1. Demographic factors (age, income, sex, etc.) |
| 2. Socioeconomic factors (social class, stage in the family life cycle) |
| 3. Geographic factors (cultural, regional, and national differences) |
| 4. Psychological factors (lifestyle, personality traits) |
| 5. Consumption patterns (heavy, moderate, and light users) |
| 6. Perceptual factors (benefit segmentation, perceptual mapping) |
| **Industrial Markets** |
| 1. End-use segments (identified by SIC code) |
| 2. Product segments (based on technological differences or production economics) |
| 3. Geographic segments (defined by boundaries between countries or by regional differences within them) |
| 4. Common buying factor segments (cut across product market and geographic segments) |
| 5. Customer size segments |

Source: Based on information in S. C. Jain, 2009, *Marketing Planning and Strategy*, Mason, OH: South-Western Cengage Custom Publishing.

Learn more about market segmentation.
www.cengagebrain.com

Almost any identifiable human or organizational characteristic can be used to subdivide a market into segments that differ from one another on a given characteristic. Common characteristics on which customers' needs vary are illustrated in Table 4.1.

## 4-1d What: Determining Which Customer Needs to Satisfy

After the firm decides *who* it will serve, it must identify the targeted customer group's needs that its goods or services can satisfy. In a general sense, *needs (what)* are related to a product's benefits and features. Successful firms learn how to deliver to customers what they want, when they want it. Having close and frequent interactions with both current and potential customers helps the firm identify those individuals' and groups' current and future needs.[32]

From a strategic perspective, a basic need of all customers is to buy products that create value for them. The generalized forms of value that goods or services provide are either low cost with acceptable features or highly differentiated features with acceptable cost. The most effective firms continuously strive to anticipate changes in customers' needs. The firm that fails to anticipate and certainly to recognize changes in its customers' needs may lose its customers to competitors whose products can provide more value to the focal firm's customers. It is also recognized that consumer needs and desires have been changing in recent years. For example, more consumers desire to have an experience rather than to simply purchase a good or service. As a result, one of Starbucks' goals has been to provide an experience, not just a cup of coffee. Customers also prefer to receive customized goods and services. Again, Starbucks has been doing this for some time, allowing customers to design their own drinks, within their menus (which have become rather extensive over time).

They also demand fast service. Consumers in the United States have been known for their impatience, but rapid service is now expected by most consumers.[33] Unhappy consumers lead to lost sales—both theirs and those of others who learn of their dissatisfaction. Therefore, it is important to maintain customer satisfaction by meeting and satisfying their needs.[34]

## 4-1e How: Determining Core Competencies Necessary to Satisfy Customer Needs

After deciding *who* the firm will serve and the specific *needs* of those customers, the firm is prepared to determine how to use its capabilities and competencies to develop products that can satisfy the needs of its target customers. As explained in Chapters 1 and 3, *core competencies* are resources and capabilities that serve as a source of competitive advantage for the firm over its rivals. Firms use core competencies (*how*) to implement value-creating strategies

M. Stasy

and thereby satisfy customers' needs. Only those firms with the capacity to continuously improve, innovate, and upgrade their competencies can expect to meet and hopefully exceed customers' expectations across time.[35] Firms must continuously upgrade their capabilities to ensure that they maintain the advantage over their rivals by providing customers with a superior product.[36] Often these capabilities are difficult for competitors to imitate partly because they are constantly being upgraded but also because they are integrated and used as configurations of capabilities to perform an important activity (e.g., R&D).[37]

Companies draw from a wide range of core competencies to produce goods or services that can satisfy customers' needs. For example, Merck is a large pharmaceutical firm well-known for its R&D capabilities. In recent times, Merck has been building on these capabilities by investing heavily in R&D. In 2012, Merck invested $7.9 billion to conduct research and identify major new drugs, which was almost 17 percent of its total sales revenue.[38] These new drugs are intended to meet the needs of consumers and to sustain Merck's competitive advantage in the industry.

SAS Institute is the world's largest privately owned software company and is the leader in business intelligence and analytics. Customers use SAS programs for data warehousing, data mining, and decision support purposes. SAS serves 60,000 sites in 135 countries and serves 90 percent of the top *Fortune* 100 firms. Allocating approximately 25 percent of revenues to research and development (R&D), a percentage that exceeds percentages allocated by its competitors, SAS relies on its core competence in R&D to satisfy the data-related needs of such customers as the U.S. Census Bureau and a host of consumer goods firms (e.g., hotels, banks, and catalog companies).[39]

Sometimes, firms may find it necessary to use their core competencies as the foundation for producing new goods or services for new customers. This may be the case for some small automobile parts suppliers in the United States. Given that U.S. auto production in recent years declined about one third from more typical levels, a number of these firms are seeking to diversify their operations, perhaps exiting the auto parts supplier industry as a result of doing so. Some analysts believe that the first rule for these small manufacturers is to determine how their current capabilities and competencies might be used to produce value-creating products for different customers. One analyst gave the following example of how this might work: "There may be no reason that a company making auto door handles couldn't make ball-and-socket joints for artificial shoulders."[40]

Find out more about innovations at Alaska Airlines.
www.cengagebrain.com

As explained in the Strategic Focus, many types of firms now emphasize innovation, not only those in high technology industries (e.g., Dell). This innovation appears to be driven by customers along with providing customers a product or service that satisfies their needs in a manner superior to that of rivals' products or services to gain or sustain a competitive advantage. In fact, the information in the Strategic Focus suggests that both Alaska Airlines and L'Oréal have gained competitive advantages due to their innovations.

Our discussion about customers shows that all organizations must use their capabilities and core competencies (the *how*) to satisfy the needs (the *what*) of the target group of customers (the *who*) the firm has chosen to serve. Next, we describe the different business-level strategies that are available to firms to use to satisfy customers as the foundation for earning above-average returns.

## 4-2 The Purpose of a Business-Level Strategy

The purpose of a business-level strategy is to create differences between the firm's position and those of its competitors.[41] To position itself differently from competitors, a firm must decide whether it intends to *perform activities differently* or to *perform different activities*.

M. Stasy

## Strategic Focus TECHNOLOGY

### Continuously Innovating to Satisfy Customers' Needs

The competitive landscape has changed in recent years such that companies in many industries have to continue to innovate to maintain their competitive advantage by providing superior value to their customers. This requirement has existed in high technology industries for years but has now spread to consumer products industries such as cosmetics and airlines. Clayton Christiansen, a noted Harvard professor, suggested that many leading firms are afraid to change because of the fear of losing their current customers. He called this the "innovator's dilemma". In fact, these firms seemed to be captive to their current customers, which allows new entrants in the industry to introduce new technologies and innovative products that capture many of the customers served by the incumbent firms.

However, firms are learning from the mistakes of others. For example, L'Oréal has established a research center in Shanghai to develop new products and tailor existing products to the particular needs of Chinese customers. These products range from lipstick to shampoo. L'Oréal is using traditional herbal remedies in several of their products for the Chinese market. Its innovations have been successful, capturing some market share from the market leader, Procter & Gamble (P&G). The Chinese market is lucrative and growing, with the beauty and personal-care products market estimated at $34 billion in 2013. The growth in this market is demonstrated by the fact that although P&G has experienced a small decline in market share, its overall business has increased by approximately 50 percent in the last three years. P&G has also been innovative in this market.

Airlines have not been known for being innovative, but Alaska Airlines introduced a novel innovation that has contributed to its success in recent years—especially in providing better service to its customers. This innovation may revolutionize the air traffic control system in the United States. Alaska Airlines developed and implemented a satellite guidance system to help pilots land planes at Alaskan airports, which often have challenging weather conditions. It has greatly aided safe landings but also helped the airline to avoid costly delays and cancelled flights, thereby offering quality service to its customers. In fact, in 2012, Alaska Airlines had the best on-time performance in the industry, with 87 percent of its flights landing on time.

Of course, being innovative means that firms as well as their employees must take risks. Jeff Bezos, founder and CEO of Amazon.com, has propelled his company into a leadership position through innovation. Bezos claims that one of the major reasons for his firm's innovation has been the promotion of experimentation. Bezos feels that one of his jobs as a leader is to encourage Amazon employees to experiment with new ideas.

*World Expo 2010 site opening ceremony in Shanghai, China. L'Oreal's Shanghai research center develops products to satisfy the needs of Chinese customers.*

Even Dell, which emphasized its highly efficient supply chain to maintain a competitive advantage in the past, is now investing significant resources in R&D to develop new products and services to satisfy customer needs. Dell executives claim that their company is selling solutions rather than specific products and focusing on the small and medium-sized business market. Dell is trying to quickly move its products and services to a cloud computing environment.

Many companies are trying to increase their innovation and in the process encourage employees to take more risks and experiment with new ideas. The new business landscape is now considerably different from the traditional one where employees were encouraged to "think inside the box".

Sources: L. Lin, 2013, L'Oréal tailors new cosmetics for China's beauty market, *Bloomberg Businessweek*, www.businessweek.com, March 28; H. Gregersen, 2013, Amazon's Jeff Bezos and Apollo 11. He's still innovating, *Bloomberg Businessweek*, www.businessweek.com, March 25; L. Kwoh, 2013, Memo to staff: Take more risks, *Wall Street Journal*, www.wsj.com, March 20; J. Mouawad, 2013, Alaska Airlines, flying above an industry's troubles, *New York Times*, www.nytimes.com, March 2; Q. Hardy, 2012, For Dell, consolidation is innovation, *New York Times—The Business of Technology*, http://bits.blogs.nytimes.com, October 18; N. Bilton, 2012, Disruptions: Innovation isn't easy, especially midstream, *New York Times—The Business of Technology*, http://bits.blogs.nytimes.com, April 15.

Strategy defines the path which provides the direction of actions to be taken by leaders of the organization.[42] In fact, "choosing to perform activities differently or to perform different activities than rivals" is the essence of business-level strategy.[43] Thus, the firm's business-level strategy is a deliberate choice about how it will perform the value chain's primary and support activities to create unique value. Indeed, in the current complex competitive landscape, successful use of a business-level strategy results from the firm learning how to integrate the activities it performs in ways that create superior value for customers.

Firms develop an activity map to show how they integrate the activities they perform. The manner in which Southwest Airlines has integrated its activities is the foundation for the successful use of its primary cost leadership strategy (this strategy is discussed later in the chapter) but also includes differentiation through the unique services provided to customers. The tight integration among Southwest's activities is a key source of the firm's ability to at least historically operate more profitably than its competitors.

Southwest Airlines has configured the activities it performs into six areas of strategic intent—limited passenger service; frequent, reliable departures; lean, highly productive ground and gate crews; high aircraft utilization; very low ticket prices; and short-haul, point-to-point routes between mid-sized cities and secondary airports. Individual clusters of tightly linked activities make it possible to achieve its strategic intent. For example, no meals, no seat assignments, and no baggage transfers form a cluster of individual activities that support the strategic intent to offer limited passenger service.

Southwest's tightly integrated activities make it difficult for competitors to imitate the firm's cost leadership strategy. The firm's unique culture and customer service are sources of competitive advantage that rivals have been unable to imitate, although some have tried and largely failed (e.g., US Airways' MetroJet subsidiary, United Airlines' United Shuttle, Delta's Song, and Continental Airlines' Continental Lite). Hindsight shows that these competitors offered low prices to customers, but weren't able to operate at costs close to those of Southwest or to provide customers with any notable sources of differentiation, such as a unique experience while in the air. The key to Southwest's success has been its ability to continuously maintain low costs while providing customers with *acceptable* levels of differentiation such as an engaging culture. Firms using the cost leadership strategy must understand that in terms of sources of differentiation accompanying the cost leader's product, the customer defines *acceptable*. Fit among activities is a key to the sustainability of competitive advantage for all firms, including Southwest Airlines. Strategic fit among the many activities is critical for competitive advantage. It is more difficult for a competitor to match a configuration of integrated activities than to imitate a particular activity such as sales promotion, or a process technology.[44]

## 4-3 Types of Business-Level Strategies

Firms choose between five business-level strategies to establish and defend their desired strategic position against competitors: *cost leadership, differentiation, focused cost leadership, focused differentiation,* and *integrated cost leadership/differentiation* (see Figure 4.1). Each business-level strategy can help the firm to establish and exploit a particular *competitive advantage* within a particular *competitive scope.* How firms integrate the activities they perform within each different business-level strategy demonstrates how they differ from one another.[45] For example, firms have different activity maps, and thus, a Southwest Airlines activity map differs from those of competitors JetBlue, Continental, American Airlines, and so forth. Superior integration of activities increases the likelihood of being able to gain an advantage over competitors and to earn above-average returns.

When selecting a business-level strategy, firms evaluate two types of potential competitive advantages: "lower cost than rivals, or the ability to differentiate and command a premium price that exceeds the extra cost of doing so."[46] Having lower cost derives from the firm's ability to perform activities differently than rivals; being able to differentiate indicates the firm's capacity to perform different (and valuable) activities. Thus, based on the nature and quality of its internal resources, capabilities, and core competencies, a firm seeks to form either a cost competitive advantage or a distinctiveness competitive advantage as the basis for implementing its business-level strategy.[47]

Two types of target markets are broad market and narrow market segment(s) (see Figure 4.1). Firms serving a broad market seek to use their capabilities to create value for customers on an industry-wide basis. A narrow market segment means that the firm intends to serve the needs of a narrow customer group. With focus strategies, the firm "selects a segment or group of segments in the industry and tailors its strategy to serving them to the exclusion of others."[48] Buyers with special needs and buyers located in specific geographic regions are examples of narrow customer groups.[49] As shown in Figure 4.1, a firm could also strive to develop a combined low cost/distinctiveness value creation approach as the foundation for serving a target customer group that is larger than a narrow market segment but not as comprehensive as a broad (or industry-wide) customer group. In this instance, the firm uses the integrated cost leadership/differentiation strategy.

None of the five business-level strategies shown in Figure 4.1 is inherently or universally superior to the others.[50] The effectiveness of each strategy is contingent both on the opportunities and threats in a firm's external environment and on the strengths and weaknesses derived from the firm's resource portfolio. It is critical, therefore, for the firm to select a

**Figure 4.1** Five Business-Level Strategies

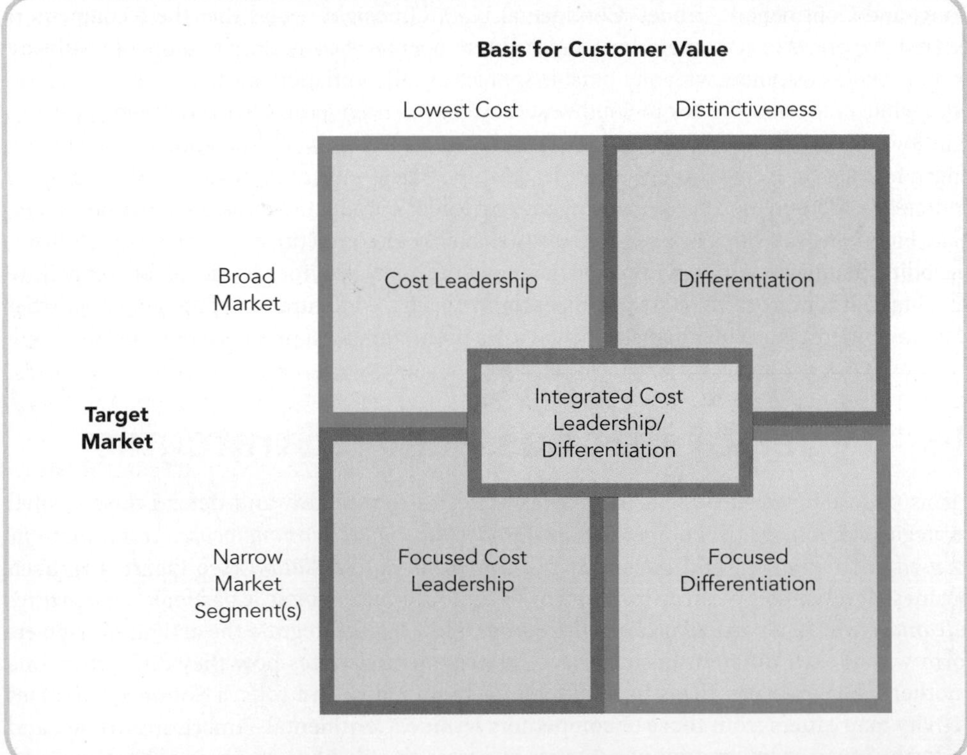


Source: Based on M. E. Porter, 1998, *Competitive Advantage: Creating and Sustaining Superior Performance*, New York: The Free Press; D. G. Sirmon, M. A. Hitt, & R. D. Ireland, 2007, Managing firm resources in dynamic environments to create value: Looking inside the black box, *Academy of Management Review*, 32: 273–292; D. G. Sirmon, M. A. Hitt, R. D. Ireland, & B. A. Gilbert, 2011, Resource orchestration to create competitive advantage: Breadth, depth and life cycles effects, *Journal of Management*, 37(5): 1390-1412.

business-level strategy that represents an effective match between the opportunities and threats in its external environment and the strengths of its internal organization based on its core competencies.[51] After the firm chooses its strategy, it should consistently emphasize actions that are required to successfully use it.

## 4-3a Cost Leadership Strategy

The **cost leadership strategy** is an integrated set of actions taken to produce goods or services with features that are acceptable to customers at the lowest cost, relative to those of competitors.[52] Firms using the cost leadership strategy commonly sell standardized goods or services (but with competitive levels of differentiation) to the industry's most typical customers. Process innovations, which are newly designed production and distribution methods and techniques that allow the firm to operate more efficiently, are critical to successful use of the cost leadership strategy. In recent years, firms have developed sourcing strategies to find low-cost suppliers to which they outsource various functions (e.g., manufacturing goods) in order to keep their costs very low.[53]

As noted, cost leaders' goods and services must have competitive levels of differentiation that create value for customers. For example, in recent years Kia Motors has emphasized the design of its cars in the U.S. market as a source of differentiation while implementing a cost leadership strategy.[54] Called "cheap chic," some analysts had a positive view of this decision, saying that "When they're done, Kia's cars will still be low-end (in price), but they won't necessarily look like it."[55] It is important for firms using the cost leadership strategy to ensure that they are concerned about the quality and attractiveness of the product for customers rather than solely concentrating on reducing costs because it could result in the firm efficiently producing products that no customer wants to purchase.[56] In fact, such extremes could limit the potential for important process innovations and lead to employment of lower-skilled workers, poor conditions on the production line, accidents, and a poor quality of work life for employees.[57]

As shown in Figure 4.1, the firm using the cost leadership strategy targets a broad customer segment or group. Cost leaders concentrate on finding ways to lower their costs relative to competitors by constantly rethinking how to complete their primary and support activities (such as highly efficient information systems) to reduce or maintain low costs while maintaining competitive levels of differentiation.[58]

For example, cost leader Greyhound Lines Inc. continuously seeks ways to reduce the costs it incurs to provide bus service while offering customers an acceptable level of differentiation. Greyhound offers additional services to customers trying to enhance the value of the experience customers have while they pay low prices for their service package. Interestingly, a number of customers now "insist on certain amenities that they receive on planes and trains—such as Internet access and comfortable seats, not to mention cleanliness." To maintain competitive levels of differentiation while using the cost leadership strategy, Greyhound has several "motor coaches" in its fleet that have leather seats, additional legroom, Wi-Fi access, and power outlets in every row.[59]

Greyhound enjoys economies of scale by serving more than 18 million passengers annually with about 3,800 destinations in North America, which produces 5.5 billion passenger miles. These scale economies allow the firm to keep its costs low while offering some of the differentiated services today's customers seek from the company. Demonstrating the firm's commitment to the physical environment segment of the general environment is the fact that "one Greyhound bus takes an average of 19 cars off the road for every 170 passengers."[60]

As primary activities, inbound logistics (e.g., materials handling, warehousing, and inventory control) and outbound logistics (e.g., collecting, storing, and distributing products to customers) often account for significant portions of the total cost to produce some goods and services. Research suggests that having a competitive advantage in logistics

The **cost leadership strategy** is an integrated set of actions taken to produce goods or services with features that are acceptable to customers at the lowest cost, relative to that of competitors.

creates more value with a cost leadership strategy than with a differentiation strategy.[61] Thus, cost leaders seeking competitively valuable ways to reduce costs may want to concentrate on the primary activities of inbound logistics and outbound logistics. In so doing many firms choose to outsource their manufacturing operations to low-cost firms with low-wage employees (e.g., China).[62] However, care must be taken because outsourcing also makes the firm more dependent on firms over which they have little control. Outsourcing creates interdependencies between the outsourcing firm and the suppliers. If dependencies become too great, it gives the supplier more power with which the supplier may increase prices of the goods and services provided. Such actions could harm the firm's ability to maintain a low-cost competitive advantage.[63]

Cost leaders also carefully examine all support activities to find additional potential cost reductions. Developing new systems for finding the optimal combination of low cost and acceptable levels of differentiation in the raw materials required to produce the firm's goods or services is an example of how the procurement support activity can facilitate successful use of the cost leadership strategy.

Big Lots Inc. uses the cost leadership strategy. With its vision of being "The World's Best Bargain Place," Big Lots is the largest closeout retailer in the United States with annual sales approaching $5 billion from more than 1,400 stores. For Big Lots, closeout goods are brand-name products from 3,000 manufacturers provided for sale at substantially lower prices than sold by other retailers.[64]

As described in Chapter 3, firms use value-chain analysis to identify the parts of the company's operations that create value and those that do not. Figure 4.2 demonstrates the value-chain activities and support functions that allow a firm to create value through the cost leadership strategy. Companies unable to effectively integrate the activities and functions shown in this figure typically lack the core competencies needed to successfully use the cost leadership strategy.

Effective use of the cost leadership strategy allows a firm to earn above-average returns in spite of the presence of strong competitive forces (see Chapter 2). The next sections (one for each of the five forces) explain how firms implement a cost leadership strategy.

### Rivalry with Existing Competitors

Having the low-cost position is valuable when dealing with rivals. Because of the cost leader's advantageous position, rivals hesitate to compete on the basis of price, especially before evaluating the potential outcomes of such competition.[65] The changes Walmart made to attract upscale customers created vulnerability in its low-cost position to rivals. Dollar Store, Amazon.com, and others took advantage of the opportunity. Amazon appears to have become a low-cost leader, and the Dollar Stores provide low costs and easy access for customers. Both of these rivals have siphoned off some of Walmart's customers.

The degree of rivalry present is based on a number of different factors such as size and resources of rivals, their dependence on the particular market, and location and prior competitive interactions, among others.[66] Firms may also take actions to reduce the amount of rivalry that they face. For example, firms sometimes form joint ventures to reduce rivalry and increase the amount of profitability enjoyed by firms in the industry.[67] In China they build strong relationships, often referred to as guanxi, with key stakeholders such as important government officials and units, suppliers, and customers, thereby restraining rivalry.[68]

### Bargaining Power of Buyers (Customers)

Powerful customers can force a cost leader to reduce its prices, but not below the level at which the cost leader's next-most-efficient industry competitor can earn average returns. Although powerful customers might be able to force the cost leader to reduce prices even below this level, they probably would choose not to do so. Prices that are low enough to

**Figure 4.2** Examples of Value-Creating Activities Associated with the Cost Leadership Strategy

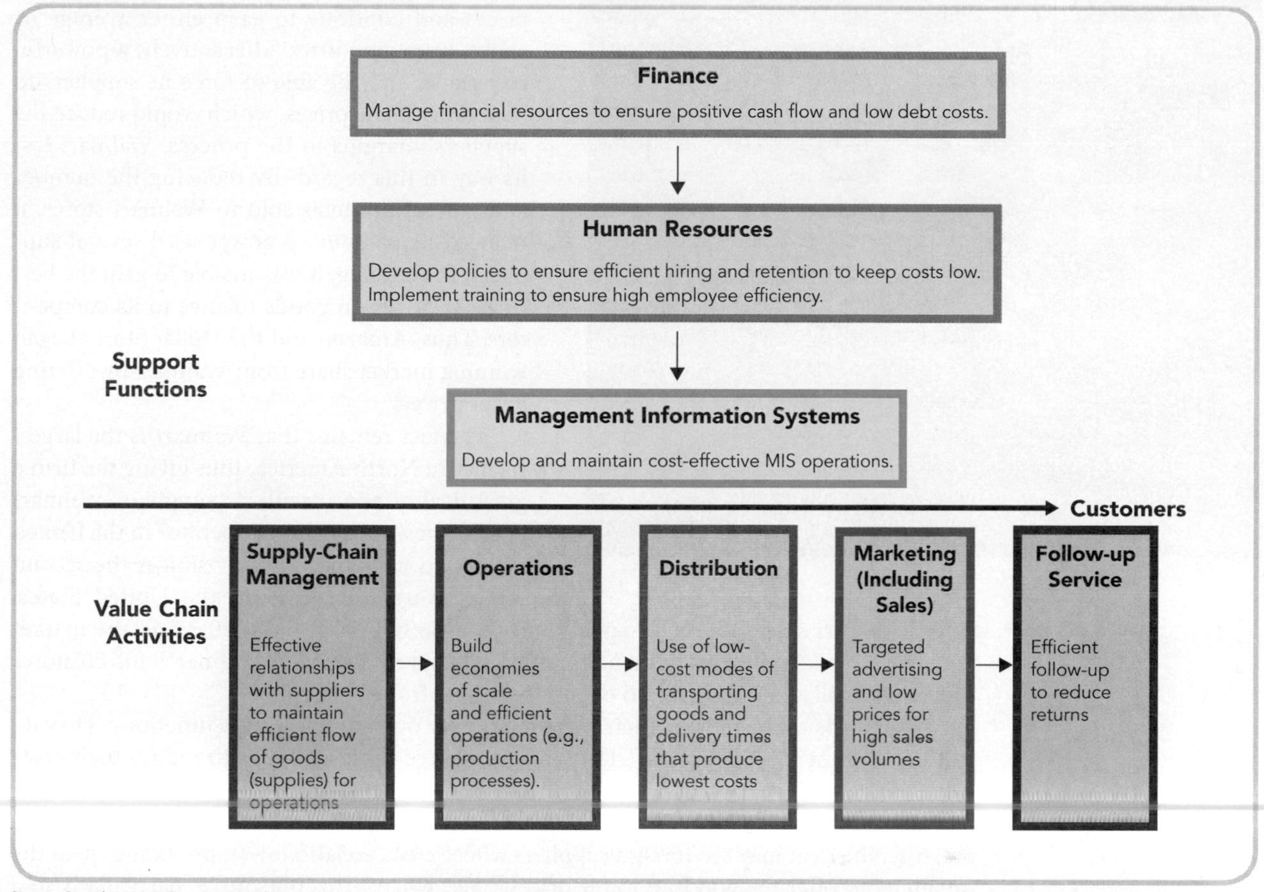


Source: Based on M. E. Porter, 1998, *Competitive Advantage: Creating and Sustaining Superior Performance,* New York: The Free Press; D. G. Sirmon, M. A. Hitt, & R. D. Ireland, 2007, Managing firm resources in dynamic environments to create value: Looking inside the black box, *Academy of Management Review,* 32: 273–292; D. G. Sirmon, M. A. Hitt, R. D. Ireland, & B. A. Gilbert, 2011, Resource orchestration to create competitive advantage: Breadth, depth and life cycles effects, *Journal of Management,* 37(5): 1390–1412.

prevent the next-most-efficient competitor from earning average returns would force that firm to exit the market, leaving the cost leader with less competition and in an even stronger position. Customers would thus lose their power and pay higher prices if they were forced to purchase from a single firm operating in an industry without rivals. In some cases, rather than forcing firms to reduce their prices, powerful customers may pressure firms to provide innovative products and services as explained in the earlier Strategic Focus.

Buyers can also develop a counterbalancing power to the customers' power by thoroughly analyzing and understanding each of their customers. To help in obtaining information and understanding the customers, buyers can participate in customers' networks. In so doing, they share information, build trust, and participate in joint problem solving with their customers.[69] In turn, they use the information obtained to provide a product that provides superior value to customers by most effectively satisfying their needs.

## Bargaining Power of Suppliers

The cost leader generally operates with margins greater than those of competitors and often tries to increase its margins by driving costs lower. Among other benefits, higher gross margins relative to those of competitors make it possible for the cost leader to absorb its suppliers' price increases. When an industry faces substantial increases in the cost of its supplies,

MELANIE BURFORD/KRT/Newscom

*Customers at a Sam's Club warehouse in Plano, Texas. The combined purchasing strength of Walmart and Sam's Club gives them a great deal of bargaining power with their suppliers.*

only the cost leader may be able to pay the higher prices and continue to earn either average or above-average returns. Alternatively, a powerful cost leader may be able to force its suppliers to hold down their prices, which would reduce the suppliers' margins in the process. Walmart lost its way in this regard. By reducing the number and type of products sold in Walmart stores, it reduced its bargaining power with several suppliers. In so doing, it was unable to gain the best (lowest) prices on goods relative to its competitors. Thus, Amazon and the Dollar Stores began winning market share from Walmart by offering lower prices.

The fact remains that Walmart is the largest retailer in North America, thus giving the firm a great deal of power with its suppliers. Walmart is the largest supermarket operator in the United States and its Sam's Club division is the second largest warehouse club in the United States. Collectively, its sales volume of approximately $466 billion in fiscal 2013 and the market penetration it suggests (more than 200 million people visit one of Walmart's 10,700 stores each week) still allow Walmart to obtain low prices from its suppliers.[70]

Some firms create dependencies on suppliers by outsourcing whole functions. They do so to reduce their overall costs.[71] They may outsource these activities to reduce their costs because of earnings pressures from stakeholders (e.g., institutional investors who own a major stock holding in the company) in the industry.[72] Often when there is such earnings pressure, the firm may see foreign suppliers whose costs are also lower, providing them the capability to offer the goods at lower prices.[73] Yet, when firms outsource, particularly to a foreign supplier, they also need to invest time and effort into building a good relationship, hopefully developing trust between the firms. Such efforts facilitate the integration of the supplier into the firm's value chain.[74]

## Potential Entrants

Through continuous efforts to reduce costs to levels that are lower than competitors, a cost leader becomes highly efficient. Because increasing levels of efficiency (e.g., economies of scale) enhance profit margins, they serve as a significant entry barrier to potential competitors.[75] New entrants must be willing to accept no-better-than-average returns until they gain the experience required to approach the cost leader's efficiency. To earn even average returns, new entrants must have the competencies required to match the cost levels of competitors other than the cost leader. The low profit margins (relative to margins earned by firms implementing the differentiation strategy) make it necessary for the cost leader to sell large volumes of its product to earn above-average returns. However, firms striving to be the cost leader must avoid pricing their products so low that they cannot operate profitably, even though volume increases.

## Product Substitutes

Compared with its industry rivals, the cost leader also holds an attractive position relative to product substitutes. A product substitute becomes a concern for the cost leader when its features and characteristics, in terms of cost and differentiation, are potentially attractive to the firm's customers. When faced with possible substitutes, the cost leader has more flexibility than its competitors. To retain customers, it often can reduce the price of its good or service. With still lower prices and competitive levels of differentiation, the cost leader increases the probability that customers prefer its product rather than a substitute.

### Competitive Risks of the Cost Leadership Strategy

The cost leadership strategy is not risk free. One risk is that the processes used by the cost leader to produce and distribute its good or service could become obsolete because of competitors' innovations.[76] These innovations may allow rivals to produce at costs lower than those of the original cost leader, or to provide additional differentiated features without increasing the product's price to customers.

A second risk is that too much focus by the cost leader on cost reductions may occur at the expense of trying to understand customers' perceptions of "competitive levels of differentiation." Walmart, for example, has been criticized for having too few salespeople available to help customers and too few individuals at checkout registers. These complaints suggest that there might be a discrepancy between how Walmart's customers define "minimal acceptable levels of service" and the firm's attempts to drive its costs increasingly lower.

Imitation is a final risk of the cost leadership strategy. Using their own core competencies, competitors sometimes learn how to successfully imitate the cost leader's strategy. When this happens, the cost leader must increase the value its good or service provides to customers. Commonly, value is increased by selling the current product at an even lower price or by adding differentiated features that create value for customers while maintaining price.

## 4-3b Differentiation Strategy

The **differentiation strategy** is an integrated set of actions taken to produce goods or services (at an acceptable cost) that customers perceive as being different in ways that are important to them.[77] While cost leaders serve a typical customer in an industry, differentiators target customers for whom value is created by the manner in which the firm's products differ from those produced and marketed by competitors. Product innovation, which is "the result of bringing to life a new way to solve the customer's problem—through a new product or service development—that benefits both the customer and the sponsoring company"[78] is critical to successful use of the differentiation strategy.[79]

Firms must be able to produce differentiated products at competitive costs to reduce upward pressure on the price that customers pay. When a product's differentiated features are produced at noncompetitive costs, the price for the product may exceed what the firm's target customers are willing to pay. If the firm has a thorough understanding of what its target customers value, the relative importance they attach to the satisfaction of different needs, and for what they are willing to pay a premium, the differentiation strategy can be effective in helping it earn above-average returns. Of course, to achieve these returns, the firm must apply its knowledge capital (knowledge held by its employees and managers) to provide customers with a differentiated product that provides them with superior value.[80]

Through the differentiation strategy, the firm produces nonstandardized (that is, distinctive) products for customers who value differentiated features more than they value low cost. For example, superior product reliability and durability and high-performance sound systems are among the differentiated features of Toyota Motor Corporation's Lexus products. However, Lexus offers its vehicles to customers at a competitive purchase price relative to other luxury automobiles. As with Lexus products, a product's unique attributes, rather than its purchase price, provide the value for which customers are willing to pay.

To maintain success with the differentiation strategy results, the firm must consistently upgrade differentiated features that customers value and/or create new valuable features (innovate) without significant cost increases.[81] This approach requires firms to constantly change their product lines.[82] These firms may also offer a portfolio of products

The **differentiation strategy** is an integrated set of actions taken to produce goods or services (at an acceptable cost) that customers perceive as being different in ways that are important to them.

that complement each other, thereby enriching the differentiation for the customer and perhaps satisfying a portfolio of consumer needs.[83] Because a differentiated product satisfies customers' unique needs, firms following the differentiation strategy are able to charge premium prices. The ability to sell a good or service at a price that substantially exceeds the cost of creating its differentiated features allows the firm to outperform rivals and earn above-average returns. Rather than costs, a firm using the differentiation strategy primarily concentrates on investing in and developing features that differentiate a product in ways that create value for customers.[84] Overall, a firm using the differentiation strategy seeks to be different from its competitors on as many dimensions as possible. The less similarity between a firm's goods or services and those of competitors, the more buffered it is from rivals' actions. Commonly recognized differentiated goods include Toyota's Lexus, Ralph Lauren's wide array of product lines, Caterpillar's heavy-duty earth-moving equipment, and McKinsey & Co.'s differentiated consulting services.

A good or service can be differentiated in many ways. Unusual features, responsive customer service, rapid product innovations and technological leadership, perceived prestige and status, different tastes, and engineering design and performance are examples of approaches to differentiation.[85] While the number of ways to reduce costs may be finite, virtually anything a firm can do to create real or perceived value is a basis for differentiation. Consider product design as a case in point. Because it can create a positive experience for customers, design is an important source of differentiation (even for cost leaders seeking to find ways to add functionalities to their low-cost products as a way of differentiating their products from competitors) and hopefully, for firms emphasizing it, of competitive advantage.[86] Apple is often cited as the firm that sets the standard in design, with the iPod, iPhone, and iPad demonstrating Apple's product design capabilities. Apple's extremely successful new product launches and market share captured with them has invited competition, the most significant of which is Samsung, as described in the Strategic Focus. As described in Chapter 3 Samsung has some strong capabilities and thus has become a formidable competitor. Although it largely imitates Apple's products, it also improves on them by adding features attractive to customers (imperfect imitation).[87] Therefore, Samsung is partially differentiating from Apple's unique (differentiated) products.

The value chain can be analyzed to determine if a firm is able to link the activities required to create value by using the differentiation strategy. Examples of value chain activities and support functions that are commonly used to differentiate a good or service are shown in Figure 4.3. Companies without the skills needed to link these activities cannot expect to successfully use the differentiation strategy. Next, we explain how firms using the differentiation strategy can successfully position themselves in terms of the five forces of competition (see Chapter 2) to earn above-average returns.

### Rivalry with Existing Competitors

Customers tend to be loyal purchasers of products differentiated in ways that are meaningful to them. As their loyalty to a brand increases, customers' sensitivity to price increases is reduced. The relationship between brand loyalty and price sensitivity insulates a firm from competitive rivalry. Thus, reputations can sustain the competitive advantage of firms following a differentiation strategy.[88] Alternatively, when highly capable rivals such as Samsung practice imperfect imitation by imitating and improving on products, companies such as Apple must pay attention. Thus, Apple must try to incrementally improve its iPhone and iPad products to exploit its investments. However, it must also invest in exploring highly novel and valuable products to establish new markets to remain ahead of Samsung.[89]

### Bargaining Power of Buyers (Customers)

The distinctiveness of differentiated goods or services reduces customers' sensitivity to price increases. Customers are willing to accept a price increase when a product still satisfies

# Strategic Focus TECHNOLOGY

## Apple vs. Samsung: Apple Differentiates and Samsung Imperfectly Imitates

Apple is not only a product innovator; it creates new markets and then dominates them as a first mover. Apple has done this with the iPod, iPhone, and iPad. Almost none of its high-tech rivals, such as Dell, Hewlett-Packard, Nokia, and BlackBerry, have offered a serious challenge. However, in recent times Samsung has become a successful challenger of Apple. In fact, it has been so successful that Apple took Samsung to court with a lawsuit for patent infringement. Apple won the lawsuit and a $1 billion judgment against Samsung. Thus, Samsung appears to be a very good imitator—perhaps too good.

Actually, Samsung invests in R&D to design products for existing markets. As such, it is identified as a fast second mover in existing markets. In this regard, Samsung is effective at imitating but changing features. In fact, it improves on features that are attractive to customers. For example, it recently introduced the Galaxy 4 smartphone, which has a five-inch screen. This screen is larger than that of the iPhone 5S and supposedly produces sharper photos.

*Samsung Galaxy Tab 10.1. Even though Samsung trails Apple in several product categories, R&D spending suggests that it plans to keep pressure on the industry leader.*

The rivalry between the two electronic product companies seems to focus on attempts to produce dominant designs. Samsung has acquired the services of one of the top designers in the world, Chris Bangle, who gained fame with his designs of autos for BMW. The design and product battles are now playing out in other product markets, such as tablets, and perhaps smart TVs and smart watches in the near future. During the 2012 Christmas holiday season, Apple sold 22.9 million iPads and Samsung sold 7.6 million tablets. Although Samsung appears to be an imitator, it spends far more money on R&D than does Apple. Samsung invests about three times as much money in R&D than Apple and, importantly, its R&D represents about 5.4 percent of its annual sales, whereas Apple invests about 2.2 percent of its annual sales in R&D.

All of this suggests that Samsung is a formidable competitor. Knowledgeable sources predict that Apple will settle its suit against Samsung, as it cannot afford to invest heavily in the litigation and appeals and forgo investing the money in R&D if it wishes to remain ahead of Samsung.

Sources: M.-J. Lee, 2013, Samsung vs. Apple's next battleground: Watches? *Wall Street Journal,* http://blog.wsj.com, March 19; R. Pendola, 2013, Apple vs. Samsung explained with a burger and fries on Facebook, *The Street,* www.thestreet.com, March 18; H. Shaughnessy, 2013, Samsung vs. Apple, the battle for design dominance, *Forbes,* www.forbes.com, March 17; B. X. Chen, 2013, Samsung's new 8-inch tablet takes on the iPad Mini, *New York Times—The Business of Technology,* http://bits.blogs.nytimes.com, February 23; B. X. Chen, 2013, Samsung emerges as a potent rival to apple's cool, *New York Times,* February 10; M. Veverka, 2013, Unplugged: Apple-Samsung showdown has diaper whiff, *USA Today,* www.usatoday.com, January 22; K. Eaton, 2013, Apple rumor patrol: 2013 iPhone edition, *Fast company,* www.fastcompany.com, January 11.



their unique needs better than does a competitor's offering. Thus, the golfer whose needs are specifically satisfied by Callaway golf clubs will likely continue buying those products even if their cost increases. Purchasers of brand-name food items (e.g., Heinz ketchup and Kleenex tissues) accept price increases in those products as long as they continue to perceive that the product satisfies their distinctive needs at an acceptable cost. In all of these instances, the customers are relatively insensitive to price increases because they do not think that an acceptable product alternative exists.

Learn about NOKIA, a competitor of Apple.
www.cengagebrain.com

### Bargaining Power of Suppliers

Because the firm using the differentiation strategy charges a premium price for its products, suppliers must provide high-quality components, driving up the firm's costs. However, the

**Figure 4.3** Examples of Value-Creating Activities Associated with the Differentiation Strategy

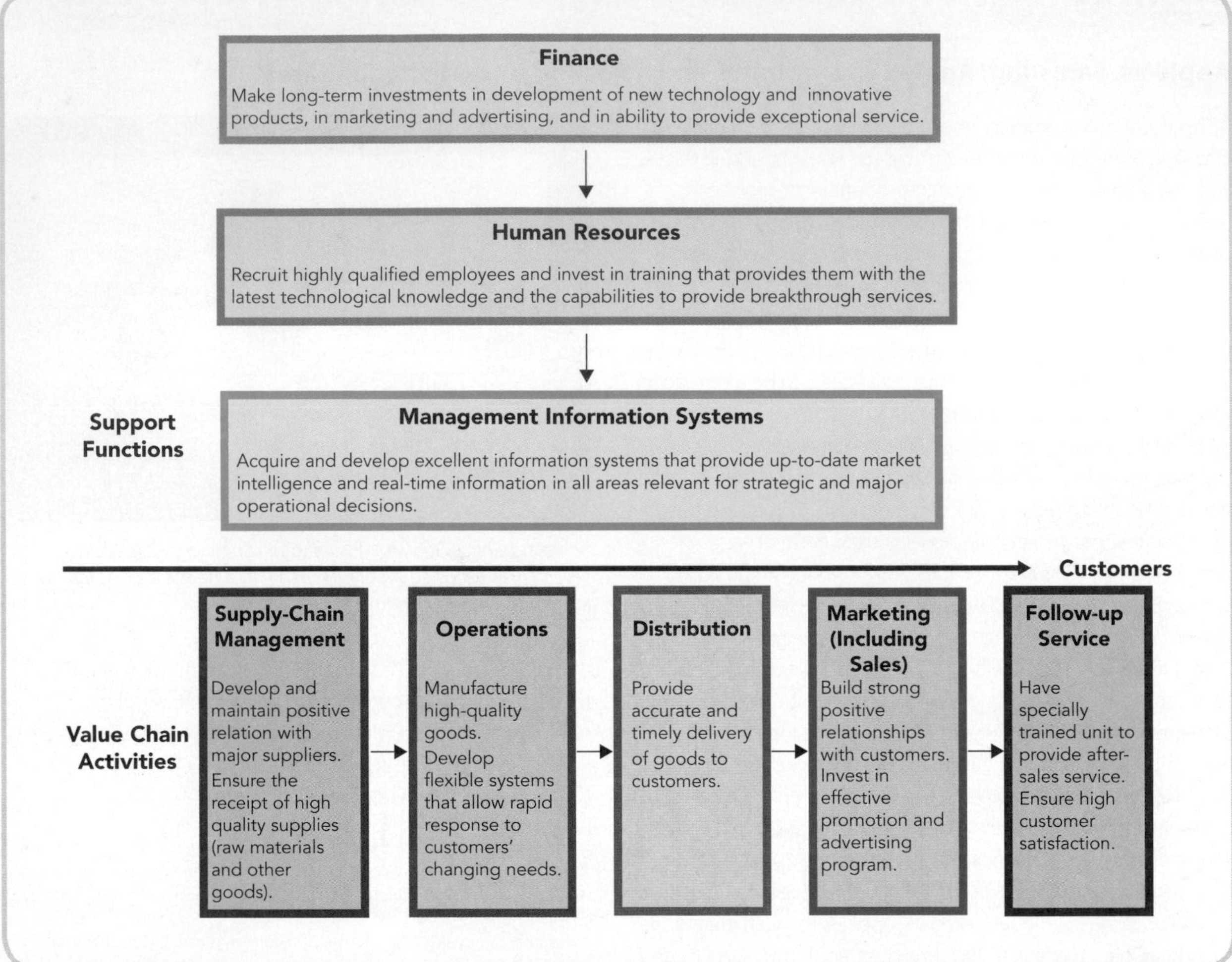


Source: Based on information from M. E. Porter, 1998, *Competitive Advantage: Creating and Sustaining Superior Performance*, New York: The Free Press; D. G. Sirmon, M. A. Hitt, & R. D. Ireland, 2007, Managing firm resources in dynamic environments to create value: Looking inside the black box, *Academy of Management Review*, 32: 273–292; D. G. Sirmon, M. A. Hitt, R. D. Ireland, & B. A. Gilbert, 2011, Resource orchestration to create competitive advantage: Breadth, depth and life cycles effects, *Journal of Management*, 37(5): 1390–1412.

high margins the firm earns in these cases partially insulate it from the influence of suppliers in that higher supplier costs can be paid through these margins.[90] Alternatively, because of buyers' relative insensitivity to price increases, the differentiated firm might choose to pass the additional cost of supplies on to the customer by increasing the price of its unique product. However, when buyers outsource the total function or large portions of it to a supplier, especially R&D for a firm following a differentiation strategy, they can become dependent on and thus vulnerable to that supplier.[91]

## Potential Entrants

Customer loyalty and the need to overcome the uniqueness of a differentiated product create substantial barriers to potential entrants. Entering an industry under these conditions typically demands significant investments of resources and patience while seeking customers' loyalty. In these cases, some potential entrants decide to make smaller investments to see if they can gain a "foothold" in the market. If it does not work they will not lose major resources, but if it works they can then invest greater resources to enhance their competitive position.[92]

### Product Substitutes

Firms selling brand-name goods and services to loyal customers are positioned effectively against product substitutes. In contrast, companies without brand loyalty face a higher probability of their customers switching either to products which offer differentiated features that serve the same function (particularly if the substitute has a lower price) or to products that offer more features and perform more attractive functions. As such, they may be vulnerable to innovations from outside the industry that better satisfy customers' needs (e.g., Apple's iPod in the music industry)[93]

### Competitive Risks of the Differentiation Strategy

One risk of the differentiation strategy is that customers might decide that the price differential between the differentiator's product and the cost leader's product is too large. In this instance, a firm may be offering differentiated features that exceed target customers' needs. The firm then becomes vulnerable to competitors that are able to offer customers a combination of features and price that is more consistent with their needs.

This risk is generalized across a number of companies producing different types of products during an economic recession—a time when sales of luxury goods (e.g., jewelry and leather goods) often suffer. A decision made during the last economic recession by Coach Inc., a maker of high-quality, luxurious accessories and gifts for women and men, demonstrates one firm's reaction to the predicted decline in the sales of luxury goods. With an interest in providing products to increasingly cost conscious customers without "cheapening" the firm's image, Coach introduced a new line of its products called "Poppy"; the average price of items in this line is approximately 20 percent lower than the average price of Coach's typical products.[94]

Richard Levine / Alamy

*A woman carries a Coach Poppy handbag in New York's Times Square. Poppy was introduced during the recent economic recession to appeal to cost-conscious customers without cheapening Coach's image.*

Another risk of the differentiation strategy is that a firm's means of differentiation may cease to provide value for which customers are willing to pay. A differentiated product becomes less valuable if imitation by rivals causes customers to perceive that competitors offer essentially the same good or service, but at a lower price.[95] A third risk of the differentiation strategy is that experience can narrow customers' perceptions of the value of a product's differentiated features. For example, customers having positive experiences with generic tissues may decide that the differentiated features of the Kleenex product are not worth the extra cost. To counter this risk, firms must continue to meaningfully differentiate their product (e.g., through innovation) for customers at a price they are willing to pay.[96]

Counterfeiting is the differentiation strategy's fourth risk. "Counterfeits are those products bearing a trademark that is identical to or indistinguishable from a trademark registered to another party, thus infringing the rights of the holder of the trademark."[97] Companies such as Hewlett-Packard must take actions to deal with the problems counterfeit goods create for them when their rights are infringed upon.

## 4-3c Focus Strategies

The **focus strategy** is an integrated set of actions taken to produce goods or services that serve the needs of a particular competitive segment. Thus, firms use a focus strategy when they utilize their core competencies to serve the needs of a particular industry segment or

The **focus strategy** is an integrated set of actions taken to produce goods or services that serve the needs of a particular competitive segment.

niche to the exclusion of others. Examples of specific market segments that can be targeted by a focus strategy include (1) a particular buyer group (e.g., youths or senior citizens), (2) a different segment of a product line (e.g., products for professional painters or the do-it-yourself group), or (3) a different geographic market (e.g., northern or southern Italy by using a foreign subsidiary).[98]

There are many specific customer needs firms can serve by using a focus strategy. For example, Goya Foods is the largest U.S.-based Hispanic-owned food company in the United States. Segmenting the Hispanic market into unique groups, Goya offers more than 1,500 products to consumers. The firm is a leading authority on Hispanic food and seeks "to be the premier source for authentic Latin cuisine."[99] By successfully using a focus strategy, firms such as Goya gain a competitive advantage in specific market niches or segments, even though they do not possess an industry-wide competitive advantage.

Although the breadth of a target is clearly a matter of degree, the essence of the focus strategy "is the exploitation of a narrow target's differences from the balance of the industry."[100] Firms using the focus strategy intend to serve a particular segment of an industry more effectively than can industry-wide competitors. In fact, entrepreneurial firms commonly serve a specific market niche or segment, partly because they do not have the knowledge or resources to serve the broader market. In fact, they generally prefer to operate "below the radar" of larger and more resource rich firms that serve the broader market.[101] They succeed when they effectively serve a segment whose unique needs are so specialized that broad-based competitors choose not to serve that segment or when they satisfy the needs of a segment being served poorly by industry-wide competitors.

Firms can create value for customers in specific and unique market segments by using the focused cost leadership strategy or the focused differentiation strategy.

## Focused Cost Leadership Strategy

Based in Sweden, IKEA, a global furniture retailer with locations in 35 countries and territories and sales revenue of 27.5 billion euros in 2012, uses the focused cost leadership strategy. Young buyers desiring style at a low cost are IKEA's target customers.[102] For these customers, the firm offers home furnishings that combine good design, function, and acceptable quality with low prices. According to the firm, "Low cost is always in focus. This applies to every phase of our activities."[103]

IKEA emphasizes several activities to keep its costs low. For example, instead of relying primarily on third-party manufacturers, the firm's engineers design low-cost, modular furniture ready for assembly by customers. To eliminate the need for sales associates or decorators, IKEA positions the products in its stores so that customers can view different living combinations (complete with sofas, chairs, tables, etc.) in a single room-like setting, which helps the customer imagine how furniture will look in the home. A third practice that helps keep IKEA's costs low is requiring customers to transport their own purchases rather than providing delivery service.

Although it is a cost leader, IKEA also offers some differentiated features that appeal to its target customers, including its unique furniture designs, in-store playrooms for children, wheelchairs for customer use, and extended hours. Thus, IKEA's focused cost leadership strategy also includes some differentiated features with its low-cost products.

## Focused Differentiation Strategy

Other firms implement the focused differentiation strategy. As noted earlier, there are many dimensions on which firms can differentiate their good or service. For example, the new generation of lunch trucks populating cities such as New York, San Francisco, Los Angeles, and even College Station, Texas, use the focused differentiation strategy. Serving "high-end fare such as grass-fed hamburgers, escargot and crème brulee," highly trained chefs and well-known restaurateurs own and operate many of these trucks. In fact, "the new breed of lunch truck is aggressively gourmet, tech-savvy and politically correct." Selling sustainably harvested fish tacos in a vehicle that is fueled by vegetable oil, the Green Truck, located in Los Angeles, demonstrates these characteristics. Moreover, the owners of these trucks often use Twitter and Facebook to inform customers of their locations as they move from point to point in their focal city.[104]

With a focus strategy, firms must be able to complete various primary value chain activities and support functions in a competitively superior manner to develop and sustain a competitive advantage and earn above-average returns. The activities required to use the focused cost leadership strategy are virtually identical to those of the industry-wide cost leadership strategy (see Figure 4.2), and activities required to use the focused differentiation strategy are largely identical to those of the industry-wide differentiation strategy (see Figure 4.3). Similarly, the manner in which each of the two focus strategies allows a firm to deal successfully with the five competitive forces parallels those of the two broad strategies. The only difference is in the firm's competitive scope; the firm focuses on a narrow industry segment. Thus, Figures 4.2 and 4.3 and the text describing the five competitive forces also explain the relationship between each of the two focus strategies and competitive advantage. However, the competitive forces in a given industry often favor either a cost leadership or a differentiation strategy.[105]

### Competitive Risks of Focus Strategies

With either focus strategy, the firm faces the same general risks as does the company using the cost leadership or the differentiation strategy, respectively, on an industry-wide basis. However, focus strategies have three additional risks.

First, a competitor may be able to focus on a more narrowly defined competitive segment and thereby "out-focus" the focuser. This would happen to IKEA if another firm found a way to offer IKEA's customers (young buyers interested in stylish furniture at a low cost) additional sources of differentiation while charging the same price or to provide the same service with the same sources of differentiation at a lower price. Second, a company competing on an industry-wide basis may decide that the market segment served by the firm using a focus strategy is attractive and worthy of competitive pursuit.[106] For example, women's clothiers such as Chico's, Ann Taylor, and Liz Claiborne might conclude that the profit potential in the narrow segment being served by Anne Fontaine is attractive and decide to design and sell competitively similar clothing items. Initially, Anne Fontaine designed and sold only white shirts for women. However, the shirts were distinctive. They were quite differentiated on the basis of their design, craftsmanship, and high quality of raw materials.[107] The third risk involved with a focus strategy is that the needs of customers within a narrow competitive segment may become more similar to those of industry-wide customers as a whole over time. As a result, the advantages of a focus strategy are either reduced or eliminated. At some point, for example, the needs of Anne Fontaine's customers for high-quality, uniquely designed white shirts could dissipate. If this were to happen, Anne Fontaine's customers might choose to buy white shirts from chains such as Liz Claiborne that sell clothing items with some differentiation, but at a lower cost.

## 4-3d Integrated Cost Leadership/Differentiation Strategy

Most consumers have high expectations when purchasing a good or service. In general, it seems that most consumers want to pay a low price for products with somewhat highly differentiated features. Because of these customer expectations, a number of firms engage in primary value chain activities and support functions that allow them to simultaneously pursue low cost and differentiation. Firms seeking to do this use the **integrated cost leadership/differentiation strategy**. The objective of using this strategy is to efficiently produce products with some differentiated features. Efficient production is the source of maintaining

The **integrated cost leadership/differentiation strategy** involves engaging in primary value chain activities and support functions that allow a firm to simultaneously pursue low cost and differentiation.

Beaustock/Dreamstime.com

*Preparing a Target store for opening in Quebec, Canada. Target successfully uses the integrated low cost/differentiation strategy.*

low costs while differentiation is the source of creating unique value. Firms that successfully use the integrated cost leadership/differentiation strategy usually adapt quickly to new technologies and rapid changes in their external environments. Simultaneously concentrating on developing two sources of competitive advantage (cost and differentiation) increases the number of primary value chain activities and support functions in which the firm must become competent. Such firms often have strong networks with external parties that perform some of the value chain activities and/or support functions.[108] In turn, having skills in a larger number of activities and functions makes a firm more flexible.

Concentrating on the needs of its core customer group (higher-income, fashion-conscious discount shoppers), Target Stores uses an integrated cost leadership-differentiation strategy as shown by its "Expect More. Pay Less." brand promise. Target's annual report describes this strategy: "Our enduring 'Expect More. Pay Less.' brand promise helped us to deliver greater convenience, increased savings and a more personalized shopping experience." In 2012, Target celebrated its fiftieth anniversary and opened its first stores in Canada.[109]

The failed strategy implemented by J.C. Penney appeared to be an attempt to integrate low cost, reducing pricing on most goods in the store, with differentiation, creating specialized stores for name-brand goods within each store. It likely failed because this strategy is very difficult to implement effectively. Often firms are "caught in the middle" and do not differentiate effectively or provide lowest-cost goods. J. C. Penney is a prime example of this failure. It could not compete with the low-cost leaders such as Walmart and Dollar Stores, nor could it compete effectively with the more upscale and differentiated department stores, such as Target and Macy's.

Interestingly, most emerging market firms have competed using the cost leadership strategy. Their labor and other supply costs tend to be considerably lower than multinational firms based in developed countries. However, in recent years some of the emerging market firms are building their capabilities to produce innovation. Coupled with their capabilities to produce lower cost goods, they may be able to gain an advantage on large multinational firms. As such, some of the emerging market firms are beginning to use an integrated low cost-differentiation strategy.[110]

Flexibility is required for firms to complete primary value chain activities and support functions in ways that allow them to use the integrated cost leadership/differentiation strategy in order to produce somewhat differentiated products at relatively low costs. Chinese auto manufacturers have developed a means of product design that provides a flexible architecture that allows low-cost manufacturing but also car designs that are differentiated from competitors.[111] Flexible manufacturing systems, information networks, and total quality management systems are three sources of flexibility that are particularly useful for firms trying to balance the objectives of continuous cost reductions and continuous enhancements to sources of differentiation as called for by the integrated strategy.

## Flexible Manufacturing Systems

Using a flexible manufacturing system (FMS), the firm integrates human, physical, and information resources to create relatively differentiated products at relatively low costs.

A significant technological advance, the FMS is a computer-controlled process used to produce a variety of products in moderate, flexible quantities with a minimum of manual intervention.[112] Often the flexibility is derived from modularization of the manufacturing process (and sometimes other value chain activities as well).[113]

The goal of an FMS is to eliminate the "low cost versus product variety" trade-off that is inherent in traditional manufacturing technologies. Firms use an FMS to change quickly and easily from making one product to making another. Used properly, an FMS allows the firm to respond more effectively to changes in its customers' needs, while retaining low-cost advantages and consistent product quality.[114] Because an FMS also enables the firm to reduce the lot size needed to manufacture a product efficiently, the firm's capacity to serve the unique needs of a narrow competitive scope is higher. In industries of all types, effective combinations of the firm's tangible assets (e.g., machines) and intangible assets (e.g., people's skills) facilitate implementation of complex competitive strategies, especially the integrated cost leadership/differentiation strategy.

## Information Networks

By linking companies with their suppliers, distributors, and customers, information networks provide another source of flexibility. These networks, when used effectively, help the firm satisfy customer expectations in terms of product quality and delivery speed.[115]

Earlier, we discussed the importance of managing the firm's relationships with its customers in order to understand their needs. Customer relationship management (CRM) is one form of an information-based network process that firms use for this purpose.[116] An effective CRM system provides a 360-degree view of the company's relationship with customers, encompassing all contact points, business processes, and communication media and sales channels.[117] The firm can then use this information to determine the trade-offs its customers are willing to make between differentiated features and low cost—an assessment that is vital for companies using the integrated cost leadership/differentiation strategy. Such systems help firms to monitor their markets and stakeholders and allow them to better predict future scenarios. This capability helps firms to adjust their strategies to be better prepared for the future.[118] Thus, to make comprehensive strategic decisions with effective knowledge of the organization's context, good information flow is essential. Better quality managerial decisions require accurate information on the firm's environment.

## Total Quality Management Systems

**Total quality management (TQM)** is a managerial process that emphasizes an organization's commitment to the customer and to continuous improvement of all processes through problem-solving approaches based on empowerment of employees.[119] Firms develop and use TQM systems to (1) increase customer satisfaction, (2) cut costs, and (3) reduce the amount of time required to introduce innovative products to the marketplace.[120]

Firms able to simultaneously reduce costs while enhancing their ability to develop innovative products increase their flexibility, an outcome that is particularly helpful to firms implementing the integrated cost leadership/differentiation strategy. Exceeding customers' expectations regarding quality is a differentiating feature, and eliminating process inefficiencies to cut costs allows the firm to offer that quality to customers at a relatively low price. Thus, an effective TQM system helps the firm develop the flexibility needed to identify opportunities to simultaneously increase differentiation and reduce costs. Research has found that TQM systems facilitate cost leadership strategies more effectively than they do differentiating strategies when the strategy is implemented alone.[121] However, it facilitates the potential synergy between the two strategies when they are integrated into one. TQM systems are available to all competitors so they may help firms maintain competitive parity, but rarely alone will they lead to a competitive advantage.[122]

**Total quality management (TQM)** is a managerial process that emphasizes an organization's commitment to the customer and to continuous improvement of all processes through problem-solving approaches based on empowerment of employees.

### Competitive Risks of the Integrated Cost Leadership/Differentiation Strategy

The potential to earn above-average returns by successfully using the integrated cost leadership/differentiation strategy is appealing. However, it is a risky strategy, because firms find it difficult to perform primary value chain activities and support functions in ways that allow them to produce relatively inexpensive products with levels of differentiation that create value for the target customer. Moreover, to properly use this strategy across time, firms must be able to simultaneously reduce costs incurred to produce products (as required by the cost leadership strategy) while increasing product differentiation (as required by the differentiation strategy).

Firms that fail to perform the value chain activities and support functions in an optimum manner become "stuck in the middle."[123] Being stuck in the middle means that the firm's cost structure is not low enough to allow it to attractively price its products and that its products are not sufficiently differentiated to create value for the target customer. This appears to be the problem experienced by J.C. Penney. At least as perceived by the customers, its prices were not low enough and the differentiation not great enough to attract the customers needed. In fact, its declining sales suggest that it lost many of its current customers without attracting others to offset the loss. These firms will not earn above-average returns and will earn average returns only when the structure of the industry in which it competes is highly favorable.[124] Thus, companies implementing the integrated cost leadership/differentiation strategy must be able to produce (or offer) products that provide the target customer some differentiated features at a relatively low cost/price.

Firms can also become stuck in the middle when they fail to successfully implement *either* the cost leadership *or* the differentiation strategy. In other words, industry-wide competitors too can become stuck in the middle. Trying to use the integrated strategy is costly in that firms must pursue both low costs and differentiation.

Firms may need to form alliances with other companies to achieve differentiation, yet alliance partners may extract prices for the use of their resources that make it difficult to meaningfully reduce costs.[125] Firms may be motivated to make acquisitions to maintain their differentiation through innovation or to add products to their portfolio not offered by competitors.[126] Research suggests that firms using "pure strategies," either cost leadership or differentiation, often outperform firms attempting to use a "hybrid strategy" (i.e., integrated cost leadership/differentiation strategy). This research suggests the risky nature of using an integrated strategy.[127] However, the integrated strategy is becoming more common and perhaps necessary in many industries because of technological advances and global competition. This strategy often necessitates a long-term perspective to make it work effectively, and therefore requires dedicated owners that allow the implementation of a long-term strategy that can require several years to produce positive returns.[128]

## SUMMARY

- A business-level strategy is an integrated and coordinated set of commitments and actions the firm uses to gain a competitive advantage by exploiting core competencies in specific product markets. Five business-level strategies (cost leadership, differentiation, focused cost leadership, focused differentiation, and integrated cost leadership/differentiation) are examined in the chapter.
- Customers are the foundation of successful business-level strategies. When considering customers, a firm simultaneously examines three issues: *who*, *what*, and *how*. These issues, respectively, refer to the customer groups to be served, the needs those customers have that the firm seeks to satisfy, and the core competencies the firm will use to satisfy customers' needs. Increasing segmentation of markets throughout the global economy creates opportunities for firms to identify more distinctive customer needs they can serve with one of the business-level strategies.
- Firms seeking competitive advantage through the cost leadership strategy produce no-frills, standardized products for an

industry's typical customer. However, these low-cost products must be offered with competitive levels of differentiation. Above-average returns are earned when firms continuously emphasize efficiency such that their costs are lower than those of their competitors, while providing customers with products that have acceptable levels of differentiated features.

- Competitive risks associated with the cost leadership strategy include (1) a loss of competitive advantage to newer technologies, (2) a failure to detect changes in customers' needs, and (3) the ability of competitors to imitate the cost leader's competitive advantage through their own distinct strategic actions.
- Through the differentiation strategy, firms provide customers with products that have different (and valued) features. Differentiated products must be sold at a cost that customers believe is competitive relative to the product's features as compared to the cost/feature combinations available from competitors' goods. Because of their distinctiveness, differentiated goods or services are sold at a premium price. Products can be differentiated on any dimension that some customer group values. Firms using this strategy seek to differentiate their products from competitors' goods or services on as many dimensions as possible. The less similarity to competitors' products, the more buffered a firm is from competition with its rivals.
- Risks associated with the differentiation strategy include (1) a customer group's decision that the unique features provided by the differentiated product over the cost leader's goods or services are no longer worth a premium price, (2) the inability of a differentiated product to create the type of value for which customers are willing to pay a premium price, (3) the ability of competitors to provide customers with products that have features similar to those of the differentiated product, but at a lower cost, and (4) the threat of counterfeiting, whereby firms produce a cheap imitation of a differentiated good or service.
- Through the cost leadership and the differentiated focus strategies, firms serve the needs of a narrow market segment (e.g., a buyer group, product segment, or geographic area). This strategy is successful when firms have the core competencies required to provide value to a specialized market segment that exceeds the value available from firms serving customers across the total market (industry).
- The competitive risks of focus strategies include (1) a competitor's ability to use its core competencies to "outfocus" the focuser by serving an even more narrowly defined market segment, (2) decisions by industry-wide competitors to focus on a customer group's specialized needs, and (3) a reduction in differences of the needs between customers in a narrow market segment and the industry-wide market.
- Firms using the integrated cost leadership/differentiation strategy strive to provide customers with relatively low-cost products that also have valued differentiated features. Flexibility is required for firms to learn how to use primary value chain activities and support functions in ways that allow them to produce differentiated products at relatively low costs. The primary risk of this strategy is that a firm might produce products that do not offer sufficient value in terms of either low cost or differentiation. In such cases, the company becomes "stuck in the middle." Firms stuck in the middle compete at a disadvantage and are unable to earn more than average returns.

# REVIEW QUESTIONS

1. What is a business-level strategy?
2. What is the relationship between a firm's customers and its business-level strategy in terms of *who*, *what*, and *how*? Why is this relationship important?
3. What are the differences among the cost leadership, differentiation, focused cost leadership, focused differentiation, and integrated cost leadership/differentiation business-level strategies?
4. How can each of the business-level strategies be used to position the firm relative to the five forces of competition in a way that helps the firm earn above-average returns?
5. What are the specific risks associated with using each business-level strategy?

# EXPERIENTIAL EXERCISES

## EXERCISE 1: MARKET SEGMENTATION THROUGH BRANDING

The "who" in a firm's target market is an extremely important decision. As discussed in the chapter, firms divide customers into groups based upon differences in customer needs, which is the heart of market segmentation. For example, if you owned a restaurant and your target market was college-aged students, your strategy would be very different than if your target market was business professionals.

In this exercise, your team will be identifying market segmentation strategies used by various companies. Remember that market segmentation "is a process used to cluster people with similar needs into individual and identifiable groups."

### Part One

Your team should select an advertised and prominent brand. You may choose a business or consumer product. However, you should choose a brand that is widely known and widely advertised. Once you have chosen the brand, find and collect at least four instances of this brand being advertised in print or digital media. Find your four or more instances from different publications, if possible.

### Part Two

Assemble a poster with the images you collected from your research. Be prepared to present your findings to the class as regards:

1. Why did you choose this brand?
2. Review each of the criteria discussed in Table 4.1 for either your consumer market or industrial market.

## EXERCISE 2: HOW INDUSTRIES DIFFER IN THEIR BUSINESS-LEVEL STRATEGY

This assignment brings together elements from the previous chapters. Accordingly, you and your team will create a business-level strategy for a firm in the hotel industry. The instructor will assign you a strategy (from the list below) and you will create a strategy for entering that industry using one of the five potential business-level strategies below:

- Cost leadership
- Differentiation
- Focused cost leadership
- Focused differentiation
- Integrated cost leadership/differentiation

### Part One

Research the hotel industry and describe the general environment and the forces in the industry. Using the dimensions of the general environment, identify some factors for each dimension that are influential for your industry. Next, describe the industry environment using the Five Forces model. Database services like Mint Global, Datamonitor, or IBIS World can be helpful in this regard. If those are not available to you, consult your local librarian for assistance. You should be able to clearly articulate the opportunities and the threats that exist.

### Part Two

Create on a poster the business-level strategy assigned to your team. Be prepared to describe the following in class:

- Mission statement
- Description of your target customer
- Picture of your business. Where is it located (downtown, suburb, rural, etc.)?
- Describe trends that provide opportunities and threats for your intended strategy.
- List the resources, both tangible and intangible, required to compete successfully in this market.
- How will you go about creating a sustainable competitive advantage?

You will find it interesting to note the difference in the hotel industry between the various business level strategies and the way in which firms compete essentially in the same industry. Remember that your text authors describe business level strategy as "an integrated and coordinated set of commitments and actions the firm uses to gain a competitive advantage by exploiting core competencies in specific product markets. Business-level strategy indicates the choices the firm has made about how it intends to compete in individual product markets."

# VIDEO CASE ▶

## DIFFERENTIATION STRATEGY IN TOUGH ECONOMIC TIMES

### Howard Schultz/CEO/Starbucks

Starbucks, 17,000 stores strong worldwide, offers 70,000 different ways to order coffee. Unfortunately, Starbucks has announced the closing of 900 underperforming stores in the United States and will cut more than 1,000 jobs. Howard Schultz, Starbucks CEO, admits that Starbucks may have grown too big too fast given today's economy, and a business plan was not in place to deal with the severity of the economic downturn. During this time, competitors like Dunkin Donuts are offering an upgraded coffee experience at a lower cost. However, Schultz maintains that Starbucks will not cut corners but will reduce waste to save the company more than $400 million and continue to sell more than a cup of coffee.

The 2012 annual report shows a turnaround for Starbucks, with global revenues reaching $13.3 billion, a 14 percent increase. In the China and Asia Pacific region, through 2012 Starbucks posted 11 consecutive quarters of double-digit growth. With nearly 3,300 stores, plus hundreds more planned throughout Asia Pacific, Starbucks is transferring is core attributes and expertise, while respecting and reflecting regional customs.

Be prepared to discuss the following concepts and questions in class:

## Concepts

- Business-level strategy
- Managing relationship with customers
- Market segmentation
- Differentiation strategy
- Five forces of competition

## Questions

1. Describe Starbucks' business-level strategy.
2. How is Starbucks managing its relationship with customers?
3. How would you describe the market segment(s) that Starbucks serves?
4. Is the differentiation strategy appropriate for Starbucks, now or in the future? Why or why not?
5. Using the five forces model of competition, how should Starbucks plan to position itself in these economic times?

# NOTES


1. R. D. Ireland, R. E. Hoskisson, & M. A. Hitt, 2012. *Understanding Business Strategy*. Mason, OH: Cengage Learning.
2. H. Greve, 2009, Bigger and safer: The diffusion of competitive advantage, *Strategic Management Journal*, 30: 1–23.
3. M. A. Delmas & M. W. Toffel, 2008, Organizational responses to environmental demands: Opening the black box, *Strategic Management Journal*, 29: 1027–1055; S. Elbanna & J. Child, 2007, The influence of decision, environmental and firm characteristics on the rationality of strategic decision-making, *Journal of Management Studies*, 44: 561–591.
4. M. G. Jacobides, S. G. Winter, & S. M. Kassberger, 2012, The dynamics of wealth, profit, and sustainable advantage, *Strategic Management Journal*, 33: 1384–1410; D. G. Sirmon, M. A. Hitt, R. D. Ireland, & B. A. Gilbert, 2011, Resource orchestration to create competitive advantage: Breadth, depth and life cycle effects, *Journal of Management*, 37: 1390–1412.
5. J. Schmidt & T. Keil, 2013, What makes a resource valuable? Identifying the drivers of firm-idiosyncratic resource value, *Academy of Management Review*, 38: 208–228; C. Zott & R. Amit, 2008, The fit between product market strategy and business model: Implications for firm performance, *Strategic Management Journal*, 29: 1–26.
6. S. Kaplan, 2008, Framing contests: Strategy making under uncertainty, *Organization Science*, 19: 729–752.
7. L. A. Costa, K. Cool, & I. Dierickx, 2013, The competitive implications of the deployment of unique resources, *Strategic Management Journal*, 34: 445–463; K. Shimizu & M. A. Hitt, 2004, Strategic flexibility: Organizational preparedness to reverse ineffective strategic decisions, *Academy of Management Executive*, 18(4): 44–59.
8. B. Chakravarthy & P. Lorange, 2008, Driving renewal: The entrepreneur-manager, *Journal of Business Strategy*, 29: 14–21.
9. J. A. Lamberg, H. Tikkanen, T. Nokelainen, & H. Suur-Inkeroinen, 2009, Competitive dynamics, strategic consistency, and organizational survival, *Strategic Management Journal*, 30: 45–60; R. D. Ireland & C. C. Miller, 2005, Decision-making and firm success, *Academy of Management Executive*, 18(4): 8–12.
10. I. Goll, N. B. Johnson, & A. A. Rasheed, 2008, Top management team demographic characteristics, business strategy, and firm performance in the U.S. airline industry: The role of managerial discretion, *Management Decision*, 40: 201–222; J. R. Hough, 2006, Business segment performance redux: A multilevel approach, *Strategic Management Journal*, 27: 45–61.
11. J. W. Spencer, 2008, The impact of multinational enterprise strategy on indigenous enterprises: Horizontal spillovers and crowding out in developing countries, *Academy of Management Review*, 33: 341–361.
12. Myspace, 2013, *Wikipedia*, http://en.wikipedia.org, April 8.
13. R. E. Hoskisson, M. A. Hitt, R. D. Ireland, & J. S. Harrison, 2013, *Competing for Advantage*, Mason, OH: Cengage Learning.
14. C. Senn, 2012, The booster zone: How to accelerate growth with strategic customers, *Journal of Business Strategy*, 33(6): 31–39; R. J. Harrington & A. K. Tjan, 2008, Transforming strategy one customer at a time, *Harvard Business Review*, 86(3): 62–72.
15. K. R. Fabrizio & L. G. Thomas, 2012, The impact of local demand on innovation in a global industry, *Strategic Management Journal*, 33: 42–64; M. Pynnonen, P. Ritala, & J. Hallikas, 2011, The new meaning of customer value: A systemic perspective, *Journal of Business Strategy*, 32(1): 51–57.
16. M. E. Porter, 1980, *Competitive Strategy*, New York: Free Press.
17. M. Baghai, S. Smit, & P. Viguerie, 2009, Is your growth strategy flying blind? *Harvard Business Review*, 87(5): 86–96.
18. D. G. Sirmon, S. Gove, & M. A. Hitt, 2008, Resource management in dyadic competitive rivalry: The effects of resource bundling and deployment, *Academy of Management Journal*, 51: 919–935; D. G. Sirmon, M. A. Hitt, & R. D. Ireland, 2007, Managing firm resources in dynamic environments to create value: Inside the black box, *Academy of Management Review*, 32: 273–292.
19. J. Singh, P. Lentz, & E. J. Nijssen, 2011, First- and second-order effects of institutional logics on firm-consumer relationships: A cross-market comparative analysis, *Journal of International Business Studies*, 42: 307–333.
20. 2013, Company Information, Caesar's Entertainment, www.caesars.com, April 9.
21. Y. Liu & R. Yang, 2009, Competing loyalty programs: Impact of market saturation, market share, and category expandability, *Journal of Marketing*, 73: 93–108.
22. P. E. Frown & A. F. Payne, 2009, Customer relationship management: A strategic perspective, *Journal of Business Market Management*, 3: 7–27.
23. H. Green, 2009, How Amazon aims to keep you clicking, *BusinessWeek*, March 2: 34–35.
24. Myspace, 2013, *Wikipedia*, http://en.wikipedia.org, April 8; Facebook, 2013, *Wikipedia*, http://en.wikipedia.org, April 8.
25. 2013, Netflix Quarter 4 2012 Letter to Shareholders, Netflix, www.netflix.com, January 23.
26. S. E. Sampson & M. Spring, 2012, Customer roles in service supply chains and opportunities for innovation, *Journal of Supply Chain Management*, 48(4): 30–50; M. Bogers, A. Afuah, & B. Bastian, 2010, Users as innovators: A review, critique and future research directions, *Journal of Management*, 36: 857–875.
27. L-Y Jin, 2010, Determinants of customers' complaint intention, *Nankai Business Review International*, 1: 87–99.
28. 2013, MSN Autos, www.autos.msn.com, April 8.
29. S. F. Slater, E. M. Olson, & G. T. Hult, 2010, Worried about strategy implementation? Don't overlook marketing's role, *Business*

*Horizons*, 53: 469–479; I. C. MacMillan & L. Selden, 2008, The incumbent's advantage, *Harvard Business Review*, 86(10): 111–121.

30. P. Riefler, A. Diamantopoulos, & J. A. Siguaw, 2012, Cosmopolitan consumers as a target group for segmentation, *Journal of International Business Studies*, 43: 285–305.
31. 2013, About Hill's pet nutrition, Hill's Pet Nutrition, www.hillspet.com, April 8.
32. L. Tournois, 2013, Mass market leadership and shampoo wars: The L'Oréal strategy, *Journal of Business Strategy*, 34(1): 4–14.
33. R. Lewis & M. Dart, 2010, *The New Rules of Retail*, New York: Palgrave Macmillan.
34. S. E. Fawcett, A. M. Fawcett. B. J. Watdson, & G. M. Manan, 2012, Peeking inside the black box: Toward as understanding of supply chain collaboration dynamics, *Journal of Supply Chain Management*, 48(1): 44–72; C. A. Funk, J. D. Arthurs, L. J. Trevino, & J. Joireman, 2010, Consumer animosity in the global value chain: The effect of international shifts on willingness to purchase hybrid products. *Journal of International Business Studies*, 41: 639–651.
35. K. Z. Zhou & C. B. Li, 2012, How knowledge affects radical innovation: Knowledge base, market knowledge acquisition and internal knowledge sharing, *Strategic Management Journal*, 33: 1090–1102; T. Y. Eng & J. G. Spickett-Jones, 2009, An investigation of marketing capabilities and upgrading performance of manufacturers in Mainland China and Hong Kong, *Journal of World Business*, 44(4): 463–475.
36. D. J. Teece, 2012, Dynamic capabilities: Routines versus entrepreneurial action, *Journal of Management Studies*, 49: 1395–1401; P. L. Drnevich & A. P. Kriauciunas, 2011, Clarifying the conditions and limits of the contributions of ordinary and dynamic capabilities to relative firm performance, *Strategic Management Journal*, 32: 254–279.
37. M. Gruber, F. Heinimann, M. Brietel, & S. Hungeling, 2010, Configurations of resources and capabilities and their performance implications: An exploratory study on technology ventures, *Strategic Management Journal*, 31: 1337–1356.
38. Merck Company fact sheet, 2013, Merck, www.merck.com, accessed April 8.
39. 2013, About SAS, www.sas.com, April 8.
40. K. E. Klein, 2009, Survival advice for auto parts suppliers, *Wall Street Journal*, www.wsj.com, June 16.
41. M. E. Porter, 1985, *Competitive Advantage*, New York: Free Press, 26.
42. R. Rumelt, 2011, *Good Strategy/Bad Strategy*, New York: Crown Business.
43. M. E. Porter, 1996, What is strategy? *Harvard Business Review*, 74(6): 61–78.
44. Porter, What is strategy?
45. J. S. Srai & L. S. Alinaghian, 2013, Value chain reconfiguration in highly disaggregated industrial systems: Examining the emergence of health care diagnostics, *Global Strategy Journal*, 3: 88–108; M. Reitzig & P. Puranam, 2009, Value appropriation as an organizational capability: The case of IP protection through patents, *Strategic Management Journal*, 30: 765–789.
46. M. E. Porter, 1994, Toward a dynamic theory of strategy, in R. P. Rumelt, D. E. Schendel, & D. J. Teece (Eds.), *Fundamental Issues in Strategy*, Boston: Harvard Business School Press: 423–461.
47. Porter, What is strategy?, 62.
48. Porter, *Competitive Advantage*, 15.
49. S. Sun, 2009, An analysis on the conditions and methods of market segmentation, *International Journal of Business and Management*, 4: 63–70.
50. J. Gonzales-Benito & I. Suarez-Gonzalez, 2010, A study of the role played by manufacturing strategic objectives and capabilities in understanding the relationship between Porter's generic strategies and business performance, *British Journal of Management*, 21(4): 1027–1043.
51. Ireland, Hoskisson, & Hitt, *Understanding Business Strategy;* G. B. Voss, D. Sirdeshmukh, & Z. G. Voss, 2008, The effects of slack resources and environmental threat on product exploration and exploitation, *Academy of Management Journal*, 51: 147–158.
52. Porter, *Competitive Strategy*, 35–40.
53. P. D. Orberg Jensen & B. Petersen, 2013, Global sourcing of services: Risk, process, and collaborative architecture, *Global Strategy Journal*, 3: 67–87; C. Weigelt, 2013, Leveraging supplier capabilities: The role of locus of capability deployment, *Strategic Management Journal*, 34: 1–21.
54. 2013, Explore Kia USA, Kia USA, www.kia.com, accessed April 10.
55. M. Ihlwan, 2009, Kia Motors: Still cheap, now chic, *BusinessWeek*, June 1, 58.
56. D. S. K. Lim, N. Celly, & E. A. Morse, 2013, Rethinking the effectiveness of asset and cost retrenchment: The contingency effects of a firm's rent creation mechanism, *Strategic Management Journal*, 34: 42–61.
57. D. Mehri, 2006, The dark side of lean: An insider's perspective on the realities of the Toyota production system, *Academy of Management Perspectives*, 20(2): 21–42.
58. C. Garcia-Olaverri & E. Huerta, 2012, Why do some companies adopt advanced management systems? The Spanish case, *Management Research*, 10: 99–124; N. T. Sheehan & G. Vaidyanathan, 2009, Using a value creation compass to discover "Blue Oceans," *Strategy & Leadership*, 37: 13–20.
59. A. M. Chaker, 2009, Planes, trains… and buses? *Wall Street Journal*, www.wsj.com, June 18.
60. 2013, Greyhound facts and figures, www.greyhound.com, accessed on April 10.
61. J.-K. Park & Y. K. Ro, 2013, Product architectures and sourcing decisions: Their impact on performance, *Journal of Management*, 39: 814–846; M. Kotabe & R. Mudambi, 2009, Global sourcing and value creation: Opportunities and challenges, *Journal of International Management*, 15: 121–125.
62. R. Liu, D. J. Feils, & B. Scholnick, 2011, Why are different services outsources to different countries? *Journal of International Business Studies*, 42: 558–571; J. Hatonen & T. Erikson, 2009, 30+ years of research and practice of outsourcing—exploring the past and anticipating the future, *Journal of International Management*, 15: 142–155.
63. M. J. Lennox, S. F. Rockart, & A. Y. Lewin, 2010, Does interdependency affect firm and industry profitability? An empirical test, *Strategic Management Journal*, 31: 121–139.
64. 2013, Corporate overview, Big Lots, www.biglots.com, April 10.
65. J. Morehouse, B. O'Mera, C. Hagen, & T. Huseby, 2008, Hitting back: Strategic responses to low-cost rivals, *Strategy & Leadership*, 36: 4–13; L. K. Johnson, 2003, Dueling pricing strategies, *The McKinsey Quarterly*, 44(3): 10–11.
66. G. J. Kilduff, H. A. Elfenbein, & B. W. Staw, 2010, The psychology of rivalry: A relationally dependent analysis of competition, *Academy of Management Journal*, 53: 943–969.
67. T. W. Tong & J. J. Reuer, 2010, Competitive consequences of interfirm collaboration: How joint ventures shape industry profitability, *Journal of International Business Studies*, 41: 1056–1073.
68. Y. Luo, Y. Huang, & S. L. Wang, 2011, Guanxi and organizational performance: A meta-analysis, *Management and Organization Review*, 8: 139–172.
69. O. D. Fjeldstad & A. Sasson, 2010, Membership matters: On the value of being embedded in customer networks, *Journal of Management Studies*, 47: 944–966.
70. 2013, Our story, http://corporate.walmart.com, accessed April 10.
71. F. J. Contractor, V. Kumar, S. K. Kundu, & T. Pedersen, 2010, Reconceptualizing the firm in a world of outsourcing and offshoring: The organizational and geographical relocation of high-value company functions. *Journal of Management Studies*, 47: 1417–1433.
72. Y. Zhang & J. Gimeno, 2010, Earnings pressure and competitive behavior: Evidence from the U.S. electricity industry, *Academy of Management Journal*, 53: 743–768.
73. B. Flynn, 2010, Introduction to the special topic forum on global supply chain management, *Journal of Supply Chain Management*, 46(2): 3–4.
74. T. J. Kull, S. C. Ellis, & R. Narasimhan, 2013, Reducing behavioral constraints to supplier integration: A socio-technical systems perspective, *Journal of Supply Chain Management*, 49(1): 64–86; J. Dyer & W. Chu, 2011, The determinants of trust in supplier-automaker relations in the U.S., Japan and Korea: A retrospective, *Journal of International Business Studies*, 42: 28–34; M-S. Cheung, M. B. Myers, & J. T. Mentzer, 2011, The value of relational learning in global buyer-supplier exchanges: A dyadic perspective and test of the pie-sharing

hypothesis, *Strategic Management Journal*, 32(10): 1061–1082.

75. O. Ormanidhi & O. Stringa, 2008, Porter's model of generic competitive strategies, *Business Economics*, 43: 55–64; J. Bercovitz & W. Mitchell, 2007, When is more better? The impact of business scale and scope on long-term business survival, while controlling for profitability, *Strategic Management Journal*, 28: 61–79.
76. A. Kaul, 2012, Technology and corporate scope: Firm and rival innovation as antecedents of corporate transactions, *Strategic Management Journal*, 33: 347–367; K. Z. Zhou & F. Wu, 2010, Technological capability, strategic flexibility and product innovation, *Strategic Management Journal*, 31: 547–561.
77. Porter, *Competitive Strategy*, 35–40.
78. 2009, Product innovation, www.1000ventures.com, June 19.
79. C. A. Siren, M. Kohtamaki, & A. Kuckertz, 2012, Exploration and exploitation strategies, profit performance and the mediating role of strategic learning: Escaping the exploitation trap, *Strategic Entrepreneurship Journal*, 6: 18–41; D. Dunlap-Hinkler, M. Kotabe, & R. Mudambi, 2010, A story of breakthrough versus incremental innovation: Corporate entrepreneurship in the global pharmaceutical industry, *Strategic Entrepreneurship Journal*, 4: 106–127.
80. U. Lichtenthaler & H. Ernst, 2012, Integrated knowledge exploitation: The complementarity of product development and technology licensing, *Strategic Management Journal*, 33: 513–534; Z. Simsek & C. Heavy, 2011, The mediating role of knowledge-based capital for corporate entrepreneurship effects on performance: A study of small-to medium sized firms, *Strategic Entrepreneurship Journal*, 5: 81–100.
81. R. Kotha, Y. Zheng, & G. George, 2011, Entry into new niches: The effects of firm age and the expansion of technological capabilities on innovative output and impact, *Strategic Management Journal*, 32(9): 1011–1024; D. Ashmos Plowman, L. T. Baker, T. E. Beck, M. Kulkarni, S. Thomas-Solansky, & D. V. Travis, 2007, Radical change accidentally: The emergence and amplification of small change, *Academy of Management Journal*, 50: 515–543.
82. J. T. Macher & C. Boerner, 2012, Technological development at the boundaries of the firm: A knowledge-based examination in drug development, *Strategic Management Journal*, 33: 1016–1036; R. Agarwal, D. Audretsch, & M. B. Sarkar, 2010, Knowledge spillovers and strategic entrepreneurship, *Strategic Entrepreneurship Journal*, 4: 271–283.
83. N. Kim & S. Min, 2012, Impact of industry incumbency and product newness on pioneer leadtime, *Journal of Management*, 38: 695–718; F. T. Rothaermel, M. A. Hitt, & L. A. Jobe, 2006, Balancing vertical integration and strategic outsourcing: Effects on product portfolio, product success and firm performance, *Strategic Management Journal*, 27: 1033–1056.
84. D. Somaya, 2012, Patent strategy and management: An integrative review and research agenda, *Journal of Management*, 38: 1084–1114; A. Cuervo-Cazurra & C. A. Un, 2010, Why some firms never invest in R&D, *Strategic Management Journal*, 31: 759–779.
85. N. E. Levitas & T. Chi, 2010, A look at the value creation effects of patenting and capital investment through a real-option lens: The moderation role of uncertainty, *Strategic Entrepreneurship Journal*, 4: 212–233; L. A. Bettencourt & A. W. Ulwick, 2008, The customer-centered innovation map, *Harvard Business Review*, 86(5): 109–114.
86. M. Abbott, R. Holland, J. Giacomin, & J. Shackleton, 2009, Changing affective content in brand and product attributes, *Journal of Product & Brand Management*, 18: 17–26.
87. H. E. Posen, J. Lee, & S. Yi, 2013, The power of imperfect imitation, *Strategic Management Journal*, 34: 149–164.
88. B. K. Boyd, D. D. Bergh, & D. J. Ketchen, 2010, Reconsidering the reputation-performance relationship: A resource-based view, *Journal of Management*, 36: 588–609; V. P. Rindova, I. O. Williamson, & A. P. Petkova, 2010, Reputation as an intangible asset: Reflections on theory and methods in two empirical studies of business school reputations, *Journal of Management*, 36: 610–619.
89. R. Mudambi & T. Swift, 2013, Knowing when to leap: Transitioning between exploitative and explorative R&R, *Strategic Management Journal*, in press.
90. O. Chatain, 2011, Value creation, competition and performance in buyer-supplier relationships, *Strategic Management Journal*, 32: 76–102.
91. A. Marinez-Noya, E. Garcia-Canal, & M. F. Guillen, 2013, R&D outsourcing and the effectiveness of intangible investments: Is proprietary core knowledge walking out the door? *Journal of Management Studies*, 5: 67–91.
92. J. W. Upson, S. J. Ketchen, B. L. Connelly, & A. L. Ranft, 2012, Competitor analysis and foothold moves, *Academy of Management Journal*, 55: 93–110.
93. S. Anokhin & J. Wincent, 2012, Start-up rates and innovation: A cross-country examination, *Journal of International Business Studies*, 43: 41–60.
94. S. Berfield, 2009, Coach's new bag, *BusinessWeek*, June 29: 41–43; S. Berfield, 2009, Coach's Poppy line is luxury for recessionary times, *BusinessWeek*, www.businessweek.com, June 18.
95. D. G. Sirmon, J.-L. Arregle, M. A. Hitt, & J. W. Webb, 2008, The role of family influence in firms' strategic responses to threat of imitation, *Entrepreneurship Theory and Practice*, 32: 979–998; F. K. Pil & S. K. Cohen, 2006, Modularity: Implications for imitation, innovation, and sustained advantage, *Academy of Management Review*, 31: 995–1011.
96. M. M. Crossan & M. Apaydin, 2010, A multi-dimensional framework of organizational innovation: A systematic review of the literature, *Journal of Management Studies*, 47: 1154–1180.
97. X. Bian & L. Moutinho, 2009, An investigation of determinants of counterfeit purchase consideration, *Journal of Business Research*, 62: 368–378.
98. Porter, *Competitive Strategy*; K. Blomkvist, P. Kappen, & I. Zander, 2010, Quo vadis? The entry into new technologies in advanced foreign subsidiaries of the multinational enterprise, *Journal of International Business Studies*, 41: 525–549.
99. 2013, About Goya foods, www.goyafoods.com, April 11.
100. Porter, *Competitive Advantage*, 15.
101. J. P. Eggers, 2012, All experience is not created equal: Learning, adapting, and focusing in product portfolio management, *Strategic Management Journal*, 33: 315–335; R. Katila, E. L. Chen, & H. Piezunka, 2012, All the right moves: How entrepreneurial firms compete effectively, *Strategic Entrepreneurship Journal*, 6: 116–132.
102. K. Kling & I. Goteman, 2003, IKEA CEO Andres Dahlvig on international growth and IKEA's unique corporate culture and brand identity, *Academy of Management Executive*, 17(1): 31–37.
103. 2013, About IKEA, IKEA, www.ikea.com, April 11.
104. K. McLaughlin, 2009, Food truck nation, *Wall Street Journal*, www.wsj.com, June 5.
105. A. Barroso & M. S. Giarratana, 2013, Product proliferation strategies and firm performance: The moderating role of product space complexity, *Strategic Management Journal*, in press.
106. C. E. Armstrong, 2012, Small retailer strategies for battling the big boxes: A "Goliath" victory?, *Journal of Strategy and Management*, 5: 41–56.
107. 2013, Ann Fontaine: History, www.annfontaine.com, accessed April 11; 2011, Anne Fontaine, www.factio-magazine.com, May 6.
108. H. A. Ndofor, D. G. Sirmon, & X. He, 2011, Firm resources, competitive actions and performance: Investigating a mediated model with evidence from the in-vitro diagnostics industry, *Strategic Management Journal*, 32: 640–657; R. A. D'Aveni, G. B. Dagnino, & K. G. Smith, 2010, The age of temporary advantage, *Strategic Management Journal*, 31: 1371–1385.
109. 2010, Letter to our shareholders, Target Annual Report, www.target.com, March 11.
110. G. A. Shinkle, A. P. Kriauciunas, & G. Hundley, 2013, Why pure strategies may be wrong for transition economy firms, *Strategic Management Journal*, in press; S. Awate, M. M. Larsen, & R. Mudambi, EMNE

catch-up strategies in the wind turbine industry: Is there a trade-off between output and innovation capabilities? *Global Strategy Journal*, 2: 205–223.

111. H. Wang & C. Kimble, 2010, Low-cost strategy through product architecture: Lessons from China, *Journal of Business Strategy*, 31(3): 12–20.

112. M. I. M. Wahab, D. Wu, and C.-G. Lee, 2008, A generic approach to measuring the machine flexibility of manufacturing systems, *European Journal of Operational Research*, 186: 137–149.

113. M. Kotabe, R. Parente, & J. Y. Murray, 2007, Antecedents and outcomes of modular production in the Brazilian automobile industry: A grounded theory approach, *Journal of International Business Studies*, 38: 84–106.

114. T. Raj, R. Shankar, & M. Sunhaib, 2009, An ISM approach to analyse interaction between barriers of transition to flexible manufacturing systems, *International Journal of Manufacturing Technology and Management*, 16: 417–438; E. K. Bish, A. Muriel, & S. Biller, 2005, Managing flexible capacity in a make-to-order environment, *Management Science*, 51: 167–180.

115. P. Theodorou & G. Florou, 2008, Manufacturing strategies and financial performance—the effect of advanced information technology: CAD/CAM systems, *Omega*, 36: 107–121.

116. N. A. Morgan & L. L. Rego, 2009, Brand portfolio strategy and firm performance, *Journal of Marketing*, 73: 59–74.

117. D. Elmuti, H. Jia, & D. Gray, 2009, Customer relationship management strategic application and organizational effectiveness: An empirical investigation, *Journal of Strategic Marketing*, 17: 75–96.

118. C. O. Scharmer & K. Kaeufer, 2010, In front of blank canvas: Sensing emerging futures, *Journal of Business Strategy*, 31(4): 21–29.

119. J. D. Westphal, R. Gulati, & S. M. Shortell, 1997, Customization or conformity: An institutional and network perspective on the content and consequences of TQM adoption, *Administrative Science Quarterly*, 42: 366–394.

120. S. Modell, 2009, Bundling management control innovations: A field study of organisational experimenting with total quality management and the balanced scorecard, *Accounting, Auditing & Accountability Journal*, 22: 59–90.

121. C. D. Zatzick, T. P. Moliterno, & T. Fang, 2012, Strategic (mis)fit: The implementation of TQM in manufacturing organizations, *Strategic Management Journal*, 33: 1321–1330.

122. A. Keramati & A. Albadvi, 2009, Exploring the relationship between use of information technology in total quality management and SMEs performance using canonical correlation analysis: A survey on Swedish car part supplier sector, *International Journal of Information Technology and Management*, 8: 442–462; R. J. David & S. Strang, 2006, When fashion is fleeting: Transitory collective beliefs and the dynamics of TQM consulting, *Academy of Management Journal*, 49: 215–233.

123. Porter, *Competitive Advantage*, 16.

124. Ibid., 17.

125. M. A. Hitt, L. Bierman, K. Uhlenbruck, & K. Shimizu, 2006, The importance of resources in the internationalization of professional service firms: The good, the bad, and the ugly, *Academy of Management Journal*, 49: 1137–1157.

126. P. Puranam, H. Singh, & M. Zollo, 2006, Organizing for innovation: Managing the coordination-autonomy dilemma in technology acquisitions, *Academy of Management Journal*, 49: 263–280.

127. S. Thornhill & R. E. White, 2007, Strategic purity: A multi-industry evaluation of pure vs. hybrid business strategies, *Strategic Management Journal*, 28: 553–561.

128. B. Connelly, L. Tihanyi, S. T. Certo, & M. A. Hitt, 2010, Marching to the beat of different drummers: The influence of institutional owners on competitive actions, *Academy of Management Journal*, 53: 723–742.

# 5

# Competitive Rivalry and Competitive Dynamics

***Studying this chapter should provide you with the strategic management knowledge needed to:***

**1** Define competitors, competitive rivalry, competitive behavior, and competitive dynamics.

**2** Describe market commonality and resource similarity as the building blocks of a competitor analysis.

**3** Explain awareness, motivation, and ability as drivers of competitive behavior.

**4** Discuss factors affecting the likelihood a competitor will take competitive actions.

**5** Describe factors affecting the likelihood a competitor will respond to actions taken by its competitors.

**6** Explain competitive dynamics in slow-cycle, in fast-cycle, and in standard-cycle markets.

## TESCO PLC: A CASE STUDY IN COMPETITIVE BEHAVIOR

Tesco PLC is the world's third-largest retailer, a fact that suggests its ability to compete successfully against companies both in the United Kingdom (its home market) and throughout the world. However, the firm's recent competitive struggles both domestically and globally appear to highlight the fact that, as noted in Chapter 1, no company's success at a point in time guarantees its future success.

So what are some descriptors of the situation Tesco is encountering? From a financial perspective, the firm reported a decline in profits in 2012 for the first time in approximately two decades. In 2013, Tesco closed its Fresh & Easy stores in the United States and also took a write-down of 804 million pounds to reflect the then-current value of its U.K. properties. In all, Tesco wrote down the value of its global operations by $3.5 billion in 2013. (The global write-down of $3.5 billion accounts for the firm's troubled operations in countries such as Turkey, China, and India as well as the closing of its U.S. operations.)

Another issue is that revenue is declining in Tesco's home market where the company still generates roughly two-thirds of its sales and profits. Part of the reason for the revenue decline is related to customer service, as suggested by the fact that the results from a recent survey of U.K. consumers "found that despite £1 billion of investment in the U.K. in FY2012/13 customer perceptions of Tesco's quality, prices, promotions and overall value for money had all deteriorated quarter on quarter and year on year." In light of these results, the firm is taking a number of actions, including adding more and better-trained staff members in its stores, refurbishing those stores, and revamping its product lines and the prices it charges for them.

Revamping product lines and changing the prices charged for items are tactical actions. In contrast, entering the U.S. market with the Fresh & Easy concept was a strategic action (strategic and tactical actions and responses are defined later in this chapter). On the surface, entering the large U.S. market seems to be a reasonable course of action for a successful global retailer to take. As is often the case though, execution of that strategic action appears to be where problems were encountered. Fresh & Easy stores were sized to be handy neighborhood stores such as those found in many European cities. This did not appeal to American consumers, as suggested by an analyst: "My sense is that what they tried to do was make a European model. Europeans tend to make more frequent trips to grocery stores, maybe every day or every other day, where Americans are used to going for bigger trips less frequently." Additionally, products carried in stores located in different parts of the United States were not customized to any degree, meaning that the potentially unique needs of any local consumers who might choose to shop daily were not being identified and satisfied.

Tesco is taking additional strategic actions as part of its current array of competitive behaviors. For example, it is taking positions in other companies for the purpose of being able to turn their stores into compelling retail destinations for customers. "Investments in the Harris & Hoole coffee chain, working with the Euphorium bakery brand in London and acquiring the Giraffe restaurant chain" are examples of the competitive behavior Tesco is displaying as a foundation for improving its performance and trying to outcompete its rivals in the process of doing so.

Sources: J. Davey & K. Holton, 2013, Tesco quits U.S. and takes $3.5 billion global writedown, *Reuters*, www.reuters.com, April 17; K. Gordon, 2013, No bonus for Tesco bosses until profit improves, *Wall Street Journal*, www.wsj.com, May 23; K. Gordon, 2013, Tesco leans on outside brands, *Wall Street Journal*, www.wsj.com, April 18; R. Head, 2013, Can Tesco outperform Wal-Mart stores? *Daily Finance*, www.dailyfinance.com, March 21; N. Pratley, 2013, Tesco's era of rolling out its aisles is over, for now, *The Guardian*, www.guardian.co.uk, April 17; A. Felsted, 2012, American dream that died for Tesco, *Financial Times*, www.ft.com, December 5.

**Learn more about Giraffe, another company acquired by Tesco.**
**www.cengagebrain.com**

Firms operating in the same market, offering similar products, and targeting similar customers are **competitors**.[1] Southwest Airlines, Delta, United, and JetBlue are competitors as are Hulu, iTunes, and Netflix. J Sainsbury PLC and WM Morrison Supermarkets PLC are the primary domestic competitors for Tesco PLC, the focal firm of the Opening Case. However, Tesco also competes with global giants such as France's Carrefour SA, Germany's Metro, and the U.S.-based Wal-Mart Stores, Inc., meaning that the firm engages in a significant amount of competitive behavior (defined fully below, competitive behavior is essentially the set of actions and responses a firm takes as it competes against its rivals).

Firms interact with their competitors as part of the broad context within which they operate while attempting to earn above-average returns.[2] Another way to consider this is to note that no firm competes in a vacuum; rather, each firm's actions are part of a mosaic of competitive actions and responses taking place among a host of companies seeking the same objective—superior performance. And evidence shows that the decisions firms make about their interactions with competitors significantly affect their ability to earn above-average returns.[3] Because of this, firms seek to reach optimal decisions when considering how to compete against their rivals.[4]

**Competitors** are firms operating in the same market, offering similar products, and targeting similar customers.

**Competitive rivalry** is the ongoing set of competitive actions and competitive responses that occur among firms as they maneuver for an advantageous market position.

**Competitive behavior** is the set of competitive actions and responses a given firm takes to build or defend its competitive advantages and to improve its market position.

**Competitive rivalry** is the ongoing set of competitive actions and competitive responses that occur among firms as they maneuver for an advantageous market position.[5] Especially in highly competitive industries, firms constantly jockey for advantage as they launch strategic actions and respond or react to rivals' moves.[6] It is important for those leading organizations to understand competitive rivalry, in that the reality is that some firms learn how to outperform their competitors, meaning that competitive rivalry influences an individual firm's ability to gain and sustain competitive advantages.[7] A sequence of firm-level moves, rivalry results from firms initiating their own competitive actions and then responding to actions taken by competitors.[8]

Zara, a clothing unit owned by Spanish retailer Inditex SA, which is the world's largest fashion retailer by sales, engages in competitive rivalry with a number of firms but especially Swedish-based Hennes & Mauritz AB (H&M). (Mango and Topshop are other important Zara competitors.) As explained in the Strategic Focus, Zara and H&M engage in a continuous stream of competitive actions and responses as they each seek the most advantageous positions in the many markets in which they are competitors. Zara uses its core competencies as the basis for competing against its rivals. Because the global retail clothing industry is highly competitive, the constant competitive jockeying between Zara and H&M is not surprising.

**Competitive behavior** is the set of competitive actions and responses a given firm takes to build or defend its competitive advantages and to improve its market position.[9] As explained in the Strategic Focus, Zara and H&M engage in competitive behavior to defend their advantages and to improve the attractiveness of their market positions.

M. Stasy

## Strategic Focus — TECHNOLOGY

### Competitive Rivalry in *Fast Fashion*: A Constant Stream of Actions and Responses

In our discussion of Zara in the Opening Case in Chapter 3, we noted that this company competing in the *fast fashion* segment of the retailing clothing industry "uses its resources and capabilities as the foundation for its core competencies." We also indicated that its core competencies allow Zara to "give customers what they want and get it to them faster than anyone else." Quick designs and its supply chain are two core competencies that remain critical to Zara's success.

In terms of design, analysts say that Zara gives customers decently made fashion items that are based on the latest looks from runways throughout the world yet are also sold at affordable prices—hence, the reason to ascribe the term "cheap chic" to the firm's clothes and to those produced by its major competitors as well. With respect to the supply chain competence, this is framed around the fact that parent-company Inditex owns a number of brands in addition to Zara, such as Massimo Dutti, Bershka, Pull & Bear, Stradivarius, and Oysho. In total, the clothing giant has over 6,000 stores located in close to 90 countries. Serving the product needs of all of its units, some say that "Inditex is something of a supply chain marvel: clothes move from concept to design to the Zara stores in a matter of days. And they move out of Zara stores within weeks."

*A window display from a Zara store. Zara's supply chain gives it a competitive advantage and underlies its ability to take competitive actions.*

With close to 3,000 stores located in almost 50 countries, H&M is another very large global clothing retailer. This firm also concentrates on the fast fashion market; and Zara and H&M compete on some of the same dimensions such as supply chain. But as discussed in Chapter 3, firms' resources are unique or idiosyncratic and as such do not yield identical capabilities and core competencies. This uniqueness is the foundation for how firms compete against one another. Relative to H&M, Zara's supply chain appears to be an advantage and a means of taking competitive actions. In the words of an analyst: "Zara has a lightning-fast supply chain with 50 percent of its clothes made in Western Europe. That allows it to capture catwalk and luxury trends and put product in its stores within weeks—something customers are willing to pay a premium for." While H&M's supply chain is impressive, it does not allow the firm to achieve competitive parity with Zara with respect to this competitive dimension. "H&M with its longer supply chain can't keep pace in terms of fashion, so it tries to compete on price instead: H&M's offerings are on average about 60 percent cheaper than Zara's. But the Stockholm-based chain is still more expensive than budget competitors such as Primark, owned by Associated British Foods PLC and U.S. chain Forever 21, leaving H&M struggling to position itself." Thus, in terms of competitive rivalry, Zara uses its supply chain advantage while H&M uses price as a competitive action to try to reduce the value Zara generates by emphasizing its supply chain.

There are additional examples of competitive rivalry between Zara and H&M. Recently H&M along with other retailers including Gap, American Eagle Outfitters, and Forever 21 established units in Mexico. Steadily increasing incomes of Mexican citizens and the country's sizable and youthful population are reasons for these entries. However, Zara is a first mover in Mexico, having established its first unit there in 1992 and expanding that initial location to 246 stores currently. Thus, entry now by some additional clothing retailers is a competitive response to the competitive action Zara took long ago. On the other hand, H&M currently is seeking to expand more rapidly in India compared to Zara. In this instance, H&M is taking a competitive action to which Zara may have to respond.

The Internet is a growing source of competitive rivalry between Zara and H&M. More specifically, H&M announced that it would establish a significant online shopping presence in the United States. However, this intended action appears to be at least in part a response to Zara's increasing Internet-related success. In commenting about its Web site, a Zara official noted that the number of visitors to the site recently doubled and that the site is receiving over 2 million hits per day.

Overall, the never-ending string of competitive actions and responses occurring between Zara & H&M provide an interesting "picture" of competitive rivalry.

Sources: C. Bjork, 2013, Inditex profit rises as global expansion continues, *Wall Street Journal*, www.wsj.com, March 13; J. Cartner-Morley, 2013, How Zara took over the high street, *The Guardian*, www.guardian.co.uk, February 15; L. Dishman, 2013, H&M's competitive advantage: Expansion in India, *Forbes*, www.forbes.com, April 29; J. Hansegard, 2013, H&M plans U.S. online store in summer, *Wall Street Journal*, www.wsj.com, March 21; M. Moffett, 2013, Soul-searching in Spanish fashion after Bangladesh factory details, *Wall Street Journal*, www.wsj.com, May 23; M. Sanchantra & L. Burkitt, 2013, Asia gravitates to cheap chic, *Wall Street Journal*, www.wsj.com, April 23; M. J. Deschamps, 2012, Just-style management briefing: Fast fashion's competitive advantages, *Just-Style*, www.just-style.com, July 2; S. Hansen, 2012, How Zara grew into the world's largest fashion retailer, *New York Times*, www.nytimes.com, November 9.

Learn more about Primark. www.cengagebrain.com

Through competitive behavior, each of these firms seeks to successfully position itself relative to the five forces of competition (see Chapter 2) and to defend its current competitive advantages while building advantages for the future (see Chapter 3).

Increasingly, competitors engage in competitive actions and responses in more than one market.[10] Firms competing against each other in several product or geographic markets are engaged in **multimarket competition**.[11] All competitive behavior—that is, the total set of actions and responses taken by all firms competing within a market—is called **competitive dynamics**. The relationships among all of these key concepts are shown in Figure 5.1.

**Multimarket competition** occurs when firms compete against each other in several product or geographic markets.

**Competitive dynamics** refer to all competitive behaviors—that is, the total set of actions and responses taken by all firms competing within a market.

This chapter focuses on competitive rivalry and competitive dynamics. A firm's strategies are dynamic in nature because actions taken by one firm elicit responses from competitors that, in turn, typically result in responses from the firm that took the initial action.[12] For example, the strategies cigarette manufacturers are implementing today include actions related to electronic cigarettes as a relatively new product. Commonly called e-cigarettes and with their health benefits still unknown, this product is a battery-powered device that converts heated, nicotine-laced liquid into vapor. Altria Group and Reynolds American, Inc. (the two largest U.S. cigarette manufacturers) updated their "e-cigarette strategies" in mid-2013. Influencing these updates were the increasing size of the market for this product and the more prominent position Lorillard Inc., the third-largest U.S. tobacco firm, had already established in it. Additional competitive actions and responses among these firms and with international cigarette manufacturers as well are expected in the foreseeable future.[13]

Competitive rivalries affect a firm's strategies, as shown by the fact that a strategy's success is determined not only by the firm's initial competitive actions but also by how well it anticipates competitors' responses to them *and* by how well the firm anticipates and responds to its competitors' initial actions (also called attacks).[14] Although competitive

**Figure 5.1** From Competition to Competitive Dynamics

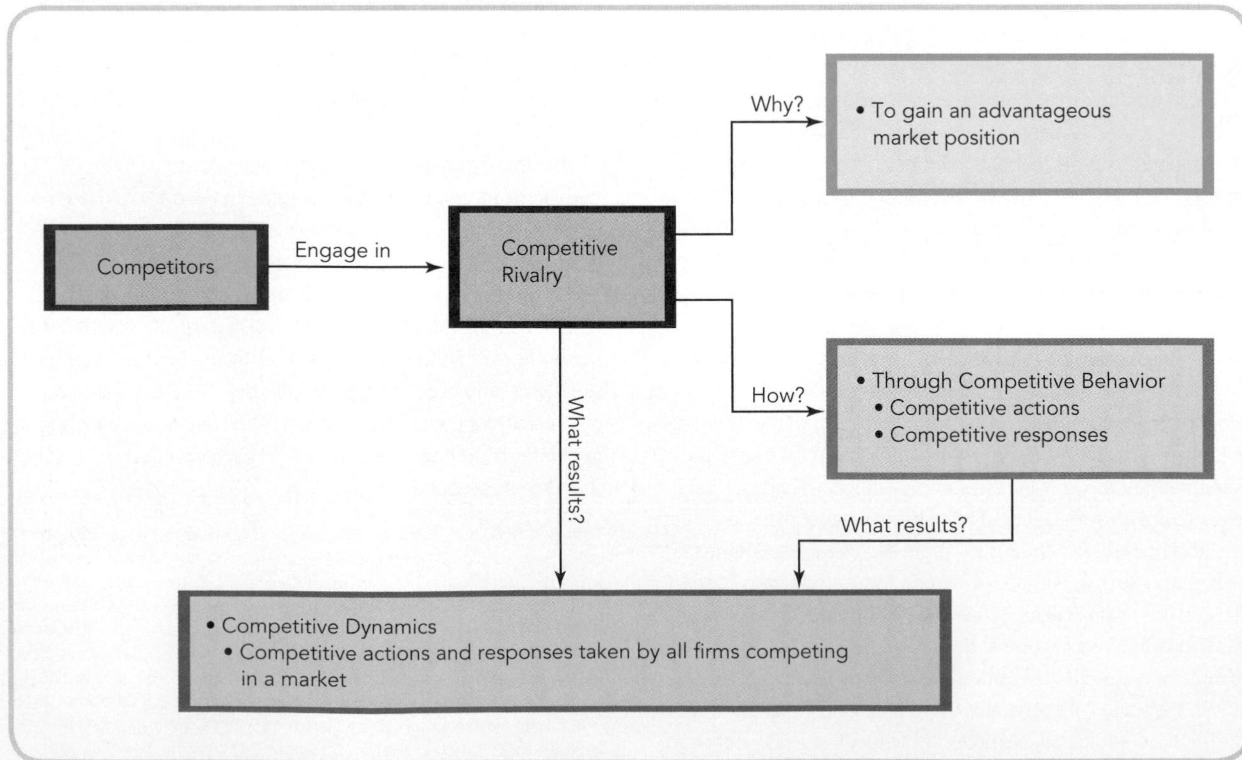


Source: Adapted from M. J. Chen, 1996, Competitor analysis and interfirm rivalry: Toward a theoretical integration, *Academy of Management Review*, 21: 100-134.

M. Stasy

rivalry affects all types of strategies (e.g., corporate-level, merger and acquisition, and international), its dominant influence is on the firm's business-level strategy or strategies. Indeed, firms' actions and responses to those of their rivals are part of the basic building blocks of business-level strategies.[15]

Recall from Chapter 4 that business-level strategy is concerned with what the firm does to successfully use its core competencies in specific product markets. In the global economy, competitive rivalry is intensifying,[16] meaning that the significance of its effect on firms' strategies is increasing. However, firms that develop and use effective business-level strategies tend to outperform competitors in individual product markets, even when experiencing intense competitive rivalry.[17]

## 5-1 A Model of Competitive Rivalry

Competitive rivalry evolves from the pattern of actions and responses as one firm's competitive actions have noticeable effects on competitors, eliciting competitive responses from them.[18] This pattern suggests that firms are mutually interdependent, that they are affected by each other's actions and responses, and that marketplace success is a function of both individual strategies and the consequences of their use.[19]

Increasingly, executives recognize that competitive rivalry can have a major effect on the firm's financial performance[20] and market position.[21] For example, research shows that intensified rivalry within an industry results in decreased average profitability for the competing firms.[22] Although Apple essentially created the smartphone market in 2007 by launching the iPhone, some believe that Google's Android has rapidly reshaped the market, as evidenced by the fact that nearly half of all smartphones shipped in 2012 ran on the Android platform. Another indicator of rivalry's effect on profitability is Symbian's virtual disappearance as a platform provider even though it was "the primary mobile operating system used by Nokia, Samsung, Motorola and Sony throughout the mid-2000s."[23]

Figure 5.2 presents a straightforward model of competitive rivalry at the firm level; this type of rivalry is usually dynamic and complex.[24] The competitive actions and responses the firm takes are the foundation for successfully building and using its capabilities and core competencies to gain an advantageous market position.[25]

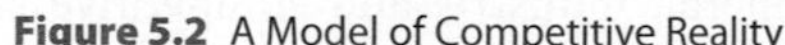

**Figure 5.2** A Model of Competitive Reality

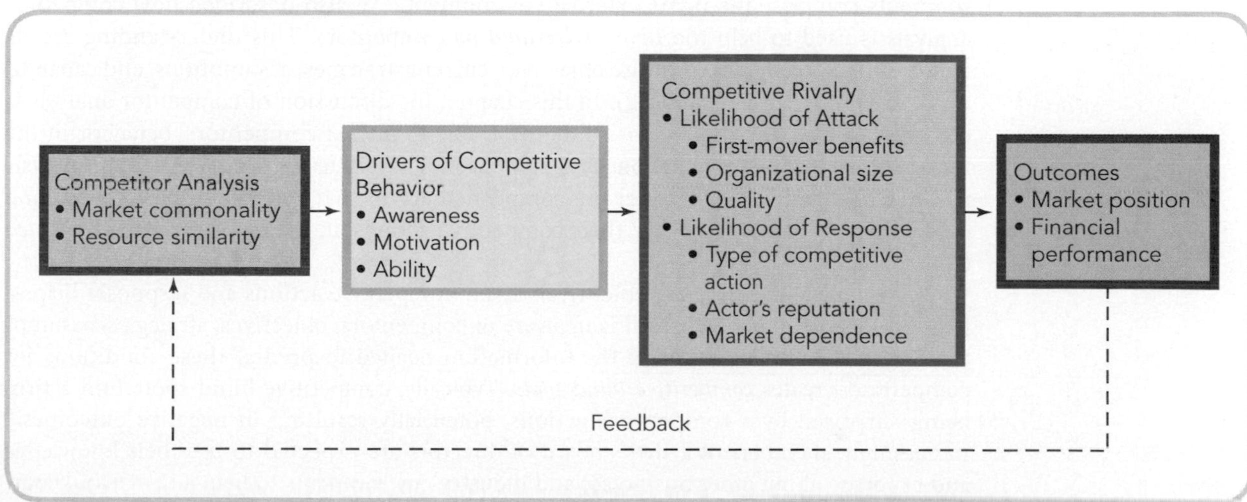


Source: Adapted from M. J. Chen, 1996, Competitor analysis and interfirm rivalry: Toward a theoretical integration, *Academy of Management Review*, 21: 100-134.

The model in Figure 5.2 presents the sequence of activities commonly involved in competition between a firm and its competitors. Companies use this model to understand how to be able to predict a competitor's behavior and reduce the uncertainty associated with it.[26] Being able to predict competitors' actions and responses has a positive effect on the firm's market position and its subsequent financial performance.[27] The total of all the individual rivalries modeled in Figure 5.2 that occur in a particular market reflect the competitive dynamics in that market.

The remainder of the chapter explains components of the model shown in Figure 5.2. We first describe market commonality and resource similarity as the building blocks of a competitor analysis. Next, we discuss the effects of three organizational characteristics—awareness, motivation, and ability—on the firm's competitive behavior. We then examine competitive (interfirm) rivalry between firms. To do this, we explain the factors that affect the likelihood a firm will take a competitive action and the factors that affect the likelihood a firm will respond to a competitor's action. In the chapter's final section, we turn our attention to competitive dynamics to describe how market characteristics affect competitive rivalry in slow-cycle, fast-cycle, and standard-cycle markets.

## 5-2 Competitor Analysis

As previously noted, a competitor analysis is the first step the firm takes to be able to predict the extent and nature of its rivalry with each competitor. Competitor analyses are especially important when entering a foreign market in that firms doing so need to understand the local competition and foreign competitors currently operating in that market.[28] Without such analyses, they are less likely to be successful.

The number of markets in which firms compete against each other is called market commonality while the similarity in their resources is called resource similarity (both terms will be discussed later). These two dimensions of competition determine the extent to which firms are competitors. Firms with high market commonality and highly similar resources are direct and mutually acknowledged competitors.[29] The drivers of competitive behavior—as well as factors influencing the likelihood that a competitor will initiate competitive actions and will respond to its competitors' actions—influence the intensity of rivalry.[30]

In Chapter 2, we discussed competitor analysis as a technique firms use to understand their competitive environment. Together, the general, industry, and competitive environments comprise the firm's external environment. We also described how competitor analysis is used to help the firm *understand* its competitors. This understanding results from studying competitors' future objectives, current strategies, assumptions, and capabilities (see Figure 2.3 in Chapter 2). In this chapter, the discussion of competitor analysis is extended to describe what firms study to be able to *predict* competitors' behavior in the form of their competitive actions and responses. The discussions of competitor analysis in Chapter 2 and in this chapter are complementary in that firms must first *understand* competitors (Chapter 2) before their competitive actions and responses can be *predicted* (this chapter).

Being able to accurately predict rivals' likely competitive actions and responses helps a firm avoid situations in which it is unaware of competitors' objectives, strategies, assumptions, and capabilities. Lacking the information needed to predict these conditions for competitors creates *competitive blind spots*. Typically, competitive blind spots find a firm being surprised by a competitor's actions, potentially resulting in negative outcomes.[31] Increasingly, members of a firm's board of directors are expected to use their knowledge and expertise about other businesses and industry environments to help a firm avoid competitive blind spots.[32]

## 5-2a Market Commonality

Every industry is composed of various markets. The financial services industry has markets for insurance, brokerage services, banks, and so forth. To concentrate on the needs of different, unique customer groups, markets can be further subdivided. The insurance market could be broken into market segments (such as commercial and consumer), product segments (such as health insurance and life insurance), and geographic markets (such as Southeast Asia and Western Europe). In general, the capabilities the Internet's technologies generate help to shape the nature of industries' markets along with patterns of competition within those industries. For example, according to a Procter and Gamble (P&G) official: "Facebook is both a marketing and a distribution channel, as P&G has worked to develop 'f-commerce' capabilities on its fan pages, fulfilled by Amazon, which has become a top 10 retail account for Pampers," a disposable diaper product.[33]

Competitors tend to agree about the different characteristics of individual markets that form an industry. For example, in the transportation industry, the commercial air travel market differs from the ground transportation market, which is served by such firms as YRC Worldwide (one of the largest, most comprehensive less-than-truckload (LTL) carriers in North America) and major YRC competitors Arkansas Best, Con-way Inc., and FedEx Freight.[34] Although differences exist, many industries' markets are partially related in terms of technologies used or core competencies needed to develop a competitive advantage. For example, although railroads and truck ground transport compete in a different segment and can be substitutes, different types of transportation companies need to provide reliable and timely service. Commercial air carriers such as Southwest, United, and Jet Blue must therefore develop service competencies to satisfy their passengers while YRC, railroads, and their major competitors must develop such competencies to serve the needs of those using their services to ship goods.

Firms sometimes compete against each other in several markets, a condition called market commonality. More formally, **market commonality** is concerned with the number of markets with which the firm and a competitor are jointly involved and the degree of importance of the individual markets to each.[35] Firms competing against one another in several or many markets are said to be engaging in multimarket competition.[36] As we noted in Chapter 2's Opening Case, Coca-Cola and PepsiCo compete across a number of product markets (e.g., soft drinks, bottled water) as well as geographic markets (throughout North America and in many other countries throughout the world). Airlines, chemicals, pharmaceuticals, and consumer foods are examples of other industries with firms often competing against each other in multiple markets.

Firms competing in several of the same markets have the potential to respond to a competitor's actions not only within the market in which a given set of actions are taken, but also in other markets where they compete with the rival. This potential creates a complicated mosaic in which the competitive actions or responses a firm takes in one market may be designed to affect the outcome of its rivalry with a particular competitor in a second market.[37] This potential complicates the rivalry between competitors. In fact, research suggests that a firm with greater multimarket contact is less likely to initiate an attack, but more likely to move (respond) aggressively when attacked. For instance, research in the computer industry found that "firms respond to competitive attacks by introducing new products but do not use price as a retaliatory weapon."[38] Thus in general, multimarket competition reduces competitive rivalry, but some firms will still compete when the potential rewards (e.g., potential market share gain) are high.[39]

**Market commonality** is concerned with the number of markets with which the firm and a competitor are jointly involved and the degree of importance of the individual markets to each.

**Resource similarity** is the extent to which the firm's tangible and intangible resources are comparable to a competitor's in terms of both type and amount.

## 5-2b Resource Similarity

**Resource similarity** is the extent to which the firm's tangible and intangible resources are comparable to a competitor's in terms of both type and amount.[40] Firms with similar types

Find out more about the United States Postal Service.
www.cengagebrain.com

and amounts of resources are likely to have similar strengths and weaknesses and use similar strategies on the basis of their strengths to pursue what may be similar opportunities in the external environment.

As we discuss in the Strategic Focus, "resource similarity" describes part of the relationship between FedEx and United Parcel Service (UPS). In addition though, these companies compete in many of the same markets, and thus are also accurately described as having market commonality. In terms of resources, to mention only a few, the firms have similar types of truck and airplane fleets, similar levels of financial capital, and rely on equally talented reservoirs of human capital along with sophisticated information technology systems to complete their work. In addition to competing aggressively against each other in North America, the firms share many other markets in common, as FedEx delivers shipments in roughly 220 countries while UPS does so in approximately 200 countries. These comparisons between the two firms suggest why the rivalry between them is intense.

When performing a competitor analysis, a firm analyzes each of its competitors with respect to market commonality and resource similarity. The results of these analyses can be mapped for visual comparisons. In Figure 5.3, we show different hypothetical intersections between the firm and individual competitors in terms of market commonality and resource similarity. These intersections indicate the extent to which the firm and those with which it compares itself are competitors. For example, the firm and its competitor displayed in quadrant I have similar types and amounts of resources (i.e., the two firms have a similar portfolio of resources). The firm and its competitor in quadrant I would use their similar resource portfolios to compete against each other in many markets that are important to each. These conditions lead to the conclusion that the firms modeled in quadrant I are direct and mutually acknowledged competitors.

As discussed in the Strategic Focus, this is the case for FedEx and UPS, meaning that these firms would map each other as direct competitors and place themselves along with that competitor in quadrant I of Figure 5.3. In contrast, the firm and its competitor shown in quadrant III share few markets and have little similarity in their resources, indicating that they aren't direct and mutually acknowledged competitors. Thus a small, local,

**Figure 5.3** A Framework of Competitor Analysis



Source: Adapted from M. J. Chen, 1996, Competitor analysis and inferfirm rivalry: Toward a theoretical integration, *Academy of Management Review*, 21: 100-134.

M. Stasy

## Strategic Focus — GLOBALIZATION

### FedEx and United Parcel Service (UPS): Maintaining Success While Competing Aggressively

Identified recently as one of the 50 greatest or most intense competitive rivalries of all time, FedEx and UPS are similar in many ways, including their resources, the markets they serve, and the competitive dimensions they emphasize to implement similar strategies. These similarities mean that the firms are direct competitors and that they are keenly *aware* of each other and have the *motivation* and *ability* to respond to the competitive actions they take against each other. (Awareness, motivation, and ability and their importance in terms of competitive rivalry are discussed later.) The two firms are the largest global courier delivery companies in what is a highly competitive industry on a global basis.

FedEx and UPS compete in many of the same product markets including next day delivery, cheaper ground delivery, time-guaranteed delivery (both domestically and internationally), and freight services. However, the firms concentrate on different segments in attempting to create superior stakeholder value and avoid direct, head-to-head competition in a host of product segments and markets. In this regard, FedEx "intends to leverage and extend the FedEx brand and to provide customers with seamless access to its entire portfolio of integrated transportation services" while UPS "seeks to position itself as the primary coordinator of the flow of goods, information and funds throughout the entire supply chain (the movement from the raw materials and parts stage through final consumption of the finished product)."

Thus, while these firms are similar, they also seek to differentiate themselves in ways that enhance the possibility of being able to gain strategic competitiveness and earn above-average returns. In broad-stroke terms, FedEx concentrates more on transportation services and international markets (recently, FedEx was generating 48 percent of revenue internationally while UPS was earning 22 percent of its revenue from international markets) while UPS concentrates more on the entire value chain while competing domestically. FedEx is the world's largest international air shipping firm while UPS is the world's largest package delivery company.

There are many actions the firms have recently taken to sharpen their ability to outcompete their primary competitor. In mid-2013, FedEx learned that its contract to fly domestic mail for the U.S. Postal Service had been selected for renewal. UPS also bid on the contract, meaning that it lost this competitive battle to its rival. To support its strength in logistics as part of the entire supply chain, UPS recently agreed to buy "Hungary-based pharmaceutical-logistics company Cemelog Zrt for an undisclosed amount in a deal to strengthen its health-care business in Europe, giving it access to the increasingly important markets of Central and Eastern Europe." UPS is also emphasizing trans-border European Union services as a growth engine for the foreseeable future. To enhance its ability to compete against UPS and other rivals as well, FedEx is restructuring some of its operations to increase efficiency. Similarly, the firm is increasing its emphasis on finding ways for its independent express, ground, and freight networks to work together more synergistically.

*Back view of a UPS postal courier delivery van. UPS and FedEx share high degrees of both market commonality and resource similarity.*



Although the rivalry between FedEx and UPS is intense and aggressive, it is also likely that it makes each firm stronger and more agile in that each has to be at its best in order to outperform the other. Thus in many ways, each of these firms is a "good competitor" for the other one.

Sources: 2013, FedEx Corp., *Standard & Poor's Stock Report*, www.standardandpoors.com, May 25; 2013, United Parcel Service, Inc., *Standard & Poor's Stock Report*, www.standardandpoors.com, May 25; L. Eaton, 2013, FedEx CEO: Truck fleets to shift to natural gas from diesel, *Wall Street Journal*, www.wsj.com, March 8; V. Mock, 2013, UPS to appeal EU's block of TNT merger, *Wall Street Journal*, www.wsj.com, April 7; B. Morris & B. Sechler, 2013, FedEx customers like slower and cheaper, *Wall Street Journal*, www.wsj.com, March 20; B. Sechler, 2013, Online shopping boosts profit for UPS, *Wall Street Journal*, www.wsj.com, April 25; B. Sechler, 2013, FedEx fends off rivals for U.S. Postal, *Wall Street Journal*, www.wsj.com, April 23.

family-owned restaurant concentrating on selling "gourmet" hamburgers does not compete directly against McDonald's. The mapping of competitive relationships is fluid as companies enter and exit markets and as rivals' resources change in type and amount, meaning that the companies with which a given firm is a direct competitor change over time.

## 5-3 Drivers of Competitive Behavior

Market commonality and resource similarity influence the drivers (awareness, motivation, and ability) of competitive behavior (see Figure 5.2). In turn, the drivers influence the firm's actual competitive behavior, as revealed by the actions and responses it takes while engaged in competitive rivalry.[41]

*Awareness*, which is a prerequisite to any competitive action or response taken by a firm, refers to the extent to which competitors recognize the degree of their mutual interdependence that results from market commonality and resource similarity.[42] (As suggested in the Strategic Focus, FedEx and UPS recognize the high degree of mutual dependence that exists between them.) Awareness affects the extent to which the firm understands the consequences of its competitive actions and responses. A lack of awareness can lead to excessive competition, resulting in a negative effect on all competitors' performance.[43]

Awareness tends to be greatest when firms have highly similar resources (in terms of types and amounts) to use while competing against each other in multiple markets. Komatsu Ltd., Japan's top construction machinery maker, and U.S.-based Caterpillar Inc. have similar resources and are aware of each other's actions given that they compete against each other in markets throughout the world. Founded in 1925, Caterpillar is the world's leading manufacturer of construction and mining equipment, diesel and natural gas engines, and industrial gas turbines, while Komatsu is the world's second largest seller of construction and mining machinery behind Caterpillar.[44] Over the years, these firms have competed aggressively against each other for market share in multiple countries and regions.

*Motivation*, which concerns the firm's incentive to take action or to respond to a competitor's attack, relates to perceived gains and losses. Thus, a firm may be aware of competitors but may not be motivated to engage in rivalry with them if it perceives that its position will not improve or that its market position won't be damaged if it doesn't respond.[45] A benefit of not having the motivation to engage in rivalry at a point in time with a competitor is that the unmotivated firm retains resources that can be used for other purposes including choosing to compete against a rival with whom there is more motivation to do so.

Market commonality affects the firm's perceptions and resulting motivation. For example, a firm is generally more likely to attack the rival with whom it has low market commonality than the one with whom it competes in multiple markets. The primary reason is the high stakes involved in trying to gain a more advantageous position over a rival with whom the firm shares many markets. As mentioned earlier, multimarket competition can result in a competitor responding to the firm's action in a market different from the one in which that action was taken. Actions and responses of this type can cause both firms to lose focus on core markets and to battle each other with resources that had been allocated for other purposes. Because of the high stakes of competition under the condition of market commonality, the probability is high that the attacked firm will respond to its competitor's action in an effort to protect its position in one or more markets.[46]

In some instances, the firm may be aware of the markets it shares with a competitor and be motivated to respond to an attack by that competitor, but lack the ability to do so. *Ability* relates to each firm's resources and the flexibility they provide. Without available resources (such as financial capital and people), the firm is not able to attack a competitor or respond to its actions. For example, smaller and newer firms tend to be more innovative but generally have fewer resources to attack larger and established competitors. Likewise, foreign firms often are at a disadvantage against local firms because of the local firms' social capital (relationships) with consumers, suppliers, and government officials.[47] However, similar resources suggest similar abilities to attack and respond. When a firm faces a competitor with similar resources, careful study of a possible attack before initiating it is essential because the similarly resourced competitor is likely to respond to that action.[48]

Resource *dissimilarity* also influences competitive actions and responses between firms, in that the more significant the difference between resources owned by the acting firm and those against whom it has taken action, the longer is the delay by the firm with a resource disadvantage.[49] For example, Walmart initially used a focused cost leadership strategy to compete only in small communities (those with a population of 25,000 or less). Using sophisticated logistics systems and efficient purchasing practices, among other methods, to gain competitive advantages, Walmart created a new type of value (primarily in the form of wide selections of products at the lowest competitive prices) for customers in small retail markets. Local competitors lacked the ability to marshal needed resources at the pace required to respond to Walmart's actions quickly and effectively. However, even when facing competitors with greater resources (greater ability) or more attractive market positions, firms should eventually respond, no matter how daunting the task seems. Choosing not to respond can ultimately result in failure, as happened with at least some local retailers who didn't respond to Walmart's competitive actions. Today, with Walmart as the world's largest retailer, it is indeed difficult for smaller competitors to have the resources required to effectively respond to its competitive actions or competitive responses.



*A Walmart store in Los Angeles, California. Walmart has developed resource dissimilarities that allow it to take actions to which competitors find it difficult to respond.*

## 5-4 Competitive Rivalry

The ongoing competitive action/response sequence between a firm and a competitor affects the performance of both firms. Because of this, it is important for companies to carefully analyze and understand the competitive rivalry present in the markets in which they compete.[50]

As we described earlier, the predictions drawn from studying competitors in terms of awareness, motivation, and ability are grounded in market commonality and resource similarity. These predictions are fairly general. The value of the final set of predictions the firm develops about each of its competitors' competitive actions and responses is enhanced by studying the "Likelihood of Attack" factors (such as first-mover benefits and organizational size) and the "Likelihood of Response" factors (such as the actor's reputation) that are shown in Figure 5.2. Evaluating and understanding these factors allow the firm to refine the predictions it makes about its competitors' actions and responses.

### 5-4a Strategic and Tactical Actions

Firms use both strategic and tactical actions when forming their competitive actions and competitive responses in the course of engaging in competitive rivalry.[51] A **competitive action** is a strategic or tactical action the firm takes to build or defend its competitive advantages or improve

A **competitive action** is a strategic or tactical action the firm takes to build or defend its competitive advantages or improve its market position.

its market position. A **competitive response** is a strategic or tactical action the firm takes to counter the effects of a competitor's competitive action. A **strategic action** or a **strategic response** is a market-based move that involves a significant commitment of organizational resources and is difficult to implement and reverse. A **tactical action** or a **tactical response** is a market-based move that is taken to fine-tune a strategy; it involves fewer resources and is relatively easy to implement and reverse. When engaging rivals in competition, firms must recognize the differences between strategic and tactical actions and responses and develop an effective balance between the two types of competitive actions and responses.

Nokia Corp. has completed a number of strategic actions in the past few years, none of which has more potentially significant possibilities than does its partnership with Microsoft. As part of this relationship, Nokia has adopted Windows Phone as its principal smartphone strategy. In announcing this collaboration, an official noted that "Nokia and Microsoft will combine our strengths to deliver an ecosystem with unrivalled global reach and scale."[52] This relationship may be at least in part a strategic response to Apple's success. An example of a recent strategic action taken relative to Nokia is Samsung's decision to locate its newest research and development center in Finland, Nokia's home market. Some analysts thought this action signaled even stiffer competition for Nokia, a firm that has now lost its market leadership position in the sales of smartphones to Samsung in its native country.[53]

Walmart prices aggressively as a means of increasing revenues and gaining market share at the expense of competitors. In this regard, the firm engages in a continuous stream of tactical actions to attack rivals by changing some of its products' prices and tactical responses to respond to price changes taken by competitors such as Costco and Target.

# 5-5 Likelihood of Attack

In addition to market commonality, resource similarity, and the drivers of awareness, motivation, and ability, other factors affect the likelihood a competitor will use strategic actions and tactical actions to attack its competitors. Three of these factors—first-mover benefits, organizational size, and quality—are discussed next. Second and late movers are considered as part of the discussion of first-mover benefits.

A **competitive response** is a strategic or tactical action the firm takes to counter the effects of a competitor's competitive action.

A **strategic action** or a **strategic response** is a market-based move that involves a significant commitment of organizational resources and is difficult to implement and reverse.

A **tactical action** or a **tactical response** is a market-based move that is taken to fine-tune a strategy; it involves fewer resources and is relatively easy to implement and reverse.

A **first mover** is a firm that takes an initial competitive action in order to build or defend its competitive advantages or to improve its market position.

## 5-5a First-Mover Benefits

A **first mover** is a firm that takes an initial competitive action in order to build or defend its competitive advantages or to improve its market position. The first-mover concept has been influenced by the work of the famous economist Joseph Schumpeter, who argued that firms achieve competitive advantage by taking innovative actions[54] (innovation is defined and discussed in Chapter 13). In general, first movers emphasize research and development (R&D) as a path to develop innovative goods and services that customers will value.[55]

The benefits of being a successful first mover can be substantial.[56] Especially in fast-cycle markets (discussed later in the chapter), where changes occur rapidly and where it is virtually impossible to sustain a competitive advantage for any length of time, a first mover can experience many times the valuation and revenue of a second mover.[57] This evidence suggests that although first-mover benefits are never absolute, they are often critical to a firm's success in industries experiencing rapid technological developments and relatively short product life cycles.[58] In addition to earning above-average returns until its competitors respond to its successful competitive action, the first mover can gain (1) the loyalty of customers who may become committed to the goods or services of the firm that first made them available, and (2) market share that can be difficult for competitors to take during future competitive rivalry.[59] The general evidence that first movers have greater survival rates than later market entrants is perhaps the culmination of first-mover benefits.[60]

The firm trying to predict its rivals' competitive actions might conclude that they will take aggressive strategic actions to gain first movers' benefits. However, even though a firm's competitors might be motivated to be first movers, they may lack the ability to do so. First movers tend to be aggressive and willing to experiment with innovation and take higher yet reasonable levels of risk, and their long-term success depends on retaining the ability to do so.[61]

To be a first mover, the firm must have readily available the resources to significantly invest in R&D as well as to rapidly and successfully produce and market a stream of innovative products.[62] Organizational slack makes it possible for firms to have the ability (as measured by available resources) to be first movers. *Slack* is the buffer or cushion provided by actual or obtainable resources that aren't currently in use and are in excess of the minimum resources needed to produce a given level of organizational output.[63] As a liquid resource, slack can quickly be allocated to support competitive actions, such as R&D investments and aggressive marketing campaigns that lead to first-mover advantages. This relationship between slack and the ability to be a first mover allows the firm to predict that a first-mover competitor likely has available slack and will probably take aggressive competitive actions to continuously introduce innovative products. Furthermore, the firm can predict that as a first mover, a competitor will try to rapidly gain market share and customer loyalty in order to earn above-average returns until its competitors are able to effectively respond to its first move.

Firms evaluating their competitors should realize that being a first mover carries risk. For example, it is difficult to accurately estimate the returns that will be earned from introducing product innovations to the marketplace.[64] Additionally, the first mover's cost to develop a product innovation can be substantial, reducing the slack available to support further innovation. Thus, the firm should carefully study the results a competitor achieves as a first mover. Continuous success by the competitor suggests additional product innovations, while lack of product acceptance over the course of the competitor's innovations may indicate less willingness in the future to accept the risks of being a first mover.[65]

A **second mover** is a firm that responds to the first mover's competitive action, typically through imitation. More cautious than the first mover, the second mover studies customers' reactions to product innovations. In the course of doing so, the second mover also tries to find any mistakes the first mover made so that it can avoid them and the problems they created. Often, successful imitation of the first mover's innovations allows the second mover to avoid the mistakes and the major investments required of the pioneering first movers.[66]

Second movers have the time to develop processes and technologies that are more efficient than those used by the first mover or that create additional value for consumers.[67] The most successful second movers rarely act too fast (so they can fully analyze the first mover's actions) nor too slow (so they do not give the first mover time to correct its mistakes and "lock in" customer loyalty). Overall, the outcomes of the first mover's competitive actions may provide a blueprint for second and even late movers as they determine the nature and timing of their competitive responses.[68]

Determining whether a competitor is an effective second mover (based on its past actions) allows a first-mover firm to predict that the competitor will respond quickly to successful, innovation-based market entries. The first mover can expect a successful second-mover competitor to study its market entries and to respond with a new entry into the market within a short time period. As a second mover, the competitor will try to respond with a product that provides greater customer value than does the first mover's product. The most successful second movers are able to rapidly and meaningfully interpret market feedback to respond quickly yet successfully to the first mover's successful innovations.

A **second mover** is a firm that responds to the first mover's competitive action, typically through imitation.

Home-improvement rating site Angie's List was founded roughly two decades ago. More than two million U.S. households are using the service to gain information about the quality

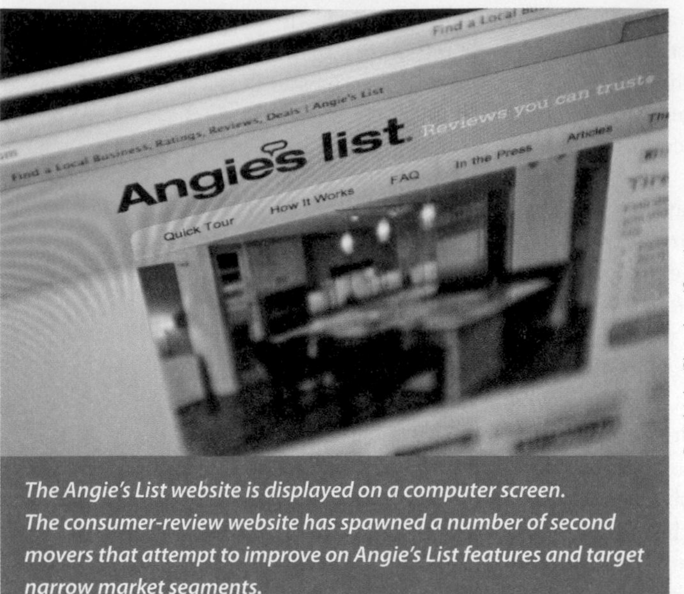

Daniel Acker/Bloomberg/Getty Images

*The Angie's List website is displayed on a computer screen. The consumer-review website has spawned a number of second movers that attempt to improve on Angie's List features and target narrow market segments.*

of 700-plus services (plumbing, electrical work, and so forth) provided by local companies. Angie's List members submit reviews at the rate of over 60,000 per month. The firm's success is suggested by the fact that it generates roughly $220 million in annual revenue.

The fact that "a growing number of websites are taking aim at the giant home-improvement rating site" suggests that second movers are responding to Angie's List as a successful first mover.[69] Each of the second movers offers a slightly different service to customers, trying to improve on the quality, breath, and/or depth of what Angie's List offers. HomeAdvisor.com, for example, differs from the first mover through its exclusive focus on home projects. Houzz.com provides users with an archive of home improvement and design images as well as access to an extensive list of articles concerned with decorating and remodeling. Of course, Angie's List is responding to the challenge of second movers through several actions including an effort to improve the method through which members seek bids from professional providers.

A **late mover** is a firm that responds to a competitive action a significant amount of time after the first mover's action and the second mover's response. Typically, a late response is better than no response at all, although any success achieved from the late competitive response tends to be considerably less than that achieved by first and second movers. However, on occasion, late movers can be successful if they develop a unique way to enter the market and compete. For firms from emerging economies this often means a niche strategy with lower-cost production and manufacturing.[70]

The firm competing against a late mover can predict that the competitor will likely enter a particular market only after both the first and second movers have achieved success in that market. Moreover, on a relative basis, the firm can predict that the late mover's competitive action will allow it to earn average returns only after the considerable time required for it to understand how to create at least as much customer value as that offered by the first and second movers' products.

## 5-5b Organizational Size

An organization's size affects the likelihood it will take competitive actions as well as the types and timing of those actions.[71] In general, small firms are more likely than large companies to launch competitive actions and tend to do it more quickly. Smaller firms are thus perceived as nimble and flexible competitors who rely on speed and surprise to defend their competitive advantages or develop new ones while engaged in competitive rivalry, especially with large companies, to gain an advantageous market position.[72] Small firms' flexibility and nimbleness allow them to develop variety in their competitive actions; large firms tend to limit the types of competitive actions used.[73]

A **late mover** is a firm that responds to a competitive action a significant amount of time after the first mover's action and the second mover's response.

Large firms, however, are likely to initiate more competitive actions along with more strategic actions during a given period.[74] Thus, when studying its competitors in terms of organizational size, the firm should use a measurement such as total sales revenue or total number of employees. The competitive actions the firm likely will encounter from competitors larger than it is will be different from the competitive actions it will encounter from smaller competitors.

The organizational size factor adds another layer of complexity. When engaging in competitive rivalry, firms prefer to be able to have the capabilities required to take a large number of unique competitive actions. For this to be the case, a firm needs to have the amount of slack resources that a large, successful company typically holds if it is to be able to launch a greater *number* of competitive actions. Simultaneously though, the firm needs to be flexible when considering competitive actions and responses it might take if it is to be able to launch a greater *variety* of competitive actions. Collectively then, firms are best served competitively when their size permits them to take an appropriate number of unique or diverse competitive actions and responses.

## 5-5c Quality

Quality has many definitions, including well-established ones relating it to the production of goods or services with zero defects[75] and as a cycle of continuous improvement.[76] From a strategic perspective, we consider quality to be the outcome of how a firm competes through its value chain activities and support functions (see Chapter 3). Thus, **quality** exists when the firm's goods or services meet or exceed customers' expectations. Some evidence suggests that quality may be the most critical component in satisfying the firm's customers.[77]

In the eyes of customers, quality is about doing the right things relative to performance measures that are important to them.[78] Customers may be interested in measuring the quality of a firm's goods and services against a broad range of dimensions. Sample quality dimensions in which customers commonly express an interest are shown in Table 5.1. Quality is possible only when top-level managers support it and when its importance is

**Quality** exists when the firm's goods or services meet or exceed customers' expectations.

**Table 5.1** Quality Dimentions of Products and Services

| Product Quality Dimensions |
|---|
| 1. *Performance*—Operating characteristics |
| 2. *Features*—Important special characteristics |
| 3. *Flexibility*—Meeting operating specifications over some period of time |
| 4. *Durability*—Amount of use before performance deteriorates |
| 5. *Conformance*—Match with preestablished standards |
| 6. *Serviceability*—Ease and speed of repair |
| 7. *Aesthetics*—How a product looks and feels |
| 8. *Perceived quality*—Subjective assessment of characteristics (Product image) |
| **Service Quality Dimensions** |
| 1. *Timeliness*—Performed in the promised period of time |
| 2. *Courtesy*—Performed cheerfully |
| 3. *Consistency*—Giving all customers similar experiences each time |
| 4. *Convenience*—Accessibility to customers |
| 5. *Completeness*—Fully serviced, as required |
| 6. *Accuracy*—Performed correctly each time |

Source: Adapted from J. Evans, 2008, *Managing for Quality and Performance*, 7th Ed., Mason, OH: Thomson Publishing.

institutionalized throughout the entire organization and its value chain.[79] When quality is institutionalized and valued by all, employees and managers alike become vigilant about continuously finding ways to improve it.[80]

Quality is a universal theme in the global economy and is a necessary but insufficient condition for competitive success.[81] Without quality, a firm's products lack credibility, meaning that customers don't think of them as viable options. Indeed, customers won't consider buying a product or using a service until they believe that it can satisfy at least their base-level expectations in terms of quality dimensions that are important to them.[82]

This was the case recently with Boeing's new 787 aircraft. This plane's lithium-ion battery system proved to be of questionable quality when parts of it were found to sometimes catch fire. In response to this quality-related problem, the U.S. Federal Aviation Administration (FAA) grounded the airplane for what turned out to be 123 days while Boeing corrected the problem in a way that satisfied the FAA. An indication of the depth of the problem is the fact that Boeing invested "200,000 hours of engineering, design, analysis and testing in the ultimate package of fixes." After meeting the FAA's expectations, airlines around the world, including those in the China, Japan, and the United States, began ordering additional 787s and prepared to receive some of those already ordered. At the time of its "re-launch," some wondered if passengers would believe the plane is "safe enough" to fly. Thus, Boeing suffered in terms of sales revenue and reputation until it was able to correct the 787's quality-related deficiencies.[83] Moreover, during this time, major competitor Airbus benefitted as customers ordered larger quantities of its A330.[84]

Quality affects competitive rivalry. The firm evaluating a competitor whose products suffer from poor quality can predict declines in the competitor's sales revenue until the quality issues are resolved. In addition, the firm can predict that the competitor likely won't be aggressive in its competitive actions until the quality problems are corrected in order to gain credibility with customers.[85] However, after the problems are corrected, that competitor is likely to take more aggressive competitive actions.

# 5-6 Likelihood of Response

The success of a firm's competitive action is affected by the likelihood that a competitor will respond to it as well as by the type (strategic or tactical) and effectiveness of that response. As noted earlier, a competitive response is a strategic or tactical action the firm takes to counter the effects of a competitor's competitive action. In general, a firm is likely to respond to a competitor's action when (1) the action leads to better use of the competitor's capabilities to develop a stronger competitive advantage or an improvement in its market position, (2) the action damages the firm's ability to use its core competencies to create or maintain an advantage, or (3) the firm's market position becomes harder to defend.[86]

In addition to market commonality and resource similarity and awareness, motivation, and ability, firms evaluate three other factors—type of competitive action, actor's reputation, and market dependence—to predict how a competitor is likely to respond to competitive actions (see Figure 5.2).

## 5-6a Type of Competitive Action

Competitive responses to strategic actions differ from responses to tactical actions. These differences allow the firm to predict a competitor's likely response to a competitive action that has been launched against it. Strategic actions commonly receive strategic responses and tactical actions receive tactical responses. In general, strategic actions elicit fewer total competitive responses because strategic responses, such as market-based moves, involve a significant commitment of resources and are difficult to implement and reverse.[87]

Another reason that strategic actions elicit fewer responses than do tactical actions is that the time needed to implement a strategic action and to assess its effectiveness can delay the competitor's response to that action.[88] In contrast, a competitor likely will respond quickly to a tactical action, such as when an airline company almost immediately matches a competitor's tactical action of reducing prices in certain markets. Either strategic actions or tactical actions that target a large number of a rival's customers are likely to elicit strong responses.[89] In fact, if the effects of a competitor's strategic action on the focal firm are significant (e.g., loss of market share, loss of major resources such as critical employees), a response is likely to be swift and strong.[90]

## 5-6b Actor's Reputation

In the context of competitive rivalry, an *actor* is the firm taking an action or a response while *reputation* is "the positive or negative attribute ascribed by one rival to another based on past competitive behavior."[91] A positive reputation may be a source of above-average returns, especially for consumer goods producers.[92] Thus, a positive corporate reputation is of strategic value[93] and affects competitive rivalry. To predict the likelihood of a competitor's response to a current or planned action, firms evaluate the responses that the competitor has taken previously when attacked—past behavior is assumed to be a predictor of future behavior.

Competitors are more likely to respond to strategic or tactical actions when they are taken by a market leader.[94] In particular, evidence suggests that commonly successful actions, especially strategic actions, will be quickly imitated. For example, although a second mover, IBM committed significant resources to enter the information service market. Competitors such as Hewlett-Packard (HP), Dell Inc., and others responded with strategic actions to enter this market as well.[95]

In a never-ending cascade of competitive actions and responses, these competitors continue jockeying among themselves for the most favorable market positions. Dell still trails IBM and HP in the worldwide server market share. However, the firm "commands the market for hyperscale servers which (are) 'density optimized' machines that companies use to support large data centers."[96] Dell's position in this market is a result of a strategic decision it made in 2007 to develop and sell "efficient, bare-bones" servers to firms such as Microsoft Corp., Amazon.com, and Salesforce.com Inc. Hyperscale servers are not pre-loaded with costly redundancy and availability capabilities, a fact that appeals to a number of customers. Because of the attractiveness of the hyperscale server space and Dell's enhanced reputation in overall server sales, competitors such as IBM and HP may respond with their own strategic actions.

In contrast to a firm with a strong reputation, competitors are less likely to respond to actions taken by a company with a reputation for risky, complex, and unpredictable competitive behavior. For example, the firm with a reputation as a price predator (an actor that frequently reduces prices to gain or maintain market share) generates few responses to its pricing tactical actions because price predators, which typically increase prices once their market share objective is reached, lack credibility with their competitors.[97]

*The Dell exhibit at the 2013 CeBIT Technology Trade Fair in Hannover, Germany. Through strategic actions it has taken, Dell has become the market leader in hyperscale servers.*

Sean Gallup/Getty mages news/Getty Images

### 5-6c Market Dependence

*Market dependence* denotes the extent to which a firm's revenues or profits are derived from a particular market.[98] In general, competitors with high market dependence are likely to respond strongly to attacks threatening their market position.[99] Interestingly, the threatened firm in these instances may not always respond quickly, even though an effective response to an attack on the firm's position in a critical market is important.

At an annual compound growth rate of 11 percent, recent predictions are that e-commerce sales will grow more than any other segment of the retail industry through at least 2017. Obviously, this growth rate is attractive to firms of all kinds including, as it turns out, Walmart. Established in 2000 as part of the world's largest firm by sales volume (with revenue of roughly $469 billion in 2012), Walmart.com is the giant retailer's attempt to become extremely successful in the e-commerce space. Today, over 1 million products are available through Walmart.com, with additional ones being regularly added to the site. Of course, competing in e-commerce pits Walmart.com squarely in competition with Amazon.com the largest online store on the planet.[100]

To date, Walmart's e-commerce business is generating roughly $9 billion per year in sales, which is just a bit over 2 percent of the firm's total revenue. Thus, Walmart currently has very little dependence for its success on the e-commerce market. Of course, Walmart is taking actions such as trying to better integrate its physical stores with its technological and logistics skills[101] and "considering a radical plan to have store customers deliver packages to online buyers, a new twist on speedier delivery services that the company hopes will enable it to better compete with Amazon.com, Inc."[102]

In contrast to Walmart, Amazon.com currently derives a strong majority of its sales volume from the e-commerce market, meaning that it has a high degree of market dependence. With $61 billion in revenue in 2012, the firm is substantially smaller than Walmart, although its total e-commerce sales revenue dwarfs that of Walmart.com's $9 billion. Given its dominant market position in e-commerce and in light of its dependence on the e-commerce market, it is virtually guaranteed that Amazon.com will continue responding to Walmart.com's competitive actions and responses.

## 5-7 Competitive Dynamics

Whereas competitive rivalry concerns the ongoing actions and responses between a firm and its direct competitors for an advantageous market position, *competitive dynamics* concerns the ongoing actions and responses among *all* firms competing within a market for advantageous positions.

To explain competitive dynamics, we explore the effects of varying rates of competitive speed in different markets (called slow-cycle, fast-cycle, and standard-cycle markets) on the behavior (actions and responses) of all competitors within a given market. Competitive behaviors as well as the reasons for taking them are similar within each market type, but differ across types of markets. Thus, competitive dynamics differ in slow-cycle, fast-cycle, and standard-cycle markets.

As noted in Chapter 1, firms want to sustain their competitive advantages for as long as possible, although no advantage is permanently sustainable. However, as we discuss next, the sustainability of the firm's competitive advantages differs by market type. In the main though, the degree of sustainability is affected by how quickly competitors can imitate a rival's competitive advantages and how costly it is to do so.

**Slow-cycle markets** are markets in which the firm's competitive advantages are shielded from imitation, commonly for long periods of time, and where imitation is costly.

### 5-7a Slow-Cycle Markets

**Slow-cycle markets** are markets in which the firm's competitive advantages are shielded from imitation, commonly for long periods of time, and where imitation is costly.[103] Thus, competitive advantages are sustainable over longer periods of time in slow-cycle markets.

Building a unique and proprietary capability produces a competitive advantage and success in a slow-cycle market. This type of advantage is difficult for competitors to understand. As discussed in Chapter 3, a difficult-to-understand and costly-to-imitate capability usually results from unique historical conditions, causal ambiguity, and/or social complexity. Copyrights and patents are examples of these types of capabilities. After a proprietary advantage is developed on the basis of using its capabilities, the competitive actions and responses a firm takes in a slow-cycle market are oriented to protecting, maintaining, and extending that advantage. Major strategic actions in these markets, such as acquisitions, usually carry less risk than in faster-cycle markets.[104]

Walt Disney Co. continues to extend its proprietary characters, such as Mickey Mouse, Minnie Mouse, and Goofy. These characters have a unique historical development as a result of Walt and Roy Disney's creativity and vision for entertaining people. Products based on the characters seen in Disney's animated films are sold through Disney's theme park shops as well as freestanding retail outlets called Disney Stores. Because copyrights shield it, the proprietary nature of Disney's advantage in terms of animated character trademarks protects the firm from imitation by competitors.

Consistent with another attribute of competition in a slow-cycle market, Disney protects its exclusive rights to its characters and their use. As with all firms competing in slow-cycle markets, Disney's competitive actions (such as building theme parks in France, Japan, and China) and responses (such as lawsuits to protect its right to fully control use of its animated characters) maintain and extend its proprietary competitive advantage while protecting it.

Patent laws and regulatory requirements such as those in the United States requiring FDA (Food and Drug Administration) approval to launch new products shield pharmaceutical companies' positions. Competitors in this market try to extend patents on their drugs to maintain advantageous positions that patents provide. However, after a patent expires, the firm is no longer shielded from competition, allowing generic imitations and usually leading to a loss of sales and profits. This was the case for Pfizer when Lipitor (which is the bestselling drug in history) went off patent in the fall of 2011. The firm's profits declined 19 percent in the first quarter after that event. The loss of patents is an industry-level concern too, as suggested by the fact that roughly $38.5 billion in sales revenue was lost in 2012 as a result of drugs going off patent.[105]

The competitive dynamics generated by firms competing in slow-cycle markets are shown in Figure 5.4. In slow-cycle markets, firms launch a product (e.g., a new drug) that

**Figure 5.4** Gradual Erosion of a Sustained Competitive Advantage

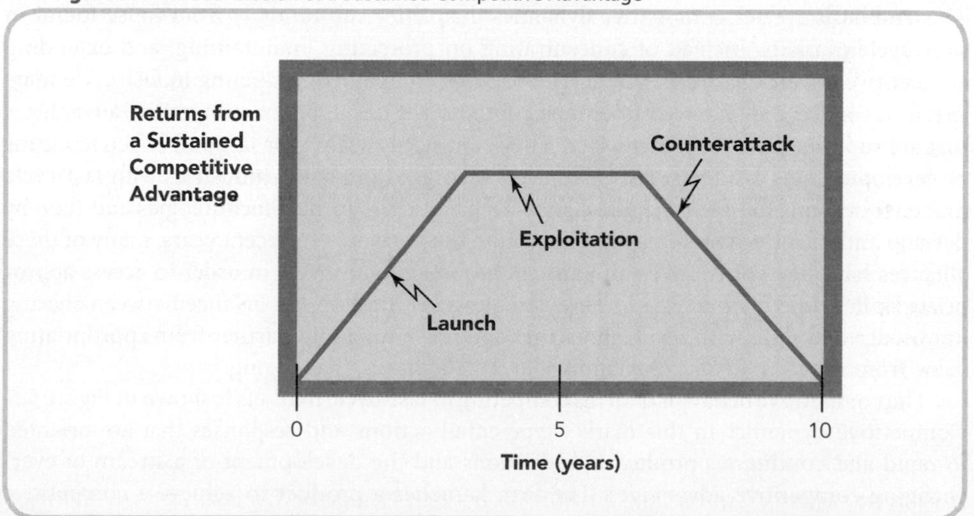


Source: Adapted from I. C. MacMillan, 1988, Controlling competitive dynamics by taking strategic initiative, *Academy of Management Executive*, II(2): 111–118.

has been developed through a proprietary advantage (e.g., R&D) and then exploit it for as long as possible while the product is shielded from competition. Eventually, competitors respond to the action with a counterattack. In markets for drugs, this counterattack commonly occurs as patents expire or are broken through legal means, creating the need for another product launch by the firm seeking a protected market position.

## 5-7b Fast-Cycle Markets

**Fast-cycle markets** are markets in which the firm's capabilities that contribute to competitive advantages aren't shielded from imitation and where imitation is often rapid and inexpensive.[106] Thus, competitive advantages aren't sustainable in fast-cycle markets. Firms competing in fast-cycle markets recognize the importance of speed; these companies appreciate that "time is as precious a business resource as money or head count—and that the costs of hesitation and delay are just as steep as going over budget or missing a financial forecast."[107] Such high-velocity environments place considerable pressures on top managers to quickly make strategic decisions that are also effective. The often substantial competition and technology-based strategic focus make the strategic decision complex, increasing the need for a comprehensive approach integrated with decision speed, two often-conflicting characteristics of the strategic decision process.[108]

Reverse engineering and the rate of technology diffusion facilitate the rapid imitation that takes place in fast-cycle markets. A competitor uses reverse engineering to quickly gain the knowledge required to imitate or improve the firm's products. Technology is diffused rapidly in fast-cycle markets, making it available to competitors in a short period. The technology often used by fast-cycle competitors isn't proprietary, nor is it protected by patents as is the technology used by firms competing in slow-cycle markets. For example, only a few hundred parts, which are readily available on the open market, are required to build a PC. Patents protect only a few of these parts, such as microprocessor chips. Interestingly, research also demonstrates that showing what an incumbent firm knows and its research capability can be a deterrent to other firms to enter a market, even a fast-cycle market.[109]

Fast-cycle markets are more volatile than slow-cycle and standard-cycle markets. Indeed, the pace of competition in fast-cycle markets is almost frenzied, as companies rely on innovations as the engines of their growth. Because prices often decline quickly in these markets, companies need to profit rapidly from their product innovations.

Recognizing this reality, firms avoid "loyalty" to any of their products, preferring to cannibalize their own before competitors learn how to do so through successful imitation. This emphasis creates competitive dynamics that differ substantially from those found in slow-cycle markets. Instead of concentrating on protecting, maintaining, and extending competitive advantages, as in slow-cycle markets, companies competing in fast-cycle markets focus on learning how to rapidly and continuously develop new competitive advantages that are superior to those they replace. They commonly search for fast and effective means of developing new products. For example, it is common in some industries with fast-cycle markets for firms to use strategic alliances to gain access to new technologies and thereby develop and introduce more new products into the market.[110] In recent years, many of these alliances have been offshore (with partners in foreign countries) in order to access appropriate skills while maintaining lower costs. However, finding the balance between sharing knowledge and skills with a foreign partner and preventing that partner from appropriating value from the focal firm's contributions to the alliance is challenging.[111]

**Fast-cycle markets** are markets in which the firm's capabilities that contribute to competitive advantages aren't shielded from imitation and where imitation is often rapid and inexpensive.

The competitive behavior of firms competing in fast-cycle markets is shown in Figure 5.5. Competitive dynamics in this market type entail actions and responses that are oriented to rapid and continuous product introductions and the development of a stream of ever-changing competitive advantages. The firm launches a product to achieve a competitive advantage and then exploits the advantage for as long as possible. However, the firm also

**Figure 5.5** Developing Temporary Advantages to Create Sustained Advantage

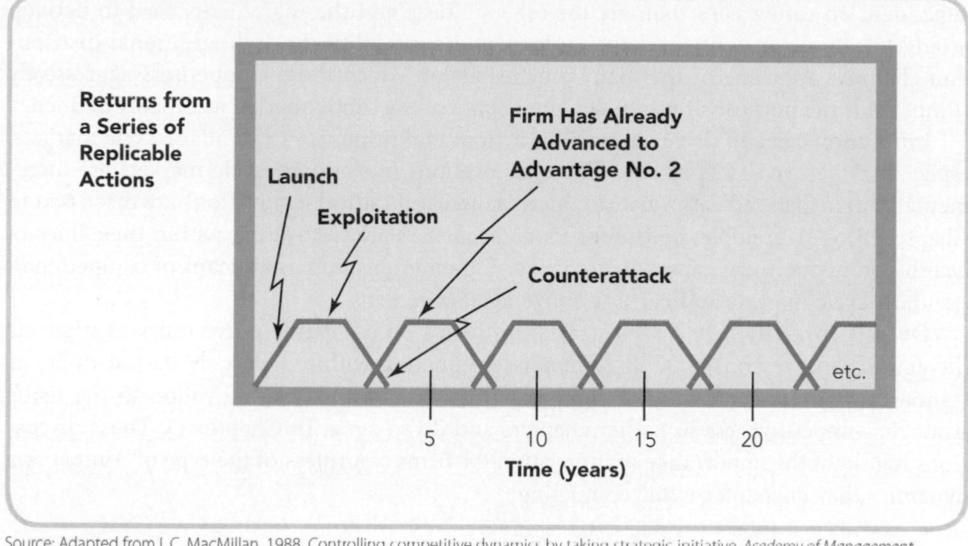


Source: Adapted from I. C. MacMillan, 1988, Controlling competitive dynamics by taking strategic initiative, *Academy of Management Executive*, II(2): 111–118.

tries to develop another temporary competitive advantage before competitors can respond to the first one. Thus, competitive dynamics in fast-cycle markets often result in rapid product upgrades as well as quick product innovations.[112]

As our discussion suggests, innovation plays a critical role in the competitive dynamics in fast-cycle markets. For individual firms then, innovation is a key source of competitive advantage. Through innovation, the firm can cannibalize its own products before competitors successfully imitate them and still maintain an advantage through next-generation products.

## 5-7c Standard-Cycle Markets

**Standard-cycle markets** are markets in which the firm's competitive advantages are partially shielded from imitation and imitation is moderately costly. Competitive advantages are partially sustainable in standard-cycle markets, but only when the firm is able to continuously upgrade the quality of its capabilities as a foundation for being able to stay ahead of competitors. The competitive actions and responses in standard-cycle markets are designed to seek large market shares, to gain customer loyalty through brand names, and to carefully control a firm's operations in order to consistently provide the same positive experience for customers.[113]

Companies competing in standard-cycle markets tend to serve many customers in what are typically highly competitive markets. Because the capabilities and core competencies on which their competitive advantages are based are less specialized, imitation is faster and less costly for standard-cycle firms than for those competing in slow-cycle markets. However, imitation is slower and more expensive in these markets than in fast-cycle markets. Thus, competitive dynamics in standard-cycle markets rest midway between the characteristics of dynamics in slow-cycle and fast-cycle markets. Imitation comes less quickly and is more expensive for standard-cycle competitors when a firm is able to develop economies of scale by combining coordinated and integrated design and manufacturing processes with a large sales volume for its products.

**Standard-cycle markets** are markets in which the firm's competitive advantages are partially shielded from imitation and imitation is moderately costly.

Because of large volumes, the size of mass markets, and the need to develop scale economies, the competition for market share is intense in standard-cycle markets. This form of competition is readily evident in the battles among consumer foods' producers, such as candy makers and major competitors Hershey Co.; Nestle, SA; Mondelez International, Inc.

(the new name for the former Kraft Foods Inc.); and Mars. (Of the firms, Hershey is far more dependent on candy sales than are the others.) Taste and the ingredients used to develop it, advertising campaigns, package designs, and availability through additional distribution channels are some of the many dimensions on which these competitors aggressively compete for the purpose of increasing their share of the candy market as broadly defined.[114]

Innovation can also drive competitive actions and responses in standard-cycle markets, especially when rivalry is intense. Some innovations in standard-cycle markets are incremental rather than radical in nature (incremental and radical innovations are discussed in Chapter 13). For example, consumer foods producers are innovating within their lines of healthy products. Today, many firms are relying on innovation as a means of competing in standard-cycle markets and earning above-average returns.

Overall, innovation has a substantial influence on competitive dynamics as it affects the actions and responses of all companies competing within a slow-cycle, fast-cycle, or standard-cycle market. We have emphasized the importance of innovation to the firm's strategic competitiveness in earlier chapters and do so again in Chapter 13. These discussions highlight the importance of innovation for firms regardless of the type of competitive dynamics they encounter while competing.

## SUMMARY

- Competitors are firms competing in the same market, offering similar products, and targeting similar customers. Competitive rivalry is the ongoing set of competitive actions and responses occurring between competitors as they compete against each other for an advantageous market position. The outcomes of competitive rivalry influence the firm's ability to sustain its competitive advantages as well as the level (average, below average, or above average) of its financial returns.
- Competitive behavior is the set of competitive actions and responses an individual firm takes while engaged in competitive rivalry. Competitive dynamics is the set of actions and responses taken by all firms that are competitors within a particular market.
- Firms study competitive rivalry in order to predict the competitive actions and responses each of their competitors are likely to take. Competitive actions are either strategic or tactical in nature. The firm takes competitive actions to defend or build its competitive advantages or to improve its market position. Competitive responses are taken to counter the effects of a competitor's competitive action. A strategic action or a strategic response requires a significant commitment of organizational resources, is difficult to successfully implement, and is difficult to reverse. In contrast, a tactical action or a tactical response requires fewer organizational resources and is easier to implement and reverse. For example, for an airline company, entering major new markets is an example of a strategic action or a strategic response; changing its prices in a particular market is an example of a tactical action or a tactical response.
- A competitor analysis is the first step the firm takes to be able to predict its competitors' actions and responses. In Chapter 2, we discussed what firms do to *understand* competitors. This discussion was extended in this chapter to describe what the firm does to *predict* competitors' market-based actions. Thus, understanding precedes prediction. Market commonality (the number of markets with which competitors are jointly involved and their importance to each) and resource similarity (how comparable competitors' resources are in terms of type and amount) are studied to complete a competitor analysis. In general, the greater the market commonality and resource similarity, the more firms acknowledge that they are direct competitors.
- Market commonality and resource similarity shape the firm's awareness (the degree to which it and its competitors understand their mutual interdependence), motivation (the firm's incentive to attack or respond), and ability (the quality of the resources available to the firm to attack and respond). Having knowledge of these characteristics of a competitor increases the quality of the firm's predictions about that competitor's actions and responses.
- In addition to market commonality and resource similarity and awareness, motivation, and ability, three more specific factors affect the likelihood a competitor will take competitive actions. The first of these concerns first-mover benefits. First movers, those taking an initial competitive action, often gain loyal customers and earn above-average returns until competitors can successfully respond to their action. Not all firms can be first movers in that they may lack the awareness, motivation, or ability required to engage in this type of competitive behavior. Moreover, some firms prefer to be a second mover (the firm responding to the first mover's action). One reason for this is that second movers, especially those acting quickly, can successfully compete against the first mover. By evaluating the first mover's product, customers' reactions to it, and the responses of other competitors to the first mover, the second mover may be able to avoid the early entrant's mistakes and

find ways to improve upon the value created for customers by the first mover's good or service. Late movers (those that respond a long time after the original action was taken) commonly are lower performers and are much less competitive.

- Organizational size tends to reduce the variety of competitive actions that large firms launch while it increases the variety of actions undertaken by smaller competitors. Ideally, the firm would prefer to initiate a large number of diverse actions when engaged in competitive rivalry. The third factor, quality, is a base denominator to competing successfully in the global economy. It is a necessary prerequisite to achieving competitive parity. It is a necessary but insufficient condition for establishing an advantage.
- The type of action (strategic or tactical) the firm took, the competitor's reputation for the nature of its competitor behavior, and that competitor's dependence on the market in which the action was taken are studied to predict a competitor's response to the firm's action. In general, the number of tactical responses taken exceeds the number of strategic responses. Competitors respond more frequently to the actions taken by the firm with a reputation for predictable and understandable competitive behavior, especially if that firm is a market leader. In general, the firm can predict that when its competitor is highly dependent for its revenue and profitability in the market in which the firm took a competitive action, that competitor is likely to launch a strong response. However, firms that are more diversified across markets are less likely to respond to a particular action that affects only one of the markets in which they compete.
- In slow-cycle markets, where competitive advantages can be maintained for at least a period of time, competitive dynamics often include firms taking actions and responses intended to protect, maintain, and extend their proprietary advantages. In fast-cycle markets, competition is substantial as firms concentrate on developing a series of temporary competitive advantages. This emphasis is necessary because firms' advantages in fast-cycle markets aren't proprietary and, as such, are subject to rapid and relatively inexpensive imitation. Standard-cycle markets have a level of competition between that in slow-cycle and fast-cycle markets; firms are moderately shielded from competition in these markets as they use capabilities that produce competitive advantages that are moderately sustainable. Competitors in standard-cycle markets serve mass markets and try to develop economies of scale to enhance their profitability. Innovation is vital to competitive success in each of the three types of markets. Companies should recognize that the set of competitive actions and responses taken by all firms differs by type of market.

## REVIEW QUESTIONS

1. Who are competitors? How are competitive rivalry, competitive behavior, and competitive dynamics defined in the chapter?
2. What is market commonality? What is resource similarity? What does it mean to say that these concepts are the building blocks for a competitor analysis?
3. How do awareness, motivation, and ability affect the firm's competitive behavior?
4. What factors affect the likelihood a firm will take a competitive action?
5. What factors affect the likelihood a firm will initiate a competitive response to a competitor's action(s)?
6. What competitive dynamics can be expected among firms competing in slow-cycle markets? In fast-cycle markets? In standard-cycle markets?

## EXPERIENTAL EXERCISES

### EXERCISE 1: TRAGEDY OF THE COMMONS

The tragedy of the commons is a dilemma that encompasses elements from social psychology and competitive behavior, among other fields. The concept first appeared in 1968 in an article by Garrett Hardin in the journal *Science*. The dilemma arises from a situation in which individuals act in ways that may not necessarily be in everyone's long-term interests. In general, the tragedy of the commons occurs when individuals all have equal access to a shared resource and each individual seeks to maximize his or her own self-interest. For a contemporary example, think about global warming in general or localized pollution in particular as instances of the dilemma: there is a distinct advantage for one country/state/business to pollute, which in turn imperils society as a whole.

As explained by R. De Young (1999, Tragedy of the commons, in D. E. Alexander and R. W. Fairbridge [Eds.] *Encyclopedia of Environmental Science*. Hingham, MA: Kluwer Academic Publishers), ecologist Garrett Hardin's parable involves a pasture "open to all." He asks us to imagine the grazing of animals on a common ground. Individuals are motivated to add to their flocks to increase personal wealth. Yet, every animal added to the total degrades the commons a small amount. Although the degradation for each additional animal is small relative to the gain in wealth for the owner, if all owners follow this pattern, the commons will ultimately be destroyed. And, being rational actors, all owners are motivated to add to their flock:

> *Therein is the tragedy. Each man is locked into a system that compels him to increase his herd without limit—in a world that is limited. Ruin is the destination toward which all men rush, each pursuing his own interest in a society that believes in the freedom of the commons (Hardin, 1968).*

In this exercise, the instructor needs four volunteers to participate. You will be asked to come to the front of the class and demonstrate the concept through a short exercise.

You should be familiar with the "Tragedy of the Commons". There are many good resources in the library, and you are encouraged to read Hardin's original 1968 article in *Science*, volume 162, pages 1243–1248, titled "The Tragedy of the Commons" before attending class.

## EXERCISE 2: IS BEING THE FIRST MOVER USUALLY ADVANTAGEOUS?

Henry Ford is often credited with saying that he would rather be the first person to be second. This is strange coming from the innovator of the mass-produced automobile in the United States. So is the first-mover advantage really a myth, or is it something for which every firm should strive?

First movers are typically considered to be the ones that initially introduce an innovative product or service into a market segment (in other words, first to market in a new segment). The notion subscribed to first movers is that being one creates an almost impenetrable competitive advantage that later entrants find difficult to overcome. However, history is replete with situations where second or later movers find success. If the best way to succeed in the future is to understand the past, then an understanding of why certain first movers succeeded and others failed should be instructive. Accordingly, this exercise requires you to investigate a first mover and identify specifically why, or why not, it was able to hold onto its first-mover advantage.

### Part One

This assignment can be done individually or in a team. Select an industry that interests you or your team. Research that industry and identify one or two instances of a first mover; research the introduction of a new offering into new market segments. For example, you might pick consumer electronics and look for firms that initiated new products in new market segments. Your choice of industry must be approved in advance by your instructor as duplication of industries is to be avoided.

### Part Two

Each individual or team is to present their findings with the discussion centering on the following at a minimum:

- Brief history and description of the industry chosen (e.g., was this a fast-, standard-, or slow-cycle market at the time the first mover initiated its strategic action)?
- How has innovation of new products traditionally been accomplished in this industry: through new firms entering the market or by existing firms launching new offerings?
- Identify one or two first movers and provide a review of what happened. If the product or offering is still considered successful, describe why. If not, why not?
- What did you learn as a result of this exercise? Do you consider trying to be the first mover a wise competitive action to take? Is your answer dependent upon industry, timing, or luck?

# VIDEO CASE

## A FOCUS ON COMPETITIVE DYNAMICS: HYUNDAI SOUTH KOREA

With an objective "to sell more cars for less than the competition," consumers are flocking to Hyundai dealerships, causing the firm to recently experience an increase in its sales volume in the U.S. market. Auto executives both inside and outside the company recognize Hyundai's ability and desire to dominate the market through top-level quality. Durability, as evidenced by longer warranties and greater consumer awareness through major advertising, is foundational to Hyundai's strong rebound.

Be prepared to discuss the following concepts and questions in class:

### Concepts

- Competitive behavior
- Competitive dynamics
- Multimarket competition
- Competitive response
- Strategic actions
- Late movers

### Questions

1. How would you describe Hyundai's competitive behavior?
2. What kind of competitive dynamics might you expect from Hyundai and other automakers?
3. Is Hyundai involved in multimarket competition? Why or why not?
4. What impact will market commonality have on competitive responses in the auto industry?
5. What strategic actions and/or responses might occur as a result of your answer to question 4?
6. Can Hyundai be identified as a late mover? If so, why? If you determine that Hyundai is a late mover, what consequences should the company be aware of that result from being a late mover?

# NOTES


1. S. Carnahan & D. Somaya, 2013, Alumni effects and relational advantage: The impact of outsourcing when your buyer hires employees from your competitors, *Academy of Management Journal*, in press; M.-J. Chen & D. Miller, 2012, Competitive dynamics: Themes, trends, and a prospective research platform, *Academy of Management Annals*, 6: 135–210; M.-J. Chen, 1996, Competitor analysis and interfirm rivalry: Toward a theoretical integration, *Academy of Management Review*, 21: 100–134.
2. P. C. Patel, S. A. Fernhaber, P. P. McDougall-Covin, & R. P. van der Have, 2013, Beating competitors to international markets: The value of geographically balanced networks for innovation, *Strategic Management Journal*, in press.
3. J. Bloodgood, 2013, Crowdsourcing: Useful for problem solving, but what about value capture? *Academy of Management Review*, 38: 455–457; T. Zahavi & D. Lavie, 2013, Intra-industry diversification and firm performance, *Strategic Management Journal*, 34: 978–998; M. Chen, H. Lin, & J. Michel, 2010, Navigating in a hypercompetitive environment: The roles of action aggressiveness and TMT integration, *Strategic Management Journal*, 31: 1410–1430.
4. P. T. M. Ingenbleek & I. A. van der Lans, 2013, Relating price strategies and price-setting practices, *European Journal of Marketing*, 47: 27–48; A. Eapen, 2012, Social structure and technology spillovers from foreign to domestic firms, *Journal of International Business Studies*, 43: 244–263.
5. F. J. Mas-Ruiz, F. Ruiz-Moreno, & A. L. de Guevara Martinez, 2013, Asymmetric rivalry within and between strategic groups, *Strategic Management Journal*, in press; P. J. Derfus, P. G. Maggitti, C. M. Grimm, & K. G. Smith, 2008, The red queen effect: Competitive actions and firm performance, *Academy of Management Journal*, 51: 61–80; C. M. Grimm, H. Lee, & K. G. Smith, 2006, *Strategy as Action: Competitive Dynamics and Competitive Advantage*, New York: Oxford University Press.
6. R. B. Mackay & R. Chia, 2012, Choice, chance, and unintended consequences in strategic change: A process understanding of the rise and fall of NorthCo Automotive, *Academy of Management Journal*, 56: 1–13; D. Di Gregorio, D. Thomas, & F. de Castilla, 2008, Competition between emerging market and multinational firms: Wal-Mart and Mexican retailers, *International Journal of Management*, 25: 532–545, 593.
7. M. Srivastava, A. Frankly, & L. Martinette, 2013, Building a sustainable competitive advantage, *Journal of Technology Management & Innovation*, 8: 47–60; G. J. Kilduff, H. A. Elfenbein, & B. M. Staw, 2010, The psychology of rivalry: A relationally dependent analysis of competition, *Academy of Management Journal*, 53: 943–969; D. G. Sirmon, S. Gove, & M. A. Hitt, 2008, Resource management in dyadic competitive rivalry: The effects of resource bundling and deployment, *Academy of Management Journal*, 51: 919–935.
8. S.-J. Chang & S. H. Park, 2012, Winning strategies in China: Competitive dynamics between MNCs and local firms, *Long Range Planning*, 45: 1–15; S. K. Ethitaj & D. H. Zhu, 2008, Performance effects of imitative entry, *Strategic Management Journal*, 29: 797–817.
9. A. Nair & D. D. Selover, 2012, A study of competitive dynamics, *Journal of Business Research*, 65: 355–361; Grimm, Lee, & Smith, *Strategy as Action*.
10. R. Chellappa, V. Sambamurthy, & N. Saraf, 2010, Competing in crowded markets: Multimarket contact and the nature of competition in the enterprise systems software industry, *Information Systems Research*: *Special Issue on Digital Systems and Competition*, 21: 614–630.
11. T. Yu, M. Subramaniam, & A. A. Cannella, 2009, Rivalry deterrence in international markets: Contingencies governing the mutual forbearance hypothesis, *Academy of Management Journal*, 52: 127–147; K. G. Smith, W. J. Ferrier, & H. Ndofor, 2001, Competitive dynamics research: Critique and future directions, in M. A. Hitt, R. E. Freeman, & J. S. Harrison (eds.), *Handbook of Strategic Management*, Oxford, UK: Blackwell Publishers, 326.
12. F. Bridoux, K. G. Smith, & C. M. Grimm, 2011, The management of resources: Temporal effects of different types of actions on performance, *Journal of Management*, 33: 1281–1310; G. Young, K. G. Smith, & C. M. Grimm, 1996, "Austrian" and industrial organization perspectives on firm-level competitive activity and performance, *Organization Science*, 73: 243–254.
13. M. Esteri, 2013, Big tobacco is about to dive into e-cigarettes, *Wall Street Journal*, www.wsj.com, May 29; C. Lobello, 2013, E-cigarettes: Could they change the tobacco industry forever? *The Week*, www.wsj.theweek.com, April 26.
14. R. Katila, E. L. Chen, & H. Piezunka, 2012, All the right moves: How entrepreneurial firms compete effectively, *Strategic Entrepreneurship Journal*, 6: 116–132; J. Marcel, P. Barr, & I. Duhaime, 2011, The influence of executive cognition on competitive dynamics, *Strategic Management Journal*, 32: 115–138.
15. R. Casadesus-Masanell & F. Zhu, 2013, Business model innovation and competitive imitation: The case of sponsor-based business models, *Strategic Management Journal*, 34: 464–482; M.-J. Chen & D. C. Hambrick, 1995, Speed, stealth, and selective attack: How small firms differ from large firms in competitive behavior, *Academy of Management Journal*, 38: 453–482.
16. J. M. Mol & N. M. Wijnberg, 2011, From resources to value and back: Competition between and within organizations, *British Journal of Management*, 22: 77–95.
17. V. K. Patel, T. M. Pieper, & J. F. Hair, Jr., 2012, The global family business: Challenges and drivers for cross-border growth, *Business Horizons*, 55: 231–239.
18. M. A. Abebe & A. Angriawan, 2013, Organizational and competitive influences of exploration and exploitation activities in small firms, *Journal of Business Research*, in press; V. Rindova, W. Ferrier, & R. Wiltbank, 2010, Value from gestalt: How sequences of competitive actions create advantage for firms in nascent markets, *Strategic Management Journal*, 31: 1474–1497; T. Yu & A. A. Cannella, Jr., Rivalry between multinational enterprises: An event history approach, *Academy of Management Journal*, 50: 665–686.
19. J. Villanueva, A. H. Van de Ven, & H. Sapienza, 2012, Resource mobilization in entrepreneurial firms, *Journal of Business Venturing*, 27: 19–30; Smith, Ferrier, & Ndofor, Competitive dynamics research, 319.
20. C. Boone, F. C. Wezel, & A. van Witteloostuijn, 2013, Joining the pack or going solo? A dynamic theory of new firm positioning, *Journal of Business Venturing*, 28: 511–527; H. Ndofor, D. G. Sirmon, & X. He, 2011, Firm resources, competitive actions and performance: Investigating a mediated model with evidence from the in-vitro diagnostics industry, *Strategic Management Journal*, 32: 640–657.
21. M. Gruber, I. C. MacMillan, & J. D. Thompson, 2013, Escaping the prior knowledge corridor: What shapes the number and variety of market opportunities identified before market entry of technology start-ups? *Organization Science*, 24: 280–300.
22. L. M. Ellram, W. L. Tate, & E. G. Feitzinger, 2013, Factor-market rivalry and competition for supply chain resources, *Journal of Supply Chain Management*, 49: 29–46; D. G. Sirmon, M. A. Hitt, J. Arregle, & J. Campbell, 2010, The dynamic interplay of capability strengths and weaknesses: Investigating the bases of temporary competitive advantage, *Strategic Management Journal*, 31: 1386–1409.
23. S. Crowly, 2013, The smartphone market's radical shakeup, *CNNMoney*, www.money.cnn.com, January 29.

24. W. Shi & J. E. Prescott, 2012, Rhythm and entrainment of acquisition and alliance initiatives and firm performance: A temporal perspective, *Organization Studies*, 33: 1281–1310.
25. H. Rahmandad, 2012, Impact of growth opportunities and competition on firm-level capability development trade-offs, *Organization Science*, 34: 138–154; Y. Y. Kor & J. T. Mahoney, 2005, How dynamics, management, and governance of resource deployments influence firm-level performance, *Strategic Management Journal*, 26: 489–496.
26. L. Mulotte, P. Dussauge, & W. Mitchell, 2013, Does pre-entry licensing undermine the performance of subsequent independent activities? Evidence from the global aerospace industry, 1944–2000, *Strategic Management Journal*, 34: 358–372; K. G. Fouskas & D. A. Drossos, 2010, The role of industry perceptions in competitive responses, *Industrial Management & Data Systems*, 110: 477–494.
27. L. K. S. Lim, 2013, Mapping competitive prediction capability: Construct conceptualization and performance payoffs, *Journal of Business Research*, 66: 1576–1586; J. C. Baum & A. Satorra, 2007, The persistence of abnormal returns at industry and firm levels: Evidence from Spain, *Strategic Management Journal*, 28: 707–722.
28. J.-L. Arregle, T. L. Miller, M. A. Hitt, & P. W. Beamish, 2013, Do regions matter? An integrated institutional and semiglobalization perspective on the internationalization of MNEs, *Strategic Management Journal*, 34: 910–934; B. I. Park & P. N. Ghauri, 2011, Key factors affecting acquisition of technological capabilities from foreign acquiring firms by small and medium sized local firms, *Journal of World Business*, 46: 116–125.
29. N. Zhou, S. H. Park, & G. R. Ungson, 2013, Profitable growth: Avoiding the 'growth fetish' in emerging markets, *Business Horizons*, 56: 473–481; Chen, Competitor analysis, 108.
30. O. Alexy, G. George, & A. Salter, 2013, Cui Bono? The selective revealing of knowledge and its implications for innovative activity, *Academy of Management Review*, in press; Chen, Competitor analysis, 109.
31. T. Lawton, T. Rajwani, & P. Reinmoeller, 2012, Do you have a survival instinct? Leveraging genetic codes to achieve fit in hostile business environments, *Business Horizons*, 55: 81–91; 2011, The power of blindspots. What companies don't know, surprises them. What they don't want to know, kills them, *Strategic Direction*, 27(4): 3–4; D. Ng, R. Westgren, & S. Sonka, 2009, Competitive blind spots in an institutional field, *Strategic Management Journal*, 30: 349–369.
32. E. Metayer, 2013, How intelligent is your company? *Competia*, www.competia.com, March.
33. J. Neff, 2011, P&G e-commerce chief sees blurring of sales, marketing, *Advertising Age*, April 11, 8.
34. 2013, About YRC, YRC homepage, www.yrc.com, May 29.
35. J. W. Upson, D. J. Ketchen, Jr., B. L. Connelly, & A. L. Ranft, 2012, Competitor analysis and foothold moves, *Academy of Management Journal*, 55: 93–110; Chen, Competitor analysis, 106.
36. T. Yu & A. A. Cannella, Jr., 2013, A comprehensive review of multimarket competition research, *Journal of Management*, 39: 76–109; J. Anand, L. F. Mesquita, & R. S. Vassolo, 2009, The dynamics of multimarket competition in exploration and exploitation activities, *Academy of Management Journal*, 52: 802–821.
37. A. Nair & D. D. Selover, 2012, A study of competitive dynamics, *Journal of Business Research*, 65: 355–361.
38. W. Kang, B. Bayus, & S. Balasubramanian, 2010, The strategic effects of multimarket contact: Mutual forbearance and competitive response in the personal computer industry, *Journal of Marketing Research*, 47: 415–427.
39. V. Bilotkach, 2011, Multimarket contact and intensity of competition: Evidence from an airline merger, *Review of Industrial Organization*, 38: 95–115; H. R. Greve, 2008, Multimarket contact and sales growth: Evidence from insurance, *Strategic Management Journal*, 29: 229–249; J. Gimeno, 1999, Reciprocal threats in multimarket rivalry: Staking out "spheres of influence" in the U.S. airline industry, *Strategic Management Journal*, 20: 101–128.
40. L. A. Costa, K. Cool, & I. Dierickx, 2013, The competitive implications of the deployment of unique resources, *Strategic Management Journal*, 34: 445–463; Chen, Competitor analysis, 107.
41. J. Haleblian, G. McNamara, K. Kolev, & B. J. Dykes, 2012, Exploring firm characteristics that differentiate leaders from followers in industry merger waves: A competitive dynamics perspective, *Strategic Management Journal*, 33: 1037–1052; Chen, Competitor analysis, 110.
42. C. Flammer, 2013, Corporate social responsibility and shareholder reaction: The environmental awareness of investors, *Academy of Management Journal*, in press.
43. J. Tang & B. S.-C. Liu, 2012, Strategic alignment and foreign entry performance: A holistic approach of the impact of entry timing, mode and location, *Business and Systems Research*, 6: 456–478; R. S. Livengood & R. K. Reger, 2010, That's our turf! Identity domains and competitive dynamics, *Academy of Management Review*, 35: 48–66.
44. B. Tita, 2013, Caterpillar expected to cut 2013 forecasts, *Wall Street Journal*, www.wsj.com, April 21.
45. Nair & Selover, *A study of competitive dynamics*; S. H. Park & D. Zhou, 2005, Firm heterogeneity and competitive dynamics in alliance formation, *Academy of Management Review*, 30: 531–554.
46. T.-J. A. Peng, S. Pike, J. C.-H. Yang, & G. Roos, 2012, Is cooperation with competitors a good idea? An example in practice, *British Journal of Management*, 23: 532–560; Chen, Competitor analysis, 113.
47. C. Williams & S. Lee, 2011, Entrepreneurial contexts and knowledge coordination within the multinational corporation, *Journal of World Business*, 46: 253–264; M. Leiblein & T. Madsen, 2009, Unbundling competitive heterogeneity: Incentive structures and capability influences on technological innovation, *Strategic Management Journal*, 30: 711–735.
48. R. Makadok, 2010, The interaction effect of rivalry restraint and competitive advantage on profit: Why the whole is less than the sum of the parts, *Management Science*, 56: 356–372.
49. C. M. Grimm & K. G. Smith, 1997, *Strategy as Action: Industry Rivalry and Coordination*, Cincinnati: South-Western Publishing Co., 125.
50. J. Alcacer, C. L. Dezso, & M. Zhao, 2013, Firm rivalry, knowledge accumulation, and MNE location choices, *Journal of International Business Studies*, 44: 504–520; B. Markens, 2011, Be aware of your competition to increase market share, *Paperboard Packaging*, 96(1): 11.
51. G. Gavetti, 2012, Perspective—Toward a behavioral theory of strategy, *Organization Science*, 23: 267–285; B. L. Connelly, L. Tihanyi, S. T. Certo, & M. A. Hitt, 2010, Marching to the beat of different drummers: The influence of institutional owners on competitive actions, *Academy of Management Journal*, 53: 723–742.
52. 2011, Nokia and Microsoft announce plans for a broad strategic partnership to build a new global mobile ecosystem, Microsoft Home Page, www.microsoft.com, February 10.
53. M.-J. Lee, 2013, Samsung makes space on Nokia's turf, *Wall Street Journal*, www.wsj.com, May 30; J. D. Stoll, 2013, Nokia loses lead in home market, *Wall Street Journal*, www.wsj.com, May 28.
54. J. Schumpeter, 1934, *The Theory of Economic Development*, Cambridge, MA: Harvard University Press.
55. S. Bakker, H. van Lente, & M. T. H. Meeus, 2012, Dominance in the prototyping phase—The case of hydrogen passenger cars, *Research Policy*, 41: 871–883.
56. L. Sleuwaegen & J. Onkelinx, 2013, International commitment, post-entry growth and survival of international new ventures, *Journal of Business Venturing*, in press; F. F. Suarez & G. Lanzolla, 2007, The role of environmental dynamics in building a first mover advantage theory, *Academy of Management Review*, 32: 377–392.
57. G. M. McNamara, J. Haleblian, & B. J. Dykes, 2008, The performance implications of participating in an acquisition wave: Early mover advantages, bandwagon effects, and the moderating influence

of industry characteristics and acquirer tactics, *Academy of Management Journal*, 51, 113–130.
58. R. K. Sinha & C. H. Noble, 2008, The adoption of radical manufacturing technologies and firm survival, *Strategic Management Journal*, 29: 943–962; D. P. Forbes, 2005, Managerial determinants of decision speed in new ventures, *Strategic Management Journal*, 26: 355–366.
59. H. R. Greve, 2009, Bigger and safer: The diffusion of competitive advantage, *Strategic Management Journal*, 30: 1–23; W. T. Robinson & S. Min, 2002, Is the first to market the first to fail? Empirical evidence for industrial goods businesses, *Journal of Marketing Research*, 39: 120–128.
60. J. C. Short & G. T. Payne, 2008, First-movers and performance: Timing is everything, *Academy of Management Review*, 33: 267–270.
61. E. de Oliveira & W. B. Werther, Jr., 2013, Resilience: Continuous renewal of competitive advantages, *Business Horizons*, 56: 333–342.
62. N. M. Jakopin & A. Klein, 2012, First-mover and incumbency advantages in mobile telecommunications, *Journal of Business Research*, 65: 362–370.
63. H. Wang, J. Choi, G. Wan, & J. Q. Dong, 2013, Slack resources and the rent-generating potential of firm-specific knowledge, *Journal of Management*, in press; K. Mellahi & A. Wilkinson, 2010, A study of the association between level of slack reduction following downsizing and innovation output, *Journal of Management Studies*, 47: 483–508.
64. R. Mudambi & T. Swift, 2013, Knowing when to leap: Transitioning between exploitative and explorative R&D, *Strategic Management Journal*, 34: in press; M. B. Lieberman & D. B. Montgomery, 1988, First-mover advantages, *Strategic Management Journal*, 9: 41–58.
65. A. Hawk, G. Pacheco-De-Almeida, & B. Yeung, 2013, Fast-mover advantages: Speed capabilities and entry into the emerging submarket of Atlantic basin LNG, *Strategic Management Journal*, 34: in press; G. Pacheco-De- Almeida, 2010, Erosion, time compression, and self-displacement of leaders in hypercompetitive environments, *Strategic Management Journal*, 31: 1498–1526.
66. F. Zhu & M. Iansiti, 2012, Entry into platform-based markets, *Strategic Management Journal*, 33: 88–106; S. Jonsson & P. Regnér, 2009, Normative barriers to imitation: Social complexity of core competences in a mutual fund industry, *Strategic Management Journal*, 30: 517–536.
67. M. A. Stanko & J. D. Bohlmann, 2013, Demand-side inertia factors and their benefits for innovativeness, *Journal of the Academy of Marketing Science*, in press; M. Poletti, B. Engelland, & H. Ling, 2011, An empirical study of declining lead times: Potential ramifications on the performance of early market entrants, *Journal of Marketing Theory and Practice*, 19(1): 27–38.
68. S. Bin, 2011, First-mover advantages: Flexible or not?, *Journal of Management & Marketing Research*, 7: 1–13; J. Gimeno, R. E. Hoskisson, B. B. Beal, & W. P. Wan, 2005, Explaining the clustering of international expansion moves: A critical test in the U.S. telecommunications industry, *Academy of Management Journal*, 48: 297–319; K. G. Smith, C. M. Grimm, & M. J. Gannon, 1992, *Dynamics of Competitive Strategy*, Newberry Park, CA: Sage Publications.
69. M. Weiker, 2013, Competitors challenge top rater Angie's List, *The Columbus Dispatch*, www.dispatch.com, May 19.
70. A. Yaprak, 2012, Market entry barriers in China: A commentary essay, *Journal of Business Research*, 65: 1216–1218; A. Fleury & M. Fleury, 2009, Understanding the strategies of late-movers in international manufacturing, *International Journal of Production Economics*, 122: 340–350; J. Li & R. K. Kozhikode, 2008, Knowledge management and innovation strategy: The challenge for latecomers in emerging economies, *Asia Pacific Journal of Management*, 25: 429–450.
71. F. Karakaya & P. Yannopoulos, 2011, Impact of market entrant characteristics on incumbent reactions to market entry, *Journal of Strategic Marketing*, 19(2): 171–185; S. D. Dobrev & G. R. Carroll, 2003, Size (and competition) among organizations: Modeling scale based selection among automobile producers in four major countries, 1885–1981, *Strategic Management Journal*, 24: 541–558.
72. W. Stam, S. Arzianian, & T. Elfring, 2013, Social capital of entrepreneurs and small firm performance: A meta-analysis of contextual and methodological moderators, *Journal of Business Venturing*, in press; L. F. Mesquita & S. G. Lazzarini, 2008, Horizontal and vertical relationships in developing economies: Implications for SMEs access to global markets, *Academy of Management Journal*, 51: 359–380.
73. C. Zhou & A. Van Witteloostuijn, 2010, Institutional constraints and ecological processes: Evolution of foreign-invested enterprises in the Chinese construction industry, 1993–2006, *Journal of International Business Studies*, 41: 539 556; M. A. Hitt, L. Bierman, & J. D. Collins, 2007, The strategic evolution of U.S. law firms, *Business Horizons*, 50: 17–28; D. Miller & M. J. Chen, 1996, The simplicity of competitive repertoires: An empirical analysis, *Strategic Management Journal*, 17: 419–440.
74. Young, Smith, & Grimm, "Austrian" and industrial organization perspectives.
75. P. B. Crosby, 1980, *Quality Is Free*, New York: Penguin.
76. W. E. Deming, 1986, *Out of the Crisis*, Cambridge, MA: MIT Press.
77. R. C. Ford & D. R. Dickson, 2012, Enhancing customer self-efficacy in co-producing service experiences, *Business Horizons*, 55: 179–188; G. C. Avery & H. Bergsteiner, 2011, Sustainable leadership practices for enhancing business resilience and performance, *Strategy & Leadership*, 39(3): 5–15.
78. L. A. Bettencourt & S. W. Brown, 2013, From goods to great: Service innovation in a product-dominated company, *Business Horizons*, 56: 277–283; X. Luo, 2010, Product competitiveness and beating analyst earnings target, *Journal of the Academy of Marketing Science*, 38: 253–264.
79. F. Pakdil, 2010, The effects of TQM on corporate performance. *The Business Review*, 15: 242–248; A. Azadegan, K. J. Dooley, P. L. Carter, & J. R. Carter, 2008, Supplier innovativeness and the role of interorganizational learning in enhancing manufacturing capabilities, *Journal of Supply Chain Management*, 44(4): 14–35.
80. M. Terziovski & P. Hermel, 2011, The role of quality management practice in the performance of integrated supply chains: A multiple cross-case analysis, *The Quality Management Journal*, 18(2): 10–25; K. E. Weick & K. M. Sutcliffe, 2001, *Managing the Unexpected*, San Francisco: Jossey-Bass, 81–82.
81. D. P. McIntyre, 2011, In a network industry, does product quality matter? *Journal of Product Innovation Management*, 28: 99–108; G. Macintosh, 2007, Customer orientation, relationship quality, and relational benefits to the firm, *Journal of Services Marketing*, 21: 150–159.
82. Q. Liu & D. Zhang, 2013, Dynamic pricing competition with strategic customers under vertical product differentiation, *Management Science*, 59: 84–101; S. Thirumalai & K. K. Sinha, 2011, Product recalls in the medical device industry: An empirical exploration of the sources and financial consequences, *Management Science*, 57: 376–392.
83. J. Chiu & D. Cameron, 2013, China clears Boeing 787 for commercial service, *Wall Street Journal*, www.wsj.com, May 23; P. LeBeau, 2013, Boeing dreamliners back in the air after lengthy grounding, *NBC News Business*, www.nbcnews.com, May 20; A. Pasztor, 2013, How Boeing rescued the 787, *Wall Street Journal*, www.wsj.com, April 20.
84. R. Aboulafia, 2013, 787 delays continue to boost Airbus, *Forbes*, www.forbes.com, May 24.
85. M. Su & V. R. Rao, 2011, Timing decisions of new product preannouncement and launch with competition, *International Journal of Production Economics*, 129(1): 51–64.
86. M. L. Sosa, 2013, Decoupling market incumbency from organizational prehistory: Locating the real sources of competitive advantage in R&D for radical innovation, *Strategic Management Journal*, 34: 245–255; T. R. Crook, D. J. Ketchen, J. G. Combs, & S. Y. Todd, 2008, Strategic resources and

performance: A meta-analysis, *Strategic Management Journal*, 29: 1141–1154.

87. R. K. Kozhikode & J. Li, 2012, Political pluralism, public policies, and organizational choices: Banking branch expansion in India, 1948–2003, *Academy of Management Journal*, 55: 339–359; C. Lutz, R. Kemp, & S. Gerhard Dijkstra, 2010, Perceptions regarding strategic and structural entry barriers, *Small Business Economics*, 35: 19–33; M. J. Chen & I. C. MacMillan, 1992, Nonresponse and delayed response to competitive moves, *Academy of Management Journal*, 35: 539–570.
88. S. M. Ben-Menahern, Z. Kwee, H. W. Volberda, & F. A. J. Van Den Bosch, 2013, Strategic renewal over time: The enabling role of potential absorptive capacity in aligning internal and external rates of change, *Long Range Planning*, 46: 216–235; M. J. Chen, K. G. Smith, & C. M. Grimm, 1992, Action characteristics as predictors of competitive responses, *Management Science*, 38: 439–455.
89. S. Ansari & P. Krop, 2012, Incumbent performance in the face of a radical innovation: Towards a framework for incumbent challenger dynamics, *Research Policy*, 41: 1357–1374; M. J. Chen & D. Miller, 1994, Competitive attack, retaliation and performance: An expectancy-valence framework, *Strategic Management Journal*, 15: 85–102.
90. K. Muller, K. Huschelrath, & V. Bilotkach, 2012, The construction of a low-cost airline network—facing competition and exploring new markets, *Managerial and Decision Economics*, 33: 485–499; N. Huyghebaert & L. M. van de Gucht, 2004, Incumbent strategic behavior in financial markets and the exit of entrepreneurial start-ups, *Strategic Management Journal*, 25: 669–688.
91. Smith, Ferrier, & Ndofor, Competitive dynamics research, 333.
92. V. Babic-Hodovic, M. Arlsanagic, & E. Mehic, 2013, Importance of internal marketing for service companies corporate reputation and customer satisfaction, *Journal of Business Administration Research*, 2: 49–57; T. Obloj & L. Capron, 2011, Role of resource gap and value appropriation: Effect of reputation gap on price premium in online auctions, *Strategic Management Journal*, 32: 447–456; V. P. Rindova, A. P. Petkova, & S. Kotha, 2007, Standing out: How firms in emerging markets build reputation, *Strategic Organization*, 5: 31–70.
93. Q. Gu & X. Lu, 2013, Unraveling the mechanisms of reputation and alliance formation: A study of venture capital syndication in China, *Strategic Management Journal*, 34: in press; D. D. Bergh & P. Gibbons, 2011, The stock market reaction to the hiring of management consultants: A signalling theory approach, *Journal of Management Studies*, 48: 544–567; P. W. Roberts & G. R. Dowling, 2003, Corporate reputation and sustained superior financial performance, *Strategic Management Journal*, 24: 1077–1093.
94. B. Larraneta, S. A. Zahra, & J. L. G. Gonzalez, 2013, Strategic repertoire variety and new venture growth: The moderating effects of origin and industry dynamism, *Strategic Management Journal*, in press; W. J. Ferrier, K. G. Smith, & C. M. Grimm, 1999, The role of competitive actions in market share erosion and industry dethronement: A study of industry leaders and challengers, *Academy of Management Journal*, 42: 372–388.
95. R. Karlgaard, 2011, Transitions: Michael reinvents Dell, *Forbes*, www.forbes.com, May 9.
96. 2013, Dell floats clout with 'hyperscale' servers, *Wall Street Journal*, www.blogs.wsj.com, May 21.
97. M. Fassnacht & S. El Husseini, 2013, EDLP versus Hi-Lo pricing strategies in retailing—a state of the art article, *Journal of Business Economics*, 83: 259–289; Smith, Grimm, & Gannon, *Dynamics of Competitive Strategy*.
98. J. Xia & S. Li, 2013, The divestiture of acquired subunits: A resource dependence approach, *Strategic Management Journal*, 34: 131–148; A. Karnani & B. Wernerfelt, 1985, Multiple point competition, *Strategic Management Journal*, 6: 87–97.
99. L. Kwanghui, H. Chesbrough, & R. Yi, 2010, Open innovation and patterns of R&D competition, *International Journal of Technology Management*, 52: 295–321; Smith, Ferrier, & Ndofor, Competitive dynamics research, 330.
100. C. O'Connor, 2013, Wal-Mart vs. Amazon: World's biggest e-commerce battle could boil down to vegetables, *Forbes*, www.forbes.com, April 23.
101. J. Wohl & A. Barr, 2013, Wal-Mart steps up its online game with help from stores, *Reuters*, www.reuters.com, March 26.
102. A. Barr & J. Wohl, 2013, Exclusive: Wal-Mart may get customers to deliver packages to online buyers, *Reuters*, www.reuters.com, March 28.
103. C. Boone, F. C. Wezel, & A. van Witleloostuijn, 2013, Joining the pack or going solo? A dynamic theory of new firm positioning, *Journal of Business Venturing*, 28: 511–527; J. R. Williams, 1992, How sustainable is your competitive advantage? *California Management Review*, 34(3): 29–51.
104. R. A. D'Aveni, G. Dagnino, & K. G. Smith, 2010, The age of temporary advantage, *Strategic Management Journal*, 31: 1371–1385; N. Pangarkar & J. R. Lie, 2004, The impact of market cycle on the performance of Singapore acquirers, *Strategic Management Journal*, 25: 1209–1216.
105. K. Thomas, 2012, Pfizer races to reinvent itself, *New York Times*, www.nytimes.com, May 1.
106. L.-C. Hsu & C.-H. Wang, 2012, Clarifying the effect of intellectual capital on performance: The mediating role of dynamic capability, *British Journal of Management*, 23: 179–205.
107. 2003, How fast is your company? *Fast Company*, June, 18.
108. R. Klingebiel & A. De Meyer, 2013, Becoming aware of the unknown: Decision making during the implementation of a strategic initiative, *Organization Science*, 24: 133–153; C. Hall & D. Lundberg, 2010, Competitive knowledge and strategy in high velocity environments, *IUP Journal of Knowledge Management*, 8(1/2): 7–17.
109. G. Clarkson & P. Toh, 2010, 'Keep out' signs: The role of deterrence in the competition for resources, *Strategic Management Journal*, 31: 1202–1225.
110. M. Kumar, 2011, Are joint ventures positive sum games? The relative effects of cooperative and noncooperative behavior, *Strategic Management Journal*, 32: 32–54; D. Li, L. Eden, M. A. Hitt, & R. D. Ireland, 2008, Friends, acquaintances or strangers? Partner selection in R&D alliances, *Academy of Management Journal*, 51: 315–334.
111. M. M. Larsen, S. Manning, & T. Pedersen, 2013, Uncovering the hidden costs of offshoring: The interplay of complexity, organizational design, and experience, *Strategic Management Journal*, 34: 533–552; F. Zirpoli & M. C. Becker, 2011, What happens when you outsource too much?, *MIT Sloan Management Review*, 52(2): 59–64.
112. D. Desai, 2013, The competitive advantage of adaptive networks: An extension of the dynamic capability view, *International Journal of Business Environment*, 5: 379–397; P. Carbonell & A. I. Rodriguez, 2006, The impact of market characteristics and innovation speed on perceptions of positional advantage and new product performance, *International Journal of Research in Marketing*, 23(1): 1–12.
113. S. P. Gudergan, T. Devinney, N. F. Richter, & R. S. Ellis, 2012, Strategic implications for (non-equity) alliance performance, *Long Range Planning*, 45: 451–476; V. Kumar, F. Jones, R. Venkatesan, & R. Leone, 2011, Is market orientation a source of sustainable competitive advantage or simply the cost of competing?, *Journal of Marketing*, 75: 16–30.
114. L. Josephs, 2011, Candy lovers face bitter Easter, *Wall Street Journal*, February 18, C10.

# 6

# Corporate-level Strategy

***Studying this chapter should provide you with the strategic management knowledge needed to:***

1. Define corporate-level strategy and discuss its purpose.
2. Describe different levels of diversification achieved using different corporate-level strategies.
3. Explain three primary reasons firms diversify.
4. Describe how firms can create value by using a related diversification strategy.
5. Explain the two ways value can be created with an unrelated diversification strategy.
6. Discuss the incentives and resources that encourage diversification.
7. Describe motives that can encourage managers to overdiversify a firm.

## GENERAL ELECTRIC: THE CLASSIC DIVERSIFIED FIRM

General Electric (GE) competes in many different industries ranging from appliances, aviation, and consumer electronics, to energy, financial services, health care, oil, and wind turbines. These industries are quite diverse, but there are similarities among several of them. In fact, GE's businesses are grouped in four divisions: GE Capital, GE Energy, GE Technology Infrastructure, and GE Home & Business Solutions. In recent years, more than 50 percent of GE's annual revenue has come from its financial services businesses. However, GE has reduced its assets in financial services—GE Capital provides approximately one-third of its total earnings. In 2012, much of GE's growth in revenues came from the manufacture and sale of jet engines for major airliners and from its increasing business in the oil and gas industry. In 2013 (based on 2012 data), GE was ranked the eighth largest corporation in the *Fortune* 500. Additionally, in 2013 it was ranked eleventh in *Fortune* magazine's list of the 50 most admired companies. Thus, GE has been a highly successful company.

GE has an impressive history and is one of the few widely diversified firms to achieve such success. GE is a highly influential global corporation. Its CEO, Jeffrey Immelt, was selected by President Obama to chair an advisory group on economic and job creation concerns. However, GE has experienced some "bumps in the road" along the way. This is to be expected because it is difficult to manage a large, widely diversified set of businesses. For example, GE never achieved the desired success with its NBC assets and sold them in 2012. In addition, it experienced significant declines in revenues and profits from its financial services businesses with the substantial problems that occurred in that industry beginning in 2008. In 2012, GE Capital rebounded and added revenue growth and profits but with a lower emphasis within the GE groups of businesses. Finally, partly because of these problems, it experienced reductions in stock value during the first decade of the twenty-first century.

GE has bounced back from these problems. Today, it is becoming a major player in the energy equipment industry, making several recent acquisitions. Additionally, GE is making large investments to be a major player in the new industrial Internet industry that is developing. GE has developed a new software R&D center in San Francisco with plans to have 400 computer scientists and software developers and invest $1 billion by 2015. The intent of GE is to develop and market Internet-connected machines that are designed to collect data and communicate it for a variety of purposes (e.g., servicing needs, quality control, etc.). GE is also beginning to experience strong growth from its investments in emerging economies such as China, India and Brazil.

A common strategy to achieve growth (and diversification) for GE over the years has been mergers and acquisitions. For example, in 2013, GE acquired Lufkin Industries for $3.3 billion. This company provides support equipment for oil and natural gas production industry. In addition, GE has at least $6 to $9 billion in cash to use for additional acquisitions in the near term from its sale of NBC Universal to Comcast. GE is also reversing its strategy of outsourcing to ensure it has the parts needed to fulfill its large amount of backorders of jet engines. For example, it acquired Avio, an Italian parts supplier, for $4.4 billion. It also plans to expand its new vertical integration strategy across its other businesses to provide it more control over the quality and timing of the output.

Sources: 2013, General Electric, 2012, Annual Report, www.ge.com/ar2012/, accessed on April 26; 2013, General Electric: The long game, *Financial Times*, www.ft.com, April 8; M. J. De La Merced, 2013, GE to buy Lufkin Industries for $3.3 billion, *New York Times DealBook*, http://dealbook.nytimes.com, April 8; 2013, The world's most admired companies, *Fortune*, March 18, 137, 142–147; S. Choudhury, 2013, GE expects India business to grow 15%–20%, *Wall Street Journal*, http://wsj.com, February 22; D. Benoit & B. Sechler, 2013, GE has cash for $6 billion to $9 billion in 2013 acquisitions, *Wall Street Journal*, http://wsj.com, February 13; K. Linebaugh, 2013, GE brings engine work back, *Wall Street Journal*, http://wsj.com, February 6; 2013, Jet engines and energy equipment lift profit at GE, *New York Times*, www.nytimes.com, January 18; S. Lohr, 2012, Looking to industry for the next digital disruption, *New York Times*, www.nytimes.com, November 23.

Learn more about Avio, another company acquired by GE.
www.cengagebrain.com

Our discussions of business-level strategies (Chapter 4) and the competitive rivalry and competitive dynamics associated with them (Chapter 5) have concentrated on firms competing in a single industry or product market.[1] In this chapter, we introduce you to corporate-level strategies, which are strategies firms use to *diversify* their operations from a single business competing in a single market into several product markets—most commonly, into several businesses. Thus, a **corporate-level strategy** specifies actions a firm takes to gain a competitive advantage by selecting and managing a group of different businesses competing in different product markets. Corporate-level strategies help companies to select new strategic positions—positions that are expected to increase the firm's value.[2] As explained in the Opening Case, General Electric competes in a number of widely diverse industries. In fact, as the title to the Opening Case suggests, some believe that GE is the classic diversified firm.[3]

As is the case with GE, firms use corporate-level strategies as a means to grow revenues and profits, but there can be additional strategic intents to growth. Firms can pursue defensive or offensive strategies that realize growth but have different strategic intents. Firms can also pursue market development by entering different geographic markets (this approach is discussed in Chapter 8). Firms can acquire competitors (horizontal integration) or buy a supplier or customer (vertical integration). As described in the Opening Case, GE has acquired a supplier of parts for the jet engines it manufactures, thereby increasing its vertical integration in this business. These strategies are discussed in Chapter 7. The basic corporate strategy, the topic of this chapter, focuses on diversification.

The decision to pursue growth is not a risk-free choice for firms. Indeed, as the Opening Case explored, GE experienced difficulty in its media businesses, especially with NBC, which it eventually sold. It also suffered significant revenue declines in its financial services businesses and thus reduced its assets in that area, choosing to seek growth in other businesses such as equipment for the oil industry and equipment for using the industrial Internet. Effective firms carefully evaluate their growth options (including the different corporate-level strategies) before committing firm resources to any of them.

A **corporate-level strategy** specifies actions a firm takes to gain a competitive advantage by selecting and managing a group of different businesses competing in different product markets.

Because the diversified firm operates in several different and unique product markets and likely in several businesses, it forms two types of strategies: corporate-level (or company-wide) and business-level (or competitive).[4] Corporate-level strategy is concerned with two key issues: in what product markets and businesses the firm should compete and how corporate headquarters should manage those businesses.[5] For the diversified company, a business-level strategy (see Chapter 4) must be selected for each of the businesses in which the firm has decided to compete. In this regard, each of GE's product divisions uses different business-level strategies; while most focus on differentiation, its consumer electronics

M. Stasy

business has products that compete in market niches to include some that are intended to serve the average income consumer. Thus, cost must also be an issue along with some level of quality.

As is the case with a business-level strategy, a corporate-level strategy is expected to help the firm earn above-average returns by creating value.[6] Some suggest that few corporate-level strategies actually create value.[7] As the Opening Case indicates, realizing value through a corporate strategy can be achieved but it is challenging to do so. In fact, GE is one of the few large, widely diversified firms that has been successful over time.

Evidence suggests that a corporate-level strategy's value is ultimately determined by the degree to which "the businesses in the portfolio are worth more under the management of the company than they would be under any other ownership."[8] Thus, an effective corporate-level strategy creates, across all of a firm's businesses, aggregate returns that exceed what those returns would be without the strategy[9] and contributes to the firm's strategic competitiveness and its ability to earn above-average returns.[10]

Product diversification, a primary form of corporate-level strategies, concerns the scope of the markets and industries in which the firm competes as well as "how managers buy, create and sell different businesses to match skills and strengths with opportunities presented to the firm."[11] Successful diversification is expected to reduce variability in the firm's profitability as earnings are generated from different businesses.[12] Diversification can also provide firms with the flexibility to shift their investments to markets where the greatest returns are possible rather than being dependent on only one or a few markets.[13] Because firms incur development and monitoring costs when diversifying, the ideal portfolio of businesses balances diversification's costs and benefits. CEOs and their top-management teams are responsible for determining the best portfolio for their company.[14]

We begin this chapter by examining different levels of diversification (from low to high). After describing the different reasons firms diversify their operations, we focus on two types of related diversification (related diversification signifies a moderate to high level of diversification for the firm). When properly used, these strategies help create value in the diversified firm, either through the sharing of resources (the related constrained strategy) or the transferring of core competencies across the firm's different businesses (the related linked strategy). We then examine unrelated diversification, which is another corporate-level strategy that can create value. Thereafter, the chapter shifts to the incentives and resources that can stimulate diversification which is value neutral. However, managerial motives to diversify, the final topic in the chapter, can actually destroy some of the firm's value.

# 6-1 Levels of Diversification

Diversified firms vary according to their level of diversification and the connections between and among their businesses. Figure 6.1 lists and defines five categories of businesses according to increasing levels of diversification. The single and dominant business categories denote no or relatively low levels of diversification; more fully diversified firms are classified into related and unrelated categories. A firm is related through its diversification when its businesses share several links; for example, businesses may share product markets (goods or services), technologies, or distribution channels. The more links among businesses, the more "constrained" is the level of diversification. "Unrelated" refers to the absence of direct links between businesses.

## 6-1a Low Levels of Diversification

A firm pursuing a low level of diversification uses either a single-or a dominant-business, corporate-level diversification strategy. A *single-business diversification strategy* is a

**Figure 6.1** Levels and Types of Diversification

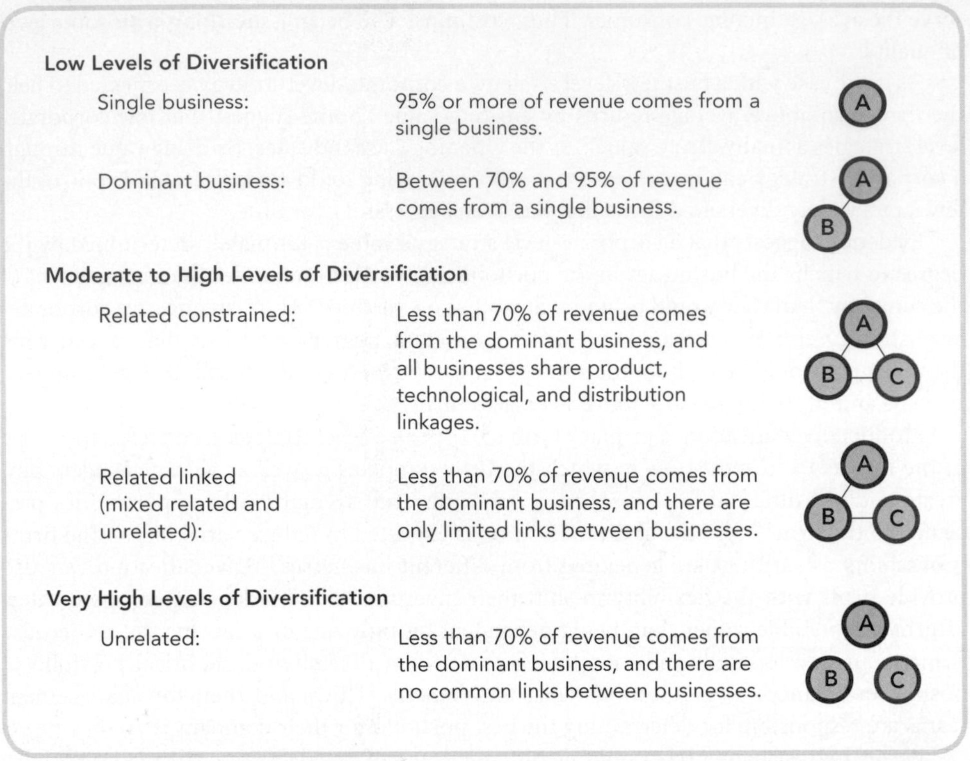

| | | |
|---|---|---|
| **Low Levels of Diversification** | | |
| Single business: | 95% or more of revenue comes from a single business. | A |
| Dominant business: | Between 70% and 95% of revenue comes from a single business. | A–B |
| **Moderate to High Levels of Diversification** | | |
| Related constrained: | Less than 70% of revenue comes from the dominant business, and all businesses share product, technological, and distribution linkages. | A, B, C (all linked) |
| Related linked (mixed related and unrelated): | Less than 70% of revenue comes from the dominant business, and there are only limited links between businesses. | A–B–C |
| **Very High Levels of Diversification** | | |
| Unrelated: | Less than 70% of revenue comes from the dominant business, and there are no common links between businesses. | A B C |

Source: Adapted from R. P. Rumelt, 1974, *Strategy, Structure and Economic Performance*, Boston: Harvard Business School.

corporate-level strategy wherein the firm generates 95 percent or more of its sales revenue from its core business area.[15] For example, Wm. Wrigley Jr. Company, the world's largest producer of chewing and bubble gums, historically used a single-business strategy while operating in relatively few product markets. Wrigley's trademark chewing gum brands include Spearmint, Doublemint, and Juicy Fruit, although the firm produces other products as well. Sugar-free Extra, which currently holds the largest share of the U.S. chewing gum market, was introduced in 1984.

In 2005, Wrigley shifted from its traditional focused strategy when it acquired the confectionary assets of Kraft Foods Inc., including the well-known brands Life Savers and Altoids. As Wrigley expanded, it may have intended to use the dominant-business strategy with the diversification of its product lines beyond gum; however, Wrigley was acquired in 2008 by Mars, a privately held global confection company (the maker of Snickers and M&Ms).[16]

With the *dominant-business diversification strategy*, the firm generates between 70 and 95 percent of its total revenue within a single business area. United Parcel Service (UPS) uses this strategy. Recently UPS generated 61 percent of its revenue from its U.S. package delivery business and 22 percent from its international package business, with the remaining 17 percent coming from the firm's non-package business.[17] Though the U.S. package delivery business currently generates the largest percentage of UPS's sales revenue, the firm anticipates that in the future its other two businesses will account for the majority of revenue growth. This expectation suggests that UPS may become more diversified, both in terms of its goods and services and in the number of countries in which those goods and services are offered.

Firms that focus on one or very few businesses and markets can earn positive returns, because they develop capabilities useful for these markets and can provide superior service to

# Strategic Focus GLOBALIZATION

## Sany's Highly Related Core Businesses

A look inside one of Sany's manufacturing facilities. Sany is a global company in the construction machinery industry.

The Sany Heavy Industry Company, Limited is China's largest producer of heavy equipment. In fact, it is the fifth largest producer of this type of equipment globally. Sany's total sales revenue in 2012 was $12.9 billion, well behind industry leader Caterpillar at $65.9 billion. However, Sany has a goal of eventually unseating Caterpillar as the industry leader. Sany plans to achieve $47 billion in annual sales within 10 years. Sany has surpassed Caterpillar as a leader in its Chinese domestic markets.

Sany has four core businesses: (1) cranes, (2) road construction machinery, (3) port machinery, and (4) pumpover machinery. While each is distinct, some similar technologies are used in the production and equipment. Furthermore, similar technologies allow similarities in production processes and equipment for certain parts. Therefore, there is a transfer of knowledge across these businesses. In addition, customers and markets share some similarities because all relate to some form of construction. For this reason, in the United States Sany has become a major sponsor of a Chevrolet on the NASCAR auto racing circuit. Sany America's marketing director, Joe Hanneman, said that research showed NASCAR racing events to be the primary recreation event for people in the U.S. construction industry.

Sany invests 5 percent of its annual sales in R&D to continuously improve the quality of existing products, identify new technologies, and develop new products. Through the end of 2012, Sany held 3,303 patents as a result of its R&D efforts. Indicative of its intent to be a technological leader in its industry, Sany has developed new postdoctoral research centers to attract top research scientists. In 2013, the company was awarded China's National Technology Invention Prize for its "super-length-boom" technology.

Sany continues to grow organically and through acquisitions. For example, in 2012, it acquired Putzmeister, a well-known concrete machine manufacturer. In addition, it has established subsidiaries in many countries, including the United States and Brazil, to enhance its international equipment sales and broaden its market reach. Largely because of its major goal of internationalization, it is moving its corporate headquarters from Changsha to Beijing, for enriched international connections.

Sources: 2013, Sany Heavy industry C. Ltd. Web site, www.sanygroup.com, accessed on April 26; 2013, Yellow Table Survey: Sany ranks no. 5 among construction machinery manufacturers in 2013, China Construction Machinery Online, www.cmbol.com, April 15; M. Barris, 2013, Sany turns to NASCAR to fuel sales, *China Daily*, www.chinadaily.com, April 4; 2013, Awarded National Technology Invention Prize, *Get to Know Sany*, 15th issue, February 15; L. Hooks, P. J. Davis, & N. Munshi, 2013, Caterpillar digs into trouble in China, *Financial Times*, www.ft.com, February 12; J. R. Hagerty & C. Murphy, 2013, Sany tries to gain traction in the U.S., *Wall Street Journal*, http://wsj.com, January 28; 2013, Sany Heavy Industry Co. Ltd: Sany Group's top 10 events in 2012, *$-traders*, www.4-traders.com, January 22; Z. Yangpeng & F. Zhiwei, 2012, Sany to move HQ to Beijing from Changsha, *China Daily*, http://usa.chinadaily.com, November 11.

Learn more about Zoomlion Co.
www.cengagebrain.com

their customers. Additionally, there are fewer challenges in managing one or a very small set of businesses, allowing them to gain economies of scale and efficiently use their resources.[18] Family-owned and controlled businesses are commonly less diversified. They prefer the focus because the family's reputation is related closely to that of the business. Thus, family members prefer to provide quality goods and services which a focused strategy better allows.[19]

Sany, the company described in the Strategic Focus, might be evaluated by some to be using a single business corporate strategy because of its focus on heavy equipment manufacturing. If this is the case, it has a series of differentiated products and is likely following a product proliferation strategy. A product proliferation strategy represents a form of intra-industry diversification.[20] Yet, Sany also has four business divisions, one for each type of heavy equipment it manufactures. Thus, it might also be considered by some to engage in moderate diversification in the form of highly related constrained diversification.

## 6-1b Moderate and High Levels of Diversification

A firm generating more than 30 percent of its revenue outside a dominant business and whose businesses are related to each other in some manner uses a related diversification corporate-level strategy. When the links between the diversified firm's businesses are rather direct, it is a *related constrained diversification strategy*. Campbell Soup, Procter & Gamble, and Merck & Company all use a related constrained strategy. With a related constrained strategy, a firm shares resources and activities across its businesses.

For example, the Publicis Groupe uses a related constrained strategy, deriving value from the potential synergy across its various groups, especially the digital capabilities in its advertising business. Given its recent performance, the related constrained strategy has created value for Publicis customers and its shareholders.[21]

The diversified company with a portfolio of businesses that have only a few links between them is called a mixed related and unrelated firm and is using the *related linked diversification strategy* (see Figure 6.1). As displayed in the Opening Case, GE uses a related-linked corporate-level diversification strategy. Compared with related constrained firms, related linked firms share fewer resources and assets between their businesses, concentrating instead on transferring knowledge and core competencies between the businesses. GE has four strategic business units (see Chapter 11 for a definition of SBUs) it calls "divisions," each composed of related businesses. There are no relationships across the strategic business units, only within them. As with firms using each type of diversification strategy, companies implementing the related linked strategy constantly adjust the mix in their portfolio of businesses as well as make decisions about how to manage these businesses.[22] Managing a diversified firm such as GE is highly challenging, but GE appears to have been well managed over the years given its success.

A highly diversified firm that has no relationships between its businesses follows an *unrelated diversification strategy*. United Technologies, Textron, Samsung, and Hutchison Whampoa Limited (HWL) are examples of firms using this type of corporate-level strategy. Commonly, firms using this strategy are called *conglomerates*. HWL is a leading international corporation with five core businesses: ports and related services; property and hotels; retail; energy, infrastructure, investments and others; and telecommunications. These businesses are not related to each other, and the firm makes no efforts to share activities or to transfer core competencies between or among them. Each of these five businesses is quite large; for example, the retailing arm of the retail and manufacturing business has more than 9,300 stores in 33 countries. Groceries, cosmetics, electronics, wine, and airline tickets are some of the product categories featured in these stores. This firm's size and diversity suggest the challenge of successfully managing the unrelated diversification strategy. However, Hutchison's CEO Li Ka-shing has been successful at not only making smart acquisitions, but also at divesting businesses with good timing.[23]

M. Stasy

# 6-2 Reasons for Diversification

A firm uses a corporate-level diversification strategy for a variety of reasons (see Table 6.1). Typically, a diversification strategy is used to increase the firm's value by improving its overall performance. Value is created either through related diversification or through unrelated diversification when the strategy allows a company's businesses to increase revenues or reduce costs while implementing their business-level strategies.[24]

Other reasons for using a diversification strategy may have nothing to do with increasing the firm's value; in fact, diversification can have neutral effects or even reduce a firm's value. Value-neutral reasons for diversification include a desire to match and thereby neutralize a competitor's market power (such as to neutralize another firm's advantage by acquiring a similar distribution outlet). Decisions to expand a firm's portfolio of businesses to reduce managerial risk can have a negative effect on the firm's value. Greater amounts of diversification reduce managerial risk in that if one of the businesses in a diversified firm fails, the top executive of that business does not risk total failure by the corporation. As such, this reduces the top executives' employment risk. In addition, because diversification can increase a firm's size and thus managerial compensation, managers have motives to diversify a firm to a level that reduces its value.[25] Diversification rationales that may have a neutral or negative effect on the firm's value are discussed later in the chapter.

Operational relatedness and corporate relatedness are two ways diversification strategies can create value (see Figure 6.2). Studies of these independent relatedness dimensions show the importance of resources and key competencies.[26] The figure's vertical dimension depicts opportunities to share operational activities between businesses (operational relatedness) while the horizontal dimension suggests opportunities for transferring corporate-level core competencies (corporate relatedness). The firm with a strong capability in managing

**Table 6.1** Reasons for Diversification

| Value-Creating Diversification |
|---|
| • Economies of scope (related diversification)<br>  • Sharing activities<br>  • Transferring core competencies<br>• Market power (related diversification)<br>  • Blocking competitors through multipoint competition<br>  • Vertical integration<br>• Financial economies (unrelated diversification)<br>  • Efficient internal capital allocation<br>  • Business restructuring |
| **Value-Neutral Diversification** |
| • Antitrust regulation<br>• Tax laws<br>• Low performance<br>• Uncertain future cash flows<br>• Risk reduction for firm<br>• Tangible resources<br>• Intangible resources |
| **Value-Reducing Diversification** |
| • Diversifying managerial employment risk<br>• Increasing managerial compensation |

**Figure 6.2** Value-Creating Diversification Strategies: Operational and Corporate Relatedness

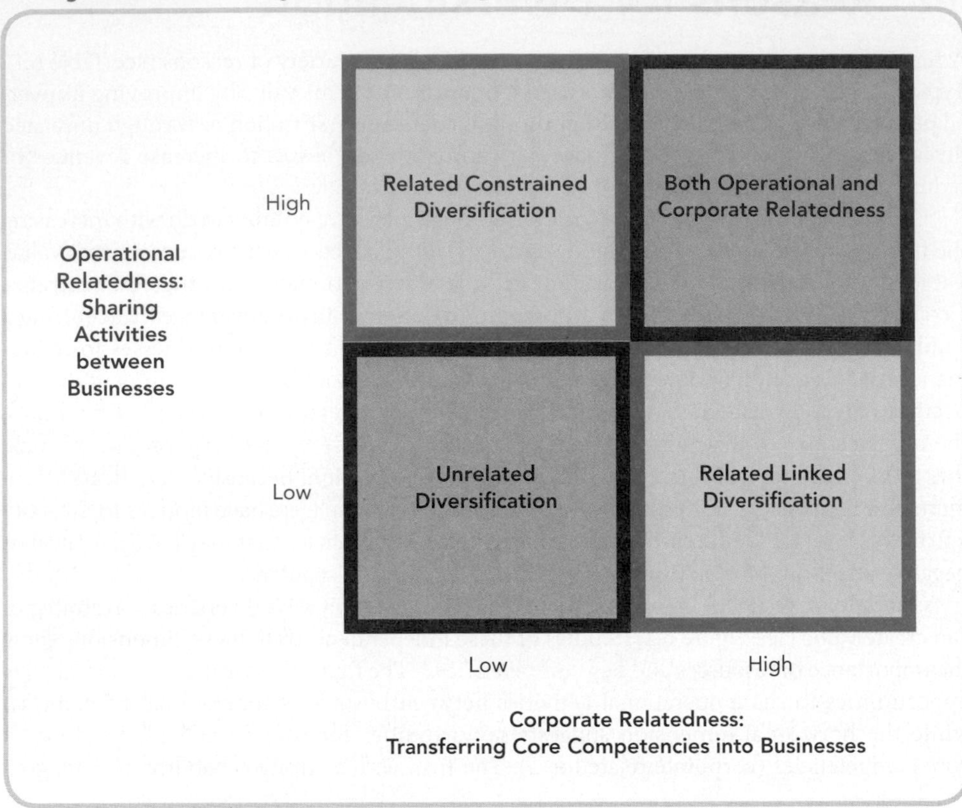




operational synergy, especially in sharing assets between its businesses, falls in the upper left quadrant, which also represents vertical sharing of assets through vertical integration. The lower right quadrant represents a highly developed corporate capability for transferring one or more core competencies across businesses.

This capability is located primarily in the corporate headquarters office. Unrelated diversification is also illustrated in Figure 6.2 in the lower-left quadrant. Financial economies (discussed later), rather than either operational or corporate relatedness, are the source of value creation for firms using the unrelated diversification strategy.

## 6-3 Value-Creating Diversification: Related Constrained and Related Linked Diversification

**Economies of scope** are cost savings that the firm creates by successfully sharing some of its resources and capabilities or transferring one or more corporate-level core competencies that were developed in one of its businesses to another of its businesses.

With the related diversification corporate-level strategy, the firm builds upon or extends its resources and capabilities to build a competitive advantage by creating value for customers.[27] The company using the related diversification strategy wants to develop and exploit economies of scope between its businesses.[28] In fact, even nonprofit organizations have found that carefully planned and implemented related diversification can provide value to them.[29] Available to companies operating in multiple product markets or industries, **economies of scope** are cost savings that the firm creates by successfully sharing some of its resources and capabilities or transferring one or more corporate-level core competencies that were developed in one of its businesses to another of its businesses.[30]

As illustrated in Figure 6.2, firms seek to create value from economies of scope through two basic kinds of operational economies: sharing activities (operational relatedness) and transferring corporate-level core competencies (corporate relatedness). The difference between sharing activities and transferring competencies is based on how separate resources are jointly used to create economies of scope. To create economies of scope tangible resources, such as plant and equipment or other business-unit physical assets, often must be shared. Less tangible resources, such as manufacturing know-how and technological capabilities, can also be shared.[31] However, know-how transferred between separate activities with no physical or tangible resource involved is a transfer of a corporate-level core competence, not an operational sharing of activities.[32]

## 6-3a Operational Relatedness: Sharing Activities

Firms can create operational relatedness by sharing either a primary activity (such as inventory delivery systems) or a support activity (such as purchasing practices)—see Chapter 3's discussion of the value chain. Firms using the related constrained diversification strategy share activities in order to create value. Procter & Gamble uses this corporate-level strategy. Sany, described in the Strategic Focus, also shares activities. For example, its various businesses share marketing activities because all of their equipment is sold to firms in the construction industry. This is evidenced by the sponsorship of an auto in NASCAR in an attempt to reach executives in the construction industry.

Activity sharing is also risky because ties among a firm's businesses create links between outcomes. For instance, if demand for one business's product is reduced, it may not generate sufficient revenues to cover the fixed costs required to operate the shared facilities. These types of organizational difficulties can reduce activity-sharing success. Additionally, activity sharing requires careful coordination between the businesses involved. The coordination challenges must be managed effectively for the appropriate sharing of activities.[33]

**Corporate-level core competencies** are complex sets of resources and capabilities that link different businesses, primarily through managerial and technological knowledge, experience, and expertise.

Although activity sharing across businesses is not risk-free, research shows that it can create value. For example, studies of acquisitions of firms in the same industry (horizontal acquisitions), such as the banking industry and software, found that sharing resources and activities and thereby creating economies of scope contributed to post-acquisition increases in performance and higher returns to shareholders.[34] Additionally, firms that sold off related units in which resource sharing was a possible source of economies of scope have been found to produce lower returns than those that sold off businesses unrelated to the firm's core business.[35] Still other research discovered that firms with closely related businesses have lower risk.[36] These results suggest that gaining economies of scope by sharing activities across a firm's businesses may be important in reducing risk and in creating value. Further, more attractive results are obtained through activity sharing when a strong corporate headquarters office facilitates it.[37]

*In 2013 Sany America became a major NASCAR sponsor partner for Tommy Baldwin Racing. The NASCAR sponsorship illustrates how Sany's businesses share marketing activities to reach executives in various segments of the construction industry.*

Jared Wickerham/Getty Images

## 6-3b Corporate Relatedness: Transferring of Core Competencies

Over time, the firm's intangible resources, such as its know-how, become the foundation of core competencies. **Corporate-level core competencies** are complex sets of resources and capabilities that link different businesses, primarily through managerial and technological knowledge, experience, and expertise.[38] Firms seeking to create value through corporate relatedness use the related linked diversification strategy as exemplified by GE.

In at least two ways, the related linked diversification strategy helps firms to create value.[39] First, because the expense of developing a core competence has already been incurred in one of the firm's businesses, transferring this competence to a second business eliminates the need for that business to allocate resources to develop it. Resource intangibility is a second source of value creation through corporate relatedness. Intangible resources are difficult for competitors to understand and imitate. Because of this difficulty, the unit receiving a transferred corporate-level competence often gains an immediate competitive advantage over its rivals.[40]

A number of firms have successfully transferred one or more corporate-level core competencies across their businesses. Virgin Group Ltd. transfers its marketing core competence across airlines, cosmetics, music, drinks, mobile phones, health clubs, and a number of other businesses.[41] Honda has developed and transferred its competence in engine design and manufacturing among its businesses making products such as motorcycles, lawnmowers, and cars and trucks. Company officials state that Honda is a major manufacturer of engines and is focused on providing products for all forms of human mobility.[42]

One way managers facilitate the transfer of corporate-level core competencies is by moving key people into new management positions.[43] However, the manager of an older business may be reluctant to transfer key people who have accumulated knowledge and experience critical to the business's success. Thus, managers with the ability to facilitate the transfer of a core competence may come at a premium, or the key people involved may not want to transfer. Additionally, the top-level managers from the transferring business may not want the competencies transferred to a new business to fulfill the firm's diversification objectives.[44] Research also suggests too much dependence on outsourcing can lower the usefulness of core competencies and thereby reduce their useful transferability to other business units in the diversified firm.[45]

## 6-3c Market Power

Firms using a related diversification strategy may gain market power when successfully using a related constrained or related linked strategy. **Market power** exists when a firm is able to sell its products above the existing competitive level or to reduce the costs of its primary and support activities below the competitive level, or both.[46] Mars' acquisition of the Wrigley assets was part of its related constrained diversification strategy and added market share to the Mars/Wrigley integrated firm, as it realized 14.4 percent of the market share. This catapulted Mars/Wrigley above Cadbury and Nestle, which had 10.1 and 7.7 percent of the market share, respectively, at the time and left Hershey with only 5.5 percent of the market.[47]

As explained in the Strategic Focus, Ericsson has the largest share of the global market in telecommunications equipment, and for many years its leadership position has afforded the company considerable market power. That market power and its leadership position in research helped it garner major contracts in 2012 for telecommunications equipment from the four largest providers of mobile broadband networks in the United States (Verizon, AT&T, Sprint, and T-Mobile).[48]

In addition to efforts to gain scale as a means of increasing market power, firms can create market power through multipoint competition and vertical integration. **Multipoint competition** exists when two or more diversified firms simultaneously compete in the same product areas or geographic markets.[49] The actions taken by UPS and FedEx in two markets, overnight delivery and ground shipping, illustrate multipoint competition. UPS moved into overnight delivery, FedEx's stronghold; in turn, FedEx bought trucking and ground shipping assets to move into ground shipping, UPS's stronghold. Moreover, geographic

**Market power** exists when a firm is able to sell its products above the existing competitive level or to reduce the costs of its primary and support activities below the competitive level, or both.

**Multipoint competition** exists when two or more diversified firms simultaneously compete in the same product areas or geographical markets.

## Strategic Focus TECHNOLOGY

### Ericsson's Substantial Market Power

*Ericsson offices, Mississauga, Ontario, Canada. One of the ways Ericsson retains its market power is through significant investments in research and development.*

Ericsson was founded in 1876 as a shop to repair telegraph equipment in Sweden. From that humble beginning, it has grown into the largest global manufacturer of equipment for mobile telecommunications networks. In 2012, it had a 38 percent share of the global market for telecommunications equipment. It has a presence in more than 180 countries and its business unit support systems provide charging and billing service for 1.6 billion people. Ericsson also holds the largest market share in global services.

Ericsson has three primary businesses: business unit networks, business unit support systems, and business unit global services. Until 2012, it also had a "devices" business unit, which was a joint venture with Sony to produce mobile phones, as well as accessories and PC cards. However, this is a highly competitive market with Apple's iPhones as well as strong-selling smartphones from Samsung, Nokia, and others. So, Ericsson sold its portion of this business to Sony. Although each of the other three business units represents a separate business market, they are complementary; because of this, Ericsson creates synergy across them. They are highly interrelated, so Ericsson uses the related-constrained diversification strategy to create synergy across the business units and thereby achieve greater market power.

Ericsson has several strong competitors, but the two primary ones are Huawei and Samsung. Huawei now holds the second largest market share in telecommunications equipment. Ericsson and Huawei's total corporate sales revenues are very similar but they serve a few distinct markets. For example, Huawei has major sales in smartphones and corporate communications grids, while 43 percent of Ericsson's sales come from managing wireless networks. However, Huawei's sales in telecommunications equipment are growing.

One way Ericsson is fighting the competition is through major investments in research and development. This research is designed to develop new technologies and products to help Ericsson maintain its competitive advantage. For example, Ericsson's researchers predict that 5G wireless access will be needed by 2020. The R&D scientists are also targeting the development of a federated networked cloud to provide such services as computation, storage, and networking. Finally, they are working on the development of 3D visual communications. Therefore, the market leader intends to maintain its market power by sustaining its competitive advantage.

Sources: 2013, Ericsson Annual Report 2012, Ericsson, www.ericsson.com, accessed April 26; 2013, Ericsson, Wikipedia, http://en.wikipedia.org/wiki/ericsson, accessed April 26; 2013, What's next in Ericsson research, Ericsson Web site, www.ericsson.com, accessed April 26; K. J. O'Brien, 2013, Ericsson finds a Chinese rival hot on its wheels, *New York Times*, www.nytimes.com, February 24; B. McCarthy & D. Thomas, 2013, Ericsson shows signs of recovery, *Financial Times*, www.ft.com, January 31; 2012, Samsung hits back at Ericsson with its own request for U.S. import ban over wireless patents, Foss patents, www.fosspatents.com, December 24.

Find out more about Sony.
www.cengagebrain.com

competition for markets increases. The strongest shipping company in Europe is DHL. All three competitors (UPS, FedEx, and DHL) entered large foreign markets to either gain a stake or to expand their existing share. If one of these firms successfully gains strong positions in several markets while competing against its rivals, its market power will increase. Interestingly, DHL had to exit the U.S. market because it was too difficult to compete against UPS and FedEx, which are dominant there.

Some firms using a related diversification strategy engage in vertical integration to gain market power. **Vertical integration** exists when a company produces its own inputs (backward integration) or owns its own source of output distribution (forward integration). In some instances, firms partially integrate their operations, producing and selling their products by using company businesses as well as outside sources.[50]

Vertical integration is commonly used in the firm's core business to gain market power over rivals. Market power is gained as the firm develops the ability to save on its operations, avoid market costs, improve product quality, possibly protect its technology from imitation by rivals, and potentially exploit underlying capabilities in the marketplace. Vertically integrated firms are better able to improve product quality and improve or create new technologies than specialized firms because they have access to more information and knowledge that are complementary.[51] Market power also is created when firms have strong ties between their assets for which no market prices exist. Establishing a market price would result in high search and transaction costs, so firms seek to vertically integrate rather than remain separate businesses.[52]

Vertical integration has its limitations. For example, an outside supplier may produce the product at a lower cost. As a result, internal transactions from vertical integration may be expensive and reduce profitability relative to competitors.[53] Also, bureaucratic costs can be present with vertical integration.[54] Because vertical integration can require substantial investments in specific technologies, it may reduce the firm's flexibility, especially when technology changes quickly. Finally, changes in demand create capacity balance and coordination problems. If one business is building a part for another internal business but achieving economies of scale requires the first division to manufacture quantities that are beyond the capacity of the internal buyer to absorb, it would be necessary to sell the parts outside the firm as well as to the internal business. Thus, although vertical integration can create value, especially through market power over competitors, it is not without risks and costs.[55]

Around the turn of the twenty-first century, de-integration became the focus of most manufacturing firms, such as Intel and Dell, and even some large auto companies, such as Ford and General Motors, as they developed independent supplier networks.[56] Flextronics, an electronics contract manufacturer, is a large contract manufacturer that helps to support this approach to supply-chain management.[57] Such firms often manage their customers' entire product lines and offer services ranging from inventory management to delivery and after-sales service. Interestingly, however, some firms are beginning to reintegrate in order to gain better control over the quality and timing of their supplies. The opening case described GE's actions to reintegrate some areas of their businesses (e.g., manufacture of jet engines) to ensure that they could meet their contractual obligations in the delivery of the goods.

## 6-3d Simultaneous Operational Relatedness and Corporate Relatedness

As Figure 6.2 suggests, some firms simultaneously seek operational and corporate relatedness to create economies of scope.[58] The ability to simultaneously create economies of scope by sharing activities (operational relatedness) and transferring core competencies (corporate relatedness) is difficult for competitors to understand and learn how to imitate. However, if the cost of realizing both types of relatedness is not offset by the benefits created, the result is diseconomies because the cost of organization and incentive structure is very expensive.[59]

**Vertical integration** exists when a company produces its own inputs (backward integration) or owns its own source of output distribution (forward integration).

M. Stasy

Walt Disney Co. uses a related diversification strategy to simultaneously create economies of scope through operational and corporate relatedness. Disney has five separate but related businesses: Media Networks, Parks and Resorts, Studio Entertainment, Consumer Products, and Interactive Media. Within the firm's Studio Entertainment business, for example, Disney can gain economies of scope by sharing activities among its different movie distribution companies, such as Touchstone Pictures, Hollywood Pictures, and Dimension Films. Broad and deep knowledge about its customers is a capability on which Disney relies to develop corporate-level core competencies in terms of advertising and marketing. With these competencies, Disney is able to create economies of scope through corporate relatedness as it cross-sells products that are highlighted in its movies through the distribution channels that are part of its Parks and Resorts and Consumer Products businesses. Thus, characters created in movies become figures that are marketed through Disney's retail stores (which are part of the Consumer Products business). In addition, themes established in movies become the source of new rides in the firm's theme parks, which are part of the Parks and Resorts business, and provide themes for clothing and other retail business products.[60]

Learn more about vertical integration.
www.cengagebrain.com

Thus, Walt Disney Co. has been able to successfully use related diversification as a corporate-level strategy through which it creates economies of scope by sharing some activities and by transferring core competencies. However, it can be difficult for investors to identify the value created by a firm (such as Walt Disney Co.) as it shares activities and transfers core competencies. For this reason, the value of the assets of a firm using a diversification strategy to create economies of scope often is discounted by investors.

## 6-4 Unrelated Diversification

Firms do not seek either operational relatedness or corporate relatedness when using the unrelated diversification corporate-level strategy. An unrelated diversification strategy (see Figure 6.2) can create value through two types of financial economies. **Financial economies** are cost savings realized through improved allocations of financial resources based on investments inside or outside the firm.[61]

**Financial economies** are cost savings realized through improved allocations of financial resources based on investments inside or outside the firm.

Efficient internal capital allocations can lead to financial economies. Efficient internal capital allocations reduce risk among the firm's businesses—for example, by leading to the development of a portfolio of businesses with different risk profiles. The second type of financial economy concerns the restructuring of acquired assets. Here, the diversified firm buys another company, restructures that company's assets in ways that allow it to operate more profitably, and then sells the company for a profit in the external market.[62] Next, we discuss the two types of financial economies in greater detail.

*The renowned Hollywood sign in Los Angeles, California. Walt Disney Co. uses a related diversification strategy to create economies of scope by sharing activities and transferring core competencies among its entertainment-focused businesses.*

© Dan Breckwoldt/Shutterstock.com

### 6-4a Efficient Internal Capital Market Allocation

In a market economy, capital markets are believed to efficiently allocate capital. Efficiency results as investors take equity

M. Stasy

positions (ownership) with high expected future cash-flow values. Capital is also allocated through debt as shareholders and debt holders try to improve the value of their investments by taking stakes in businesses with high growth and profitability prospects.

In large diversified firms, the corporate headquarters office distributes capital to its businesses to create value for the overall corporation. The nature of these distributions can generate gains from internal capital market allocations that exceed the gains that would accrue to shareholders as a result of capital being allocated by the external capital market.[63] Because those in a firm's corporate headquarters generally have access to detailed and accurate information regarding the actual and potential future performance of the company's portfolio of businesses, they have the best information to make capital distribution decisions.

Compared with corporate office personnel, external investors have relatively limited access to internal information and can only estimate the performances of individual businesses as well as their future prospects. Moreover, although businesses seeking capital must provide information to potential suppliers (such as banks or insurance companies), firms with internal capital markets can have at least two informational advantages. First, information provided to capital markets through annual reports and other sources may not include negative information, instead emphasizing positive prospects and outcomes. External sources of capital have a limited ability to understand the operational dynamics within large organizations. Even external shareholders who have access to information are unlikely to receive full and complete disclosure.[64] Second, although a firm must disseminate information, that information also becomes simultaneously available to the firm's current and potential competitors. With insights gained by studying such information, competitors might attempt to duplicate a firm's value-creating strategy. Thus, an ability to efficiently allocate capital through an internal market helps the firm protect the competitive advantages it develops while using its corporate-level strategy as well as its various business-unit–level strategies.

If intervention from outside the firm is required to make corrections to capital allocations, only significant changes are possible because the power to make changes by outsiders is often indirect (e.g., through members of the board of directors). External parties can try to make changes by forcing the firm into bankruptcy or changing the top management team. Alternatively, in an internal capital market, the corporate headquarters office can fine-tune its corrections, such as choosing to adjust managerial incentives or encouraging strategic changes in one of the firm's businesses.[65] Thus, capital can be allocated according to more specific criteria than is possible with external market allocations. Because it has less accurate information, the external capital market may fail to allocate resources adequately to high-potential investments. The corporate headquarters office of a diversified company can more effectively perform such tasks as disciplining underperforming management teams through resource allocations.[66] GE (discussed in the Opening Case) has done an exceptionally good job of allocating capital across its many businesses. Although a related linked firm, it differentially allocates capital across its four major strategic business units. Although GE Capital produced the high returns for GE over the last few decades, it received a healthy amount of capital from internal allocations. However, as described in the case, its performance has suffered in recent years, and GE has reduced the resources provided to this business (increasing the resources for other businesses such as energy).

Large, highly diversified businesses often face what is known as the "conglomerate discount." This discount results from analysts not knowing how to value a vast array of large businesses with complex financial reports. To overcome this discount, many unrelated diversified or industrial conglomerates have sought to convince investors that the company is strong and will produce strong returns. For instance, United Technologies increased the dividend it paid to shareholders and divested some businesses that were not related closely to one of its five businesses. The CEO's letter to shareholders in the 2012 Annual Report suggested that these changes along with an acquisition of businesses complementary to its current portfolio and the new corporate structure implemented in 2011 would return the company to double-digit growth in the near term.[67] In spite of the challenges associated with it, a number of corporations continue to use the unrelated diversification strategy, especially in Europe and in emerging markets. As an example, Siemens is a large diversified German conglomerate that engages in substantial diversification in order to balance its economic risk. In economic downturns, diversification can help some companies improve future performance.[68]

The Achilles' heel for firms using the unrelated diversification strategy in a developed economy is that competitors can imitate financial economies more easily than they can replicate the value gained from the economies of scope developed through operational relatedness and corporate relatedness. This issue is less of a problem in emerging economies, in which the absence of a "soft infrastructure" (including effective financial intermediaries, sound regulations, and contract laws) supports and encourages use of the unrelated diversification strategy.[69] In fact, in emerging economies such as those in Korea, India, and Chile, research has shown that diversification increases the performance of firms affiliated with large diversified business groups.[70]

### 6-4b Restructuring of Assets

Financial economies can also be created when firms learn how to create value by buying, restructuring, and then selling the restructured companies' assets in the external market.[71] As in the real estate business, buying assets at low prices, restructuring them, and selling them at a price that exceeds their cost generates a positive return on the firm's invested capital.

Unrelated diversified companies that pursue this strategy try to create financial economies by acquiring and restructuring other companies' assets but it involves significant trade-offs. For example, Danaher's success requires a focus on mature manufacturing businesses because of the uncertainty of demand for high-technology products. It has acquired 400 businesses since 1984 and applied the Danaher Business System to reduce costs and create a lean organization.[72] In high-technology businesses, resource allocation decisions are highly complex, often creating information-processing overload on the small corporate headquarters offices that are common in unrelated diversified firms. High-technology businesses are often human-resource dependent; these people can leave or demand higher pay and thus appropriate or deplete the value of an acquired firm.[73]

Buying and then restructuring service-based assets so they can be profitably sold in the external market is also difficult. Thus, for both high-technology firms and service-based companies, relatively few tangible assets can be restructured to create value and sell profitably. It is difficult to restructure intangible assets such as human capital and effective relationships that have evolved over time between buyers (customers) and sellers (firm personnel). Ideally, executives will follow a strategy of buying businesses when prices are lower, such as in the midst of a recession, and selling them at late stages in an expansion.[74] Because of the increases in global economic activity, including more cross-border acquisitions, there is also a growing number of foreign divestitures and restructuring in internal markets (e.g., partial or full privatization of state-owned enterprises). Foreign divestitures are even more complex than domestic ones and must be managed carefully.[75]

## 6-5 Value-Neutral Diversification: Incentives and Resources

The objectives firms seek when using related diversification and unrelated diversification strategies all have the potential to help the firm create value through the corporate-level strategy. However, these strategies, as well as single-and dominant-business diversification strategies, are sometimes used with objectives that are value-neutral. Different incentives to diversify sometimes exist, and the quality of the firm's resources may permit only diversification that is value neutral rather than value creating.

## 6-5a Incentives to Diversify

Incentives to diversify come from both the external environment and a firm's internal environment. External incentives include antitrust regulations and tax laws. Internal incentives include low performance, uncertain future cash flows, and the pursuit of synergy and reduction of risk for the firm.

### Antitrust Regulation and Tax Laws

Government antitrust policies and tax laws provided incentives for U.S. firms to diversify in the 1960s and 1970s.[76] Antitrust laws prohibiting mergers that created increased market power (via either vertical or horizontal integration) were stringently enforced during that period.[77] Merger activity that produced conglomerate diversification was encouraged primarily by the Celler-Kefauver Antimerger Act (1950), which discouraged horizontal and vertical mergers. As a result, many of the mergers during the 1960s and 1970s were "conglomerate" in character, involving companies pursuing different lines of business. Between 1973 and 1977, 79.1 percent of all mergers were conglomerate in nature.[78]

During the 1980s, antitrust enforcement lessened, resulting in more and larger horizontal mergers (acquisitions of target firms in the same line of business, such as a merger between two oil companies).[79] In addition, investment bankers became more open to the kinds of mergers facilitated by regulation changes; as a consequence, takeovers increased to unprecedented numbers.[80] The conglomerates, or highly diversified firms, of the 1960s and 1970s became more "focused" in the 1980s and early 1990s as merger constraints were relaxed and restructuring was implemented.[81]

In the 2000s, antitrust concerns emerged again with the large volume of mergers and acquisitions (see Chapter 7).[82] Mergers are now receiving more scrutiny than they did in the 1980s, 1990s, and the first decade of the 2000s.[83]

The tax effects of diversification stem not only from corporate tax changes, but also from individual tax rates. Some companies (especially mature ones) generate more cash from their operations than they can reinvest profitably. Some argue that *free cash flows* (liquid financial assets for which investments in current businesses are no longer economically viable) should be redistributed to shareholders as dividends.[84] However, in the 1960s and 1970s, dividends were taxed more heavily than were capital gains. As a result, before 1980, shareholders preferred that firms use free cash flows to buy and build companies in high-performance industries. If the firm's stock value appreciated over the long term, shareholders might receive a better return on those funds than if the funds had been redistributed as dividends, because returns from stock sales would be taxed more lightly than would dividends.

*Google CEO Larry Page testifies at a U.S. Senate hearing on antitrust policy.*

Bloomberg/Getty Images

Under the 1986 Tax Reform Act, however, the top individual ordinary income tax rate was reduced from 50 to 28 percent, and the special capital gains tax was changed to treat capital gains as ordinary income. These changes created an incentive for shareholders to stop encouraging firms to retain funds for purposes of diversification. These tax law changes also influenced an increase in divestitures of unrelated business units after 1984. Thus, while individual tax rates for capital gains and dividends created a shareholder incentive to increase diversification before 1986, they encouraged lower diversification after 1986, unless it was funded by tax-deductible debt. Yet, there have been changes in the maximum individual tax rates since the 1980s. The top individual tax rate has varied from 31 percent in 1992 to 39.6 percent in 2013. There have also been some changes in the capital gains tax rates.

Corporate tax laws also affect diversification. Acquisitions typically increase a firm's depreciable asset allowances. Increased depreciation (a non-cash-flow expense) produces lower taxable income, thereby providing an additional incentive for acquisitions. At one time, acquisitions were an attractive means for securing tax benefits, but changes recommended by the Financial Accounting Standards Board eliminated the "pooling of interests" method to account for the acquired firm's assets. It also eliminated the write-off for research and development in process, and thus reduced some of the incentives to make acquisitions, especially acquisitions in related high-technology industries (these changes are discussed further in Chapter 7).[85]

Thus, regulatory changes such as the ones we have described create incentives or disincentives for diversification. Interestingly, European antitrust laws have historically been stricter regarding horizontal mergers than those in the United States, but recently have become more similar.[86]

## Low Performance

Some research shows that low returns are related to greater levels of diversification.[87] If high performance eliminates the need for greater diversification, then low performance may provide an incentive for diversification. In 2005, eBay acquired Skype for $3.1 billion in hopes that it would create synergies and improve communication between buyers and sellers. However, within three years, eBay decided to sell Skype because it has failed to increase cash flow for its core e-commerce business and the expected synergies were not realized. In 2011, eBay sold Skype to Microsoft for $8.5 billion. Although analysts thought the premium paid by Microsoft may have been too high, one review in the *Financial Times* suggested that Skype could play a prominent role in Microsoft's multimedia strategy. Thus, the potential synergies between Skype and Microsoft may be greater than those with eBay.[88] The poor performance may be because of errors made by top managers (such as eBay's original acquisition of Skype), and that lead to divestitures similar to eBay's action.[89]

Research evidence and the experience of a number of firms suggest that an overall curvilinear relationship, as illustrated in Figure 6.3, may exist between diversification and performance.[90] Although low performance can be an incentive to diversify, firms that are more broadly diversified compared to their competitors may have overall lower performance.

## Uncertain Future Cash Flows

As a firm's product line matures or is threatened, diversification may be an important defensive strategy.[91] Small firms and companies in mature or maturing industries sometimes find it necessary to diversify for long-term survival.[92]

Diversifying into other product markets or into other businesses can reduce the uncertainty about a firm's future cash flows. Merck decided to expand into the biosimilars business (production of drugs that are similar to approved drugs) in hopes of stimulating its prescription drug business due to lower expected results as many of its drug patents expire.[93] Thus, in 2009 it purchased Insmed's portfolio of follow-on biologics for $130 million. It will

**Figure 6.3** The Curvilinear Relationship between Diversification and Performance

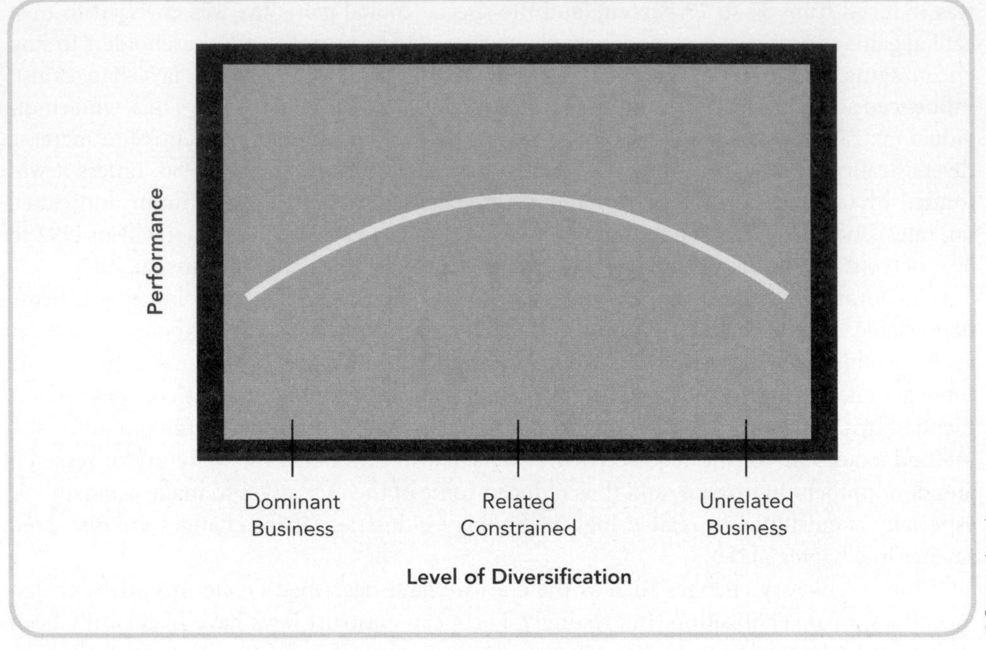




carry out the development of biologics that prevent infections in cancer patients receiving chemotherapy. One such drug, INS-19, is in late-stage trials, while INS-20 is in early-stage development.[94]

## Synergy and Firm Risk Reduction

Diversified firms pursuing economies of scope often have investments that are too inflexible to realize synergy between business units. As a result, a number of problems may arise. **Synergy** exists when the value created by business units working together exceeds the value that those same units create working independently. However, as a firm increases its relatedness between business units, it also increases its risk of corporate failure because synergy produces joint interdependence between businesses that constrains the firm's flexibility to respond. This threat may force two basic decisions.

First, the firm may reduce its level of technological change by operating in environments that are more certain. This behavior may make the firm risk averse and thus uninterested in pursuing new product lines that have potential but are not proven. Alternatively, the firm may constrain its level of activity sharing and forgo potential benefits of synergy. Either or both decisions may lead to further diversification.[95] The former will likely lead to related diversification into industries in which more certainty exists[96] while the latter may produce additional, but unrelated, diversification. Research suggests that a firm using a related diversification strategy is more careful in bidding for new businesses, whereas a firm pursuing an unrelated diversification strategy may be more likely to overprice its bid because an unrelated bidder is less likely to have full information about the acquired firm.[97] However, firms using either a related or an unrelated diversification strategy must understand the consequences of paying large premiums.[98] These problems often cause managers to become more risk averse and focus on achieving short-term returns. When they do, they are less likely to be concerned about social problems and in making long-term investments (e.g., to develop innovation). Alternatively, diversified firms (related and unrelated) can be innovative.[99]

**Synergy** exists when the value created by business units working together exceeds the value that those same units create working independently.

## 6-5b Resources and Diversification

As already discussed, firms may have several value-neutral incentives as well as value-creating incentives (such as the ability to create economies of scope) to diversify. However, even when incentives to diversify exist, a firm must have the types and levels of resources and capabilities needed to successfully use a corporate-level diversification strategy.[100] Although both tangible and intangible resources facilitate diversification, they vary in their ability to create value. Indeed, the degree to which resources are valuable, rare, difficult to imitate, and nonsubstitutable (see Chapter 3) influences a firm's ability to create value through diversification. For instance, free cash flows are a tangible financial resource that may be used to diversify the firm. However, compared with diversification that is grounded in intangible resources, diversification based on financial resources only is more visible to competitors and thus more imitable and less likely to create value on a long-term basis.[101] Tangible resources usually include the plant and equipment necessary to produce a product and tend to be less-flexible assets. Any excess capacity often can be used only for closely related products, especially those requiring highly similar manufacturing technologies. For example, large computer makers such as Dell and Hewlett-Packard have underestimated the demand for tablet computers, especially Apple's iPad. Apple developed the iPad and many expect it to eventually replace the personal computer (PC). In fact, HP's and Dell's sales of their PCs have been declining since the introduction of the iPad. Apple sold 42.4 million iPads in in the last quarter of 2012 and the first quarter of 2013. Samsung and competitors have developed rival pads and are selling a considerable number. Most analysts believe that the days of the personal computer are numbered, suggesting that Dell and HP must diversify into other product lines to make up for the loss of revenue from laptop sales.[102]

Excess capacity of other tangible resources, such as a sales force, can be used to diversify more easily. Again, excess capacity in a sales force is more effective with related diversification, because it may be utilized to sell products in similar markets (e.g., same customers). The sales force would be more knowledgeable about related product characteristics, customers, and distribution channels.[103] Tangible resources may create resource interrelationships in production, marketing, procurement, and technology, defined earlier as activity sharing. Intangible resources are more flexible than tangible physical assets in facilitating diversification. Although the sharing of tangible resources may induce diversification, intangible resources such as tacit knowledge could encourage even more diversification.[104]

Sometimes, however, the benefits expected from using resources to diversify the firm for either value-creating or value-neutral reasons are not gained.[105] For example, Sara Lee executives found that they could not realize synergy between elements of their company's diversified portfolio, and subsequently shed businesses accounting for 40 percent of company revenue to focus on food and food-related products and more readily achieve synergy.[106]

*Author to supply photo caption in first-pass pages.*

© iStockPhoto.com/Chesky_W

## 6-6 Value-Reducing Diversification: Managerial Motives to Diversify

Managerial motives to diversify can exist independent of value-neutral reasons (i.e., incentives and resources) and value-creating reasons (e.g., economies of scope). The desire for increased compensation and reduced managerial risk are two motives for top-level executives to diversify their firm beyond value-creating and value-neutral levels.[107] In slightly different words, top-level executives may diversify a firm in order to diversify their own employment risk, as long as profitability does not suffer excessively.[108]

Diversification provides additional benefits to top-level managers that shareholders do not enjoy. Research evidence shows that diversification and firm size are highly correlated, and as firm size increases, so does executive compensation.[109] Because large firms are complex, difficult-to-manage organizations, top-level managers commonly receive substantial levels of compensation to lead them, but the amounts vary across countries.[110] Greater levels of diversification can increase a firm's complexity, resulting in still more compensation for executives to lead an increasingly diversified organization. Governance mechanisms, such as the board of directors, monitoring by owners, executive compensation practices, and the market for corporate control, may limit managerial tendencies to overdiversify. These mechanisms are discussed in more detail in Chapter 10.

In some instances, though, a firm's governance mechanisms may not be strong, allowing executives to diversify the firm to the point that it fails to earn even average returns.[111] The loss of adequate internal governance may result in relatively poor performance, thereby triggering a threat of takeover. Although takeovers may improve efficiency by replacing ineffective managerial teams, managers may avoid takeovers through defensive tactics, such as "poison pills," or may reduce their own exposure with "golden parachute" agreements.[112] Therefore, an external governance threat, although restraining managers, does not flawlessly control managerial motives for diversification.[113]

Most large publicly held firms are profitable because the managers leading them are positive stewards of firm resources, and many of their strategic actions, including those related to selecting a corporate-level diversification strategy, contribute to the firm's success.[114] As mentioned, governance mechanisms should be designed to deal with exceptions to the managerial norms of making decisions and taking actions that increase the firm's ability to earn above-average returns. Thus, it is overly pessimistic to assume that managers usually act in their own self-interest as opposed to their firm's interest.[115]

Top-level executives' diversification decisions may also be held in check by concerns for their reputation. If a positive reputation facilitates development and use of managerial power, a poor reputation can reduce it. Likewise, a strong external market for managerial talent may deter managers from pursuing inappropriate diversification.[116] In addition, a diversified firm may acquire other firms that are poorly managed in order to restructure its own asset base. Knowing that their firms could be acquired if they are not managed successfully encourages executives to use value-creating diversification strategies.

As shown in Figure 6.4, the level of diversification with the greatest potential positive effect on performance is based partly on the effects of the interaction of resources, managerial motives, and incentives on the adoption of particular diversification strategies. As indicated earlier, the greater the incentives and the more flexible the resources, the higher the level of expected diversification. Financial resources (the most flexible) should have a stronger relationship to the extent of diversification than either tangible or intangible resources. Tangible resources (the most inflexible) are useful primarily for related diversification.

As discussed in this chapter, firms can create more value by effectively using diversification strategies. However, diversification must be kept in check by corporate governance

**Figure 6.4** Summary Model of the Relationship between Diversification and Firm Performance

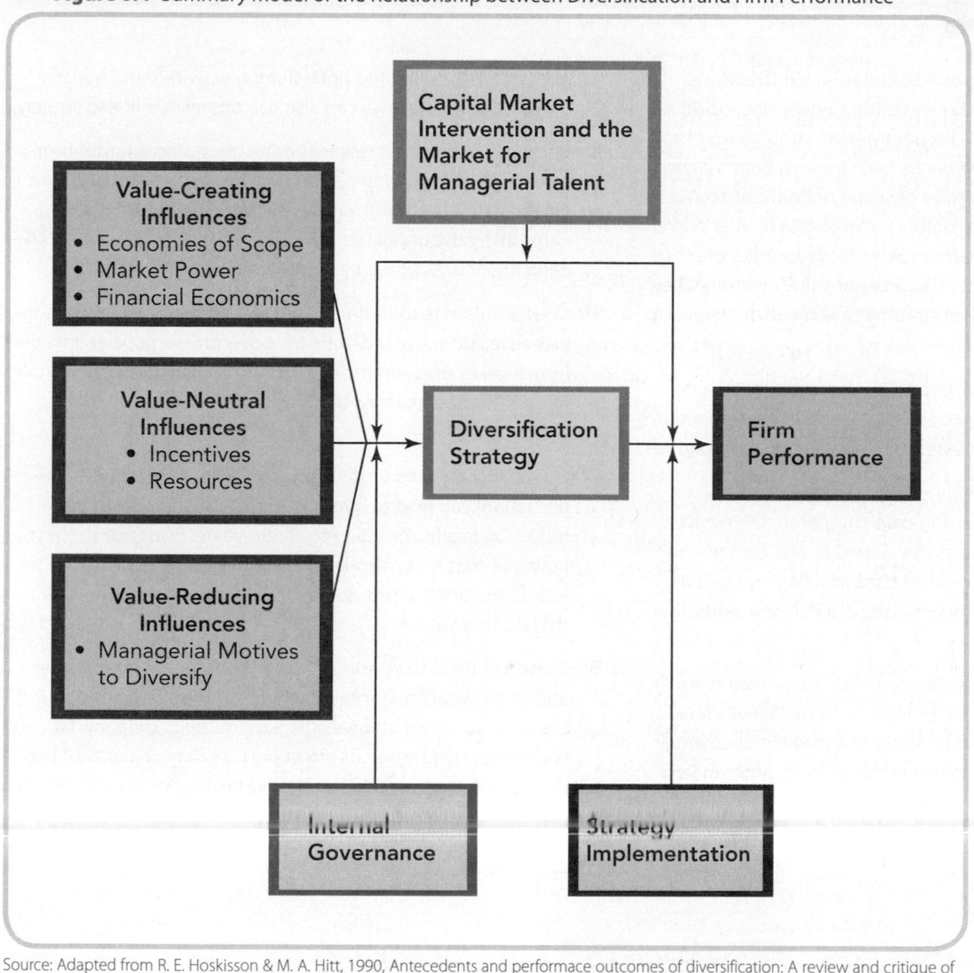


Source: Adapted from R. E. Hoskisson & M. A. Hitt, 1990, Antecedents and performace outcomes of diversification: A review and critique of theoretical perspectives, *Journal of Management*, 16: 498.

(see Chapter 10). Appropriate strategy implementation tools, such as organizational structures, are also important for the strategies to be successful (see Chapter 11).

We have described corporate-level strategies in this chapter. In the next chapter, we discuss mergers and acquisitions as prominent means for firms to diversify and to grow profitably. These trends toward more diversification through acquisitions, which have been partially reversed due to restructuring (see Chapter 7), indicate that learning has taken place regarding corporate-level diversification strategies.[117] Accordingly, firms that diversify should do so cautiously, choosing to focus on relatively few, rather than many, businesses. In fact, research suggests that although unrelated diversification has decreased, related diversification has increased, possibly due to the restructuring that continued into the 1990s and early twenty-first century. This sequence of diversification followed by restructuring has occurred in Europe and in countries such as Korea, following actions of firms in the United States and the United Kingdom.[118] Firms can improve their strategic competitiveness when they pursue a level of diversification that is appropriate for their resources (especially financial resources) and core competencies and the opportunities and threats in their country's institutional and competitive environments.[119]

# SUMMARY

- The primary reason a firm uses a corporate-level strategy to become more diversified is to create additional value. Using a single-or dominant-business corporate-level strategy may be preferable to seeking a more diversified strategy, unless a corporation can develop economies of scope or financial economies between businesses, or unless it can obtain market power through additional levels of diversification. Economies of scope and market power are the main sources of value creation when the firm uses a corporate-level strategy to achieve moderate to high levels of diversification.
- The related diversification corporate-level strategy helps the firm create value by sharing activities or transferring competencies between different businesses in the company's portfolio.
- Sharing activities usually involves sharing tangible resources between businesses. Transferring core competencies involves transferring core competencies developed in one business to another business. It also may involve transferring competencies between the corporate headquarters office and a business unit.
- Sharing activities is usually associated with the related constrained diversification corporate-level strategy. Activity sharing is costly to implement and coordinate, may create unequal benefits for the divisions involved in the sharing, and can lead to fewer managerial risk-taking behaviors.
- Transferring core competencies is often associated with related linked (or mixed related and unrelated) diversification, although firms pursuing both sharing activities and transferring core competencies can also use the related linked strategy.
- Efficiently allocating resources or restructuring a target firm's assets and placing them under rigorous financial controls are two ways to accomplish successful unrelated diversification. Firms using the unrelated diversification strategy focus on creating financial economies to generate value.
- Diversification is sometimes pursued for value-neutral reasons. Incentives from tax and antitrust government policies, low performance, or uncertainties about future cash flow are examples of value-neutral reasons that firms choose to become more diversified.
- Managerial motives to diversify (including to increase compensation) can lead to overdiversification and a subsequent reduction in a firm's ability to create value. Evidence suggests, however, that many top-level executives seek to be good stewards of the firm's assets and avoid diversifying the firm in ways that destroy value.
- Managers need to consider their firm's internal organization and its external environment when making decisions about the optimum level of diversification for their company. Of course, internal resources are important determinants of the direction that diversification should take. However, conditions in the firm's external environment may facilitate additional levels of diversification, as might unexpected threats from competitors.

# REVIEW QUESTIONS

1. What is corporate-level strategy and why is it important?
2. What are the different levels of diversification firms can pursue by using different corporate-level strategies?
3. What are three reasons firms choose to diversify their operations?
4. How do firms create value when using a related diversification strategy?
5. What are the two ways to obtain financial economies when using an unrelated diversification strategy?
6. What incentives and resources encourage diversification?
7. What motives might encourage managers to overdiversify their firm?

# EXPERIENTIAL EXERCISES

## EXERCISE 1: WHAT'S MY CORPORATE-LEVEL STRATEGY AND HOW DID I GET THIS WAY?

Your text defines corporate-level strategy as "actions a firm takes to gain a competitive advantage by selecting and managing a group of different businesses competing in different product markets." However, these actions are dynamic and longitudinal—they evolve over time. How did Ford Motor Company or IBM arrive at the corporate-level strategies they use today, and what are those strategies?

### Part One

Form teams of four or five students and select a publicly traded firm, preferably one that has been in existence for a few decades. A comprehensive listing of all U.S. publicly traded firms may be found at the Investor Guide Web site (http://www.investorguide.com/stocklist.php) as well as links to each firm's homepage and other financial data. You will also want to access the firm's SEC filings, which could be available at your library or through the Securities and Exchange Commission's Web site at http://www.sec.gov/edgar.shtml.

### Part Two

Complete a poster that can be displayed in class. Your poster should represent the firm and its evolution as far back in its history as you can get on one poster. The goal is to highlight the firm's beginnings, its acquisitions and divestiture activity, and its movement from one corporate-level strategy to another. You will need to do some extensive research on the firm to identify common linkages between operating units.

Be prepared to answer the following questions:

- How has the firm's corporate-level strategy evolved over time?
- What is the current corporate-level strategy and what links, if any, exist between operating units?
- Critique the current corporate-level strategy (e.g., too much diversification, too little, just right, and why).

## EXERCISE 2: WHAT DOES THIS ANNOUNCEMENT MEAN?

Form 8K of the Securities and Exchange Commission is often called the current report due to the SEC requirement that companies must report or announce any major events that shareholders should know about. Many times the reporting is rather common such as the departure of an executive or changing of the firm's auditor. However, an important firm notification on their 8K filing is due to the announcement of a merger or acquisition which, as mentioned in the preceding chapter, has a significant impact on corporate level strategy.

This exercise requires teams of students to analyze 8K filings in the last 12 months. You can find many sources of this information but a good place to start is your university library. Contact your reference librarian for databases and financial analysis sites that will help you efficiently identify some good candidates. Teams are to pick one 8K filing that represents a firm's announced acquisition. It does not particularly matter if the acquisition was consummated, as the announcement in and of itself is sufficient. Once the team has identified the acquisition they must be prepared to at a minimum answer the following questions in the form of a presentation to the class:

1. Describe the acquiring firm in terms of its corporate level strategy.
2. Analyze the firm's press releases regarding the announced acquisition. How is the firm categorizing the event?
3. Describe the target in terms of its corporate level strategy.
4. Now analyze the announced acquisition in terms of its new corporate level strategy. How do you categorize the proposed entity? Does this match with press reports?
5. Rate the acquisition. Does this combination of two firms make sense in your team's opinion?

## VIDEO CASE

### THE ROAD TO DIVERSIFICATION

#### Barry Diller/Senior Executive/IAC

Barry Diller, once the chairman and CEO of Paramount Pictures and Fox and intrigued by interactive commerce, purchased QVC only to lose it in other business acquisition attempts, particularly his bid to purchase Paramount. Losing the bid to own Paramount as well as other organizations, Barry Diller purchased QVC competitor HSN and began an interactive conglomerate from financial services to matchmaking services such as Match.com. Along the way, Diller discovered that his many businesses related to one another and united all his brands under one corporate headquarters. Barry Diller, driven by vision and the ability to grasp new and difficult concepts, insists that IAC/InterActiveCorp is a brand-by-brand endless multiproduct company similar to Procter & Gamble.

Be prepared to discuss the following concepts and questions in class:

### Concepts

- Corporate-level strategy
- Levels of diversification
- Value-creating diversification
- Operational and corporate relatedness
- Related and unrelated diversification
- Motivations to overdiversify

### Questions

1. Describe Diller's corporate-level strategy.
2. Describe IAC's level of diversification.
3. What do you think was Diller's reason to diversify?
4. Is Diller's approach value-creating diversification? Why or why not?
5. Explain how IAC businesses and brands are related. Do they have related diversification?
6. Is Diller in a position to overdiversify?

# NOTES


1. M. E. Porter, 1980, *Competitive Strategy*, New York: The Free Press, xvi.
2. M. D. R. Chari, S. Devaraj, & P. David, 2008, The impact of information technology investments and diversification strategies on firm performance, *Management Science*, 54: 224–234; A. Pehrsson, 2006, Business relatedness and performance: A study of managerial perceptions, *Strategic Management Journal*, 27: 265–282.
3. J. Joseph & W. Ocasio, 2012, Architecture, attention and adaptation in the multibusiness firm: General Electric from 1951 to 2001, *Strategic Management Journal*, 33: 633–660.
4. M. E. Porter, 1987, From competitive advantage to corporate strategy, *Harvard Business Review*, 65(3): 43–59.
5. Ibid.; M. E. Raynor, 2007, What is corporate strategy, really? *Ivey Business Journal*, 71(8): 1–3.
6. W. P. Wan, R. E. Hoskisson, J. C. Short, & D. W. Yiu, 2011, Resource-based theory and corporate diversification: Accomplishments and opportunities, *Journal of Management*, 37(5): 1335–1368; A. A. Calart & J. E. Ricart, 2007, Corporate strategy: An agent-based approach, *European Management Review*, 4: 107–120.
7. K. Lee, M. W. Peng, & K. Lee, 2008, From diversification premium to diversification discount during institutional transitions, *Journal of World Business*, 43(1): 47–65; M. Ammann & M. Verhofen, 2006, The conglomerate discount: A new explanation based on credit risk, *International Journal of Theoretical & Applied Finance*, 9(8): 1201–1214; S. A. Mansi & D. M. Reeb, 2002, Corporate diversification: What gets discounted? *Journal of Finance*, 57: 2167–2183.
8. A. Campbell, M. Goold, & M. Alexander, 1995, Corporate strategy: The question for parenting advantage, *Harvard Business Review*, 73(2): 120–132.
9. K. Favaro, 2013, We're from corporate and we are here to help: Understanding the real value of corporate strategy and the head office, *Strategy+Business Online*, www.strategy-business.com, April 8; D. Collis, D. Young, & M. Goold, 2007, The size, structure, and performance of corporate headquarters, *Strategic Management Journal*, 28: 283–405.
10. G. Kenny, 2012, Diversification: Best practices of the leading companies, *Journal of Business Strategy*, 33: 12-20; D. Miller, 2006, Technological diversity, related diversification performance, *Strategic Management Journal*, 27: 601–619.
11. D. D. Bergh, 2001, Diversification strategy research at a crossroads: Established, emerging and anticipated paths, in M. A. Hitt, R. E. Freeman, & J. S. Harrison (eds.), *Handbook of Strategic Management*, Oxford, UK: Blackwell Publishers, 363–383.
12. S. F. Matusik & M. A. Fitza, 2012, Diversification in the venture capital industry: Leveraging knowledge under uncertainty, *Strategic Management Journal*, 33: 407–426; H. C. Wang & J. B. Barney, 2006, Employee incentives to make firm-specific investments: Implications for resource-based theories of corporate diversification, *Academy of Management Journal*, 31: 466–476.
13. A. Kaul, 2012, Technology and corporate scope: Firm and rival innovation as antecedents of corporate transactions, *Strategic Management Journal*, 33: 347–367; K. Z. Zhou & F. Wu, 2010, Technological capability, strategic flexibility and product innovation, *Strategic Management Journal*, 31: 547–561.
14. J. J. Marcel, 2009, Why top management team characteristics matter when employing a chief operating officer: A strategic contingency perspective, *Strategic Management Journal*, 30(6): 647–658; A. J. Ward, M. J. Lankau, A. C. Amason, J. A. Sonnenfeld, & B. R. Agle, 2007, Improving the performance of top management teams, *MIT Sloan Management Review*, 48(3): 85–90.
15. R. P. Rumelt, 1974, *Strategy, Structure, and Economic Performance*, Boston: Harvard Business School; L. Wrigley, 1970, *Divisional Autonomy and Diversification* (Ph.D. dissertation), Harvard Business School.
16. P. Gogoi, N. Arndt, & J. Crown, 2008, A bittersweet deal for Wrigley: Selling the family business wasn't William Wrigley Jr.'s plan, but the Mars offer was too good to refuse, *BusinessWeek*, May 12, 34.
17. 2013, United Parcel Service 2010 Annual Report, www.ups.com, May 7.
18. R. Rumelt, 2011, *Good Strategy/Bad Strategy: The Difference and Why it Matters*, New York: Crown Business Publishing.
19. M. Spriggs, A. Yu, D. Deeds, & R. L. Sorenson, 2012, Too many cooks in the kitchen: Innovative capacity, collaborative network orientation and performance in small family businesses, *Family Business Review*, 26: 32–50; L. R. Gomez-Mejia, M. Makri, & M. L. Kintana, 2010, Diversification decisions in family controlled firms, *Journal of Management Studies*, 47: 223–252.
20. A. Barroso & M. S. Giarratana, 2013, Product proliferation strategies and firm performance: The moderating role of product space complexity, *Strategic Management Journal*, in press.
21. 2013, Publicis Groupe, Wikipedia, http://en.wikipedia.org/wiki/Publicis, May 8.
22. J. L. Stimpert, I. M. Duhaime, & J. Chesney, 2010, Learning to manage a large diversified firm, *Journal of Leadership and Organizational Studies*, 17: 411–425.
23. 2013, Hutchison Whampoa Limited 2012 Annual Report, www.hutchison whampoa.com, accessed May 8; 2013, Hutchison Whampoa Limited, *Wikipedia*, http://en.wikipedia.org/wiki/Hutchison_Whampoa_Limited, accessed on May 8.
24. C.-N. Chen & W. Chu, 2012, Diversification, resource concentration and business group performance: Evidence from Taiwan, *Asia Pacific Journal of Management*, 29: 1045–1061.
25. D. H. Ming Chng, M. S. Rodgers, E. Shih, & X.-B. Song, 2012, When does incentive compensation motivate managerial behavior? An experimental investigation of the fit between incentive compensation, executive core self-evaluation and firm performance, *Strategic Management Journal*, 33: 1343–1362; J. E. Core & W. R. Guay, 2010, Is CEO pay too high and are incentives too low? A wealth-based contracting framework, *Academy of Management Perspectives*, 24(1): 5–19; I. Filatotchev & D. Allcock, 2010, Corporate governance and executive remuneration: A contingency framework, *Academy of Management Perspectives*, 24(1): 20–33.
26. D. G. Sirmon, M. A. Hitt, R. D. Ireland, & B. A. Gilbert, 2011, Resource orchestration to create competitive advantage: Breadth, depth and life cycle effects, *Journal of Management*, 37(5): 1390–1412; D. J. Miller, M. J. Fern, & L. B. Cardinal, 2007, The use of knowledge for technological innovation within diversified firms, *Academy of Management Journal*, 50: 308–326.
27. R. A. D'Aveni, G. B. Dagnino, & K. G. Smith, 2010. The age of temporary advantage, *Strategic Management Journal*, 31: 1371–1385; H. Tanriverdi & C.-H. Lee, 2008, Within-industry diversification and firm performance in the presence of network externalities: Evidence from the software industry, *Academy of Management Journal*, 51(2): 381–397.
28. M. E. Graebner, K. M. Eisenhardt, & P. T. Roundy, 2010, Success and failure of technology acquisitions: Lessons for buyers and sellers, *Academy of Management Perspectives*, 24(3): 73–92; M. D. R. Chari, S. Devaraj, & P. David, 2008, The impact of information technology investments and diversification strategies on firm performance, *Management Science*, 54(1): 224–234.
29. G. M. Kistruck, I. Qureshi, & P. W. Beamish, 2013, Geographic and product diversification in charitable organizations, *Journal of Management*, 39: 496–530.
30. F. Neffke & M. Henning, 2013, Skill relatedness and firm diversification, *Strategic Management Journal*, 34: 297–316.
31. M. Makri, M. A. Hitt, & P. J. Lane, 2010, Complementary technologies, knowledge relatedness and invention outcomes in high technology mergers and acquisitions, *Strategic Management Journal*, 31: 602–628.
32. N. Shin, 2009, Information technology and diversification: How their relationship

affects firm performance. *International Journal of E-Collaboration*, 5(1): 69–83; D. Miller, 2006, Technological diversity, related diversification, and firm performance, *Strategic Management Journal*, 27: 601–619.

33. M. V. S. Kumar, 2013, The costs of related diversification: The impact of core business on the productivity of related segments, *Organization Science*, in press; Y. M. Zhou, 2011, Synergy, coordination costs, and diversification choices, *Strategic Management Journal*, 32: 624–639.
34. M. A. Hitt, D. King, H. Krishnan, M. Makri, M. Schijven, K. Shimizu, & H. Zhu, 2012, Creating value through mergers and acquisitions: Challenges and opportunities, in D. Faulkner, S. Teerikangas, & R. Joseph (Eds.), *Oxford Handbook of Mergers and Acquisitions*, Oxford, UK: Oxford University Press, 2012, 71–113; P. Puranam & K. Srikanth, 2007, What they know vs. what they do: How acquirers leverage technology acquisitions, *Strategic Management Journal*, 28: 805–825.
35. L. B. Lien, 2013, Can the survivor principle survive diversification? *Organization Science*, in press; D. D. Bergh, 1995, Size and relatedness of units sold: An agency theory and resource-based perspective, *Strategic Management Journal*, 16: 221–239.
36. M. Lubatkin & S. Chatterjee, 1994, Extending modern portfolio theory into the domain of corporate diversification: Does it apply? *Academy of Management Journal*, 37: 109–138.
37. E. Dooms & A. A. Van Oijen, 2008, The balance between tailoring and standardizing control, *European Management Review*, 5(4): 245–252; T. Kono, 1999, A strong head office makes a strong company, *Long Range Planning*, 32(2): 225.
38. I.-C. Hsu & Y.-S. Wang, 2008, A model of intraorganizational knowledge sharing: Development and initial test. *Journal of Global Information Management*, 16(3): 45–73; Puranam & Srikanth, What they know vs. what they do; F. T. Rothaermel, M. A. Hitt, & L. A. Jobe, 2006, Balancing vertical integration and strategic outsourcing: Effects on product portfolio, product success, and firm performance, *Strategic Management Journal*, 27: 1033–1056.
39. A. Rodríguez-Duarte, F. D. Sandulli, B. Minguela-Rata, & J. I. López-Sánchez, 2007, The endogenous relationship between innovation and diversification, and the impact of technological resources on the form of diversification, *Research Policy*, 36: 652–664; L. Capron & N. Pistre, 2002, When do acquirers earn abnormal returns? *Strategic Management Journal*, 23: 781–794.
40. Miller, Fern, & Cardinal, The use of knowledge for technological innovation within diversified firms; J. W. Spencer, 2003, Firms' knowledge-sharing strategies in the global innovation system: Empirical evidence from the flat panel display industry, *Strategic Management Journal*, 24: 217–233.
41. J. Thottam, 2008, Branson's flight plan, *Time*, April 28, 40.
42. 2013, Operations overview, Honda Motor Company, www.honda.com, May 9.
43. L. C. Thang, C. Rowley, T. Quang, & M. Warner, 2007, To what extent can management practices be transferred between countries?: The case of human resource management in Vietnam, *Journal of World Business*, 42(1): 113–127; G. Stalk Jr., 2005, Rotate the core, *Harvard Business Review*, 83(3): 18–19.
44. J. A. Martin & K. M. Eisenhardt, 2010, Rewiring: Cross-business unit collaborations in multibusiness organizations, *Academy of Management Journal*, 53: 265–301.
45. S. Gupta, A. Woodside, C. Dubelaar, & D. Bradmore, 2009, Diffusing knowledge-based core competencies for leveraging innovation strategies: Modeling outsourcing to knowledge process organizations (KPOs) in pharmaceutical networks, *Industrial Marketing Management*, 38(2): 219–227.
46. A. Pehrsson, 2010, Business-relatedness and the strategy of moderations: Impacts on foreign subsidiary performance, *Journal of Strategy and Management*, 3: 110–133; S. Chatterjee & J. Singh, 1999, Are trade-offs inherent in diversification moves? A simultaneous model for type of diversification and mode of expansion decisions, *Management Science*, 45: 25–41.
47. J. Wiggins, 2008, Mars' move for Wrigley leaves rivals trailing, *Financial Times*, April 29, 24.
48. K. J. O'Brien, 2013, Despite sales growth, Ericsson profit plunges, *New York Times*, www.nytimes.com, April 24.
49. L. Fuentelsaz & J. Gomez, 2006, Multipoint competition, strategic similarity and entry into geographic markets, *Strategic Management Journal*, 27: 477–499; J. Gimeno & C. Y. Woo, 1999, Multimarket contact, economies of scope, and firm performance, *Academy of Management Journal*, 42: 239–259..
50. T. A. Shervani, G. Frazier, & G. Challagalla, 2007, The moderating influence of firm market power on the transaction cost economics model: An empirical test in a forward channel integration context, *Strategic Management Journal*, 28: 635–652; R. Gulati, P. R. Lawrence, & P. Puranam, 2005, Adaptation in vertical relationships: Beyond incentive conflict, *Strategic Management Journal*, 26: 415–440.
51. N. Lahiri & S. Narayanan, 2013, Vertical integration, innovation and alliance portfolio size: Implications for firm performance, *Strategic Management Journal*, 34: 1042–1064; D.J. Teece, 2012, *Strategy, Innovation and the Theory of the Firm*, Northampton, MA: Edward Elgar Publishing Ltd.
52. R. Carter & G. M. Hodgson, 2006, The impact of empirical tests of transaction cost economics on the debate on the nature of the firm, *Strategic Management Journal*, 27: 461–476; O. E. Williamson, 1996, Economics and organization: A primer, *California Management Review*, 38(2): 131–146.
53. R. Kapoor, 2013, Persistence of integration in the face of specialization: How firms navigated the winds of disintegration and shaped the architecture of the semiconductor industry, *Organization Science*, 24: 1195–1213; S. Novak & S. Stern, 2008, How does outsourcing affect performance dynamics? Evidence from the automobile industry, *Management Science*, 54: 1963–1979.
54. E. Rawley, 2010, Diversification, coordination costs and organizational rigidity: Evidence from microdata, *Strategic Management Journal*, 31: 873–891.
55. C. Wolter & F. M. Veloso, 2008, The effects of innovation on vertical structure: Perspectives on transaction costs and competences, *Academy of Management Review*, 33(3): 586–605; M. G. Jacobides, 2005, Industry change through vertical disintegration: How and why markets emerged in mortgage banking, *Academy of Management Journal*, 48: 465–498.
56. T. Hutzschenreuter & F. Grone, 2009, Changing vertical integration strategies under pressure from foreign competition: The case of U.S. and German multinationals, *Journal of Management Studies*, 46: 269–307.
57. 2011, Flextronics International Ltd., www.flextronics.com, May 31.
58. K. M. Eisenhardt & D. C. Galunic, 2000, Coevolving: At last, a way to make synergies work, *Harvard Business Review*, 78(1): 91–111.
59. P. David, J. P. O'Brien, T. Yoshikawa, & A. Delios, 2010, Do shareholders or stakeholders appropriate the rents from corporate diversification? The influence of ownership structure, *Academy of Management Journal*, 53: 636–654; J. A. Nickerson & T. R. Zenger, 2008, Envy, comparison costs, and the economic theory of the firm, *Strategic Management Journal*, 13: 1429–1449.
60. 2013, Corporate overview, Walt Disney company, http://corporate.disney.go.com, May 10; L Greene, 2009, Adult nostalgia for childhood brands, *Financial Times*, www.ft.com, February 14; M. Marr, 2007, The magic kingdom looks to hit the road, *Wall Street Journal*, www.wsj.com, February 8.
61. D. Lee & R. Madhaven, 2010, Divestiture and firm performance: A meta-analysis, *Journal of Management*, 36: 1345–1371; D. W. Ng, 2007, A modern resource-based approach to unrelated diversification. *Journal of Management Studies*, 44(8): 1481–1502; D. D. Bergh, 1997, Predicting divestiture of unrelated acquisitions: An integrative model of ex ante conditions, *Strategic Management Journal*, 18: 715–731.
62. Porter, *Competitive Advantage*.
63. S. Lee, K. Park, H. H. Shin, 2009, Disappearing internal capital markets:

Evidence from diversified business groups in Korea. *Journal of Banking & Finance*, 33(2): 326–334; D. Collis, D. Young, & M. Goold, 2007, The size, structure, and performance of corporate headquarters, *Strategic Management Journal*, 28: 283–405; O. E. Williamson, 1975, *Markets and Hierarchies: Analysis and Antitrust Implications*, New York: Macmillan Free Press.

64. R. Aggarwal & N. A. Kyaw, 2009, International variations in transparency and capital structure: Evidence from European firms. *Journal of International Financial Management & Accounting*, 20(1): 1–34; R. J. Indjejikian, 2007, Discussion of accounting information, disclosure, and the cost of capital, *Journal of Accounting Research*, 45(2): 421–426.

65. J. T. Campbell, T. C. Campbell, D. G. Sirmon, L. Bierman, & C. S. Tuggle, 2012, Shareholder influence over director nomination via proxy access: Implications for agency conflict and stakeholder value, *Strategic Management Journal*, 33: 1431–1451; A. Capezio, J. Shields, & M. O'Donnell, 2011, Too good to be true: Board structural independence as a moderator of CEO pay-for-performance, *Journal of Management Studies*, 48: 487–513.

66. A. Mackey, 2008, The effect of CEOs on firm performance, *Strategic Management Journal*, 29: 1357–1367; Dooms & Van Oijen, The balance between tailoring and standardizing control; D. Miller, R. Eisenstat, & N. Foote, 2002, Strategy from the inside out: Building capability-creating organizations, *California Management Review*, 44(3): 37–54; M. E. Raynor & J. L. Bower, 2001, Lead from the center: How to manage divisions dynamically, *Harvard Business Review*, 79(5): 92–100.

67. 2013, Shareowner letter, United Technologies 2012 Annual Report, http://2012ar.utc.com/letter, accessed May 10.

68. B. Quint. 2009, Companies deal with tough times through diversification, *Information Today*, 26(3): 7–8.

69. S. L. Sun, X. Zhoa, & H. Yang, 2010, Executive compensation in Asia: A critical review, *Asia Pacific Journal of Management*, 27: 775–802; A. Delios, D. Xu, & P. W. Beamish, 2008, Within-country product diversification and foreign subsidiary performance, *Journal of International Business Studies*, 39(4): 706–724.

70. Lee, Park, Shin, Disappearing internal capital markets: Evidence from diversified business groups in Korea; A. Chakrabarti, K. Singh, & I. Mahmood, 2006, Diversification and performance: Evidence from East Asian firms, *Strategic Management Journal*, 28: 101–120.

71. D. D. Bergh, R. A. Johnson, & R. L. Dewitt, 2008, Restructuring through spin-off or sell-off: Transforming information asymmetries into financial gain, *Strategic Management Journal*, 29(2): 133–148; C. Decker & M. Mellewigt, 2007, Thirty years after Michael E. Porter: What do we know about business exit? *Academy of Management Perspectives*, 2: 41–55; S. J. Chang & H. Singh, 1999, The impact of entry and resource fit on modes of exit by multibusiness firms, *Strategic Management Journal*, 20: 1019–1035.

72. 2013, About us, Danaher, www.danaher.com, May 10.

73. R. Coff, 2003, Bidding wars over R&D-intensive firms: Knowledge, opportunism, and the market for corporate control, *Academy of Management Journal*, 46: 74–85.

74. J. Xia & S. Li, 2013, The divestiture of acquired subunits: A resource-dependence approach, *Strategic Management Journal*, 34: 131–148; C. Moschieri & J. Mair, 2012, Managing divestitures through time—Expanding current knowledge, *Academy of Management Perspectives*, 26(4): 35–50.

75. H. Berry, 2013, When do firms divest foreign operations? *Organization Science*, in press; D. Ma, 2012, A relational view of organizational restructuring: The case of transitional China, *Management and Organization Review*, 8: 51–75.

76. M. Lubatkin, H. Merchant, & M. Srinivasan, 1997, Merger strategies and shareholder value during times of relaxed antitrust enforcement: The case of large mergers during the 1980s, *Journal of Management*, 23: 61–81.

77. D. P. Champlin & J. T. Knoedler, 1999, Restructuring by design? Government's complicity in corporate restructuring, *Journal of Economic Issues*, 33(1): 41–57.

78. R. M. Scherer & D. Ross, 1990, *Industrial Market Structure and Economic Performance*, Boston: Houghton Mifflin.

79. A. Shleifer & R. W. Vishny, 1994, Takeovers in the 1960s and 1980s: Evidence and implications, in R. P. Rumelt, D. E. Schendel, & D. J. Teece (Eds.), *Fundamental Issues in Strategy*, Boston: Harvard Business School Press, 403–422.

80. S. Chatterjee, J. S. Harrison, & D. D. Bergh, 2003, Failed takeover attempts, corporate governance and refocusing, *Strategic Management Journal*, 24: 87–96; Lubatkin, Merchant, & Srinivasan, Merger strategies and shareholder value; D. J. Ravenscraft & R. M. Scherer, 1987, *Mergers, Sell-Offs and Economic Efficiency*, Washington, DC: Brookings Institution, 22.

81. D. A. Zalewski, 2001, Corporate takeovers, fairness, and public policy, *Journal of Economic Issues*, 35: 431–437; P. L. Zweig, J. P. Kline, S. A. Forest, & K. Gudridge, 1995, The case against mergers, *BusinessWeek*, October 30, 122–130.

82. E. J. Lopez, 2001, New anti-merger theories: A critique, *Cato Journal*, 20: 359–378; 1998, The trustbusters' new tools, *The Economist*, May 2, 62–64.

83. D. Bush & D. D. Gelb, 2012 Anti-trust enforcement: An inflection point? *Journal of Business Strategy*, 33(6): 15–21.

84. M. C. Jensen, 1986, Agency costs of free cash flow, corporate finance, and takeovers, *American Economic Review*, 76: 323–329.

85. M. A. Hitt, J. S. Harrison, & R. D. Ireland 2001, *Mergers and Acquisitions: A Guide to Creating Value for Stakeholders*, New York: Oxford University Press.

86. M. T. Brouwer, 2008, Horizontal mergers and efficiencies; theory and antitrust practice, *European Journal of Law and Economics*, 26(1): 11–26.

87. T. Afza, C. Slahudin, & M. S. Nazir, 2008, Diversification and corporate performance: An evaluation of Pakistani firms, *South Asian Journal of Management*, 15(3): 7–18; J. M. Shaver, 2006, A paradox of synergy: Contagion and capacity effects in mergers and acquisitions, *Academy of Management Journal*, 31: 962–976.

88. M. Palmer & T. Bradshaw, 2011, Skype can be the "glue" in Microsoft's multimedia strategy, *Financial Times*, http://blogs.ft.com, May 14.

89. K. Shimizu & M. A. Hitt, 2011, Errors at the top of the hierarchy, in D. A. Hofmann & M. Friese (Eds.), *Errors in Organizations*, New York: Routledge.

90. L. E. Palich, L. B. Cardinal, & C. C. Miller, 2000, Curvilinearity in the diversification-performance linkage: An examination of over three decades of research, *Strategic Management Journal*, 21: 155–174.

91. Sirmon, Hitt, Ireland, & Gilbert, Resource orchestration to create competitive advantage; A. E. Bernardo & B. Chowdhry, 2002, Resources, real options, and corporate strategy, *Journal of Financial Economics*, 63: 211–234.

92. W. H. Tsai, Y. C. Kuo, J.-H. Hung, 2009, Corporate diversification and CEO turnover in family businesses: Self-entrenchment or risk reduction? *Small Business Economics, 32*(1): 57–76; N. W. C. Harper & S. P. Viguerie, 2002, Are you too focused? *McKinsey Quarterly*, Mid-Summer, 29–38.

93. L. Jarvis, 2008, Pharma strategies: Merck launches into the bio-similars business, *Chemical & Engineering News*, December, 86(50): 7.

94. J. Carroll, 2009, Merck acquires bio-similars in $130M pact, *Fierce Biotech*, www.fiercebiotech.com, February 12.

95. T. B. Folta & J. P. O'Brien, 2008, Determinants of firm-specific thresholds in acquisition decisions, *Managerial and Decision Economics*, 29(2/3): 209–225.

96. N. M. Kay & A. Diamantopoulos, 1987, Uncertainty and synergy: Towards a formal model of corporate strategy, *Managerial and Decision Economics*, 8: 121–130.

97. R. W. Coff, 1999, How buyers cope with uncertainty when acquiring firms in knowledge-intensive industries: Caveat emptor, *Organization Science*, 10: 144–161.

98. P. B. Carroll & C. Muim 2008, 7 ways to fail big, *Harvard Business Review*, 86(9): 82–91.

99. S. K. Kim, J. D. Arthurs, A. Sahaym, & J. B. Cullen, 2013, Search behavior of the diversified firm: The impact of fit on innovation, *Strategic Management Journal*, 34: 999–1009; J. Kang, 2013, The relationship

between corporate diversification and corporate social performance, *Strategic Management Journal*, 34: 94–109.

100. D. G. Sirmon, S. Gove, & M. A. Hitt, 2008, Resource management in dyadic competitive rivalry: The effects of resource bundling and deployment, *Academy of Management Journal*, 51(5): 919–935; S. J. Chatterjee & B. Wernerfelt, 1991, The link between resources and type of diversification: Theory and evidence, *Strategic Management Journal*, 12: 33–48.
101. E. N. K. Lim, S. S. Das, & A. Das, 2009, Diversification strategy, capital structure, and the Asian financial crisis (1997–1998): Evidence from Singapore firms, *Strategic Management Journal*, 30(6): 577–594; W. Keuslein, 2003, The Ebitda folly, *Forbes*, March 17, 165–167.
102. 2013, Apple's hot news, Apple Inc., www.apple.com, accessed May 10.
103. L. Capron & J. Hull 1999, Redeployment of brands, sales forces, and general marketing management expertise following horizontal acquisitions: A resource-based view, *Journal of Marketing*, 63(2): 41–54.
104. M. V. S. Kumar, 2009, The relationship between product and international diversification: The effects of short-run constraints and endogeneity. *Strategic Management Journal*, 30(1): 99–116; C. B. Malone & L. C. Rose, 2006. Intangible assets and firm diversification, *International Journal of Managerial Finance*, 2(2): 136–153.
105. C. Moschieri, 2011, The implementation and structuring of divestitures: The unit's perspective, *Strategic Management Journal*, 32: 368–401; K. Shimizu & M. A. Hitt, 2005, What constrains or facilitates divestitures of formerly acquired firms? The effects of organizational inertia, *Journal of Management*, 31: 50–72.
106. D. Cimilluca & J. Jargon, 2009, Corporate news: Sara Lee weighs sale of European business, *Wall Street Journal*, March 13, B3; J. Jargon & J. Vuocolo, 2007, Sara Lee CEO challenged on antitakeover defenses, *Wall Street Journal*, May 11, B4.
107. A. J. Nyberg, I. S. Fulmer, B. Gerhart, & M. A. Carpenter, 2010, Agency theory revisited: CEO return, and shareholder interest alignment, *Academy of Management Journal*, 53: 1029–1049; J. G. Combs & M. S. Skill, 2003, Managerialist and human capital explanation for key executive pay premiums: A contingency perspective, *Academy of Management Journal*, 46: 63–73.
108. D. Souder, Z. Simsek, & S. G. Johnson, 2012, The differing effects of agent and founder CEOs on the firm's market expansion, *Strategic Management Journal*, 33: 23–41; L. L. Lan & L. Heracleous, 2010, Rethinking agency theory: The view from law, *Academy of Management Review*, 35: 294–314; R. E. Hoskisson, M. W. Castleton, & M. C. Withers, 2009, Complementarity in monitoring and bonding: More intense monitoring leads to higher executive compensation, *Academy of Management Perspectives*, 23(2): 57–74.
109. Geiger & Cashen, Organizational size and CEO compensation; J. J. Cordeiro & R. Veliyath, 2003, Beyond pay for performance: A panel study of the determinants of CEO compensation, *American Business Review*, 21(1): 56–66; Wright, Kroll, & Elenkov, Acquisition returns, increase in firm size, and chief executive officer compensation.
110. M. van Essen, P. P. Heugens, J. Otto, & J. van Oosterhout, 2012, An institution-based view of executive compensation: A multilevel meta-analytic test, *Journal of International Business Studies*, 43: 396–423; Y. Deutsch, T. Keil, & T. Laamanen, 2011, A dual agency view of board compensation: The joint effects of outside director and CEO options on firm risk, *Strategic Management Journal*, 32: 212–227.
111. A. J. Wowak & D. C. Hambrick, 2010, A model of person-pay interaction: How executives vary in their responses to compensation arrangements, *Strategic Management Journal*, 31: 803–821; J. Bogle, 2008, Reflections on CEO compensation, *Academy of Management Perspectives*, 22(2): 21–25.
112. M. Kahan & E. B. Rock, 2002, How I learned to stop worrying and love the pill: Adaptive responses to takeover law, *University of Chicago Law Review*, 69(3): 871–915.
113. R. C. Anderson, T. W. Bates, J. M. Bizjak, & M. L. Lemmon, 2000, Corporate governance and firm diversification, *Financial Management*, 29(1): 5–22; J. D. Westphal, 1998, Board games: How CEOs adapt to increases in structural board independence from management, *Administrative Science Quarterly*, 43: 511–537.
114. S. M. Campbell, A. J. Ward, J. A. Sonnenfeld, & B. R. Agle, 2008, Relational ties that bind: Leader-follower relationship dimensions and charismatic attribution, *Leadership Quarterly*, 19(5): 556–568; M. Wiersema, 2002, Holes at the top: Why CEO firings backfire, *Harvard Business Review*, 80(12): 70–77.
115. D. Allcock & I. Filatotchev, 2010, Executive incentive schemes in initial public offerings: The effects of multiple-agency conflicts and corporate governance, *Journal of Management*, 36: 663–686; J. M. Bizjak, M. L. Lemmon, & L. Naveen, 2008, Does the use of peer groups contribute to higher pay and less efficient compensation?, *Journal of Financial Economics*, 90(2): 152–168; N. Wasserman, 2006, Stewards, agents, and the founder discount: Executive compensation in new ventures, *Academy of Management Journal*, 49: 960–976.
116. E. F. Fama, 1980, Agency problems and the theory of the firm, *Journal of Political Economy*, 88: 288–307.
117. M. Y. Brannen & M. F. Peterson, 2009, Merging without alienating: Interventions promoting cross-cultural organizational integration and their limitations, *Journal of International Business Studies*, 40(3): 468–489; M. L. A. Hayward, 2002, When do firms learn from their acquisition experience? Evidence from 1985–1995, *Strategic Management Journal*, 23: 21–39.
118. R. E. Hoskisson, R. A. Johnson, L. Tihanyi, & R. E. White, 2005, Diversified business groups and corporate refocusing in emerging economies, *Journal of Management*, 31: 941–965.
119. C. N. Chung & X. Luo, 2008, Institutional logics or agency costs: The influence of corporate governance models on business group restructuring in emerging economies, *Organization Science*, 19(5): 766–784; W. P. Wan & R. E. Hoskisson, 2003, Home country environments, corporate diversification strategies, and firm performance, *Academy of Management Journal*, 46: 27–45.

# 7

# Merger and Acquisition Strategies

***Studying this chapter should provide you with the strategic management knowledge needed to:***

1. Explain the popularity of merger and acquisition strategies in firms competing in the global economy.
2. Discuss reasons why firms use an acquisition strategy to achieve strategic competitiveness.
3. Describe seven problems that work against achieving success when using an acquisition strategy.
4. Name and describe the attributes of effective acquisitions.
5. Define the restructuring strategy and distinguish among its common forms.
6. Explain the short- and long-term outcomes of the different types of restructuring strategies.

## STRATEGIC ACQUISITIONS AND ACCELERATED INTEGRATION OF THOSE ACQUISITIONS ARE A VITAL CAPABILITY OF CISCO SYSTEMS

Cisco Systems is in the business of building the infrastructure that allows the Internet to work. As the Internet evolved, however, Cisco's business was required to change with this evolution. As part of its advancement, Cisco Systems has used an acquisition strategy to build network products and extend their reach into new areas, both related and unrelated. In the beginning, digital connectivity was important through e-mail and Web browsing and searches. This evolved into a network economy facilitating ecommerce, digital supply chains, and digital collaboration. Subsequently, the digital interaction phase moved Cisco into developing infrastructure for social media, mobile and cloud computing, and digital video. The next stage seems to be "the Internet of everything" connecting people, processes, data, and things. This will require the basic core in routing, switching, and services, as well as large data centers to facilitate visualization through cloud computing. Video and collaboration as well as basic architecture of the business will be transforming to become the base strategic business blocks. Furthermore, the need to have strong digital security will be paramount.

Cisco has entered many aspects of this business through acquisitions. For instance, in 2012, Cisco acquired TV software developer NDS for $5 billion. NDS Group develops software for television networks. In particular, its solutions allow pay-TV providers to deliver digital content to TVs, DVRs, PCs, and other multimedia devices. It provides solutions that protect digital content so that only paid subscribers can access it. Because of Cisco's customer-driven focus, it has sought to help its customers capture these market transitions and meet their particular needs. Of course, Cisco also builds the routers that allow video data and e-mail communications to come together through their blade servers (individual and modular servers that cut down on cabling). These routers and servers support cloud computing for the mobile devices that deliver the video that NDS software enables on desktop and mobile devices.

Also in 2012, Cisco purchased Meraki for $1.2 billion. Meraki provides solutions that optimize services in the cloud. For instance, it offers mid-sized customers Wi-Fi, switching, security, and mobile device management centrally from a set of cloud servers. For instance, if you are a guest at a university or other company campus it supports, you can bring your own personal device into the network, which allows guest networking and facilitates application controls. It manages the firewall and other advanced networking services to protect security as well.

John Chambers, Cisco CEO, has helped the firm move through the many transitions noted earlier. In the IT sector, 90 percent of acquisitions fail. However, as Chambers notes, "although Cisco does better than anyone else, we know that a third of our acquisitions won't work." Chambers worked for companies that did not successfully make transitions. Wang Laboratories missed a transition, and after experiencing this as an executive, Chambers learned to have a "healthy paranoia." He adds: "More than anything, I've tried to make Cisco a company that can see big transitions and move." One way they do this is to "listen to the customers very closely" to understand the necessary changes.

As Cisco makes the transition into the all-everything network, not only must it manage the cloud, but it also must provide service to the mobile devices that work in cellular networks. Accordingly, Cisco also acquired Intucell, a self-optimizing network software developer, for $475 million. It likewise acquired Truviso, Inc., a provider of network data analysis and reporting software, for an undisclosed price (it was partly owned by venture capital firms and was headquartered in Israel). Most recently it acquired Ubiquisys, which cuts cellular carriers' costs "by shifting traffic from congested towers to more targeted locations inside an office, home or public space, which also boosts the service's reliability." This approach is especially efficient when seeking to improve "coverage in crowded areas such as stadiums, convention centers and subway stations." These acquisitions help cellular network customers manage their products in the network more efficiently in the delivery of data, e-mail, and video services. As you can see, for this series of acquisitions Cisco has used acquisitions strategically to move into new areas as its environment changes, to learn about new technologies, and to gain knowledge on new technologies as it experiences these transitions.

In the process of this rapid change, it has developed a distinct ability to integrate acquisitions. When Cisco contemplates an acquisition, along with financial due diligence to make sure that it is paying the right price, it also develops a detailed plan for possible post-merger integration. It begins communicating early with stakeholders about integration plans and conducts rigorous post-mortems to identify ways "to make subsequent integrations more efficient and effective." Once a deal is completed, this allows the company to hit the ground running when the deal becomes public. Cisco is ready "from Day 1 to explain how the two companies are going to come together and provide unique value and how the integration effort itself will be structured to realize value." The firm does not "want the [acquired] organization to go in limbo," which can happen if the integration process is not well thought out. Also, during the integration process, it is important to know how far the integration should go. Sometimes integration is too deep, and value is destroyed that was being sought in the acquisition. Sometimes it may even pay to keep the business separate from Cisco's other operations to allow the business to function without integration until the necessary learning is complete. "Cisco learned the hard way that complex deals require you to know at a high level of detail how you're going to drive value."

Sources: L. Capron, 2013, Cisco's corporate development portfolio: A blend of building, borrowing and buying, *Strategy & Leadership*, 41(2): 27–30; D. FitzGerald & S. Chaudhuri, 2013, Corporate news: Cisco doubles down on small-cell transmitters with Ubiquisys, *Wall Street Journal*, April 4, B7; T. Geron, 2012, Meraki-Cisco deal a boost for Sequoia, Google-connected VCs, *Forbes*, November 19, 18; R. Karlgaard, 2012, Cisco's Chambers: Driving change, *Forbes*, February 22, 68; A. Moscaritolo, 2012, Cisco to acquire TV software developer NDS for $5 billion, *PC Magazine*, March 1; B. Worthen, D. Cimilluca, & A. Das, 2012, Cisco hedges bet on video delivery, *Wall Street Journal*, March 16, B1; R. Myers, 2011, Integration acceleration, *CFO*, 27(1): 52–57.

**Learn more about Meraki, another company acquired by Cisco.**
**www.cengagebrain.com**

We examined corporate-level strategy in Chapter 6, focusing on types and levels of product diversification strategies that firms derive from their core competencies to create competitive advantages and value for stakeholders. As noted in that chapter, diversification allows a firm to create value by productively using excess resources to exploit new opportunities.[1] In this chapter, we explore merger and acquisition strategies. Firms throughout the world use these strategies, often in concert with diversification strategies, to become more diversified. As noted in the Opening Case, merger and acquisition strategies remain popular as a source of firm growth to meet new challenges and opportunities, and hopefully of above-average returns.

M. Stasy

Most corporations are very familiar with merger and acquisition strategies. For example, as the opening case on Cisco Systems illustrates, the latter half of the twentieth century found major companies using these strategies to grow and to deal with the competitive challenges in their domestic markets as well as those emerging from global competitors. Today, smaller firms also use merger and acquisition strategies to grow in their existing markets and to enter new markets.[2]

Not unexpectedly, some mergers and acquisitions fail to reach their promise.[3] Accordingly, explaining how firms can successfully use merger and acquisition strategies to create stakeholder value[4] is a key purpose of this chapter. To do this, we first explain the continuing popularity of merger and acquisition strategies as a choice firms evaluate when seeking growth and strategic competitiveness. As part of this explanation, we describe the differences between mergers, acquisitions, and takeovers. We next discuss specific reasons firms choose to use acquisition strategies and some of the problems organizations may encounter when implementing them. We then describe the characteristics associated with effective acquisitions before closing the chapter with a discussion of different types of restructuring strategies. Restructuring strategies are commonly used to correct or deal with the results of ineffective mergers and acquisitions.

# 7-1 The Popularity of Merger and Acquisition Strategies

Merger and acquisition (M&A) strategies have been popular among U.S. firms for many years. Some believe that these strategies played a central role in the restructuring of U.S. businesses during the 1980s and 1990s and that they continue generating these types of benefits in the twenty-first century.[5]

Although popular, and appropriately so, as a means of growth with the potential to lead to strategic competitiveness, it is important to emphasize that changing conditions in the external environment influence the type of M&A activity firms pursue. During the recent financial crisis, tightening credit markets made it more difficult for firms to complete "megadeals" (those costing $10 billion or more). Although the flow of deals picked up in 2011 and 2012 in the United States, the global deal flow has not reached the number and overall total value realized in 2007. In the first quarter of 2013, deals valued at more than US$5 billion totaled US$542.8 billion, a 10 percent increase over 2012. However, "over 8,100 worldwide deals were announced during the first quarter of 2013, a 16 percent decline from 2012 and the slowest quarter for M&A, by number of deals, since the third quarter of 2004."[6] Worries over the U.S. budget deficit and the associated sequester and the overall health of government finances in the European region created uncertainty about the wisdom of pursuing deals. However, one analyst noted that "European companies have strong balance sheets and low economic growth in their markets, which means they have to acquire to grow."[7] For example, Heineken NV, a large beer producer headquartered in Europe, noted a revenue increase from 2012, but the increase "was entirely due to acquisitions, notably of Asia Pacific Breweries, maker of Tiger beer. Heineken acquired the bulk of the company for $6.4 billion" in late 2012.[8]

In the final analysis, firms use merger and acquisition strategies to improve their ability to create more value for all stakeholders, including shareholders. As suggested by Figure 1.1, this reasoning applies equally to all of the other strategies (e.g., business-level, corporate-level, international, and cooperative) a firm may formulate and then implement.

However, evidence suggests that using merger and acquisition strategies in ways that consistently create value is challenging. This is particularly true for acquiring firms in that some research results indicate that shareholders of acquired firms often earn above-average returns from acquisitions, while shareholders of acquiring firms typically earn returns that are close to zero.[9] Moreover, in approximately two-thirds of all acquisitions, the acquiring firm's stock price falls immediately after the intended transaction is announced. This negative response reflects investors' skepticism about the likelihood that the acquirer will be able to achieve the synergies required to justify the premium.[10] Premiums can sometimes appear to be excessive, as in the potential acquisition of Illumina (a biotech firm) by Roche (a Swiss pharmaceutical firm). One analyst suggested that "Roche was willing to pay 30.1 times Illumina's expected 2012 earnings and a 61 percent premium to its share price before takeover speculation gripped the stock, a much higher premium than in recent pharma deals."[11] Obviously, creating the amount of value required to account for this type of premium is not going to be easy. In fact, Roche ultimately dropped its offer because Illumina's board wanted an even larger premium. Franz Humer, chairman at Roche, noted: "Roche doesn't do acquisitions that don't create added value. We have self-discipline."[12] Overall then, those leading firms that are using merger and acquisition strategies must recognize that creating more value for their stakeholders by doing so is indeed difficult.[13]

A **merger** is a strategy through which two firms agree to integrate their operations on a relatively coequal basis.

An **acquisition** is a strategy through which one firm buys a controlling, or 100 percent, interest in another firm with the intent of making the acquired firm a subsidiary business within its portfolio.

A **takeover** is a special type of acquisition wherein the target firm does not solicit the acquiring firm's bid; thus, takeovers are unfriendly acquisitions.

### 7-1a Mergers, Acquisitions, and Takeovers: What Are the Differences?

A **merger** is a strategy through which two firms agree to integrate their operations on a relatively coequal basis. Glencore and Xstrata announced their "merger of equals" in February 2012. Glencore was the larger coming in, headquartered in Switzerland, and is one of the world's largest commodity mining and trading companies in the world. Xstrata was an Anglo-Swiss company focused on mining commodities such as coal, nickel, and zinc. Together, they are an integrated mining and commodity trading power player.[14]

Even though the transaction between Glencore and Xstrata appears to be a merger, the reality is that few true mergers actually take place. The main reason for this is that one party to the transaction is usually dominant in regard to various characteristics such as market share, size, or value of assets. In this case the transaction is slanted more towards Glencore.[15]

An **acquisition** is a strategy through which one firm buys a controlling, or 100 percent, interest in another firm with the intent of making the acquired firm a subsidiary business within its portfolio. After completing the transaction, the management of the acquired firm reports to the management of the acquiring firm.

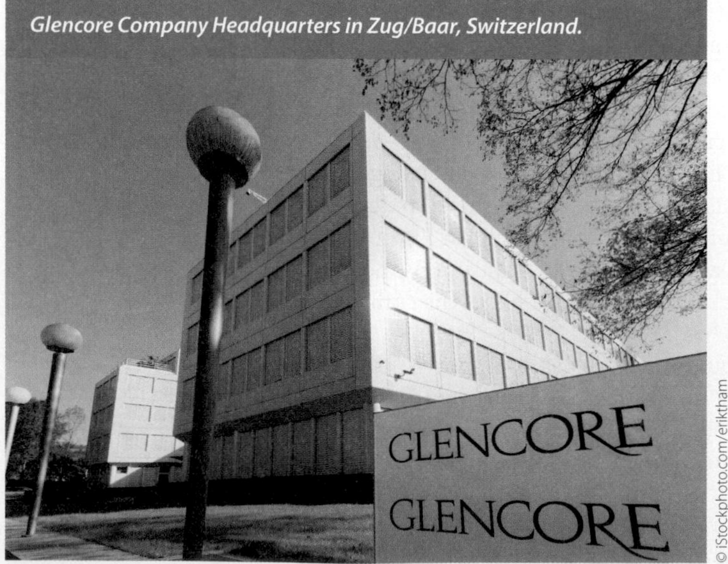

Glencore Company Headquarters in Zug/Baar, Switzerland.

© iStockphoto.com/erikthan

Although most of the mergers that are completed are friendly in nature, acquisitions can be friendly or unfriendly. A **takeover** is a special type of acquisition wherein the target firm does not solicit the acquiring firm's bid; thus, takeovers are unfriendly acquisitions. As explained in Chapter 10, firms have developed takeover defenses (mostly corporate governance devices) for preventing hostile takeovers when such a bid is undesired by the target's board of directors.[16] For example, the previously mentioned Illumina takeover attempt by Roche was a hostile bid.

Research evidence reveals that "pre-announcement returns" of hostile takeovers "are largely anticipated and associated with a significant increase in the bidder's and target's share prices."[17] This evidence provides a rationale why some firms are willing to pursue buying another company even when that firm is not interested in being bought. Often, determining the price the acquiring firm is willing to pay to "take over" the target firm is the core issue in these transactions. As noted above, the Roche bid failed because they could not agree on an appropriate price.

On a comparative basis, acquisitions are more common than mergers and takeovers. Accordingly, we focus the remainder of this chapter's discussion on acquisitions.

# 7-2 Reasons for Acquisitions

In this section, we discuss reasons firms decide to acquire another company. Although each reason can provide a legitimate rationale, acquisitions are not always as successful as the involved parties want them to be. Later in the chapter, we examine problems firms may encounter when seeking growth and strategic competitiveness through acquisitions.

## 7-2a Increased Market Power

Achieving greater market power is a primary reason for acquisitions.[18] Defined in Chapter 6, *market power* exists when a firm is able to sell its goods or services above competitive levels or when the costs of its primary or support activities are lower than those of its competitors. Market power usually is derived from the size of the firm and its resources and capabilities to compete in the marketplace;[19] it is also affected by the firm's share of the market. Therefore, most acquisitions that are designed to achieve greater market power entail buying a competitor, a supplier, a distributor, or a business in a highly related industry to allow the exercise of a core competence and to gain competitive advantage in the acquiring firm's primary market.

If a firm achieves enough market power, it can become a market leader, which is the goal of many firms. For example, in December 2012, Delta Airlines announced that it was purchasing a 49 percent stake in Virgin Atlantic Airways for $360 million as it seeks to boost its market share of transatlantic flights between Europe and the United States.[20]

Next, we discuss how firms use horizontal, vertical, and related types of acquisitions to increase their market power.

### Horizontal Acquisitions

The acquisition of a company competing in the same industry as the acquiring firm is a *horizontal acquisition*. Horizontal acquisitions increase a firm's market power by exploiting cost-based and revenue-based synergies.[21] For instance, the combination of Delta and Virgin Atlantic noted above brings together two large players that increase the competitiveness of both carriers as they compete with other airlines.

Research suggests that horizontal acquisitions result in higher performance when the firms have similar characteristics,[22] such as strategy, managerial styles, and resource allocation patterns. Similarities in these characteristics, as well as previous alliance management experience, support efforts to integrate the acquiring and the acquired firm. Horizontal acquisitions are often most effective when the acquiring firm integrates the acquired firm's assets with its own assets, but only after evaluating and divesting excess capacity and assets that do not complement the newly combined firm's core competencies.[23] The Glencore and Xstrata deal noted above is a horizontal acquisition, and it also necessitates some asset divestiture to please antitrust authorities as well as layoffs of duplicate personnel performing the same function.

### Vertical Acquisitions

A *vertical acquisition* refers to a firm acquiring a supplier or distributor of one or more of its goods or services. Through a vertical acquisition, the newly formed firm controls additional parts of the value chain (see Chapters 3 and 6),[24] which is how vertical acquisitions lead to increased market power.

Bob Evans Farms, Inc. is primarily known for its Bob Evans and Mimi's restaurants. It also produces meat and side items for sale in retail grocery stores in all 50 U.S. states. In 2012, it acquired Kettle Creations, which co-manufactured side dishes to Bob Evans' specifications. This represents a vertical acquisition as Kettle Creations is a supplier of prepared products for both restaurants and retail sales items under the Bob Evans label. In an environment where there can be disruptions in the supply chain, vertical acquisitions create better predictability and less disruption in the supply chain, especially when there is growth in the restaurant chain and in the food retail segment businesses to support the increased vertical capacity. Kettle Creations has been making mashed potatoes and macaroni and cheese for Bob Evans since 2009 and will be integrated with BEF Foods Inc., a subsidiary of Bob Evans Farms, Inc.[25]

### Related Acquisitions

Acquiring a firm in a highly related industry is called a *related acquisition*. Through a related acquisition, firms seek to create value through the synergy that can be generated by integrating some of their resources and capabilities. For example, Oracle has been acquiring related acquisitions in telecommunications. Oracle, a dominant software provider, has focused on overall enterprise management software with a concentration on managing inventories, ledgers, and other business operations. It is now beginning to target facilitating networks that managers have to use external to the firm. For example, it recently acquired Tekelec from a private equity group led by Siris Capital Group LLC. This acquisition followed previous deals to buy Acme Packet Inc. and Xsigo Systems Inc., both telecom gear producers, to broaden its footprint to facilitate large corporate data centers in managing their external networks. Many of these deals are to compete with cloud offerings such as those from competitor Salesforce.com Inc. that provide Internet management software, which help firms manage and better target customers through Internet sales and distribution.[26]

Horizontal, vertical, and related acquisitions that firms complete to increase their market power are subject to regulatory review as well as to analysis by financial markets.[27] For example, UPS agreed to purchase Thomas Nationwide Transport (TNT) Express for over $6 billion. However, the European Commission questioned whether the merger would meet antitrust guidelines and lower the competitiveness of the package delivery business in Europe. After this ruling, in January 2013 the United Parcel Service (UPS) officially disbanded its attempt to purchase TNT Express.[28] Thus, firms seeking growth and market power through acquisitions must understand the political/legal segment of the general environment (see Chapter 2) in order to successfully use an acquisition strategy.

## 7-2b Overcoming Entry Barriers

*Barriers to entry* (introduced in Chapter 2) are factors associated with a market or with the firms currently operating in it that increase the expense and difficulty new firms encounter when trying to enter that particular market. For example, well-established competitors may have economies of scale in the manufacture or service of their products. In addition, enduring relationships with customers often create product loyalties that are difficult for new entrants to overcome. When facing differentiated products, new entrants typically must spend considerable resources to advertise their products and may find it necessary to sell below competitors' prices to entice new customers.

Facing the entry barriers that economies of scale and differentiated products create, a new entrant may find acquiring an established company to be more effective than entering the market as a competitor offering a product that is unfamiliar to current buyers. In fact, the higher the barriers to market entry, the greater the probability that a firm will acquire an existing firm to overcome them. For example, many video content consumers want to watch such content on mobile devices. However, DirecTV and Dish Network, two of the largest satellite television companies, do not have a way to readily produce and distribute content to mobile devices such as smartphones through their satellite networks. However, some firms can do this through software. Comcast, a cable TV firm, can use its Xfinity mobile app software to distribute televised content to their cable customers' mobile devices. As such, to overcome this barrier to entry, Dish Network has proposed an acquisition of Sprint Nextel, a mobile service provider. SoftBank is also bidding on Sprint Nextel as a way to enter into the U.S. market as a mobile service provider. As will be discussed later, SoftBank is the third largest mobile carrier in Japan.[29]

As this discussion suggests, a key advantage of using an acquisition strategy to overcome entry barriers is that the acquiring firm gains immediate access to a market. This advantage can be particularly attractive for firms seeking to overcome entry barriers associated with entering international markets.[30] Multinational corporations from developing economies seek to enter developed and other emerging economies because they are among the fastest-growing firms in the world.[31] As discussed next, completing a cross-border acquisition of a local target allows a firm to quickly enter fast-growing economies such as these.

## Cross-Border Acquisitions

Acquisitions made between companies with headquarters in different countries are called *cross-border acquisitions*.[32] For example, as noted above, the third largest mobile operator in Japan in regard to market share, SoftBank, is seeking to buy a 70 percent stake in Sprint Nextel for $20.1 billion. SoftBank is seeking to extend its reach beyond its domestic market because Japan's growth is limited relative to other countries.[33]

There are other interesting changes taking place in terms of cross-border acquisition activity. Historically, North American and European companies were the most active acquirers of companies outside their domestic markets. However, the current global competitive landscape is one in which firms from other nations may use an acquisition strategy more frequently than do their counterparts in North America and Europe. In this regard, Chinese companies, in particular, are well positioned for cross-border acquisitions. Chinese corporations are well capitalized with strong balance sheets and cash reserves, and they have learned from their past failures, as indicated in the Strategic Focus.[34] In the Strategic Focus, we also describe recent cross-border acquisitions by emerging market companies and how their approaches differ. For example, Bimbo, a Mexican bakery operator, recently purchased bakery operations, Weston Foods, from Sara Lee in the U.S. As you will see, many of the deals cited are horizontal, vertical, or related acquisitions through which the acquiring companies seek to increase their market power.

As noted in the Strategic Focus, firms headquartered in mid-range developing economies such as China and Brazil are also completing more cross-border acquisitions than in the past. The weak U.S. dollar and more favorable government policies toward cross-border acquisitions are supporting such companies' desires to rapidly become more global.

Firms using an acquisition strategy to complete cross-border acquisitions should understand that these transactions are not risk free. For example, firms seeking to acquire companies in China must recognize that China remains a challenging environment for foreign investors. Political and legal obstacles make acquisitions in China risky and difficult.[35] Due diligence is problematic as well because corporate governance and transparency of financial statements are often obscure. For instance, Caterpillar, an earthmoving equipment company, acquired Chinese manufacturing company Siwei, but after the purchase discovered the company's accounting was fraudulent and as such the price it paid was misrepresented by management.[36] Thus, firms must carefully study the risks as well as the potential benefits when contemplating cross-border acquisitions.

## Strategic Focus GLOBALIZATION

### Cross-Border Acquisitions by Firms from Emerging Economies: Leveraging Resources to Gain a Larger Global Footprint and Market Power

Historically, large multinational firms from North America and Europe have pursued international acquisitions in emerging and developing countries in order to establish stronger economies of scale for domestic brands as well as provide opportunities for sourcing of scarce resources. Although the Spanish economy is in the doldrums, Spanish firms have used this strategy relatively recently to expand, first into Latin America and then into other European countries. Telefónica and Banco Santander are Spanish companies that have extended their reach, especially through cross-border acquisitions. For instance, Telefónica is now the world's fifth largest telecommunication provider in terms of revenue, and Santander is the fourth largest bank on the same metric and has become Latin America's largest retail bank.

Like many Spanish firms, many emerging economy firms are seeking to build a global footprint through acquisitions. For example, after China was accepted into the World Trade Organization in 2000, many Chinese cross-border mergers and acquisitions were attempted. However, many Chinese companies who made cross-border acquisitions saw them end in failure in their first attempts. In 2003, there was $1.6 billion spent on acquisitions, which swelled to $18.2 billion by 2006. However, TLC Corporation's acquisition of France's Thomson Electronics, SAIC's takeover of South Korea's Ssangyong Motor Company, Ping An's investment in the Belgium-Dutch financial services group Fortis, and Ningbo Bird's strategic partnership with France's Sajan ended in stunning failures, where the Chinese either pulled out or had to sell off much of their acquired assets. The Chinese, however, have learned from their mistakes. Instead of buying global brands, sales networks, and goodwill in branded products, they are now mainly trying to acquire concrete assets such as mineral deposits, state of the art technologies, or R&D facilities. This strategy was encouraged by the government after pulling back from the failed acquisitions just mentioned. As the economy around the world depreciated assets and as the RMB (China's currency) appreciated relative to developed economies, the strategy focused on hard assets because it made better investing sense rather than seeking to buy established branded products in which they did not always have managerial capability to realize successful performance. Interestingly, research suggests that India's acquiring companies (comparative to Chinese companies) have focused on buying competitors (horizontal acquisitions) in less-developed nations to build global market power.

Bimbo is the world's largest bakery company, formed in 1945 by a Spanish immigrant to Mexico. Initially, Bimbo expanded its operations throughout Latin America from its Mexican base.

*Spanish telecommunications company Telefonica has extended its market reach through cross-border acquisitions.*

However, in 1996 it made its first acquisition in the United States. By 2012, it had acquired more than a dozen U.S. firms, including the bakery operations of Sara Lee, Weston Foods. Under Sara Lee, Weston Foods had declined because of a lack of focus on efficient execution in the low-margin bread and bakery business. Bimbo's leaders are continually on the road looking for ways to improve productivity. For instance, in China they used tricycle delivery bikes in urban areas where streets are too narrow for trucks, a practice first honed and implemented in Latin America. At the same time, their trucks are equipped with sophisticated computer systems that optimize delivery routes. In the process of developing better strategic execution, it has also created better ways of integrating new acquisitions into its operating procedures honed in emerging economies. As such, Bimbo is likely to increase the efficiency of the Weston baker operations.

Similarly, Orascom, a Cairo-based Egyptian conglomerate, has used the construction business as a base platform and has prospered by pursuing acquisitions in countries that others shun. Orascom Group has entered a set of turbulent countries, including Jordan, Yemen, Pakistan, Zimbabwe, Algeria, Tunisia, Iraq, Bangladesh, North Korea, Burundi, Central African Republic, Namibia, and Lebanon. For example, its entry into North Korea in 2007 was due to the desire to use North Korean labor on a project already underway in China. Orascom agreed to a $150 million modernization of a North Korean cement plant in exchange for a 50 percent equity in its operation and permission to use North Korean labor. Through this agreement, Orascom built trust with North Korean officials and, more importantly, gained insight into Korea's infrastructure plans. Since 2007, it has diversified into partial ownership of a North Korean bank and also helped build the Ryugyong Hotel, a 105-floor skyscraper in Pyongyang. Other diversifications have included a large mobile phone business in Egypt as well as other emerging countries' economies, mostly through acquisitions and subsequent internal development.

Brazil is another country with a large emerging economy whose companies have significant acquisition activity. In 2013, Natura Cosméticos, a Brazilian beauty products firm, acquired 65 percent ownership of Australian-based Emeis Holdings, owner of luxury beauty brand Aesop. Emeis sells Aesop branded products in more than 60 stores in 11 countries. In 2010, Marfrig, a Brazilian meat packer, acquired Keystone Foods for $1.25 billion. Keystone is a top supplier to American fast food chains such as Subway and McDonald's. JBS, now the world's largest meat packer, bought Pilgrim's Pride for $800 million as well as Swift for $1.4 billion. Both of these firms are meat packing operations, which gives JBS significant exposure in the United States. These acquisitions in large part were made possible by Brazil's national development bank (BNDES), which supports Brazilian firms in developing their international operations.

Although acquisitions allow emerging market firms to enter foreign developed country markets as well as industries outside their domestic market, such acquisitions come at a price. Research suggests that emerging economy firms pay a higher premium than other firms. Perhaps these firms feel they have to pay this premium in order to win the deal and persuade regulators that they are not a threat, especially in industries which [illegible] suggests that government ownership leads firms to overpay and that the overpayment reduces value for minority shareholders (nongovernment shareholders). Many of these acquisitions are also becoming less focused on infrastructure development and more on consumer market acquisitions because the firms cannot only extend their power into developed companies, but they can help to improve technology in their own domestic market, where a large middle class is emerging with consumers having more buying power. It is expected that this trend of acquisitions from emerging economies to developed economies will continue.

Sources: F. Bonifacio, 2013, Natura acquires majority stake in Australian skin care company, *Global Cosmetic Industry*, March: 22–23; B. Grant & G. Stieglitz, 2013, Equipment maker crumbles as baking industry consolidates, *Journal of Corporate Renewal*, 26(3): 10–13; V. Chen, J. Li, & D. M. Shapiro, 2012, International reverse spillover effects on parent firms: Evidences from emerging-market MNEs in developed markets, *European Management Journal*, 30(3): 204–218; F. De Beule & J. Duanmu, 2012, Locational determinants of internationalization: A firm-level analysis of Chinese and Indian acquisitions, *European Management Journal*, 30(3): 264–277; M. F. Guillén & E. García-Canal, 2012, Execution as strategy, *Harvard Business Review*, 90(10): 103–107; G. Jones, 2012, The growth opportunity that lies next door, *Harvard Business Review*, 90(7/8): 141–145; B. Kedia, N. Gaffney, & J. Clampit, 2012, EMNEs and knowledge-seeking FDI, *Management International Review*, 52(2): 155–173; S. A. Nonis & C. Relyea, 2012, Business innovations from emerging market countries into developed countries: Implications for multinationals from developed countries, *Thunderbird International Business Review*, 54(3): 291–298; L. Rabbiosi, S. Elia, & F. Bertoni, 2012, Acquisitions by EMNCs in developed markets, *Management International Review*, 52(2): 193–212; P. J. Williamson & A. P. Raman, 2011, How China reset its global acquisition agenda, *Harvard Business Review*, 89(4): 109–114; J. Zhang, C. Zhou, & H. Ebbers, 2011, Completion of Chinese overseas acquisitions: Institutional perspective and evidence, *International Business Review*, 20(2): 226–238.

## 7-2c Cost of New Product Development and Increased Speed to Market

Developing new products internally and successfully introducing them into the marketplace often requires significant investment of a firm's resources, including time, making it difficult to quickly earn a profitable return.[37] Because an estimated 88 percent of innovations fail to achieve adequate returns, firm managers are also concerned with achieving adequate returns from the capital invested to develop and commercialize new products. Potentially contributing to these less-than-desirable rates of return is the successful imitation of approximately 60 percent of innovations within four years after the patents are obtained. These types of outcomes may lead managers to perceive internal product development as a high-risk activity.[38]

Learn more about Bimbo.
www.cengagebrain.com

Acquisitions are another means a firm can use to gain access to new products and to current products that are new to the firm. Compared with internal product development processes, acquisitions provide more predictable returns as well as faster market entry. Returns are more predictable because the performance of the acquired firm's products can be assessed prior to completing the acquisition.[39]

Medtronic is the world's largest medical device maker. While pharmaceutical firms invent many of their products internally, most of Medtronic's products are acquired from surgeons or other outside inventors.[40] Research confirms that it can be a good strategy to buy early stage products, especially if you have strong R&D capability, even though there is

M. Stasy

risk and uncertainty in doing so.[41] Acquisitions can enable firms to enter markets quickly and to increase the predictability of returns on their investments.

### 7-2d **Lower Risk Compared to Developing New Products**

Because the outcomes of an acquisition can be estimated more easily and accurately than the outcomes of an internal product development process, managers may view acquisitions as being less risky.[42] However, firms should exercise caution when using acquisitions to reduce their risks relative to the risks the firm incurs when developing new products internally. Indeed, even though research suggests acquisition strategies are a common means of avoiding risky internal ventures (and therefore risky R&D investments), acquisitions may also become a substitute for innovation. Accordingly, acquisitions should always be strategic rather than defensive in nature. For example, the proposed Dish Network acquisition of Sprint Nextel, a mobile service provider, needs to be done with great care because Dish does not have experience operating a cellular service, given its operational experience as a satellite TV service provider.

### 7-2e **Increased Diversification**

Acquisitions are also used to diversify firms. Based on experience and the insights resulting from it, firms typically find it easier to develop and introduce new products in markets they are currently serving. In contrast, it is difficult for companies to develop products that differ from their current lines for markets in which they lack experience.[43] Thus, it is relatively uncommon for a firm to develop new products internally to diversify its product lines.[44]

For example, Xerox purchased Affiliated Computer Services, an outsourcing firm, to bolster its services business. Xerox is seen primarily as a hardware technology company, selling document management equipment. However, over time, Xerox has sought to diversify into helping firms to manage business processes and technology services. As such, through this acquisition it seeks to have more and more of its business in the technology service sector. In this way, Xerox seeks to take care of the document-intensive business processes behind the scenes.[45]

Acquisition strategies can be used to support use of both unrelated and related diversification strategies (see Chapter 6).[46] For example, United Technologies Corp. (UTC) uses acquisitions as the foundation for implementing its unrelated diversification strategy. Since the mid-1970s it has been building a portfolio of stable and noncyclical businesses, including Otis Elevator Co. (elevators, escalators, and moving walkways) and Carrier Corporation (heating and air conditioning systems) in order to reduce its dependence on the volatile aerospace industry. Pratt & Whitney (aircraft engines), Hamilton Sundstrand (aerospace and industrial systems), Sikorsky (helicopters), UTC Fire & Security (fire safety and security products and services), and UTC Power (fuel cells and power systems) are the other businesses in which UTC competes as a result of using its acquisition strategy. While each business UTC acquires manufactures industrial and/or commercial products, many have a relatively low focus on technology (e.g., elevators, air conditioners, and security systems). It has recently run into trouble, however, with its acquisition of Goodrich, a defense contractor, and a downturn in Europe and emerging economies.[47]

In contrast to UTC, Cisco Systems pursues mostly related acquisitions, as illustrated in the Opening Case. Cisco wants to make the transition into the "all-everything network"; as such, not only must it manage transfers between computing devices and the cloud, but it also must provide service to the mobile devices that work in cellular networks.[48] Historically, these acquisitions have helped the firm build its network components business, which is focused on producing network backbone hardware. These recent acquisitions have helped Cisco diversify its operations beyond its original expertise in network hardware and network management software into network connection software among a large variety of devices, including mobile devices and cellular networks and helping client firms manage cloud computing applications.[49]

Firms using acquisition strategies should be aware that, in general, the more related the acquired firm is to the acquiring firm, the greater is the probability the acquisition will be successful.[50] Thus, horizontal acquisitions and related acquisitions tend to contribute more to the firm's strategic competitiveness than do acquisitions of companies operating in product markets that are quite different from those in which the acquiring firm competes, although complementary acquisitions in different industries can help expand a firm's capabilities.

### 7-2f Reshaping the Firm's Competitive Scope

As discussed in Chapter 2, the intensity of competitive rivalry is an industry characteristic that affects the firm's profitability.[51] To reduce the negative effect of an intense rivalry on their financial performance, firms may use acquisitions to lessen their dependence on one or more products or markets. Reducing a company's dependence on specific markets shapes the firm's competitive scope.

Each time UTC pursues a new acquisition (Goodrich, its latest acquisition, focuses on the growing commercial aerospace market), it helps to reshape its competitive scope. In a more subtle manner, P&G's acquisition of Gillette reshaped its competitive scope by giving P&G a stronger presence in some products for whom men are the target market. Xerox's purchase of Affiliated Computer Services likewise has reshaped Xerox's competitive scope to focus more on services, and Cisco has become more focused on software to facilitate inter-network connections through its latest acquisitions. Thus, using an acquisition strategy reshaped the competitive scope of each of these firms.

### 7-2g Learning and Developing New Capabilities

Firms sometimes complete acquisitions to gain access to capabilities they lack. For example, acquisitions may be used to acquire a special technological capability. Research shows that firms can broaden their knowledge base and reduce inertia through acquisitions[52] and increase the potential of their capabilities when they acquire diverse talent through cross-border acquisitions.[53] Of course, firms are better able to learn these capabilities if they share some similar properties with the firm's current capabilities. Thus, firms should seek to acquire companies with different but related and complementary capabilities in order to build their own knowledge base.[54]

A number of large pharmaceutical firms are acquiring the ability to create "large molecule" drugs, also known as biological drugs, by buying biotechnology firms. Thus, these firms are seeking access to both the pipeline of possible drugs and the capabilities that these firms have to produce them. Such capabilities are important for large pharmaceutical firms because these biological drugs are more difficult to duplicate by chemistry alone (the historical basis on which most pharmaceutical firms have expertise).[55] For example, in 2012 Bristol-Myers Squibb acquired a biopharmaceutical firm, Amylin Pharmaceuticals, Inc., for $5.3 billion. Amylin focuses on diabetes drugs and will give Bristol-Myers more sales opportunities as many of its drugs have lost patent protection.[56] Biotech firms are focused on DNA research and have a biology base rather than a chemistry base. If the acquisition is successful, there is added capability and possibly new competitive advantage. Biological drugs must clear more regulatory barriers or hurdles which, when accomplished, add more to the advantage the acquiring firm develops through such acquisitions.

## 7-3 Problems in Achieving Acquisition Success

Acquisition strategies based on reasons described in this chapter can increase strategic competitiveness and help firms earn above-average returns. However, even when pursued for value-creating reasons, acquisition strategies are not problem-free. Reasons for the use of acquisition strategies and potential problems with such strategies are shown in Figure 7.1.

**Figure 7.1** Reasons for Acquisitions and Problems in Achieving Success

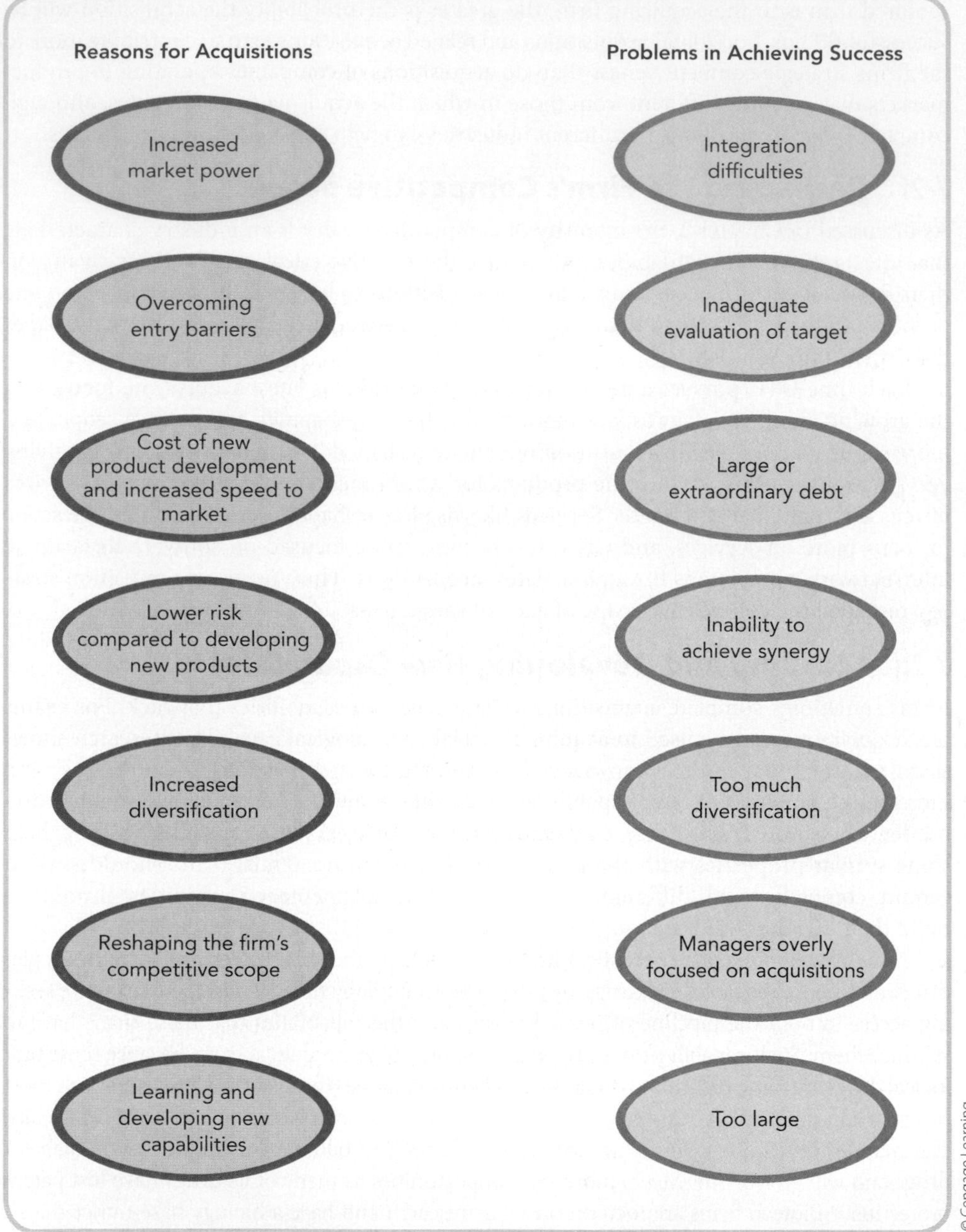




Research suggests that perhaps 20 percent of all mergers and acquisitions are successful, approximately 60 percent produce disappointing results, and the remaining 20 percent are clear failures; evidence on technology acquisitions reports even higher failure rates.[57] In general, though, companies appear to be increasing their ability to effectively use acquisition strategies. One analyst suggests that "Accenture research and subsequent work with clients show that half of large corporate mergers create at least marginal returns—an improvement from a decade ago, when many studies concluded that as many as three-quarters of all mergers destroyed shareholder value as measured two years after the merger announcement."[58] Greater acquisition success accrues to firms able to (1) select the "right" target,

(2) avoid paying too high a premium (doing appropriate due diligence), and (3) effectively integrate the operations of the acquiring and target firms.[59] In addition, retaining the target firm's human capital is foundational to efforts by employees of the acquiring firm to fully understand the target firm's operations and the capabilities on which those operations are based.[60] The Bristol-Myers acquisition of Amylin is an example of the importance of retaining the right employees because of Amylin's employees' expertise in biotechnology. As shown in Figure 7.1, several problems may prevent successful acquisitions.

## 7-3a Integration Difficulties

The importance of a successful integration should not be underestimated.[61] Post-merger integration is often a complex organizational process that is difficult and challenging to the managers involved. The processes tend to generate uncertainty and often resistance because of cultural clashes and organizational politics.[62] There is also a sense of fairness and unfairness as people get rewarded or laid off depending on how the employees involved experience a sense of fairness or distributive justice.[63] As suggested by a researcher studying the process, "Managerial practice and academic writings show that the post-acquisition integration phase is probably the single most important determinant of shareholder value creation (and equally of value destruction) in mergers and acquisitions."[64]

Although critical to acquisition success, firms should recognize that integrating two companies following an acquisition can be quite difficult. Melding two corporate cultures, linking different financial and control systems, building effective working relationships (particularly when management styles differ), and resolving problems regarding the status of the newly acquired firm's executives are examples of integration challenges firms often face.[65]

Integration is complex and involves a large number of activities, which if overlooked can lead to significant difficulties.[66] For example, when United Parcel Service (UPS) acquired Mail Boxes Etc., a large retail shipping chain, it appeared to be a merger that would generate benefits for both firms. The problem is that most of the Mail Boxes Etc. outlets were owned by franchisees. Following the merger, the franchisees lost the ability to deal with other shipping companies such as FedEx, which reduced their competitiveness. Furthermore, franchisees complained that UPS often built company-owned shipping stores close by franchisee outlets of Mail Boxes Etc. Additionally, a culture clash evolved between the free-wheeling entrepreneurs who owned the franchises of Mail Boxes Etc. and the efficiency-oriented corporate approach of the UPS operation, which focused on managing a large fleet of trucks and an information system to efficiently pick up and deliver packages. Also, Mail Boxes Etc. was focused on retail traffic, whereas UPS was focused more on the logistics of wholesale pickup and delivery. Although 87 percent of Mail Boxes Etc. franchisees decided to rebrand under the UPS name, many formed an owner's group and even filed suit against UPS in regard to the unfavorable nature of the franchisee contract.[67] In 2012, the Mail Boxes Etc. store brand has been dropped and the name changed to The UPS Store, Inc., and today UPS only franchises The UPS Store branded stores in the United States.[68]

*Once an acquisition has been completed, the difficult task of integrating two companies begins.*

## 7-3b Inadequate Evaluation of Target

*Due diligence* is a process through which a potential acquirer evaluates a target firm for acquisition. In an effective due diligence process, hundreds of items are examined in areas as diverse as the financing for the intended transaction, differences in cultures between the acquiring and target firm, tax consequences of the transaction, and actions that would be necessary to successfully meld the two workforces. Due diligence is commonly performed by investment bankers such as Deutsche Bank, Goldman Sachs, and Morgan Stanley, as well as accountants, lawyers, and management consultants specializing in that activity, although firms actively pursuing acquisitions may form their own internal due diligence team. Firms almost always work with intermediaries like large investment banks to facilitate the due diligence of the transaction. Interestingly, research suggests that acquisition performance increases with the number of transactions facilitated by an investment bank but decreases when the relationship with a particular investment bank becomes exclusive.[69] As previously noted, Caterpillar's due diligence before its acquisition of Siwei in China was obviously inadequate.[70] Although due diligence often focuses on evaluating the accuracy of the financial position and accounting standards used (a financial audit), due diligence also needs to examine the quality of the strategic fit and the ability of the acquiring firm to effectively integrate the target to realize the potential gains from the deal.[71]

The failure to complete an effective due diligence process may easily result in the acquiring firm paying an excessive premium for the target company. Acquisition of Autonomy, which provides software to help customers analyze data, has burdened HP since it was acquired for $11 billion in 2011. There were claims of "serious accounting improprieties, disclosure failures and outright misrepresentations at Autonomy Corporation plc," which occurred prior to the acquisition.[72] Interestingly, research shows that in times of high or increasing stock prices due diligence is relaxed; firms often overpay during these periods, and long-run performance of the newly formed firm suffers.[73] The way boards pay CEOs indicates confidence or a lack of confidence in the value-creation potential of an announced acquisition. Often acquiring firms' CEOs' equity-based holdings (incentive compensation) "do not appear to anticipate long-term value creation from their acquisitions."[74] In other words, the incentive pay suggests that acquisitions may not be worth as much because CEOs have to be incented to make them pay off.

In addition, firms sometimes allow themselves to enter a "bidding war" for a target, even though they realize that their successive bids exceed the parameters identified through due diligence. Assumptions in financing deals suggest that investors are rational in regard to evaluating acquisition announcements. However, research in strategic management suggests that investors draw information from managers who have been shown to be biased; they often overpay, have escalation of commitment, experience hubris (feeling that they can manage a target firm better than the current management), and can be self-interest-seeking in such deals.[75] Earlier, we mentioned that Roche was willing to pay a 61 percent premium to acquire Illumina. We cannot be sure that Roche would have overpaid had the deal been consummated, but the point is that rather than enter a bidding war, firms should only extend bids that are consistent with the results of their due diligence process. It could be that Illumina would have provided Roche with a new platform for growth and over time this deal would look cheap, but the key is doing a strategic analysis along with rational due diligence so that both the strategic fit and financials make sense.

## 7-3c Large or Extraordinary Debt

To finance a number of acquisitions completed during the 1980s and 1990s, some companies significantly increased their levels of debt. A financial innovation called junk bonds helped make this possible. *Junk bonds* are a financing option through which risky acquisitions are financed with money (debt) that provides a large potential return to lenders (bondholders). Because junk bonds are unsecured obligations that are not tied to specific assets for collateral, interest rates for these high-risk debt instruments sometimes reached between 18 and 20 percent during the 1980s.[76] Some prominent financial economists viewed debt as a means to discipline managers, causing them to act in the shareholders' best interests.[77] Managers holding this view are less concerned about the amount of debt their firm assumes when acquiring other companies.

Junk bonds are now used less frequently to finance acquisitions, and the conviction that debt disciplines managers is less strong.[78] Nonetheless, firms sometimes still take on what turns out to be too much debt when acquiring companies. As noted, both Dish Network and SoftBank have provided offers to buy Sprint Nextel. Interestingly, SoftBank brings a large cash infusion for Sprint, but does not provide synergy or possible additional spectrum for Sprint's cellular network. On the other hand, Dish provides better potential synergy but also would require a large load of debt. Dish needs to raise an additional $9.3 billion of debt to execute the deal. It is expected that the vast majority of this debt will be secured by Sprint assets. This could put Sprint at a disadvantage, especially considering that Sprint is a capital-intensive business that will require significant investment to keep up with its cellular competitors—AT&T and Verizon.[79] Thus, firms using an acquisition strategy must be certain that their purchases do not create a debt load that overpowers the company's ability to accomplish its strategic objectives while remaining solvent.

## 7-3d **Inability to Achieve Synergy**

Derived from *synergos*, a Greek word that means "working together," *synergy* exists when the value created by units working together exceeds the value those units could create working independently (see Chapter 6). That is, synergy exists when assets are worth more when used in conjunction with each other than when they are used separately. For shareholders, synergy generates gains in their wealth that they could not duplicate or exceed through their own portfolio diversification decisions.[80] Synergy is created by the efficiencies derived from economies of scale and economies of scope and by sharing resources (e.g., human capital and knowledge) across the businesses in the merged firm.[81]

A firm develops a competitive advantage through an acquisition strategy only when a transaction generates private synergy. *Private synergy* is created when combining and integrating the acquiring and acquired firms' assets, yield capabilities, and core competencies that could not be developed by combining and integrating either firm's assets with another company. Danone, a French diversified food producer and distributor, has made an acquisition of 92 percent of Happy Family, an organic food business launched in 2006. Happy Family has a 4 percent share of the U.S. baby foods market with such product labels as Amaranth Ratatouille, Orange Mango Coconut Smoothie, and Greek-Style Yogurt. This appears to be a good strategic acquisition for Danone because baby food is one of its fastest-growing portfolio areas.[82] However, it is not yet known what the private synergy might be. Private synergy is possible when firms' assets are complementary in unique ways; that is, the unique type of asset complementarity is not always possible simply by combining two companies' sets of assets with each other.[83] Because of its uniqueness, private synergy is difficult for competitors to understand and imitate, and it is also difficult to create.

A firm's ability to account for costs that are necessary to create anticipated revenue and cost-based synergies affects its efforts to create private synergy. Firms experience several expenses when trying to create private synergy through acquisitions. Called transaction costs, these expenses are incurred when firms use acquisition strategies to create synergy.[84] Transaction costs may be direct or indirect. Direct costs include legal fees and charges from investment bankers who complete due diligence for the acquiring firm. Indirect costs include managerial time to evaluate target firms and then to complete negotiations, as well as the loss of key managers and employees following an acquisition.[85] Firms tend to underestimate the sum of indirect costs when the value of the synergy that may be created by combining and integrating the acquired firm's assets with the acquiring firm's assets is calculated.

### 7-3e Too Much Diversification

As explained in Chapter 6, diversification strategies can lead to strategic competitiveness and above-average returns. In general, firms using related diversification strategies outperform those employing unrelated diversification strategies. However, conglomerates formed by using an unrelated diversification strategy also can be successful, as demonstrated by United Technologies Corp.

At some point, however, firms can become over-diversified. The level at which over-diversification occurs varies across companies because each firm has different capabilities to manage diversification. Recall from Chapter 6 that related diversification requires more information processing than does unrelated diversification. Because of this additional information processing, related diversified firms become over-diversified with a smaller number of business units than do firms using an unrelated diversification strategy.[86] Regardless of the type of diversification strategy implemented, however, over-diversification leads to a decline in performance, after which business units are often divested.[87] Commonly, such divestments, which tend to reshape a firm's competitive scope, are part of a firm's restructuring strategy. (We discuss the strategy in greater detail later in the chapter.)

Even when a firm is not over-diversified, a high level of diversification can have a negative effect on its long-term performance. For example, the scope created by additional amounts of diversification often causes managers to rely on financial rather than strategic controls to evaluate business units' performance (we define and explain financial and strategic controls in Chapters 11 and 12). Top-level executives often rely on financial controls to assess the performance of business units when they do not have a rich understanding of business units' objectives and strategies. Using financial controls, such as return on investment (ROI), causes individual business-unit managers to focus on short-term outcomes at the expense of long-term investments. When long-term investments are reduced to increase short-term profits, a firm's overall strategic competitiveness may be harmed.[88]

*Over-diversification can have a negative effect on long-term firm performance. Well-conceived and effectively executed strategies only occur when leaders have a rich understanding of their businesses.*

Larry Washburn/Getty Images

Another problem resulting from too much diversification is the tendency for acquisitions to become substitutes for innovation. As we noted earlier, pharmaceutical firms such as Roche must be aware of this tendency as they acquire other firms to gain access to their products and capabilities. Typically, managers have no interest in acquisitions substituting for internal R&D efforts and the innovative outcomes that they can produce. However, a reinforcing cycle evolves. Costs associated with acquisitions may result in fewer allocations to activities, such as R&D, that are linked to innovation. Without adequate support, a firm's innovation skills begin to atrophy. Without internal innovation skills, the only option available to a firm to gain access to innovation is to complete still more acquisitions. Evidence suggests that a firm using acquisitions as a substitute for internal innovations eventually encounters performance problems.[89]

### 7-3f Managers Overly Focused on Acquisitions

Typically, a considerable amount of managerial time and energy is required for acquisition strategies to be used successfully.

Activities with which managers become involved include (1) searching for viable acquisition candidates, (2) completing effective due diligence processes, (3) preparing for negotiations, and (4) managing the integration process after completing the acquisition.

Top level managers do not personally gather all of the data and information required to make acquisitions. However, these executives do make critical decisions on the firms to be targeted, the nature of the negotiations, and so forth. Company experiences show that participating in and overseeing the activities required for making acquisitions can divert managerial attention from other matters that are necessary for long-term competitive success, such as identifying and taking advantage of other opportunities and interacting with important external stakeholders.[90]

Both theory and research suggest that managers can become overly involved in the process of making acquisitions.[91] One observer suggested, "Some executives can become preoccupied with making deals—and the thrill of selecting, chasing and seizing a target."[92] The over-involvement can be surmounted by learning from mistakes and by not having too much agreement in the boardroom. Dissent is helpful to make sure that all sides of a question are considered (see Chapter 10). For example, research suggests that there may be group bias in the decision making of boards of directors regarding acquisitions. The research suggests that possible group polarization leads to either higher premiums paid or lower premiums paid after group discussions about potential premiums for target firms paid.[93] When failure does occur, leaders may be tempted to blame the failure on others and on unforeseen circumstances rather than on their excessive involvement in the acquisition process.

The acquisitions strategy of Citigroup is a case in point. In 1998, Citigroup's CEO John Reed, in a merger between Citicorp and Travelers Group (CEO Sanford I. Weill), set out to cross-sell financial services to the same customer and thereby reduce sales costs (Weill ultimately became the CEO). To accomplish this goal, the merged firm focused on a set of acquisitions, including insurance and private equity investing beyond traditional banking services. However, as noted by one commentator, "More than once, ambitious executives, such as Sanford Weill of Citigroup fame, have assembled 'financial supermarkets,' and thinking that customers' needs for credit cards, checking accounts, wealth management services, insurance, and stock brokerage could be furnished most efficiently and effectively by the same company. Those efforts have failed, over and over again. Each function fulfills a different job that arises at a different point in a customer's life, so a single source for all of them holds no advantage."[94] Vikram Pandit, the CEO who took over after Charles Prince at Citigroup, was forced to sell off a lot of those peripheral financial service businesses during the financial crisis. However, most of the divestiture was handled by the subsequent CEO, Michael Corbat.[95]

## 7-3g **Too Large**

Most acquisitions create a larger firm, which should help increase its economies of scale. These economies can then lead to more efficient operations—for example, two sales organizations can be integrated using fewer sales representatives because such sales personnel can sell the products of both firms (particularly if the products of the acquiring and target firms are highly related).[96] However, size can also increase the complexity of the management challenge and create diseconomies of scope; that is, not enough economic benefit to outweigh the costs of managing the more complex organization created through acquisitions. This was also the case in the failed merger between DaimlerChrysler and Mitsubishi; it became too costly to integrate the operations of Mitsubishi to derive the necessary benefits of economies of scale in the merged firm.[97]

Many firms seek increases in size because of the potential economies of scale and enhanced market power (discussed earlier). At some level, the additional costs required to manage the larger firm will exceed the benefits of the economies of scale and additional market power. The complexities generated by the larger size often lead managers to implement more bureaucratic controls to manage the combined firm's operations. *Bureaucratic controls* are formalized supervisory and behavioral rules and policies designed to ensure consistency of decisions and actions across different units of a firm. However, through time, formalized controls often lead to relatively rigid and standardized managerial behavior.[98] Certainly, in the long run, the diminished flexibility that accompanies rigid and standardized managerial behavior may produce less innovation. Because of innovation's importance to competitive success, the bureaucratic controls resulting from a large organization (i.e., built by acquisitions) can have a detrimental effect on performance. For this reason, Cisco announced an internal restructuring to reduce bureaucracy after its numerous acquisitions; "it will dispense with most of a network of internal councils and associated boards that have been criticized for adding layers of bureaucracy and wasting managers' time."[99] As one analyst noted, "Striving for size per se is not necessarily going to make a company more successful. In fact, a strategy in which acquisitions are undertaken as a substitute for organic growth has a bad track record in terms of adding value."[100]

## 7-4 Effective Acquisitions

Earlier in the chapter, we noted that acquisition strategies do not always lead to above-average returns for the acquiring firm's shareholders.[101] Nonetheless, some companies are able to create value when using an acquisition strategy.[102] The probability of success increases when the firm's actions are consistent with the "attributes of successful acquisitions" shown in Table 7.1.

As illustrated in the Opening Case, Cisco Systems appears to pay close attention to Table 7.1's attributes when using its acquisition strategy. In fact, Cisco is admired for its ability to complete successful acquisitions and integrate them quickly, although as noted this has created a larger firm.[103] A number of other network companies pursued acquisitions to build up their ability to sell into the network equipment buying binge associated with the Internet's development, but only Cisco retained much of its value in the post-bubble era. Many firms, such as

**Table 7.1** Attributes of Successful Acquisitions

| Attributes | Results |
|---|---|
| 1. Acquired firm has assets or resources that are complementary to the acquiring firm's core business | 1. High probability of synergy and competitive advantage by maintaining strengths |
| 2. Acquisition is friendly | 2. Faster and more effective integration and possibly lower premiums |
| 3. Acquiring firm conducts effective due diligence to select target firms and evaluate the target firm's health (financial, cultural, and human resources) | 3. Firms with strongest complementarities are acquired and overpayment is avoided |
| 4. Acquiring firm has financial slack (cash or a favorable debt position) | 4. Financing (debt or equity) is easier and less costly to obtain |
| 5. Merged firm maintains low to moderate debt position | 5. Lower financing cost, lower risk (e.g., of bankruptcy), and avoidance of trade-offs that are associated with high debt |
| 6. Acquiring firm has sustained and consistent emphasis on R&D and innovation | 6. Maintain long-term competitive advantage in markets |
| 7. Acquiring firm manages change well and is flexible and adaptable | 7. Faster and more effective integration facilitates achievement of synergy |

Lucent, Nortel, and Ericsson, teetered on the edge of bankruptcy after the dot-com bubble burst. When it makes an acquisition, "Cisco has gone much further in its thinking about integration. Not only is retention important, but Cisco also works to minimize the distractions caused by an acquisition. This is important, because the speed of change is so great that if the target firm's product development teams are distracted, they will be slowed, contributing to acquisition failure. So, integration must be rapid and reassuring."[104] For example, Cisco facilitates acquired employees' transitions to their new organization through a link on its Web site called "Cisco Acquisition Connection." This Web site has been specifically designed for newly acquired employees and provides up-to-date materials tailored to their new jobs.[105]

Results from a research study shed light on the differences between unsuccessful and successful acquisition strategies and suggest that a pattern of actions improves the probability of acquisition success.[106] The study shows that when the target firm's assets are complementary to the acquired firm's assets, an acquisition is more successful. With complementary assets, the integration of two firms' operations has a higher probability of creating synergy. In fact, integrating two firms with complementary assets frequently produces unique capabilities and core competencies. With complementary assets, the acquiring firm can maintain its focus on core businesses and leverage the complementary assets and capabilities from the acquired firm. In effective acquisitions, targets are often selected and "groomed" by establishing a working relationship prior to the acquisition.[107] As discussed in Chapter 9, strategic alliances are sometimes used to test the feasibility of a future merger or acquisition between the involved firms.[108]

The study's results also show that friendly acquisitions facilitate integration of the firms involved in an acquisition. The influence that target firms feel regarding their willingness to sell to an acquiring firm influences the likelihood of a friendly transaction taking place. For instance, the likelihood of a transaction in the Chinese beer industry has been the source for some research. The research showed that firms in the beer industry who established state-owned enterprises were more likely to be party to a transaction than firms that were able to attract more private investment.[109] Through friendly acquisitions, firms work together to find ways to integrate their operations to create synergy.[110] In hostile takeovers, animosity often results between the two top-management teams, a condition that in turn affects working relationships in the newly created firm. As a result, more key personnel in the acquired firm may be lost, and those who remain may resist the changes necessary to integrate the two firms.[111] With effort, cultural clashes can be overcome, and fewer key managers and employees will become discouraged and leave.[112]

Additionally, effective due diligence processes involving the deliberate and careful selection of target firms and an evaluation of the relative health of those firms (financial health, cultural fit, and the value of human resources) contribute to successful acquisitions.[113] Financial slack in the form of debt equity or cash, in both the acquiring and acquired firms, also frequently contributes to acquisition success. Even though financial slack provides access to financing for the acquisition, it is still important to maintain a low or moderate level of debt after the acquisition to keep debt costs low. When substantial debt was used to finance the acquisition, companies with successful acquisitions reduced the debt quickly, partly by selling off assets from the acquired firm, especially noncomplementary or poorly performing assets. For these firms, debt costs do not prevent long-term investments such as R&D, and managerial discretion in the use of cash flow is relatively flexible.

Another attribute of successful acquisition strategies is an emphasis on innovation, as demonstrated by continuing investments in R&D activities.[114] As noted earlier, Xerox purchased Affiliated Computer Services, which facilitated its transition from strictly a hardware producer focused on copiers to business services and processing. However, the company's research facility, Xerox PARC in Palo Alto, facilitated this transition.[115] This research facility helped to create the laser printer and ethernet cable, and early on developed the graphic user interface that Steve Jobs encountered in late 1979 and discerned to be the future of personal computing technology. This idea led to the founding of Apple Computer. Significant R&D investments show a strong managerial commitment to innovation, a characteristic that is increasingly important to overall competitiveness in the global economy as well as to acquisition success.

Flexibility and adaptability are the final two attributes of successful acquisitions. When executives of both the acquiring and the target firms have experience in managing change and learning from acquisitions, they will be more skilled at adapting their capabilities to new environments.[116] As a result, they will be more adept at integrating the two organizations, which is particularly important when firms have different organizational cultures.

As we have learned, firms use an acquisition strategy to grow and achieve strategic competitiveness. Sometimes, though, the actual results of an acquisition strategy fall short of the projected results. When this happens, firms consider using restructuring strategies.

## 7-5 Restructuring

**Restructuring** is a strategy through which a firm changes its set of businesses or its financial structure.[117] Restructuring is a global phenomenon.[118] From the 1970s into the 2000s, divesting businesses from company portfolios and downsizing accounted for a large percentage of firms' restructuring strategies. Commonly, firms focus on fewer products and markets following restructuring. The words of an executive describe this typical outcome: "Focus on your core business, but don't be distracted, let other people buy assets that aren't right for you."[119]

Although restructuring strategies are generally used to deal with acquisitions that are not reaching expectations, firms sometimes use these strategies because of changes they have detected in their external environment.[120] For example, opportunities sometimes surface in a firm's external environment that a diversified firm can pursue because of the capabilities it has formed by integrating firms' operations. In such cases, restructuring may be appropriate to position the firm to create more value for stakeholders given the environmental changes.[121]

As discussed next, firms use three types of restructuring strategies: downsizing, downscoping, and leveraged buyouts.

### 7-5a Downsizing

*Downsizing* is a reduction in the number of a firm's employees and, sometimes, in the number of its operating units, but it may or may not change the composition of businesses in the company's portfolio. Thus, downsizing is an intentional proactive management strategy whereas "decline is an environmental or organizational phenomenon that occurs involuntarily and results in erosion of an organization's resource base."[122] Downsizing is often a part of acquisitions that fail to create the value anticipated when the transaction was completed. Downsizing is often used when the acquiring firm paid too high of a premium to acquire the target firm.[123] Once thought to be an indicator of organizational decline, downsizing is now recognized as a legitimate restructuring strategy.

Reducing the number of employees and/or the firm's scope in terms of products produced and markets served occurs in firms to enhance the value being created as a result of completing an acquisition. When integrating the operations of the acquired firm and the acquiring firm, managers may not at first appropriately downsize. This is understandable in that "no one likes to lay people off or close facilities."[124] However, downsizing may be necessary because acquisitions often create a situation in which the newly formed firm has duplicate organizational functions such as sales, manufacturing, distribution, human

**Restructuring** is a strategy through which a firm changes its set of businesses or its financial structure.

resource management, and so forth. Failing to downsize appropriately may lead to too many employees doing the same work and prevent the new firm from realizing the cost synergies it anticipated.[125] Managers should remember that as a strategy, downsizing will be far more effective when they consistently use human resource practices that ensure procedural justice and fairness in downsizing decisions.[126]

## 7-5b Downscoping

*Downscoping* refers to divestiture, spin-off, or some other means of eliminating businesses that are unrelated to a firm's core businesses. Downscoping has a more positive effect on firm performance than does downsizing[127] because firms commonly find that downscoping causes them to refocus on their core business.[128] Managerial effectiveness increases because the firm has become less diversified, allowing the top management team to better understand and manage the remaining businesses.[129] Interestingly, sometimes the divested unit can also take advantage of unforeseen opportunities not recognized while under the leadership of the parent firm.[130] Interestingly, acquisitions of divested assets in the U.S. software industry performed better than acquisitions of privately held firms, and even better than acquisitions of publicly held firms. One can argue that when firms sell because of distress, this enhances the positive returns for the acquirers of these divested assets and the relative bargaining power of the acquiring firm over the price paid.[131] However, research also suggests that investors face considerable uncertainty in evaluating firms' divestiture decisions, and thus may look at social context to infer the quality of the decisions. That is, the divestitures take place in waves, as do acquisitions; if firms are leading the waves, the market will respond positively, but if they are following the waves (following other firms' leads in regard to divestiture activity), such later acquisitions generate the lowest stock market returns.[132]

Firms often use the downscoping and the downsizing strategies simultaneously. In Citigroup's restructuring (noted earlier) it used both downscoping and downsizing, as have many large financial institutions in the recession.[133] However, when doing this, firms need to avoid layoffs of key employees, as such layoffs might lead to a loss of one or more core competencies. Instead, a firm that is simultaneously downscoping and downsizing becomes smaller by reducing the diversity of businesses in its portfolio to focus on core areas.[134]

In general, U.S. firms use downscoping as a restructuring strategy more frequently than do European companies—in fact, the trend in Europe, Latin America, and Asia has been to build conglomerates. In Latin America, these conglomerates are called *grupos*. Many Asian and Latin American conglomerates have begun to adopt Western corporate strategies in recent years and have been refocusing on their core businesses. This downscoping has occurred simultaneously with increasing globalization and with more open markets that have greatly enhanced competition. By downscoping, these firms have been able to focus on their core businesses and improve their competitiveness.[135]

Learn more about Downscoping.
www.cengagebrain.com

## 7-5c Leveraged Buyouts

A *leveraged buyout* (LBO) is a restructuring strategy whereby a party (typically a private equity firm) buys all of a firm's assets in order to take the firm private. The Strategic Focus on the strategic positioning of private equity firms' general partners expands on their overall approach to structuring their portfolio of firms. The Strategic Focus illustrates how private equity firms have been evolving into a number of different strategic types.

As explained in the Strategic Focus, once a PE firm completes the transaction of a new portfolio firm, the target firm's company stock is no longer traded publicly. Traditionally, leveraged buyouts were used as a restructuring strategy to correct for managerial mistakes or because the firm's managers were making decisions that primarily served their own interests rather than those of shareholders.[136] However, some firms use buyouts to build firm resources and expand rather than simply restructure distressed assets.

M. Stasy

## Strategic Focus SUCCESS

### Strategic Positioning of Private Equity Buyout Firms (General Partners)

Private equity (PE) is equity capital which is not traded on public equity exchanges such as the New York Stock Exchange. In general, PE firms can include investments in early stage by "angel investors" and venture capitalists but is more readily known for late-stage mature enterprise buyout, or acquisition, strategies. These late-stage PE buyout firms used to be called leveraged buyout associations (or LBO associations). General partners in PE firms manage funds contributed by PE investors (usually labeled limited partners and composed mostly of institutional investors). General partners orchestrate the acquisition of portfolio firms. Most firms use the capital provided by limited partners to leverage money from banks and debt markets to make the acquisitions. These acquired firms are often publicly traded firms that are taken private. Accordingly, PE firms have five general players: general partners who play the most important role as they solicit investor funds and choose target firms to acquire or invest in; limited partners, who provide equity capital; target portfolio firms purchased by general partners; and banks and other debt suppliers who provide additional finance for buyout deals. In this example, we will discuss four strategic positions that general partners use to establish their portfolio of acquired firms. Figure 7.2 depicts the strategic positions of PE firms (general partners).

As Figure 7.2 illustrates, there are two basic dimensions of the strategic positioning of these firms—the financial structure emphasis and the diversified scope of the portfolio firms acquired. The financial structure emphasis has two basic categories, one focused on debt provided by banks or other debt providers, and the other focused on equity providers such as limited partners (institutional investors). This vertical dimension (financial structure) emphasizes a long-term vs. short-term orientation. Usually debt providers have a shorter-term orientation and are more conservative, whereas limited partners/owners may have a longer-term partnership arrangement with the general partners, given the funding arrangement of targeted funds provided to the general partner by limited partners. The horizontal dimension focuses on the diversified scope of the portfolio firms. Some PE firms have a very focused scope—for example, in a particular industry; whereas others have a very diversified scope across a wide range of industries and sectors. Those firms with a narrow scope usually provide more professional guidance and nurture in-house cooperation between buyout firms and do many add-on acquisitions to bolster the viability of firms in the longer term.

The lower-left quadrant focuses on short-term efficiency players, where buyout firms seek to restructure operations of an acquired portfolio firm and, as quickly as possible through financial engineering, to put the firm back on the open market

*Martin C. Halusa, CEO of Apax Partners Worldwide LLP, at the 38th Annual World Economic Forum in Davos, Switzerland. Apax Partners looks for long-term investments in growth companies with a strategy that is geared toward releasing potential of the firms in which it invests.*

through an IPO or sale to another company. Many PE buyout firms seek to reduce the holding period for a portfolio firm. For example, in 2000, the average holding period was 3.57 years, whereas in 2011 it was 4.81 years. This is because the exit opportunities for buyout firms in the financial downturn were more limited. More recently, many of the buyouts have been secondary buyouts; that is, one PE firm buying a portfolio firm from another PE firm rather than through an IPO or sale to another firm.

The upper-left quadrant representing niche players has more investment from limited partners with longer-term equity positions, and the holding period is longer than the mean-reported years for a portfolio firm. SCF Partners is an example of such a niche player. SCF Partners has made $1.6 billion in investments in portfolio companies and has produced approximately 10 IPOs as exits. However, SCF Partners' investments are relatively small compared to KKR, which as of 2010 had managed more than $60 billion in investments in portfolio firms. SCF Partners has focused its portfolio in "energy services, manufacturing, and energy equipment industry segments." With its narrow focus, it can develop expertise, cultivate its networks, and build a solid reputation in its chosen industry. SCF Partners collaborates with entrepreneurial owners of buyout firms to implement reforms and pursue complementary acquisitions to build up both the size and breadth of services for portfolio firms. They also seek to keep the entrepreneurial owners in place in order to maintain the emphasis on business growth. They recently had an IPO of Form Energy Technologies, which provides technologies and products

**Figure 7.2** Strategic Positioning of Private Equity Firm General Partner Portfolios

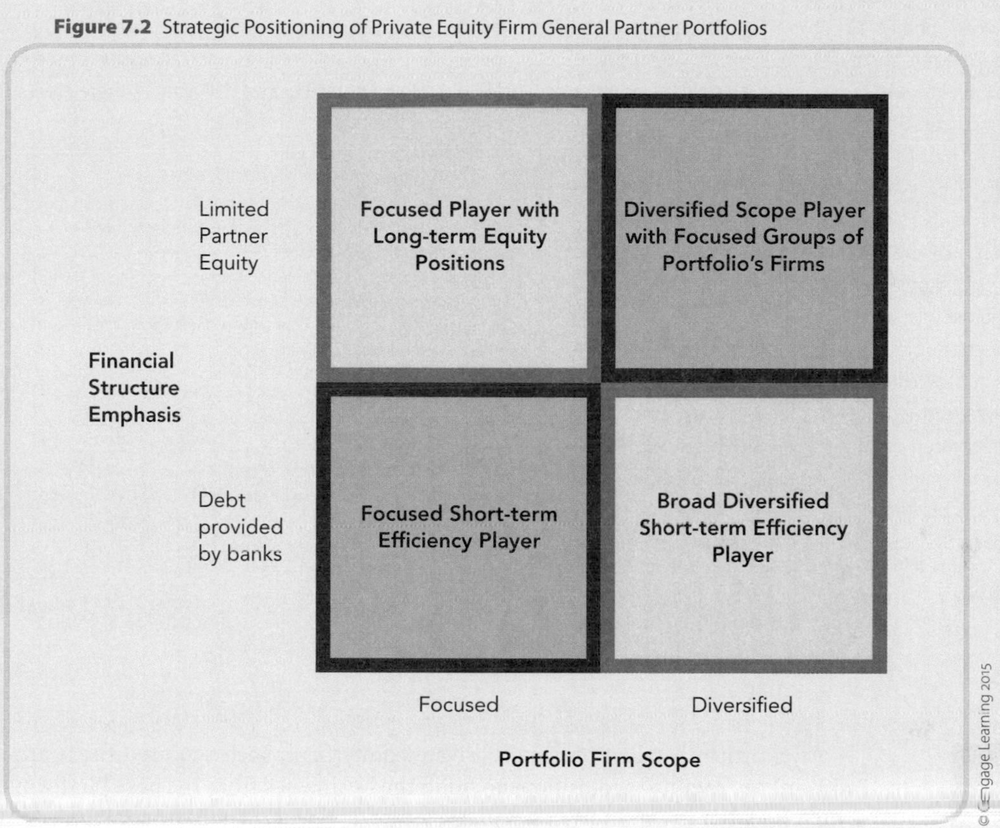


to undersea drilling and extraction operations, such as selling remote operating vehicles for inspection and survey of deep water well construction.

PE firms in the upper-right quadrant are diversified players with focused groups of portfolio firms and pursue more of a related diversification approach among portfolio firms (see Chapter 6). Furthermore, they have operational expertise that is provided to the firms, and usually the holding period for portfolio firms is longer than average. Apax Partners examples this type of portfolio firm. They invest in only five industries (financial services, health care, media, retailing, and telecom). Apax encourages the growth of its buyout firms to maximize value in its portfolio before pursuing an exit strategy.

PE firms in the lower-right quadrant focus on short-term efficiency but often have very large and diversified portfolios of firms. They might be represented by well-known firms such as KKR, Blackstone, and Carlyle. Interestingly, these particular general partner firms are publicly traded as well. As these large firms grow in size, they grow beyond the scope of particular industries and need to diversify to find new deals. Also, the size of the deal is increased because to have an impact on performance and overall value creation they generally have to do large publicly traded firm buyouts. Although these firms have had to pay attention to operational improvement because holding times have grown longer, their focus on operational improvement is necessitated because they lack exit opportunities rather than from a desire to exchange better operational engineering for financial engineering. Also, as noted, this has also led to a major trend toward secondary buyouts of portfolio firms (one PE firm buying another PE firm's portfolio assets).

Finally, PE firms in the lower-left quadrant are focused on more short-term efficiency plays but in a more focused target market. Bain Capital is a good representative of this quadrant. Although the company is a typical short-term efficiency, it has historically focused on services industries (e.g., SunGard in business services, Toys"R"Us in retailing services, and Dunkin' Brands in the dining services industry). Because it has global reach, its focused strategy has enabled it to successfully implement corporate capital restructuring, operating earnings improvements, and acquisition development across countries.

Overall, PE firms provide advantages and disadvantages to portfolio firms. Some of the advantages are that there is stronger alignment between owners and managers because debt obligations constrain managerial discretion. Managers can take a longer-term perspective because they don't have to worry about quarterly earnings reports. Also, PE firms provide growth capital for firms unable to access public equity markets or other sources of financing. They also provide exit opportunities and enhance liquidity for small and medium-sized business owners, as illustrated in the SCF Partners example. However, PE firms have some drawbacks. Their high debt loads prevent portfolio firms from pursuing potentially valuable opportunities, especially long-term investment opportunities, and focus on high technology firms with R&D intensity.

There may also be some general advantages for the economy. PE firms facilitate consolidation and rationalizing of industries, and help to catalyze restructuring and removing excess capacity in mature industries when needed. Their investment approach also enhances diversification opportunities for limited partner institutional investors by creating a new class of investment. Finally, the approach they use broadens the market for corporate control, especially for distressed firms, leading to improved asset pricing and more efficient resource allocation in the economy at large. However, as Figure 7.2 illustrates, there are a wide range of approaches that are illustrated by the various examples in the quadrants associated with this figure.

Sources: 2013, PitchBook & Grant Thornton: Private equity exits report 2012 annual edition, www.grantthornton.com, Web site accessed May 7; N. Bacon, M. Wright, R. Ball, & M. Meuleman, 2013, Private equity, HRM, and employment, *Academy of Management Perspectives*, 27(1): 7–21; F. Cornelli, Z. Kominek, & A. Ljungqvist, 2013, Monitoring managers: Does it matter? *Journal of Finance*, 68(2): 431–481; R. Dezember, 2013, Carlyle Group lowers velvet rope – Offering allows some people to invest as little as $50,000 with the giant private-equity firm, *Wall Street Journal*, March 13, C1; R. E. Hoskisson, W. Shi, X. Yi, & J. Jin, 2013, The evolution and strategic positioning of private equity firms, *Academy of Management Perspectives*, 27(1): 22–38; P. G. Klein, J. L. Chapman, & M. P. Mondelli, 2013, Private equity and entrepreneurial governance: Time for a balanced view, *Academy of Management Perspectives*, 27(1): 39–51; H. Touryalai, 2013, A kinder, gentler KKR, *Forbes*, February 11, 82–87; J. Chang, 2012, Private equity revives in chemical M&A, *ICIS Chemical Business*, October 1, 16–17; R. Dezember & S. Terlep, 2012, Buyouts boom, but not like '07, *Wall Street Journal*, August 23, C1–C2; N. Vardi, 2012, The kings of capital, *Forbes*, October 22, 78–83.

Find out more about Apax Partners.
**www.cengagebrain.com**

After a firm is taken over by a private equity firm, such acquired firms are free to do "add-on" or "role-up" acquisitions to build the businesses from the base platform of a single acquisition. For example, as noted in the Strategic Focus, SCF Partners acquires mostly private and often founder-dominated firms, who have deep knowledge about and emotional connections with their ventures and are committed to growing their businesses. In other words, these entrepreneurial founder-owners are the key to buyout businesses' success by SCF Partners. As a result, in the post-buyout period, most top executives remain in the firm, and the role of SCF Partners is to assist these executives in improving firm performance. For example, the rapid growth of the tar sands industry in Canada requires increased investment in infrastructure (e.g., roads and metal buildings to accommodate workers), as most tar sands resources are located in the Canadian wilderness. Recognizing opportunities associated with this boom, SCF Partners established Site Energy Services Ltd. to acquire small energy services firms, consolidating local infrastructure services firms in Calgary by acquiring these local firms and getting them to partner with each other to increase scale and scope through joint operations.[137]

However, significant amounts of debt are commonly incurred to finance a buyout; hence the term *leveraged* buyout. To support debt payments and to downscope the company to concentrate on the firm's core businesses, the new owners may immediately sell a number of assets.[138] It is not uncommon for those buying a firm through an LBO to restructure the firm to the point that it can be sold at a profit within a five- to eight-year period.

Management buyouts (MBOs), employee buyouts (EBOs), and whole-firm buyouts, in which one company or partnership purchases an entire company instead of a part of it, are the three types of LBOs. In part because of managerial incentives, MBOs, more so than EBOs and whole-firm buyouts, have been found to lead to downscoping, increased strategic focus, and improved performance.[139] Research shows that management buyouts can lead to greater entrepreneurial activity and growth.[140] As such, buyouts can represent a form of firm rebirth to facilitate entrepreneurial efforts and stimulate strategic growth and productivity.[141]

M. Stasy

## 7-5d Restructuring Outcomes

The short- and long-term outcomes associated with the three restructuring strategies are shown in Figure 7.3. As indicated, downsizing typically does not lead to higher firm performance.[142] In fact, some research results show that downsizing contributes to lower returns for both U.S. and Japanese firms. The stock markets in the firms' respective nations evaluated downsizing negatively, believing that it would have long-term negative effects on the firms' efforts to achieve strategic competitiveness. Investors also seem to conclude that downsizing occurs as a consequence of other problems in a company.[143] This assumption may be caused by a firm's diminished corporate reputation when a major downsizing is announced.[144]

The loss of human capital is another potential problem of downsizing (see Figure 7.3). Losing employees with many years of experience with the firm represents a major loss of knowledge. As noted in Chapter 3, knowledge is vital to competitive success in the global economy. Research also suggests that such loss of human capital can also spill over into dissatisfaction of customers.[145] Thus, in general, research evidence and corporate experience suggest that downsizing may be of more tactical (or short-term) value than strategic (or long-term) value,[146] meaning that firms should exercise caution when restructuring through downsizing.

Downscoping generally leads to more positive outcomes in both the short and long term than does downsizing or a leveraged buyout. Downscoping's desirable long-term outcome of higher performance is a product of reduced debt costs and the emphasis on strategic controls derived from concentrating on the firm's core businesses. In so doing, the refocused firm should be able to increase its ability to compete.[147]

Although whole-firm LBOs have been hailed as a significant innovation in the financial restructuring of firms, they can involve negative trade-offs.[148] First, the resulting large debt

**Figure 7.3** Restructuring and Outcomes

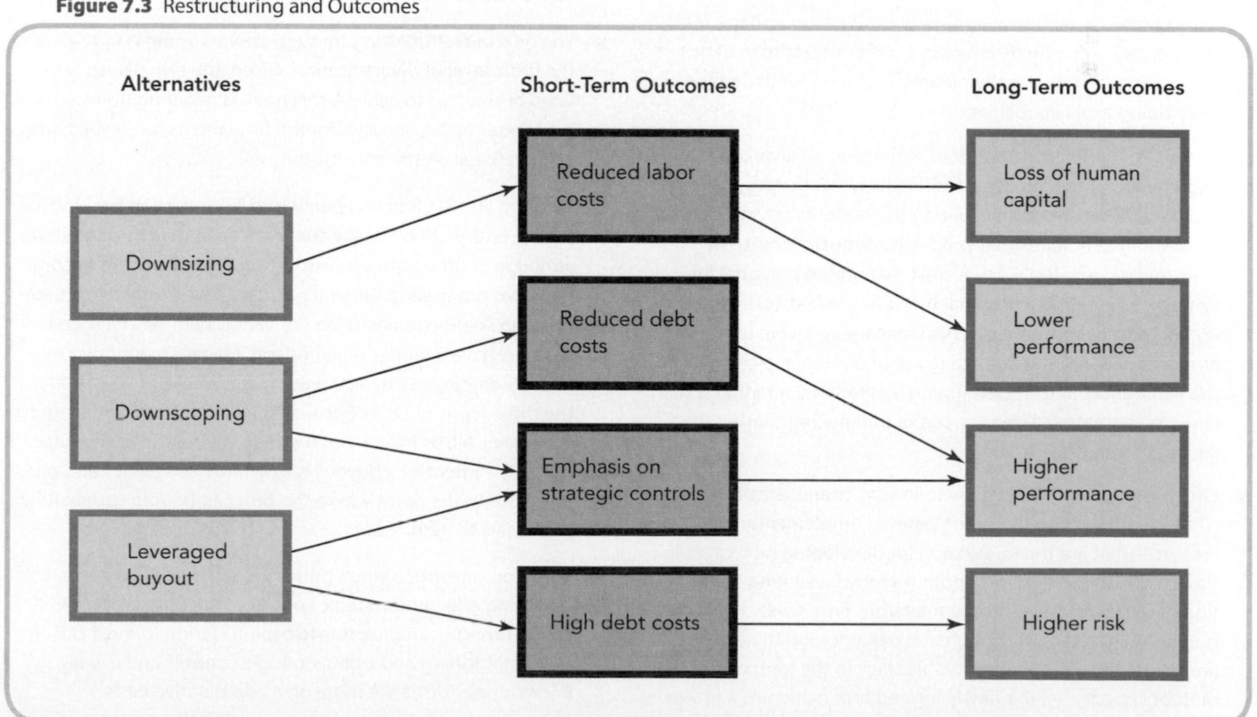

increases the firm's financial risk, as is evidenced by the number of companies that filed for bankruptcy in the 1990s after executing a whole-firm LBO. Sometimes, the intent of the owners to increase the efficiency of the bought-out firm and then sell it within five to eight years creates a short-term and risk-averse managerial focus.[149] As a result, these firms may fail to invest adequately in R&D or take other major actions designed to maintain or improve the company's core competence.[150] Research also suggests that in firms with an entrepreneurial mindset, buyouts can lead to greater innovation, especially if the debt load is not too great.[151] However, because buyouts more often result in significant debt, most LBOs have been completed in mature industries where stable cash flows are normal, which can help the PE to meet the debt obligations.

## SUMMARY

- Although the number of mergers and acquisitions completed declined in 2008 and 2009, largely because of the global financial crisis, merger and acquisition strategies became more frequent in 2010 and 2011 as a path to firm growth and earning strategic competitiveness. Globalization and deregulation of multiple industries in many economies are two of the factors making mergers and acquisitions attractive to large corporations and small firms.
- Firms use acquisition strategies to (1) increase market power, (2) overcome entry barriers to new markets or regions, (3) avoid the costs of developing new products and increase the speed of new market entries, (4) reduce the risk of entering a new business, (5) become more diversified, (6) reshape their competitive scope by developing a different portfolio of businesses, and (7) enhance their learning as the foundation for developing new capabilities.
- Among the problems associated with using an acquisition strategy are (1) the difficulty of effectively integrating the firms involved, (2) incorrectly evaluating the target firm's value, (3) creating debt loads that preclude adequate long-term investments (e.g., R&D), (4) overestimating the potential for synergy, (5) creating a firm that is too diversified, (6) creating an internal environment in which managers devote increasing amounts of their time and energy to analyzing and completing the acquisition, and (7) developing a combined firm that is too large, necessitating extensive use of bureaucratic, rather than strategic, controls.
- Effective acquisitions have the following characteristics: (1) the acquiring and target firms have complementary resources that are the foundation for developing new capabilities; (2) the acquisition is friendly, thereby facilitating integration of the firms' resources; (3) the target firm is selected and purchased based on thorough due diligence; (4) the acquiring and target firms have considerable slack in the form of cash or debt capacity; (5) the newly formed firm maintains a low or moderate level of debt by selling off portions of the acquired firm or some of the acquiring firm's poorly performing units; (6) the acquiring and acquired firms have experience in terms of adapting to change; and (7) R&D and innovation are emphasized in the new firm.
- Restructuring is used to improve a firm's performance by correcting for problems created by ineffective management. Restructuring by downsizing involves reducing the number of employees and hierarchical levels in the firm. Although it can lead to short-term cost reductions, they may be realized at the expense of long-term success, because of the loss of valuable human resources (and knowledge) and overall corporate reputation.
- The goal of restructuring through downscoping is to reduce the firm's level of diversification. Often, the firm divests unrelated businesses to achieve this goal. Eliminating unrelated businesses makes it easier for the firm and its top-level managers to refocus on the core businesses.
- Through an LBO, a firm is purchased so that it can become a private entity. LBOs usually are financed largely through debt, although limited partners (institutional investors) are becoming more prominent. General partners have a variety of strategies and some emphasize equity versus debt when limited partners have a longer time horizon. Management buyouts (MBOs), employee buyouts (EBOs), and whole-firm LBOs are the three types of LBOs. Because they provide clear managerial incentives, MBOs have been the most successful of the three. Often, the intent of a buyout is to improve efficiency and performance to the point where the firm can be sold successfully within five to eight years.
- Commonly, restructuring's primary goal is gaining or reestablishing effective strategic control of the firm. Of the three restructuring strategies, downscoping is aligned most closely with establishing and using strategic controls and usually improves performance more on a comparative basis.

# REVIEW QUESTIONS

1. Why are merger and acquisition strategies popular in many firms competing in the global economy?
2. What reasons account for firms' decisions to use acquisition strategies as a means to achieving strategic competitiveness?
3. What are the seven primary problems that affect a firm's efforts to successfully use an acquisition strategy?
4. What are the attributes associated with a successful acquisition strategy?
5. What is the restructuring strategy, and what are its common forms?
6. What are the short- and long-term outcomes associated with the different restructuring strategies?

# EXPERIENTIAL EXERCISES

## EXERCISE 1: HOW DID THE DEAL WORK OUT?

The text argues that mergers and acquisitions are a popular strategy for businesses both in the United States and across borders. However, returns for acquiring firms do not always live up to expectations. This exercise seeks to address this notion by analyzing, pre- and post hoc, the results of actual acquisitions. By looking at the notifications of a deal beforehand, categorizing that deal, and then following it for a year, you will be able to learn about actual deals and their implications for strategists.

Working in teams, identify a merger or acquisition that was completed in the last few years. This may be a cross-border acquisition or a U.S.-centered one. A couple of possible sources for this information are Reuters' online M&A section or Yahoo! Finance's U.S. Mergers and Acquisitions Calendar. Each team must get their M&A choice approved in advance so as to avoid duplicates.

To complete this assignment, you should be prepared to answer the following questions:

1. Describe the environment for this arrangement at the time it was completed. Using concepts discussed in the text, focus on management's representation to shareholders, the industry environment, and the overall rationale for the deal.
2. Did the acquirer pay a premium for the target firm? If so, how much? In addition, search for investor comments regarding the wisdom of this agreement. Attempt to identify how the market reacted at the announcement of the deal (LexisNexis typically provides an article that will address this issue).
3. Describe the merger or acquisition going forward. Use the concepts from the text such as, but not limited to:
   a. The reason for the merger or acquisition (i.e., market power, overcoming entry barriers, etc.)
   b. Were there problems in achieving acquisition success?
   c. Would you categorize this deal as successful as of the time of your research? Give the reasons why or why not.

Plan on presenting your findings to the class in a 10- to 15-minute presentation. Organize the presentation as if you were updating the shareholders of the newly combined firm.

## EXERCISE 2: WHAT REALLY GOES INTO A DUE DILIGENCE CHECKLIST?

Due diligence, according to your text, can potentially be a main determinant of whether or not an acquisition bucks the trend of unsatisfactory results. Since a significant number of acquisitions fail to live up to expectations, how is it that a due diligence process can provide such a benefit? An inadequate evaluation of the target seems hard to believe, noting that many times very sophisticated entities or individuals carry out this process like management consulting firms, investment banks, legal specialists, etc. Your assignment in this exercise is to research and produce a due diligence checklist that if implemented will provide to the extent possible a robust assessment of a target firm and attempt to prevent the aforementioned inadequate evaluation.

Working in teams, utilize library databases, trade associations, merger and acquisition clearing houses and the like to develop by category a due diligence checklist. This checklist is to be comprehensive in that it should cover the important topics as well as dive into the details underneath each one. Simply copying a checklist found on the internet will not suffice. You are to provide your checklist as a composite of the various readings, research, and examples you are able to find (make sure to provide references).

Be prepared to present to the class your findings and at a minimum explore:

1. What references went into your checklist?
2. Which areas do you feel would be the most difficult to quantify?
3. How long should this process take for an average acquisition?
4. How much will it cost?
5. Why do you think there are so many different varieties of due diligence checklists that are in use by various entities? Does this variety help or hurt accuracy? In other words, would a standard template across industries lead to a better process?

## VIDEO CASE ▶

### THE POWER OF A MERGER: SOUTHWEST

Southwest, long recognized for its discount airfares and its targeting of the price-conscious consumer, has combined forces with another discount carrier—AirTran. AirTran asserts that with such a merger the potential exists for the expansion of discount airfares in the industry. In an industry where profit motive is high, consolidation is not uncommon even among major airlines, but the air traveler still sees fewer seats and higher prices. While major carriers seek profits, particularly in add-on fees, Southwest continues to press the competition by refraining from excessive fees.

Be prepared to discuss the following concepts and questions in class:

### Concepts

- Mergers
- Acquisitions
- Restructuring

### Questions

1. What would make the arrangement between Southwest and AirTran a merger and not an acquisition?
2. What were the reasons that Southwest and AirTran had for merging? What approach(es) did these companies use?
3. What would cause the Southwest/AirTran merger not to be successful?
4. What strategies would you recommend to Southwest should it need to restructure?

## NOTES


1. M. Gruber, I. C. MacMillan, & J. D. Thompson, 2012, From minds to markets: How human capital endowments shape market opportunity identification of technology start-ups, *Journal of Management*, 38(5): 1421–1449; D. J. Teece, 2010, Alfred Chandler and "capabilities" theories of strategy and management, *Industrial and Corporate Change*, 19: 297–316.
2. H. R. Greve, 2011, Positional rigidity: Low performance and resource acquisition in large and small firms, *Strategic Management Journal*, 32(1): 103–114; R. Ragozzino & J. J. Reuer, 2010, The opportunities and challenges of entrepreneurial acquisitions, *European Management Review*, 7(2): 80–90.
3. K. Muehlfeld, P. Rao Sahib, & A. Van Witteloostuijn, 2012, A contextual theory of organizational learning from failures and successes: A study of acquisition completion in the global newspaper industry, 1981–2008, *Strategic Management Journal*, 33(8): 938–964; M. A. Hitt, D. King, H. Krishnan, M. Makri, M. Schijven, K. Shimizu, & H. Zhu, 2009, Mergers and acquisitions: Overcoming pitfalls, building synergy and creating value, *Business Horizons*, 52(6): 523–529.
4. A. S. Gaur, S. Malhotra, & P. Zhu, 2013, Acquisition announcements and stock market valuations of acquiring firms' rivals: A test of the growth probability hypothesis in China, *Strategic Management Journal*, 34(2): 215–232; C. M. Christensen, R. Alton, C. Rising, & A. Waldeck, 2011, The new M&A playbook, *Harvard Business Review*, 89(3): 48–57; G. M. McNamara, J. Haleblian, & B. J. Dykes, 2008, The performance implications of participating in an acquisition wave: Early mover advantages, bandwagon effects, and the moderating influence of industry characteristics and acquirer tactics, *Academy of Management Journal*, 51: 113–130.
5. J. J. Reuer, T. W. Tong, & C. Wu, 2012, A signaling theory of acquisition premiums: Evidence from IPO targets, *Academy of Management Journal*, 55(3): 667–683; R. Dobbs & V. Tortorici, 2007, Cool heads will bring in the best deals; boardroom discipline is vital if the M&A boom is to benefit shareholders, *Financial Times*, February 28, 6.
6. 2013, Mergers & acquisitions review – financial advisors Q1 2013, www.thomsonreuters.com, April 4.
7. A. Kirchfeld & S. Saitto, 2012, Fourth-quarter M&A surge spurs optimism after 2012 deals decline, www.bloomberg.com, December 26.
8. 2013, Heineken reports rise in first quarter profits due to acquisitions; sees weaker 2013 growth, www.yahoofinance.com, April 24.
9. M. Cornett, B. Tanyeri, & H. Tehranian, 2011, The effect of merger anticipation on bidder and target firm announcement period returns, *Journal of Corporate Finance*, 17(3): 595–611; J. J. Reuer, 2005, Avoiding lemons in M&A deals, *MIT Sloan Management Review*, 46(3): 15–17.
10. C. Quinn Trank, J. E. Stambaugh, & H. Bemis, 2012, Capturing success, not taking the blame, *People & Strategy*, 35(3): 30–37; K. Cools & M. van de Laar, 2006, The performance of acquisitive companies in the U.S., in L. Renneboog (ed.), *Advances in Corporate Finance and Asset Pricing*, Amsterdam, Netherlands: Elsevier Science, 77–105.
11. A. Peaple, 2012, Roche is getting personal with Illumina, *Wall Street Journal*, January 26, C10.
12. N. Kresge & A. Edney, 2013, Illumina falls as Roche drops deal to buy U.S. company, www.bloomberg.com, January 13.
13. V. Ambrosini, C. Bowman, & R. Schoenberg, 2011, Should acquiring firms pursue more than one value creation strategy? An empirical test of acquisition performance, *British Journal of Management*, 22(1): 173–185; K. J. Martijn Cremers, V. B. Nair, & K. John, 2009, Takeovers and the cross-section of returns, *Review of Financial Studies*, 22: 1409–1445.
14. A. MacDonald, 2013, Glencore Xstrata unveils integration plan, *Wall Street Journal*, May 6, B3.
15. Ibid.
16. M. Humphery-Jenner, 2013, Takeover defenses as drivers of innovation and value-creation, *Strategic Management Journal*, in press.
17. M. Martynova & L. Renneboog, 2011, The performance of the European market for corporate control: Evidence from the

fifth takeover wave, *European Financial Management*, 17(2): 208–259; S. Sudarsanam & A. A. Mahate, 2006, Are friendly acquisitions too bad for shareholders and managers? Long-term value creation and top management turnover in hostile and friendly acquirers, *British Journal of Management: Supplement*, 17(1): S7–S30.

18. S. Bhattacharyya & A. Nain, 2011, Horizontal acquisitions and buying power: A product market analysis, *Journal of Financial Economics*, 99(1): 97–115; E. Akdogu, 2009, Gaining a competitive edge through acquisitions: Evidence from the telecommunications industry, *Journal of Corporate Finance*, 15: 99–112; E. Devos, P.-R. Kadapakkam, & S. Krishnamurthy, 2009, How do mergers create value? A comparison of taxes, market power, and efficiency improvements as explanations for synergies, *Review of Financial Studies*, 22: 1179–1211.

19. M. A. Hitt, D. King, H. Krishnan, M. Makri, M. Schijven, K. Shimizu, & H. Zhu, 2012, Creating value through mergers and acquisitions: Challenges and opportunities, in D. Faulkner, S. Teerikangas, & R. Joseph (Eds.), *Oxford Handbook of Mergers and Acquisitions,* Oxford, UK: Oxford University Press, 71–113; T. Hamza, 2011, Determinants of short-term value creation for the bidder: Evidence from France, *Journal of Management & Governance*, 15(2): 157–186; J. Haleblian, C. E. Devers, G. McNamara, M. A. Carpenter, & R. B. Davison, 2009, Taking stock of what we know about mergers and acquisitions: A review and research agenda, *Journal of Management*, 35: 469–502.

20. C. Winter, 2012, Bid & ask, *Bloomberg Businessweek*, December 17, 50.

21. Gaur, Malhotra, & Zhu, Acquisition announcements and stock market valuations of acquiring firms' rivals; K. E. Meyer, S. Estrin, S. K. Bhaumik, & M. W. Peng, 2009, Institutions, resources, and entry strategies in emerging economies, *Strategic Management Journal*, 30: 61–80; D. K. Oler, J. S. Harrison, & M. R. Allen, 2008, The danger of misinterpreting short-window event study findings in strategic management research: An empirical illustration using horizontal acquisitions, *Strategic Organization*, 6: 151–184.

22. M. Zollo & J. J. Reuer, 2010, Experience spillovers across corporate development activities, *Organization Science*, 21(6): 1195–1212; C. E. Fee & S. Thomas, 2004, Sources of gains in horizontal mergers: Evidence from customer, supplier, and rival firms, *Journal of Financial Economics*, 74: 423–460.

23. G. E. Halkos & N. G. Tzeremes, 2013, Estimating the degree of operational efficiency gains from a potential bank merger and acquisition: A DEA bootstrapped approach, *Journal of Banking & Finance*, 37(5): 1658–1668; L. Capron, W. Mitchell, & A. Swaminathan, 2001, Asset divestiture following horizontal acquisitions: A dynamic view, *Strategic Management Journal*, 22: 817–844.

24. J. Shenoy, 2012, An examination of the efficiency, foreclosure, and collusion rationales for vertical takeovers, *Management Science*, 58(8): 1482–1501; M. F. Guillén & E. García-Canal, 2010, How to conquer new markets with old skills, *Harvard Business Review*, 88(11): 118–122; A. Parmigiani, 2007, Why do firms both make and buy? An investigation of concurrent sourcing, *Strategic Management Journal*, 28: 285–311.

25. D. Eaton, 2012, Bob Evans paying $50M for Kettle Creations, supplier of mashed potatoes and macaroni and cheese, *The Business Journal's Digital Network*, www.bizjournals.com, August 14.

26. D. FitzGerald, 2013, Oracle expands telecomm footprint with Tekelec buy, *Wall Street Journal*, www.wsj.com, March 25.

27. J. W. Brock & N. P. Obst, 2009, Market concentration, economic welfare, and antitrust policy, *Journal of Industry, Competition and Trade*, 9: 65–75; M. T. Brouwer, 2008, Horizontal mergers and efficiencies: Theory and antitrust practice, *European Journal of Law and Economics*, 26: 11–26.

28. J. Berman, 2013, UPS' planned acquisition of TNT Express officially withdrawn, *Logistics Management*, February, 14–15.

29. A. Sherman, 2013, Why DirecTV will take a pass on mobile, *Bloomberg Businessweek*, May 13–19, 44.

30. P. Zhu, V. Jog, & I. Otchere, 2011, Partial acquisitions in emerging markets: A test of the strategic market entry and corporate control hypotheses, *Journal of Corporate Finance*, 17(2): 288–305; K. E. Meyer, M. Wright, & S. Pruthi, 2009, Managing knowledge in foreign entry strategies: A resource-based analysis, *Strategic Management Journal*, 30: 557–574.

31. R. E. Hoskisson, M. Wright, I. Filatotchev, & M. W. Peng, 2013, Emerging multinationals from mid-range economies: The influence of institutions and factor markets, *Journal of Management Studies*, 50: in press; C. Y. Tseng, 2009, Technological innovation in the BRIC economies, *Research-Technology Management*, 52: 29–35; S. McGee, 2007, Seeking value in BRICs, *Barron's*, July 9, L10–L11.

32. I. Erel, R. C. Liao, & M. S. Weisbach, 2012, Determinants of cross-border mergers and acquisitions, *Journal of Finance*, 67(3): 1045–1082; K. Boeh, 2011, Contracting costs and information asymmetry reduction in cross-border M&A, *Journal of Management Studies*, 48(3): 568–590; R. Chakrabarti, N. Jayaraman, & S. Mukherjee, 2009, Mars-Venus marriages: Culture and cross-border M&A, *Journal of International Business Studies*, 40: 216–237.

33. I. Boudway, 2012, Bid & ask, *Bloomberg Businessweek*, October 22, 56.

34. F. De Beule & J. Duanmu, 2012, Locational determinants of internationalization: A firm-level analysis of Chinese and Indian acquisitions, *European Management Journal*, 30(3): 264–277; P. J. Williamson & A. P. Raman, 2011, How China reset its global acquisition agenda, *Harvard Business Review*, 89(4): 109–114; E. Zabinski, D. Freeman, & X. Jian, 2009, Navigating the challenges of cross-border M&A, *The Deal Magazine*, www.thedeal.com, May 29.

35. J. Lahart, 2012, Emerging risk for multinationals, *Wall Street Journal*, November 15, C12; Y. W. Chin, 2011, M&A under China's Anti-Monopoly Law, *Business Law Today*, 19(7): 1–5.

36. S. Montlake, 2013, Cat scammed, *Forbes*, March 4, 36–38.

37. L. Capron & W. Mitchell, 2012, *Build, Borrow or Buy: Solving the Growth Dilemma*, Cambridge: Harvard Business Review Press; G. K. Lee & M. B. Lieberman, 2010, Acquisition vs. internal development as modes of market entry, *Strategic Management Journal*, 31(2): 140–158; C. Homburg & M. Bucerius, 2006, Is speed of integration really a success factor of mergers and acquisitions? An analysis of the role of internal and external relatedness, *Strategic Management Journal*, 27: 347–367.

38. H. Evanschitzky, M. Eisend, R. J. Calantone, & Y. Jiang, 2012, Success factors of product innovation: An updated meta-analysis, *Journal of Product Innovation Management*, 29: 21–37; H. K. Ellonen, P. Wikström, & A. Jantunen, 2009, Linking dynamic-capability portfolios and innovation outcomes, *Technovation*, 29: 753–762; S. Karim, 2006, Modularity in organizational structure: The reconfiguration of internally developed and acquired business units, *Strategic Management Journal*, 27: 799–823.

39. M. Makri, M. A. Hitt, & P. J. Lane, 2010, Complementary technologies, knowledge relatedness, and invention outcomes in high technology M&As, *Strategic Management Journal*, 31: 602–628; R. E. Hoskisson & L. W. Busenitz, 2002, Market uncertainty and learning distance in corporate entrepreneurship entry mode choice, in M. A. Hitt, R. D. Ireland, S. M. Camp, & D. L. Sexton (eds.), *Strategic Entrepreneurship: Creating a New Mindset*, Oxford, U.K.: Blackwell Publishers, 151–172; M. A. Hitt, R. E. Hoskisson, R. A. Johnson, & D. D. Moesel, 1996, The market for corporate control and firm innovation, *Academy of Management Journal*, 39: 1084–1119.

40. A. DeRosa, 2012, Medtronic grows global reach, *Plastics News*, December 10, 11; M. Herper, 2010, Medtronic's bionic battle, *Forbes*, www.forbes.com, December 12.

41. S. Ransbotham & S. Mitra, 2010, Target age and the acquisition of innovation in high-technology industries, *Management Science*, 56(11): 2076–2093.

42. W. P. Wan & D. W. Yiu, 2009, From crisis to opportunity: Environmental jolt,

corporate acquisitions, and firm performance, *Strategic Management Journal*, 30: 791–801; G. Ahuja & R. Katila, 2001, Technological acquisitions and the innovation performance of acquiring firms: A longitudinal study, *Strategic Management Journal*, 22: 197–220.

43. J. R. Clark & R. S. Huckman, 2012, Broadening focus: Spillovers, complementarities, and specialization in the hospital industry, *Management Science*, 58(4): 708–722; X. Dean, Z. Changhui, & P. H. Phan, 2010, A real options perspective on sequential acquisitions in China, *Journal of International Business Studies*, 41(1): 166–174.

44. N. Zhou & A. Delios, 2012, Diversification and diffusion: A social networks and institutional perspective, *Asia Pacific Journal of Management*, 29(3): 773–798; U. Zander & L. Zander, 2010, Opening the grey box: Social communities, knowledge and culture in acquisitions, *Journal of International Business Studies*, 41(1): 27–37; F. Vermeulen, 2005, How acquisitions can revitalize companies, *MIT Sloan Management Review*, 46(4): 45–51; M. A. Hitt, R. E. Hoskisson, R. D. Ireland, & J. S. Harrison, 1991, Effects of acquisitions on R&D inputs and outputs, *Academy of Management Journal*, 34: 693–706.

45. S. Gamm, 2012, Xerox works to duplicate copier glory in digital services model, *Forbes*, July 19, 59; G. Colvin, 2010, Ursula Burns, *Fortune*, May 3, 161(6): 96–102.

46. H. Prechel, T. Morris, T. Woods, & R. Walden, 2008, Corporate diversification revisited: The political-legal environment, the multilayer-subsidiary form, and mergers and acquisitions, *The Sociological Quarterly*, 49: 849–878; C. E. Helfat & K. M. Eisenhardt, 2004, Inter-temporal economies of scope, organizational modularity, and the dynamics of diversification, *Strategic Management Journal*, 25: 1217–1232.

47. Z. Asher, 2012, X-ray: United Technologies, *Money*, September, 56; E. Crooks, 2011, United Technologies seeks emerging market expansion, *Financial Times*, April 28, 15.

48. B. Worthen, D. Cimilluca, & A. Das, 2012, Cisco hedges bet on video delivery, *Wall Street Journal*, March 16.

49. R. Kirkland, 2013, Connecting everything: A conversation with Cisco's Padmasree Warrior, *McKinsey Quarterly*, www.mckinseyquarterly.com, May.

50. Makri, Hitt, & Lane, Complementary technologies, knowledge relatedness, and invention outcomes in high technology M&As; T. Laamanen & T. Keil, 2008, Performance of serial acquirers: Toward an acquisition program perspective, *Strategic Management Journal*, 29: 663–672.

51. Bhattacharyya & Nain, Horizontal acquisitions and buying power; T. Yu, M. Subramaniam, & A. A. Cannella, Jr., 2009, Rivalry deterrence in international markets: Contingencies governing the mutual forbearance hypothesis, *Academy of Management Journal*, 52: 127–147; D. G. Sirmon, S. Gove, & M. A. Hitt, 2008, Resource management in dyadic competitive rivalry: The effects of resource bundling and deployment, *Academy of Management Journal*, 51: 919–933.

52. A. Kaul, 2012, Technology and corporate scope: Firm and rival innovation as antecedents of corporate transactions, *Strategic Management Journal*, 33(4): 347–367; M. Zollo & J. J. Reuer, 2010, Experience spillovers across corporate development activities, *Organization Science*, 21(6): 1195–1212; P. Puranam & K. Srikanth, 2007, What they know vs. what they do: How acquirers leverage technology acquisitions, *Strategic Management Journal*, 28: 805–825.

53. T. Gantumur & A. Stephan, 2012, Mergers & acquisitions and innovation performance in the telecommunications equipment industry, *Industrial & Corporate Change*, 21(2): 277–314; B. Park & P. N. Ghauri, 2011, Key factors affecting acquisition of technological capabilities from foreign acquiring firms by small and medium-sized local firms, *Journal of World Business*, 46(1): 116–125; S. A. Zahra & J. C. Hayton, 2008, The effect of international venturing on firm performance: The moderating influence of absorptive capacity, *Journal of Business Venturing*, 23: 195–220.

54. Makri, Hitt, & Lane, Complementary technologies, knowledge relatedness, and invention outcomes in high technology mergers and acquisitions; J. S. Harrison, M. A. Hitt, R. E. Hoskisson, & R. D. Ireland, 2001, Resource complementarity in business combinations: Extending the logic to organizational alliances, *Journal of Management*, 27: 679–690.

55. M. Friesl, 2012, Knowledge acquisition strategies and company performance in young high technology companies, *British Journal of Management*, 23(3): 325–343.

56. J. D. Rockoff, 2012, Bristol to buy Amylin in $5.3 billion deal, *Wall Street Journal*, www.wsj.com, July 1.

57. M. E. Graebner, K. M. Eisenhardt, & P. T. Roundy, 2010, Success and failure in technology acquisitions: Lessons for buyers and sellers, *Academy of Management Perspectives*, 24(3), 73–92; J. A. Schmidt, 2002, Business perspective on mergers and acquisitions, in J. A. Schmidt (ed.), *Making Mergers Work*, Alexandria, VA: Society for Human Resource Management, 23–46.

58. T. Herd, 2010, M&A success beating the odds, *Bloomberg Businessweek*, www.businessweek.com, June 23.

59. Muehlfeld, Rao Sahib, & Van Witteloostuijn, A contextual theory of organizational learning from failures and successes; M. Cording, P. Christmann, & D. R. King, 2008, Reducing causal ambiguity in acquisition integration: Intermediate goals as mediators of integration decisions and acquisition performance, *Academy of Management Journal*, 51: 744–767.

60. S. Teerikangas, 2012, Dynamics of acquired firm pre-acquisition employee reactions, *Journal of Management*, 38(2): 599–639; D. S. Siegel & K. L. Simons, 2010, Assessing the effects of mergers and acquisitions on firm performance, plant productivity, and workers: New evidence from matched employer-employee data, *Strategic Management Journal*, 31(8): 903–916; N. Kumar, 2009, How emerging giants are rewriting the rules of M&A, *Harvard Business Review*, 87(5): 115–121; M. C. Sturman, 2008, The value of human capital specificity versus transferability, *Journal of Management*, 34: 290–316.

61. A. Zaheer, X. Castañer, & D. Souder, 2013, Synergy sources, target autonomy, and integration in acquisitions, *Journal of Management*, 39(3): 604–632; K. M. Ellis, T. H. Reus, & B. T. Lamont, 2009, The effects of procedural and informational justice in the integration of related acquisitions, *Strategic Management Journal*, 30: 137–161.

62. T. H. Reus, 2012, Culture's consequences for emotional attending during cross-border acquisition implementation, *Journal of World Business*, 47(3): 342–351.

63. P. Monin, N. Noorderhaven, E. Vaara, & D. Kroon, 2013, Giving sense to and making sense of justice in postmerger integration, *Academy of Management Journal*, 56(1): 256–284.

64. M. Zollo, 1999, M&A—The challenge of learning to integrate: Mastering strategy (part eleven), *Financial Times*, December 6, 14–15.

65. J. Q. Barden, 2012, The influences of being acquired on subsidiary innovation adoption, *Strategic Management Journal*, 33(11): 1269–1285; E. Clark & M. Geppert, 2011, Subsidiary integration as identity construction and institution building: A political sensemaking approach, *Journal of Management Studies*, 48(2): 395–416; H. G. Barkema & M. Schijven, 2008, Toward unlocking the full potential of acquisitions: The role of organizational restructuring, *Academy of Management Journal*, 51: 696–722.

66. A. E. Rafferty & S. L. D. Restburg, 2010, The impact of change process and context on change reactions and turnover during a merger, *Journal of Management*, 36: 1309–1338.

67. R. Gibson, 2006, Package deal; UPS's purchase of Mail Boxes Etc. looked great on paper. Then came the culture clash, *Wall Street Journal*, May 8, R13.

68. 2013, Mail Boxes Etc., Wikipedia, www.wikipedia.org, accessed on May 17.

69. A. Sleptsov, J. Anand, & G. Vasudeva, 2013, Relationship configurations with information intermediaries: The effect of firm-investment bank ties on expected acquisition performance, *Strategic Management Journal*, 34(8): 957–977.

70. Montlake, Cat scammed.

71. R. Duchin & B. Schmidt, 2013, Riding the merger wave: Uncertainty, reduced

monitoring, and bad acquisitions, *Journal of Financial Economics*, 107(1): 69–88; J. DiPietro, 2010, Responsible acquisitions yield growth, *Financial Executive*, 26(10): 16–19.

72. A. Noto, 2013, HP assets conjure offers from tech buyers, *Mergers & Acquisitions Report*, January 21, 32.

73. T. B. Folta & J. P. O'Brien, 2008, Determinants of firm-specific thresholds in acquisition decisions, *Managerial and Decision Economics*, 29: 209–225; R. J. Rosen, 2006, Merger momentum and investor sentiment: The stock market reaction to merger announcements, *Journal of Business*, 79: 987–1017.

74. C. E. Devers, G. McNamara, J. Haleblian, & M. E. Yoder, 2013, Do they walk the talk or just talk the talk? Gauging acquiring CEO and director confidence in the value-creation potential of announced acquisitions, *Academy of Management Journal*, in press.

75. M. Schijven & M. A. Hitt, 2012, The vicarious wisdom of crowds: Toward a behavioral perspective on investor reactions to acquisition announcements, *Strategic Management Journal*, 33(11): 1247–1268.

76. G. Yago, 1991, *Junk Bonds: How High Yield Securities Restructured Corporate America*, New York: Oxford University Press, 146–148.

77. M. C. Jensen, 1986, Agency costs of free cash flow, corporate finance, and takeovers, *American Economic Review*, 76: 323–329.

78. S. Guo, E. S. Hotchkiss, & W. Song, 2011, Do buyouts (still) create value? *Journal of Finance*, 66(2): 479–517.

79. M. Gottfried, 2013, Debt Dish could give Sprint indigestion, *Wall Street Journal*, April 26, C8.

80. S. W. Bauguess, S. B. Moeller, F. P. Schlingemann, & C. J. Zutter, 2009, Ownership structure and target returns, *Journal of Corporate Finance*, 15: 48–65; H. Donker & S. Zahir, 2008, Takeovers, corporate control, and return to target shareholders, *International Journal of Corporate Governance*, 1: 106–134.

81. Zaheer, Castañer, & Souder, Synergy sources, target autonomy, and integration in acquisitions; Y. M. Zhou, 2011, Synergy, coordination costs, and diversification choices, *Strategic Management Journal*, 32: 624–639; A. B. Sorescu, R. K. Chandy, & J. C. Prabhu, 2007, Why some acquisitions do better than others: Product capital as a driver of long-term stock returns, *Journal of Marketing Research*, 44(1): 57–72.

82. S. Daneshkhu, 2013, Danone buys US organic baby food maker Happy Family, *Financial Times*, www.ft.com, May 13.

83. J. B. Barney, 1988, Returns to bidding firms in mergers and acquisitions: Reconsidering the relatedness hypothesis, *Strategic Management Journal*, 9 (Special Issue): 71–78.

84. O. E. Williamson, 1999, Strategy research: Governance and competence perspectives, *Strategic Management Journal*, 20: 1087–1108.

85. S. Snow, 2013, How to avoid a post-acquisition idea slump, *Fast Company*, February, 50; M. Cleary, K. Hartnett, & K. Dubuque, 2011, Road map to efficient merger integration, *American Banker*, March 22, 9; S. Chatterjee, 2007, Why is synergy so difficult in mergers of related businesses? *Strategy & Leadership*, 35(2): 46–52.

86. W. P. Wan, R. E. Hoskisson, J. C. Short, & D. W. Yiu, 2011, Resource-based theory and corporate diversification: Accomplishments and opportunities, *Journal of Management*, 37(5): 1335–1368; E. Rawley, 2010, Diversification, coordination costs and organizational rigidity: Evidence from microdata, *Strategic Management Journal*, 31: 873–891; C. W. L. Hill & R. E. Hoskisson, 1987, Strategy and structure in the multiproduct firm, *Academy of Management Review*, 12: 331–341.

87. S. Pathak, R. E. Hoskisson, & R. A. Johnson, 2013, Settling up in CEO compensation: The impact of divestiture intensity and contextual factors in refocusing firms, *Strategic Management Journal*, in press; M. L. A. Hayward & K. Shimizu, 2006, De-commitment to losing strategic action: Evidence from the divestiture of poorly performing acquisitions, *Strategic Management Journal*, 27: 541–557; R. A. Johnson, R. E. Hoskisson, & M. A. Hitt, 1993, Board of director involvement in restructuring: The effects of board versus managerial controls and characteristics, *Strategic Management Journal*, 14 (Special Issue): 33–50.

88. J. Hagedoorn & N. Wang, 2012, Is there complementarity or substitutability between internal and external R&D strategies? *Research Policy*, 41(6): 1072–1083; P. David, J. P. O'Brien, T. Yoshikawa, & A. Delios, 2010, Do shareholders or stakeholders appropriate the rents from corporate diversification? The influence of ownership structure, *Academy of Management Journal*, 53: 636–654; R. E. Hoskisson & R. A. Johnson, 1992, Corporate restructuring and strategic change: The effect on diversification strategy and R&D intensity, *Strategic Management Journal*, 13: 625–634.

89. R. D. Banker, S. Wattal, & J. M. Plehn-Dujowich, 2011, R&D versus acquisitions: Role of diversification in the choice of innovation strategy by information technology firms, *Journal of Management Information Systems*, 28(2): 109–144; J. L. Stimpert, I. M. Duhaime, & J. Chesney, 2010, Learning to manage a large diversified firm, *Journal of Leadership and Organizational Studies*, 17: 411–425; T. Keil, M. V. J. Maula, H. Schildt, & S. A. Zahra, 2008, The effect of governance modes and relatedness of external business development activities on innovative performance, *Strategic Management Journal*, 29: 895–907; K. H. Tsai & J. C. Wang, 2008, External technology acquisition and firm performance: A longitudinal study, *Journal of Business Venturing*, 23. 91–112.

90. A. Kacperczyk, 2009, With greater power comes greater responsibility? Takeover protection and corporate attention to stakeholders, *Strategic Management Journal*, 30: 261–285; L. H. Lin, 2009, Mergers and acquisitions, alliances and technology development: An empirical study of the global auto industry, *International Journal of Technology Management*, 48: 295–307; M. L. Barnett, 2008, An attention-based view of real options reasoning, *Academy of Management Review*, 33: 606–628.

91. J. A. Martin & K. J. Davis, 2010, Learning or hubris? Why CEOs create less value in successive acquisitions, *Academy of Management Perspectives*, 24(1): 79–81; M. L. A. Hayward & D. C. Hambrick, 1997, Explaining the premiums paid for large acquisitions: Evidence of CEO hubris, *Administrative Science Quarterly*, 42: 103–127; R. Roll, 1986, The hubris hypothesis of corporate takeovers, *Journal of Business*, 59: 197–216.

92. F. Vermeulen, 2007, Business insight (a special report): Bad deals: Eight warning signs that an acquisition may not pay off, *Wall Street Journal*, April 28, R10.

93. D. H. Zhu, 2013, Group polarization on corporate boards: Theory and evidence on board decisions about acquisition premiums, *Strategic Management Journal*, 34(7): 800–822.

94. Christensen, Alton, Rising, & Waldeck, The new M&A playbook.

95. J. Reingold & D. Burke, 2013, Citigroup's new CEO is a banker. Imagine that, *Fortune*, May 20, 176–181.

96. V. Swaminathan, F. Murshed, & J. Hulland, 2008, Value creation following merger and acquisition announcements: The role of strategic emphasis alignment, *Journal of Marketing Research*, 45: 33–47.

97. J. Begley & T. Donnelly, 2011, The DaimlerChrysler Mitsubishi merger: A study in failure, *International Journal of Automotive Technology and Management*, 11(1): 36–48.

98. M. Wagner, 2011, To explore or to exploit? An empirical investigation of acquisitions by large incumbents, *Research Policy*, 40(9): 1217–1225; H. Greve, 2011, Positional rigidity: Low performance and resource acquisition in large and small firms, *Strategic Management Journal*, 32(1): 103–114.

99. D. Clark & S. Tibken, 2011, Corporate news: Cisco to reduce its bureaucracy, *Wall Street Journal*, May 6, B4.

100. Vermeulen, Business insight (a special report): Bad deals: Eight warning signs that an acquisition may not pay off.

101. E. Gomes, D. N. Angwin, Y. Weber, & S. Tarba, 2013, Critical success factors through the mergers and acquisitions process: Revealing pre- and post-M&A

connections for improved performance, *Thunderbird International Business Review*, 55(1): 13–35; M. Cording, P. Christmann, & C. Weigelt, 2010, Measuring theoretically complex constructs: The case of acquisition performance, *Strategic Organization*, 8(1): 11–41; H. G. Barkema & M. Schijven, 2008, How do firms learn to make acquisitions? A review of past research and an agenda for the future, *Journal of Management*, 34: 594–634.

102. A. Riviezzo, 2013, Acquisitions in knowledge-intensive industries: Exploring the distinctive characteristics of the effective acquirer, *Management Research Review*, 36(2): 183–212; S. Chatterjee, 2009, The keys to successful acquisition programmes, *Long Range Planning*, 42: 137–163.
103. R. Karlgaard, 2012, Driving change: Cisco's Chambers, *Forbes*, February 13, 32; R. Myers, 2011, Integration acceleration, *CFO*, 27(1): 52–57.
104. D. Mayer & M. Kenney, 2004, Economic action does not take place in a vacuum: Understanding Cisco's acquisition and development strategy, *Industry and Innovation*, 11(4): 299–325.
105. 2013, Business management case study: How Cisco applies companywide expertise for integrating acquired companies, www.cisco.com, accessed May 17.
106. M. A. Hitt, R. D. Ireland, J. S. Harrison, & A. Best, 1998, Attributes of successful and unsuccessful acquisitions of U.S. firms, *British Journal of Management*, 9: 91–114.
107. K. Uhlenbruck, M. A. Hitt, & M. Semadeni, 2006, Market value effects of acquisitions involving Internet firms: A resource-based analysis, *Strategic Management Journal*, 27: 899–913.
108. A. Zaheer, E. Hernandez, & S. Banerjee, 2010, Prior alliances with targets and acquisition performance in knowledge-intensive industries, *Organization Science*, 21: 1072–1094; P. Porrini, 2004, Can a previous alliance between an acquirer and a target affect acquisition performance? *Journal of Management*, 30: 545–562.
109. Y. Zeng, T. J. Douglas, & C. Wu, 2013, The seller's perspective on determinants of acquisition likelihood: Insights from China's beer industry, *Journal of Management Studies*, 50(4): 673–698.
110. A. Rouzies & H. L. Colman, 2012, Identification processes in post-acquisition integration: The role of social interactions, *Corporate Reputation Review*, 15(3): 143–157; D. K. Ellis, T. Reus, & B. Lamont, 2009, The effects of procedural and informational justice in the integration of related acquisitions, *Strategic Management Journal*, 30(2): 137–161; R. J. Aiello & M. D. Watkins, 2000, The fine art of friendly acquisition, *Harvard Business Review*, 78(6): 100–107.
111. J. Krug, P. Wright, & M. Kroll, 2013, Top management turnover following mergers and acquisitions: Solid research to date but still much to be learned, *Academy of Management Perspectives*, in press; D. D. Bergh, 2001, Executive retention and acquisition outcomes: A test of opposing views on the influence of organizational tenure, *Journal of Management*, 27: 603–622; J. P. Walsh, 1989, Doing a deal: Merger and acquisition negotiations and their impact upon target company top management turnover, *Strategic Management Journal*, 10: 307–322.
112. D. A. Waldman & M. Javidan, 2009, Alternative forms of charismatic leadership in the integration of mergers and acquisitions, *The Leadership Quarterly*, 20: 130–142; F. J. Froese, Y. S. Pak, & L. C. Chong, 2008, Managing the human side of cross-border acquisitions in South Korea, *Journal of World Business*, 43: 97–108.
113. R. Agarwal, J. Anand, J. Bercovitz, & R. Croson, 2012, Spillovers across organizational architectures: The role of prior resource allocation and communication in post-acquisition coordination outcomes, *Strategic Management Journal*, 33(6): 710–733; K. Marmenout, 2010, Employee sensemaking in mergers: How deal characteristics shape employee attitudes, *Journal of Applied Behavioral Science*, 46(3): 329–359; M. E. Graebner, 2009, Caveat venditor: Trust asymmetries in acquisitions of entrepreneurial firms, *Academy of Management Journal*, 52: 435–472; N. J. Morrison, G. Kinley, & K. L. Ficery, 2008, Merger deal breakers: When operational due diligence exposes risk, *Journal of Business Strategy*, 29: 23–28.
114. Y. Suh, J. You, & P. Kim, 2013, The effect of innovation capabilities and experience on cross-border acquisition performance, *Global Journal of Business Research*, 7(3): 59–74; J. Jwu-Rong, H. Chen-Jui, & L. Hsieh-Lung, 2010, A matching approach to M&A, R&D, and patents: Evidence from Taiwan's listed companies, *International Journal of Electronic Business Management*, 8(3): 273–280.
115. E. McGirt, 2012, Fresh copy: How Ursala Burns reinvented Xerox, *Fast Company*, January, 132–138.
116. K. H. Heimeriks, M. Schijven, & S. Gates, 2013, Manifestations of higher-order routines: The underlying mechanisms of deliberate learning in the context of postacquisition integration, *Academy of Management Journal*, 55(3): 703–726; J. M. Shaver & J. M. Mezias, 2009, Diseconomies of managing in acquisitions: Evidence from civil lawsuits, *Organization Science*, 20: 206–222; M. L. McDonald, J. D. Westphal, & M. E. Graebner, 2008, What do they know? The effects of outside director acquisition experience on firm acquisition performance, *Strategic Management Journal*, 29: 1155–1177.
117. C. Moschieri & J. Mair, 2012, Managing divestitures through time—Expanding current knowledge, *Academy of Management Perspectives*, 26(4): 35–50; D. Lee & R. Madhaven, 2010, Divestiture and firm performance: A meta-analysis, *Journal of Management*, 36: 1345–1371; D. D. Bergh & E. N.-K. Lim, 2008, Learning how to restructure: Absorptive capacity and improvisational views of restructuring actions and performance, *Strategic Management Journal*, 29: 593–616.
118. Y. Zhou, X. Li, & J. Svejnar, 2011, Subsidiary divestiture and acquisition in a financial crisis: Operational focus, financial constraints, and ownership, *Journal of Corporate Finance*, 17(2): 272–287; Y. G. Suh & E. Howard, 2009, Restructuring retailing in Korea: The case of Samsung-Tesco, *Asia Pacific Business Review*, 15: 29–40; Z. Wu & A. Delios, 2009, The emergence of portfolio restructuring in Japan, *Management International Review*, 49: 313–335.
119. S. Thurm, 2008, Who are the best CEOs of 2008? *Wall Street Journal*, www.wsj.com, December 15.
120. J. Xia & S. Li, 2013, The divestiture of acquired subunits: A resource-dependence approach, *Strategic Management Journal*, 34: 131–148; L. Diestre & N. Rajagopalan, 2011, An environmental perspective on diversification: The effects of chemical relatedness and regulatory sanctions, *Academy of Management Journal*, 54: 97–115.
121. A. Fortune & W. Mitchell, 2012, Unpacking firm exit at the firm and industry levels: The adaptation and selection of firm capabilities, *Strategic Management Journal*, 33(7): 794–819; J. L. Morrow, Jr., D. G. Sirmon, M. A. Hitt, & T. R. Holcomb, 2007, Creating value in the face of declining performance: Firm strategies and organizational recovery, *Strategic Management Journal*, 28: 271–283; J. L. Morrow, Jr., R. A. Johnson, & L. W. Busenitz, 2004, The effects of cost and asset retrenchment on firm performance: The overlooked role of a firm's competitive environment, *Journal of Management*, 30: 189–208.
122. G. J. Castrogiovanni & G. D. Bruton, 2000, Business turnaround processes following acquisitions: Reconsidering the role of retrenchment, *Journal of Business Research*, 48: 25–34; W. McKinley, J. Zhao, & K. G. Rust, 2000, A sociocognitive interpretation of organizational downsizing, *Academy of Management Review*, 25: 227–243.
123. J. D. Evans & F. Hefner, 2009, Business ethics and the decision to adopt golden parachute contracts: Empirical evidence of concern for all stakeholders, *Journal of Business Ethics*, 86: 65–79; H. A. Krishnan, M. A. Hitt, & D. Park, 2007, Acquisition premiums, subsequent workforce reductions and post-acquisition performance, *Journal of Management*, 44: 709–732.
124. K. McFarland, 2008, Four mistakes leaders make when downsizing, *BusinessWeek Online*, www.businessweek.com, October 24.

125. D. K. Lim, N. Celly, E. A. Morse, & W. Rowe, 2013, Rethinking the effectiveness of asset and cost retrenchment: The contingency effects of a firm's rent creation mechanism, *Strategic Management Journal*, 34(1): 42–61.
126. R. Iverson & C. Zatzick, 2011, The effects of downsizing on labor productivity: The value of showing consideration for employees' morale and welfare in high-performance work systems, *Human Resource Management*, 50(1): 29–43; C. O. Trevor & A. J. Nyberg, 2008, Keeping your headcount when all about you are losing theirs: Downsizing, voluntary turnover rates, and the moderating role of HR practices, *Academy of Management Journal*, 51: 259–276.
127. Bergh & Lim, Learning how to restructure; R. E. Hoskisson & M. A. Hitt, 1994, *Downscoping: How to Tame the Diversified Firm*, New York: Oxford University Press.
128. A. T. Nicolai, A. Schulz, & T. W. Thomas, 2010, What Wall Street wants – Exploring the role of security analysts in the evolution and spread of management concepts, *Journal of Management Studies*, 47(1): 162–189; L. Dranikoff, T. Koller, & A. Schneider, 2002, Divestiture: Strategy's missing link, *Harvard Business Review*, 80(5): 74–83.
129. R. E. Hoskisson & M. A. Hitt, 1990, Antecedents and performance outcomes of diversification: A review and critique of theoretical perspectives, *Journal of Management*, 16: 461–509.
130. C. Moschieri, 2011, The implementation and structuring of divestitures: The unit's perspective, *Strategic Management Journal*, 32: 368–401.
131. T. Laamanen, M. Brauer, & O. Junna, 2013, Performance of acquirers of divested assets: Evidence from the U.S. software industry, *Strategic Management Journal*, in press.
132. M. F. Brauer & M. F. Wiersema, 2012, Industry divestiture waves: How a firm's position influences investor returns, *Academy of Management Journal*, 55(6): 1472–1492.
133. Reingold & Burke, Citigroup's new CEO is a banker; 2010, Citi to shrink its consumer-lending unit, *American Banker*, June 2, 16.
134. Pathak, Hoskisson, & Johnson, Settling up in CEO compensation: The impact of divestiture intensity and contextual factors in refocusing firms; A. Kambil, 2008, What is your recession playbook? *Journal of Business Strategy*, 29: 50–52.
135. H. Berry, 2013, When do firms divest foreign operations? *Organization Science*, 24(1): 246–261; C. Chi-Nien & L. Xiaowei, 2008, Institutional logics or agency costs: The influence of corporate governance models on business group restructuring in emerging economies, *Organization Science*, 19(5): 766–784; R. E. Hoskisson, R. A. Johnson, L. Tihanyi, & R. E. White, 2005, Diversified business groups and corporate refocusing in emerging economies, *Journal of Management*, 31: 941–965.
136. S. N. Kaplan & P. Stromberg, 2009, Leveraged buyouts and private equity, *Journal of Economic Perspectives*, 23: 121–146; C. Moschieri & J. Mair, 2008, Research on corporate divestures: A synthesis, *Journal of Management & Organization*, 14: 399–422.
137. R. E. Hoskisson, W. Shi, X. Yi, & J. Jin, 2013, The evolution and strategic positioning of private equity firms, *Academy of Management Perspectives*, 27(1): 22–38.
138. K. H. Wruck, 2009, Private equity, corporate governance, and the reinvention of the market for corporate control, *Journal of Applied Corporate Finance*, 20: 8–21; M. F. Wiersema & J. P. Liebeskind, 1995, The effects of leveraged buyouts on corporate growth and diversification in large firms, *Strategic Management Journal*, 16: 447–460.
139. N. Wilson, M. Wright, D. S. Siegel, & L. Scholes, 2012, Private equity portfolio company performance during the global recession, *Journal of Corporate Finance*, 18(1): 193–205; R. Harris, D. S. Siegel, & M. Wright, 2005, Assessing the impact of management buyouts on economic efficiency: Plant-level evidence from the United Kingdom, *Review of Economics and Statistics*, 87: 148–153.
140. H. Bruining, E. Verwaal, & M. Wright, 2013, Private equity and entrepreneurial management in management buy-outs, *Small Business Economics*, 40(3): 591–605; M. Meuleman, K. Amess, M. Wright, & L. Scholes, 2009, Agency, strategic entrepreneurship, and the performance of private equity-backed buyouts, *Entrepreneurship Theory and Practice*, 33: 213–239.
141. Moschieri, The implementation and structuring of divestitures: The unit's perspective; Siegel & Simons, Assessing the effects of mergers and acquisitions on firm performance, plant productivity, and workers; W. Kiechel III, 2007, Private equity's long view, *Harvard Business Review*, 85(8): 18–20; M. Wright, R. E. Hoskisson, & L. W. Busenitz, 2001, Firm rebirth: Buyouts as facilitators of strategic growth and entrepreneurship, *Academy of Management Executive*, 15(1): 111–125.
142. E. G. Love & M. Kraatz, 2009, Character, conformity, or the bottom line? How and why downsizing affected corporate reputation, *Academy of Management Journal*, 52: 314–335; J. P. Guthrie & D. K. Datta, 2008, Dumb and dumber: The impact of downsizing on firm performance as moderated by industry conditions, *Organization Science*, 19: 108–123.
143. H. A. Krishnan & D. Park, 2002, The impact of work force reduction on subsequent performance in major mergers and acquisitions: An exploratory study, *Journal of Business Research*, 55(4): 285–292; P. M. Lee, 1997, A comparative analysis of layoff announcements and stock price reactions in the United States and Japan, *Strategic Management Journal*, 18: 879–894.
144. D. J. Flanagan & K. C. O'Shaughnessy, 2005, The effect of layoffs on firm reputation, *Journal of Management*, 31: 445–463.
145. P. Williams, K. M. Sajid, & N. Earl, 2011, Customer dissatisfaction and defection: The hidden costs of downsizing, *Industrial Marketing Management*, 40(3): 405–413.
146. P. Galagan, 2010, The biggest losers: The perils of extreme downsizing, *T+D*, November, 27–29; D. S. DeRue, J. R. Hollenbeck, M. D. Johnson, D. R. Ilgen, & D. K. Jundt, 2008, How different team downsizing approaches influence team-level adaptation and performance, *Academy of Management Journal*, 51: 182–196; C. D. Zatzick & R. D. Iverson, 2006, High-involvement management and workforce reduction: Competitive advantage or disadvantage? *Academy of Management Journal*, 49: 999–1015.
147. C. Moschieri & J. Mair, 2011, Adapting for innovation: Including divestitures in the debate, *Long Range Planning*, 44(1): 4–25; K. Shimizu & M. A. Hitt, 2005, What constrains or facilitates divestitures of formerly acquired firms? The effects of organizational inertia, *Journal of Management*, 31: 50–72.
148. P. G. Klein, J. L. Chapman, & M. P. Mondelli, 2013, Private equity and entrepreneurial governance: Time for a balanced view, *Academy of Management Perspectives*, 27(1): 39–51; D. T. Brown, C. E. Fee, & S. E. Thomas, 2009, Financial leverage and bargaining power with suppliers: Evidence from leveraged buyouts, *Journal of Corporate Finance*, 15: 196–211.
149. S. B. Rodrigues & J. Child, 2010, Private equity, the minimalist organization and the quality of employment relations, *Human Relations*, 63(9): 1321–1342; G. Wood & M. Wright, 2009, Private equity: A review and synthesis, *International Journal of Management Reviews*, 11: 361–380; A.-L. Le Nadant & F. Perdreau, 2006, Financial profile of leveraged buy-out targets: Some French evidence, *Review of Accounting and Finance*, (4): 370–392.
150. M. Goergen, N. O'Sullivan, & G. Wood, 2011, Private equity takeovers and employment in the UK: Some empirical evidence, *Corporate Governance: An International Review*, 19(3): 259–275; G. D. Bruton, J. K. Keels, & E. L. Scifres, 2002, Corporate restructuring and performance: An agency perspective on the complete buyout cycle, *Journal of Business Research*, 55: 709–724; W. F. Long & D. J. Ravenscraft, 1993, LBOs, debt, and R&D intensity, *Strategic Management Journal*, 14 (Special Issue): 119–135.
151. S. A. Zahra, 1995, Corporate entrepreneurship and financial performance: The case of management leveraged buyouts, *Journal of Business Venturing*, 10: 225–248.

# 8

# International Strategy

***Studying this chapter should provide you with the strategic management knowledge needed to:***

1. Explain incentives that can influence firms to use an international strategy.
2. Identify three basic benefits firms achieve by successfully implementing an international strategy.
3. Explore the determinants of national advantage as the basis for international business-level strategies.
4. Describe the three international corporate-level strategies.
5. Discuss environmental trends affecting the choice of international strategies, particularly international corporate-level strategies.
6. Explain the five modes firms use to enter international markets.
7. Discuss the two major risks of using international strategies.
8. Discuss the strategic competitiveness outcomes associated with international strategies, particularly with an international diversification strategy.
9. Explain two important issues firms should have knowledge about when using international strategies.

## AN INTERNATIONAL STRATEGY POWERS ABB'S FUTURE

ABB is a major competitor in the power and automation technologies industries across the major markets globally. It has 145,000 employees operating in almost 100 countries. In fact, it has five major businesses—power products, power systems, discrete automation, low voltage products, and process automation. It operates in eight major regions: (1) Northern Europe, (2) Central Europe, (3) the Mediterranean, (4) North America, (5) South America, (6) India, the Middle East, and Africa, (7) North Asia, and (8) South Asia. Over time, ABB has been a successful company using its geographic diversification across the globe to its advantage. However, it also exemplifies the difficulty of managing an international strategy and operations. For example, its power systems business has experienced performance problems in recent years due to poor performance in some countries. As a result, it recently announced that it was going to reduce or eliminate operations in Lithuania, Nigeria, the Philippines, Slovakia, and six additional countries. The CEO stated that the returns from these operations had not justified the investments made.

In recent years, most of ABB's entries to new markets and expansions in existing markets have come from acquisitions of existing businesses in those markets. Recently, it acquired Siemens' solar energy business, Power-One, and U.S.-based Los Gatos Research, a manufacturer of gas analyzers used in environmental monitoring and research. The purchase of Power-One represents a major risk as the solar power industry is in a downturn, yet some analysts predict a brighter future for the industry over the long term. ABB also uses other modes of entry and expansion, exemplified by the 2013 joint venture with China's Jiangsu Jinke Smart Electric Company to design, manufacture, and provide follow-up service on high voltage instrument transformers. It also recently procured major contracts for business in Brazil and South Africa.

Partly due to the global economic recession that began in 2008, recent weak economic performance, and some poor expansion decisions, ABB's performance has been weaker than expected. As a result, the CEO and chief technology officer announced their resignations in 2013. Despite these changes, ABB is a highly respected global brand and after its recent changes (e.g., closing some country operations), its revenues and earnings have started to rise. These positive changes have been largely attributed to the success of its North American businesses. Its acquisitions of Baldor (maker of industrial motors) in 2010 and Thomas & Betts in 2012 greatly enhanced its North American operations and revenues. Therefore, even in turbulent times, ABB's future looks bright.

Sources: 2013, ABB procures contract in Brazil, *Zacks Equity Research*, www.zacks.com, May 14; 2013, ABB's South African project, *Zacks Equity Research*, www.zacks.com, May 13; P. Winters, 2013, ABB loses Banerjee after Hogan's decision to step down, *Bloomberg Businessweek*, www.businessweek.com, May 13; J. Revill & A. Morse, 2013, ABB CEO to resign, *Wall Street Journal*, www.wsj.com, May 10; 2013, ABB strengthens footprints in China, *Zacks Equity Research*, www.zacks.com, May 10; J. Revill, 2013, ABB buys US gas analyzer company Los Gatos Research, *Wall Street Journal*, www.wsj.com, May 3; 2013, ABB/Power-One: Shining example, *Financial Times*, www.ft.com, April 22; W. Pentland, 2013, ABB gambles big on solar power, *Forbes*, www.forbes.com, April 22; M. Scott, 2013, ABB to buy Power-One for $1 billion, *New York Times Dealbook*, http://dealbook.nytimes.com, April 22; J. Shotter, 2013, ABB boosted by US ventures, *Financial Times*, www.ft.com, February 14; J. Shotter, 2012, ABB overhauls power systems division, *Financial Times*, www.ft.com, December 14.

Learn more about Baldor, another company acquired by ABB.
www.cengagebrain.com

Our description of ABB's competitive actions in this chapter's Opening Case (e.g., expansion in North American markets) highlights the importance of international markets for this firm. It is using its returns in the North American markets to overcome weaknesses in its European markets. Being able to effectively compete in countries and regions outside a firm's domestic market is increasingly important to firms of all types, as exemplified by ABB. One reason for this is that the effects of globalization continue to reduce the number of industrial and consumer markets in which only domestic firms can compete successfully. In place of what historically were relatively stable and predictable domestic markets, firms across the globe find they are now competing in globally oriented industries—industries in which firms must compete in all world markets where a consumer or commercial good or service is sold in order to be competitive.[1] Unlike domestic markets, global markets are relatively unstable and much less predictable.

The purpose of this chapter is to discuss how international strategies can be a source of strategic competitiveness for firms competing in global markets. To do this, we examine a number of topics (see Figure 8.1). After describing incentives that influence firms to identify international opportunities, we discuss three basic benefits that can accrue to firms that successfully use international strategies. We then turn our attention to the international strategies available to firms. Specifically, we examine both international business-level strategies

**Figure 8.1** Opportunities and Outcomes of International Strategy

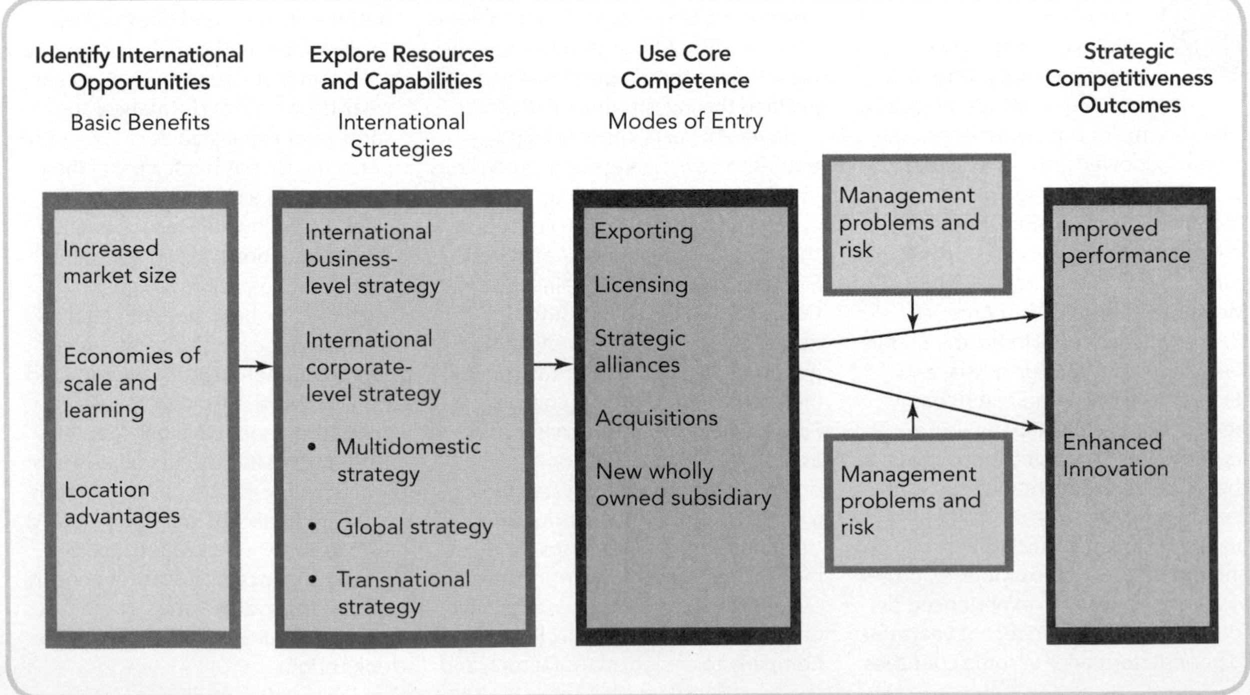

and international corporate-level strategies. The five modes of entry firms can use to enter international markets for implementing their international strategies are then examined. Firms encounter economic and political risks when using international strategies. Some refer to these as economic and political institutions.[2] These risks must be effectively managed if the firm is to achieve the desired outcomes of higher performance and enhanced innovation. After discussing the outcomes firms seek when using international strategies, the chapter closes with mention of two cautions about international strategy that should be kept in mind.

# 8-1 Identifying International Opportunities

An **international strategy** is a strategy through which the firm sells its goods or services outside its domestic market.[3] In some instances, firms using an international strategy become quite diversified geographically as they compete in numerous countries or regions outside their domestic market. This is the case for ABB in that it competes in about 100 countries. In other cases, firms engage in less international diversification in that they only compete in a small number of markets outside their "home" market.

There are incentives for firms to use an international strategy and to diversify their operations geographically, and they can gain three basic benefits when they successfully do so.[4] We show international strategy's incentives and benefits in Figure 8.2.

## 8-1a Incentives to Use International Strategy

Raymond Vernon expressed the classic rationale for an international strategy.[5] He suggested that typically a firm discovers an innovation in its home-country market, especially in advanced economies such as those in Germany, France, Japan, Sweden, Canada, and the United States. Often demand for the product then develops in other countries, causing a firm to export products from its domestic operations to fulfil that demand. Continuing increases in demand can subsequently justify a firm's decision to establish operations outside of its domestic base. As Vernon noted, engaging in an international strategy has the potential to help a firm extend the life cycle of its product(s).

Gaining access to needed and potentially scarce resources is another reason firms use an international strategy. Key supplies of raw material—especially minerals and energy—are critical to firms' efforts in some industries to manufacture their products. Of course energy and mining companies have operations throughout the world to gain access to the raw materials they in turn sell to manufacturers requiring those resources. Rio Tinto is a leading international mining group. Operating as a global organization, the firm has 71,000 employees across six continents to include Australia, North America, Europe, South America, Asia and Africa. Rio Tinto uses its capabilities of technology and innovation (see first incentive noted above), exploration, marketing, and operational processes to identify, extract, and market mineral resources throughout the world.[6] In other industries where labor costs account for a significant portion of a company's expenses, firms may choose to establish facilities in other countries to gain access to less expensive labor. Clothing and electronics manufacturers are examples of firms pursuing an international strategy for this reason.

Increased pressure to integrate operations on a global scale is another factor influencing firms to pursue an international strategy. As nations industrialize, the demand for some products and commodities appears to become more similar. This borderless demand for globally branded products may be due to similarities in lifestyle in developed nations. Increases in global communications also facilitate the ability of people in different countries to visualize and model lifestyles in different cultures.[7] In an increasing number of industries,

An **international strategy** is a strategy through which the firm sells its goods or services outside its domestic market.

**Figure 8.2** Incentives and Basic Benefits of International Strategy

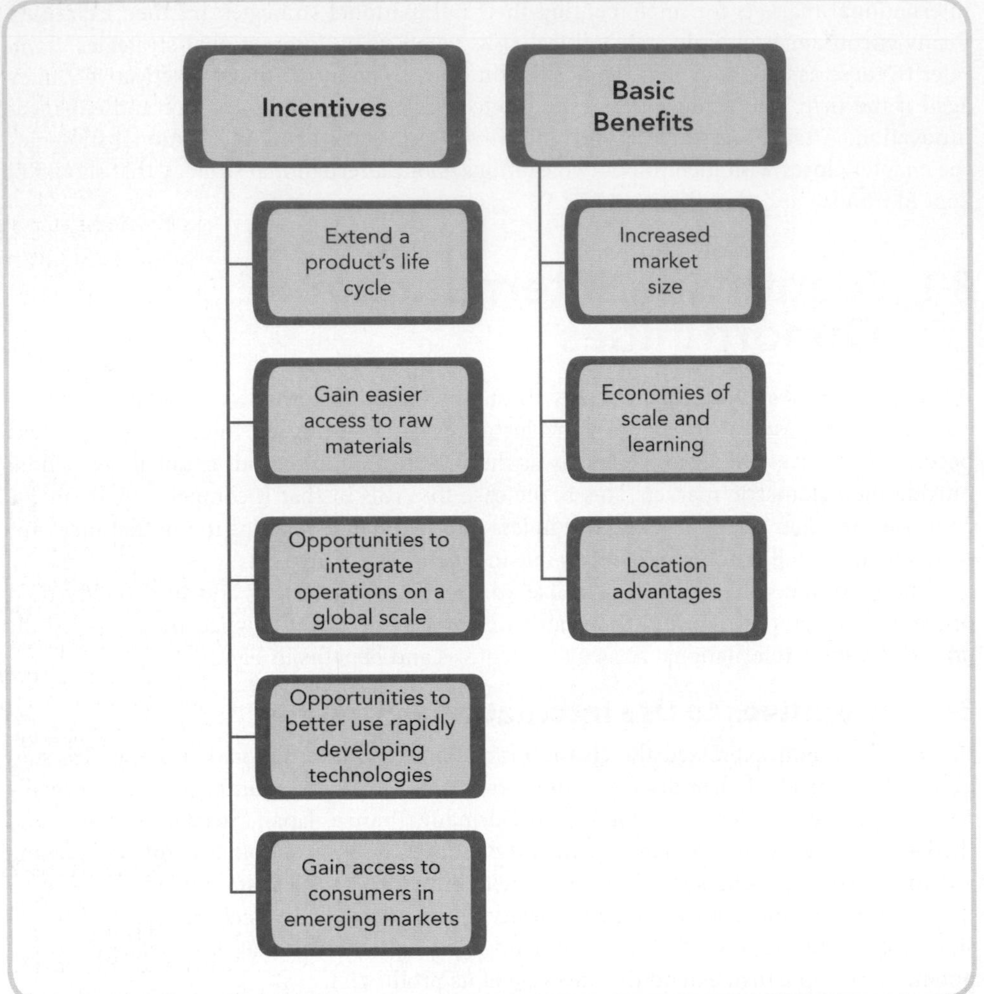


technology drives globalization because the economies of scale necessary to reduce costs to the lowest level often require an investment greater than that needed to meet domestic market demand. Moreover, in emerging markets the increasingly rapid adoption of technologies such as the Internet and mobile applications permits greater integration of trade, capital, culture, and labor. In this sense, technologies are the foundation for efforts to bind together disparate markets and operations across the world. International strategy makes it possible for firms to use technologies to organize their operations into a seamless whole.[8]

The potential of large demand for goods and services from people in emerging markets such as China and India is another strong incentive for firms to use an international strategy.[9] This is the case for French-based Carrefour Group. This firm is the world's second-largest retailer (behind only Walmart) and the largest in Europe. Carrefour operates five main grocery store formats—hypermarkets, supermarkets, cash & carry, hypercash stores, and convenience stores. The firm also sells products online.[10] In 2011, Carrefour acquired minority stakes in three mainland Chinese retailers to strengthen its presence there, as this market is critical to its growth plans.[11]

Even though India, another emerging market economy, differs from Western countries in many respects, including culture, politics, and the precepts of its economic system, it also offers a huge potential market and its government is becoming more supportive of foreign direct investment.[12] However, differences among Chinese, Indian, and Western-style economies and cultures make the successful use of an international strategy challenging. In particular, firms seeking to meet customer demands in emerging markets must learn how to manage an array of political and economic risks,[13] such as those we discuss later in the chapter.

Learn more about Globalization.
www.cengagebrain.com

We've now discussed incentives that influence firms to use international strategies. Firms derive three basic benefits by successfully using international strategies: (1) increased market size; (2) increased economies of scale and learning; and (3) development of a competitive advantage through location (e.g., access to low-cost labor, critical resources, or customers). These benefits will be examined here in terms of both their costs (such as higher coordination expenses and limited access to knowledge about host country political influences)[14] and their challenges.

## 8-1b Three Basic Benefits of International Strategy

As noted, effectively using one or more international strategies can result in three basic benefits for the firm. These benefits facilitate the firm's effort to achieve strategic competitiveness (see Figure 8.1) when using an international strategy.

### Increased Market Size

Firms can expand the size of their potential market—sometimes dramatically—by using an international strategy to establish stronger positions in markets outside their domestic market. As noted, access to additional consumers is a key reason Carrefour sees China as a major source of growth.

Takeda, a large Japanese pharmaceutical company, acquired Swiss drug maker Nycomed in 2011, which exemplifies one form of its growth strategy. Buying Nycomed made Takeda a major player in European markets. More significantly, the acquisition broadened Takeda's distribution capability in emerging markets. The company is focusing on the development of its global business operations in emerging markets and developed economy countries, and organic growth through scientific and business process innovation.[15] Along with Starbucks, Carrefour and Takeda are two additional companies relying on international strategy as the path to increased market size in China and other regions of the world.

Firms such as Starbucks, Carrefour, and Takeda understand that effectively managing different consumer tastes and practices linked to cultural values or traditions in different markets is challenging. Nonetheless, they accept this challenge because of the potential to enhance the firm's performance. Other firms accept the challenge of successfully implementing an international strategy largely because of limited growth opportunities in their domestic market. This appears to be at least partly the case for major competitors Coca-Cola and PepsiCo, firms that have not been able to generate significant growth in their U.S. domestic (and North America) markets for some time. Indeed, most of these firms' growth is occurring in international markets. An international market's overall size also has the potential to affect the degree of benefit a firm can accrue as a result of using an international strategy. In general, larger international markets offer higher potential returns and thus pose less risk for the firm choosing to invest in those markets. Relatedly, the strength of the science base of the international markets in which a firm may compete is important in that scientific knowledge and the human capital needed to use that knowledge can facilitate efforts to more effectively sell and/or produce products that create value for customers.[16]

M. Stasy

An SAS Airbus A319. Airbus and Boeing achieve economies of scale by manufacturing in several regions of the world.

Hady Khandani/vario images/Alamy

## Economies of Scale and Learning

By expanding the number of markets in which they compete, firms may be able to enjoy economies of scale, particularly in their manufacturing operations. More broadly, firms able to standardize the processes used to produce, sell, distribute, and service their products across country borders enhance their ability to learn how to continuously reduce costs while hopefully increasing the value their products create for customers. For example, rivals Airbus SAS and Boeing have multiple manufacturing facilities and outsource some activities to firms located throughout the world, partly for the purpose of developing economies of scale as a source of being able to create value for customers.

Economies of scale are critical in a number of settings in addition to the airline manufacturing industry. Automobile manufacturers certainly seek economies of scale as a benefit of their international strategies. Ford employs 166,000 people worldwide and operates in six global regions: North America, Europe, Central and South America, Middle East, Africa, and Asia Pacific. Competing in these global markets, Ford Motor Company is planning on increasing sales in each region but especially in Asia.[17] Overall, Ford seeks to increase the annual number of products it sells outside of North America. For example, it increased its market share in Europe in 2013. Demonstrating the use of this international strategy is the fact that Ford is now run as a single global business developing cars and trucks that can be built and sold throughout the world.[18] Firms may also be able to exploit core competencies in international markets through resource and knowledge sharing between units and network partners across country borders.[19] By sharing resources and knowledge in this manner, firms can learn how to create synergy, which in turn can help each firm learn how to produce higher-quality products at a lower cost.

Working in multiple international markets also provides firms with new learning opportunities,[20] perhaps even in terms of research and development activities. Increasing the firm's R&D ability can contribute to its efforts to enhance innovation, which is critical to both short- and long-term success. However, research results suggest that to take advantage of international R&D investments, firms need to already have a strong R&D system in place to absorb knowledge resulting from effective R&D activities.[21]

## Location Advantages

Locating facilities in markets outside their domestic market can sometimes help firms reduce costs. This benefit of an international strategy accrues to the firm when its facilities in international locations provide easier access to lower-cost labor, energy, and other natural resources. Other location advantages include access to critical supplies and to customers. Once positioned in an attractive location, firms must manage their facilities effectively to gain the full benefit of a location advantage.[22]

A firm's costs, particularly those dealing with manufacturing and distribution, as well as the nature of international customers' needs, affect the degree of benefit it can capture through a location advantage.[23] Cultural influences may also affect location advantages and disadvantages. International business transactions are less difficult for a firm to complete when there is a strong match among the cultures with which the firm is involved while implementing its international strategy.[24] Finally, physical distances influence firms' location choices as well as how to manage facilities in the chosen locations.[25]

# 8-2 International Strategies

Firms choose to use one or both basic types of international strategy: business-level international strategy and corporate-level international strategy. At the business level, firms select from among the generic strategies of cost leadership, differentiation, focused cost leadership, focused differentiation, and integrated cost leadership/differentiation. At the corporate level, multidomestic, global, and transnational international strategies (the transnational is a combination of the multidomestic and global strategies) are considered. To contribute to the firm's efforts to achieve strategic competitiveness in the form of improved performance and enhanced innovation (see Figure 8.1), each international strategy the firm uses must be based on one or more core competencies.[26]

## 8-2a International Business-Level Strategy

Firms considering the use of any international strategy first develop domestic-market strategies (at the business level and at the corporate level if the firm has diversified at the product level). One reason this is important is that the firm may be able to use some of the capabilities and core competencies it has developed in its domestic market as the foundation for competitive success in international markets.[27] However, research results indicate that the value created by relying on capabilities and core competencies developed in domestic markets as a source of success in international markets diminishes as a firm's geographic diversity increases.[28]

**Figure 8.3** Determinants of National Advantage

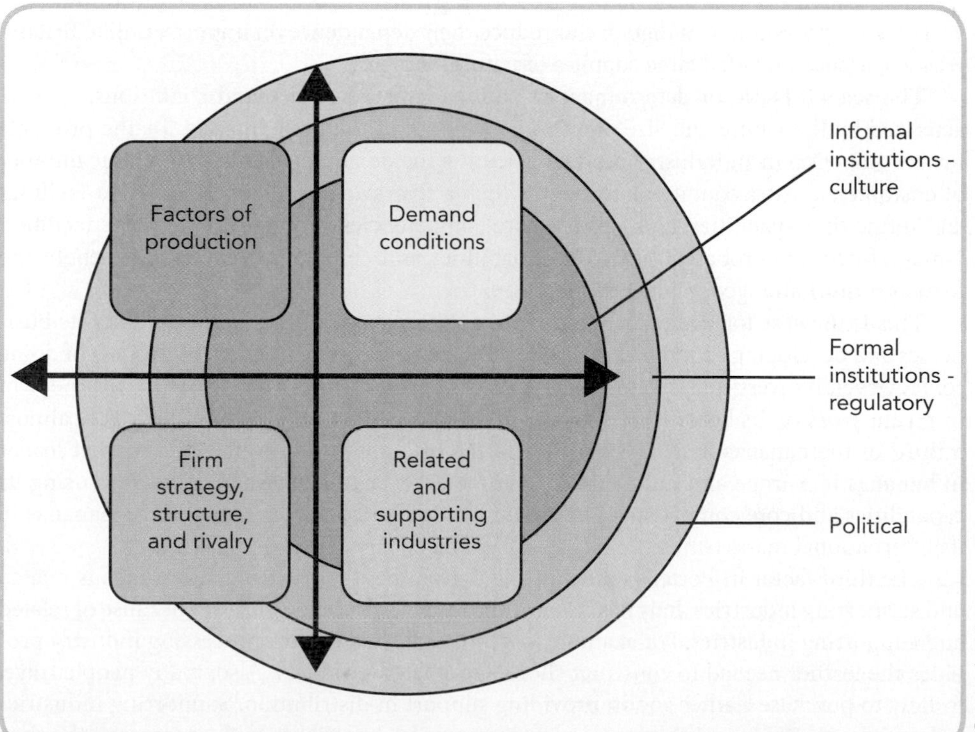

As we know from our discussion of competitive dynamics in Chapter 5, firms do not select and then use strategies in isolation of market realities. In the case of international strategies, conditions in a firm's domestic market affect the degree to which the firm can build on capabilities and core competencies it established in that market to create capabilities and core competencies in international markets. The reason for this is grounded in Michael Porter's analysis of why some nations are more competitive than other nations and why and how some industries within nations are more competitive relative to those industries in other nations. Porter's core argument is that conditions or factors in a firm's home base—that is, in its domestic market—either hinder the firm's efforts to use an international business-level strategy for the purpose of establishing a competitive advantage in international markets or support those efforts. Porter identifies four factors as determinants of a national advantage that some countries possess (see Figure 8.3).[29] Interactions among these four factors influence a firm's choice of international business-level strategy.

The first determinant of national advantage is factors of production. This determinant refers to the inputs necessary for a firm to compete in any industry. Labor, land, natural resources, capital, and infrastructure (such as transportation, postal, and communication systems) represent such inputs. There are basic factors (for example, natural and labor resources) and advanced factors (such as digital communication systems and a highly educated workforce). Other factors of production are generalized (highway systems and the supply of debt capital) and specialized (skilled personnel in a specific industry, such as the workers in a port that specialize in handling bulk chemicals). If a country possesses advanced and specialized production factors, it is likely to serve an industry well by spawning strong home-country competitors that also can be successful global competitors.

Ironically, countries often develop advanced and specialized factors because they lack critical basic resources. For example, some Asian countries, such as South Korea, lack abundant natural resources but have a workforce with a strong work ethic, a large number of engineers, and systems of large firms to create an expertise in manufacturing. Similarly, Germany developed a strong chemical industry, partially because Hoechst and BASF spent years creating a synthetic indigo dye to reduce their dependence on imports, unlike Britain, whose colonies provided large supplies of natural indigo.[30]

The second factor or determinant of national advantage, demand conditions, is characterized by the nature and size of customers' needs in the home market for the products firms competing in an industry produce. Meeting the demand generated by a large number of customers creates conditions through which a firm can develop scale-efficient facilities and refine the capabilities, and perhaps core competencies, required to use those facilities. Once refined, the probability that the capabilities and core competencies will benefit the firm as it diversifies geographically increases.

This is the case for Chiquita Brands International, which spent years building its businesses and developing economies of scale and scale efficient facilities in the process of doing so. However, it diversified into too many different product lines and has refocused the firm in recent years on its bananas and packaged salads product lines. Now, it produces almost a third of the bananas it sells on its own farms in Latin America. It is the market leader in bananas in Europe and number two in the market in North America. So, it is using its capabilities and core competencies in growing and distributing Chiquita brand bananas in its international markets.[31]

The third factor in Porter's model of the determinants of national advantage is related and supporting industries. Italy has become the leader in the shoe industry because of related and supporting industries. For example, a well-established leather-processing industry provides the leather needed to construct shoes and related products. Also, many people travel to Italy to purchase leather goods, providing support in distribution. Supporting industries in leather-working machinery and design services also contribute to the success of the shoe industry. In fact, the design services industry supports its own related industries, such as ski boots, fashion apparel, and furniture. In Japan, cameras and copiers are related industries. Similarly, Germany is known for the quality of its machine tools, and Eastern Belgium is known for skilled manufacturing (supporting and related industries are important in these two settings too).[32]

Pixel Memoirs/Alamy

*High quality shoes on sale at a shop in Florence, Italy. Related and supporting industries contribute to Italy's national advantage in the shoe industry.*

Firm strategy, structure, and rivalry make up the final determinant of national advantage and also foster the growth of certain industries. The types of strategy, structure, and rivalry among firms vary greatly from nation to nation. The excellent technical training system in Germany fosters a strong emphasis on continuous product and process improvements. In Italy, the national pride of the country's designers spawns strong industries not only in shoes but also sports cars, fashion apparel, and furniture. In the United States, competition among computer manufacturers and software producers contributes to further development of these industries.

The four determinants of national advantage (see Figure 8.3) emphasize the structural characteristics of a specific economy that contribute to some degree to national advantage and influence the firm's selection of an international business-level strategy. Individual governments' policies also affect the nature of the determinants as well as how firms compete within the boundaries governing bodies establish and enforce within a particular economy.[33] While studying their external environment (see Chapter 2), firms considering the possibility of using an international strategy need to gather information and data that will allow them to understand the effects of governmental policies and their enforcement on their nation's ability to establish advantages relative to other nations as well as the relative degree of competitiveness on a global basis of the industry in which firms might compete on a global scale.

Those leading companies should recognize that a firm based in a country with a national competitive advantage is not guaranteed success as it implements its chosen international business-level strategy. The actual strategic choices managers make may be the most compelling reasons for success or failure as firms diversify geographically. Accordingly, the factors illustrated in Figure 8.3 are likely to produce the foundation for a firm's competitive advantages only when it develops and implements an appropriate international business-level strategy that takes advantage of distinct country factors. Thus, these distinct country factors should be thoroughly considered when making a decision about the international business-level strategy to use. The firm will then make continuous adjustments to its international business-level strategy in light of the nature of competition it encounters in different international markets and in light of customers' needs. Lexus, for example, does not have the share of the luxury car market in China that it desires. Accordingly, Toyota (Lexus' manufacturer) is adjusting how it implements its international differentiation business-level strategy in China to better serve customers. The firm is doing this by "turning to the feature that cemented its early success in the United States: extreme customer service. Showroom amenities such as cappuccino machines, Wi-Fi, Lego tables for the kids, and airport shuttles for busy executives dropping off their cars for servicing are examples of the services now being offered to customers in China."[34] Time will tell if this adjustment to Lexus' strategy in China will lead to the success the firm desires.

## 8-2b International Corporate-Level Strategy

A firm's international business-level strategy is also based at least partially on its international corporate-level strategy. Some international corporate-level strategies give individual country units the authority to develop their own business-level strategies, while others dictate the business-level strategies in order to standardize the firm's products and sharing of resources across countries.[35]

International corporate-level strategy focuses on the scope of a firm's operations through geographic diversification.[36] International corporate-level strategy is required when the firm operates in multiple industries that are located in multiple countries or regions (e.g., Southeast Asia or the European Union) and in which they sell multiple products. The headquarters unit guides the strategy, although as noted, business- or country-level managers can have substantial strategic input depending on the type of international corporate-level strategy the firm uses. The three international corporate-level strategies are shown in Figure 8.4; the international corporate-level strategies vary in terms of two dimensions—the need for global integration and the need for local responsiveness.

### Multidomestic Strategy

A **multidomestic strategy** is an international strategy in which strategic and operating decisions are decentralized to the strategic business units in individual countries or regions for the purpose of allowing each unit the opportunity to tailor products to the local market.[37]

**Figure 8.4** International Corporate-Level Strategies

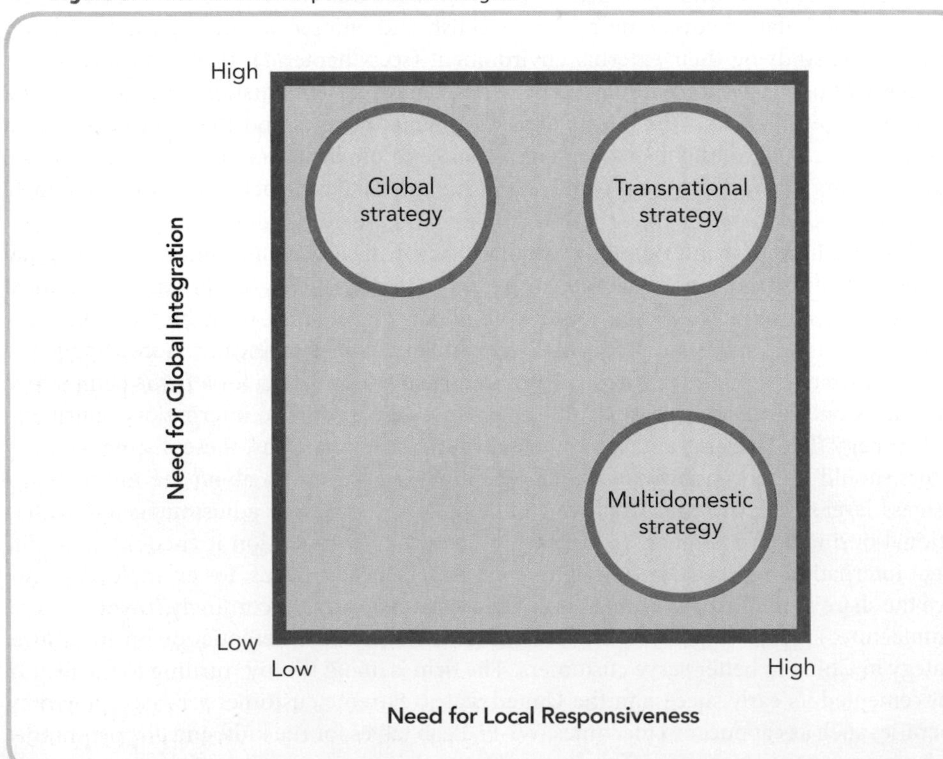


A **multidomestic strategy** is an international strategy in which strategic and operating decisions are decentralized to the strategic business units in individual countries or regions for the purpose of allowing each unit the opportunity to tailor products to the local market.

With this strategy, the firm's need for local responsiveness is high while its need for global integration is low. Influencing these needs is the firm's belief that consumer needs and desires, industry conditions (e.g., the number and type of competitors), political and legal structures, and social norms vary by country. Thus, a multidomestic strategy focuses on competition within each country because market needs are thought to be segmented by country boundaries. To meet the specific needs and preferences of local customers, country or regional managers have the autonomy to customize the firm's products. Therefore, these strategies should maximize a firm's competitive response to the idiosyncratic requirements of each market.[38] The multidomestic strategy is most appropriate for use when the differences between the markets a firm serves and the customers in them are significant.

The use of multidomestic strategies usually expands the firm's local market share because the firm can pay attention to the local clientele's needs. However, using a multidomestic strategy results in less knowledge sharing for the corporation as a whole because of the differences across markets, decentralization, and the different international business-level strategies employed by local units.[39] Moreover, multidomestic strategies do not allow the development of economies of scale and thus can be more costly.

Unilever is a large European consumer products company selling products in over 180 countries. The firm has more than 400 global brands that are grouped into three business units—foods, home care, and personal care. Historically, Unilever has used a highly decentralized approach for the purpose of managing its global brands. This approach allows regional managers considerable autonomy to adapt the characteristics of specific products to satisfy the unique needs of customers in different markets. However, more recently, Unilever has sought to increase the coordination between its independent subsidiaries in order to establish an even stronger global brand presence. Part of the way it achieves some coordination is by having the presidents of each of the five global regions serve as members of the top management team.[40] As such, Unilever may be transitioning from a multidomestic strategy to a transnational strategy.

## Global Strategy

A **global strategy** is an international strategy in which a firm's home office determines the strategies business units are to use in each country or region.[41] This strategy indicates that the firm has a high need for global integration and a low need for local responsiveness. These needs indicate that compared to a multidomestic strategy, a global strategy seeks greater levels of standardization of products across country markets. The firm using a global strategy seeks to develop economies of scale as it produces the same or virtually the same products for distribution to customers throughout the world who are assumed to have similar needs. The global strategy offers greater opportunities to take innovations developed at the corporate level or in one market and apply them in other markets.[42] Improvements in global accounting and financial reporting standards facilitate use of this strategy.[43] A global strategy is most effective when the differences between markets and the customers the firm is serving are insignificant.

Efficient operations are required to successfully implement a global strategy. Increasing the efficiency of a firm's international operations mandates resource sharing and greater coordination and cooperation across market boundaries. Centralized decision making as designed by headquarters details how resources are to be shared and coordinated across markets. Research results suggest that the outcomes a firm achieves by using a global strategy become more desirable when the strategy is used in areas in which regional integration among countries is occurring.[44]

A **global strategy** is an international strategy in which a firm's home office determines the strategies business units are to use in each country or region.

CEMEX is a global building materials company that uses the global strategy. CEMEX is the world's leading supplier of ready-mix concrete and one of the world's largest producers of white Portland cement. CEMEX sells to customers in more than 50 countries in multiple regions, including North America, Latin America, Europe, the Mediterranean, and Asia. With annual sales of approximately $15 billion, the firm employs more than 44,000 people.[45]

To implement its global strategy, CEMEX has centralized a number of its activities. The Shared Services Model is a recent example of how this firm centralizes operations in order to gain scale economies, among other benefits. It uses its vertical integration to promote cooperation among the businesses to provide value-creating service for its customers[46] In essence, the Shared Services Model integrates and centralizes some support functions from the firm's value chain (see Chapter 3). This integration and centralization brings about the types of benefits sought by firms when using a global strategy. Significant cost savings, increases in the productivity of the involved support functions, the fostering of economies of scale, and the freeing up of resources all provide benefits to CEMEX.

Because of increasing global competition and the need to simultaneously be cost efficient and produce differentiated products, the number of firms using a transnational international corporate-level strategy is increasing.

## Transnational Strategy

A **transnational strategy** is an international strategy through which the firm seeks to achieve both global efficiency and local responsiveness. With this strategy, the firm has strong needs for both global integration and local responsiveness. In the Opening Case, we discussed ABB's international strategy. It is known, however, for using the transnational strategy to pursue profitable growth in international markets. For example, ABB focuses on power and automation technologies that allow it to achieve some economies of scale through coordination of its technology development and application and by sharing resources to satisfy customer needs in different parts of the world. In doing so, it achieves a form of global integration. However, it also simultaneously decentralizes decisions to the country level to allow a local business to tailor products, and especially services, to local customers' needs (local responsiveness).

Realizing the twin goals of global integration and local responsiveness is difficult in that global integration requires close global coordination while local responsiveness requires local flexibility. "Flexible coordination"—building a shared vision and individual commitment through an integrated network—is required to implement the transnational strategy. Such integrated networks allow a firm to manage its connections with customers, suppliers, partners, and other parties more efficiently rather than using arm's-length transactions.[47] The transnational strategy is difficult to use because of its conflicting goals (see Chapter 11 for more on the implementation of this and other corporate-level international strategies). On the positive side, effectively implementing a transnational strategy often produces higher performance than does implementing either the multidomestic or global strategies.[48]

Transnational strategies are becoming increasingly necessary to successfully compete in international markets. Reasons for this include the fact that continuing increases in the number of viable global competitors challenge firms to reduce their costs. Simultaneously, the increasing sophistication of markets with greater information flows made possible largely by the diffusion of the Internet and the desire for specialized products to meet consumers' unique needs pressures firms to differentiate their products in local markets. Differences in culture and institutional environments also require firms to adapt their products and approaches to local environments. However, some argue that transnational strategies are not required to successfully compete in international markets. Those holding this view suggest that most multinational firms try to compete at the regional level (e.g., the European Union) rather than at the country level. To the degree this is the case, the need for the firm to simultaneously offer relatively unique products that are adapted to local markets and to produce those products at lower costs permitted by developing scale economies is reduced.[49]

A **transnational strategy** is an international strategy through which the firm seeks to achieve both global efficiency and local responsiveness.

The complexities of competing in global markets increase the need for the use of a transnational strategy, as shown in the discussion of Mondelez International in the Strategic Focus. In fact, Kraft Foods made a decision to spin off its domestic grocery products into a separate business in order to focus on its high-growth snack foods business, in which 80 percent of sales come from foreign markets. Mondelez is a $35 billion company that has power brands (brands that are globally known and respected) and local brands. So, it

## Strategic Focus GLOBALIZATION

### Mondelez International: A Global Leader in Snack Foods Markets

In 2012, with 80 percent of its sales in faster-growing international markets, Kraft Foods decided that it needed to split into two separate companies—a North American grocery business and an international snack foods company. The business focused on North America will sell well-known, traditional Kraft brands such as Velveeta, Kraft Macaroni & Cheese, and Oscar Mayer. These goods are profitable despite being low growth. The snack food company will focus on such power brands as Oreo, Cadbury, and Ritz. It will also promote local brands tailored to the idiosyncratic needs of local markets.

The snack foods business was named Mondelez by combining two words: monde (meaning world) and delez (new word to mean delicious) to communicate the meaning of products that are "world delicious". The separation into different businesses allows each to use its own specialized strategy that best suits its products and markets, and the competitive landscape it faces. Mondelez International is the global market leader in biscuits, chocolate, candy, and powdered beverages and holds the number two position in the global markets for chewing gum and coffee. About 45 percent of its sales come from fast growing emerging markets. Some of the local brands designed for customers in the emerging markets include Barni (soft biscuits) sold in Russia, Bubbalo (bubble gum) sold in India, Mexico, Portugal, and Spain, and Corte Noire (coffee) sold in France, Ireland, Russia, Ukraine, and the U.K. Mondelez is reinvesting profits into emerging markets seeking more growth. In 2012, the combined net revenues for Asia-Pacific, Eastern Europe, Africa, Latin America, and the Middle East grew by 8 percent (excluding the effects of foreign currency valuation changes). Performance was especially strong in the BRIC countries (the large emerging markets of Brazil, Russia, India, and China), with double-digit growth.

Despite its success in the emerging markets, Mondelez's net income has declined recently due to lower coffee prices and a reduction in demand for gum and candy. The CEO and other top executives suggested that volatility in global markets also has affected the firm's results. These are problems experienced by most of the companies that enter and compete in global markets.

*Juergen Leisse, head of the German Division of Kraft Foods, Inc., at the company's headquarters in Bremen, Germany. The name "Kraft Foods" will disappear from German supermarkets and be replaced with "Mondelez International."*

Sources: 2013, Unleashing a global snacking powerhouse, Mondelez International, www.mondelezinternational.com, accessed on May 21; N. Munshi, 2013, Mondelez tergets emerging markets growth, *Financial Times*, www.ft.com, May 7; 2013, Mondelez International's CEO discusses Q1 2013 results – Earnings call transcript, Mondelez International, www.mondelezinternational.com, May 7; D. Gelles, D. McCrum & N. Munshi, Activists hope to profit when cookie crumbles, *Financial Times*, www.ft.com, April 14; 2013, Kraft and Mondelez: Snacks and snags, *Financial Times*, www.ft.com, April 8; S. Strom, 2012, For Oreo, Cadbury and Ritz, a new parent company, *New York Times*, www.nytimes.com, May 23; 2012, Kraft Foods proposes Mondelez International Inc. as new name for global snacks company, *PR Newswire*, www.printthis.clickability.com, March 21; M.J. de la Merced, 2012, Kraft, 'Mondelez' and the art of corporate rebranding, *New York Times Dealbook*, http://dealbook.nytimes.com, March 21.

Learn more about Corte Noire (coffee).
www.cengagebrain.com

globally integrates its operations to standardize and maintain its power brands while simultaneously developing and marketing local brands that are specialized to meet the needs of local customers. In Chapter 5, we referenced the significant competitive rivalry that Mondelez encounters in its consumer markets.

Next we discuss trends in the global environment that are affecting the choices firms make when deciding which international corporate-level strategies to use and in which international markets to compete.

## 8-3 Environmental Trends

Although the transnational strategy is difficult to implement, an emphasis on global efficiency is increasing as more industries and the companies competing within them encounter intensified global competition. Magnifying the scope of this issue is the fact that, simultaneously, firms are experiencing demands for local adaptations of their products. These demands can be from customers (for products to satisfy their tastes and preferences) and from governing bodies (for products to satisfy a country's regulations). In addition, most multinational firms desire coordination and sharing of resources across country markets to hold down costs, as illustrated by the CEMEX example.[50]

Because of these conditions, some large multinational firms with diverse products use a multidomestic strategy with certain product lines and a global strategy with others when diversifying geographically. Many multinational firms may require this type of flexibility if they are to be strategically competitive, in part due to trends that change over time.

Liability of foreignness and regionalization are two important trends influencing a firm's choice and use of international strategies, particularly international corporate-level strategies. We discuss these trends next.

### 8-3a Liability of Foreignness

The dramatic success of Japanese firms such as Toyota and Sony in the United States and other international markets in the 1980s was a powerful jolt to U.S. managers and awakened them to the importance of international competition and the fact that many markets were rapidly becoming globalized. In the twenty-first century, Brazil, Russia, India, and China (BRIC) represent major international market opportunities for firms from many countries, including the United States, Japan, Korea, and members of the European Union.[51] However, even if foreign markets seem attractive, as appears to be the case with the BRIC countries, there are legitimate concerns for firms considering entering these markets. This is the *liability of foreignness*,[52] a set of costs associated with various issues firms face when entering foreign markets, including unfamiliar operating environments; economic, administrative, and cultural differences; and the challenges of coordination over distances.[53] Four types of distances commonly associated with liability of foreignness are cultural, administrative, geographic, and economic.[54]

Walt Disney Company's experience while opening theme parks in foreign countries demonstrates the liability of foreignness. For example, Disney suffered "lawsuits in France, at Disneyland Paris, because of the lack of fit between its transferred personnel policies and the French employees charged to enact them."[55] Disney executives learned from this experience in building the firm's theme park in Hong Kong as the company "went out of its way to tailor the park to local tastes."[56] Thus, as with Walt Disney Company, firms thinking about using an international strategy to enter foreign markets must be aware of the four types of distances they'll encounter when doing so and determine actions to take to reduce the potentially negative effects associated with those distances.

## 8-3b Regionalization

Regionalization is a second global environmental trend influencing a firm's choice and use of international strategies. This trend is becoming prominent largely because where a firm chooses to compete can affect its strategic competitiveness.[57] As a result, the firm considering using international strategies must decide if it should enter individual country markets or if it would be better served by competing in one or more regional markets rather than in individual country markets.

Currently, the global strategy is used less frequently. It remains difficult to successfully implement even when the firm uses Internet-based strategies.[58] In addition, the amount of competition vying for a limited amount of resources and customers can limit firms' focus to a specific region rather than on country-specific markets that are located in multiple parts of the world. A regional focus allows firms to marshal their resources to compete effectively rather than spreading their limited resources across multiple country-specific international markets.[59]

However, a firm that competes in industries where the international markets differ greatly (in which it must employ a multidomestic strategy) may wish to narrow its focus to a particular region of the world. In so doing, it can better understand the cultures, legal and social norms, and other factors that are important for effective competition in those markets. For example, a firm may focus on Far East markets only rather than competing simultaneously in the Middle East, Europe, and the Far East. Or the firm may choose a region of the world where the markets are more similar and some coordination and sharing of resources would be possible. In this way, the firm may be able not only to better understand the markets in which it competes, but also to achieve some economies, even though it may have to employ a multidomestic strategy. For instance, research suggests that most large retailers are better at focusing on a particular region rather than being truly global.[60] Firms commonly focus much of their international market entries on countries adjacent to their home country, which might be referred to as their home region.[61]

Countries that develop trade agreements to increase the economic power of their regions may promote regional strategies. The European Union (EU) and South America's Organization of American States (OAS) are country associations that developed trade agreements to promote the flow of trade across country boundaries within their respective regions.[62] Many European firms acquire and integrate their businesses in Europe to better coordinate pan-European brands as the EU tries to create unity across the European markets. With this process likely to continue as new countries are added to the agreement, some international firms may prefer to focus on regions rather than multiple country markets when entering international markets.

The North American Free Trade Agreement (NAFTA), signed by the United States, Canada, and Mexico, facilitates free trade across country borders in North America. NAFTA loosens restrictions on international strategies within this region and provides greater opportunity for regional international strategies.[63]

Most firms enter regional markets sequentially, beginning in markets with which they are more familiar. They also introduce their largest and strongest lines of business into these markets first, followed by other product lines once the initial efforts are deemed successful. The additional product lines typically are introduced in the original investment location.[64] However, research also suggests that the size of the market and industry characteristics can influence this decision.[65]

Regionalization is important to most multinational firms, even those competing in many regions across the globe. For example, most large multinational firms have organizational structures that group operations within the same region (across countries) for managing and coordination purposes. As explained in the Opening Case, ABB has eight regional managers to which country operations in each of the regions report. Managing businesses by regions helps multinational enterprises (MNEs) deal with the complexities and challenges of operating in multiple international markets.

After selecting its business- and corporate-level international strategies, the firm determines how it will enter the international markets in which it has chosen to compete. We turn to this topic next.

## 8-4 Choice of International Entry Mode

Five modes of entry into international markets are available to firms. We show these entry modes and their characteristics in Figure 8.5. Each means of market entry has its advantages and disadvantages, suggesting that the choice of entry mode can affect the degree of success

**Figure 8.5** Modes of Entry and their Characteristics

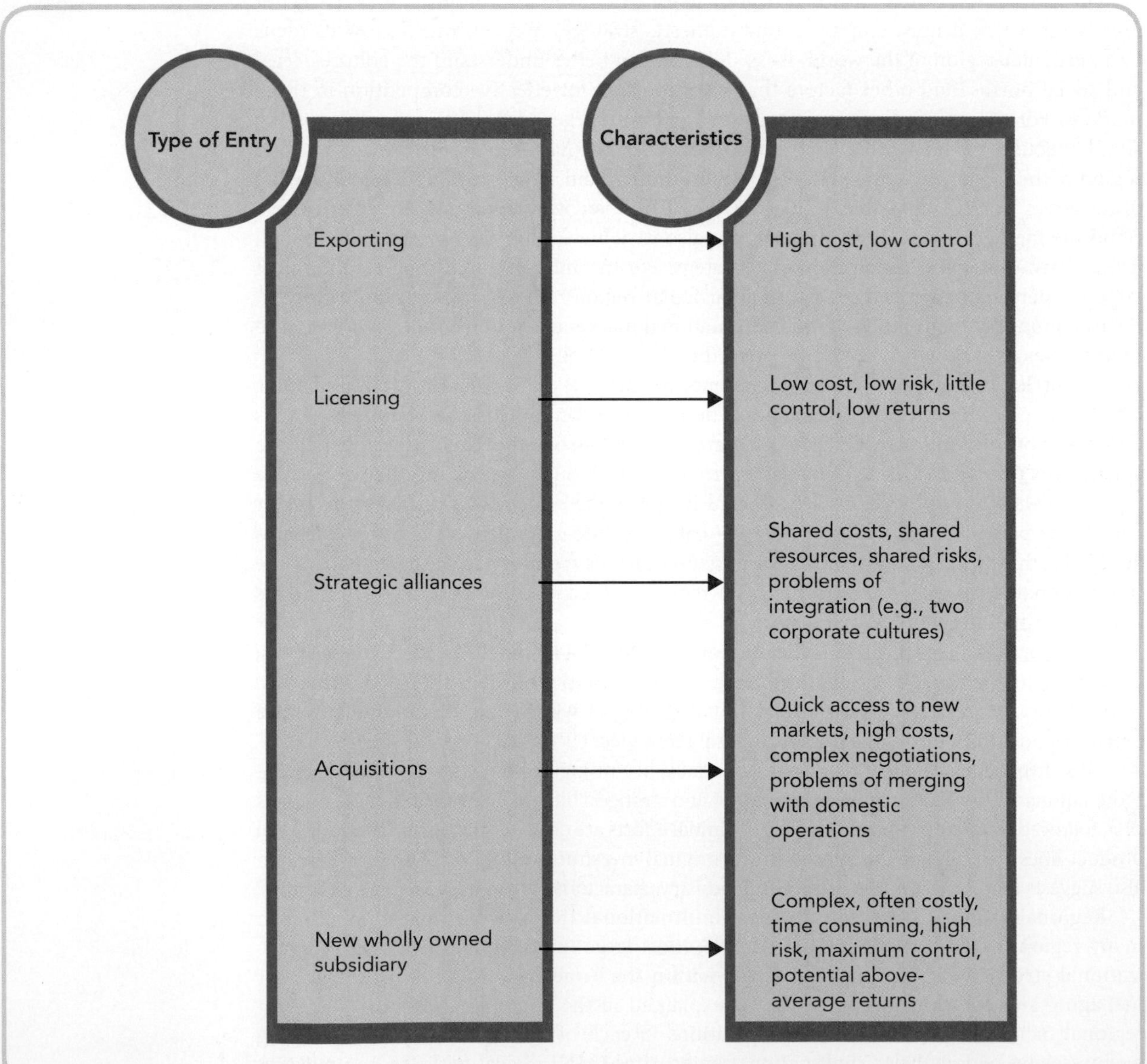

the firm achieves by implementing an international strategy.[66] Many firms competing in multiple markets commonly use more than one and may use all five entry modes.[67]

## 8-4a Exporting

For many firms, exporting is the initial mode of entry used.[68] *Exporting* is an entry mode through which the firm sends products it produces in its domestic market to international markets. Selection of exporting as the way of entering international markets is a popular entry mode choice for small businesses.[69]

The number of small U.S. firms using an international strategy is increasing, with some predicting that up to 50 percent of small U.S. firms will be involved in international trade by 2018, most of them through export.[70] By exporting, firms avoid the expense of establishing operations in host countries (that is, in countries outside their home country) in which they have chosen to compete. However, firms must establish some means of marketing and distributing their products when exporting. Usually, contracts are formed with host-country firms to handle these activities. Potentially high transportation costs to export products to international markets and the expense of tariffs placed on the firm's products as a result of host countries' policies are examples of exporting costs. The loss of some control when the firm contracts with local companies located in host countries for marketing and distribution purposes is another disadvantage of exporting. Moreover, contracting with local companies can be expensive, making it harder for the exporting firm to earn profits.[71] Evidence suggests that, in general, using an international cost leadership strategy when exporting to developed countries has the most positive effect on firm performance while using an international differentiation strategy with larger scale when exporting to emerging economies leads to the greatest amount of success. In either case, firms with strong market orientation capabilities are more successful.[72]

Firms export mostly to countries that are closest to their facilities because of the lower transportation costs and the usually greater similarity between geographic neighbors. For example, the United States' NAFTA partners Mexico and Canada account for more than half of the goods exported from Texas. The Internet has also made exporting easier. Firms of any size can use the Internet to access critical information about foreign markets, examine a target market, research the competition, and find lists of potential customers.[73] Governments also use the Internet to support the efforts of those applying for export and import licenses, facilitating international trade among countries while doing so.

## 8-4b Licensing

*Licensing* is an entry mode in which an agreement is formed that allows a foreign company to purchase the right to manufacture and sell a firm's products within a host country's market or a set of host countries' markets.[74] The licensor is normally paid a royalty on each unit produced and sold. The licensee takes the risks and makes the monetary investments in facilities for manufacturing, marketing, and distributing products. As a result, licensing is possibly the least costly form of international diversification. As with exporting, licensing is an attractive entry mode option for smaller firms, and potentially for newer firms as well.[75]

China, a country accounting for almost one-third of all cigarettes smoked worldwide, is obviously a huge market for this product. U.S. cigarette firms want to have a strong presence in China but have had trouble entering this market, largely because of successful lobbying by state-owned tobacco firms against such entry. Because of these conditions, cigarette manufacturer Philip Morris International (PMI) had an incentive to form a deal with these state-owned firms. Accordingly, PMI and the China National Tobacco Corporation (CNTC) completed a licensing agreement at the end of 2005. This agreement provides CNTC access to the most famous brand in the world, Marlboro.[76] Because it is a licensing agreement rather than a foreign direct investment by PMI, China maintains control of distribution. The Marlboro brand was launched at two Chinese manufacturing plants in 2008. The Chinese state-owned tobacco monopoly, as part of the agreement, also receives PMI's help through a joint venture in distributing its own brands in select foreign markets. To date, the Chinese cigarettes have been distributed in the Czech Republic and Poland.[77]

Another potential benefit of licensing as an entry mode is the possibility of earning greater returns from product innovations by selling the firm's innovations in international markets as well as in the domestic market.[78] Firms can obtain a larger market for their innovative new products, which helps them to pay off their R&D costs to develop them and to earn a return faster on the innovations than if they only sell them in domestic markets. And they do this with little risk without additional investment costs.

Licensing also has disadvantages. For example, after a firm licenses its product or brand to another party, it has little control over selling and distribution. Developing licensing agreements that protect the interests of both parties while supporting the relationship embedded within an agreement helps prevent this potential disadvantage.[79] In addition, licensing provides the least potential returns because returns must be shared between the licensor and the licensee. Another disadvantage is that the international firm may learn the technology of the party with whom it formed an agreement and then produce and sell a similar competitive product after the licensing agreement expires. In a classic example, Komatsu first licensed much of its technology from International Harvester, Bucyrus-Erie, and Cummins Engine to compete against Caterpillar in the earthmoving equipment business. Komatsu then dropped these licenses and developed its own products using the technology it had gained from the U.S. companies.[80] Because of potential disadvantages, the parties to a licensing arrangement should finalize an agreement only after they are convinced that both parties' best interests are protected.

## 8-4c Strategic Alliances

Increasingly popular as an entry mode among firms using international strategies,[81] a *strategic alliance* finds a firm collaborating with another company in a different setting in order to enter one or more international markets.[82] Firms share the risks and the resources required to enter international markets when using strategic alliances.[83] Moreover, because partners bring their unique resources together for the purpose of working collaboratively, strategic alliances can facilitate developing new capabilities and possibly core competencies that may contribute to the firm's strategic competitiveness.[84] Indeed, developing and learning how to use new capabilities and/or competencies (particularly those related to technology) is often a key purpose for which firms use strategic alliances as an entry mode.[85] Firms should be aware that establishing trust between partners is critical for developing and managing technology-based capabilities while using strategic alliances.[86]

French-based Limagrain is the fourth largest seed company in the world through its subsidiary Vilmorin & Cie. An international agricultural cooperative group specializing in field seeds, vegetable seeds, and cereal products, part of Limagrain's strategy calls for it to continue to enter and compete in additional international markets. Limagrain is using strategic alliances as an entry mode. In 2011, the firm formed a strategic alliance with the Brazilian seed company Sementes Guerra in Brazil. The joint venture is named Limagrain Guerra do Brasil. Corn is the focus of the joint venture between these companies. Guerra is a family-owned company engaged in seed research, the production of corn, wheat, and soybeans, and the distribution of those products to farmers in Brazil and neighboring countries. Limagrain also had an earlier, successful joint venture with KWS in the United States. This venture, called AgReliant Genetics, focused primarily on corn and soybeans.[87]

Not all alliances formed for the purpose of entering international markets are successful.[88] Incompatible partners and conflict between the partners are primary reasons for failure when firms use strategic alliances as an entry mode. Another issue here is that international strategic alliances are especially difficult to manage. Trust is an important aspect of alliances and must be carefully managed. The degree of trust between partners strongly influences alliance success. The probability of alliance success increases as the amount of trust between partners expands. Efforts to build trust are affected by at least four fundamental issues: the initial condition of the relationship, the negotiation process to arrive at an agreement, partner interactions, and external events.[89] Trust is also influenced by the country cultures involved and the relationships between the countries' governments (e.g., degree of political differences) where the firms in the alliance are home based.[90] Firms should be aware of these issues when trying to appropriately manage trust.

Research has shown that equity-based alliances over which a firm has more control are more likely to produce positive returns.[91] (We discuss equity-based and other types of strategic alliances in Chapter 9.) However, if trust is required to develop new capabilities through an alliance, equity positions can serve as a barrier to the necessary relationship building. And trust can be an especially important issue when firms have multiple partners supplying raw materials and/or services in their value chain (often referred to as outsourcing).[92] If conflict in a strategic alliance formed as an entry mode is not manageable, using acquisitions to enter international markets may be a better option.[93]

## 8-4d **Acquisitions**

When a firm acquires another company to enter an international market, it has completed a cross-border acquisition. Specifically, a *cross-border acquisition* is an entry mode through which a firm from one country acquires a stake in or purchases all of a firm located in another country.

As free trade expands in global markets, firms throughout the world are completing a larger number of cross-border acquisitions. The ability of cross-border acquisitions to provide rapid access to new markets is a key reason for their growth. In fact, of the five entry modes, acquisitions often are the quickest means for firms to enter international markets.[94]

Today, there is a broad range of cross-border acquisitions being completed by a diverse set of companies. DJO Global is a market leader in providing orthopaedic rehabilitation services. It has achieved significant growth since its founding in the late 1970s through mergers. It was founded in the United States (California) but was acquired by a major British medical devices conglomerate, Smith & Nephew, in 1987. Thereafter, it made several acquisitions. In 2007, it was acquired by The Blackstone Group and another company involved in the same industry and was merged into DJO Global. Since that time, DJO has continued to grow through acquisitions in countries such as Canada, South Africa, and Tunisia. DJO now distributes its products in more than 36 countries and has approximately $1 billion in annual sales.[95] Interestingly, firms use cross-border acquisitions less frequently to enter markets where corruption affects business transactions and, hence, the use of international strategies. Firms' preference is to use joint ventures to enter markets in which corruption is an issue rather than using acquisitions. (Discussed fully in Chapter 9, a joint venture is a type of strategic alliance in which two or more firms create a legally independent company and share their resources and capabilities to operate it.) However, these ventures fail more often, although this is less frequently the case for firms experienced with entering "corrupt" markets. When acquisitions are made in such countries, acquirers commonly pay smaller premiums to buy firms in different markets.[96]

Although increasingly popular, acquisitions as an entry mode are not without costs, nor are they easy to successfully complete and operate. Cross-border acquisitions have some of the disadvantages of domestic acquisitions (see Chapter 7). In addition, they often require debt financing to complete, which carries an extra cost. Another issue for firms to consider is that negotiations for cross-border acquisitions can be exceedingly complex and are generally more complicated than are the negotiations associated with domestic

*The CEOs of British Airways (Willie Walsh) and Iberia (Antonio Vazquez) merged their companies in 2011 to form the International Airlines Group (IAG). The multi-billion-euro merger created Europe's third largest airline.*

acquisitions. Dealing with the legal and regulatory requirements in the target firm's country and obtaining appropriate information to negotiate an agreement are also frequent problems. Finally, the merging of the new firm into the acquiring firm is often more complex than is the case with domestic acquisitions. The firm completing the cross-border acquisition must deal not only with different corporate cultures, but also with potentially different social cultures and practices.[97] These differences make integrating the two firms after the acquisition more challenging; it is difficult to capture the potential synergy when integration is slowed or stymied because of cultural differences.[98] Therefore, while cross-border acquisitions are popular as an entry mode primarily because they provide rapid access to new markets, firms considering this option should be fully aware of the costs and risks associated with using it.

## 8-4e New Wholly Owned Subsidiary

A **greenfield venture** is an entry mode through which a firm invests directly in another country or market by establishing a new wholly owned subsidiary. The process of creating a greenfield venture is often complex and potentially costly, but this entry mode affords maximum control to the firm and has the greatest amount of potential to contribute to the firm's strategic competitiveness as it implements international strategies. This potential is especially true for firms with strong intangible capabilities that might be leveraged through a greenfield venture.[99] Moreover, having additional control over its operations in a foreign market is especially advantageous when the firm has proprietary technology.

Research also suggests that "wholly owned subsidiaries and expatriate staff are preferred" in service industries where "close contacts with end customers" and "high levels of professional skills, specialized know-how, and customization" are required.[100] Other research suggests that as investments, greenfield ventures are used more prominently when the firm's business relies significantly on the quality of its capital-intensive manufacturing facilities. In contrast, cross-border acquisitions are more likely to be used as an entry mode when a firm's operations are human capital intensive—for example, if a strong local union and high cultural distance would cause difficulty in transferring knowledge to a host nation through a greenfield venture.[101]

The risks associated with greenfield ventures are significant in that the costs of establishing a new business operation in a new country or market can be substantial. To support the operations of a newly established operation in a foreign country, the firm may have to acquire knowledge and expertise about the new market by hiring either host-country nationals, possibly from competitors, or through consultants, which can be costly. This new knowledge and expertise often is necessary to facilitate the building of new facilities, establishing distribution networks, and learning how to implement marketing strategies that can lead to competitive success in the new market.[102] Importantly, while taking these actions the firm maintains control over the technology, marketing, and distribution of its products. Research also suggests that when the country risk is high, firms prefer to enter

A **greenfield venture** is an entry mode through which a firm invests directly in another country or market by establishing a new wholly owned subsidiary.

with joint ventures instead of greenfield investments. However, if firms have previous experience in a country, they prefer to use a wholly owned greenfield venture rather than a joint venture.[103]

China has been an attractive market for foreign retailers (e.g., Walmart) because of its large population, the growing economic capabilities of Chinese citizens, and the opening of the Chinese market to foreign firms. For example, by 2005 more than 300 foreign retailers had entered China, many of them using greenfield ventures. Of course, China is a unique environment partly because of its culture but more so because of the government control and intervention. Good relationships with local and national government officials are quite important to foreign firms' success in China. Because of these complexities and the challenges they present, foreign retailers' success in this market has been mixed despite the substantial opportunities that exist there. Thus great care should be exercised when selecting the best mode for entering particular markets, as we discuss next.[104]

## 8-4f Dynamics of Mode of Entry

Several factors affect the firm's choice about how to enter international markets. Market entry is often achieved initially through exporting, which requires no foreign manufacturing expertise and investment only in distribution. Licensing can facilitate the product improvements necessary to enter foreign markets, as in the Komatsu example. Strategic alliances are a popular entry mode because they allow a firm to connect with an experienced partner already in the market. Partly because of this, geographically diversifying firms often use alliances in uncertain situations, such as an emerging economy where there is significant risk (e.g., Venezuela and Columbia).[105] However, if intellectual property rights in the emerging economy are not well protected, the number of firms in the industry is growing fast, and the need for global integration is high, other entry modes such as a joint venture (see Chapter 9) or a wholly owned subsidiary are preferred.[106] In the final analysis though, all three modes—export, licensing, and strategic alliance—can be effective means of initially entering new markets and for developing a presence in those markets.

Acquisitions, greenfield ventures, and sometimes joint ventures are used when firms want to establish a strong presence in an international market. Aerospace firms Airbus and Boeing have used joint ventures, especially in large markets, to facilitate entry, while military equipment firms such as Thales SA have used acquisitions to build a global presence. Japanese auto manufacturer Toyota has established a presence in the United States through both greenfield ventures and joint ventures. Because of Toyota's highly efficient manufacturing processes, the firm wants to maintain control over manufacturing when possible. To date, Toyota has established 52 manufacturing facilities in 27 countries. Demonstrating the importance of greenfield ventures and joint ventures to Toyota's international diversification strategy is the fact that in 2012 the firm opened its first new manufacturing plant in Japan in over 20 years.[107] Both acquisitions and greenfield ventures are likely to come at later stages in the development of a firm's international strategies.

Thus, to enter a global market, a firm selects the entry mode that is best suited to its situation. In some instances, the various options will be followed sequentially, beginning with exporting and eventually leading to greenfield ventures. In other cases, the firm may use several, but not all, of the different entry modes, each in different markets. The decision regarding which entry mode to use is primarily a result of the industry's competitive conditions, the country's situation and government policies, and the firm's unique set of resources, capabilities, and core competencies.

FEMSA, the large multibusiness Mexican firm, has been expanding its operations into multiple countries in recent years, as described in the Strategic Focus. Most of its expansion has been into other Latin American countries (where it better understands the culture and markets). But, it very recently expanded into the Philippines, a dramatic

## Strategic Focus

### Mexico's FEMSA: Building its International Prowess

Fomento Economico Mexicano SAB de CV has a market capitalization of $39.02 billion. It has more than 180,000 employees and is a major competitor in the beverage industry, convenience stores, and drugstores/pharmacies. In fact, Coca-Cola FEMSA SAB is the largest bottler of Coke not only in Latin America but in the entire world. In 2013, it continued to add to its strength in this business with a purchase of a regional bottler, Grupo Yoli, which was the largest soft-drink bottler in southern Mexico. In 2008, FEMSA decided to expand its convenience store chain, Oxxo, to other countries outside of Mexico. It now operates more than 10,600 stores in Mexico and Columbia. In 2012, it opened 1,040 new stores, which amounts to almost three per day. Oxxo is the largest and fastest-growing chain of convenience stores in Latin America.

Until 2010, FEMSA was a major beer producer in Mexico with operations in Brazil (which it entered through an acquisition of Kaiser Brewery) as well. However, Heineken acquired the FEMSA brewery business at that time. Yet, because the sale involved and exchange of equity, FEMSA now holds 20 percent of the equity in the Heineken Group (the second largest equity stake in this company).

Although FEMSA continues to promote organic growth, most of its major advances in size have come from acquisitions. For example, in 2013 FEMSA made its first foray outside of Latin America. It acquired a 51 percent stake (controlling interest) in Coca-Cola's bottling operations in the Philippines. It now has operations in nine countries, including eight in Latin America.

In 2013, it also expanded its drugstore/pharmacy chain with an acquisition by its retail subsidiary, FEMSA Comercio, of Farmacias FM Moderno. At the time of its acquisition, Farmacias FM Moderno operated more than 100 stores in Mexico's western state of Sinaloa.

Therefore, FEMSA is a multi-billion-dollar business that has used its stash of cash to build substantial growth through acquisitions. It has expanded its presence in Mexico but also in all of the most prominent economies in Latin America (e.g., Brazil, Argentina, Colombia, and Venezuela in addition to Mexico).

*A Filipino worker collects empty Coca-Cola bottles in Manila. In 2013 FEMSA acquired the controlling interest in Coca-Cola Bottling Company's operations in the Philippines.*



Sources: 2013, Strategic business, FEMSA Web site, http://femsa.com.en, Accessed on May 30; Sources:2013, Business units, FEMSA Web site, http://femsa.com.en, Accessed on May 30; 2013, Fomento Economico Mexicano SAB de CV, *DealBook, New York Times*, http://dealbook.on.nytimes.com, May 16; E. Garcis, 2013, Mexico's FEMSA: From convenience stores to pharmacies, *Financial Times*, http://blogs.ft.com, May 15; 2013, FEMSA expands drugstore chain, *Zacks Equity Research*, http://finance.yahoo.com, May 14; 2013, FEMSA announces acquisition of Farmacias FM Moderno, *Market Wire*, www.nbcnews.com, May 13; B. Case, 2013, Coca-Cola FEMSA expands with $700 million Yoli purchase, *Bloomberg Businessweek*, www.businessweek.com, January 18; A. Thomson, 2012, Mexico's FEMSA eyes Coca-Cola's Philippines unit, *Financial Times*, http://blogs.ft.com, February 21; M. J. de la Merced & C. V. Nicholson, 2010, Heineken in deal to buy a big Mexican Brewer, *New York Times*, www.nytimes.com, January 12; D. D. Stanford & T. Black, 2008, Mexico's Oxxo convenience stores to branch out, *Houston Chronicle*, www.chron.com, February 22.

entry into Asia. Its most common mode of entry has been acquisitions. It has considerable experience with acquisitions given that a large amount of its domestic growth has also come from acquisitions. Its latest acquisition in the Philippines will cause the executives to deal with unique institutions and new political and economic risks that they have not previously encountered.

## 8-5 Risks in an International Environment

International strategies are risky, particularly those that would cause a firm to become substantially more diversified in terms of geographic markets served. Firms entering markets in new countries encounter a number of complex institutional risks.[108] Political and economic risks cannot be ignored by firms using international strategies (see specific examples of political and economic risks in Figure 8.6).

### 8-5a Political Risks

*Political risks* "denote the probability of disruption of the operations of multinational enterprises by political forces or events whether they occur in host countries, home country, or result from changes in the international environment."[109] Possible disruptions to a firm's operations when seeking to implement its international strategy create numerous problems, including uncertainty created by government regulation; the existence of many, possibly conflicting, legal authorities or corruption; and the potential nationalization of private assets.[110] Firms investing in other countries when implementing their international strategy may have concerns about the stability of the national government and the effects of unrest and government instability on their investments or assets.[111] To deal with these concerns, firms should conduct a political risk analysis of the countries or regions they may enter using one of the five entry modes. Through political risk analysis, the firm examines potential sources and factors of noncommercial disruptions of their foreign investments and the operations flowing from them.[112] However, occasionally firms might use political (institutional) weaknesses as an opportunity to transfer activities or practices that stakeholders see as undesirable for their operations in the home country to a new market so they can continue earning returns on these questionable practices.[113]

**Figure 8.6** Risks in the International Environment

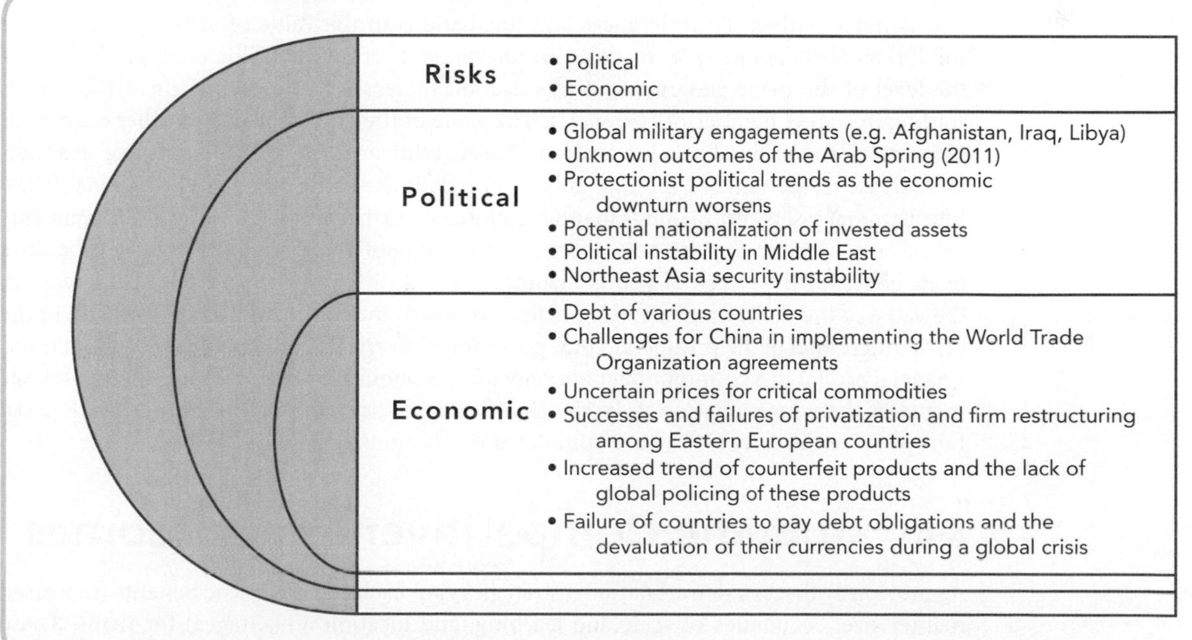

Russia has experienced a relatively high level of institutional instability in the years following its revolutionary transition to a more democratic government. Decentralized political control and frequent changes in policies created chaos for many, but especially for those in the business landscape. In an effort to regain more central control and reduce the chaos, Russian leaders took actions such as prosecuting powerful private firm executives, seeking to gain state control of firm assets, and not approving some foreign acquisitions of Russian businesses. The initial institutional instability, followed by the actions of the central government, caused some firms to delay or avoid significant foreign direct investment in Russia. Although leaders in Russia have tried to reassure potential investors about their property rights, prior actions, the fact that other laws (e.g., environmental and employee laws) are weak, and commonplace government corruption make firms leery of investing in Russia. In fact, the *2013 World Economic Forum Competitiveness Report* suggested that the largest impediments to business in Russia are corruption, inefficient government bureaucracy, and weak access to financing.[114]

### 8-5b Economic Risks

*Economic risks* include fundamental weaknesses in a country or region's economy with the potential to cause adverse effects on firms' efforts to successfully implement their international strategies. As illustrated in the example of Russian institutional instability and property rights, political risks and economic risks are interdependent. If firms cannot protect their intellectual property, they are highly unlikely to use a means of entering a foreign market that involves significant and direct investments. Therefore, countries need to create, sustain, and enforce strong intellectual property rights in order to attract foreign direct investment.

Another economic risk is the perceived security risk of a foreign firm acquiring firms that have key natural resources or firms that may be considered strategic in regard to intellectual property. For instance, many Chinese firms have been buying natural resource firms in Australia and Latin America as well as manufacturing assets in the United States. This has made the governments of the key resource firms nervous about such strategic assets falling under the control of state-owned Chinese firms.[115] Terrorism has also been of concern. Indonesia has difficulty competing for investment against China and India, countries that are viewed as having fewer security risks.

As noted earlier, the differences and fluctuations in the value of currencies is among the foremost economic risks of using an international strategy.[116] This is especially true as the level of the firm's geographic diversification increases to the point where the firm is trading in a large number of currencies. The value of the dollar relative to other currencies determines the value of the international assets and earnings of U.S. firms; for example, an increase in the value of the U.S. dollar can reduce the value of U.S. multinational firms' international assets and earnings in other countries. Furthermore, the value of different currencies can at times dramatically affect a firm's competitiveness in global markets because of its effect on the prices of goods manufactured in different countries.[117] An increase in the value of the dollar can harm U.S. firms' exports to international markets because of the price differential of the products. Thus, government oversight and control of economic and financial capital in a country affect not only local economic activity, but also foreign investments in the country.[118] Certainly, the significant political and policy changes in Eastern Europe since the early 1990s have stimulated much more FDI there.[119]

## 8-6 Strategic Competitiveness Outcomes

As previously discussed, international strategies can result in three basic benefits (increased market size, economies of scale and learning, and location advantages) for firms. These basic benefits are gained when the firm successfully manages political, economic, and other institutional risks while implementing its international strategies; in turn, these benefits are critical to the firm's efforts to achieve strategic competitiveness (as measured by improved performance and enhanced innovation—see Figure 8.1).

Overall, the degree to which firms achieve strategic competitiveness through international strategies is expanded or increased when they successfully implement an international diversification strategy. As an extension or elaboration of international strategy, an **international diversification strategy** is a strategy through which a firm expands the sales of its goods or services across the borders of global regions and countries into a potentially large number of geographic locations or markets. Instead of entering one or just a few markets, the international diversification strategy finds firms using international business-level and international corporate-level strategies for the purpose of entering multiple regions and markets in order to sell their products.

## 8-6a International Diversification and Returns

Evidence suggests numerous reasons for firms to use an international diversification strategy,[120] meaning that international diversification should be related positively to firms' performance as measured by the returns it earns on its investments. Research has shown that as international diversification increases, a firm's returns decrease initially but then increase quickly as it learns how to manage the increased geographic diversification it has created.[121] In fact, the stock market is particularly sensitive to investments in international markets. Firms that are broadly diversified into multiple international markets usually achieve the most positive stock returns, especially when they diversify geographically into core business areas.[122]

Many factors contribute to the positive effects of international diversification, such as private versus government ownership, potential economies of scale and experience, location advantages, increased market size, and the opportunity to stabilize returns. The stabilization of returns helps reduce a firm's overall risk.[123] Large, well-established firms and entrepreneurial ventures can both achieve these positive outcomes by successfully implementing an international diversification strategy.

As described in the earlier Strategic focus, FEMSA was using an acquisition strategy to increase its international diversification. FEMSA's financial results suggest that it has achieved positive returns from this strategy. Of course, its recent entry into Asian markets with an acquisition of operations in the Philippines may pose greater challenges.

## 8-6b Enhanced Innovation

In Chapter 1, we indicated that developing new technology is at the heart of strategic competitiveness. As noted in our discussion of the determinants of national advantage (see Figure 8.3), a nation's competitiveness depends, in part, on the capacity of its industries to innovate. Eventually and inevitably, competitors outperform firms that fail to innovate. Therefore, the only way for individual nations and individual firms to sustain a competitive advantage is to upgrade it continually through innovation.[124]

An international diversification strategy and the geographic diversification it brings about create the potential for firms to achieve greater returns on their innovations (through larger or more numerous markets) while reducing the often substantial risks of R&D investments. Additionally, international diversification may be necessary to generate the resources required to sustain a large-scale R&D operation. An environment of rapid technological obsolescence makes it difficult to invest in new technology and the capital-intensive operations necessary to compete in such an environment. Firms operating solely in domestic markets may find such investments difficult because of the length of time required to recoup the original investment. However, diversifying into a number of international markets improves a firm's ability to appropriate additional returns from innovation before competitors can overcome the initial competitive advantage created by the innovation.[125] In addition, firms

An **international diversification strategy** is a strategy through which a firm expands the sales of its goods or services across the borders of global regions and countries into a potentially large number of geographic locations or markets.

moving into international markets are exposed to new products and processes. If they learn about those products and processes and integrate this knowledge into their operations, further innovation can be developed. To incorporate the learning into their own R&D processes, firms must manage those processes effectively in order to absorb and use the new knowledge to create further innovations.[126] For a number of reasons then, international strategies and certainly an international diversification strategy provide incentives for firms to innovate.[127]

The relationship among international geographic diversification, innovation, and returns is complex. Some level of performance is necessary to provide the resources the firm needs to diversify geographically; in turn, geographic diversification provides incentives and resources to invest in R&D. Effective R&D should enhance the firm's returns, which then provide more resources for continued geographic diversification and investment in R&D.[128] Of course, the returns generated from these relationships increase through effective managerial practices. Evidence suggests that more culturally diverse top management teams often have a greater knowledge of international markets and their idiosyncrasies, but their orientation to expand internationally can be affected by the nature of their incentives.[129] Moreover, managing the business units of a geographically diverse multinational firm requires skill, not only in managing a decentralized set of businesses, but also coordinating diverse points of view emerging from businesses located in different countries and regions. Firms able to do this increase the likelihood of outperforming their rivals.[130]

# 8-7 The Challenge of International Strategies

Effectively using international strategies creates basic benefits and contributes to the firm's strategic competitiveness. However, for several reasons, attaining these positive outcomes is difficult.

## 8-7a Complexity of Managing International Strategies

Pursuing international strategies, particularly an international diversification strategy, typically leads to growth in a firm's size and the complexity of its operations. In turn, larger size and greater operational complexity make a firm more difficult to manage. At some point, size and complexity either cause firms to become virtually unmanageable or increase the cost of their management beyond the value using international strategies creates. Different cultures and institutional practices (such as those associated with governmental agencies) that are part of the countries in which a firm competes when using an international strategy also can create difficulties.[131]

*Toyota's FT-86 on display at the 2010 Paris Motor Show.*

Toyota's experiences over the past few years appear to demonstrate the relationship between firm size and managerial complexity. Toyota became the world's largest car manufacturer at the end of 2008, surpassing General Motors (GM had been the largest auto manufacturer for 77 years). Volkswagen-Porsche briefly replaced Toyota as the world's largest car and truck manufacturer, but in 2013 Toyota again became the largest. As always is the case though, larger size makes a firm harder to manage successfully. In spite of its legendary focus on and reputation for quality, over the past few years and after becoming the world's largest manufacturer, Toyota experienced product quality problems, particularly in the all-important U.S. market. Perhaps the increased difficulty of managing a larger firm contributed to Toyota's product quality problems. However, Toyota seems to have recovered from these difficulties and continues seeking additional growth through its international strategy. For example, its sales revenues in fiscal year 2013 increased by 18.7 percent over fiscal year 2012. Its net income increased by 239.3 percent for the same time period. And, international sales are quite important to Toyota, as they account for slightly more than 81 percent of its total vehicle sales.[132]

Firms have to build on their capabilities and other advantages to overcome the challenges encountered in international markets. For example, some firms from emerging economies that hold monopolies in their home markets can invest the resources gained there to enhance their competitiveness in international markets (because they don't have to be concerned about competitors in home markets).[133] The key is for firms to overcome the various liabilities of foreignness regardless of their source.[134]

## 8-7b Limits to International Expansion

Learning how to effectively manage an international strategy improves the likelihood of achieving positive outcomes such as enhanced performance. However, at some point the degree of geographic and (possibly) product diversification the firm's international strategies bring about causes the returns from using the strategies to level off and eventually become negative.[135]

There are several reasons for the limits to the positive effects of the diversification associated with international strategies. First, greater geographic dispersion across country borders increases the costs of coordination between units and the distribution of products. This is especially true when firms have multiple locations in countries that have diverse subnational institutions. Second, trade barriers, logistical costs, cultural diversity, and other differences by country (e.g., access to raw materials and different employee skill levels) greatly complicate the implementation of an international strategy.[136]

Institutional and cultural factors can be strong barriers to the transfer of a firm's core competencies from one market to another.[137] Marketing programs often have to be redesigned and new distribution networks established when firms expand into new markets. In addition, firms may encounter different labor costs and capital expenses. In general, it becomes increasingly difficult to effectively implement, manage, and control a firm's international operations with increases in geographic diversity.[138]

The amount of diversification in a firm's international operations that can be managed varies from company to company and is affected by managers' abilities to deal with ambiguity and complexity. The problems of central coordination and integration are mitigated if the firm's international operations compete in friendly countries that are geographically close and have cultures similar to its own country's culture. In that case, the firm is likely to encounter fewer trade barriers, the laws and customs are better understood, and the product is easier to adapt to local markets.[139] For example, U.S. firms may find it less difficult to expand their operations into Mexico, Canada, and Western European countries than into Asian countries.

The relationships between the firm using an international strategy and the governments in the countries in which the firm is competing can also be constraining.[140] The reason for this is that the differences in host countries' governmental policies and practices can be substantial, creating a need for the focal firm to learn how to manage what can be a large set of different enforcement policies and practices. At some point, the differences create too many problems for the firm to be successful. Using strategic alliances is another way firms can deal with this limiting factor. Partnering with companies in different countries allows the focal firm to rely on its partner to help deal with local laws, rules, regulations, and customs. But these partnerships are not risk free and managing them tends to be difficult.[141]

## SUMMARY

- The use of international strategies is increasing. Multiple factors and conditions are influencing the increasing use of these strategies, including opportunities to (1) extend a product's life cycle, (2) gain access to critical raw materials, sometimes including relatively inexpensive labor, (3) integrate a firm's operations on a global scale to better serve customers in different countries, (4) better serve customers whose needs appear to be more alike today as a result of global communications media and the Internet's capabilities to inform, and (5) meet increasing demand for goods and services that is surfacing in emerging markets.
- When used effectively, international strategies yield three basic benefits: increased market size, economies of scale and learning, and location advantages. Firms use international business-level and international corporate-level strategies to geographically diversify their operations.
- International business-level strategies are usually grounded in one or more home-country advantages. Research suggests that there are four determinants of national advantage: factors of production; demand conditions; related and supporting industries; and patterns of firm strategy, structure, and rivalry.
- There are three types of international corporate-level strategies. A multidomestic strategy focuses on competition within each country in which the firm competes. Firms using a multidomestic strategy decentralize strategic and operating decisions to the business units operating in each country, so that each unit can tailor its products to local conditions. A global strategy assumes more standardization of products across country boundaries; therefore, a competitive strategy is centralized and controlled by the home office. Commonly, large multinational firms, particularly those with multiple diverse products being sold in many different markets, use a multidomestic strategy with some product lines and a global strategy with others.
- A transnational strategy seeks to integrate characteristics of both multidomestic and global strategies for the purpose of being able to simultaneously emphasize local responsiveness and global integration.
- Two global environmental trends—liability of foreignness and regionalization—are influencing firms' choices of international strategies as well as their implementation. Liability of foreignness challenges firms to recognize that distance between their domestic market and international markets affects how they compete. Some firms choose to concentrate their international strategies on regions (e.g., the EU and NAFTA) rather than on individual country markets.
- Firms can use one or more of five entry modes to enter international markets. Exporting, licensing, strategic alliances, acquisitions, and new wholly owned subsidiaries, often referred to as greenfield ventures, are the five entry modes. Most firms begin with exporting or licensing, because of their lower costs and risks, but later they often use strategic alliances and acquisitions as well. The most expensive and risky means of entering a new international market is establishing a new wholly owned subsidiary (greenfield venture). On the other hand, such subsidiaries provide the advantages of maximum control by the firm and, if successful, the greatest returns. Large, geographically diversified firms often use most or all five entry modes across different markets when implementing international strategies.
- Firms encounter a number of risks when implementing international strategies. The two major categories of risks firms need to understand and address when diversifying geographically through international strategies are political risks (risks concerned with the probability a firm's operations will be disrupted by political forces or events, whether they occur in the firm's domestic market or in the markets the firm has entered to implement its international strategies) and economic risks (risks resulting from fundamental weaknesses in a country's or a region's economy with the potential to adversely affect a firm's ability to implement its international strategies).
- Successful use of international strategies (especially an international diversification strategy) contributes to a firm's strategic competitiveness in the form of improved performance and enhanced innovation. International diversification facilitates innovation in a firm because it provides a larger market to gain greater and faster returns from investments in innovation. In addition, international diversification can generate the resources necessary to sustain a large-scale R&D program.
- In general, international diversification helps to achieve above-average returns, but this assumes that the diversification is effectively implemented and that the firm's international

operations are well managed. International diversification provides greater economies of scope and learning which, along with greater innovation, help produce above-average returns.

- A firm using International strategies to pursue strategic competitiveness often experience complex challenges that must be overcome. Some limits also constrain the ability to manage international expansion effectively. International diversification increases coordination and distribution costs, and management problems are exacerbated by trade barriers, logistical costs, and cultural diversity, among other factors.

# REVIEW QUESTIONS

1. What incentives influence firms to use international strategies?
2. What are the three basic benefits firms can achieve by successfully using an international strategy?
3. What four factors are determinants of national advantage and serve as a basis for international business-level strategies?
4. What are the three international corporate-level strategies? What are the advantages and disadvantages associated with these individual strategies?
5. What are some global environmental trends affecting the choice of international strategies, particularly international corporate-level strategies?
6. What five entry modes do firms consider as paths to use to enter international markets? What is the typical sequence in which firms use these entry modes?
7. What are political risks and what are economic risks? How should firms approach dealing with these risks?
8. What are the strategic competitiveness outcomes firms can reach through international strategies, and particularly through an international diversification strategy?
9. What are two important issues that can potentially affect a firm's ability to successfully use international strategies?

# EXPERIENTIAL EXERCISES

## EXERCISE 1: CROSS-BORDER EXPANSION

Should Ronco Toys expand to Mexico? One of the important reasons for expanding internationally is location advantages through which placing facilities outside one's home country can provide cost advantages. Advantages don't necessarily always have to be about cost reduction; the international country might provide access to important raw materials, logistical support, and energy or other natural resources.

For purposes of this exercise you are to consider that your team has been hired to act as a consulting company for the purposes of analyzing a potential cross-border expansion of a U.S. firm. Your client, Ronco Toys Inc., has made the decision to expand internationally to Mexico under the Maquiladora Program. Under this program American companies (and other countries as well) can establish factories in Mexico close to the Texas border and thereby gain significant cost reductions in labor. This program began in the 1960s but expanded rapidly after NAFTA was approved in 1994. By some estimates today there are over one million Mexicans working in over 3,000 factories producing goods that will most likely be exported to the United States.

Your client makes toys that are rather labor intensive and has found that demand is outstripping supply from their U.S.-based factory. In addition, cost pressures from competitors are squeezing margins uncomfortably. Therefore the CEO has decided to open up a new factory in a Mexican Maquiladora rather than expand domestically. Your challenge in this exercise is to critically examine this decision.

Provide both a list of pros and cons to help the CEO wade through the decision. Pay particular attention to the following:

1. Do you think this is the best solution possible given the limited data provided?
2. What other options should be considered?
3. What other items should go into this decision besides labor cost savings?

Be prepared to present your findings to the class.

## EXERCISE 2: WHERE NEXT?

In this exercise, consider your team to be a consultant to a multinational fast food restaurant company that is trying to increase its international exposure in the coming years. As you recall from the chapter, an international strategy is one in which "the firm sells its goods or services outside its domestic market." The choices to do so are varied and include exporting, licensing, alliance, acquisition, or creating a new wholly owned subsidiary. The reasons are just as varied as the entry modes.

To identify a suitable candidate for analysis, consult research databases such as Datamonitor or Business Source Complete. For example, Jack in the Box operates more than 2,200 units but they are all in the United States, which provides advantages as well as disadvantages. Compare this with McDonald's, the world's largest food-service retailing chain, with 34,000 restaurants operating in 119 countries as of 2013. You will also find SWOT (strengths, weaknesses, opportunities, threats) analysis on companies through databases such as those mentioned above.

Your consulting firm has been retained by the fast-food retailer to investigate the feasibility of expanding internationally. You should be prepared to address the following questions:

1. Which international location(s) seem to fit best based on your research?
2. Which entry mode seems the most reasonable for the firms to use?
3. What macro environmental and industry trends support your recommendations? Economic characteristics include gross national product, wages, unemployment, and inflation. Trend analysis of these data (e.g., are wages rising or falling, rate of change in wages, etc.) is preferable to single point-in-time snapshots.
4. What country risks seem most problematic?

The following additional Internet resources may be useful in your research:

- The Library of Congress has a collection of country studies.
- *BBC News* offers country profiles.
- *The Economist Intelligence Unit* (http://www.eiu.com) offers country profiles.
- Both the United Nations and International Monetary Fund provide statistics and research reports.
- The *CIA World Factbook* has profiles of different regions.
- The *Global Entrepreneurship Monitor* provides reports with detailed information about economic conditions and social aspects for a number of countries.
- Links can be found at http://www.countryrisk.com to a number of resources that assess both political and economic risk for individual countries.
- For U.S. data, see http://www.census.gov.
- Be prepared to discuss and defend your recommendations in class.

# VIDEO CASE ▶

## THE LURE OF AN INTERNATIONAL STRATEGY: INDIA/INFOSYS

India, home to low-cost living and resources, has become a technology mecca that maintains the second-largest software industry in the world. The country has managed to amass the presence of big-name international companies and create a few of its own, such as InfoSys. The key to luring foreign investors and workers is to create companies on par with any in the West. InfoSys, which is similar to a resort spa, continues to offer more experience and opportunity for many young Americans from U.S. colleges than would be possible in the US. Infosys was ranked India's 'Most Admired Company' in Wall Street Journal Asia 200, a listing of Asia's leading companies in 2010, a distinction achieved for nine years in a row. Established in 1981 with capital of $250, Infosys has grown to a $6.4 billion IT services and consulting company.

Be prepared to discuss the following concepts and questions in class:

### Concepts

- International strategy
- Business-level strategy
- Corporate-level strategy
- National advantage

### Questions

1. What international strategy incentives does India offer to a foreign investor? What limitations exist in India for companies desiring international expansion?
2. What benefits does InfoSys receive from its international strategy?
3. How does India's national advantage(s) influence its business-level strategy?
4. What corporate-level strategy is used by InfoSys and why?

# NOTES


1. C. N. Pitelis & D. J. Teece, 2012, Cross-border market co-creation, dynamic capabilities and the entrepreneurial theory of the multinational enterprise, in D. J. Teece (ed.), *Strategy, innovation and the theory of the firm*, Cheltenham, UK: Edward Elgar, 341–364; M. J. Nieto & A. Rodriguez, 2011, Offshoring of R&D: Looking abroad to improve innovation performance, *Journal of International Business Studies*, 42: 345–361.
2. R. M. Holmes, T. Miller, M. A. Hitt, & M. P. Salmador, 2013, The interrelationship among informal institutions, formal institutions and inward foreign direct investment, *Journal of Management*, 39: 531–566.
3. J.-L. Arregle, L. Naldi, M. Nordqvist & M. A. Hitt, 2012, Internationalization of family-controlled firms: A study of the effects of external involvement in governance, *Entrepreneurship Theory and Practice*, 36: 1115–1143; E. Golovko & G. Valentini, 2011, Exploring the complementarity between innovation and export for SMEs' growth, *Journal of International Business Studies*, 42: 362–380; M. A. Hitt, L. Tihanyi, T. Miller, & B. Connelly, 2006, International diversification: Antecedents, outcomes and moderators, *Journal of Management*, 32: 831–867.
4. M. F. Wiersema & H. P. Bowen, 2011, The relationship between international diversification and firm performance: Why it remains a puzzle, *Global Strategy Journal*, 1: 152–170.
5. R. Vernon, 1996, International investment and international trade in the product cycle, *Quarterly Journal of Economics*, 80: 190–207.
6. 2013, Our strategy, Rio Tinto homepage, www.riotinto.com, accessed on May 27.
7. E. Ko, C. R. Taylor, H. Sung, J. Lee, U. Wagner, D. Martin-Consuega Navarro, & F. Wang, 2012, Global marketing segmentation usefulness in the sportswear industry, *Journal of Business Research*, 65(11): 1565–1575.
8. J. Li, Y. Li, & D. Shapiro, 2012, Knowledge seeking and outward FDI of emerging market firms: The moderating effect of inward FDI, *Global Strategy Journal*, 2: 277–295; 2011, The globalization index 2010, Ernst & Young, http://www.ey.com, January.
9. B. Michael & S. H. Park, 2013, Who is your company? Where to locate to compete in emerging markets, *IEMS Market Brief*, Sklokovo Institute for Emerging Market Studies, vol. 13-03, February; K. E. Meyer, R. Mudambi, & R. Nanula, 2011, Multinational enterprises and local contexts: The opportunities and challenges of multiple embeddedness, *Journal of Management Studies*, 48: 235–252.
10. 2013, Our stores, Carrefour Group homepage, www.carrefour.com, May 28.
11. M. Colchester, 2011, Carrefour documents remain sealed, *Wall Street Journal*, www.wsj.com, June 24.
12. T. R. Annamalai & A. Deshmukh, 2011, Venture capital and private equity in India: An analysis of investments and exits, *Journal of Indian Business Research*, 3: 6–21; P. Zheng, 2009, A comparison of FDI determinants in China and India, *Thunderbird International Business Review*, 51: 263–279.
13. R. Ramamurti, 2012, What is really different about emerging market multinationals? *Global Strategy Journal*, 2: 41–47; S. Athreye & S. Kapur, 2009, Introduction: The internationalization of Chinese and Indian firms—trends, motivations and strategy, *Industrial and Corporate Change*, 18: 209–221.
14. M. Carney, E. R. Gedajlovic, P. M. A. R. Heugens, M. van Essen, & J. van Oosterhout, 2011, Business group affiliation, performance, context, and strategy: A meta-analysis, *Academy of Management Journal*, 54: 437–460; B. Elango, 2009, Minimizing effects of "liability of foreignness": Response strategies of foreign firm in the United States, *Journal of World Business*, 44: 51–62.
15. 2013, Midrange growth strategy starting from fiscal year 2013, News Release, www.takeda.com, May 9; K. Inagaki & J. Osawa, 2011, Takeda, Toshiba make $10 billion M&A push, *Wall Street Journal*, www.wsj.com, May 20; K. Iagaki, 2011, Takeda buys Nycomed for $14 billion, *Wall Street Journal*, www.wsj.com, May 20.
16. A. Verbeke & W. Yuan, 2013, The drivers of multinational enterprise subsidiary entrepreneurship in China: A resource-based view perspective, *Journal of Management Studies*, 50: 236–258; S. B. Choi, S. H. Lee, & C. Williams, 2011, Ownership and firm innovation in transition economy: Evidence from China, *Research Policy*, 40: 441–452.
17. 2013, Corporate, Ford Motor Company, www.ford.com, accessed May 28; N. E. Boudette, 2011, Ford forecasts sharp gains from Asian sales, *Wall Street Journal*, www.wsj.com, June 8.
18. 2013. Investor relations news, Ford Motor Company, www.ford.com, accessed May 28.
19. A. H. Kirka, G. T. Hult, S. Deligonul, M. Z. Perry, & S. T. Cavusgil, 2012, A multilevel examination of the drivers of firm multinationality: A meta-analysis, *Journal of Management*, 38: 502–530; L. Nachum & S. Song, 2011, The MNE as a portfolio: Interdependencies in MNE growth trajectory, *Journal of International Business Studies*, 42: 381–405.
20. G. Qian, T. A. Khoury, M. W. Peng, & Z. Qian, 2010, The performance implications of intra- and inter-regional geographic diversification, *Strategic Management Journal*, 31: 1018–1030; H. Zou & P. N. Ghauri, 2009, Learning through international acquisitions: The process of knowledge acquisition in China, *Management International Review*, 48: 207–226.
21. Y. Zhang, H. Li, Y. Li, & L.-A. Zhou, 2010, FDI spillovers in an emerging market: The role of foreign firms' country origin diversity and domestic firms' absorptive capacity, *Strategic Management Journal*, 31: 969–989; J. Song & J. Shin, 2008, The paradox of technological capabilities: A study of knowledge sourcing from host countries of overseas R&D operations, *Journal of International Business Studies*, 39: 291–303.
22. F. J. Froese, 2013, Work values of the next generation of business leaders in Shanghai, Tokyo and Seoul, *Asia Pacific Journal of Management*, 30: 297–315; H. Hoang & F. T. Rothaermel, 2010, Leveraging internal and external experience: Exploration, exploitation, and R&D project performance, *Strategic Management Journal*, 31: 734–758.
23. A. Gambardella & M. S. Giarratana, 2010, Localized knowledge spillovers and skill-based performance, *Strategic Entrepreneurship Journal*, 4: 323–339; A. M. Rugman & A. Verbeke, 2009, A new perspective on the regional and global strategies of multinational services firms, *Management International Review*, 48: 397–411.
24. O. Shenkar, 2012, Cultural distance revisited: Towards a more rigorous conceptualization and measurement of cultural differences, *Journal of International Business Studies*, 43: 1–11; R. Chakrabarti, Gupta-Mukherjee, & N. Jayaraman, 2009, Mars-Venus marriages: Culture and cross-border M&A, *Journal of International Business Studies*, 40: 216–236.
25. B. T. McCann & G. Vroom, 2010, Pricing response to entry and agglomeration effects, *Strategic Management Journal*, 31: 284–305; C. C. J. M. Millar & C. J. Choi, 2009, Worker identity, the liability of foreignness, the exclusion of local managers and unionism: A conceptual analysis, *Journal of Organizational Change Management*, 21: 460–470.
26. Y. Y. Chang, Y. Gong, & M. Peng, 2013, Expatriate knowledge transfer, subsidiary absorptive capacity and subsidiary performance, *Academy of Management Journal*, in press; P. Kappen, 2011, Competence-creating overlaps and subsidiary technological evolution in the multinational corporation, *Research Policy*, 40: 673–686.
27. A. Cuervo-Cazurra & M. Genc, 2008, Transforming disadvantages into advantages: Developing-country MNEs in the least developed countries, *Journal of International Business Studies*, 39: 957–979; M. A. Hitt, L. Bierman, K. Uhlenbruck, &

K. Shimizu, 2006, The importance of resources in the internationalization of professional service firms: The good, the bad and the ugly, *Academy of Management Journal*, 49: 1137–1157.

28. A. Arino, 2011, Building the global enterprise: Strategic assembly, *Global Strategy Journal*, 1: 47–49; P. Dastidar, 2009, International corporate diversification and performance: Does firm self-selection matter? *Journal of International Business Studies*, 40: 71–85.
29. M. E. Porter, 1990, *The Competitive Advantage of Nations*, New York: The Free Press.
30. Ibid., 84.
31. D. Englander, 2013, Chiquita Brands—Stocks with appeal, *Wall Street Journal*, www.wsj.com, April 28.
32. 2011, New building blocks for jobs and economic growth, Global competition and collaboration conference, Georgetown University, May 16 and 17.
33. C. Wang, J. Hong, M. Kafouros, & M. Wright, 2012, Exploring the role of government involvement in outward FDI from emerging economies, *Journal of International Business Studies*, 43: 655–676; J. Nishimura & H. Okamuro, 2011, Subsidy and networking: The effects of direct and indirect support programs of the cluster policy, *Research Policy*, 40: 714–727; S. Sheng, K. Z. Zhou, & J. J. Li, 2011, The effects of business and political ties on firm performance: Evidence from China, *Journal of Marketing*, 75: 1–15.
34. M. Kitamura, A. Ohnsman, & Y. Hagiwara, 2011, Why Lexus doesn't lead the pack in China, *Bloomberg Businessweek*, April 3, 32–33.
35. J. M. Shaver, 2011, The benefits of geographic sales diversification: How exporting facilitates capital investment, *Strategic Management Journal*, 32: 1046–1060.
36. L. Diestre & N. Rajagopalan, 2011, An environmental perspective on diversification: The effects of chemical relatedness and regulatory sanctions, *Academy of Management Journal*, 54: 97–115.
37. S. A. Appelbaum, M. Roy, & T. Gilliland, 2011, Globalization of performance appraisals: Theory and applications, *Management Decision*, 49: 570–585; D. A. Ralson, D. H. Holt, R. H. Terpstra, & Y. K. Cheng, 2008, The impact of national culture and economic ideology on managerial work values: A study of the United States, Russia, Japan, and China, *Journal of International Business Studies*, 39: 8–26.
38. S. Zaheer & L. Nachum, 2011, Sense of place: From location resources to MNE locational capital, *Global Strategy Journal*, 1: 96–108; N. Guimaraes-Costs & M. P. E. Cunha, 2009, Foreign locals: A liminal perspective of international managers, *Organizational Dynamics*, 38: 158–166.
39. J.-S. Chen & A. S. Lovvorn, 2011, The speed of knowledge transfer within multinational enterprises: The role of social capital, *International Journal of Commerce and Management*, 21: 46–62; H. Kasper, M. Lehrer, J. Muhlbacher, & B. Muller, 2009, Integration-responsiveness and knowledge-management perspectives on the MNC: A typology and field study of cross-site knowledge-sharing practices, *Journal of Leadership & Organizational Studies*, 15: 287–303.
40. 2013, Introduction to Unilever global, Unilever homepage, www.unilever.com, accessed on May 28; J. Neff, 2008, Unilever's CMO finally gets down to business, *Advertising Age*, July 11.
41. M. P. Koza, S. Tallman, & A. Ataay, 2011, The strategic assembly of global firms: A microstructural analysis of local learning and global adaptation, *Global Strategy Journal*, 1: 27–46; P. J. Buckley, 2009, The impact of the global factory on economic development, *Journal of World Business*, 44: 131–143.
42. A. Zaheer & E. Hernandez, 2011, The geographic scope of the MNC and its alliance portfolio: Resolving the paradox of distance, *Global Strategy Journal*, 1: 109–126.
43. L. Hail, C. Leuz, & P. Wysocki, 2010, Global accounting convergence and the potential adoption of IFRS by the U.S. (part II): Political factors and future scenarios for U.S. accounting standards, *Accounting Horizons*, 24: 567–581; R. G. Barker, 2003, Trend: Global accounting is coming, *Harvard Business Review*, 81(4): 24–25.
44. J.-L. Arregle, T. Miller, M. A. Hitt, & P. W. Beamish, 2013, Do regions matter? An integrated institutional and semiglobalization perspective on the internationalization of MNEs, *Strategic Management Journal*, 34: 910–934; L. H. Shi, C. White, S. Zou, & S. T. Cavusgil, 2010, Global account management strategies: Drivers and outcomes, *Journal of International Business Studies*, 41: 620–638.
45. 2013, About us, CEMEX, www.cemex.com, accessed on May 28.
46. 2012, 2012 CEMEX Annual Report, www.cemex.com, accessed on May 28.
47. R. Greenwood, S. Fairclough, T. Morris, & M. Boussebaa, 2010, The organizational design of transnational professional service firms, *Organizational Dynamics*, 39: 173–183.
48. C. Stehr, 2010, Globalisation strategy for small and medium-sized enterprises, *International Journal of Entrepreneurship and Innovation Management*, 12: 375–391; A. M. Rugman & A. Verbeke, 2008, A regional solution to the strategy and structure of multinationals, *European Management Journal*, 26: 305–313.
49. 2010, Regional resilience: Theoretical and empirical perspectives, *Cambridge Journal of Regions, Economy and Society*, 3–10; Rugman & Verbeke, A regional solution to the strategy and structure of multinationals.
50. M. W. Peng & Y. Jiang, 2010, Institutions behind family ownership and control in large firms, *Journal of Management Studies*, 47: 253–273; A. M. Rugman & A. Verbeke, 2003, Extending the theory of the multinational enterprise: Internationalization and strategic management perspectives, *Journal of International Business Studies*, 34: 125–137.
51. D. Klonowski, 2011, Private equity in emerging markets: Stacking up the BRICs, *Journal of Private Equity*, 14: 24–37.
52. J. Mata & E. Freitas, 2012, Foreignness and exit over the life cycle of firms, *Journal of International Business Studies*, 43: 615–630. R. G. Bell, I. Filatotchev & A. A. Rasheed, 2012, The liability of foreignness, in capital markets: Sources and remedies, *Journal of International Business Studies*, 43: 107–122.
53. R. Salomon & Z. Wu, 2012, Institutional distance and local isomorphism strategy, *Journal of International Business Studies*, 43: 347–367.
54. J. T. Campbell, L. Eden, & S. R. Miller, 2012, Multinationals and corporate social responsibility in host countries: Does distance matter? *Journal of International Business Studies*, 43: 84–106; P. Ghemawat, 2001, Distance still matters, *Harvard Business Review*, 79(8): 137–145.
55. N. Y. Brannen, 2004, When Mickey loses face: Recontextualization, semantic fit and semiotics of foreignness, *Academy of Management Review*, 29: 593–616.
56. M. Schuman, 2006, Disney's Hong Kong headache, *Time*, www.time.com, May 8.
57. Arregle, Miller, Hitt, & Beamish, Do regions matter?; J. Cantwell & Y. Zhang, 2011, Innovation and location in the multinational firm, *International Journal of Technology Management*, 54: 116–132.
58. K. Ito & E. L. Rose, 2010, The implicit return on domestic and international sales: An empirical analysis of U.S. and Japanese firms, *Journal of International Business Studies*, 41: 1074–1089; A. M. Rugman & A. Verbeke, 2007, Liabilities of foreignness and the use of firm-level versus country-level data: A response to Dunning et al. (2007), *Journal of International Business Studies*, 38: 200–205.
59. Arregle, Miller, Hitt, & Beamish, Do regions matter?; E. R. Banalieva, M. D. Santoro, & R. J. Jiang, 2012, Home region focus and technical efficiency of multinational enterprises: The moderating role of regional integration, *Management International Review*, 52(4): 493–518.
60. A. M. Rugman & S. Girod, 2003, Retail multinationals and globalization: The evidence is regional, *European Management Journal*, 21: 24–37.
61. D. E. Westney, 2006, Review of the regional multinationals: MNEs and global strategic management (book review), *Journal of International Business Studies*, 37: 445–449.
62. R. D. Ludema, 2002, Increasing returns, multinationals and geography of preferential trade agreements, *Journal of International Economics*, 56: 329–358.

63. M. Aspinwall, 2009, NAFTA-ization: Regionalization and domestic political adjustment in the North American economic area, *Journal of Common Market Studies*, 47: 1–24.
64. D. Zu & O. Shenar, 2002, Institutional distance and the multinational enterprise, *Academy of Management Review*, 27: 608–618.
65. A. Ojala, 2008, Entry in a psychically distant market: Finnish small and medium-sized software firms in Japan, *European Management Journal*, 26: 135–144.
66. K. D. Brouthers, 2013, Institutional, cultural and transaction cost influences on entry mode choice and performance, *Journal of International Business Studies*, 44: 1–13.
67. B. Maekelburger, C. Schwens, & R. Kabst, 2012, Asset specificity and foreign market entry mode choice of small and medium-sized enterprises: The moderating influence of knowledge safeguards and institutional safeguards, *Journal of International Business Studies*, 43: 458–476.
68. J. M. Shaver, The benefits of geographic sales diversification; C. A. Cinquetti, 2009, Multinationals and exports in a large and protected developing country, *Review of International Economics*, 16: 904–918.
69. P. Ganotakis & J. H. Love, 2012, Export propensity, export intensity and firm performance: The role of the entrepreneurial founding team, *Journal of International Business Studies*, 43: 693–718.
70. M. Bandyk, 2008, Now even small firms can go global, *U.S. News & World Report*, March 10, 52.
71. B. Cassiman & E. Golovko, 2010, Innovation and internationalization through exports, *Journal of International Business Studies*, 42: 56–75.
72. X. He, K. D. Brouthers, & I. Filatotchev, 2013, Resource-based and institutional perspectives on export channel selection and export performance, *Journal of Management*, 39: 27–47; M. Hughes, S. L. Martin, R. E. Morgan, & M. J. Robson, 2010, Realizing product-market advantage in high-technology international new ventures: The mediating role of ambidextrous innovation, *Journal of International Marketing*, 18: 1–21.
73. P. Ganotakis & J. H. Love, 2011, R&D, product innovation, and exporting: Evidence from UK new technology-based firms, *Oxford Economic Papers*, 63: 279–306; M. Gabrielsson & P. Gabrielsson, 2011, Internet-based sales channel strategies of born global firms, *International Business Review*, 20: 88–99.
74. P. S. Aulakh, M. Jiang, & Y. Pan, 2010, International technology licensing: Monopoly rents transaction costs and exclusive rights, *Journal of International Business Studies*, 41: 587–605; R. Bird & D. R. Cahoy, 2008, The impact of compulsory licensing on foreign direct investment: A collective bargaining approach, *American Business Law Journal*, 45: 283–330.
75. M. S. Giarratana & S. Torrisi, 2010, Foreign entry and survival in a knowledge-intensive market: Emerging economy countries' international linkages, technology competences, and firm experience, *Strategic Entrepreneurship Journal*, 4: 85–104; U. Lichtenthaler, 2008, Externally commercializing technology assets: An examination of different process stages, *Journal of Business Venturing*, 23: 445–464.
76. N. Byrnes & F. Balfour, 2009, Philip Morris unbound, *BusinessWeek*, May 4, 38–42.
77. 2013, PMI around the world, Philip Morris International homepage, www.pmi.com, accessed on May 29.
78. E. Dechenaux, J. Thursby, & M. Thursby, 2011, Inventor moral hazard in university licensing: The role of contracts, *Research Policy*, 40: 94–104; S. Hagaoka, 2009, Does strong patent protection facilitate international technology transfer? Some evidence from licensing contrasts of Japanese firms, *Journal of Technology Transfer*, 34: 128–144.
79. U. Lichtenthaler, 2011, The evolution of technology licensing management: Identifying five strategic approaches, *R&D Management*, 41: 173–189; M. Fiedler & I. M. Welpe, 2010, Antecedents of cooperative commercialisation strategies of nanotechnology firms, *Research Policy*, 39: 400–410.
80. C. A. Barlett & S. Rangan, 1992, Komatsu Limited, in C. A. Bartlett & S. Ghoshal (eds.), *Transnational Management: Text, Cases and Readings in Cross Border Management*, Homewood, IL: Irwin, 311–326.
81. S. Veilleux, N. Haskell, & F. Pons, 2012, Going global: How smaller enterprises benefit from strategic alliances, *Journal of Business Strategy*, 33(5): 22–31; C. Schwens, J. J. Eiche, & R. Kabst, 2011, The moderating impact of informal institutional distance and formal institutional risk on SME entry mode choice, *Journal of Management Business Studies*, 48: 330–351.
82. T. Barnes, S. Raynor, & J. Bacchus, 2012, A new typology of forms of international collaboration, *Journal of Business and Strategy*, 5: 81–102; S. Prashantham & S. Young, 2011, Post-entry speed of international new ventures, *Entrepreneurship Theory and Practice*, 35: 275–292.
83. Z. Bhanji & J. E. Oxley, 2013, Overcoming the dual liability of foreignness and privateness in international corporate citizenship partnerships, *Journal of International Business Studies*, 44: 290–311; J. S. Harrison, M. A. Hitt, R. E. Hoskisson, & R. D. Ireland, 2001, Resource complementarity in business combinations: Extending the logic to organization alliances, *Journal of Management*, 27: 679–690.
84. R. A. D'Aveni, G. B. Dagnino, & K. G. Smith, 2010, The age of temporary advantage, *Strategic Management Journal*, 31: 1371–1385; M. A. Hitt, D. Ahlstrom, M. T. Dacin, E. Levitas, & L. Svobodina, 2004, The institutional effects on strategic alliance partner selection in transition economies: China versus Russia, *Organization Science*, 15: 173–185.
85. G. Vasudeva, J. W. Spencer, & H. J. Teegen, 2013, Bringing the institutional context back in: A cross-national comparison of alliance partner selection and knowledge acquisition, *Organization Science*, in press; R. A. Corredoira & L. Rosenkopf, 2010, Should auld acquaintance be forgot? The reverse transfer of knowledge through mobility ties, *Strategic Management Journal*, 31: 159–181.
86. J-P. Roy, 2012, IJV partner trustworthy behavior: The role of host country governance and partner selection criteria, *Journal of Management Studies*, 49: 332–355; M. J. Robson, C. S. Katsikeas, & D. C. Bello, 2008, Drivers and performance outcomes of trust in international strategic alliances: The role of organizational complexity, *Organization Science*, 19: 647–668.
87. 2013, Our activities: Partnerships, Limagrain, www.limagrain.com, accessed on May 30; 2011, Limagrain signs strategic alliance to enter Brazilian corn market, *Great Lakes Hybrids*, www.greatlakeshybrids.com, February 14.
88. S. Kotha & K. Srikanth, 2013, Managing a global partnership model: Lessons from the Boeing 787 'dreamliner' program, *Global Strategy Journal*, 3: 41–66; C. Schwens, J. Eiche, & R. Kabst, 2011, The moderating impact of informal institutional distance and formal institutional risk on SME entry mode choice, *Journal of Management Studies*, 48: 330–351.
89. Y. Luo, O. Shenkar, & H. Gurnani, 2008, Control-cooperation interfaces in global strategic alliances: A situational typology and strategic responses, *Journal of International Business Studies*, 39: 428–453.
90. I. Arikan & O. Shenkar, 2013, National animosity and cross-border alliances, *Academy of Management Journal*, in press; T. K. Das, 2010, Interpartner sensemaking in strategic alliances: Managing cultural differences and internal tensions, *Management Decision*, 48: 17–36.
91. B. B. Nielsen, 2010, Strategic fit, contractual, and procedural governance in alliances, *Journal of Business Research*, 63: 682–689; D. Li, L. Eden, M. A. Hitt, & R. D. Ireland, 2008, Friends, acquaintances and stranger? Partner selection in R&D alliances, *Academy of Management Journal*, 51: 315–334.
92. P. D. O. Jensen & B. Petersen, 2013, Global sourcing of services: Risk, process and collaborative architecture, *Global Strategy Journal*, 3: 67–87.
93. S.-F. S. Chen, 2010, A general TCE model of international business institutions; market failure and reciprocity, *Journal of International Business Studies*, 41: 935–959; J. Wiklund & D. A. Shepherd, 2009, The effectiveness of alliances and acquisitions: The role of resource combination activities,

*Entrepreneurship Theory and Practice*, 33: 193–212.
94. A. Guar, S. Malhotra, & P. Zhu, 2013, Acquisition announcements and stock market valuations of acquiring firms' rivals: A test of the growth probability hypothesis in China, *Strategic Management Journal*, 34: 215–232; M. A. Hitt & V. Pisano, 2003, The cross-border merger and acquisition strategy, *Management Research*, 1: 133–144.
95. 2013, Corporate information—Our company history, DJO Global, www.djoglobal.com accessed on May 15.
96. S. Malhotra, P.-C. Zhu, & W. Locander, 2010, Impact of host-country corruption on U.S. and Chinese cross-border acquisitions, *Thunderbird International Business Review*, 52: 491–507; P. X. Meschi, 2009, Government corruption and foreign stakes in international joint ventures in emerging economies, *Asia Pacific Journal of Management*, 26: 241–261.
97. J. Li & C. Qian, 2013, Principal-principal conflicts under weak institutions: A study of corporate takeovers in China, *Strategic Management Journal*, 34: 498–508; A. Madhok & M. Keyhani, 2012, Acquisitions as entrepreneurship: Asymmetries, opportunities, and the internationalization of multinationals from emerging economies, *Global Strategy Journal*, 2: 26–40.
98. E. Vaara, R. Sarala, G. K. Stahl, & I. Bjorkman, 2012, *Journal of Management Studies*, 49: 1–27; D. R. Denison, B. Adkins, & A. Guidroz, 2011, Managing cultural integration in cross-border mergers and acquisitions, in W. H. Mobley, 2011, M. Li, & Y. Wang (eds.), *Advances in Global Leadership*, vol. 6, Bingley, UK: Emerald Publishing Group, 95–115.
99. S.-J. Chang, J. Chung, & J. J. Moon, 2013, When do wholly owned subsidiaries perform better than joint ventures? *Strategic Management Journal*, 34: 317–337; Y. Fang, G.-L. F. Jiang, S. Makino, & P. W. Beamish, 2010, Multinational firm knowledge, use of expatriates, and foreign subsidiary performance, *Journal of Management Studies*, 47: 27–54.
100. C. Bouquet, L. Hebert, & A. Delios, 2004, Foreign expansion in service industries: Separability and human capital intensity, *Journal of Business Research*, 57: 35–46.
101. C. Schwens, J. Eiche, & R. Kabst, 2011, The moderating impact of informal institutional distance and formal institutional risk on SME entry mode choice, *Journal of Management Studies*, 48: 330–351; K. F. Meyer, S. Estrin, S., Bhaumik, & M. W. Peng, 2009, Institutions, resources, and entry strategies in emerging economics, *Strategic Management Journal*, 30: 61–80.
102. Chang, Chung, & Moon, When do wholly owned subsidiaries perform better than joint ventures?; K. D. Brouthers & D. Dikova, 2010, Acquisitions and real options: The greenfield alternative, *Journal of Management Studies*, 47: 1048–1071.
103. Y. Parke & B. Sternquist, 2008, The global retailer's strategic proposition and choice of entry mode, *International Journal of Retail & Distribution Management*; 36: 281–299.
104. L. Q. Siebers, 2012, Foreign retailers in China: The first ten years, *Journal of Business Strategy*, 33: 27–38.
105. J. Anand, R. Oriani, & R. S. Vassolo, 2010, Alliance activity as a dynamic capability in the face of a discontinuous technological change, *Organization Science*, 21: 1213–1232; R. Farzad, 2007, Extreme investing: Inside Colombia, *BusinessWeek*, May 28, 50–58.
106. A. M. Rugman, 2010, Reconciling internalization theory and the eclectic paradigm, *Multinational Business Review*, 18: 1–12; J. Che & G. Facchini, 2009, Cultural differences, insecure property rights and the mode of entry decision, *Economic Theory*, 38: 465–484.
107. 2013, Company profile-facilities, Toyota Motor Corporation, www.toyota-global.com, accessed on May 30.
108. B. Batjargal, M. Hitt, A. Tsui, J.-L. Arregle, J. Webb, & T. Miller, 2013, Institutional polycentrism, entrepreneurs' social networks and new venture growth, *Academy of Management Journal*, in press.
109. C. Giersch, 2011, Political risk and political due diligence, *Global Risk Affairs*, www.globalriskaffairs.com, March 4.
110. J. Li & Y. Tang, 2010, CEO hubris and firm risk taking in China: The moderating role of managerial discretion, *Academy of Management Journal*, 53: 45–68; I. Alon & T. T. Herbert, 2009, A stranger in a strange land: Micro political risk and the multinational firm, *Business Horizons*, 52: 127–137; P. Rodriguez, K. Uhlenbruck, & L. Eden, 2003, Government corruption and the entry strategies of multinationals, *Academy of Management Review*, 30: 383–396.
111. D. Quer, E. Claver, & L. Rienda, 2012, Political risk, cultural distance, and outward foreign direct investment: Empirical evidence from large Chinese firms, *Asia Pacific Journal of Management*, 29: 1089–1104; O. Branzei & S. Abdelnour, 2010, Another day, another dollar: Enterprise resilience under terrorism in developing countries, *Journal of International Business Studies*, 41: 804–825; F. Wu, 2009, Singapore's sovereign wealth funds: The political risk of overseas investment, *World Economics*, 9(3): 97–122.
112. Giersch, Political risk and political due diligence.
113. J. Surroca, J. A. Tribo, & S. A. Zahra, 2013, Stakeholder pressure on MNEs and the transfer of socially irresponsible practices to subsidiaries, *Academy of Management Journal*, 56: 549–572.
114. K. Schwab, 2012, *The global competitiveness report, 2012–2013, World Economic Forum*, Geneva, Switzerland; M. D. Hanous & A. Prazdnichnyky, 2011, The Russia competitiveness report 2011, *World Economic Forum*, January.
115. G. Fornes & A. Butt-Philip, 2011, Chinese MNEs and Latin America: A review, *International Journal of Emerging Markets*, 6: 98–117; S. Globerman & D. Shapiro, 2009, Economic and strategic considerations surrounding Chinese FDI in the United States, *Asia Pacific Journal of Management*, 26: 163–183.
116. C. R. Goddard, 2011, Risky business: Financial-sector liberalization and China, *Thunderbird International Business Review*, 53: 469–482; I. G. Kawaller, 2009, Hedging currency exposures by multinationals: Things to consider, *Journal of Applied Finance*, 18: 92–98.
117. C. C. Chung, S.-H. Lee, P. W. Beamish, & T. Ksobe, 2010, Subsidiary expansion/contraction during times of economic crisis, *Journal of International Business Studies*, 41: 500–516.
118. R. G. Bell, I. Filatotchev, & R. V. Aguilera, 2013, Corporate governance and investors' perceptions of foreign IPO value: An institutional perspective, *Academy of Management Journal*, in press.
119. V. Monatiriotis & R. Alegria, 2011, Origin of FDI and intra-industry domestic spillovers: The case of Greek and European FDI in Bulgaria, *Review of Development Economics*, 15: 326–339; N. Bandelj, 2009, The global economy as instituted process: The case of Central and Eastern Europe, *American Sociological Review*, 74: 128–149; L. Tihanyi & W. H. Hegarty, 2007, Political interests and the emergence of commercial banking in transition economies, *Journal of Management Studies*, 44: 789–813.
120. F. J. Contractor, 2012, Why do multinational firms exist? A theory note about the effect of multinational expansion on performance and recent methodological critiques, *Global Strategy Journal*, 2: 318–331; P. David, J. P. O'Brien, T. Yoshikawa, & A. Delios, 2010, Do shareholders or stakeholders appropriate the rents from corporate diversification? The influence of ownership structure, *Academy of Management Journal*, 53: 636–654.
121. L. Li, 2007, Multinationality and performance: A synthetic review and research agenda, *International Journal of Management Reviews*, 9: 117–139; J. A. Doukas & O. B. Kan, 2006, Does global diversification destroy firm value? *Journal of International Business Studies*, 37: 352–371.
122. J. H. Fisch, 2012, Information costs and internationalization performance, *Global Strategy Journal*, 2: 296–312; S. E. Christophe & H. Lee, 2005, What matters about internationalization: A market-based assessment, *Journal of Business Research*, 58: 636–643.
123. H. Berry, 2013, When do firms divest foreign operations? *Organization Science*, in press; T. J. Andersen, 2011, The risk implications of multinational enterprise, *International Journal of Organizational Analysis*, 19: 49–70.

124. H. Berry, 2013, Global integration and innovation: Multi country knowledge generation within MNCs, *Strategic Management Journal*, in press; A. Y. Lewin, S. Massini, & C. Peeters, 2011, Microfoundations of internal and external absorptive capacity routines, *Organization Science*, 22: 81-98.
125. P. C. Patel, S. A. Fernhaber, P. P. McDougal-Covin, & R. P. van der Have, 2013, Beating competitors to international markets: The value of geographically balanced networks for innovation, *Strategic Management Journal*, in press.
126. O. Bertrand & M. J. Mol, 2013, The antecedents and innovation effects of domestic and offshore R&D outsourcing: The contingent impact of cognitive distance and absorptive capacity, *Strategic Management Journal*, 34: 751–760; B. S. Reiche, 2012, Knowledge benefits of social capital upon repatriation: A longitudinal study of international assignees, *Journal of Management Studies*, 49: 1052–1072; H. A. Ndofor, D. G. Sirmon, & X. He, 2011, Firm resources, competitive actions and performance: Investigating a mediated model with evidence from the in-vitro diagnostics industry, *Strategic Management Journal*, 32: 81–98; 640–657.
127. G. R. G. Benito, R. Lunnan & S. Tomassen, 2011, Distant encounters of the third kind: Multinational companies locating divisional headquarters abroad, *Journal of Management Studies*, 48: 373–394; M. A. Hitt, L. Tihanyi, T. Miller, & B. Connelly, 2006, International diversification: Antecedents, outcomes, and moderators, *Journal of Management*, 32: 831–867.
128. I. Guler & A. Nerkar, 2012, The impact of global and local cohesion on innovation in the pharmaceutical industry, *Strategic Management Journal*, 33: 535–549.
129. X. Fu, 2012, Foreign direct investment and managerial knowledge spillovers through diffusion of management practices, *Journal of Management Studies*, 49: 970–999; D. Holtbrugge & A. T. Mohr, 2011, Subsidiary interdependencies and international human resource management practices in German MNCs, *Management International Review*, 51: 93–115.
130. M. Halme, S. Lindeman, & P. Linna, 2012, Innovation for inclusive business: Intrapreneurial bricolage in multinational corporations, *Journal of Management Studies*, 49: 743–784; I. Filatotchev & M. Wright, 2010, Agency perspectives on corporate governance of multinational enterprises, *Journal of Management Studies*, 47: 471–486.
131. J. I. Siegel & S. H. Schwartz, 2013, Egalitarianism, cultural distance and foreign direct investment: A new approach, *Organization Science*, in press; G. A. Shinkle & A. P. Kriauciunas, 2012, The impact of current and founding institutions on strength of competitive aspirations in transition economies, *Strategic Management Journal*, 33: 448–458; D. Dikova, P. R. Sahib, & A. van Witteloostuijn, 2010, Cross-border acquisition abandonment and completion: The effect of institutional differences and organizational learning in the international business service industry, 1981–2001, *Journal of International Business Studies*, 41: 223–245.
132. 2013, Earnings release presentation, Toyota Global Web site, www.toyotaglobal.com, May 8.
133. P. C. Nell & B. Ambos, 2013, Parenting advantage in the MNC: An embeddedness perspective on the value added by headquarters, *Strategic Management Journal*, in press; J.-F. Hennart, 2012, Emerging market multinationals and the theory of the multinational enterprise, *Global Strategy Journal*, 2: 168–187.
134. C. G. Asmussen & A. Goerzen, 2013, Unpacking dimensions of foreignness: Firm-specific capabilities and international dispersion in regional, cultural and institutional space, *Global Strategy Journal*, 3: 127–149.
135. Wiersema & Bowen, The relationship between international diversification and firm performance; C.-F. Wang, L.-Y. Chen, & S.-C. Change, 2011, International diversification and the market value of new product introduction, *Journal of International Management*, 17(4): 333–347.
136. R. Belderbos, T. W. Tong, & S. Wu, 2013, Multinationality and downside risk: The roles of option portfolio and organization, *Strategic Management Journal*, in press; W. Shi, S. L. Sun and M. W. Peng, 2012, Sub-national institutional contingencies, network positions and IJV partner selection, *Journal of Management Studies*, 49: 1221–1245.
137. B. Baik, J.-K. Kang, J.-M. Kim, & J. Lee, 2013, The liability of foreignness in international equity investments: Evidence from the U.S. stock market, *Journal of International Business Studies*, 44: 391–411.
138. S. H. Lee & S. Song, 2012, Host country uncertainty, intra-MNC production shifts, and subsidiary performance, *Strategic Management Journal*, 33: 1331–1340.
139. L. Berchicci, A. King, & C. L. Tucci, 2011, Does the apple always fall close to the tree? The geographical proximity choice of spin-outs, *Strategic Entrepreneurship Journal*, 5: 120–136; A. Ojala, 2008, Entry in a psychically distant market: Finnish small and medium-sized software firms in Japan, *European Management Journal*, 26: 135–144.
140. B. L. Connelly, R. E. Hoskisson, L. Tihanyi, & S. T. Certo, 2010, Ownership as a form of corporate governance, *Journal of Management Studies*, 47: 1561–1580; M. L. L. Lam, 2009, Beyond credibility of doing business in China: Strategies for improving corporate citizenship of foreign multinational enterprises in China, *Journal of Business Ethics*, 87: 137–146.
141. E. Fang & S. Zou, 2010, The effects of absorptive capacity and joint learning on the instability of international joint ventures in emerging economies, *Journal of International Business Studies*, 41: 906–924; D. Lavie & S. Miller, 2009, Alliance portfolio internationalization and firm performance, *Organization Science*, 19: 623–646.

# 9

# Cooperative Strategy

***Studying this chapter should provide you with the strategic management knowledge needed to:***

1. Define cooperative strategies and explain why firms use them.
2. Define and discuss the three major types of strategic alliances.
3. Name the business-level cooperative strategies and describe their use.
4. Discuss the use of corporate-level cooperative strategies in diversified firms.
5. Understand the importance of cross-border strategic alliances as an international cooperative strategy.
6. Explain cooperative strategies' risks.
7. Describe two approaches used to manage cooperative strategies.

# ALLIANCE FORMATION, BOTH GLOBALLY AND LOCALLY, IN THE GLOBAL AUTOMOBILE INDUSTRY

The academic literature on alliances has some interesting recent findings. One of these findings is the rationale that because firms are often located in the same country, and often in the same region of the country, it is easier for them to collaborate on major projects. As such, they compete globally, but may cooperate locally. Historically, firms have learned to collaborate by establishing strategic alliances and forming cooperative strategies when there is intensive competition. This interesting paradox is due to several reasons. First, when there is intense rivalry, it is difficult to maintain market power. As such, cooperative strategy can reduce market power through better norms of competition; this pertains to the idea of *"mutual forbearance"* (this idea will be discussed later in this chapter). Another rationale which has emerged is based on the resource-based view of the firm (see Chapter 3). To compete, firms often need resources that they don't have but may be found in other firms in or outside of the focal firm's home industry. As such, these "complementary resources" are another rationale for why large firms form joint ventures and strategic alliances within the same industry or in vertically related industries (this idea will be more clearly explained later in this chapter).

Because firms are co-located and have similar needs, it's easier for them to jointly work together, for example, to produce engines and transmissions as part of the powertrain. This is evident in the European alliance between Peugeot-Citroën and Opel-Vauxhall (owned by General Motors). It is also the reason for a recent U.S. alliance between Ford and General Motors in developing upgraded nine- and ten-speed transmissions. Furthermore, they are looking to develop together eleven- and twelve-speed automatic transmissions to improve fuel efficiency and help them to meet new federal guidelines regarding such efficiency.

In regard to resource complementarity, a very successful alliance was formed in 1999 by French-based Renault and Japan-based Nissan. Each of these firms lacked the necessary size to develop economies of scale and economies of scope that were critical to succeed in the 1990s and beyond in the global automobile industry. When the alliance was formed, each firm took an ownership stake in the other. The larger of the two companies, Renault, holds a 43.3 percent stake in Nissan, while Nissan has a 15 percent stake in Renault. It is interesting to note that Carlos Ghosn serves as the CEO of both companies. Over time, this corporate-level synergistic alliance (we discuss this type of alliance later in the chapter) has developed three values to guide their relationship: (1) *trust* (work fairly, impartially, and professionally); (2) *respect* (honor commitments, liabilities, and responsibilities; and (3) *transparency* (be open, frank, and clear). Largely due to these established principles, the Renault-Nissan alliance is a recognized success. One could argue that the main reason for the success of this alliance is the complementary assets that both firms bring to the alliance; Nissan is strong in Asia while Renault is strong in Europe. Together they have been able to establish other production locations, such as those in Latin America, which they may not have obtained independently.

Some firms enter alliances because they are "squeezed in the middle;" that is, they have moderate volumes, mostly for the mass market, but need to collaborate to establish viable economies of scale. For example, Fiat-Chrysler needs to boost its annual sales from $4.3 billion to something like $6 billion, and likewise needs to strengthen its presence in the booming Asian market to have enough global market power. As such, it is entering joint ventures with two undersized Japanese carmakers, Mazda and Suzuki; however, the past history of Mazda and Suzuki with alliances may be a reason for their not being overly enthusiastic about the prospects of the current alliances. Fiat broke up with GM, Chrysler with Daimler, and Mazda with Ford.

This is also the situation in Europe locally for Peugeot-Citroën of France, which is struggling for survival along with the GM European subsidiary, Opel-Vauxhall. More specifically, Peugeot-Citroën and Opel-Vauxhall have struck a tentative agreement to share platforms and engines to get the capital necessary for investment in future models. As such, in all these examples, they need additional market share, but also enough capital to make the investment necessary to realize more market power to compete.

In summary, there are a number of rationales why competitors not only compete but also cooperate in establishing strategic alliances and joint ventures in order to meet strategic needs for increased market power, take advantage of complementary assets, and cooperate with close neighbors, often in the same region of the country.

Sources: 2013, Markets and makers: Running harder, *Economist*, April 20, ss4–ss7; J. Boxell, 2013, Peugeot reaffirms push into BRICs, *Financial Times*, www.ft.com, February 7; D. Pearson & J. Bennett, 2013, Corporate news: GM, Peugeot pledge to deepen car alliance – Tough market in Europe has slowed progress, but automakers now see opportunities to cooperate outside the region, *Wall Street Journal*, www.wsj.com, January 10; J. B. White, 2013, Mazda uses alliances to boost sales, *Wall Street Journal*, www.wsj.com, January 27; T. Yu, M. Subramaniam, & A. A. Cannella, Jr., 2013, Competing globally, allying locally: Alliances between global rivals and host-country factors, *Journal of International Business Studies*, 44: 117–137; W. Lim, 2012, The voyage of the Renault-Nissan Alliance: A successful venture, *Advances In Management*, 5(9): 25–29.

Learn more about Peugeot-Citroën, another strategic alliance.
www.cengagebrain.com

As explained in the Opening Case, Renault and Nissan have formed a cooperative strategy as a means of improving each firm's performance. Renault and Nissan, as is the case for all companies, are trying to use their resources and capabilities in ways that will create the greatest amount of value for stakeholders.[1]

Forming a cooperative strategy like the one between Renault and Nissan, or between other global automobile companies, has the potential to be a viable engine of firm growth. Specifically, a **cooperative strategy** is a means by which firms collaborate for the purpose of working together to achieve a shared objective.[2] Cooperating with other firms is a strategy firms use to create value for a customer that it likely could not create by itself. For example, Fiat and Chrysler are in an equity alliance where Fiat has a significant ownership position in Chrysler. In describing a Fiat-designed and developed compact car that Chrysler will build and sell in the United States under its own name, an auto industry analyst said that a product such as this is "why the two auto makers…have a relationship."[3]

A **cooperative strategy** is a means by which firms collaborate for the purpose of working together to achieve a shared objective.

Firms also try to create competitive advantages when using a cooperative strategy. A competitive advantage developed through a cooperative strategy often is called a *collaborative* or *relational* advantage,[4] denoting that the relationship that develops among collaborating partners is commonly the basis on which a competitive advantage is built. Importantly, successful use of cooperative strategies finds a firm outperforming its rivals in terms of strategic competitiveness and above-average returns,[5] often because they've been able to form a competitive advantage.

M. Stasy

We examine several topics in this chapter. First, we define and offer examples of different strategic alliances as primary types of cooperative strategies. We focus on strategic alliances because firms use them more frequently than other types of cooperative relationships. Next, we discuss the extensive use of cooperative strategies in the global economy and reasons for that use. In succession, we describe business-level, corporate-level, international, and network cooperative strategies. The chapter closes with a discussion of the risks of using cooperative strategies as well as how effectively managing the strategies can reduce those risks.

## 9-1 Strategic Alliances as a Primary Type of Cooperative Strategy

A **strategic alliance** is a cooperative strategy in which firms combine some of their resources and capabilities for the purpose of creating a competitive advantage. Strategic alliances involve firms with some degree of exchange and sharing of resources and capabilities to codevelop, sell, and service goods or services.[6] In addition, firms use strategic alliances to leverage their existing resources and capabilities while working with partners to develop additional resources and capabilities as the foundation for new competitive advantages.[7] To be certain, the reality today is that "strategic alliances have become a cornerstone of many firms' competitive strategy."[8] This means that for many firms, and particularly for large global competitors, strategic alliances are potentially many in number but are always important in efforts to outperform competitors.

Consider the strategic alliance between the Syfy Cable Network and Trion Worlds to jointly create a simultaneous TV show and associated video game. Both the show and video game are focused on Syfy's new TV series, "Defiance," "about aliens who came to Earth and their prickly relationship with the current inhabitants." Because of the newness and difficulty of coordinating strategies between the partners involved, there were many hurdles in forming the project. There was disagreement about how to finance and market the project as well as the timing to launch. Many cable channels now have their own popular and critically well-regarded TV programming, such as AMC's "Mad Men" and HBO's "Game of Thrones" (among many possible examples). Likewise, Amazon.com and Netflix are in the process of producing original shows. Syfy is owned by NBCUniversal, which is majority owned by Comcast, a large cable television service provider. Each week as fans watch the "Defiance" one-hour drama, they can participate in the video game and pursue elements of what happened in the plot. The video game has attracted one million registered users since it went live on April 2, 2012. The joint project has gained advertisers such as Fiat-Chrysler through its Dodge branded products. Many Dodge products are scattered throughout the Syfy and Trion show and game platforms. Although this is an interesting innovation, it is a risky gamble because the network has spent $40M on the show's first season and has agreed to cover half of the game's $70M production costs. One analyst suggested, however, that if it is successful, it could alter the way that Comcast and other media producers develop entertainment on multiple platforms.[9]

Before describing three types of major strategic alliances and reasons for their use, we need to note that for all cooperative strategies, success is more likely when partners behave cooperatively. Actively solving problems, being trustworthy, and consistently pursuing ways to combine partners' resources and capabilities to create value are examples of cooperative behavior known to contribute to alliance success.[10] Recall that *trust*, *respect*, and *transparency* are three core values on which the Renault-Nissan corporate-level cooperative strategy is based. Perhaps these values are instrumental to the success that is credited to this cooperative relationship.

A **strategic alliance** is a cooperative strategy in which firms combine some of their resources and capabilities for the purpose of creating a competitive advantage.

## 9-1a Types of Major Strategic Alliances

Joint ventures, equity strategic alliances, and nonequity strategic alliances are the three major types of strategic alliances firms use. The ownership arrangement is a key difference among these alliances.

A **joint venture** is a strategic alliance in which two or more firms create a legally independent company to share some of their resources and capabilities for the purpose of developing a competitive advantage. Typically, partners in a joint venture own equal percentages and contribute equally to the venture's operations. Some evidence suggests that recent global economic difficulties have increased the attractiveness of this type of strategic alliance. Often formed to improve a firm's ability to compete in uncertain competitive environments, such as those associated with economic downturns, joint ventures are effective in establishing long-term relationships and in transferring tacit knowledge. Interestingly, AIG's Chinese joint venture saved it in the 2008 financial meltdown. The large insurance giant was founded in Shanghai in 1919 by C. V. Starr, a California life insurance pioneer. In 1950, after Mau's Communist takeover, AIG left China and established itself in the United States. However, it maintained a joint venture relationship (with AIA) with large real estate and insurance holdings in some of Asia's most expensive districts. To repay AIG's debt to the U.S. government it received in the global financial crisis, it sold most of its AIA joint venture holdings. Recently, AIG announced an agreement with the People's Insurance Company of China, a state-owned insurer, to invest roughly $500M in a People's Insurance public offering in Hong Kong. As part of the deal, the two companies are expected to reinitiate a joint venture to sell life insurance in China.[11]

Because it can't be codified, tacit knowledge, which is increasingly critical to firms' efforts to develop core competencies, is learned through experiences such as those taking place when people from partner firms work together in a joint venture.[12] Overall, a joint venture may be the optimal type of cooperative arrangement when firms need to combine their resources and capabilities to create a competitive advantage that is substantially different from any they possess individually and when the partners intend to enter highly uncertain, hypercompetitive markets.

Learn more about Equity Strategic Alliances.
www.cengagebrain.com

A **joint venture** is a strategic alliance in which two or more firms create a legally independent company to share some of their resources and capabilities for the purpose of developing a competitive advantage.

An **equity strategic alliance** is an alliance in which two or more firms own different percentages of the company they have formed by combining some of their resources and capabilities for the purpose of creating a competitive advantage.

Because China has potentially significant shale gas reserves, multinational companies such as Shell, Chevron, and ConocoPhillips have been pursuing joint ventures with Chinese petroleum firms. They intend to conduct exploratory drilling using hydraulic fracturing techniques to extract the shale gas. The Chinese petroleum companies do not have the "fracking" technology needed and, as such, are seeking to benefit from joint ventures with foreign firms who have expertise in these techniques. For example, Chevron recently formed a joint venture with the China National Petroleum Corp. and has begun exploratory drilling in Sichuan province. Likewise, ConocoPhillips has announced a joint venture with Sinopec. China generates 80 percent of its electricity from coal and is building coal-fired electricity generating plants at the rate of about one a week. If it could use shale gas for these generating plants, they would emit approximately half the $CO_2$ of coal.[13] Joint ventures such as these in China are not necessarily permanent in nature. There are different reasons for the lack of permanence, including dissatisfaction from one or all parties with the partnership's outcomes or changes in the strategic direction one or more partners wish to pursue. If the exploratory drilling does not create a new opportunity, the partnership may be disbanded, or circumstances may change and one partner may want to buy out the other's investment.

An **equity strategic alliance** is an alliance in which two or more firms own different percentages of the company they have formed by combining some of their resources and capabilities for the purpose of creating a competitive advantage. Many foreign direct investments in China by multinational corporations are completed through equity strategic alliances. Likewise, many Chinese firms pursuing outward foreign direct investment are doing so through equity alliances, especially when the Chinese firm is a state-owned enterprise.[14]

M. Stasy

Equity alliances can be primarily for capital infusions alone, but also for changing one's strategy. For instance, recently Club Mediterranee SA (Club Med), a resort operator and one of France's best-known international brands, wanted to partner with a private equity firm, France's AXA Private Equity, as well as with a Chinese conglomerate, Fosun International Ltd. In essence, this is a private equity deal for the managers of Club Med to gain control and capital as it upgrades its European resorts, but also to partner with Fosun as it shifts emphasis to develop more Asian outlets because the Asian customer, especially the Chinese, are the most important growing segment of the global hospitality resort market. In recent years, Fosun also has looked to increase its overseas collaboration with other buyout firms such as Carlyle Group, which sought investment in Chinese companies.[15]

Katie Orlinsky/Getty Images

*Fracking in Bradford County, Pennsylvania. Many Chinese petroleum companies are looking to form joint ventures with firms that possess fracking technology.*

A **nonequity strategic alliance** is an alliance in which two or more firms develop a contractual relationship to share some of their resources and capabilities for the purpose of creating a competitive advantage.[16] In this type of alliance, firms do not establish a separate independent company and therefore do not take equity positions. For this reason, nonequity strategic alliances are less formal, demand fewer partner commitments than do joint ventures and equity strategic alliances, and generally do not foster an intimate relationship between partners; nonetheless, research evidence indicates that they can create value for the involved firms.[17] The relative informality and lower commitment levels characterizing nonequity strategic alliances make them unsuitable for complex projects where success requires effective transfers of tacit knowledge between partners.[18] Licensing agreements, distribution agreements, and supply contracts are examples of nonequity strategic alliances.

Commonly, outsourcing commitments are specified in the form of a nonequity strategic alliance. (Discussed in Chapter 3, *outsourcing* is the purchase of a value-chain activity, or a support-function activity from another firm.) Apple Inc. and most other computer, tablet, and smartphone firms outsource most or all of their production to nonequity strategic alliance partners. Apple has traditionally outsourced most of its manufacturing to one dominant partner, Foxconn Technology Group, a large Taiwanese contract manufacturer. More recently, however, under CEO Tim Cook, Pegatron Corp., also a Taiwanese firm, Apple has diversified its manufacturing suppliers by partnering with this smaller rival to Foxconn to produce the iPad mini. Pegatron has accepted lower margins given its smaller size; its margins are 0.8 percent compared to 1.7 percent for Foxconn.[19] Interestingly, many firms that outsource introduce modularity where the contract producer only generates a part of the whole product. This approach prevents the contracting partner or outsourcee from gaining too much knowledge or from sharing certain aspects of the business the outsourcing firm does not want revealed.[20]

A **nonequity strategic alliance** is an alliance in which two or more firms develop a contractual relationship to share some of their resources and capabilities for the purpose of creating a competitive advantage.

## 9-1b Reasons Firms Develop Strategic Alliances

Cooperative strategies are an integral part of the competitive landscape and are quite important to many companies and even to educational institutions. In fact, many firms are cooperating with educational institutions to help commercialize ideas flowing from basic research projects completed at universities.[21] In for-profit organizations, many executives believe that strategic alliances are central to their firm's growth and success.[22] The fact that alliances can account for up to 25 percent or more of a typical firm's sales revenue demonstrates their importance. Also, highlighting alliances' importance is the fact that in some settings, such as the global airline industry, competition is increasingly between large alliances rather than between large companies.[23]

Among other benefits, strategic alliances allow partners to create value that they couldn't develop by acting independently and to enter markets more quickly and with greater market penetration possibilities.[24] For example, South America's largest retailer by market value, Chilean firm SACI Falabella, is seeking to establish a foothold in Brazil through its Sodimac home improvement unit by taking a 51 percent ownership position in Dicico, a chain of home improvement stores owned by Construdecor SA. Falabella owns department stores, supermarkets, shopping malls, and home improvement stores in Chile, Colombia, Peru, and Argentina. Falabella's chief executive, CEO Sandro Solari, said, "We see good value in having a [local] partner" in managing Dicico. Falabella purchased its ownership position from previous part-owner Markinvest Gestao de Participaceos Limitada. The Brazilian entry is important for Falabella because Brazil is home to half of South America's population and has a large and growing middle class.[25]

Another reason to form strategic alliances is that most (if not all) firms lack the full set of resources and capabilities needed to reach their objectives, which indicates that partnering with others will increase the probability of reaching firm-specific performance objectives. This may be especially true for small businesses—ones in which capital is scarce as well as larger ones. Given constrained resources, firms can collaborate for a number of purposes, including those of reaching new customers and broadening both the product offerings and the distribution of their products without adding significantly to their cost structures. The example noted earlier between Syfy Cable Network and Trion Worlds to create a simultaneous TV show and associated video game through a strategic alliance broadens both companies' offerings.

Unique competitive conditions characterize slow-cycle, fast-cycle, and standard-cycle markets.[26] We discussed these three market types in Chapter 5 while examining competitive rivalry and competitive dynamics. These unique conditions find firms using strategic alliances to reach objectives that differ slightly by market type (see Figure 9.1).

*Slow-cycle markets* are markets where the firm's competitive advantages are shielded from imitation for relatively long periods of time and where imitation is costly. These markets are close to monopolistic conditions. Railroads and, historically, telecommunications, utilities, and financial services are industries characterized as slow-cycle markets. In *fast-cycle markets*, the firm's competitive advantages are not shielded from imitation, preventing their long-term sustainability. Competitive advantages are moderately shielded from imitation in *standard-cycle markets*, typically allowing them to be sustained for a longer period of time than in fast-cycle market situations, but for a shorter period of time than in slow-cycle markets.

## Slow-Cycle Markets

Firms in slow-cycle markets often use strategic alliances to enter restricted markets or to establish franchises in new markets. For example, in 2013, Choice Hotels International, a large franchised hotel operator with brands such as Comfort Suites, entered into a multi-year strategic alliance agreement with Bluegreen Vacations and Bluegreen Resorts Management, both subsidiaries of Bluegreen Corp. Choice Hotels set up its Ascend Hotel Collection of historic and boutique hotels as part of its independent hotel offerings in the United States, Canada, Scandinavia, and Latin America. Bluegreen Vacations will become

**Figure 9.1** Reasons for Strategic Alliances by Market Type

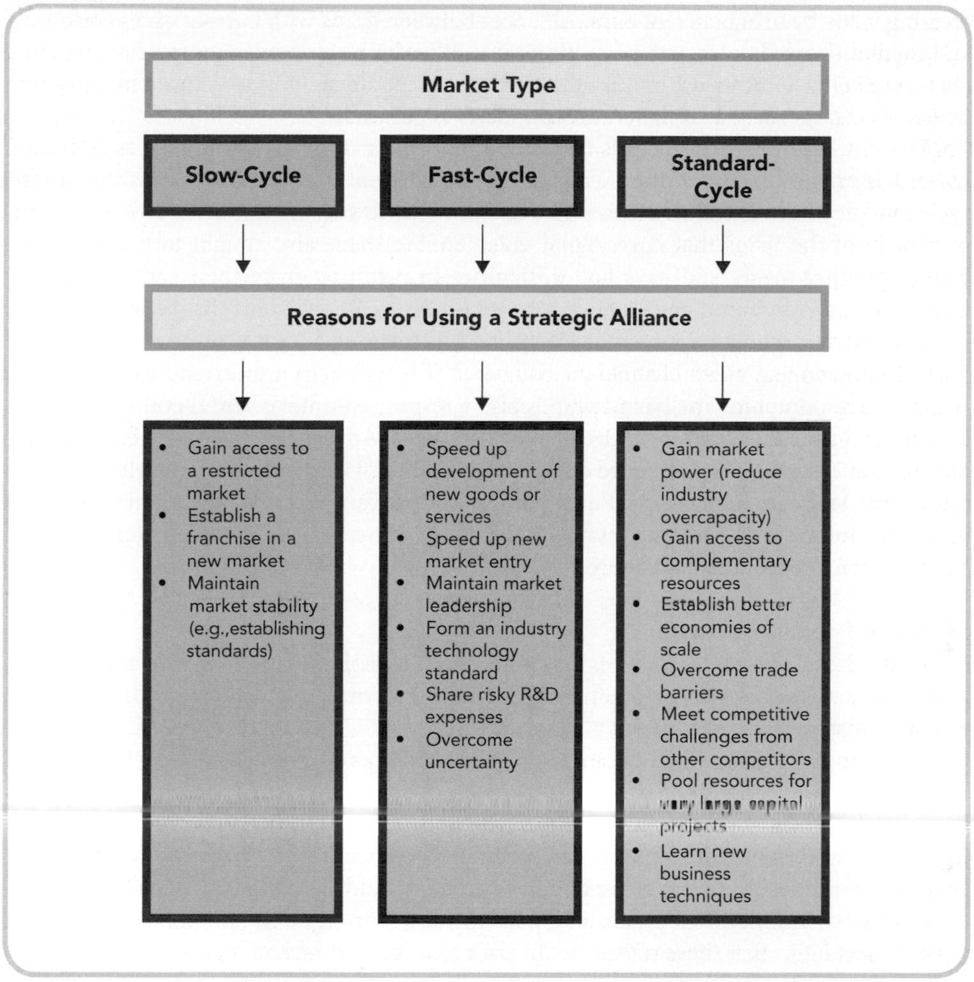

"the official vacation ownership provider of Choice Hotels." Choice Hotels' loyalty program, Choice Privileges, as well as Bluegreen's benefit program, TravelerPlus, are eligible to enroll each other's members through the alliance. For example, TravelerPlus participants will be upgraded to "Elite Gold status and receive special benefits," and will have access to all of Choice Hotels worldwide, including the 75 hotels in the Ascend Hotel Collection.[27]

Slow-cycle markets are becoming rare in the twenty-first century competitive landscape for several reasons, including the privatization of industries and economies, the rapid expansion of the Internet's capabilities for quick dissemination of information, and the speed with which advancing technologies make quickly imitating even complex products possible.[28] Firms competing in slow-cycle markets, including hotel chains, should recognize the future likelihood that they'll encounter situations in which their competitive advantages become partially sustainable (in the instance of a standard-cycle market) or unsustainable (in the case of a fast-cycle market). Cooperative strategies can help firms transition from relatively sheltered markets to more competitive ones.[29]

### Fast-Cycle Markets

Fast-cycle markets are unstable, unpredictable, and complex; in a word, hypercompetitive.[30] Combined, these conditions virtually preclude establishing long-lasting competitive advantages, forcing firms to constantly seek sources of new competitive advantages while creating value by using current ones. Alliances between firms with current excess resources and capabilities and those with promising capabilities help companies compete in fast-cycle markets to effectively transition from the present to the future and to gain rapid entry into new markets. As such, a "collaboration mindset" is paramount.[31]

The entertainment business is fast becoming a new digital marketplace as television content is now available on the Web. This has led the entertainment business into a fast-cycle market where collaboration is important not only to succeed but to survive. For example, many of the firms that have digital video content have also sought to make a profit through digital music and have had difficulties in profiting from their earlier ventures. BuzzFeed is a Web-based news source focused on 18- to 34-year-olds that receives revenue from advertisers who advertise on its Web site. It is forming a joint venture with CNN and YouTube to create a video channel on YouTube. This will help it to extend its reach to its youthful demographic. The partnership is also a response to make sure that the content on CNN's Web site is relevant to the 18 to 34 age segment. Advertisers pay BuzzFeed to create hosted-brand content that is shared over Facebook and Twitter rather than solely relying on traditional Web site banner ads. BuzzFeed will take advantage of CNN's archives of news programming such as "amazing rescue moments for miners stranded underground" to create interest for its youthful audience.[32]

### Standard-Cycle Markets

In standard-cycle markets, alliances are more likely to be made by partners that have complementary resources and capabilities. The alliances formed by airline companies are an example of standard-cycle market alliances.

When initially established decades ago, these alliances were intended to allow firms to share their complementary resources and capabilities to make it easier for passengers to fly between secondary cities in the United States and Europe. Today, airline alliances are mostly global in nature and are formed primarily so members can gain marketing clout, have opportunities to reduce costs, and have access to additional international routes.[33] Of these reasons, international expansion by having access to more international routes is the most important in that these routes are the path to increased revenues and potential profits. To support efforts to control costs, alliance members jointly purchase some items and share facilities such as passenger gates, customer service centers, and airport passenger lounges when possible. For passengers, airline alliances "offer simpler ticketing and smoother connections on intercontinental trips as well as the chance to earn and redeem frequent-flier miles on other member carriers."[34]

There are three major airline alliances operating today. Star Alliance is the largest with 28 members. With 12 members, Oneworld Alliance is the smallest while the 13-member SkyTeam Alliance has one more member. Given the geographic areas where markets are growing, these global alliances are adding partners from Asia. For example, in recent years, China Southern Airlines and China Eastern Airlines joined the SkyTeam Alliance, Air China and Shenzhen Airlines were added to the Star Alliance, and Malaysia Airlines joined OneWorld. In general, most airline alliances such as the ones we've described are formed to help firms gain economies of scale and meet competitive challenges (see Figure 9.1).

Within these large alliances and outside them as well, airlines are also forming dyadic or bilateral alliances between partners that have complementary opportunities. For example, Qantas Airways Ltd. has formed an alliance with Emirates Airline because it allows Qantas passengers to make only one stop on their way to the United States or Europe, whereas formerly, as part of its 17-year alliance with British Airlines (a Oneworld partner), they had to make two stops to get to distant continental European destinations (flying first to London Heathrow Airport). Now they can fly directly to 30 European destinations from Dubai, plus the flight time through the Mideast is two hours shorter than through Singapore, British Airways' hub. The size and the strategic positioning of the growing Mideast airlines such as Emirates, Qatar, and Etihad have been key in reframing these global travel routes and global alliances.[35]

## 9-2 Business-Level Cooperative Strategy

A **business-level cooperative strategy** is a strategy through which firms combine some of their resources and capabilities for the purpose of creating a competitive advantage by competing in one or more product markets. As discussed in Chapter 4, business-level strategy details what the firm intends to do to gain a competitive advantage in specific product markets. Thus, the firm forms a business-level cooperative strategy when it believes that combining some of its resources and capabilities with those of one or more partners will create competitive advantages that it can't create by itself and will lead to success in a specific product market. We list the four business-level cooperative strategies in Figure 9.2.

### 9-2a Complementary Strategic Alliances

**Complementary strategic alliances** are business-level alliances in which firms share some of their resources and capabilities in complementary ways for the purpose of creating a competitive advantage.[36] Vertical and horizontal are the two dominant types of complementary strategic alliances (see Figure 9.2).

#### Vertical Complementary Strategic Alliance

In a *vertical complementary strategic alliance*, firms share some of their resources and capabilities from different stages of the value chain for the purpose of creating a competitive advantage (see Figure 9.3).[37] Oftentimes, vertical complementary alliances are formed to adapt to environmental changes;[38] sometimes the changes represent an opportunity for partnering firms to innovate while adapting.[39]

China's Mengniu Dairy Company, a large state-owned enterprise, was implicated in 2008 during China's infamous food scandals, when six infants died and over 300,000 fell

**Figure 9.2** Business-Level Cooperative Strategies

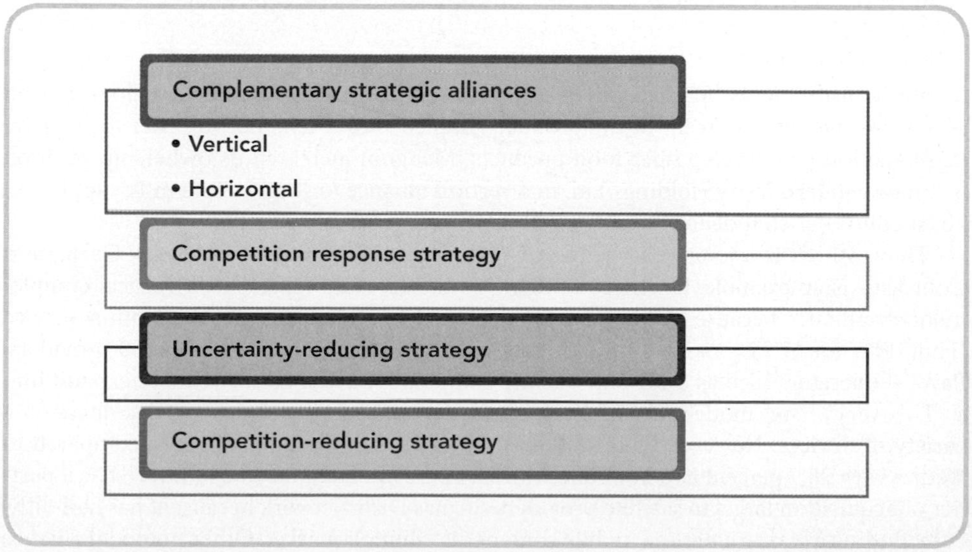

Complementary strategic alliances
- Vertical
- Horizontal

Competition response strategy

Uncertainty-reducing strategy

Competition-reducing strategy



A **business-level cooperative strategy** is a strategy through which firms combine some of their resources and capabilities for the purpose of creating a competitive advantage by competing in one or more product markets.

**Complementary strategic alliances** are business-level alliances in which firms share some of their resources and capabilities in complementary ways for the purpose of creating a competitive advantage.

**Figure 9.3** Vertical and Horizontal Complementary Strategic Alliances

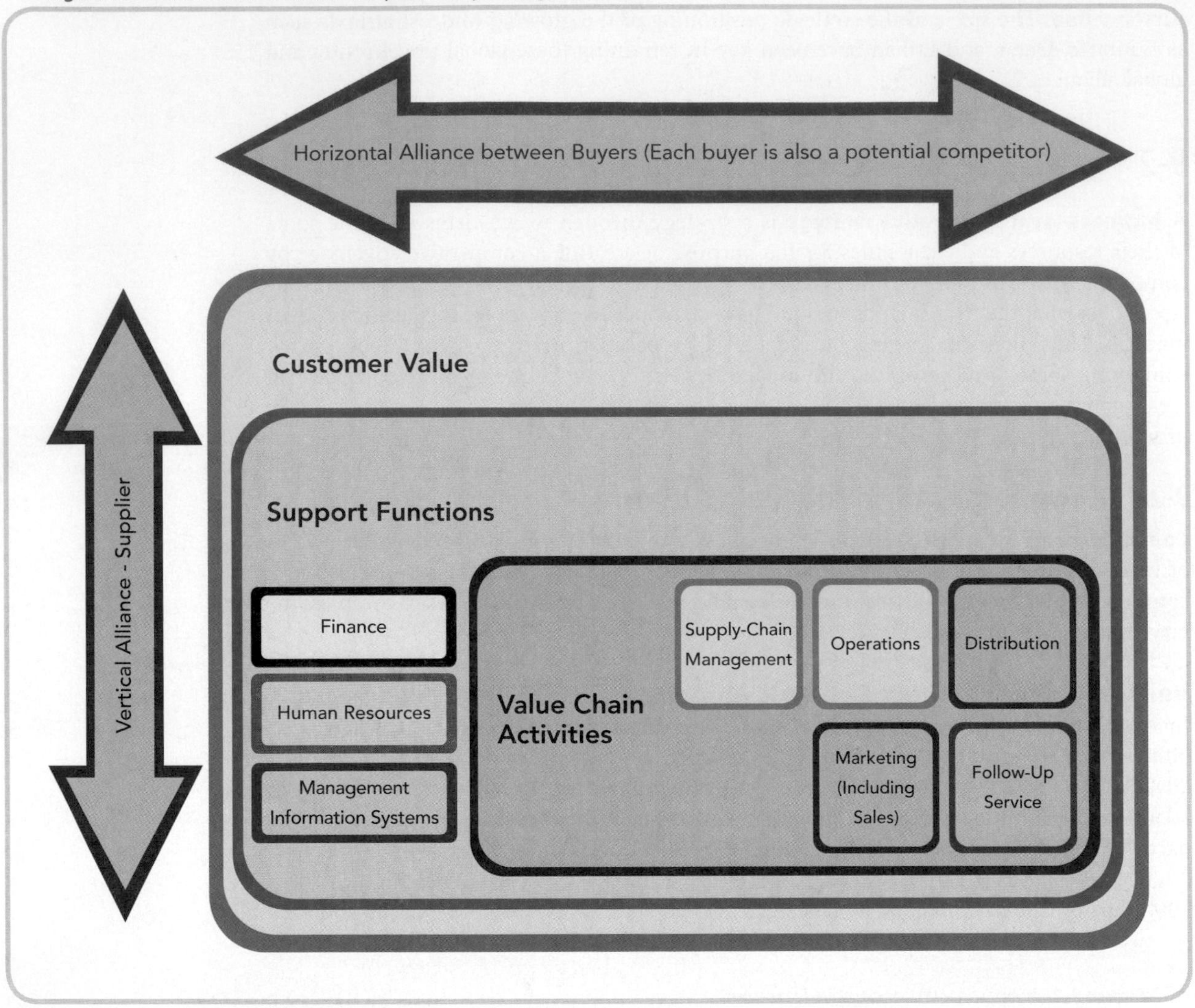

ill after consuming its branded infant formula. The chemical melamine was found as an additive in nearly 10 percent of the product sampled from Mengniu. In order to improve its reputation and develop safer food products, Mengniu increased its ownership position in China Modern Dairy Holdings Ltd. in a vertical alliance to "build a safe milk supply and boost consumer confidence."[40]

Hulu, which is a joint venture between three companies—Disney, News Corp., and Comcast—is an example. For these content producers, Hulu represents a vertical complementary alliance because Hulu is an ad-supported free platform or subscription service (Hulu Plus for $7.99 a month) to distribute video content from more than 400 providers. Pay TV operators such as cable and satellite companies have tried for years to expand into a "TV everywhere" model offering live and on-demand programming to subscribers on a variety of devices. However, Hulu only has 2.2 percent of broadband traffic compared to Netflix with 28.9 percent and YouTube with 15.4 percent. Hulu may be of interest as a partner or acquisition target to satellite providers such as Dish Network because it has had difficulty finding a way to enter the mobile content distribution market. Other potential alliance targets might be firms like Yahoo! that are also seeking better mobile access. If a paid-TV provider (such as DISH) partners with or buys the firm, however, it would limit Hulu strategically because it would want to offer it only to its own subscribers and would thereby sacrifice much of Hulu's current revenue ($695M in 2012 split roughly evenly between advertising and subscriptions).[41]

### Horizontal Complementary Strategic Alliance

A *horizontal complementary strategic alliance* is an alliance in which firms share some of their resources and capabilities from the same stage (or stages) of the value chain for the purpose of creating a competitive advantage. Commonly, firms use complementary strategic alliances to focus on joint long-term product development and distribution opportunities.[42] As noted previously, Hulu is a joint Web site that Comcast, News Corporation, and Walt Disney Company formed for the purpose of distributing video content. Through this horizontal equity strategic alliance, the alliance's partners provide content (one vertical stage of the value chain) to Hulu for distribution (another part of the value chain).

China's Mengniu Dairy Company is also forming a horizontal complementary strategic alliance with Danone SA, a large French food producer, to produce and distribute yogurt. Danone has strong brands such as Activia yogurt and Evian water. Danone is forming a joint venture with Mengniu to jointly produce and distribute yogurt branded products. Yogurt sales in China are up significantly, and Mengniu holds 17 percent while Danone holds 1.6 percent of the Chinese market share in yogurt. The joint venture will give Danone greater access to China's growing yogurt sales, and Mengniu will "gain a foreign partner in a market where foreign brands are seen as offering higher safety standards and quality."[43]

Pharmaceutical companies form a number of horizontal alliances. For example, as health care reform takes place in the United States, large pharmaceutical firms are seeking relationships with biotechnology drug producers.[44] Bristol-Myers Squibb and AstraZeneca have formed a horizontal alliance focused on diabetes. This alliance has been strengthened recently by Bristol-Myers's acquisition of Amylin Pharmaceuticals Inc. With Amylin's platform, the AstraZeneca and Bristol-Myers Squibb alliance will provide developmental strength and the ability to overcome regulatory and commercialization hurdles.[45]

As noted in the Opening Case, many horizontal complementary strategic alliances are formed in the automobile manufacturing industry. Around the world, rivals are joining forces to improve vehicle development and improve efficiency through alliances. Ford and General Motors, two of the largest auto manufacturers in the United States, have formed a partnership to "develop a new range of 9- and 10-speed automatic transmissions for cars, crossovers, and trucks." This strategic move is driven by more stringent federal efficiency standards. Interestingly, these companies previously collaborated on a 6-speed transmission, which is now used in Ford Fusion sedans, the Edge Crossover, and Escape and Explorer SUVs. GM uses them in the Chevrolet Malibu, Traverse Cruse, and other models as well. It also sounds like 11- and 12-speed transmissions may be in the near future. As competitive innovation occurs, firms often need to join together to keep up with competitive trends. Strategic alliances are a way to do this quickly and likewise share the development costs.[46] As such, cooperative strategies of all types are instrumental to automobile manufacturers' efforts to successfully compete globally.

## 9-2b Competition Response Strategy

As discussed in Chapter 5, competitors initiate competitive actions to attack rivals and launch competitive responses to their competitors' actions. Strategic alliances can be used at the business level to respond to competitors' attacks. Because they can be difficult to reverse and expensive to operate, strategic alliances are primarily formed to take strategic rather than tactical actions and to respond to competitors' actions in a like manner.

KENNELL KRISTA/SIPA/Newscom

A woman rents a DVD at a Redbox kiosk located inside a Safeway store. Redbox and Verizon are partnering to launch a video streaming service.

Coinstar is most broadly known for its Redbox subsidiary, which has kiosks at large retail outlets (such as Walmart) and drugstores (such as Walgreens) that offer dollar-a-day DVDs or video games for rent. However, the streaming video market has been threatening Redbox's business model through competitors such as Netflix, Amazon, and Hulu. Accordingly, in 2012, Redbox signed a strategic partnership agreement with Verizon to launch a streaming video service. Verizon offers broad consumer availability and service to the partnership, while Redbox offers strong relationships with media producers and has wide distribution. It seeks to be "an affordable service that will allow all consumers across the U.S. to enjoy the new and popular entertainment they want, whenever they choose, using the media and devices they prefer." It will be a subscription-based service. Customers will initially pay $8 per month and gain online access to a catalog of older films at no extra fee and have a set of newer movies available on demand for an additional fee. Additionally, patrons will get credits for four recent releases each month from Redbox's kiosks at supermarkets and drugstores around the country.[47]

## 9-2c Uncertainty-Reducing Strategy

Firms sometimes use business-level strategic alliances to hedge against risk and uncertainty, especially in fast-cycle markets.[48] These strategies are also used where uncertainty exists, such as in entering new product markets and especially those of emerging economies.

As large global auto firms manufacture more hybrid vehicles, there is insufficient industry capacity to meet the demand for the type of batteries used in these vehicles. In turn, the lack of a sufficient supply of electric batteries creates uncertainty for automobile manufacturers. To reduce this uncertainty, auto firms are forming alliances. For example, Daimler AG of Germany buys Tesla batteries to insert into its "smart" minicar as well as its Freightliner trucks because it is confident that the batteries will be of sufficient quality.[49]

## 9-2d Competition-Reducing Strategy

Used to reduce competition, collusive strategies differ from strategic alliances in that collusive strategies are often an illegal type of cooperative strategy. Explicit collusion and tacit collusion are the two types of collusive strategies.

*Explicit collusion* exists when two or more firms negotiate directly to jointly agree about the amount to produce as well as the prices for what is produced.[50] Explicit collusion strategies are illegal in the United States and most developed economies (except in regulated industries). Accordingly, companies choosing to use explicit collusion as a strategy should recognize that competitors and regulatory bodies might challenge the acceptability of their competitive actions.

*Tacit collusion* exists when several firms in an industry indirectly coordinate their production and pricing decisions by observing each other's competitive actions and responses.[51] Tacit collusion results in production output that is below fully competitive levels and above fully competitive prices. Unlike explicit collusion, firms engaging in tacit collusion do not directly negotiate output and pricing decisions. However, research suggests that joint ventures or cooperation between two firms can lead to less competition in other markets in which both firms operate.[52]

Tacit collusion tends to be used as a competition-reducing business-level strategy in industries with a high degree of concentration, such as the airline and breakfast cereal industries. Research in the airline industry suggests that tacit collusion reduces service quality and on-time performance.[53] Firms in these industries recognize their interdependence, which means that their competitive actions and responses significantly affect competitors' behavior toward them. Understanding this interdependence and carefully observing competitors can lead to tacit collusion.

Over time, four firms—Kellogg Company (producers of Kellogg's Corn Flakes, Fruit Loops, etc.), General Mills Inc. (Cheerios, Lucky Charms, etc.), Ralcorp Holdings, now owned by ConAgra Foods (producing mostly private store brands), and Quaker Foods North America, a part of PepsiCo (Quaker Oatmeal, Cap'n Crunch, etc.)—have accounted for as much as 80 percent of sales volume in the ready-to-eat segment of the U.S. cereal market.[54] Some believe that this high degree of concentration results in prices to consumers that substantially exceed the costs companies incur to produce and sell their products. If prices are above the competitive level in this industry, it may be a possibility that the dominant firms use a tacit collusion cooperative strategy.

*Mutual forbearance* is a form of tacit collusion in which firms do not take competitive actions against rivals they meet in multiple markets. Rivals learn a great deal about each other when engaging in multimarket competition, including how to deter the effects of their rivals' competitive attacks and responses. Given what they know about each other as competitors, firms choose not to engage in what could be destructive competition in multiple product markets.[55]

In general, governments in free-market economies seek to determine how rivals can form cooperative strategies for the purpose of increasing their competitiveness without violating established regulations about competition.[56] However, this task is challenging when evaluating collusive strategies, particularly tacit ones. For example, the regulation of securities analysts through Regulation Fair Disclosure (Reg-FD) promoted more potential competition through competitive parity by eliminating privileged access to proprietary firm information as a critical source of competitive advantage. In doing so, research suggests that it led to more mutual forbearance among competing firms because they had more awareness of information possessed by their competitors, thus leading to more tacit collusion.[57] However, individual companies must analyze the effect of a competition-reducing strategy on their performance and competitiveness and decide if pursuing such a strategy is an overall facilitator of their competitive success.

## 9-2e Assessing Business-Level Cooperative Strategies

Firms use business-level cooperative strategies to develop competitive advantages that can contribute to successful positions in individual product markets. Evidence suggests that complementary business-level strategic alliances, especially vertical ones, have the greatest probability of creating a competitive advantage and possibly even a sustainable one.[58] Horizontal complementary alliances are sometimes difficult to maintain because often they are formed between firms that compete against each other at the same time they are cooperating. Renault and Nissan still compete against each other with some of their products while collaborating to produce and sell other products. In a case such as this, partnering firms may feel a "push" toward and a "pull" from alliances. Airline firms, for example, want to compete aggressively against others serving their markets and target customers. However, the need to develop scale economies and to share resources and capabilities (such as scheduling systems) dictates that alliances be formed so the firms can compete by using cooperative actions and responses while they simultaneously compete against one another through competitive actions and responses. The challenge in these instances is for each firm to find ways to create the greatest amount of value from both their competitive and cooperative actions. It seems that Nissan and Renault may have learned how to achieve this balance.

Although strategic alliances designed to respond to competition and to reduce uncertainty can also create competitive advantages, these advantages often are more temporary than those developed through complementary (both vertical and horizontal) alliances. The primary reason for this is that complementary alliances have a stronger focus on creating value than do competition-reducing and uncertainty-reducing alliances, which are formed to respond to competitors' actions or reduce uncertainty rather than to attack competitors.

Of the four business-level cooperative strategies, the competition-reducing strategy has the lowest probability of creating a competitive advantage. For example, research suggests that firms following a foreign direct investment strategy using alliances as a follow-the-leader imitation approach may not have strong strategic or learning goals. Thus, such investment could be attributable to tacit collusion among the participating firms rather than trying to develop a competitive advantage (which should be the core objective).

## 9-3 Corporate-Level Cooperative Strategy

A **corporate-level cooperative strategy** is a strategy through which a firm collaborates with one or more companies for the purpose of expanding its operations. The alliance between Choice Hotels International and Bluegreen Corp. mentioned earlier is a corporate-level strategic alliance because it goes across the business-level hotel divisions of Choice and the subsidiaries of Bluegreen Corp. This alliance diversifies the lodging offering of both firms. Diversifying alliances, synergistic alliances, and franchising are the most commonly used corporate-level cooperative strategies (see Figure 9.4).

Firms use diversifying and synergistic alliances to improve their performance by diversifying their operations through a means other than or in addition to internal organic growth or a merger or acquisition.[59] When a firm seeks to diversify into markets in which the host nation's government prevents mergers and acquisitions, alliances become an especially appropriate option. Corporate-level strategic alliances are also attractive compared with mergers, and particularly acquisitions, because they require fewer resource commitments[60] and permit greater flexibility in terms of efforts to diversify partners' operations.[61] An alliance can be used as a way to determine whether the partners might benefit from a future merger or acquisition between them. This "testing" process often characterizes alliances formed to combine firms' unique technological resources and capabilities.[62]

### 9-3a Diversifying Strategic Alliance

A **diversifying strategic alliance** is a strategy in which firms share some of their resources and capabilities to engage in product and/or geographic diversification. The Strategic Focus on Samsung Electric discusses how Samsung uses diversifying alliances for a number of purposes, including reducing its dependence on Google's Android operating system for

A **corporate-level cooperative strategy** is a strategy through which a firm collaborates with one or more companies for the purpose of expanding its operations.

A **diversifying strategic alliance** is a strategy in which firms share some of their resources and capabilities to engage in product and/or geographic diversification.

**Figure 9.4** Corporate-Level Cooperative Strategies

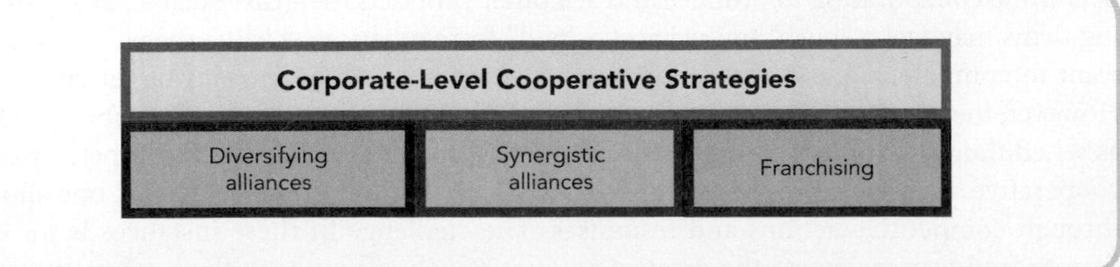

Strategic Focus TECHNOLOGY

## Samsung Electric Is Using Diversifying Alliances to Reduce Its Dependence on Google's Android Operating System

Samsung signaled that it will start selling mobile phones featuring a new operating system called Tizen that is backed by Intel Corp. This appears to be a strategy to reduce its alliance on Google's Android operating system (OS), especially after the Internet search company acquired handset maker Motorola, who could potentially be a competitor for Samsung. The Tizen association (a strategic partnership) was formed in 2012 by executives from Intel, Samsung, NTT DOCOMO Inc., and Vodafone Group PLC to support an open-source software association, which has led to the Tizen operating system being available for mobile devices. Because Google is devoting more attention to producing mobile hardware devices as its rivalry with Apple accelerates, this has led to a reaction by Samsung, Intel, and others to make sure they are not too dependent upon any one operating system.

*A Google Nexus 7 digital tablet. Samsung is partnering with other firms to develop a new operating system that will reduce its reliance on Google's Android OS.*

Samsung and Mozilla are also developing a strategic alliance to build a new mobile Web browser. It will be based on Android and ARM software architecture, and will be called Servo. It's interesting to know that Mozilla is hard at work on developing a mobile operating system. Again, it seems that Samsung is concerned about being overly dependent on Google's Android system even though it shipped 215.8 million handsets in 2012 using this operating system (OS). Furthermore, it has captured nearly 40 percent of the global market share in smartphones, so why would it be bothered with developing an alternative browser to Google Chrome as well as possibly pursuing a new mobile operating system? Additional evidence of this diversification is that Samsung intends to produce mobile devices managed by Microsoft's Windows phone OS. Again, it is seen by one analyst as a hedge against the company's overdependence on Android: "Samsung continues to have a strategic weakness in its reliance on an ecosystem that the company does not own."

Samsung also uses alliances to develop global industry standardization for products that provide reduced costs across the industry. For instance, in 2012 it established "an alliance for wireless power (A4WP) initialized between Qualcomm Inc. and Samsung Group to promote global standardization of a wireless power transfer technology, which could be utilized for cell phones, electric vehicles, and other devices." This is more of a technology alliance where the full use of technology is unknown at the start of the alliance. The partners hope that the commercialization of the technology that they jointly develop will create an industry-wide standard. Jointly developing technology suggests that it will more likely be adopted across the industry rather than if it is created by a single player.

Samsung is also developing partnerships to help sell its hardware. For instance, Samsung has developed a strategic partnership with Houghton Mifflin Harcourt Publishing Co. (HMH) through its Samsung Electronics America Inc. subsidiary. It will partner with HMH to develop "educational content and solutions on the Android-powered tablet device of Samsung." This partnership will help power technology transformation in schools in the use of educational text material. Likewise, the partnership will help promote Samsung Android-powered tablets in schools and will provide schools with "special pricing, services, and support" besides helping them to implement their mobile education goals. The Samsung devices will use the "learning hub," an exclusive Samsung platform for educational content which is available worldwide.

As can be seen from these examples, Samsung is using alliances to diversify away from its dependence on the Android OS and also to have an edge in selling new devices based on new operating systems if they become popular. Likewise, it is using alliances to develop new sources of components, such as an alliance for wireless power, and new sources of distribution, such as its alliance with HMH. As such, it uses alliances as a form of corporate strategy to diversify among various operating systems to sell devices as well as for relationships with suppliers of parts and software (Mozilla) and distributors (HMH).

Sources: 2013, HMH partners with Samsung, *Educational Marketer*, February 11, 1–7; J. Lee, 2013, Samsung to sell Tizen-based handsets after Motorola deal, *Bloomberg*, www.bloomberg.com, January 3; J. Paczkowski, 2013, Samsung buddies up with Mozilla on new Android browser tech, *All Things D*, www.allthingsd.com, April 3; J. Paczkowski, 2013, Samsung plans multiple Tizen smartphones for 2013, *All Things D*, www.allthingsd.com, January 3; 2012, Samsung, Qualcomm establish wireless charging alliance, *Energy Daily*, May 14, 4.

Learn more about Houghton Mifflin Harcourt Publishing Co., another company in partnership with Samsung.
www.cengagebrain.com

mobile phones after Google purchased a potential competitor, Motorola. Also, Samsung is diversifying with the opportunity to get new hardware parts as well as major software inputs such as Mozilla browsers instead of being dependent on Google Chrome. Likewise, it is diversifying its ability to distribute its products to new customers such as schools through an alliance with a publisher, Houghton Mifflin Harcourt Publishing Co.[63]

## 9-3b Synergistic Strategic Alliance

A **synergistic strategic alliance** is a strategy in which firms share some of their resources and capabilities to create economies of scope. Similar to the business-level horizontal complementary strategic alliance, synergistic strategic alliances create synergy across multiple functions or multiple businesses between partner firms. The Renault-Nissan collaboration we discussed in the Opening Case is a synergistic strategic alliance in that among other outcomes, the firms seek to create economies of scope by sharing their resources and capabilities to develop manufacturing platforms that can be used to produce cars that will be either a Renault or a Nissan branded product. The cooperative arrangement between Fiat and Chrysler is also a synergistic alliance. It is interesting to note that corporate synergistic alliances can be carried out at the same time as their "twin", complementary alliances at the business-unit level. For instance, Fiat has also a signed a partnership deal with Mazda "to supply the Mazda Miata roadster as the foundation for a new Alfa Romeo sports car, taking a high-profile step forward in its fight to survive in a world of global giants."[64] Without economies of scope such as those between Fiat and Chrysler and between Fiat and Mazda at the business level, the probability of success for all companies involved is reduced.

## 9-3c Franchising

**Franchising** is a strategy in which a firm (the franchisor) uses a franchise as a contractual relationship to describe and control the sharing of its resources and capabilities with its partners (the franchisees).[65] A *franchise* is a "contractual agreement between two legally independent companies whereby the franchisor grants the right to the franchisee to sell the franchisor's product or do business under its trademarks in a given location for a specified period of time."[66] Often, success is determined in these strategic alliances by how well the franchisor can replicate its success across multiple partners in a cost-effective way.[67]

Franchising is a popular strategy. Recent estimates are that in the United States alone, the gross domestic product of all franchised businesses is approximately $1.2 trillion (this is about one-third of all sales generated in the United States) and that there are more than 828,000 individual franchise store locations employing a total of 18 million people.[68] Already frequently used in developed nations, franchising is also expected to account for significant portions of growth in emerging economies in the twenty-first century.[69] As with diversifying and synergistic strategic alliances, franchising is an alternative to pursuing growth through mergers and acquisitions. McDonald's, Choice Hotels International, Hilton International, Marriott International, Mrs. Fields Cookies, Subway, and Ace Hardware are well-known firms using the franchising corporate-level cooperative strategy.

Franchising is a particularly attractive strategy to use in fragmented industries, such as retailing, hotels and motels, and commercial printing. In fragmented industries, a large number of small and medium-sized firms compete as rivals; however, no firm or small set of firms has a dominant share, making it possible for a company to gain a large market share by consolidating independent companies through the contractual relationships that are a part of a franchise agreement.

In the most successful franchising strategy, the partners (the franchisor and the franchisees) work closely together.[70] A primary responsibility of the franchisor is to develop programs to transfer the knowledge and skills to the franchisees that are needed to successfully compete at the local level.[71] In return, franchisees should provide feedback to the franchisor

A **synergistic strategic alliance** is a strategy in which firms share some of their resources and capabilities to create economies of scope.

**Franchising** is a strategy in which a firm (the franchisor) uses a franchise as a contractual relationship to describe and control the sharing of its resources and capabilities with its partners (the franchisees).

M. Stasy

regarding how their units could become more effective and efficient.[72] Working cooperatively, the franchisor and its franchisees find ways to strengthen the core company's brand name, which is often the most important competitive advantage for franchisees operating in their local markets.[73]

### 9-3d Assessing Corporate-Level Cooperative Strategies

Costs are incurred to implement each type of cooperative strategy.[74] Compared with their business-level counterparts, corporate-level cooperative strategies commonly are broader in scope and more complex, making them relatively more challenging and costly to use.

In spite of these costs, firms can create competitive advantages and value for customers by effectively using corporate-level cooperative strategies.[75] Internalizing successful alliance experiences makes it more likely that the strategy will attain the desired advantages. In other words, those involved with forming and using corporate-level cooperative strategies can also use them to develop useful knowledge about how to succeed in the future. To gain maximum value from this knowledge, firms should organize it and verify that it is always properly distributed to those involved with forming and using alliances.

We explain in Chapter 6 that firms answer two questions when dealing with corporate-level strategy—in which businesses and product markets will the firm choose to compete and how will those businesses be managed? These questions are also answered as firms form corporate-level cooperative strategies. Thus, firms able to develop corporate-level cooperative strategies and manage them in ways that are valuable, rare, imperfectly imitable, and nonsubstitutable (see Chapter 3) develop a competitive advantage that is in addition to advantages gained through the activities completed to implement business-level cooperative strategies. (Later in the chapter, we further describe alliance management as another potential competitive advantage.)

## 9-4 International Cooperative Strategy

The new competitive landscape finds firms using cross-border transactions for several purposes. In Chapter 7, we discussed cross-border acquisitions, actions through which a company located in one country acquires a firm located in a different country. In Chapter 8, we described how firms use cross-border acquisitions as a way of entering international markets. Here in Chapter 9, we examine cross-border strategic alliances as a type of international cooperative strategy. Thus, firms engage in cross-border activities to achieve several related objectives.

A **cross-border strategic alliance** is a strategy in which firms with headquarters in different countries decide to combine some of their resources and capabilities for the purpose of creating a competitive advantage. Taking place in virtually all industries, the number of cross-border alliances firms are completing continues to increase.[76] These alliances are sometimes formed instead of mergers and acquisitions, which can be riskier. Even though cross-border alliances can themselves be complex and hard to manage,[77] they have the potential to help firms use some of their resources and capabilities to create value in locations outside their home market.

Limited domestic growth opportunities and foreign government economic policies are key reasons firms use cross-border alliances. As discussed in Chapter 8, local ownership is an important national policy objective in some nations. In India and China, for example, governmental policies reflect a strong preference to license local companies. Thus, in some countries, the full range of entry mode choices we described in Chapter 8 may not be available to firms seeking to geographically diversify into a number of international markets. Indeed, investment by foreign firms in these instances may be allowed only through a partnership

A **cross-border strategic alliance** is a strategy in which firms with headquarters in different countries decide to combine some of their resources and capabilities for the purpose of creating a competitive advantage.

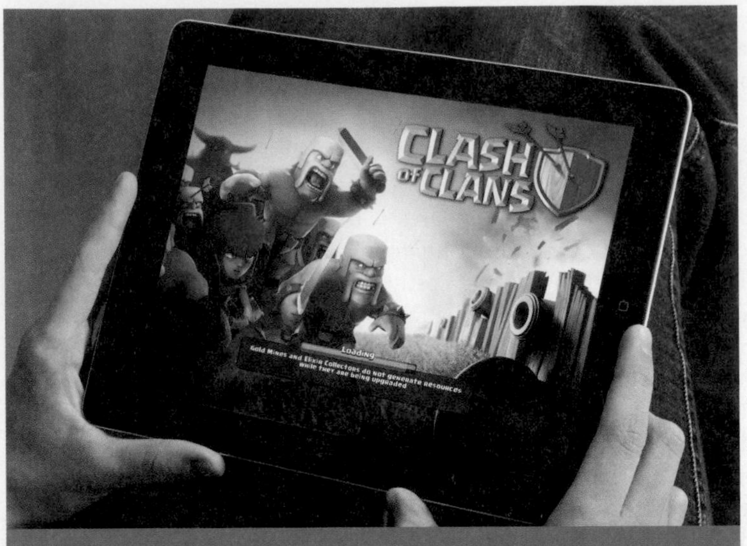


IanDagnall Computing/Alamy

*Playing Supercell's popular free game "Clash of Clans" on a 4th generation iPad. Through a cross-border strategic alliance with GungHo Online Entertainment, Inc., the game will be exposed to 14 million potential users in Japan.*

with a local firm, such as in a cross-border alliance. Important too is the fact that strategic alliances with local partners can help firms overcome certain liabilities of moving into a foreign country, including those related to a lack of knowledge of the local culture or institutional norms.[78] A cross-border strategic alliance can also help foreign partners from an operational perspective, because the local partner has significantly more information about factors contributing to competitive success such as local markets, sources of capital, legal procedures, and politics.[79] Interestingly, research results suggest that firms with foreign operations have longer survival rates than domestic-only firms, although this is reduced if there are competition problems between foreign subsidiaries.[80]

A cross-border alliance has been struck between Japan's GungHo Online Entertainment, Inc. and Finland's Supercell Oy. Supercell's "Clash of Clans" ranked as one of the top grossing apps in Apple's App Store for iPhone and iPad apps in 112 countries. Likewise, "Puzzle & Dragons" surpassed Nintendo's "Super Mario Brothers" in number of players in Japan. Each company hopes to win new users through this strategic alliance for their respective products. In Japan, piggybacking on several firms' mobile games isn't unusual, but outside of Japan's game firms it is more unusual. The agreement will include a "Clash of Clans" dungeon theme in GungHo's game, while a banner illustrated by "Puzzle & Dragons" characters will appear in Supercell's game. For Supercell, which plans to open an office in Japan in 2013, the initial campaign of the alliance will allow it to be exposed to 14 million new possible users who currently play "Puzzle & Dragons" in Japan. The idea is to help each company market where the other is weak. Furthermore, they might work together on similar marketing efforts in the future. Both firms have a similar philosophy "to put fun and creativity first."[81]

In general, cross-border strategic alliances are more complex and risky than domestic strategic alliances, especially when used in emerging economies. However, the fact that firms competing internationally tend to outperform domestic-only competitors suggests the importance of learning how to geographically diversify into international markets. Compared with mergers and acquisitions, cross-border alliances may be a better way to learn this process, especially in the early stages of a firm's geographic diversification efforts.

## 9-5 Network Cooperative Strategy

In addition to forming their own alliances with individual companies, an increasing number of firms are collaborating in multiple alliances called networks.[82] A **network cooperative strategy** is a strategy wherein several firms agree to form multiple partnerships for the purpose of achieving shared objectives.

A **network cooperative strategy** is a strategy wherein several firms agree to form multiple partnerships for the purpose of achieving shared objectives.

Through its Global Partner Network, Cisco has formed alliances with a host of individual companies including IBM, Microsoft, Infosys, Emerson, Fujitsu, Intel, and Nokia. According to Cisco, partnering allows a firm to "drive growth and differentiate (its) business by extending (its) capabilities to meet customer requirements."[83] Demonstrating the complexity of network cooperative strategies is the fact that Cisco also competes against a number of the firms with whom it has formed cooperative agreements. For example, Cisco is competing against IBM as it now sells and services servers. At the same time, Cisco and IBM's alliance is very active as the firms seek to help customers integrate "a broad range of industry-specific expertise and cutting-edge solutions, all based on respective core competencies in foundational technology architectures, software and services."[84] Overall, in spite of their complexity, the IBM/Cisco example shows how firms are using network cooperative strategies more extensively as a way of creating value for customers by offering many goods and services in many geographic (domestic and international) markets.

A network cooperative strategy is particularly effective when it is formed by geographically clustered firms,[85] as in California's Silicon Valley (where "the culture of Silicon Valley encourages collaborative webs"[86]). Effective social relationships and interactions among partners while sharing their resources and capabilities make it more likely that a network cooperative strategy will be successful,[87] as does having a productive *strategic center firm* (we discuss strategic center firms in detail in Chapter 11). Firms involved in networks gain information and knowledge from multiple sources. They can use these heterogeneous knowledge sets to produce more and better innovation. As a result, firms involved in networks of alliances tend to be more innovative.[88] However, there are disadvantages to participating in networks as a firm can be locked into its partnerships, precluding the development of alliances with others. In certain network configurations, such as Japanese *keiretsus*, firms in a network are expected to help other firms in that network whenever support is required. Such expectations can become a burden and negatively affect the focal firm's performance over time.[89] The Strategic Focus discusses industry clusters, with such geographic districts forming to focus on storage facilities for cloud computing and genomic research.

Find out more about the Human Genome Project.
www.cengagebrain.com

A new industrial district in China is focused on auto manufacturing. Volkswagen recently signed an $862 million deal to establish a gearbox production based in the Tianjin economic-technological development area (TEDA). This is a government-backed industrial park in Tianjin, a port city in China, about an hour away from Beijing by high-speed train. This is the initial investment, with a target of 450,000 units of production by 2014. Ultimately, they expect the total annual capacity to be 1.35 million units, with more than $4.8 billion invested. Other auto manufacturers in TEDA include Toyota, Great Wall Motors (which is China's top automotive exporter), and Xingma and Qingyuan (both of which make electric-powered vehicles). In 2010, 500,000 cars were manufactured in TEDA, a figure that TEDA hopes will increase to about 1.2 million by 2015. Furthermore, the park is setting up to increase suppliers who contribute parts to Toyota and Hyundai.[90] Within these districts, it is more likely that firms will become part of specific networks.

## 9-5a Alliance Network Types

An important advantage of a network cooperative strategy is that firms gain access to their partners' other partners. Having access to multiple collaborations increases the likelihood that additional competitive advantages will be formed as the set of shared resources and capabilities expands.[91] In turn, being able to develops new capabilities further stimulates product innovations that are critical to strategic competitiveness in the global economy.

The set of strategic alliance partnerships firms develop when using a network cooperative strategy is called an *alliance network*. Companies' alliance networks vary by industry characteristics. A *stable alliance network* is formed in mature industries where demand is relatively constant and predictable. Through a stable alliance network, firms try to extend their competitive advantages to other settings while continuing to profit from operations in their core, relatively mature industry. Thus, stable networks are built primarily to *exploit* the economies (scale and/or scope) that exist between the partners, such as in the airline and automobile industries.[92]

M. Stasy

# Strategic Focus GLOBALIZATION

## Industrial Clusters: Geographic Centers for Collaborative Partnering

Clusters or *industrial districts* are geographic concentrations of a set of interconnected companies, often with specialized suppliers and service providers, and with education, government and trade association institutions focused on a particular industrial sector and agglomerated in a specific geographic region. Often these clusters begin because they increase company productivity, enabling them to lower costs and facilitate innovation. Developing such regions is important to government officials looking to increase economic development, as well as for companies seeking to co-locate with other reputable companies often with government tax incentives and institutions, such as universities to facilitate training of students with increased employment opportunities for graduates.

Research, in fact, shows that where there is cluster-driven agglomeration, there is also higher employment growth and higher wage growth, growth in the number of new establishments, and an increase in innovation and patenting. The strength of a dominant cluster, such as Silicon Valley, also strengthens related clusters in the region and adjacent regions. Often new industries emerge where there is a strong cluster environment. As such, there is good reason why governments are interested in incenting strong cluster growth in their geographic area.

For instance, African nations are increasingly seeking economic growth, and some have used innovation hubs to accelerate startup company growth. Kenya, for example, has over 40 percent of its population living on $2 a day, and political corruption, crippling droughts, and power outages have plagued the country. However, the Kenyan government revised its constitution in 2010 to create more transparency and better institutions supporting business. As such, a number of high-tech companies have sought to develop an iHub in downtown Nairobi, with supporting partners from Intel, Samsung, Google, Microsoft, and others in the cluster. It has also created mLab and NaiLab as incubators to foster growth-oriented startups focused on mobile software and hardware applications.

Research, however, suggests that such clusters or hubs have been implemented around the world, with varied results. Studies indicate that specializing in one area of R&D without added diversification often leads to eventual failure. As such, clusters with businesses, suppliers, think tanks, universities, multiple industries, and trade associations co-located in an industrial park or innovation cluster work best for stimulating economic growth and innovation. Accordingly, companies with a variety of purposes and specializations co-located with network suppliers, customers, and support services facilitate new and more innovative products and services and thus are more successful.

*U.S. National Human Genome Research Institute Director Francis Collins at a press conference in Bethesda, Maryland, announcing that a six-country consortium has successfully mapped the human genome. Geographic clusters are now being developed around the world to create a database of genetic information.*

Sometimes these clusters are driven by specific regional geographic strengths. For example, large data storage centers for high-tech companies using cloud resources have located such centers in Prineville, The Dalles, and other small towns in Oregon. Such locations in Oregon allow for more natural cooling of such large computer systems. Facebook executive Jay Park states that Prineville is "an ideal location for the crew and system Facebook uses for its data storage center." Other locations were chosen for more idiosyncratic reasons. Microsoft and the software cluster associated with it in Seattle was located there because Bill Gates, Microsoft's founder, was born in Seattle.

Research suggests that workers who began their career in industrial hub locations, such as people in the hedge fund industry who previously worked in New York and London, outperformed their peers once they leave these districts. As such, there is an individual effect on the human capital development in these industrial hubs. Furthermore, research also suggests that there is a collective impact on the firms that are in centralized positions (that is, have connections to more firms, suppliers, and customers in the industrial district); the more central firms have more and better innovation. Those who connect firms to each other (bridging ties) have a positive impact on innovation, but not as impactful as those that are more centralized in the hub.

Geographic clusters are being developed around the world focused on creating a vast database of genetic information. It took nearly 13 years and almost $14 million in government and private funding for the Human Genome Project to complete the first map of a person's genome. Now, for $1,000, a company in Iceland will chart your genetic propensities for 47 different diseases and traits. New preventative measures from this project "will save patients, insurers, and employers money, and studies project genomic medicine will generate $350 billion worth of economic activity and millions of jobs." But the industry is a long way from the ability to fully utilize the data encoded in our chromosomes. The question is, where will the various clusters be found around the world? There are a number in the United States and Canada—one in Vancouver, British Columbia, and one around La Jolla, California. The one at La Jolla includes the University of California-San Diego, the Salk Institute, the Scripps Research Institute, the Venter Institute, Synthetic Genomics, and 30 or 40 companies all within a few square miles and all using genomic methods and research. There is also a cluster growing in the Boston area, the Cambridge area in the United Kingdom, and the Genomics Institute in Beijing, China. Thus, the history of industrial districts is positive overall, and they are now being planned with more precision.

Sources: C. Casanueva, I. Castro, & J. L. Galán, 2013, Information networks and innovation in mature industrial clusters, *Journal of Business Research*, 66(5): 603–613; R. J. P. De Figueiredo, P. Meyer-Doyle, & E. Rawley, 2013, Inherited agglomeration effects in hedge fund spawns, *Strategic Management Journal*, 34(7): 843–862; L. Dobusch & E. Schübler, 2013, Theorizing path dependence: A review of positive feedback mechanisms in technology markets, regional clusters, and organizations, *Industrial & Corporate Change*, 22(3): 617–647; E. Francis, 2013, Building an auto industry hub through value creation, *Automotive Industries*, January, 111–112; G. Holden, 2013, Kenya's fertile ground for tech innovation, *Research Technology Management*, 56(3): 7–8; H. Milanov & D. A. Shepherd, 2013, The importance of the first relationship: The ongoing influence of initial network on future status, *Strategic Management Journal*, 34(6): 727–750; 2012, Not a cloud in sight, *Economist*, October 27, 19–20; F. Ghadar, J. Sviokla, & D. A. Stephan, 2012, Why life science needs its own Silicon Valley, *Harvard Business Review*, 90(7/8): 25–27.

*Dynamic alliance networks* are used in industries characterized by frequent product innovations and short product life cycles.[93] For instance, the pace of innovation in the information technology (IT) industry (as well as other fast-cycle market industries) is too fast for any one company to be successful across time if it only competes independently. Another example is the movie industry, an industry in which firms participate in a number of networks for the purpose of producing and distributing movies. Also, as the alliance between Syfy Cable Network and Trion Worlds to create a simultaneous TV show and associated video game based on a new TV series, "Defiance", suggests, such networks are becoming even larger and more dynamic.[94] In dynamic alliance networks, partners typically *explore* new ideas and possibilities with the potential to lead to product innovations, entries to new markets, and the development of new markets. Research suggests that firms that help to broker relationships between firms remain important network participants as these networks change.[95] Often, large firms in industries such as software and pharmaceuticals create networks of relationships with smaller entrepreneurial startup firms in their search for innovation-based outcomes.[96] An important outcome for small firms successfully partnering with larger firms in an alliance network is the credibility they build by being associated with their larger collaborators.[97]

Network strategies of multiple partners affect the overall success of many firms. For instance, a network set of alliances formed by Samsung and Sony with suppliers, sales channels, and R&D partners from 2008 to 2011 illustrates this point. Samsung is at the center of a network with a variety of diverse partners such as Dreamworks and KT, "which do interesting things with 3-D technologies but don't typically work together." Samsung is well-placed within its network of firms to look at the future because it provides many parts for many firms, such as for Apple's iPhone, even though it competes with Apple with its own Galaxy X4 phone. For instance, the Galaxy X4 has "cutting-edge gesture- and eye-tracking features."[98]

On the other hand, Sony, a large, diversified firm, also has a web of allies, including Sharp and Toshiba, that work together. Although its allies are highly integrated with Sony, the network is less likely to yield breakthrough innovations because it is less exposed to a diverse set of partners in new areas. In dynamic networks with high levels of strategic change, it provides an advantage if a firm is at the center of a hub and spoke network. In integrated stable networks, small firms can be helped when there are external shocks to the network because the relationships help them in a downturn. But such stable integrated networks are less likely to yield breakthrough product ideas.[99]

One of the reasons that Tesla, a manufacturer of plug-in electric vehicles, has been successful when others such as Fisker have failed is its efforts to partner with other firms as it developed its new models, facilitating not only its survival but its success. Of course, Tesla's new Model S sedan is a very impressive vehicle and has won *Motor Trend* and *Automobile* magazine awards as well as strong reviews from *Consumer Reports*. Tesla's founder and CEO, Elon Musk, has degrees in physics and business and has already started and sold a successful company, PayPal, and runs SpaceX, a maker of rockets and spacecraft. As such, he has the ability and connections to partner with other firms. This allowed him to get a strong bevy of investors who often are also partners. Daimler AG of Germany buys Tesla batteries to insert into its "smart" minicar as well as its Freightliner trucks. Likewise, it also invested $50 million in the company. Also, Toyota partnered with Tesla to develop its next-generation RAV4 plug-in electric vehicle offering, and likewise invested $50 million. Accordingly, one of the reasons for Tesla's survival when others have failed is the ability to get support from other partners, which has allowed it to survive and succeed.[100]

## 9-6 Competitive Risks with Cooperative Strategies

Stated simply, many cooperative strategies fail. In fact, evidence shows that two-thirds of cooperative strategies have serious problems in their first two years and that as many as 50 percent of them fail. This failure rate suggests that even when the partnership has potential complementarities and synergies, alliance success is elusive.[101] Although failure is undesirable, it can be a valuable learning experience, meaning that firms should carefully study a cooperative strategy's failure to gain insights with respect to how to form and manage future cooperative arrangements.[102] We show prominent cooperative strategy risks in Figure 9.5.

**Figure 9.5** Managing Competitive Risks in Cooperative Strategies

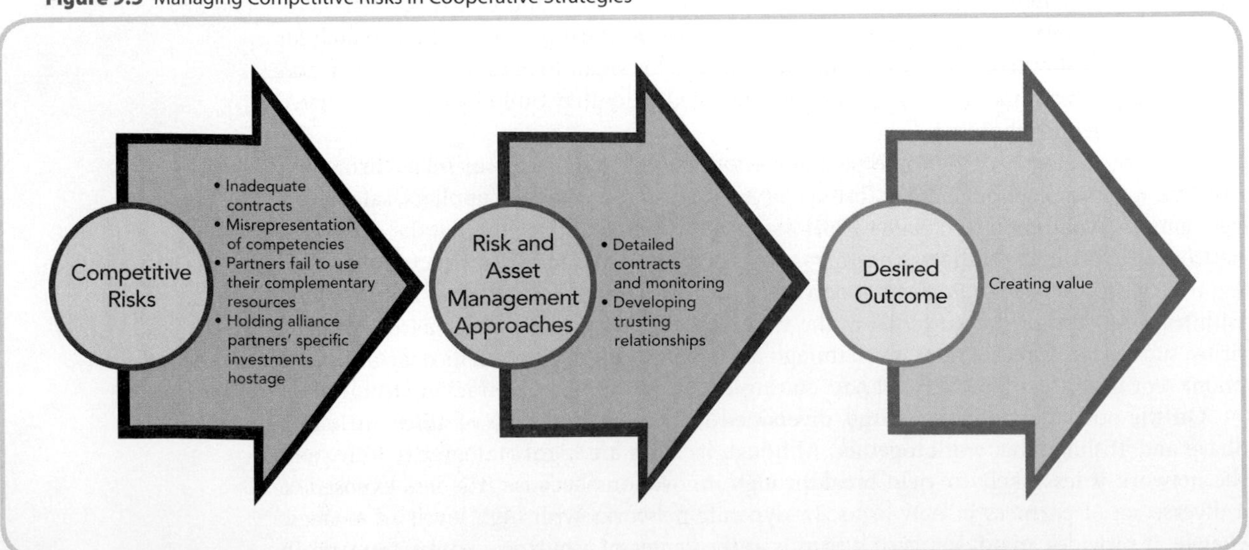

One cooperative strategy risk is that a firm may act in a way that its partner thinks is opportunistic. BP plc and OAO Rosneft developed a joint venture to explore Russia's Arctic Ocean in search of oil. However, the investment by minority partners of this joint venture was driven down in value at one point by 50 percent over concern that the Russian government, Rosneft's dominant owner, would expropriate value from the deal.[103] In general, opportunistic behaviors surface either when formal contracts fail to prevent them or when an alliance is based on a false perception of partner trustworthiness. Not infrequently, the opportunistic firm wants to acquire as much of its partner's tacit knowledge as it can.[104] Full awareness of what a partner wants in a cooperative strategy reduces the likelihood that a firm will suffer from another's opportunistic actions.[105]

Some cooperative strategies fail when it is discovered that a firm has misrepresented the competencies it can bring to the partnership. This risk is more common when the partner's contribution is grounded in some of its intangible assets. Superior knowledge of local conditions is an example of an intangible asset that partners often fail to deliver. An effective way to deal with this risk may be to ask the partner to provide evidence that it does possess the resources and capabilities (even when they are largely intangible) it will share in the cooperative strategy.[106]

A firm's failure to make available to its partners the resources and capabilities (such as the most sophisticated technologies) that it committed to the cooperative strategy is a third risk. For example, the effectiveness of a recently formed collaboration between BP plc and OAO Rosneft (the state-controlled Russian oil company) is dependent on each firm contributing some of its seismic and drilling-related resources and capabilities as the foundation for efforts to develop three areas in the Arctic Ocean.[107] A failure by either partner to contribute needed resources and capabilities to this alliance has the potential to diminish the likelihood of success. This particular risk surfaces most commonly when firms form an international cooperative strategy, especially in emerging economies.[108] In these instances, different cultures and languages can cause misinterpretations of contractual terms or trust-based expectations.

A final risk is that one firm may make investments that are specific to the alliance while its partner does not. For example, the firm might commit resources and capabilities to develop manufacturing equipment that can be used only to produce items coming from the alliance. If the partner isn't also making alliance-specific investments, the firm is at a relative disadvantage in terms of returns earned from the alliance compared with investments made to earn the returns.

## 9-7 Managing Cooperative Strategies

Cooperative strategies are an important means of firm growth and enhanced performance, but these strategies are difficult to effectively manage. Because the ability to effectively manage cooperative strategies is unevenly distributed across organizations in general, assigning managerial responsibility for a firm's cooperative strategies to a high-level executive or to a team improves the likelihood that the strategies will be well managed. In turn, being able to successfully manage cooperative strategies can itself be a competitive advantage.[109]

Those responsible for managing the firm's cooperative strategies should take the actions necessary to coordinate activities, categorize knowledge learned from previous experiences, and make certain that what the firm knows about how to effectively form and use cooperative strategies is in the hands of the right people at the right time. Firms must also learn how to manage both the tangible and intangible assets (such as knowledge) that are involved with a cooperative arrangement. Too often, partners concentrate on managing tangible assets at the expense of taking action to also manage a cooperative relationship's intangible assets.[110]

Cost minimization and opportunity maximization are the two primary approaches firms use to manage cooperative strategies[111] (see Figure 9.5). In the *cost-minimization* approach, the firm develops formal contracts with its partners. These contracts specify how the cooperative strategy is to be monitored and how partner behavior is to be controlled. The alliance mentioned earlier between Ford and General Motors to develop transmissions at a lower cost for each firm is based on such a contractual relationship. Thus it appears that at least at the outset, the cost-minimization approach is being used to manage this alliance. The goal of the cost-minimization approach is to minimize the cooperative strategy's cost and to prevent opportunistic behavior by a partner.

Maximizing a partnership's value-creating opportunities is the focus of the *opportunity-maximization* approach. In this case, partners are prepared to take advantage of unexpected opportunities to learn from each other and to explore additional marketplace possibilities. Less formal contracts, with fewer constraints on partners' behaviors, make it possible for partners to explore how their resources and capabilities can be shared in multiple value-creating ways. This is the approach Renault and Nissan use to manage their collaborative relationship. The values of *trust*, *respect*, and *transparency* on which this alliance is based facilitate use of the opportunity-maximization management approach.

Firms can successfully use both approaches to manage cooperative strategies. However, the costs to monitor the cooperative strategy are greater with cost minimization, in that writing detailed contracts and using extensive monitoring mechanisms is expensive, even though the approach is intended to reduce alliance costs. Although monitoring systems may prevent partners from acting in their own best interests, they also often preclude positive responses to new opportunities that surface to productively use alliance partners' resources and capabilities. Thus, formal contracts and extensive monitoring systems tend to stifle partners' efforts to gain maximum value from their participation in a cooperative strategy and require significant resources to be put into place and used.[112]

The relative lack of detail and formality that is a part of the contract developed when using the opportunity-maximization approach means that firms need to trust that each party will act in the partnership's best interests. The psychological state of *trust* in the context of cooperative arrangements is the belief that a firm will not do anything to exploit its partner's vulnerabilities even if it has an opportunity to do so. When partners trust each other, there is less need to write detailed formal contracts to specify each firm's alliance behaviors,[113] and the cooperative relationship tends to be more stable.[114]

On a relative basis, trust tends to be more difficult to establish in international cooperative strategies than domestic ones. Differences in trade policies, cultures, laws, and politics that are part of cross-border alliances account for the increased difficulty. When trust exists, monitoring costs are reduced and opportunities to create value are maximized. Essentially, in these cases the firms have built social capital.[115] Renault and Nissan have built social capital through their alliance by building their relationship on the mutual trust between the partners as well as their adherence to operating within the framework of agreed-upon confidentiality rules.[116]

Research showing that trust between partners increases the likelihood of success when using alliances highlights the benefits of the opportunity-maximization approach to managing cooperative strategies. Trust may also be the most efficient way to influence and control alliance partners' behaviors. Research indicates that trust can be a capability that is valuable, rare, imperfectly imitable, and often nonsubstitutable.[117] Thus, firms known to be trustworthy can have a competitive advantage in terms of how they develop and use cooperative strategies. Increasing the importance of trust in alliances is the fact that it is not possible to specify all operational details of a cooperative strategy in a formal contract. As such, being confident that its partner can be trusted reduces the firm's concern about its inability to contractually control all alliance details.

## SUMMARY

- A cooperative strategy is one through which firms work together to achieve a shared objective. Strategic alliances, where firms combine some of their resources and capabilities for the purpose of creating a competitive advantage, are the primary form of cooperative strategies. Joint ventures (where firms create and own equal shares of a new venture), equity strategic alliances (where firms own different shares of a newly created venture), and nonequity strategic alliances (where firms cooperate through a contractual relationship) are the three major types of strategic alliances. Outsourcing, discussed in Chapter 3, commonly occurs as firms form nonequity strategic alliances.
- Collusive strategies are the second type of cooperative strategies (with strategic alliances being the other). In many economies, explicit collusive strategies are illegal unless sanctioned by government policies. Increasing globalization has led to fewer government-sanctioned situations of explicit collusion. Tacit collusion, also called mutual forbearance, is a cooperative strategy through which firms tacitly cooperate to reduce industry output below the potential competitive output level, thereby raising prices above the competitive level.
- The reasons firms use cooperative strategies vary by slow-cycle, fast-cycle, and standard-cycle market conditions. To enter restricted markets (slow cycle), to move quickly from one competitive advantage to another (fast cycle), and to gain market power (standard cycle) are among the reasons firms choose to use cooperative strategies.
- Four business-level cooperative strategies are used to help the firm improve its performance in individual product markets: (1) Through vertical and horizontal complementary alliances, companies combine some of their resources and capabilities to create value in different parts (vertical) or the same parts (horizontal) of the value chain. (2) Competition response strategies are formed to respond to competitors' actions, especially strategic actions. (3) Uncertainty-reducing strategies are used to hedge against the risks created by the conditions of uncertain competitive environments (such as new product markets). (4) Competition-reducing strategies are used to avoid excessive competition while the firm marshals its resources and capabilities to improve its strategic competitiveness.Complementary alliances have the highest probability of helping a firm form a competitive advantage; competition-reducing alliances have the lowest probability.
- Firms use corporate-level cooperative strategies to engage in product and/or geographic diversification. Through diversifying strategic alliances, firms agree to share some of their resources and capabilities to enter new markets or produce new products. Synergistic alliances are ones where firms share some of their resources and capabilities to develop economies of scope. Synergistic alliances are similar to business-level horizontal complementary alliances where firms try to develop operational synergy, except that synergistic alliances are used to develop synergy at the corporate level. Franchising is a corporate-level cooperative strategy where the franchisor uses a franchise as a contractual relationship to specify how resources and capabilities will be shared with franchisees.
- As an international cooperative strategy, a cross-border strategic alliance is used for several reasons, including the performance superiority of firms competing in markets outside their domestic market and governmental restrictions on a firm's efforts to grow through mergers and acquisitions. Commonly, cross-border strategic alliances are riskier than their domestic counterparts, particularly when partners aren't fully aware of each other's purpose for participating in the partnership.
- In a network cooperative strategy, several firms agree to form multiple partnerships to achieve shared objectives. A firm's opportunity to gain access "to its partner's other partnerships" is a primary benefit of a network cooperative strategy. Network cooperative strategies are used to form either a stable alliance network or a dynamic alliance network. Used in mature industries, stable networks are used to extend competitive advantages into new areas. In rapidly changing environments where frequent product innovations occur, dynamic networks are used primarily as a tool of innovation.
- Cooperative strategies aren't risk free. If a contract is not developed appropriately, or if a partner misrepresents its competencies or fails to make them available, failure is likely. Furthermore, a firm may be held hostage through asset-specific investments made in conjunction with a partner, which may be exploited.
- Trust is an increasingly important aspect of successful cooperative strategies. Firms place high value on opportunities to partner with companies known for their trustworthiness. When trust exists, a cooperative strategy is managed to maximize the pursuit of opportunities between partners. Without trust, formal contracts and extensive monitoring systems are used to manage cooperative strategies. In this case, the interest is "cost minimization" rather than "opportunity maximization."

## REVIEW QUESTIONS

1. What is the definition of cooperative strategy, and why is this strategy important to firms competing in the twenty-first century competitive landscape?
2. What is a strategic alliance? What are the three major types of strategic alliances firms form for the purpose of developing a competitive advantage?

3. What are the four business-level cooperative strategies? What are the key differences among them?
4. What are the three corporate-level cooperative strategies? How do firms use each of these strategies for the purpose of creating a competitive advantage?
5. Why do firms use cross-border strategic alliances?
6. What risks are firms likely to experience as they use cooperative strategies?
7. What are the differences between the cost-minimization approach and the opportunity-maximization approach to managing cooperative strategies?

# EXPERIENTIAL EXERCISES

## EXERCISE 1: ALLIANCE MANAGEMENT AS A PROFESSION

According to your text, "a cooperative strategy is a means by which firms collaborate for the purpose of working together to achieve a shared objective. Cooperating with other firms is a strategy firms use to create value for a customer that it likely could not create by itself." This describes the end state and not the mechanics upon which firms rely to achieve a successful alliance partnership. So is there a career in alliance management?

This is an individual assignment and one in which you can learn more about strategic alliance as a career path to compliment your budding knowledge of the field. Begin by researching strategic alliance professionals in your library and on the Internet. You should also interview a strategic alliance management professional. You can find them through either firms that undertake alliances or consulting firms that assist them. Start your research by answering the following questions:

1. Find any trade associations of organizations or professionals that are aligned with the field.
2. Does the work get done mainly through in-company personnel or consulting firms?
3. What are the benefits, and downsides, to a career in strategic alliance management?
4. Are there entry level positions or is experience required to get into the field?
5. Put together, does this profession have an appeal to you personally? Why or why not?

## EXERCISE 2: AIRLINES AND ALLIANCES

According to your text, a strategic alliance "is a partnership between firms whereby their resources and capabilities are combined to create a competitive advantage." So why is an alliance in the best interests for an airline company such as United, American, or British Airways? In this exercise, your instructor will assign one of the three main alliances (OneWorld, Star, or SkyTeam), and your teams will be asked to investigate the alliance and be prepared to discuss the following issues:

1. In general, why do airlines form an alliance with one another (particularly internationally) rather than expanding by acquisition?
2. What is the history of the alliance to which you were assigned?
3. Describe the main benefits that airlines hope to gain through membership. What is the competitive advantage of your particular alliance, if you find there is one?
4. Categorize the alliance in terms of the three types of strategic alliances. Also describe the cooperative strategy of a member firm in relation to its business-level and corporate-level strategy.
5. Think through issues of the future of airline alliances. If you were the CEO of a major U.S. airline, what might worry you about your particular alliance, if anything?

# VIDEO CASE

## A PARTNERSHIP WITH A COOPERATIVE TWIST: MICROSOFT AND YAHOO!

In its infancy, the Microsoft/Yahoo! partnership brought a cloud of layoff and market concerns, but the priority was to compete against Google for control of the Internet search market. Media and analysts predicted benefits to partners and consumers over the long term. Yahoo! remains an independent company with control of its user interface, while Microsoft added strength to its browser and gained a greater share of Internet advertising, which all provide an alternative to the Internet search market. Statistics show that Google has 66.5 percent of the Internet search market, with Yahoo! at 12 percent and Microsoft at 17.3 percent.

Be prepared to discuss the following concepts and questions in class:

## Concepts

1. Cooperative strategy
2. Strategic alliance
3. Business-level cooperative strategies
4. Corporate-level cooperative strategies

## Questions

1. What kind of competitive advantage is created through the Microsoft/Yahoo! cooperative strategy?
2. What kind of strategic alliance has occurred between Microsoft and Yahoo!? Explain your answer. For what reasons do you think they developed such an alliance?
3. Now that Microsoft and Yahoo! have partnered, what business-level cooperative strategies do you think we can expect? Why?
4. What corporate-level cooperative strategies do you think we can expect? Why?

## NOTES


1. U. Wassmer & P. Dussauge, 2012, Network resource stocks and flows: How do alliance portfolios affect the value of new alliance formations? *Strategic Management Journal*, 33(7): 871–883; G. Schreyöegg & J. Sydow, 2011, Organizing for fluidity? Dilemmas of new organizational forms, *Organization Science*, 21: 1251–1262; D. Lavie, 2009, Capturing value from alliance portfolios, *Organizational Dynamics*, 38(1): 26–36.
2. D. Lavie, P. R. Haunschild, & P. Khanna, 2012, Organizational differences, relational mechanisms, and alliance performance, *Strategic Management Journal*, 33(13): 1453–1479; H. Yang, Z. Lin, & Y. Lin, 2010, A multilevel framework of firm boundaries: Firm characteristics, dyadic differences, and network attributes, *Strategic Management Journal*, 31: 237–261.
3. J. Bennett, 2011, Dodge will test Fiat alliance, *Wall Street Journal*, www.wsj.com, June 25.
4. J. H. Dyer & W. Chu, 2011, The determinants of trust in supplier–automaker relationships in the U.S., Japan, and Korea, *Journal of International Business Studies*, 31(2): 259–285; J. H. Dyer & H. Singh, 1998, The relational view: Cooperative strategy and sources of interorganizational competitive advantage, *Academy of Management Review*, 23: 660–679.
5. J. Walter, F. W. Kellermanns, & C. Lechner, 2012, Decision making within and between organizations: Rationality, politics, and alliance performance, *Journal of Management*, 38(5): 1582–1610; R. J. Jiang, Q. T. Tao, & M. D. Santoro, 2010, Alliance portfolio diversity and firm performance, *Strategic Management Journal*, 31: 1136–1144.
6. J. Charterina & J. Landeta, 2013, Effects of knowledge-sharing routines and dyad-based investments on company innovation and performance: An empirical study of Spanish manufacturing companies, *International Journal of Management*, 30(2): 197–216; F. Lumineau, M. Fréchet, & D. Puthod, 2011, An organizational learning perspective on the contracting process, *Strategic Organization*, 9: 8–32.
7. J. L. Cummings & S. R. Holmberg, 2012, Best-fit alliance partners: The use of critical success factors in a comprehensive partner selection process, *Long Range Planning*, 45(2/3): 136–159; S. Lahiri & B. L. Kedia, 2009, The effects of internal resources and partnership quality on firm performance: An examination of Indian BPO providers, *Journal of International Management*, 15: 209–222.
8. K. H. Heimeriks & G. Duysters, 2007, Alliance capability as a mediator between experience and alliance performance: An empirical investigation into the alliance capability development process, *Journal of Management Studies*, 44: 25–49.
9. D. Leonard, 2013, Syfy's ultimate transmedia adventure, *Bloomberg Businessweek*, May 20–May 26, 19–20.
10. J. Roy, 2012, IJV partner trustworthy behaviour: The role of host country governance and partner selection criteria, *Journal of Management Studies*, 49(2): 332–355; K. H. Heimeriks, E. Klijn, & J. J. Reuer, 2009, Building capabilities for alliance portfolios, *Long Range Planning*, 42: 96–114.
11. N. Chowdhury, 2013, AIG's Asian savior, *Fortune*, January 14, 17.
12. E. Chrysostome, R. Nigam, & C. Jarilowski, 2013, Revisiting strategic learning in international joint ventures: A knowledge creation perspective, *International Journal of Management*, 30(1): 88–98; D. Tan & K. E. Meyer, 2011, Country-of-origin and industry FDI agglomeration of foreign investors in an emerging economy, *Journal of International Business Studies*, 42: 504–520.
13. B. Dumaine, 2013, Fracking comes to China, *Fortune*, April 29, 102–107.
14. L. Cui & F. Jiang, 2012, State ownership effect on firms' FDI ownership decisions under institutional pressure: A study of Chinese outward-investing firms, *Journal of International Business Studies*, 43(3): 264–284; Z. Huang, X. Han, F. Roche, & J. Cassidy, 2011, The dilemma facing strategic choice of entry mode: Multinational hotels in China, *Global Business Review*, 12: 181–192; J. Xia, J. Tan, & D. Tan, 2008, Mimetic entry and bandwagon effect: The rise and decline of international equity joint venture in China, *Strategic Management Journal*, 29: 195–217.
15. T. Varela & L. Burkitt, 2013, Club Med gets a Chinese-backed bid: Conglomerate Fosun teams with private-equity firm for a proposed buyout of French resort operator, *Wall Street Journal*, May 28, B1.
16. A. Majocchi, U. Mayrhofer, & J. Camps, 2013, Joint ventures or non-equity alliances? Evidence from Italian firms, *Management Decision*, 51(2): 380–395; T. Das & N. Rahman, 2010, Determinants of partner opportunism in strategic alliances: A conceptual framework, *Journal of Business Psychology*, 25: 55–74; Y. Wang & S. Nicholas, 2007, The formation and evolution of non-equity strategic alliances in China, *Asia Pacific Journal of Management*, 24: 131–150.
17. S. P. Gudergan, T. Devinney, N. Richter, & R. Ellis, 2012, Strategic implications for (non-equity) alliance performance, *Long Range Planning*, 45(5/6): 451–476; J. J. Reuer, E. Klijn, F. A. J. van den Bosch, & H. W. Volberda, 2011, Bringing corporate governance to international joint ventures, *Global Strategy Journal*, 1: 54–66.
18. J. Schweitzer & S. P. Gudergan, 2011, Contractual complexity, governance and organisational form in alliances, *International Journal of Strategic Business Alliances*, 2: 26–40; C. Weigelt, 2009, The impact of outsourcing new technologies on integrative capabilities and performance, *Strategic Management Journal*, 30: 595–616.
19. E. Dou, 2013, Apple shifts from Foxconn to Pegatron, *Wall Street Journal*, May 30, B5.
20. A. Cabigiosu, F. Zirpoli, & A. Camuffo, 2013, Modularity, interfaces definition and the integration of external sources of innovation in the automotive industry, *Research Policy*, 42(3): 662–675; F. Zirpoli & M. C. Becker, 2011, The limits of design and

engineering outsourcing: Performance integration and the unfulfilled promise of modularity, *R&D Management*, 41: 21–43.

21. D. Mindruta, 2013, Value creation in university-firm research collaborations: A matching approach, *Strategic Management Journal*, 34(6): 644–665; A. L. Sherwood & J. G. Covin, 2008, Knowledge acquisition in university-industry alliances: An empirical investigation from a learning theory perspective, *Journal of Product Innovation Management*, 25: 162–179.
22. D. Faems, M. Janssens, & I. Neyens, 2012, Alliance portfolios and innovation performance: Connecting structural and managerial perspectives, *Group & Organization Management*, 37(2): 241–268; J. Kim, 2011, Alliance governance and technological performance: Some evidence from biotechnology alliances, *Industrial and Corporate Change*, 20: 969–990; P. Beamish & N. Lupton, 2009, Managing joint ventures, *Academy of Management Perspectives*, 23(2): 75–94.
23. X. Hu, R. Caldentey, & G. Vulcano, 2013, Revenue sharing in airline alliances, *Management Science*, 59(5): 1177–1195; U. Wassmer, 2010, Alliance portfolios: A review and research agenda, *Journal of Management*, 36: 141–171; S. G. Lazzarini, 2007, The impact of membership in competing alliance constellations: Evidence on the operational performance of global airlines, *Strategic Management Journal*, 28: 345–367.
24. Lavie, Haunschild, & Khanna, Organizational differences, relational mechanisms, and alliance performance; Yang, Lin, & Lin, A multilevel framework of firm boundaries: Firm characteristics, dyadic differences, and network attributes.
25. G. Ibanez, 2013, Chile's Falabella buys foothold in Brazil, *Wall Street Journal*, www.wsj.com, May 28.
26. J. R. Williams, 1998, *Renewable Advantage: Crafting Strategy Through Economic Time*, New York: Free Press.
27. 2013, BlueGreen, Choice form strategic partnership, *Hotel Management*, March, 48.
28. A. Tafti, S. Mithas, & M. S. Krishnan, 2013, The effect of information technology-enabled flexibility on formation and market value of alliances, *Management Science*, 59(1): 207–225; P. Savetpanuvong, U. Tanlamai, & C. Lursinsap, 2011, Sustaining innovation in information technology entrepreneurship with a sufficiency economy philosophy, *International Journal of Innovation Science*, 3(2): 69–82.
29. H. Ouyang, 2010, Imitator-to-innovator S curve and chasms, *Thunderbird International Business Review*, 52: 31–44; H. K. Steensma, J. Q. Barden, C. Dhanaraj, M. Lyles, & L. Tihanyi, 2008, The evolution and internalization of international joint ventures in a transitioning economy, *Journal of International Business Studies*, 39: 491–507.
30. H. E. Posen & D. A. Levinthal, 2012, Chasing a moving target: Exploitation and exploration in dynamic environments, *Management Science*, 58(3): 587–601; K. M. Eisenhardt, 2002, Has strategy changed? *MIT Sloan Management Review*, 43(2): 88–91.
31. X. Yin, J. Wu, & W. Tsai, 2012, When unconnected others connect: Does degree of brokerage persist after the formation of a multipartner alliance? *Organization Science*, 23(6): 1682–1699; S. Lahiri, L. Pérez-Nordtvedt, & R. W. Renn, 2008, Will the new competitive landscape cause your firm's decline? It depends on your mindset, *Business Horizons*, 51: 311–320.
32. W. Launder, 2013, BuzzFeed, CNN and YouTube plan online-video channel, *Wall Street Journal*, May 28, B6.
33. Hu, Caldentey, & Vulcano, Revenue sharing in airline alliances; A.-P. de Man, N. Roijakkers, & H. de Graauw, 2010, Managing dynamics through robust alliance governance structures: The case of KLM and Northwest Airlines, *European Management Journal*, 28: 171–181; C. Czipura & D. R. Jolly, 2007, Global airline alliances: Sparking profitability for a troubled industry, *Journal of Business Strategy*, 28(2): 57–64.
34. S. Stellin, 2011, The clout of air alliances, *New York Times*, www.nytimes.com, May 2.
35. D. Cameron, J. Kell, D. Michaels, & D. Pearson, 2012, Airlines shuffle marketing alliances, *Wall Street Journal*, October 9, B3; J. Flottau, 2012, Alliance blues, *Aviation Week & Space Technology*, October 9, 24.
36. G. Vasudeva, J. W. Spencer, & H. J. Teegen, 2013, Bringing the institutional context back in: A cross-national comparison of alliance partner selection and knowledge acquisition, *Organization Science*, 24(2): 319–338; D. Elmuti, A. S. Abou-Zaid, & H. Jia, 2012, Role of strategic fit and resource complementarity in strategic alliance effectiveness, *Journal of Global Business & Technology*, 8(2): 16–28; W. Shi & J. E. Prescott, 2011, Sequence patterns of firms' acquisition and alliance behavior and their performance implications, *Journal of Management Studies*, 48: 1044–1070.
37. N. Lahiri & S. Narayanan, 2013, Vertical integration, innovation and alliance portfolio size: Implications for firm performance, *Strategic Management Journal*, 34(9): 1042–1064; S. M. Mudambi & S. Tallman, 2010, Make, buy or ally? Theoretical perspectives on knowledge process outsourcing through alliances, *Journal of Management Studies*, 47: 1434–1456.
38. J. Hagedoorn & N. Wang, 2012, Is there complementarity or substitutability between internal and external R&D strategies? *Research Policy*, 41(6): 1072–1083; M. Meuleman, A. Lockett, S. Manigart, & M. Wright, 2010, Partner selection decisions in interfirm collaborations: The paradox of relational embeddedness, *Journal of Management Studies*, 47: 995–1019.
39. E. Revilla, M. Sáenz, & D. Knoppen, 2013, Towards an empirical typology of buyer–supplier relationships based on absorptive capacity, *International Journal of Production Research*, 51(10): 2935–2951; J. Zhang & C. Baden-Fuller, 2010, The influence of technological knowledge base and organizational structure on technology collaboration, *Journal of Management Studies*, 47: 679–704; J. Wiklund & D. A. Shepherd, 2009, The effectiveness of alliances and acquisitions: The role of resource combination activities, *Entrepreneurship Theory and Practice*, 33(1): 193–212.
40. L. Burkitt, 2013, Dairy giants join in China yogurt venture, *Wall Street Journal*, www.wsj.com, May 20.
41. M. Gottfried, 2013, Hulu dance partners should cut in, *Wall Street Journal*, May 24, C8.
42. C. Häeussler, H. Patzelt, & S. A. Zahra, 2012, Strategic alliances and product development in high technology new firms: The moderating effect of technological capabilities, *Journal of Business Venturing*, 27(2): 217–233; D. H. Hsu & S. Wakeman, 2011, Resource benefits and learning costs in strategic alliances, University of Pennsylvania, working paper: March; M. Makri, M. A. Hitt, & P. J. Lane, 2010, Complementary technologies, knowledge relatedness, and invention outcomes in high technology mergers and acquisitions, *Strategic Management Journal*, 31: 602–628.
43. Burkitt, Dairy giants join in China yogurt venture.
44. L. Diestre & N. Rajagopalan, 2012, Are all 'sharks' dangerous? New biotechnology ventures and partner selection in R&D alliances, *Strategic Management Journal*, 33(10): 1115–1134.
45. 2012, Two drug makers strengthen alliance, *Chain Drug Review*, 34(16): 103.
46. J. Welsh, 2013, Too many gears? GM and Ford join to build 10-speed transmissions, *Wall Street Journal*, http://blogs.wsj.com, April 15.
47. B. Stone, 2013, This theater is getting awfully crowded, *Bloomberg Businessweek*, January 21, 36–37; A. Carr, 2012, Redbox partners with Verizon to launch streaming video service, *Fast Company*, www.fastcompany.com, February 6.
48. N. Mouri, M. B. Sarkar, & M. Frye, 2012, Alliance portfolios and shareholder value in post-IPO firms: The moderating roles of portfolio structure and firm-level uncertainty, *Journal of Business Venturing*, 27(3): 355–371; C. López-Duarte & M. M. Vidal-Surez, 2010, External uncertainty and entry mode choice: Cultural distance, political risk and language diversity, *International Business Review*, 19: 575–588; J. J. Reuer & T. W. Tong, 2005, Real options

in international joint ventures, *Journal of Management*, 31: 403–423.

49. J. Mueller, 2013, The reason Tesla is still alive (and other green car companies aren't), *Forbes*, May 11, 7.

50. M. A. Fonseca & H. Normann, 2012, Explicit vs. tacit collusion—The impact of communication in oligopoly experiments, *European Economic Review*, 56(8): 1759–1772; M. Escrihuela-Villar & J. Guillén, 2011, On collusion and industry size, *Annals of Economics and Finance*, 12(1): 31–40; L. Tesfatsion, 2007, Agents come to bits: Toward a constructive comprehensive taxonomy of economic entities, *Journal of Economic Behavior & Organization*, 63: 333–346.

51. M. Van Essen & W. B. Hankins, 2013, Tacit collusion in price-setting oligopoly: A puzzle redux, *Southern Economic Journal*, 79(3): 703–726; Y. Lu & J. Wright, 2010, Tacit collusion with price-matching punishments, *International Journal of Industrial Organization*, 28: 298–306.

52. R. W. Cooper & T. W. Ross, 2009, Sustaining cooperation with joint ventures, *Journal of Law, Economics, and Organization*, 25(1): 31–54.

53. L. Zou, C. Yu, & M. Dresner, 2012, Multimarket contact, alliance membership, and prices in international airline markets, *Transportation Research Part E: Logistics and Transportation Review*, 48(2): 555–565; J. T. Prince & D. H. Simon, 2009, Multi-market contact and service quality: Evidence from on-time performance in the U.S. airline industry, *Academy of Management Journal*, 52: 336–354.

54. B. Chidmi, 2012, Vertical relationships in the ready-to-eat breakfast cereal industry in Boston, *Agribusiness*, 28(3): 241–259; N. Panteva, 2011, IBISWorld Industry Report 31123: Cereal production in the U.S., January.

55. Zou, Yu, & Dresner, Multimarket contact, alliance membership, and prices in international airline markets; Z. Guedri & J. McGuire, 2011, Multimarket competition, mobility barriers, and firm performance, *Journal of Management Studies*, 48: 857–890.

56. P. Massey & M. McDowell, 2010, Joint dominance and tacit collusion: Some implications for competition and regulatory policy, *European Competition Journal*, 6: 427–444.

57. A. H. Bowers, H. R. Greve, H. Mitsuhashi, & J. A. C. Baum, 2013, Competitive parity, status disparity, and mutual forbearance: Securities analysts' competition for investor attention, *INSEAD Working Papers Collection*, (43): 1–52

58. B. Nielsen, 2010, Strategic fit, contractual, and procedural governance in alliances, *Journal of Business Research*, 63: 682–689; P. Dussauge, B. Garrette, & W. Mitchell, 2004, Asymmetric performances: The market share impact of scale and link alliances in the global auto industry, *Strategic Management Journal*, 25: 701–711.

59. L. Capron & W. Mitchell, 2012, *Build, Borrow or Buy: Solving the Growth Dilemma*, Cambridge: Harvard Business Review Press; C. Häussler, 2011, The determinants of commercialization strategy: Idiosyncrasies in British and German biotechnology, *Entrepreneurship Theory and Practice*, 35: 653–681.

60. Y. Lew & R. R. Sinkovics, 2013, Crossing borders and industry sectors: Behavioral governance in strategic alliances and product innovation for competitive advantage, *Long Range Planning*, 46(1/2): 13–38; P. Ritala & H.-K. Ellonen, 2010, Competitive advantage in interfirm cooperation: Old and new explanations, *Competitiveness Review*, 20: 367–383.

61. H. Liu, X. Jiang, J. Zhang, & X. Zhao, 2013, Strategic flexibility and international venturing by emerging market firms: The moderating effects of institutional and relational factors, *Journal of International Marketing*, 21(2): 79–98; J. Anand, R. Oriani, & R. S. Vassolo, 2010, Alliance activity as a dynamic capability in the face of a discontinuous technological change, *Organization Science*, 21: 1213–1232; J. Li, C. Dhanaraj, & R. L. Shockley, 2008, Joint venture evolution: Extending the real options approach, *Managerial and Decision Economics*, 29: 317–336.

62. S. Chang & M. Tsai, 2013, The effect of prior alliance experience on acquisition performance, *Applied Economics*, 45(6): 765–773; A. Zaheer, E. Hernandez, & S. Banerjee, 2010, Prior alliances with targets and acquisition performance in knowledge-intensive industries, *Organization Science*, 21(5): 1072–1091.

63. J. Paczkowski, 2013, Samsung buddies up with Mozilla on new Android browser tech, *All Things D*, http://allthingsd.com, April 3; J. Paczkowski, 2013, Samsung plans multiple Tizen Smartphones for 2013, *All Things D*, http://allthingsd.com, January 3.

64. J. B. White, 2013, Mazda uses alliances to boost sales, *Wall Street Journal*, www.wsj.com, January 27.

65. V. K. Garg, R. L. Priem, & A. A. Rasheed, 2013, A theoretical explanation of the cost advantages of multi-unit franchising, *Journal of Marketing Channels*, 20(1/2): 52–72; J. G. Combs, D. J. Ketchen, Jr., C. L. Shook, & J. C. Short, 2011, Antecedents and consequences of franchising: Past accomplishments and future challenges, *Journal of Management*, 37: 99–126.

66. F. Lafontaine, 1999, Myths and strengths of franchising, "Mastering Strategy" (Part Nine), *Financial Times*, November 22, 8–10.

67. A. A. Perryman & J. G. Combs, 2012, Who should own it? An agency-based explanation for multi-outlet ownership and co-location in plural form franchising, *Strategic Management Journal*, 33(4): 368–386; D. Grewal, G. R. Iyer, R. G. Javalgi, & L. Radulovich, 2011, Franchise partnership and international expansion: A conceptual framework and research propositions, *Entrepreneurship Theory and Practice*, 35: 533–557; A. M. Hayashi, 2008, How to replicate success, *MIT Sloan Management Review*, 49(3): 6–7.

68. 2013, Building local businesses one opportunity at a time, International Franchise Association, www.buildingopportunity.com, June 6.

69. G. M. Kistruck, J. W. Webb, C. J. Sutter, & R. D. Ireland, 2011, Microfranchising in base-of-the-pyramid markets: Institutional challenges and adaptations to the franchise model, *Entrepreneurship Theory and Practice*, 35: 503–531.

70. N. Mumdziev & J. Windsperger, 2013, An extended transaction cost model of decision rights allocation in franchising: The moderating role of trust, *Managerial and Decision Economics*, 34(3–5): 170–182; J. McDonnell, A. Beatson, & C.-H. Huang, 2011, Investigating relationships between relationship quality, customer loyalty and cooperation: An empirical study of convenience stores' franchise chain systems, *Asia Pacific Journal of Marketing and Logistics*, 23: 367–385.

71. B. Merrilees & L. Frazer, 2013, Internal branding: Franchisor leadership as a critical determinant, *Journal of Business Research*, 66(2): 158–164; T. M. Nisar, 2011, Intellectual property securitization and growth capital in retail franchising, *Journal of Retailing*, 87(3): 393–405; A. K. Paswan & C. M. Wittman, 2000, Knowledge management and franchise systems, *Industrial Marketing Management*, 38: 173–180.

72. D. Grace, S. Weaven, L. Frazer, & J. Giddings, 2013, Examining the role of franchisee normative expectations in relationship evaluation, *Journal of Retailing*, 89(2): 219–230; W. R. Meek, B. Davis-Sramek, M. S. Baucus, & R. N. Germain, 2011, Commitment in franchising: The role of collaborative communication and a franchisee's propensity to leave, *Entrepreneurship Theory and Practice*, 35: 559–581.

73. N. Gorovaia & J. Windsperger, 2013, Real options, intangible resources and performance of franchise networks, *Managerial and Decision Economics*, 34(3–5): 183–194; T. W. K. Leslie & L. S. McNeill, 2010, Towards a conceptual model for franchise perceptual equity, *Journal of Brand Management*, 18: 21–33.

74. M. Onal Vural, L. Dahlander, & G. George, 2013, Collaborative benefits and coordination costs: Learning and capability development in science, *Strategic Entrepreneurship Journal*, 7: 122–137; M. J. Nieto & A. Rodríguez, 2011, Offshoring of R&D: Looking abroad to improve innovation performance, *Journal of International Business Studies*, 42: 345–361.

75. G. Ahuja, C. Morris Lampert, & E. Novelli, 2013, The second face of appropriability: Generative appropriability and its determinants, *Academy of Management*

*Review*, 38(2): 248–269; C. Choi & P. Beamish, 2013, Resource complementarity and international joint venture performance in Korea, *Asia Pacific Journal of Management*, 30(2): 561–576.

76. S. Veilleux, N. Haskell, & F. Pons, 2012, Going global: How smaller enterprises benefit from strategic alliances, *Journal of Business Strategy*, 33(5): 22–31; L. D. Qiu, 2010, Cross-border mergers and strategic alliances, *European Economic Review*, 54: 818–831; H. Ren, B. Gray, & K. Kim, 2009, Performance of international joint ventures: What factors really make a difference and how? *Journal of Management*, 35: 805–832.

77. I. Arikan & O. Shenkar, 2013, National animosity and cross-border alliances, *Academy of Management Journal*, in press; Y. Yan, D. Ding, & S. Mak, 2009, The impact of business investment on capability exploitation and organizational control in international strategic alliances, *Journal of Change Management*, 9(1): 49–65.

78. Vasudeva, Spencer, & Teegen, Bringing the institutional context back in: A cross-national comparison of alliance partner selection and knowledge acquisition; L. Li, G. Qian, & Z. Qian, 2013, Do partners in international strategic alliances share resources, costs, and risks? *Journal of Business Research*, 66(4): 489–498; A. Zaheer & E. Hernandez, 2011, The geographic scope of the MNC and its alliance portfolio: Resolving the paradox of distance, *Global Strategy Journal*, 1: 109–126.

79. Roy, IJV partner trustworthy behaviour: The role of host country governance and partner selection criteria; M. Meuleman & M. Wright, 2011, Cross-border private equity syndication: Institutional context and learning, *Journal of Business Venturing*, 26: 35–48; T. J. Wilkinson, A. R. Thomas, & J. M. Hawes, 2009, Managing relationships with Chinese joint venture partners, *Journal of Global Marketing*, 22(2): 109–120.

80. B. B. Nielsen & S. Gudergan, 2012, Exploration and exploitation fit and performance in international strategic alliances, *International Business Review*, 21(4): 558–574; D. Kronborg & S. Thomsen, 2009, Foreign ownership and long-term survival, *Strategic Management Journal*, 30: 207–219.

81. N. Negishi & I. Sherr, 2013, East meets the west in mobile game, *Wall Street Journal*, June 7, B2.

82. Lavie, Capturing value from alliance portfolios; D. Lavie, C. Lechner, & H. Singh, 2007, The performance implications of timing of entry and involvement in multipartner alliances, *Academy of Management Journal*, 50(3): 578–604.

83. 2013, Partner with Cisco, Cisco homepage, www.cisco.com, June 6.

84. 2013, Strategic alliance—IBM, Cisco homepage, www.cisco.com, June 6.

85. W. Fu, J. Revilla Diez, & D. Schiller, 2013, Interactive learning, informal networks and innovation: Evidence from electronics firm survey in the Pearl River Delta, China, *Research Policy*, 42(3): 635–646; A. T. Ankan & M. A. Schilling, 2011, Structure and governance in industrial districts: Implications for competitive advantage, *Journal of Management Studies*, 48: 772–803.

86. F. Ghadar, J. Sviokla, & D. A. Stephan, 2012, Why life science needs its own silicon valley, *Harvard Business Review*, 90(7/8): 25–27.

87. C. Casanueva, I. Castro, & J. L. Galán, 2013, Informational networks and innovation in mature industrial clusters, *Journal of Business Research*, 66(5): 603–613; J. Wincent, S. Anokhin, D. Örtqvist, & E. Autio, 2010, Quality meets structure: Generalized reciprocity and firm-level advantage in strategic networks, *Journal of Management Studies*, 47: 597–624; D. Lavie, 2007, Alliance portfolios and firm performance: A study of value creation and appropriation in the U.S. software industry, *Strategic Management Journal*, 28: 1187–1212.

88. L. Dobusch & E. Schübler, 2013, Theorizing path dependence: A review of positive feedback mechanisms in technology markets, regional clusters, and organizations, *Industrial & Corporate Change*, 22(3): 617–647; A. M. Joshi & A. Nerkar, 2011, When do strategic alliances inhibit innovation by firms? Evidence from patent pools in the global optical disc industry, *Strategic Management Journal*, 32(11): 1139–1160.

89. J. P. MacDuffie, 2011, Inter-organizational trust and the dynamics of distrust, *Journal of International Business Studies*, 42: 35–47; H. Kim, R. E. Hoskisson, & W. P. Wan, 2004, Power, dependence, diversification strategy and performance in keiretsu member firms, *Strategic Management Journal*, 25: 613–636.

90. E. Francis, 2013, Building an auto industry hub through value creation, *Automotive Industries*, January, 111–112.

91. V. Van de Vrande, 2013, Balancing your technology-sourcing portfolio: How sourcing mode diversity enhances innovative performance, *Strategic Management Journal*, 34(5): 610–621; A. V. Shipilov, 2009, Firm scope experience, historic multimarket contact with partners, centrality, and the relationship between structural holes and performance, *Organization Science*, 20: 85–106.

92. A. Cui & G. O'Connor, 2012, Alliance portfolio resource diversity and firm innovation, *Journal of Marketing*, 76(4): 24–43; P.-H. Soh, 2010, Network patterns and competitive advantage before the emergence of a dominant design, *Strategic Management Journal*, 31: 438–461.

93. G. Soda, 2011, The management of firms' alliance network positioning: Implications for innovation, *European Management Journal*, 29(5): 377–388; T. Kiessling & M. Harvey, 2008, Globalisation of internal venture capital opportunities in developing small and medium enterprises' relationships, *International Journal of Entrepreneurship and Innovation Management*, 8: 233–253; V. Shankar & B. L. Bayus, 2003, Network effects and competition: An empirical analysis of the home video game industry, *Strategic Management Journal*, 24: 375–384.

94. Leonard, Syfy's ultimate transmedia adventure.

95. Yin, Wu & Tsai, When unconnected others connect: Does degree of brokerage persist after the formation of a multipartner alliance?

96. A. G. Karamanos, 2012, Leveraging micro- and macro-structures of embeddedness in alliance networks for exploratory innovation in biotechnology, *R&D Management*, 42(1): 71–89; D. Somaya, Y. Kim, & N. S. Vonortas, 2011, Exclusivity in licensing alliances: Using hostages to support technology commercialization, *Strategic Management Journal*, 32: 159–186.

97. Veilleux, Haskell, & Pons, Going global: How smaller enterprises benefit from strategic alliances; M. J. Nieto & L. Santamaría, 2010, Technological collaboration: Bridging the innovation gap between small and large firms, *Journal of Small Business Management*, 48: 44–69; P. Ozcan & K. M. Eisenhardt, 2009, Origin of alliance portfolios: Entrepreneurs, network strategies, and firm performance, *Academy of Management Journal*, 52: 246–279.

98. H. R. Greve, T. J. Rowley, & A. V. Shipilov, 2013, How partners shape strategy, *Harvard Business Review*, 91(6): 28.

99. Ibid.

100. Mueller, The reason Tesla is still alive (and other green car companies aren't).

101. H. R. Greve, H. Mitsuhashi, & J. A. C. Baum, 2013, Greener pastures: Outside options and strategic alliance withdrawal, *Organization Science*, 24(1): 79–98; H. R. Greve, J. A. C. Baum, H. Mitsuhashi, & T. J. Rowley, 2010, Built to last but falling apart: Cohesion, friction, and withdrawal from interfirm alliances, *Academy of Management Journal*, 53: 302–322; M. Rod, 2009, A model for the effective management of joint ventures: A case study approach, *International Journal of Management*, 26(1): 3–17.

102. G. Vasudeva & J. Anand, 2011, Unpacking absorptive capacity: A study of knowledge utilization from alliance portfolios, *Academy of Management Journal*, 54: 611–623; J.-Y. Kim & A. S. Miner, 2007, Vicarious learning from the failures and near-failures of others: Evidence from the U.S. commercial banking industry, *Academy of Management Journal*, 50(2): 687–714.

103. J. Marson, 2013, TNK-BP investors appeal to Rosneft's chief over shares, *Wall Street Journal*, www.wsj.com, April 17.

104. K. Zhou & D. Xu, 2012, How foreign firms curtail local supplier opportunism in China: Detailed contracts, centralized control, and relational governance,

*Journal of International Business Studies*, 43(7): 677–692; R. Agarwal, D. Audretsch, & M. B. Sarkar, 2010, Knowledge spillovers and strategic entrepreneurship, *Strategic Entrepreneurship Journal*, 4: 271–283; Y. Li, Y. Liu, M. Li, & H. Wu, 2008, Transformational offshore outsourcing: Empirical evidence from alliances in China, *Journal of Operations Management*, 26: 257–274.

105. Cummings & Holmberg, Best-fit alliance partners: The use of critical success factors in a comprehensive partner selection process; A. V. Werder, 2011, Corporate governance and stakeholder opportunism, *Organization Science*, 22(5): 1345–1358; T. K. Das & R. Kumar, 2011, Regulatory focus and opportunism in the alliance development process, *Journal of Management*, 37: 682–708.

106. A. S. Cui, 2013, Portfolio dynamics and alliance termination: The contingent role of resource dissimilarity, *Journal of Marketing*, 77(3): 15–32; M. S. Giarratana & S. Torrisi, 2010, Foreign entry and survival in a knowledge-intensive market: Emerging economy countries' international linkages, technology competencies, and firm experience, *Strategic Entrepreneurship Journal*, 4: 85–104; M. B. Sarkar, P. S. Aulakh, & A. Madhok, 2009, Process capabilities and value generation in alliance portfolios, *Organization Science*, 20: 583–600.

107. S. Williams & J. Marson, 2013, BP nears arctic deal with Rosneft, *Wall Street Journal*, www.wsj.com, March 22.

108. M. Nippa & S. Beechler, 2013, What do we know about the success and failure of international joint ventures? In search of relevance and holism, in T. M. Devinney, T. Pedersen, & L. Tihanyi (eds.), *Philosophy of Science and Meta-knowledge in International Business and Management*, 26: 363–396; Lumineau, Fréchet, & Puthod, An organizational learning perspective on the contracting process; P.-X. Meschi, 2009, Government corruption and foreign stakes in international joint ventures in emerging economies, *Asia Pacific Journal of Management*, 26: 241–261.

109. I. Neyens & D. Faems, 2013, Exploring the impact of alliance portfolio management design on alliance portfolio performance, *Managerial & Decision Economics*, 34(3–5): 347–361; D. G. Sirmon, M. A. Hitt, R. D. Ireland, & B. A. Gilbert, 2011, Resource orchestration to create competitive advantage: Breadth, depth, and life cycle effects, *Journal of Management*, 37(5): 1390–1412; M. H. Hansen, R. E. Hoskisson, & J. B. Barney, 2008, Competitive advantage in alliance governance: Resolving the opportunism minimization-gain maximization paradox, *Managerial and Decision Economics*, 29: 191–208.

110. C. C. Chung & P. W. Beamish, 2010, The trap of continual ownership change in international equity joint ventures, *Organization Science*, 21: 995–1015.

111. Mudambi & Tallman, Make, buy or ally?; Hansen, Hoskisson, & Barney, Competitive advantage in alliance governance: Resolving the opportunism minimization-gain maximization paradox.

112. N. N. Arranz & J. C. F. de Arroyabe, 2012, Effect of formal contracts, relational norms and trust on performance of joint research and development projects, *British Journal of Management*, 23(4): 575–588; L. Poppo, K. Z. Zhou, & S. Ryu, 2008, Alternative origins to interorganizational trust: An interdependence perspective on the shadow of the past and the shadow of the future, *Organization Science*, 19: 39–55.

113. G. Ertug, I. Cuypers, N. Noorderhaven, & B. Bensaou, 2013, Trust between international joint venture partners: Effects of home countries, *Journal of International Business Studies*, 44(3): 263–282; J. J. Li, L. Poppo, & K. Z. Zhou, 2010, Relational mechanisms, formal contracts, and local knowledge acquisition by international subsidiaries, *Strategic Management Journal*, 31: 349–370.

114. S. E. Fawcett, S. L. Jones, & A. M. Fawcett, 2012, Supply chain trust: The catalyst for collaborative innovation, *Business Horizons*, 55(2): 163–178; H. C. Dekker & A. Van den Abbeele, 2010, Organizational learning and interfirm control: The effects of partner search and prior exchange experience, *Organization Science*, 21: 1233–1250; T. K. Das & R. Kumar, 2009, Interpartner harmony in strategic alliances: Managing commitment and forbearance, *International Journal of Strategic Business Alliances*, 1(1): 24–52.

115. T. A. Khoury, M. Junkunc, & D. L. Deeds, 2013, The social construction of legitimacy through signaling social capital: Exploring the conditional value of alliances and underwriters at IPO, *Entrepreneurship Theory & Practice*, 37(3): 569–601; J. W. Rottman, 2008, Successful knowledge transfer within offshore supplier networks: A case study exploring social capital in strategic alliances, *Journal of Information Technology*, 23(10): 31–43.

116. 2013, The principles of the alliance, Renault homepage, www.renault.com, June 7.

117. R. Kumar & A. Nathwani, 2012, Business alliances: Why managerial thinking and biases determine success, *Journal of Business Strategy*, 33(5): 44–50; C. C. Phelps, 2010, A longitudinal study of the influence of alliance network structure and composition on firm exploratory innovation, *Academy of Management Journal*, 53: 890–913; C. E. Ybarra & T. A. Turk, 2009, The evolution of trust in information technology alliances, *Journal of High Technology Management Research*, 20(1): 62–74.

# 10

# Corporate Governance

***Studying this chapter should provide you with the strategic management knowledge needed to:***

**1** Define corporate governance and explain why it is used to monitor and control top-level managers' decisions.

**2** Explain why ownership is largely separated from managerial control in organizations.

**3** Define an agency relationship and managerial opportunism and describe their strategic implications.

**4** Explain the use of three internal governance mechanisms to monitor and control managers' decisions.

**5** Discuss the types of compensation top-level managers receive and their effects on managerial decisions.

**6** Describe how the external corporate governance mechanism—the market for corporate control—restrains top-level managers' decisions.

**7** Discuss the nature and use of corporate governance in international settings, especially in Germany, Japan, and China.

**8** Describe how corporate governance fosters ethical decisions by a firm's top-level managers.

## THE IMPERIAL CEO, JPMORGAN CHASE'S JAMIE DIMON: IS IT THE END OF CORPORATE GOVERNANCE?

Jamie Dimon, CEO of JPMorgan Chase, is one of the very few top executives at large banks or major financial services firms who was unscathed by the substantial economic recession which began in 2008—a recession largely caused by those firms taking inappropriate risks. He is described as charismatic and an excellent leader. Yet, in 2012, JPMorgan Chase experienced its own scandal caused by exceptional risk taking. Traders in its London operations were allowed to build a huge exposure in credit derivatives that breached the acceptable risk limits of most analytical models. As a result, the bank suffered losses of more than $6 billion. It is referred to as the London Whale trading debacle.

Because of the huge loss and concerns about the lack of oversight that led to this debacle, there was a move by shareholder activists to separate the CEO and chair of the board positions, requiring Dimon to hold only the CEO title. Playing key roles were the American Federation of State, County and Municipal Employees (AFSCME) and the Institutional Shareholder Services (ISS). The AFSCME was pushing to separate the holders of the CEO and chair positions at JPMorgan Chase. The ISS was pushing for shareholders to withhold the votes for three directors currently on the Morgan's board policy committee.

Dimon described the London Whale debacle as an anomaly caused by the inappropriate behavior of a few bad employees. However, it seems to suggest serious weaknesses in the bank's oversight of activities involving significant risk.

Executives and board members of JPMorgan Chase worked hard to thwart these efforts. Lee Raymond, the former CEO of Exxon Mobil who has been on the Morgan board for 25 years, played a key role in these efforts to support Dimon and avoid a negative vote. They lobbied major institutional shareholders, and even asked former U.S. president Bill Clinton to help work out a compromise with the AFSCME (though he declined). They even suggested that Dimon would quit if he had to give up one of the roles and it would harm the stock price. In the end, Dimon and the bank won the vote with a two-thirds majority for Dimon to retain both positions.

Several analysts decried the vote and suggested that having a third of the shareholders vote against Dimon is not a major vote of confidence. One even suggested that the vote is not surprising because of the 10 largest institutional owners of the bank's stock, 7 have CEOs who also hold the chair position. So, how could they openly argue that this is bad for JPMorgan when they do it in their organizations? Furthermore, these major institutional investors want the banks to engage in high-risk activities with the potential to produce high returns. This is especially true because the downside risk of losses is low as the government cannot afford to allow the big banks to fail.

One analyst suggested that the shareholders voted out of fear (potential loss of Dimon) and for personality instead of good corporate governance. Analysts for the *Financial Times* argued that the outcome of this vote demonstrates how weak shareholder rights are in the United States. Finally, another analyst noted that while splitting the CEO and chair positions does not guarantee good governance, it is a prerequisite for it. Lee Raymond suggested that the board would take action. Several speculate that such actions will not relate to Dimon but rather to a reconfiguration of the board members on the risk and audit committees. Some have argued that certain members of these committees have little knowledge of their function and/or have financial ties to the bank thereby creating a potential conflict of interest.

Sources: J. Eisinger, 2013, Flawed system suits the shareholders just fine, *New York Times DealBook*, http://dealbook.nytimes.com, May 29; J. Plender, 2013, The divine right of the imperial CEO, *Financial Times*, www.ft.com, May 26; J. Sommer, 2013, The CEO triumphant (at least at Apple and Chase), *New York Times*, www.nytimes.com, May 25; H. Moore, 2013, JP Morgan CEO Jamie Dimon remains the Indiana Jones of corporate America, *The Guardian*, www.guardian.com, May 21; J. Silver-Greenberg & S. Craig, 2013, Strong lobbying helps Dimon thwart a shareholder challenge, *New York Times DealBook*, http://dealbook.nytimes.com, May 21; D. Fitzpatrick, J. S. Lublin, & J. Steinberg, 2013, Vote strengthens Dimon's grip, *Wall Street Journal*, www.wsj.com, May 21; A.T. Crane & A. Currie, 2013, Dimon's Pyrrhic victory, *New York Times DealBook*, http://dealbook.nytimes.com, May 21; D. Benoit, 2013, J.P. Morgan's powerful board members, *Wall Street Journal*, www.wsj.com, May 20; M. Egan, 2013, Top J.P. Morgan directors back Dimon as CEO, Chair, *Fox Business*, www.foxbusiness.com, May 10.

**Learn more about the American Federation of State, County and Municipal Employees.**
**www.cengagebrain.com**

As the Opening Case suggests, corporate governance is complex and designed to provide oversight of how firms operate. At a broader level, reflects the type of infrastructure provided by individual nations as the framework within which companies compete. Given that we are concerned with the strategic management process firms use, our focus in this chapter is on corporate governance in companies (although we do also address governance at the level of nations). The complexity and the potential problems with corporate governance, such as having true checks and balances in the system of governance, are shown by the JPMorgan Chase example in the Opening Case. In fact, it appears that there were very few checks and balances in the corporate governance of JPMorgan Chase. Company CEO Jamie Dimon appears to more like a "king" than an officer under the watchful eye of the board of directors.

Comprehensive in scope and complex in nature, corporate governance is a responsibility that challenges firms and their leaders. Successfully dealing with this challenge is important, as evidence suggests that corporate governance is critical to firms' success; because of this, governance is an increasingly important part of the strategic management process.[1] For example, if the board makes the wrong decisions in selecting, governing, and compensating the firm's CEO as its strategic leader, the shareholders and the firm suffer. When CEOs are motivated to act in the best interests of the firm—in particular, the shareholders—the company's value is more likely to increase. Additionally, effective succession plans and appropriate monitoring and direction-setting efforts by the board of directors contribute positively to a firm's performance.

**Corporate governance** is the set of mechanisms used to manage the relationships among stakeholders and to determine and control the strategic direction and performance of organizations.

**Corporate governance** is the set of mechanisms used to manage relationships among stakeholders and to determine and control the strategic direction and performance of organizations.[2] At its core, corporate governance is concerned with identifying ways to ensure that decisions (especially strategic decisions) are made effectively and that they facilitate a firm's efforts to achieve strategic competitiveness.[3] Governance can also be thought of as a means to establish and maintain harmony between parties (the firm's owners and its top-level managers) whose interests may conflict.

In modern corporations—especially those in nations with "Westernized" infrastructures and business practices such as the United States and the United Kingdom—ensuring that top-level managers' interests are aligned with other stakeholders' interests, particularly those of shareholders, is a primary objective of corporate governance. Thus, corporate governance involves oversight in areas where owners, managers, and members of boards of directors

M. Stasy

may have conflicts of interest. Processes used to elect members of the firm's board of directors, the general management of CEO pay and more focused supervision of director pay, and the corporation's overall strategic direction are examples of areas in which oversight is sought.[4] Because corporate governance is an ongoing process concerned with how a firm is to be managed, its nature evolves in light of the types of never-ending changes in a firm's external environment that we discussed in Chapter 2.

The recent global emphasis on corporate governance stems mainly from the apparent failure of corporate governance mechanisms to adequately monitor and control top-level managers' decisions (as exemplified by the Opening Case on JPMorgan Chase). In turn, undesired or unacceptable consequences resulting from using corporate governance mechanisms cause changes such as electing new members to the board of directors with the hope of providing more effective governance. A second and more positive reason for this interest comes from evidence that a well-functioning corporate governance system can create a competitive advantage for an individual firm.[5]

As noted earlier, corporate governance is of concern to nations as well as to individual firms.[6] Although corporate governance reflects company standards, it also collectively reflects the societal standards of nations.[7] Commenting about governance-related changes being made in Singapore, an official noted that, "Good corporate governance plays an important role in ensuring the effective functioning of Singapore's capital markets."[8] Ensuring the independence of board members and practices a board should follow to exercise effective oversight of a firm's internal control efforts are examples of recent changes to governance standards being applied in Singapore. Efforts such as these are important in that research shows that how nations govern their corporations affects firms' investment decisions. In other words, firms seek to invest in nations with national governance standards that are acceptable to them.[9] This is particularly the case when firms consider the possibility of geographically expanding into emerging markets.

In the chapter's first section, we describe the relationship on which the modern corporation is built—namely, the relationship between owners and managers. We use the majority of the chapter to explain various mechanisms owners use to govern managers and to ensure that they comply with their responsibility to satisfy stakeholders' needs, especially those of shareholders.

Three internal governance mechanisms and a single external one are used in the modern corporation. The three internal governance mechanisms we describe in this chapter are (1) ownership concentration, represented by types of shareholders and their different incentives to monitor managers; (2) the board of directors; and (3) executive compensation. We then consider the market for corporate control, an external corporate governance mechanism. Essentially, this market is a set of potential owners seeking to acquire undervalued firms and earn above-average returns on their investments by replacing ineffective top-level management teams.[10] The chapter's focus then shifts to the issue of international corporate governance. We briefly describe governance approaches used in several countries outside of the United States and United Kingdom. In part, this discussion suggests that the structures used to govern global companies competing in both developed and emerging economies are becoming more, rather than less, similar. Closing our analysis of corporate governance is a consideration of the need for these control mechanisms to encourage and support ethical behavior in organizations.

## 10-1 Separation of Ownership and Managerial Control

Historically, U.S. firms were managed by founder-owners and their descendants. In these cases, corporate ownership and control resided in the same people. As firms grew larger, "the managerial revolution led to a separation of ownership and control in most large corporations, where control of the firm shifted from entrepreneurs to professional managers while ownership became dispersed among thousands of unorganized stockholders who were removed from the day-to-day management of the firm."[11] These changes created the modern public corporation, which is based on the efficient separation of ownership and managerial control. Supporting the separation is a basic legal premise suggesting that the primary objective of a firm's activities is to increase the corporation's profit and, thereby, the owners' (shareholders') financial gains.[12]

The separation of ownership and managerial control allows shareholders to purchase stock, which entitles them to income (residual returns) from the firm's operations after paying expenses. This right, however, requires that shareholders take a risk that the firm's expenses may exceed its revenues. To manage this investment risk, shareholders maintain a diversified portfolio by investing in several companies to reduce their overall risk.[13] The poor performance or failure of any one firm in which they invest has less overall effect on the value of the entire portfolio of investments. Thus, shareholders specialize in managing their investment risk.

Commonly, those managing small firms also own a significant percentage of the firm. In such instances, there is less separation between ownership and managerial control. Moreover, in a large number of family-owned firms, ownership and managerial control are not separated at all. Research shows that family-owned firms perform better when a member of the family is the CEO than when the CEO is an outsider.[14]

In many regions outside the United States, such as in Latin America, Asia, and some European countries, family-owned firms dominate the competitive landscape.[15] The primary purpose of most of these firms is to increase the family's wealth, which explains why a family CEO often is better than an outside CEO. Family ownership is also significant in U.S. companies in that at least one-third of the S&P 500 firms have substantial family ownership, holding on average about 18 percent of a firm's equity.[16]

Family-controlled firms face at least two critical issues related to corporate governance. First, as they grow, they may not have access to all of the skills needed to effectively manage the firm and maximize returns for the family. Thus, outsiders may be required to facilitate growth. Also, as they grow, they may need to seek outside capital and thus give up some of the ownership. In these cases, protecting the minority owners' rights becomes important.[17] To avoid these potential problems, when family firms grow and become more complex, their owner-managers may contract with managerial specialists. These managers make major decisions in the owners' firm and are compensated on the basis of their decision-making skills. Research suggests that firms in which families own enough equity to have influence without major control tend to make the best strategic decisions.[18]

*In family-owned firms there is little, if any, separation between ownership and control.*

EIGHTFISH/The Image Bank/Getty Images

Without owner (shareholder) specialization in risk bearing and management specialization in decision making, a firm may be limited by its owners' abilities to simultaneously manage it and make effective strategic decisions relative to risk. Thus, the separation and specialization of ownership (risk bearing) and managerial control (decision making) should produce the highest returns for the firm's owners.

## 10-1a Agency Relationships

The separation between owners and managers creates an agency relationship. An agency relationship exists when one or more persons (the principal or principals) hire another person or persons (the agent or agents) as decision-making specialists to perform a service.[19] Thus, an **agency relationship** exists when one party delegates decision-making responsibility to a second party for compensation (see Figure 10.1).

In addition to shareholders and top-level managers, other examples of agency relationships are consultants and clients and insured and insurer. Moreover, within organizations, an agency relationship exists between managers and their employees, as well as between top-level managers and the firm's owners.[20] However, in this chapter we focus on the agency relationship between the firm's owners (the principals) and top-level managers (the principals' agents) because these managers are responsible for formulating and implementing the firm's strategies, which have major effects on firm performance.[21]

The separation between ownership and managerial control can be problematic. Research evidence documents a variety of agency problems in the modern corporation.[22] Problems can surface because the principal and the agent have different interests and goals or because shareholders lack direct control of large publicly traded corporations. Problems also surface when an agent makes decisions that result in pursuing goals that conflict with those of

An **agency relationship** exists when one party delegates decision-making responsibility to a second party for compensation.

**Figure 10.1** An Agency Relationship

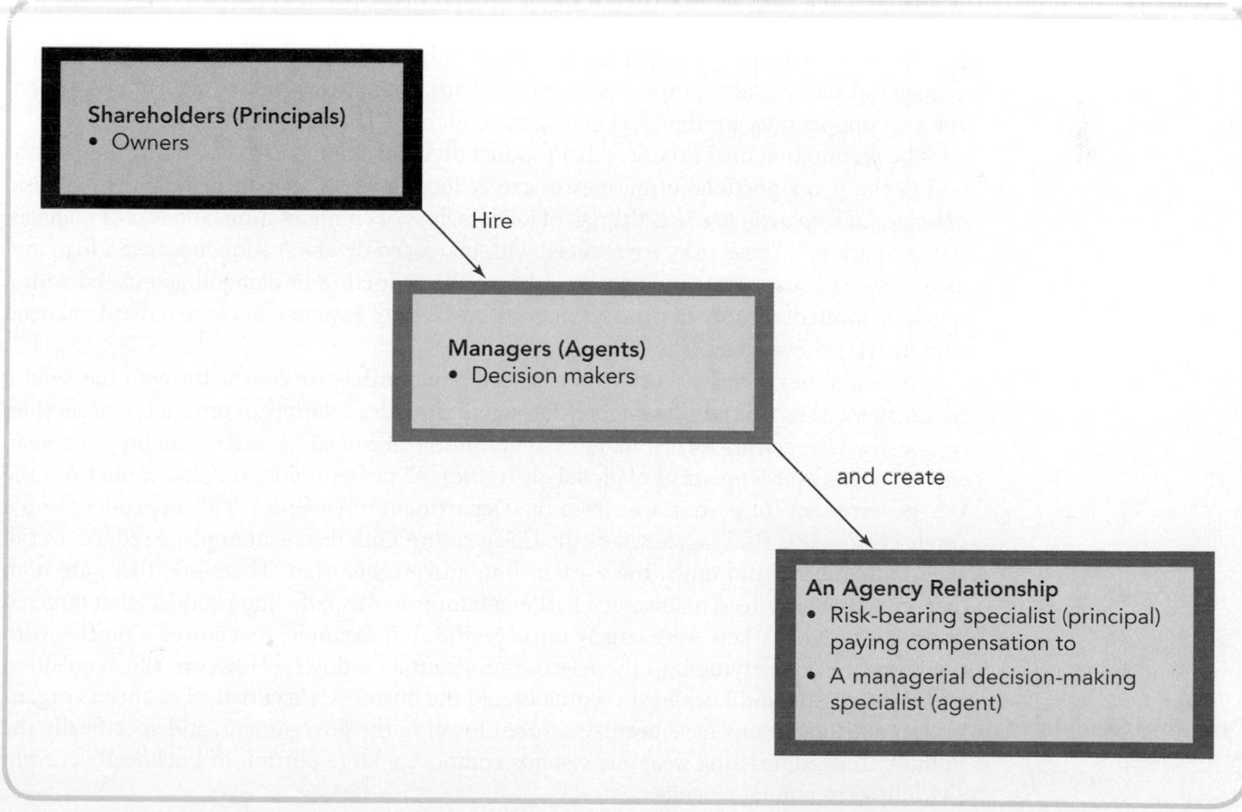

the principals. Thus, the separation of ownership and control potentially allows divergent interests (between principals and agents) to occur, which can lead to managerial opportunism.

**Managerial opportunism** is the seeking of self-interest with guile (i.e., cunning or deceit).[23] Opportunism is both an attitude (e.g., an inclination) and a set of behaviors (i.e., specific acts of self-interest).[24] Principals do not know beforehand which agents will or will not act opportunistically. A top-level manager's reputation is an imperfect predictor; moreover, opportunistic behavior cannot be observed until it has occurred. Thus, principals establish governance and control mechanisms to prevent agents from acting opportunistically, even though only a few are likely to do so. Interestingly, research suggests that when CEOs feel constrained by governance mechanisms, they are more likely to seek external advice that in turn helps them make better strategic decisions.[25]

The agency relationship suggests that any time principals delegate decision-making responsibilities to agents, the opportunity for conflicts of interest exists. Top-level managers, for example, may make strategic decisions that maximize their personal welfare and minimize their personal risk.[26] Decisions such as these prevent maximizing shareholder wealth. Decisions regarding product diversification demonstrate this situation.

## 10-1b Product Diversification as an Example of an Agency Problem

As explained in Chapter 6, a corporate-level strategy to diversify the firm's product lines can enhance a firm's strategic competitiveness and increase its returns, both of which serve the interests of all stakeholders and certainly shareholders and top-level managers. However, product diversification can create two benefits for top-level managers that shareholders do not enjoy, meaning that they may prefer product diversification more than shareholders do.[27]

The fact that product diversification usually increases the size of a firm and that size is positively related to executive compensation is the first of the two benefits of additional diversification that may accrue to top-level managers. Diversification also increases the complexity of managing a firm and its network of businesses, possibly requiring additional managerial pay because of this complexity.[28] Thus, increased product diversification provides an opportunity for top-level managers to increase their compensation.[29]

The second potential benefit is that product diversification and the resulting diversification of the firm's portfolio of businesses can reduce top-level managers' employment risk. *Managerial employment risk* is the risk of job loss, loss of compensation, and loss of managerial reputation.[30] These risks are reduced with increased diversification, because a firm and its upper-level managers are less vulnerable to the reduction in demand associated with a single or limited number of product lines or businesses. Events that occurred at Lockheed demonstrate these issues.

For a number of years, Lockheed has been a major defense contractor with the federal government as its primary customer. Although it provides a variety of products and services (processes U.S. census forms, handles $600 billion of Social Security benefits each year, and manages over 50 percent of global air traffic), 82 percent of its revenue came from the U.S. government (61 percent was from the Department of Defense). This dependence on a single customer is risky, as shown by the U.S. government's recent attempts to reduce overall spending and to wind down the wars in Iraq and Afghanistan. Therefore, there are high incentives for Lockheed to diversify. Earlier attempts to diversify into products that targeted other customer markets were largely unsuccessful. For example, it acquired Comcast with the intent of diversifying into the telecommunications industry. However, the acquisition was unsuccessful and Lockheed eventually sold the business. Essentially, Lockheed's organization and operations have been structured to serve the government, and specifically the military. Indeed, existing weapons systems compose a large portion of Lockheed's current $47 billion in annual revenue.

**Managerial opportunism** is the seeking of self-interest with guile (i.e., cunning or deceit).

Lockheed's new CEO, Marillyn Hewson, is charged with charting a future for the company that likely includes diversification. The firm's Center for Innovation is working on several potential products and services in health care and cybersecurity. So, it appears that it will try to diversify organically by developing innovations internally (using its current capabilities) rather than acquiring other firms as it did in the past. In fact, Hewson describes Lockheed as a global security enterprise, suggesting its new focus and vision. So, while previous diversification efforts were unsuccessful, Lockheed is trying again with a new CEO and emphasis on internal innovation.[31]

Free cash flow is the source of another potential agency problem. Calculated as operating cash flow minus capital expenditures, free cash flow represents the cash remaining after the firm has invested in all projects that have positive net present value within its current businesses.[32] Top-level managers may decide to invest free cash flow in product lines that are not associated with the firm's current lines of business to increase the firm's degree of diversification (as is currently being done at Lockheed). However, when managers use free cash flow to diversify the firm in ways that do not have a strong possibility of creating additional value for stakeholders and certainly for shareholders, the firm is overdiversified. Overdiversification is an example of self-serving and opportunistic managerial behavior. In contrast to managers, shareholders may prefer that free cash flow be distributed to them as dividends, so they can control how the cash is invested.[33]

In Figure 10.2, Curve *S* shows shareholders' optimal level of diversification. As the firm's owners, shareholders seek the level of diversification that reduces the risk of the firm's total failure while simultaneously increasing its value by developing economies of scale and scope (see Chapter 6). Of the four corporate-level diversification strategies shown in Figure 10.2, shareholders likely prefer the diversified position noted by point *A* on Curve *S*—a position that is located between the dominant business and related-constrained diversification strategies. Of course, the optimum level of diversification owners seek varies from firm to firm.[34] Factors that affect shareholders' preferences include the firm's primary industry, the intensity

**Figure 10.2** Manager and Shareholder Risk and Diversification

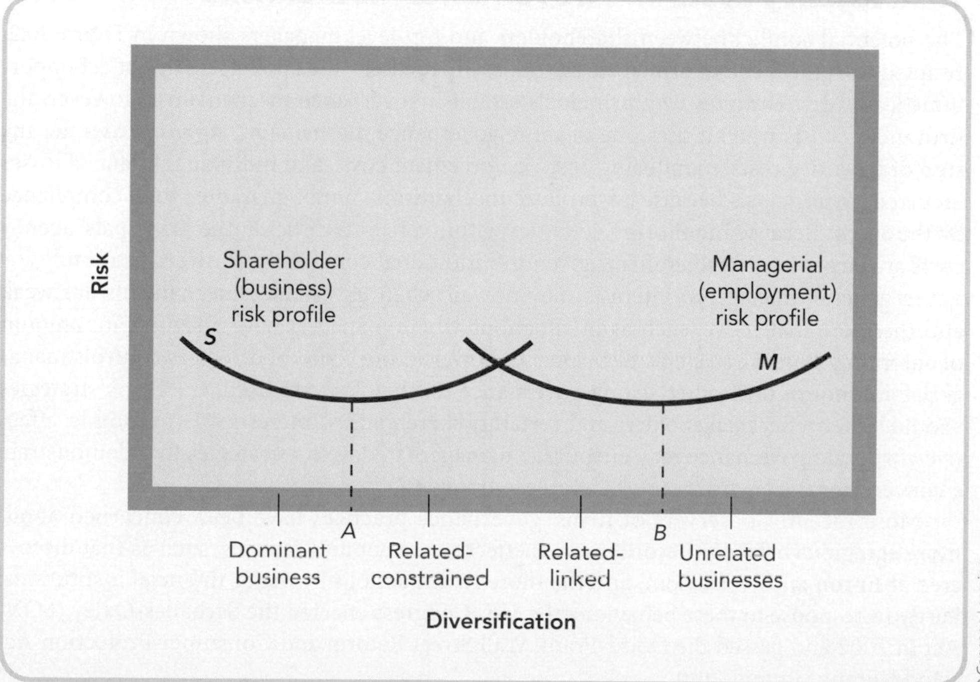

of rivalry among competitors in that industry, the top management team's experience with implementing diversification strategies, and the firm's perceived expertise in the new business and its effects on other firm strategies, such as its entry into international markets.[35]

As is the case for principals, top-level managers—as agents—also seek an optimal level of diversification. Declining performance resulting from too much diversification increases the probability that external investors (representing the market for corporate control) will purchase a substantial percentage of or the entire firm for the purpose of controlling it. If a firm is acquired, the employment risk for its top-level managers increases significantly. Furthermore, these managers' employment opportunities in the external managerial labor market (discussed in Chapter 12) are affected negatively by a firm's poor performance. Therefore, top-level managers prefer that the firms they lead be diversified. However, their preference is that the firm's diversification falls short of the point at which it increases their employment risk and reduces their employment opportunities.[36] Curve *M* in Figure 10.2 shows that top-level managers prefer higher levels of product diversification than do shareholders. Top-level managers might find the optimal level of diversification as shown by point *B* on Curve *M*.

In general, shareholders prefer riskier strategies and more focused diversification. Shareholders reduce their risk by holding a diversified portfolio of investments. Alternatively, managers cannot balance their employment risk by working for a diverse portfolio of firms; therefore, managers may prefer a level of diversification that maximizes firm size and their compensation while also reducing their employment risk. Finding the appropriate level of diversification is difficult for managers. Research has shown that too much diversification can have negative effects on the firm's ability to create innovation (managers' unwillingness to take on higher risks). Alternatively, diversification that strategically fits the firm's capabilities can enhance its innovation output.[37] However, too much or inappropriate diversification can also divert managerial attention from other important firm activities such as corporate social responsibility.[38] Product diversification, therefore, is a potential agency problem that could result in principals incurring costs to control their agents' behaviors.

### 10-1c Agency Costs and Governance Mechanisms

The potential conflict between shareholders and top-level managers shown in Figure 10.2, coupled with the fact that principals cannot easily predict which managers might act opportunistically, demonstrates why principals establish governance mechanisms. However, the firm incurs costs when it uses one or more governance mechanisms. **Agency costs** are the sum of incentive costs, monitoring costs, enforcement costs, and individual financial losses incurred by principals because governance mechanisms cannot guarantee total compliance by the agent. Because monitoring activities within a firm is difficult, the principals' agency costs are larger in diversified firms given the additional complexity of diversification.[39]

In general, managerial interests may prevail when governance mechanisms are weak and therefore ineffective, such as in situations where managers have a significant amount of autonomy to make strategic decisions. If, however, the board of directors controls managerial autonomy, or if other strong governance mechanisms are used, the firm's strategies should better reflect stakeholders and certainly shareholders' interests.[40] For example, effective corporate governance may encourage managers to develop strategies that demonstrate a concern for the environment (i.e., "green strategies").[41]

More recently, observers of firms' governance practices have been concerned about more egregious behavior beyond mere ineffective corporate strategies, such as that discovered at Enron and WorldCom, and the more recent actions by major financial institutions. Partly in response to these behaviors, the U.S. Congress enacted the Sarbanes-Oxley (SOX) Act in 2002 and passed the Dodd-Frank Wall Street Reform and Consumer Protection Act (Dodd-Frank) in mid-2010.

**Agency costs** are the sum of incentive costs, monitoring costs, enforcement costs, and individual financial losses incurred by principals because governance mechanisms cannot guarantee total compliance by the agent.

Because of these two acts, corporate governance mechanisms should receive greater scrutiny.[42] While the implementation of SOX has been controversial to some, most believe that its use has led to generally positive outcomes in terms of protecting stakeholders and certainly shareholders' interests. For example, Section 404 of SOX, which prescribes significant transparency improvement on internal controls associated with accounting and auditing, has arguably improved the internal auditing scrutiny (and thereby trust) in firms' financial reporting. Moreover, research suggests that internal controls associated with Section 404 increase shareholder value.[43] Nonetheless, some argue that the Act, especially Section 404, creates excessive costs for firms. In addition, a decrease in foreign firms listing on U.S. stock exchanges occurred at the same time as listing on foreign exchanges increased. In part, this shift may be because of the costs SOX generates for firms seeking to list on U.S. exchanges.

AP Photo/Pablo Martinez Monsivais

*President Barack Obama signing the Dodd-Frank Wall Street Reform and Consumer Protection Act. The full impact of this controversial governance mechanism has yet to be determined.*

Dodd-Frank is recognized as the most sweeping set of financial regulatory reforms in the United States since the Great Depression. The Act is intended to align financial institutions' actions with society's interests. Dodd-Frank includes provisions related to the categories of consumer protection, systemic risk oversight, executive compensation, and capital requirements for banks. Some legal analysts offer the following description of the Act's provisions: "(Dodd-Frank) creates a Financial Stability Oversight Council headed by the Treasury Secretary, establishes a new system for liquidation of certain financial companies, provides for a new framework to regulate derivatives, establishes new corporate governance requirements, and regulates credit rating agencies and securitizations. The Act also establishes a new consumer protection bureau and provides for extensive consumer protection in financial services."[44]

More intensive application of governance mechanisms as mandated by legislation such as Sarbanes-Oxley and Dodd-Frank affects firms' choice of strategies. For example, more intense governance might find firms choosing to pursue fewer risky projects, possibly decreasing shareholder wealth as a result. In considering how some provisions associated with Dodd-Frank that deal with banks might be put into practice, a U.S. federal regulator said, "To put it plainly, my view is that we are in danger of trying to squeeze too much risk and complexity out of banking."[45] As this comment suggests, determining governance practices that strike an appropriate balance between protecting stakeholders' interests and allowing firms to implement strategies with some degree of risk is difficult.

Next, we explain the effects of the three internal governance mechanisms on managerial decisions regarding the firm's strategies.

## 10-2 Ownership Concentration

**Ownership concentration** is defined by the number of large-block shareholders and the total percentage of the firm's shares they own. **Large-block shareholders** typically own

**Ownership concentration** is defined by the number of large-block shareholders and the total percentage of the firm's shares they own.

**Large-block shareholders** typically own at least 5 percent of a company's issued shares.

at least 5 percent of a company's issued shares. Ownership concentration as a governance mechanism has received considerable interest because large-block shareholders are increasingly active in their demands that firms adopt effective governance mechanisms to control managerial decisions so that they will best represent owners' interests.[46] In recent years, the number of individuals who are large-block shareholders has declined. Institutional owners have replaced individuals as large-block shareholders.

In general, diffuse ownership (a large number of shareholders with small holdings and few, if any, large-block shareholders) produces weak monitoring of managers' decisions. One reason for this is that diffuse ownership makes it difficult for owners to effectively coordinate their actions. As noted earlier, diversification beyond the shareholders' optimum level can result from ineffective monitoring of managers' decisions. Higher levels of monitoring could encourage managers to avoid strategic decisions that harm shareholder value, such as too much diversification. Research evidence suggests that ownership concentration is associated with lower levels of firm product diversification.[47] Thus, with high degrees of ownership concentration, the probability is greater that managers' decisions will be designed to maximize shareholder value.[48] However, the influence of large-block shareholders is mitigated to a degree in Europe by strong labor representation on boards of directors.[49]

As noted, ownership concentration influences decisions made about the strategies a firm will use and the value created by their use. In general, but not in every case, ownership concentration's influence on strategies and firm performance is positive. For example, when large-block shareholders have a high degree of wealth, they have power relative to minority shareholders to appropriate the firm's wealth; this is particularly the case when they are in managerial positions. Excessive appropriation at the expense of minority shareholders is somewhat common in emerging economy countries where minority shareholder rights often are not as protected as they are in the United States. In fact, in some of these countries state ownership of an equity stake (even minority ownership) can be used to control these potential problems.[50] The importance of boards of directors to mitigate excessive appropriation of minority shareholder value has been found in firms with strong family ownership where family members have incentives to appropriate shareholder wealth, especially in the second generation after the founder has departed.[51] In general, family-controlled businesses will outperform nonfamily businesses, especially smaller and nonpublic firms because of the importance of enhancing the family's wealth and maintaining the family business.[52] However, families often try to balance the pursuit of economic and noneconomic objectives such that they sometimes may be moderately risk averse (thereby influencing their innovative output).[53]

## 10-2a The Increasing Influence of Institutional Owners

A classic work published in the 1930s argued that a separation of ownership and control had come to characterize the "modern" corporation.[54] This change occurred primarily because growth prevented founders-owners from maintaining their dual positions in what were increasingly complex companies. More recently, another shift has occurred: Ownership of many modern corporations is now concentrated in the hands of institutional investors rather than individual shareholders.[55]

**Institutional owners** are financial institutions such as mutual funds and pension funds that control large-block shareholder positions. Because of their prominent ownership positions, institutional owners, as large-block shareholders, have the potential to be a powerful governance mechanism. Estimates of the amount of equity in U.S. firms held by institutional owners held range from 60 to 75 percent. Recent commentary suggests the importance of pension funds to an entire economy: "Pension funds are critical drivers of growth and economic activity in the United States because they are one of the only significant sources of long-term, patient capital."[56]

**Institutional owners** are financial institutions such as mutual funds and pension funds that control large-block shareholder positions.

These percentages suggest that as investors, institutional owners have both the size and the incentive to discipline ineffective top-level managers and that they can significantly influence a firm's choice of strategies and strategic decisions.[57] Research evidence indicates that institutional and other large-block shareholders are becoming more active in their efforts to influence a corporation's strategic decisions, unless they have a business relationship with the firm. Initially, these shareholder activists and institutional investors concentrated on the performance and accountability of CEOs and contributed to the dismissal of a number of them. Activists often target the actions of boards more directly via proxy vote proposals that are intended to give shareholders more decision rights because they believe board processes have been ineffective.[58] A rule approved by the U.S. Securities and Exchange Commission allowing large shareholders (owning 1 to 5 percent of a company's stock) to nominate up to 25 percent of a company's board of directors enhances shareholders' decision rights.[59]

The institutional investor BlackRock is the largest manager of financial assets in the world, with just under $4 trillion invested and holdings in most of the largest global corporations. Interestingly, it was once described as a "silent giant" because it did not engage in activism. However, recently the silent giant has been awakened, as it has begun asking more questions of the firms in which it holds significant investments. Most of its actions are "behind the scenes," only voting against a director or a company proposal when its unobtrusive actions have failed to change the firm's behavior. BlackRock has become more "confrontational" in order to ensure the value of its investments, and some wish that it would become even more active because of the power of its large equity holdings.[60] To date, research suggests that institutional activism may not have a strong direct effect on firm performance but may indirectly influence a targeted firm's strategic decisions, including those concerned with international diversification and innovation. Thus, to some degree at least, institutional activism has the potential to discipline managers and to enhance the likelihood of a firm taking future actions that are in shareholders' best interests.[61] However, the Opening Case suggests that large institutional owners often go along with the desires of powerful CEOs and boards such as at JPMorgan Chase.

## 10-3 Board of Directors

Shareholders elect the members of a firm's board of directors. The **board of directors** is a group of elected individuals whose primary responsibility is to act in the owners' best interests by formally monitoring and controlling the firm's top-level managers.[62] Those elected to a firm's board of directors are expected to oversee managers and to ensure that the corporation operates in ways that will best serve stakeholders' interests, and particularly the owners' interests. Helping board members reach their expected objectives are their powers to direct the affairs of the organization and reward and discipline top-level managers.

Though important to all shareholders, a firm's individual shareholders with small ownership percentages are very dependent on the board of directors to represent their interests. Unfortunately, evidence suggests that boards have not been highly effective in monitoring and controlling top-level managers' decisions and subsequent actions.[63] Because of their relatively ineffective performance and in light of the recent financial crisis, boards are experiencing increasing pressure from shareholders, lawmakers, and regulators to become more forceful in their oversight role to prevent top-level managers from acting in their own best interests. Moreover, in addition to their monitoring role, board members increasingly are expected to provide resources to the firms they serve. These resources include their personal knowledge and expertise and their relationships with a wide variety of organizations.[64]

**board of directors** is a group of elected individuals whose primary responsibility is to act in the owners' best interests by formally monitoring and controlling the firm's top-level managers.

Generally, board members (often called directors) are classified into one of three groups (see Table 10.1). *Insiders* are active top-level managers in the company who are elected to the board because they are a source of information about the firm's day-to-day operations.[65] *Related outsiders* have some relationship with the firm, contractual or otherwise, that may create questions about their independence, but these individuals are not involved with the corporation's day-to-day activities. *Outsiders* provide independent counsel to the firm and may hold top-level managerial positions in other companies or may have been elected to the board prior to the beginning of the current CEO's tenure.[66]

Historically, inside managers dominated a firm's board of directors. A widely accepted view is that a board with a significant percentage of its membership from the firm's top-level managers provides relatively weak monitoring and control of managerial decisions.[67] With weak board monitoring, managers sometimes use their power to select and compensate directors and exploit their personal ties with them. In response to the SEC's proposal to require audit committees to be composed of outside directors, in 1984 the New York Stock Exchange implemented a rule requiring outside directors to head the audit committee. Subsequently, other rules required that independent outsider directors lead important committees such as the compensation committee and the nomination committee.[68] These other requirements were instituted after the Sarbanes-Oxley Act was passed, and policies of the New York Stock Exchange now require companies to maintain boards of directors that are composed of a majority of outside independent directors and to maintain full independent audit committees. Thus, additional scrutiny of corporate governance practices is resulting in a significant amount of attention being devoted to finding ways to recruit quality independent directors and to encourage boards to take actions that fully represent shareholders' best interests.[69]

Critics advocate reforms to ensure that independent outside directors are a significant majority of a board's total membership; research suggests this has been accomplished.[70] However, others argue that having outside directors is not enough to resolve the problems in that CEO power can strongly influence a board's decision. One proposal to reduce the power of the CEO is to separate the chair's role and the CEO's role on the board so that the same person does not hold both positions.[71] A situation in which an individual holds both the CEO and chair of the board title is called *CEO duality*. As is shown with the Opening Case about CEO duality at JPMorgan Chase, it is often very difficult to separate the CEO and chair positions after they have been given to one person. Unfortunately, having a board that actively monitors top-level managers' decisions and actions does not ensure high performance. The value that the directors bring to the company also influences the outcomes. For example, boards with members having significant relevant experience and knowledge are the most likely to help the firm formulate and implement effective strategies.[72]

**Table 10.1** Classification of Board of Directors' Members

| *Insiders* |
|---|
| • **The firm's CEO and other top-level managers** |
| *Related outsiders* |
| • **Individuals not involved with the firm's day-to-day operations, but who have a relationship with the company** |
| *Outsiders* |
| • **Individuals who are independent of the firm in terms of day-to-day operations and other relationships** |

Alternatively, having a large number of outside board members can also create some problems. For example, because outsiders typically do not have contact with the firm's day-to-day operations and do not have ready access to detailed information about managers and their skills, they lack the insights required to fully and effectively evaluate their decisions and initiatives.[73] Outsiders can, however, obtain valuable information through frequent interactions with inside board members and during board meetings to enhance their understanding of managers and their decisions.

Because they work with and lead the firm daily, insiders have access to information that facilitates forming and implementing appropriate strategies. Accordingly, some evidence suggests that boards with a critical mass of insiders typically are better informed about intended strategic initiatives, the reasons for the initiatives, and the outcomes expected from pursuing them.[74] Without this type of information, outsider-dominated boards may emphasize financial, as opposed to strategic, controls to gather performance information to evaluate managers' and business units' performances. A virtually exclusive reliance on financial evaluations shifts risk to top-level managers who, in turn, may make decisions to maximize their interests and reduce their employment risk. Reducing investments in R&D, further diversifying the firm, and pursuing higher levels of compensation are some of the results of managers' actions to reach the financial goals set by outsider-dominated boards.[75] Additionally, boards can make mistakes in strategic decisions because of poor decision processes, and in CEO succession decisions because of the lack of important information about candidates as well as the firm's specific needs. Overall, knowledgeable and balanced boards are likely to be the most effective over time.[76]

## 10-3a Enhancing the Effectiveness of the Board of Directors

Because of the importance of boards of directors in corporate governance and as a result of increased scrutiny from shareholders—in particular, large institutional investors—the performances of individual board members and of entire boards are being evaluated more formally and with greater intensity.[77] The demand for greater accountability and improved performance is stimulating many boards to voluntarily make changes. Among these changes are (1) increases in the diversity of the backgrounds of board members (e.g., a greater number of directors from public service, academic, and scientific settings; a greater percentage of ethnic minorities and women; and members from different countries on boards of U.S. firms); (2) the strengthening of internal management and accounting control systems; (3) establishing and consistently using formal processes to evaluate the board's performance; (4) modifying the compensation of directors, especially reducing or eliminating stock options as a part of their package; and (5) creating the "lead director" role[78] that has strong powers with regard to the board agenda and oversight of non-management board member activities.

An increase in the board's involvement with a firm's strategic decision-making processes creates the need for effective collaboration between board members and top-level managers. Some argue that improving the processes used by boards to make decisions and monitor managers and firm outcomes is important for board effectiveness.[79] Moreover, because of the increased pressure from owners and the potential conflict among board members, procedures are necessary to help boards function effectively while seeking to discharge their responsibilities.

Increasingly, outside directors are being required to own significant equity stakes as a prerequisite to holding a board seat. In fact, some research suggests that firms perform better if outside directors have such a stake; the trend is toward higher pay for directors with more stock ownership, but with fewer stock options.[80] However, other research suggests that too much ownership can lead to lower independence for board members.[81] In addition, other research suggests that diverse boards help firms make more effective strategic

© iStockphoto.com/Photomorphic

*The Board of Directors is an important internal governance mechanism. It is widely believed that increased director independence and board member diversity lead to more effective governance.*

decisions and perform better over time.[82] Although questions remain about whether more independent and diverse boards enhance board effectiveness, the trends for greater independence and increasing diversity among board members are likely to continue.

### 10-3b Executive Compensation

The compensation of top-level managers, and especially of CEOs, generates a great deal of interest and strongly held opinions. Some believe that top-management team members and certainly CEOs have a great deal of responsibility for a firm's performance and that they should be rewarded accordingly.[83] Others conclude that these individuals (and again, especially CEOs) are greatly overpaid and that their compensation is not as strongly related to firm performance as should be the case.[84] One of the three internal governance mechanisms attempts to deal with these issues. Specifically, **executive compensation** is a governance mechanism that seeks to align the interests of managers and owners through salaries, bonuses, and long-term incentives, such as stock awards and options.[85]

Long-term incentive plans (typically involving stock options and stock awards) are an increasingly important part of compensation packages for top-level managers, especially those leading U.S. firms. Theoretically, using long-term incentives facilitates the firm's efforts (through the board of directors' pay-related decisions) to avoid potential agency problems by linking managerial compensation to the wealth of common shareholders.[86] Effectively designed long-term incentive plans have the potential to prevent large-block stockholders (e.g., institutional investors) from pressing for changes in the composition of the board of directors and the top-management team in that they assume that when exercised, the plans will ensure that top-level managers will act in shareholders' best interests. Additionally, shareholders typically assume that top-level managers' pay and the firm's performance are more properly aligned when outsiders are the dominant block of a board's membership. Research results suggesting that fraudulent behavior can be associated with stock option incentives, such as earnings manipulation,[87] demonstrate the importance of the firm's board of directors (as a governance mechanism) actively monitoring the use of executive compensation as a governance mechanism.

Effectively using executive compensation as a governance mechanism is particularly challenging for firms implementing international strategies. For example, the interests of the owners of multinational corporations may be best served by less uniformity in the firm's foreign subsidiaries' compensation plans.[88] Developing an array of unique compensation plans requires additional monitoring, potentially increasing the firm's agency costs. Importantly, pay levels vary by regions of the world. For example, managerial pay is highest in the United States and much lower in Asia. Historically, compensation for top-level managers has been lower in India partly because many of the largest firms have strong family ownership and control.[89] Also, acquiring firms in other countries increases the complexity associated with a board of directors' efforts to use executive compensation as an effective internal corporate governance mechanism.[90]

**Executive compensation** is a governance mechanism that seeks to align the interests of managers and owners through salaries, bonuses, and long-term incentives such as stock awards and options.

### 10-3c The Effectiveness of Executive Compensation

As an internal governance mechanism, executive compensation—especially long-term incentive compensation—is complicated, for several reasons. First, the strategic decisions top-level managers make are complex and nonroutine, meaning that direct supervision (even by the firm's board of directors) is likely to be ineffective as a means of judging the quality of their decisions. The result is a tendency to link top-level managers' compensation to outcomes the board can easily evaluate, such as the firm's financial performance. This leads to a second issue in that, typically, the effects of top-level managers' decisions are stronger on the firm's long-term performance than its short-term performance. This reality makes it difficult to assess the effects of their decisions on a regular basis (e.g., annually). Third, a number of other factors affect a firm's performance besides top-level managerial decisions and behavior. Unpredictable changes in segments (economic, demographic, political/legal, etc.) in the firm's general environment (see Chapter 2) make it difficult to separate out the effects of top-level managers' decisions and the effects (both positive and negative) of changes in the firm's external environment on the firm's performance.

Properly designed and used incentive compensation plans for top-level managers may increase the value of a firm in line with shareholder expectations, but such plans are subject to managerial manipulation.[91] Additionally, annual bonuses may provide incentives to pursue short-run objectives at the expense of the firm's long-term interests. Although long-term, performance-based incentives may reduce the temptation to underinvest in the short run, they increase executive exposure to risks associated with uncontrollable events, such as market fluctuations and industry decline. The longer term the focus of incentive compensation, the greater are the long-term risks top-level managers bear. Also, because long-term incentives tie a manager's overall wealth to the firm in a way that is inflexible, such incentives and ownership may not be valued as highly by a manager as by outside investors who have the opportunity to diversify their wealth in a number of other financial investments.[92] Thus, firms may have to overcompensate for managers using long-term incentives.[93]

Even though some stock option-based compensation plans are well designed with option strike prices substantially higher than current stock prices, some have been developed for the primary purpose of giving executives more compensation. Research of stock option repricing where the strike price value of the option has been lowered from its original position suggests that action is taken more frequently in high-risk situations.[94] However, repricing also happens when firm performance is poor, to restore the incentive effect for the option. Evidence also suggests that politics are often involved, which has resulted in "option backdating."[95] While this evidence shows that no internal governance mechanism is perfect, some compensation plans accomplish their purpose. For example, recent research suggests that long-term pay designed to encourage managers to be environmentally friendly has been linked to higher success in preventing pollution.[96]

The Strategic Focus summarizes some issues regarding executive compensation and the Board's ouster of one CEO and appointment of a new one at Citigroup. Vikram Pandit was awarded compensation of $14.9 million for 2011 but this action was placed before the shareholders, 55 percent of whom voted against it. A new chair of the board was appointed who clashed with the CEO over major strategic actions he took. This CEO was forced to resign in October of 2012 and was given $6.7 million in pay for his work in 2012. The newly appointed CEO was awarded a pay package of $11.5 million in compensation for 2012. The new compensation system for Citigroup executives will more closely link pay with the performance of the bank, with shareholder value relative to peer banks and return on assets as the primary factors. As the discussion suggests, this internal governance mechanism is likely to continue receiving a great deal of scrutiny in the years to come. When designed properly and used effectively, each of the three internal governance mechanisms can contribute positively to the firm operating in ways that best serve stakeholders and

# Strategic Focus

FAILURE

## CEO Pay and Performance: Board Revolution at Citigroup

Vikram Pundit was appointed as CEO of Citigroup in 2007. He had to try to correct the major problems from the financial disaster that struck Citigroup and most major banking organizations in the United States. In fact, because of the poor risk management at Citigroup that resulted in major losses from collateralized debt obligations related to bad mortgages, Citigroup received the largest federal bailout to stay afloat.

Pandit brought in a new management team and set about restructuring the bank. Approximately 11,000 jobs were eliminated and some units were sold off. These actions finally produced a small profit in 2010 and a net profit of $11 billion in 2011. Although the turnaround seemed to be successful, some analysts felt that more assets should have been sold off and the bank should become smaller and more focused. Perhaps most critical is that shareholder value decreased by 89 percent during Pandit's tenure.

A new chair of the board, Michael O'Neill, was appointed in April 2012. Shareholders and the board were displeased by two major actions taken by Pandit. First, he requested approval from the Federal Reserve to return capital to shareholders through a stock buyback (such actions commonly increase the stock price) or by issuing dividends. When the Fed did not approve this request, shareholders blamed Pandit. The second action that concerned shareholders and the board was the selloff of Citigroup's stake in Morgan Stanley at a loss.

In 2012, shareholders were given a vote on the proposed compensation package for Pandit of $14.9 million and 55 percent voted against it. Additionally, Pandit clashed with new board chair O'Neill on the executive team pay packages (presumably his own as well) and for the failure of recent strategic actions.

In October 2012, Pandit was forced to resign and awarded $6.7 million for his work as CEO during 2012. Michael Corbat, a long-time employee of Citigroup, was immediately named the new CEO. Interestingly, he was given a pay package of $11.5 million in 2012, which included a $4.2 million cash bonus. The board's compensation committee consulted the major shareholders (institutional investors) who collectively own about 30 percent of the equity in the bank to determine the compensation package for Corbat. They changed the way in which Citigroup's top executives would be paid. Instead of deferred cash compensation, the performance portion was composed of stock grants that vested three years in the future. The amount of stock award will be based on the bank's shareholder value relative to peer banks and to return on assets.

*Michael L. Corbat, CEO of Citigroup, arrives at the Planalto Palace before a meeting with Brazil's President, Dilma Rousseff, in Brasilia on April 9, 2013. Corbat is restructuring Citi in the wake of the forced resignation of his predecessor, Vikram Pandit.*



Although Corbat suggested that the bank was on the right path, he is expected to engage in additional restructuring. He also appointed a new top management team. After Corbat was on the job for slightly more than half a year, Citigroup's stock price was already up about 30 percent. So, he has had a strong start. Of course, he will have to perform well if he wishes to receive higher compensation and, indeed, keep his job as CEO.

Sources: M. Farrel, 2013, Citi's stock surges 30% under Corbat, *CNNMoney*, http://money.cnn.com, March 13; S. S. Patel, 2013, Citi on the right strategic path: CEO Corbat-restructuring mainly in the past, but more on tap if needed, *MarketWatch*, www.marketwatch.com, March 5; C. Isidore, 2013, Citigroup CEO Corbat's pay: $11.5 million, *CNNMoney*, http://money.cnn.com, February 22; D. Enrich, S. Kapner, & D. Fitzpatrick, 2012, Pandit is forced out at Citi, *Wall Steet Journal*, www.wsj.com, October 17; S. Schaefer, 2012, Meet the new boss: Citi taps Michael Corbat for CEO job after Pandit resigns, *Forbes*, www.forbes.com, October 16; R. Cox, M. Goldstein, & J. Horowitz, 2012, Citi's Pandit exits abruptly after board clash, *Reuters*, www.reuters.com, October 16; B. Protess, 2012, Adept moves in financial crisis clear Citigroup Chief's path to top job, *New York Times DealBook*, http://dealbook.nytimes.com, October 16; J. E. David, 2012, Meet Michael Corbat, Citigroup's new boss, CNBC.com, www.cnbc.com, October 16.

especially shareholders' interests. By the same token, because none of the three mechanisms are perfect in design or execution, the market for corporate control, an external governance mechanism, is sometimes needed.

Learn more about Morgan Stanley.
www.cengagebrain.com

## 10-4 Market for Corporate Control

The **market for corporate control** is an external governance mechanism that is active when a firm's internal governance mechanisms fail.[97] The market for corporate control is composed of individuals and firms that buy ownership positions in or purchase all of potentially undervalued corporations typically for the purpose of forming new divisions in established companies or merging two previously separate firms. Because the top-level managers are assumed to be responsible for the undervalued firm's poor performance, they are usually replaced. An effective market for corporate control ensures that ineffective and/or opportunistic top-level managers are disciplined.[98]

Commonly, target firm managers and board members are sensitive about takeover bids emanating from the market for corporate control in that being a target suggests that they have been ineffective in fulfilling their responsibilities. For top-level managers, a board's decision to accept an acquiring firm's offer typically finds them losing their jobs in that the acquirer usually wants different people to lead the firm. At the same time, rejection of an offer also increases the risk of job loss for top-level managers because the pressure from the board and shareholders for them to improve the firm's performance becomes substantial.[99]

A hedge fund is an investment fund that can pursue many different investment strategies, such as taking long and short positions, using arbitrage, and buying and selling undervalued securities for the purpose of maximizing investors' returns. Growing rapidly, in 2012 the top 100 hedge funds invested about $1.35 trillion in the United States alone.[100] Given investors' increasing desire to hold underperforming funds and their managers accountable, hedge funds have become increasingly active in the market for corporate control.[101]

In general, activist pension funds (as institutional investors and as an internal governance mechanism) are reactive in nature, taking actions when they conclude that a firm is underperforming. In contrast, activist hedge funds (as part of the market for corporate control) are proactive, "identifying a firm whose performance could be improved and then investing in it."[102] This means that "hedge funds are better at identifying undervalued companies, locating potential acquirers for them, and removing opposition to a takeover."[103]

In March 2013, investor Carl Icahn made a bid to purchase Dell. In January 2013, it was announced that Michael Dell was leading a group of investors to complete a management buyout of his company. Because of poor performance it had been the target of acquisition rumors, and the buyout is intended to avoid Dell losing control (although the stated purpose is to make the company stronger and more competitive). In announcing his bid, Icahn criticized Dell for what he believed was the firm's underperformance relative to its potential. Importantly, he criticized Dell's offer for being too low. Dell's buyout offer was for $13.65 per share. Icahn originally offered $15 per share for up to 58.1 percent of the shares. In May, Icahn teamed with Southwestern to offer $12 per share or additional Dell stock. Michael Dell's buyout team claims that Icahn is short of having the required money to complete the deal. Interestingly, in June 2013, Dell Inc. announced a 14 percent reduction in pay for its CEO, Michael Dell, because of its poor performance (declining sales, profits, and stock price). Regardless of who wins this battle, it seems that Dell's strategy failed and so did its governance system because performance continues to decline.[104]

The situation between Icahn and Dell demonstrates the possibility that the firm may have been underperforming and, as such, that the market for corporate control should be active to discipline managers and to represent shareholders' best interests. However, another

The **market for corporate control** is an external governance mechanism that is active when a firm's internal governance mechanisms fail.

M. Scasy

possibility is suggested by research results—namely, that as a governance mechanism, investors sometimes use the market for corporate control to take an ownership position in firms that are performing well.[105] A study of active corporate raiders in the 1980s showed that takeover attempts often were focused on above-average performance firms in an industry.[106] This work and other recent research suggest that the market for corporate control is an imperfect governance mechanism.[107] Actually, mergers and acquisitions are highly complex strategic actions with many purposes and potential outcomes. Some are successful and many are not—even when they have potential to do well—because implementation challenges when integrating two diverse firms can limit their ability to realize their potential.[108]

In summary, the market for corporate control is a blunt instrument for corporate governance; nonetheless, this governance mechanism does have the potential to represent shareholders' best interests. Accordingly, top-level managers want to lead their firms in ways that make disciplining by activists outside the company unnecessary and/or inappropriate.

There are a number of defense tactics top-level managers can use to fend off a takeover attempt. Managers leading a target firm that is performing well are almost certain to try to thwart the takeover attempt. Even in instances when the target firm is underperforming its peers, managers might use defense tactics to protect their own interests. In general, managers' use of defense tactics is considered to be self-serving in nature.

## 10-4a **Managerial Defense Tactics**

In the majority of cases, hostile takeovers are the principal means by which the market for corporate control is activated. A *hostile takeover* is an acquisition of a target company by an acquiring firm that is accomplished "not by coming to an agreement with the target company's management but by going directly to the company's shareholders or fighting to replace management in order to get the acquisition approved."[109] Dell's potential management buyout by Michael Dell and a team of investors is not a hostile bid because it has been initiated by management (namely Michael Dell). However, it can be considered as a defense tactic against potential hostile bids. Alternatively, Carl Icahn's offer represents a hostile takeover bid.

Firms targeted for a hostile takeover may use multiple defense tactics to fend off the takeover attempt. Increased use of the market for corporate control has enhanced the sophistication and variety of managerial defense tactics that are used in takeovers.

Because the market for corporate control tends to increase risk for managers, managerial pay may be augmented indirectly through golden parachutes (wherein a CEO can receive up to three years' salary if his or her firm is taken over). Golden parachutes, similar to most other defense tactics, are controversial. Another takeover defense strategy is traditionally known as a "poison pill." This strategy usually allows shareholders (other than the acquirer) to convert "shareholders' rights" into a large number of common shares if an individual or company acquires more than a set amount of the target firm's stock (typically 10 to 20 percent). Increasing the total number of outstanding shares dilutes the potential acquirer's existing stake, meaning that to maintain or expand its ownership position the potential acquirer must buy additional shares at premium prices. The additional purchases increase the potential acquirer's costs. Some firms amend the corporate charter so board member elections are staggered, resulting in only one third of members being up for reelection each year. Research shows that this results in managerial entrenchment and reduced vulnerability to hostile takeovers.[110] Additional takeover defense strategies are presented in Table 10.2.

Most institutional investors oppose the use of defense tactics. TIAA-CREF and CalPERS have taken actions to have several firms' poison pills eliminated. Many institutional investors also oppose severance packages (golden parachutes), and the opposition is increasing significantly in Europe as well.[111] However, an advantage to severance packages is that they may encourage top-level managers to accept takeover bids with the potential to best serve

**Table 10.2** Hostile Takeover Defense Strategies

| Defense strategy | Success as a strategy | Effects on shareholder wealth |
|---|---|---|
| Capital structure change Dilution of the target firm's stock, making it more costly for an acquiring firm to continue purchasing the target's shares. Employee stock option plans (ESOPs), recapitalization, issuance of additional debt, and share buybacks are actions associated with this strategy. | Medium | Inconclusive |
| Corporate charter amendment An amendment to the target firm's charter for the purpose of staggering the elections of members to its board of directors so that all are not elected during the same year. This change to the firm's charter prevents a potential acquirer from installing a completely new board in a single year. | Very low | Negative |
| Golden parachute A lump-sum payment of cash that is given to one or more top-level managers when the firm is acquired in a takeover bid. | Low | Negligible |
| Greenmail The repurchase of the target firm's shares of stock that were obtained by the acquiring firm at a premium in exchange for an agreement that the acquirer will no longer target the company for takeover. | Medium | Negative |
| Litigation Lawsuits that help the target firm stall hostile takeover attempts. Antitrust charges and inadequate disclosure are examples of the grounds on which the target firm could file. | Low | Positive |
| Poison pill An action the target firm takes to make its stock less attractive to a potential acquirer. | High | Positive |
| Standstill agreement A contract between the target firm and the potential acquirer specifying that the acquirer will not purchase additional shares of the target firm for a specified period of time in exchange for a fee paid by the target firm. | Low | Negative |

Source: R. Campbell, C. Ghosh, M. Petrova, & C. F. Sirmans, 2011, Corporate governance and performance in the market for corporate control: The case of REITS, *Journal of Real Estate Finance & Economics*, 42: 451-480; M. Ryngaert & R. Schlten, 2010, Have changing takeover defense rules and strategies entrenched management and damaged shareholders? The case of defeated takeover bids, *Journal of Corporate Finance*, 16: 16-37; N, Ruiz-Mallorqui & D. J. Santana-Martin, 2009, Ultimate institutional owner and takeover defenses in the controlling versus minority shareholders context, *Corporate Governance: An International Review*, 17: 238-254; J. A. Pearce II & R. B. Robinson, Jr., 2004, Hostile takeover defenses that maximize shareholder wealth, *Business Horizons*, 47(5): 15-24.

shareholders' interest.[112] Alternatively, research results show that using takeover defenses reduces the amount of pressure managers feel to seek short-term performance gains, resulting in them concentrating on developing strategies with a longer time horizon and a high probability of serving stakeholders' interests. Such firms are more likely to invest in and develop innovation; when they do so, the firm's market value increases, thereby rewarding shareholders.[113]

An awareness on the part of top-level managers about the existence of external investors in the form of individuals (e.g., Carl Icahn) and groups (e.g., hedge funds) often positively influences them to align their interests with those of the firm's stakeholders, especially the shareholders. Moreover, when active as an external governance mechanism, the market for corporate control has brought about significant changes in many firms' strategies and, when used appropriately, has served shareholders' interests. Of course, the goal is to have the managers develop the psychological ownership of principals.[114]

As described in the Strategic Focus, the top-level executives at Smithfield stand to profit handsomely from the sale of the company to a Chinese firm, Shuanghui International. Their personal fortunes will increase by more than $85 million with the completion of the acquisition. They will benefit even though Smithfield has been the second worst-performing food company in the United States. It has achieved negative returns and paid shareholders no dividends for five years. Their benefits come from defense tactics that immediately vest their holdings of stock options and other stock granted for future performance increases.

## Strategic Focus GLOBALIZATION

### Rewarding Top Executives of One of the Worst-Performing Food Companies in the World: The Chinese Takeover of Smithfield Foods

The proxy filing by Smithfield Foods in 2012 described how top executives of the company would profit from a change of control in the company. Specifically, if Smithfield is acquired by an external party, the senior executives of the company would have their stock options, restricted stock, and performance-based shares vest immediately. In addition, they would retain their jobs (very unusual as immediate vesting is normally allowed only when the executives lose their jobs due to the acquisition). If they lose their jobs, the benefits are even greater.

In 2012, Smithfield had $13.1 billion in annual revenues. Smithfield is vertically integrated and the largest U.S. pork producer (11 percent of its revenues are from international sales). However, the company has achieved a negative return of 18 percent over the five years ending in March 2013. It also paid no dividends to shareholders during this time. During this time, Smithfield is the second-worst performer of all U.S. food producers, with sales of more than $10 billion.

In March, one of Smithfield's largest owners, Continental Grain (it holds 6.8 percent of the company's stock), sent a letter encouraging the top executives and board to focus on creating value. The shareholders have gained little benefit in recent years with negative returns and no dividends. Competitors Tyson and Hormel have paid $429 million and $728 million in dividends, respectively, during the five years when Smithfield paid none.

A Chinese company has come to the rescue, as Shuanghui International has made an offer to acquire Smithfield and pay a 31 percent premium. Because of the "change of control" provisions, the senior executives are scheduled to receive $85.4 million if the acquisition is completed, and the executives will all be retained in their current positions. If by chance the executives' employment is terminated within two years of the acquisition, they will collectively receive a minimum of $126.4 million.

Some have expressed concerns that a Chinese company will control Smithfield. The acquisition will have to be approved by the Committee on Foreign Investment in the United States, a government group that evaluates national security risks. Others have expressed concern because of the lack of controls and scandals in the food industry in China. However, industry analysts note that pork consumption is on the decline in the United States and on the increase in China. So, Smithfield is most likely to produce pork for the Chinese market rather than import meat from China for the U.S. market. In fact, the acquisition will provide Smithfield an opportunity to sell its goods in the lucrative pork food market in China.

*In one of the largest-ever purchases of a U.S. firm, China's Shuanghui International entered into a deal to buy Smithfield Foods for $4.7 billion. Through this acquisition, Shuanghui International will secure a strong supply of U.S. pork for the Chinese market.*



Unless Continental balks at the acquisition or another suitor makes a better offer, it is expected that Smithfield will be acquired by Shuanghui. And, although the senior executives have not created value for shareholders in some time, they stand to profit handsomely from the sale of their company.

Sources: T. Biesheuvel & S. Casey, 2013, Smithfield bosses to pocket $85.4 million from Chinese deal, *Charlotte Observer*, www.charlotteobserver.com, May 31; D. Kesmodel & S. Thurm, 2013, Smithfield CEO in line for big stock payout, *Wall Street Journal*, www.wsj.com, May 30; D. Thomas & O. Oran, 2013, China's appetite for pork spurs $4.7 billion Smithfield buy, *Yahoo! Finance*, http://finance.yahoo.com, May 30; K.B. Grant, 2013, Bacon backlash unlikely over Smithfield deal, *Yahoo! Finance*, http://finance.yahoo.com, May 30; S. Montlake, 2013, Why Chinese purchase of Smithfield could be game changer for pork trade, *Forbes*, www.forbes.com, May 30; P. Kavilanz, 2013, China's expensive love affair with pork, *CNNMoney*, http://money.cnn.com, May 29; S. Strom, 2013, China's food deal extends its reach, already mighty, *New York Times*, www.nytimes.com, May 29.

And their compensation will be more than 48 percent higher if they are terminated within two years after the acquisition. So, it largely ensures they will keep their jobs as well.

Next, we describe international governance practices to explain how they differ across regions and countries.

Find out more about Tyson.
www.cengagebrain.com

# 10-5 International Corporate Governance

Corporate governance is an increasingly important issue in economies around the world, including emerging economies. Globalization in trade, investments, and equity markets increases the potential value of firms throughout the world using similar mechanisms to govern corporate activities. Moreover, because of globalization, major companies want to attract foreign investment. For this to happen, foreign investors must be confident that adequate corporate governance mechanisms are in place to protect their investments.

Although globalization is stimulating an increase in the intensity of efforts to improve corporate governance and potentially to reduce the variation in regions and nations' governance systems,[115] the reality remains that different nations do have different governance systems in place. Recognizing and understanding differences in various countries' governance systems as well as changes taking place within those systems improves the likelihood a firm will be able to compete successfully in the international markets it chooses to enter. Next, to highlight the general issues of differences and changes taking place in governance systems, we discuss corporate governance practices in two developed economies—Germany and Japan—and in China, an emerging economy.

## 10-5a Corporate Governance in Germany and Japan

In many private German firms, the owner and manager may be the same individual. In these instances, agency problems are not present.[116] Even in publicly traded German corporations, a single shareholder is often dominant. Thus, the concentration of ownership is an important means of corporate governance in Germany, as it is in the United States.[117]

Historically, banks occupied the center of the German corporate governance system. This is the case in other European countries as well, such as Italy and France. As lenders, banks become major shareholders when companies they financed seek funding on the stock market or default on loans. Although the stakes are usually less than 10 percent, banks can hold a single ownership position up to but not exceeding 15 percent of the bank's capital. Although shareholders can tell banks how to vote their ownership position, they generally do not do so. The banks monitor and control managers, both as lenders and as shareholders, by electing representatives to supervisory boards.

German firms with more than 2,000 employees are required to have a two-tiered board structure that places the responsibility for monitoring and controlling managerial (or supervisory) decisions and actions in the hands of a separate group.[118] All the functions of strategy and management are the responsibility of the management board (the Vorstand); however, appointment to the Vorstand is the responsibility of the supervisory tier (the Aufsichtsrat). Employees, union members, and shareholders appoint members to the Aufsichtsrat. Proponents of the German structure suggest that it helps prevent corporate wrongdoing and rash decisions by "dictatorial CEOs." However, critics maintain that it slows decision making and often ties a CEO's hands. The corporate governance practices in Germany make it difficult to restructure companies as quickly as can be done in the United States. Because of the role of local government (through the board structure) and the power of banks in Germany's corporate governance structure, private shareholders rarely have major ownership positions in German firms. Additionally, there is a significant amount of cross-shareholdings among firms.[119] However, large institutional investors, such as pension

M. Stasy

funds (outside of banks and insurance companies), are also relatively insignificant owners of corporate stock. Thus, at least historically, German executives generally have not been dedicated to maximizing shareholder wealth to the degree that is the case for top-level managers in the United Kingdom and the United States.[120]

However, corporate governance practices used in Germany have been changing in recent years. A manifestation of these changes is that a number of German firms are gravitating toward U.S. governance mechanisms. Recent research suggests that the traditional system in Germany produced some agency costs because of a lack of external ownership power. Interestingly, German firms with listings on U.S. stock exchanges have increasingly adopted executive stock option compensation as a long-term incentive pay policy.[121]

The concepts of obligation, family, and consensus affect attitudes toward corporate governance in Japan. As part of a company family, individuals are members of a unit that envelops their lives; families command the attention and allegiance of parties throughout corporations. In addition, Japanese firms are concerned with a broader set of stakeholders than are firms in the United States, including employees, suppliers, and customers.[122] Moreover, a *keiretsu* (a group of firms tied together by cross-shareholdings) is more than an economic concept—it, too, is a family. Some believe, though, that extensive cross-shareholdings impede the type of structural change that is needed to improve the nation's corporate governance practices.[123] Consensus, another important influence in Japanese corporate governance, calls for the expenditure of significant amounts of energy to win the hearts and minds of people whenever possible, as opposed to top-level managers issuing edicts.[124] Consensus is highly valued, even when it results in a slow and cumbersome decision-making process.

As in Germany, banks in Japan have an important role in financing and monitoring large public firms.[125] Because the main bank in the keiretsu owns the largest share of stocks and holds the largest amount of debt, it has the closest relationship with a firm's top-level managers. The main bank provides financial advice to the firm and also closely monitors managers. Thus, Japan has a bank-based financial and corporate governance structure, whereas the United States has a market-based financial and governance structure.[126]

Aside from lending money, a Japanese bank can hold up to 5 percent of a firm's total stock; a group of related financial institutions can hold up to 40 percent. In many cases, main-bank relationships are part of a horizontal keiretsu. A keiretsu firm usually owns less than 2 percent of any other member firm; however, each company typically has a stake of that size in every firm in the keiretsu. As a result, 30 to 90 percent of a firm is owned by other members of the keiretsu. Thus, a keiretsu is a system of relationship investments.

Japan's corporate governance practices have been changing in recent years. For example, because of Japanese banks' continuing development as economic organizations, their role in the monitoring and control of managerial behavior and firm outcomes is less significant than in the past.[127] Also, deregulation in the financial sector has reduced the cost of mounting hostile takeovers.[128] As such, deregulation facilitated additional activity in Japan's market for corporate control, which was nonexistent in past years. And there are pressures for more changes because of weak performance by many Japanese companies. In fact, there has been significant criticism of the corporate governance practices of the Tokyo Electric Power Company after the severe problems at the Fukushima Daiichi nuclear power plant following the earthquake and tsunami in 2011. Most Japanese firms have boards that are largely composed of internal management so they reflect the upper echelon of management. As a result, these boards exercise little monitoring of the top-level managers in Japanese firms. Independent nonexecutive board members are rare but the practice is beginning to increase in Japanese firms. A recent study showed that outside directors composed about 13.5 percent of the Japanese firm boards that are listed on the Nikkei 500.[129]

### 10-5b Corporate Governance in China

"China has a unique and large, socialist, market-oriented economy. The government has done much to improve the corporate governance of listed companies."[130] These comments suggest that corporate governance practices in China have been changing with increasing privatization of businesses and the development of equity markets. However, the stock markets in China remain young and are continuing to develop. In their early years, these markets were weak because of significant insider trading, but with stronger governance these markets have improved.[131]

There has been a gradual decline in China in the equity held in state-owned enterprises and the number and percentage of private firms have grown, but the state still relies on direct and/or indirect controls to influence the strategies firms use. Even private firms try to develop political ties with the government because of their role in providing access to resources and to the economy.[132] In terms of long-term success, these conditions may affect firms' performance in that research shows that firms with higher state ownership tend to have lower market value and more volatility in that value across time. This is because of agency conflicts in the firms and because the executives do not seek to maximize shareholder returns given that they must also seek to satisfy social goals placed on them by the government.[133] This suggests a potential conflict between the principals, particularly the state owner and the private equity owners of the state-owned enterprises.[134]

Some evidence suggests that corporate governance in China may be tilting toward the Western model. For example, recent research shows that with increasing frequency, the compensation of top-level executives in Chinese companies is closely related to prior and current financial performance of their firm.[135] Research also shows that due to the weaker institutions, firms with family CEOs experience more positive financial performance than others without the family influence.[136]

Changing a nation's governance systems is a complicated task that will encounter problems as well as successes while seeking progress. Thus, corporate governance in Chinese companies continues to evolve and likely will for some time to come as parties (e.g., the Chinese government and those seeking further movement toward free-market economies) interact to form governance mechanisms that are best for their nation, business firms, and citizens. However, along with changes in the governance systems of specific countries, multinational companies' boards and managers are also evolving. For example, firms that have entered more international markets are likely to have more top executives with greater international experience and to have a larger proportion of foreign directors on theory boards.[137]

## 10-6 Governance Mechanisms and Ethical Behavior

The three internal and one external governance mechanisms are designed to ensure that the agents of the firm's owners—the corporation's top-level managers—make strategic decisions that best serve the interests of all stakeholders. In the United States, shareholders are commonly recognized as the company's most significant stakeholders. Increasingly though, top-level managers are expected to lead their firms in ways that will also serve the needs of product market stakeholders (e.g., customers, suppliers, and host communities) and organizational stakeholders (e.g., managerial and nonmanagerial employees).[138] Therefore, the firm's actions and the outcomes flowing from them should result in at least minimal satisfaction of the interests of all stakeholders. Without at least minimal satisfaction of its interests, a dissatisfied stakeholder will withdraw its support from the firm and provide it to another (e.g., customers will purchase products from a supplier offering an acceptable substitute).

Some believe that the internal corporate governance mechanisms designed and used by ethically responsible companies increase the likelihood the firm will be able to at least minimally satisfy all stakeholders' interests.[139] Scandals at companies such as Enron, WorldCom, HealthSouth, and Satyam (a large information technology company based in India), among others, illustrate the negative effects of poor ethical behavior on a firm's efforts to satisfy stakeholders. The issue of ethical behavior by top-level managers as a foundation for best serving stakeholders' interests is being taken seriously in countries throughout the word.[140]

The decisions and actions of the board of directors can be an effective deterrent to unethical behaviors by top-level managers. Indeed, evidence suggests that the most effective boards set boundaries for their firms' business ethics and values.[141] After the boundaries for ethical behavior are determined and likely formalized in a code of ethics, the board's ethics-based expectations must be clearly communicated to the firm's top-level managers and to other stakeholders (e.g., customers and suppliers) with whom interactions are necessary for the firm to produce and sell its products. Moreover, as agents of the firm's owners, top-level managers must understand that the board, acting as an internal governance mechanism, will hold them fully accountable for developing and supporting an organizational culture in which only ethical behaviors are permitted. As explained in Chapter 12, CEOs can be positive role models for improved ethical behavior.

Learn more about ethical behavior.
www.cengagebrain.com

A major issue confronted by multinational companies operating in international markets is that of bribery.[142] As a whole, countries with weak institutions that have greater bribery activity tend to have fewer exports as a result. In addition, small and medium-sized firms are the most harmed by bribery. Thus, bribery tends to limit entrepreneurial activity that can help a country's economy grow. While larger multinational firms tend to experience fewer negative outcomes, their power to exercise more ethical leadership allows them greater flexibility in selecting which markets they will enter and how they will do so.[143]

Through effective governance that results from well-designed governance mechanisms and the appropriate country institutions, top-level managers, working with others, are able to select and use strategies that result in strategic competitiveness and earning above-average returns. While some firms' governance mechanisms are ineffective, other companies are recognized for the quality of their governance activities.

*World Finance* evaluates the corporate governance practices of companies throughout the world. For 2013, this group's "Best Corporate Governance Awards" by country were given to Royal Bank of Canada (Canada), COSCO (China), Continental AG (Germany), Royal Philips Electronics (Netherlands), GlaxoSmithKline (United Kingdom), and AECOM (United States). These awards are determined by analyzing a number of issues concerned with corporate governance, such as board accountability and financial disclosure, executive compensation, shareholder rights, ownership base, takeover provisions, corporate behavior, and overall responsibility exhibited by the company.[144]

# SUMMARY


- Corporate governance is a relationship among stakeholders that is used to determine a firm's direction and control its performance. How firms monitor and control top-level managers' decisions and actions affects the implementation of strategies. Effective governance that aligns managers' decisions with shareholders' interests can help produce a competitive advantage for the firm.
- Three internal governance mechanisms are used in the modern corporation: (1) ownership concentration, (2) the board of directors, and (3) executive compensation. The market for corporate control is an external governance mechanism influencing managers' decisions and the outcomes resulting from them.
- Ownership is separated from control in the modern corporation. Owners (principals) hire managers (agents) to make decisions that maximize the firm's value. As risk-bearing specialists, owners diversify their risk by investing in multiple corporations with different risk profiles. Owners expect their agents (the firm's top-level managers, who are decision-making specialists)


M. Stasy

to make decisions that will help to maximize the value of their firm. Thus, modern corporations are characterized by an agency relationship that is created when one party (the firm's owners) hires and pays another party (top-level managers) to use its decision-making skills.

- Separation of ownership and control creates an agency problem when an agent pursues goals that conflict with the principals' goals. Principals establish and use governance mechanisms to control this problem.
- Ownership concentration is based on the number of large-block shareholders and the percentage of shares they own. With significant ownership percentages, such as those held by large mutual funds and pension funds, institutional investors often are able to influence top-level managers' strategic decisions and actions. Thus, unlike diffuse ownership, which tends to result in relatively weak monitoring and control of managerial decisions, concentrated ownership produces more active and effective monitoring. Institutional investors are a powerful force in corporate America and actively use their positions of concentrated ownership to force managers and boards of directors to make decisions that best serve shareholders' interests.
- In the United States and the United Kingdom, a firm's board of directors, composed of insiders, related outsiders, and outsiders, is a governance mechanism expected to represent shareholders' interests. The percentage of outside directors on many boards now exceeds the percentage of inside directors. Through implementation of the SOX Act, outsiders are expected to be more independent of a firm's top-level managers compared with directors selected from inside the firm. Relatively recent rules formulated and implemented by the U.S. Securities and Exchange Commission to allow owners with large stakes to propose new directors are beginning to change the balance even more in favor of outside and independent directors. Additional governance-related regulations have resulted from the Dodd-Frank Act.
- Executive compensation is a highly visible and often criticized governance mechanism. Salary, bonuses, and long-term incentives are used for the purpose of aligning managers' and shareholders' interests. A firm's board of directors is responsible for determining the effectiveness of the firm's executive compensation system. An effective system results in managerial decisions that are in shareholders' best interests.
- In general, evidence suggests that shareholders and boards of directors have become more vigilant in controlling managerial decisions. Nonetheless, these mechanisms are imperfect and sometimes insufficient. When the internal mechanisms fail, the market for corporate control—as an external governance mechanism—becomes relevant. Although it too is imperfect, the market for corporate control has been effective resulting in corporations reducing inefficient diversification and implementing more effective strategic decisions.
- Corporate governance structures used in Germany, Japan, and China differ from each other and from the structure used in the United States. Historically, the U.S. governance structure focused on maximizing shareholder value. In Germany, employees, as a stakeholder group, take a more prominent role in governance. By contrast, until recently, Japanese shareholders played virtually no role in monitoring and controlling top-level managers. However, Japanese firms are now being challenged by "activist" shareholders. In China, the central government still plays a major role in corporate governance practices. Internationally, all these systems are becoming increasingly similar, as are many governance systems both in developed countries, such as France and Spain, and in transitional economies, such as Russia and India.
- Effective governance mechanisms ensure that the interests of all stakeholders are served. Thus, strategic competitiveness results when firms are governed in ways that permit at least minimal satisfaction of capital market stakeholders (e.g., shareholders), product market stakeholders (e.g., customers and suppliers), and organizational stakeholders (managerial and nonmanagerial employees; see Chapter 2). Moreover, effective governance produces ethical behavior in the formulation and implementation of strategies.

## REVIEW QUESTIONS

1. What is corporate governance? What factors account for the considerable amount of attention corporate governance receives from several parties, including shareholder activists, business press writers, and academic scholars? Why is governance necessary to control managers' decisions?
2. What is meant by the statement that ownership is separated from managerial control in the corporation? Why does this separation exist?
3. What is an agency relationship? What is managerial opportunism? What assumptions do owners of corporations make about managers as agents?
4. How is each of the three internal governance mechanisms—ownership concentration, boards of directors, and executive compensation—used to align the interests of managerial agents with those of the firm's owners?
5. What trends exist regarding executive compensation? What is the effect of the increased use of long-term incentives on top-level managers' strategic decisions?
6. What is the market for corporate control? What conditions generally cause this external governance mechanism to become active? How does this mechanism constrain top-level managers' decisions and actions?

7. What is the nature of corporate governance in Germany, Japan, and China?
8. How can corporate governance foster ethical decisions and behaviors on the part of managers as agents?

# EXPERIENTIAL EXERCISES

## EXERCISE 1: WHAT IS HAPPENING TO EXECUTIVE PAY?

Your text describes executive compensation as "a governance mechanism that seeks to align the interests of managers and owners through salaries, bonuses, and long-term incentives such as stock awards and options." There is a great deal of interest in setting executive compensation for public corporations. There are those with strongly held beliefs that the system is broken and pay is out of control. Those in this camp feel that Dodd-Frank finally puts some controls in place, particularly for those whose pay increases while firm performance lags. They also argue that shareholders are not well protected. Additionally those who feel Dodd-Frank is an overreach of regulation argue that free market mechanisms should allow the proper setting of executive compensation.

The Dodd-Frank Wall Street Reform and Consumer Protection Act of 2010 contained some important regulations regarding executive compensation, in particular "say-on-pay" shareholder voting requirements and provisions that companies must disclose the relationship between executive compensation and firm performance. There also is a move to link these measures to Total Shareholder Return (TSR) as a way to align executive compensation.

Many pundits on both sides predicted significant changes to executive compensation as a result of the passage of this bill. Since a few years have passed, what has been the impact? Individually, research trends in executive compensation since the passage of the law in 2010.

Be prepared to answer the following questions:

1. What has happened to executive pay packages since passage of the act?
2. What is total shareholder return and how is it calculated? Provide an example.
3. Has there been any impact on long term incentive pay for executives?
4. Do you feel that passage of Dodd-Frank as regards executive compensation has been effective?

## EXERCISE 2: GOVERNANCE: DOES IT MATTER COMPETITIVELY?

Governance mechanisms are effective when they meet the needs of all stakeholders. Governance mechanisms are also a key way in which to ensure that strategic decisions are made effectively. As a potential employee, how would you go about investigating a firm's governance structure, and would that investigation weigh in your decision to become an employee? Identify a firm that you currently would like to join or one that you just find interesting. Working individually, research the following aspects of your target firm.

- Find a copy of the firm's most recent proxy statement and 10-K. Proxy statements are sent to shareholders prior to each year's annual meeting and contain detailed information about the company's governance and issues on which a shareholder vote might be held. Proxy statements are typically available from a firm's Web site (look for an "Investors" submenu). You can also access proxy statements and other government filings such as the 10-K from the SEC's EDGAR database (http://www.sec.gov/edgar.shtml). Alongside the proxy you should also be able to access the firm's annual report. Here you will find information concerning performance, governance, and the firm's outlook, among other matters.
- Identify one of the firm's main competitors for comparison. You can find one of the firm's main competitors by using company analysis tools such as Datamonitor.

Some of the topics that you should examine include:

- Compensation plans (for both the CEO and board members–be sure to look for differences between fixed and incentive compensation)
- Board composition (e.g., board size, insiders and outsiders, interlocking directorates, functional experience, how many active CEOs, how many retired CEOs, what is the demographic makeup, and age diversity)
- Committees (e.g., number, composition, compensation)
- Stock ownership by officers and directors—identify beneficial ownership from stock owned (you will need to look through the notes of the ownership tables to comprehend this)
- Ownership concentration—how much of the firm's outstanding stock is owned by institutions, individuals, insiders? How many large-block shareholders are there (owners of 5 percent or more)?
- Does the firm utilize a dual structure for the CEO and chair of the board?
- Is there a lead director who is not an officer of the company?
- Activities by activist shareholders regarding corporate governance issues of concern
- Are there any managerial defense tactics employed by the firm? For example, what does it take for a shareholder proposal to come to a vote and be adopted?

- Does the firm have a code of ethical conduct? If so, what does it contain?

Prepare a report summarizing the results of your findings that compares your target firm and its competitor side by side. Your memo should include the following topics:

- Summarize the key aspects of the firms' governance mechanisms.
- Create a single graph covering the last 10-year historical stock performance for both companies. If applicable, find a representative index to compare both with, such as S&P or NASDAQ.
- Highlight key differences between your target firm and its competitor.
- Based on your review of the firm's governance, did you change your opinion of the firm's desirability as an employer? Why or why not? How does the target firm compare to the main competitor you identified?

## VIDEO CASE

### KNOWLEDGE BRINGS CORPORATE GOVERNANCE: WHISTLEBLOWING AT STAFFORD GENERAL HOSPITAL

Emphasizing targets rather than proper care, Stafford General Hospital created a culture that discouraged complaints and resulted in high mortality rates. The public campaigns of family members and relatives to vocalize their knowledge of Stafford's failures in basic nursing care stimulated government investigations, which revealed that doctors and nurses knew of the hospital's poor care and that their concerns were ignored. While whistleblower provisions were already in place, this investigation and new leadership has made quality of care a primary concern along with monetary commitments to staff, facilities, and training, and a "no blame whistleblowing policy" to bring poor practices out in the open. A 2011 Care Quality Commission inspection found a lack of suitably trained nurses in the emergency room, so the ER was closed at night for three months for staff development. In 2013 the hospital trust was almost insolvent following a 67 percent drop in the number of patients, due to a loss of confidence after the scandal. However, Stafford Hospital's mortality rate is now amongst the best within the West Midlands.

Be prepared to discuss the following concepts and questions in class:

### Concepts

1. Corporate governance
2. Agency relationship
3. Market for corporate control
4. International corporate governance

### Questions

1. What corporate governance mechanisms failed at Stafford General Hospital?
2. Were there possibilities of agency problems within Stafford? Why or why not? Could managerial opportunism be an issue?
3. Can the Trust Foundation for Stafford be effective as a market for corporate control?
4. What role do you think the corporate governance structure of the United Kingdom played in the problems at Stafford?
5. How do you think the situation at Stafford will impact international corporate governance?

## NOTES


1. X. Castaner & N. Kavadis, 2013, Does good governance prevent bad strategy? A study of corporate governance, financial diversification, and value creation by French corporations, 2000–2006, *Strategic Management Journal*, in press; D. R. Dalton & C. M. Dalton, 2011, Integration of micro and macro studies in governance research: CEO duality, board composition, and financial performance, *Journal of Management*, 37: 404–411.
2. A. P. Cowen & J. J. Marcel, 2011, Damaged goods: Board decisions to dismiss reputationally compromised directors, *Academy of Management Journal*, 54: 509–527; I. Okhmatovskiy & R. J. David, 2012, Setting your own standards: Internal corporate governance codes as a response to institutional pressure, *Organization Science*, 23: 155–176.
3. P. J. Davis, 2013, Senior executives and their boards: Toward a more involved director, *Journal of Business Strategy*, 34(1): 3–40; G. D. Bruton, I. Filatotchev, S. Chahine, & M. Wright, 2010, Governance, ownership structure, and performance of IPO firms: The impact of different types of private equity investors and institutional environments, *Strategic Management Journal*, 31: 491–509.
4. A. T. Arikan & M. A. Schilling, 2011, Structure and governance in industrial districts: Implications for competitive advantage, *Journal of Management Studies*, 48: 772–803; D. R. Dalton, M. A. Hitt, S. T. Certo, & C. M. Dalton, 2008, The fundamental agency problem and its mitigation: Independence, equity and the market for corporate control, in J. P. Walsh and A. P. Brief (eds.),

*The Academy of Management Annals*, New York: Lawrence Erlbaum Associates, 1–64; E. F. Fama & M. C. Jensen, 1983, Separation of ownership and control, *Journal of Law and Economics*, 26: 301–325.

5. R. V. Aguilera, 2011, Interorganizational governance and global strategy, *Global Strategy Journal*, 1: 90–95; J. S. Harrison, D. A. Bosse, & R. A. Phillips, 2010, Managing for stakeholders, stakeholder utility functions, and competitive advantage, *Strategic Management Journal*, 31: 58–74.
6. Y. Huang, A. Chen & L. Kao, 2012, *Asia Pacific Journal of Management*, 29: 39–58; T. J. Boulton, S. B. Smart, & C. J. Zutter, 2010, IPO underpricing and international corporate governance, *Journal of International Business Studies*, 41: 206–222.
7. E. Vaara, R. Sarala, G. K. Stahl, & I. Bjorkman, 2012, The impact of organizational and national cultural differences on social conflict and knowledge transfer in international acquisitions, *Journal of Management Studies*, 49: 1–27; W. Judge, 2010, Corporate governance mechanisms throughout the world, *Corporate Governance: An International Review*, 18: 159–160.
8. A. Tan, 2011, Singapore proposes corporate governance changes to shield image, *Bloomberg Businessweek*, www.businessweek.com, June 14.
9. G. Bell, I. Filatotchev, & R. Aguilera, 2013, Corporate governance and investors' perceptions of foreign IPO value: An institutional perspective, *Academy of Management Journal*, in press; W. Kim, T. Sung, & S.-J. Wei, 2011, Does corporate governance risk at home affect investment choice abroad? *Journal of International Economics*, 85: 25–41.
10. J. Lee, 2013, Dancing with the enemy? Relational hazards and the contingent value of repeat exchanges in M&A markets, *Organization Science*, 24: 1237–1256; S. Boivie, D. Lange, M. L. McDonald, & J. D. Westphal, 2011, Me or we: The effects of CEO organizational identification on agency costs, *Academy of Management Journal*, 54: 551–576; M. A. Hitt, R. E. Hoskisson, R. A. Johnson, & D. D. Moesel, 1996, The market for corporate control and firm innovation, *Academy of Management Journal*, 45: 697–716.
11. G. E. Davis & T. A. Thompson, 1994, A social movement perspective on corporate control, *Administrative Science Quarterly*, 39: 141–173.
12. V. V. Acharya, S. C. Myers, & R. G. Rajan, 2011, The internal governance of firms, *Journal of Finance*, 66: 689–720; R. Bricker & N. Chandar, 2000, Where Berle and Means went wrong: A reassessment of capital market agency and financial reporting, *Accounting, Organizations, and Society*, 25: 529–554.
13. A. M. Colpan, T. Yoshikawa, T. Hikino, & E. G. Del Brio, 2011, Shareholder heterogeneity and conflicting goals: Strategic investments in the Japanese electronics industry, *Journal of Management Studies*, 48: 591–618; R. M. Wiseman & L. R. Gomez-Mejia, 1999, A behavioral agency model of managerial risk taking, *Academy of Management Review*, 23: 133–153.
14. D. L. Deephouse & P. Jaskiewicz, 2013, Do family firms have better reputations than non-family firms? An integration of socioecomotional wealth and social identity theory, *Journal of Management Studies*, 50: 337–360; A. Minichilli, G. Corbetta, & I. C. MacMillan, 2010, Top management teams in family-controlled companies: 'Familiness', 'faultlines', and their impact on financial performance, *Journal of Management Studies*, 47: 205–222.
15. D. Miller, I. Le Breton-Miller, & R. Lester, 2013, Family firm governance, strategic conformity and performance: Institutional vs. strategic perspectives, *Organization Science*, in press; M. W. Peng & Y. Jiang, 2010, Institutions behind family ownership and control in large firms, *Journal of Management Studies*, 47: 253–273.
16. E. Gedajlovic, M. Carney, J. J. Chrisman, & F. W. Kellermans, 2012, The adolescence of family firm research: Taking stock and planning for the future, *Journal of Management*, 38: 1010–1037; R. C. Anderson & D. M. Reeb, 2004, Board composition: Balancing family influence in S&P 500 firms, *Administrative Science Quarterly*, 49: 209–237.
17. E. Lutz & S. Schrami, 2012, Family firms: Should they hire an outside CFO? *Journal of Business Strategy*, 33(1): 39–44; E.-T. Chen & J. Nowland, 2010, Optimal board monitoring in family-owned companies: Evidence from Asia, *Corporate Governance: An International Review*, 18: 3–17; M. Santiago-Castro & C. J. Brown, 2007, Ownership structure and minority rights: A Latin American view, *Journal of Economics and Business*, 59: 430–442.
18. J. L. Arregle, L. Naldi, M. Nordquvist, & M. A. Hitt, 2012, Internationalization of family controlled firm: A study of the effects of external involvement in governance, *Entrepreneurship Theory and Practice*, 36: 1115–1143; D. G. Sirmon, J.-L. Arregle, M. A. Hitt, & J. W. Webb, 2008, Strategic responses to the threat of imitation, *Entrepreneurship Theory and Practice*, 32: 979–998.
19. R. M. Wiseman, G. Cuevas-Rodriguez, & L. R. Gomez-Mejia, 2012, Towards a social theory of agency, *Journal of Management Studies*, 49: 202–222; G. Dushnitsky & Z. Shapira, 2010, Entrepreneurial finance meets organizational reality: Comparing investment practices and performance of corporate and independent venture capitalists, *Strategic Management Journal*, 31: 990–1017.
20. T. J. Quigley & D. C. Hambrick, 2012, When the former CEO stays on as board chair: Effects on successor discretion, strategic change and performance, *Strategic Management Journal*, 33: 834–859; S. Machold, M. Huse, A. Minichilli, & M. Nordqvist, 2011, Board leadership and strategy involvement in small firms: A team production approach, *Corporate Governance: An International Review*, 19: 368–383.
21. T. Yoshikawa, A. A. Rasheed, & E. B. Del Brio, 2010, The impact of firm strategy and foreign ownership on executive bonus compensation in Japanese firms, *Journal of Business Research*, 63: 1254–1260; A. Mackey, 2008, The effects of CEOs on firm performance, *Strategic Management Journal*, 29: 1357–1367.
22. W. Li & Y. Lu, 2012, CEO dismissal, institutional development and environmental dynamism, *Asia Pacific Journal of Management*, 29: 1007–1026; L. L. Lan & L. Heracleous, 2010, Rethinking agency theory: The view from law, *Academy of Management Review*, 35: 294–314; Dalton, Hitt, Certo, & Dalton, 2008, The fundamental agency problem and its mitigation: Independence, equity and the market for corporate control.
23. K. Vafai, 2010, Opportunism in organizations, *Journal of Law, Economics, and Organization*, 26: 158–181; O. E. Williamson, 1996, *The Mechanisms of Governance*, New York: Oxford University Press, 6.
24. F. Lumineau & D. Malhotra, 2011, Shadow of the contract: How contract structure shapes interfirm dispute resolution, *Strategic Management Journal*, 32: 532–555; B. E. Ashforth, D. A. Gioia, S. L. Robinnson, & L. K. Trevino, 2008, Reviewing organizational corruption, *Academy of Management Review*, 33: 670–684.
25. M. L. McDonald, P. Khanna, & J. D. Westphal, 2008, Getting them to think outside the circle: Corporate governance CEOs' external advice networks, and firm performance, *Academy of Management Journal*, 51: 453–475.
26. J. Harris, S. Johnson, & D. Souder, 2013, Model theoretic knowledge accumulation: The case of agency theory and incentive alignment, *Academy of Management Review*, 38: 442–454; L. Weber & K. J. Mayer, 2011, Designing effective contracts: Exploring the influence of framing and expectations, *Academy of Management Review*, 36: 53–75.
27. T. Hutzschenreuter & J. Horstkotte, 2013, Performance effects of top management team demographic faultlines in the process of product diversification, *Strategic Management Journal*, 34: 704–726; E. Levitas, V. L. Barker, III, & M. Ahsan, 2011, Top manager ownership levels and incentive alignment in inventively active firms, *Journal of Strategy and Management*, 4: 116–135.
28. I. K. El Medi & S. Seboui, 2011, Corporate diversification and earnings management, *Review of Accounting and Finance*, 10: 176–196; P. David, J. P. O'Brien, T. Yoshikawa, &.

A. Delios, 2010, Do shareholders or stakeholders appropriate the rents from corporate diversification? The influence of ownership structure, *Academy of Management Journal*, 53: 636–654; G. P. Baker & B. J. Hall, 2004, CEO incentives and firm size, *Journal of Labor Economics*, 22: 767–798.

29. S. W. Geiger & L. H. Cashen, 2007, Organizational size and CEO compensation: The moderating effect of diversification in downscoping organizations, *Journal of Managerial Issues*, 9: 233–252.

30. M. Larraza-Kintana, L. R. Gomez-Mejia, & R. M. Wiseman, 2011, Compensation framing and the risk-taking behavior of the CEO: Testing the influence of alternative reference points, *Management Research: The Journal of the Iberoamerican Academy of Management*, 9: 32–55; S. Rajgopal, T. Shevlin, & V. Zamaora, 2006, CEOs' outside employment opportunities and the lack of relative performance evaluation in compensation contracts, *Journal of Finance*, 61: 1813–1844.

31. B. Kowitt, 2013, Lockheed's secret weapon, *Fortune*, May 20, 196–204.

32. M. S. Jensen, 1986, Agency costs of free cash flow, corporate finance, and takeovers, *American Economic Review*, 76: 323–329.

33. R. E. Meyer & M. A. Hollerer, 2010, Meaning structures in a contested issue field: A topographic map of shareholder value in Austria, *Academy of Management Journal*, 54: 1241–1262; A. V. Douglas, 2007, Managerial opportunism and proportional corporate payout policies, *Managerial Finance*, 33(1): 26–42; M. Jensen & E. Zajac, 2004, Corporate elites and corporate strategy: How demographic preferences and structural position shape the scope of the firm, *Strategic Management Journal*, 25: 507–524.

34. S. F. Matusik & M. A. Fitza, 2012, Diversification in the venture capital industry: Leveraging knowledge under uncertainty, *Strategic Management Journal*, 33: 407–426; G. Kenny, 2012, Diversification: Best practices of the leading companies, *Journal of Business Strategy*, 33: (1): 12-20.

35. M. V. Shyam Kumar, 2013, The costs of related diversification: The impact of the core business on the productivity of related segments, *Organization Science*, in press; F. Neffke & M. Henning, Skill relatedness and firm diversification, *Strategic Management Journal*, 34: 297–316; M. V. S. Kumar, 2009, The relationship between product and international diversification: The effects of short-run constraints and endogeneity, *Strategic Management Journal*, 30: 99–116.

36. A. Milidonis & K. Stathopoulos, 2011, Managerial incentives, conservatism, and debt, Working paper, http://ssrn.com/abstract=1879186, July 5; D. D. Bergh, R. A. Johnson, & R.-L. Dewitt, 2008, Restructuring through spin-off or sell-off: Transforming information asymmetries into financial gain, *Strategic Management Journal*, 29: 133–148.

37. S. K. Kim, J. D. Arthurs, A. Sahaym, & J. B. Cullen, 2013, Search behavior of the diversified firm: The impact of fit on innovation, *Strategic Management Journal*, 34: 999–1009.

38. J. Kang, 2013, The relationship between corporate diversification and corporate social performance, *Strategic Management Journal*, 34: 94–109.

39. R. Duchin, 2010, Cash holdings and corporate diversification, *Journal of Finance*, 65: 955–992; E. Rawley, 2010, Diversification, coordination costs, and organizational rigidity: Evidence from microdata, *Strategic Management Journal*, 31: 873–891; T. K. Berry, J. M. Bizjak, M. L. Lemmon, & L. Naveen, 2006, Organizational complexity and CEO labor markets: Evidence from diversified firms, *Journal of Corporate Finance*, 12: 797–817.

40. R. Krause & M. Semadeni, 2013, Apprentice, departure and demotion: An examination of the three types of CEO-board chair separation, *Academy of Management Journal*, 56: 805–826.

41. J. L. Walls, P. Berrone, & P. H. Phan, 2012, Corporate governance and environmental performance: Is there really a link? *Strategic Management Journal*, 33: 885–913; C. J. Kock, J. Santalo, & L. Diestre, 2012, Corporate governance and the environment: What type of governance creates greener companies? *Journal of Management Studies*, 49: 492–514.

42. M. Hossain, S. Mitra, Z. Rezaee, & B. Sarath, 2011, Corporate governance and earnings management in the pre- and post-Sarbanes-Oxley act regimes: Evidence from implicated option backdating firms, *Journal of Accounting Auditing & Finance*, 28: 279–315; V. Chhaochharia & Y. Grinstein, 2007, Corporate governance and firm value: The impact of the 2002 governance rules, *Journal of Finance*, 62: 1789–1825.

43. Z. Singer & H. You, 2011, The effect of Section 404 of the Sarbanes-Oxley Act on earnings quality, *Journal of Accounting and Finance*, 26: 556–589; D. Reilly, 2006, Checks on internal controls pay off, *Wall Street Journal*, August 10, C3.

44. 2010, The Dodd-Frank Act: Financial reform update index, Faegre & Benson, www.faegre.com, September 7.

45. B. Appelmaum, 2011, Dodd-Frank supporters clash with currency chief, *New York Times*, www.nytimes.com, July 23.

46. M. Goranova, R. Dhanwadkar, & P. Brandes, 2010, Owners on both sides of the deal: Mergers and acquisitions and overlapping institutional ownership, *Strategic Management Journal*, 31: 1114–1135; F. Navissi & V. Naiker, 2006, Institutional ownership and corporate value, *Managerial Finance*, 32: 247–256.

47. B. L. Connelly, R. E. Hoskisson, L. Tihanyi, & S. T. Certo, 2010, Ownership as a form of corporate governance, *Journal of Management Studies*, 47: 1561–1589; M. Singh, I. Mathur, & K. C. Gleason, 2004, Governance and performance implications of diversification strategies: Evidence from large U.S. firms, *Financial Review*, 39: 489–526.

48. K. A. Desender, R. A. Aguilera, R. Crespi, & M. Garcia-Cestona, 2013, When does ownership matter? Board characteristics and behavior, *Strategic Management Journal*, 34: 823–842; J. Wu, D. Xu, & P. H. Phan, 2011, The effects of ownership concentration and corporate debt on corporate divestitures in Chinese listed firms, *Asia Pacific Journal of Management*, 28: 95–114.

49. M. van Essen, J. van Oosterhout, & P. Heugens, 2013, Competition and cooperation in corporate governance: The effects of labor institutions on blockholder effectiveness in 23 European countries, *Organization Science*, in press.

50. C. Inoue, S. Lazzarni, & A. Musacchio, 2013, Leviathan as a minority shareholder: Firm-level implications of equity purchases by the state, *Academy of Management Journal*, in press.

51. C. Singla, R. Veliyath, & R. George, 2013, Family firms and internationalization-governance relationships: Evidence of secondary agency issues, *Strategic Management Journal*, in press; S.-Y. Collin & J. Ahlberg, 2012, Blood in the boardroom: Family relationships influencing the functions of the board, *Journal of Family Business Strategy*, 3: 207–219.

52. D. Miller, A. Minichilli, & G. Corbetta, 2013, Is family leadership always beneficial? *Strategic Management Journal*, 34: 553–571; J. J. Chrisman, J. H. Chua, A. W. Pearson, & T. Barnett, 2012, Family involvement, family influence and family-centered non-economic goals in small firms, *Entrepreneurship Theory and Practice*, 36: 1103–1113.

53. A. Konig, N. Kammerlander, & A Enders, 2013, The family innovator's dilemma: How family influence affects the adoption of discontinuous technologies by incumbent firms, *Academy of Management Review*, 38: 418–441; J. J. Chrisman & P. C. Patel, 2012, Variations in R&D investments of family and nonfamily firms: Behavioral agency and myopic loss aversion perspectives, *Academy of Management Journal*, 55: 976–997; A. Stewart & M. A. Hitt, 2012, Why can't a family business be more like a nonfamily business? Modes of professionalization in family firms, *Family Business Review*, 25: 58–86.

54. A. Berle & G. Means, 1932, *The Modern Corporation and Private Property*, New York: Macmillan.

55. R. A. Johnson, K. Schnatterly, S. G. Johnson, & S.-C. Chiu, 2010, Institutional investors and institutional environment: A comparative analysis and review, *Journal*

*of Management Studies*, 47: 1590–1613; M. Gietzmann, 2006, Disclosure of timely and forward-looking statements and strategic management of major institutional ownership, *Long Range Planning*, 39: 409–427.

56. D. Marchick, 2011, Testimony of David Marchick—The power of pensions: Building a strong middle class and a strong economy, The Carlyle Group homepage, www.carlyle.com, July 12.
57. J. Chou, L. Ng, V. Sibilkov, & Q. Wang, 2011, Product market competition and corporate governance, *Review of Development Finance*, 1: 114–130; S. D. Chowdhury & E. Z. Wang, 2009, Institutional activism types and CEO compensation: A time-series analysis of large Canadian corporations, *Journal of Management*, 35: 5–36.
58. Y. Ertimur, F. Ferri, & S. R. Stubben, 2010, Board of directors' responsiveness to shareholders: Evidence from shareholder proposals, *Journal of Corporate Finance*, 16: 53–72; T. W. Briggs, 2007, Corporate governance and the new hedge fund activism: An empirical analysis, *Journal of Corporation Law*, 32: 681–723.
59. D. Brewster, 2009, U.S. investors get to nominate boards, *Financial Times*, www.ft.com, May 20.
60. P. Barnett, 2013, Are BlackRock's actions a sign that short-termism can be defeated? *Strategy Snack*, Strategic Management Bureau, May 23; S. Craig, 2013, The giant of shareholders, quietly stirring, *New York Times*, www.nytimes.com, May 18; 2013, About us, BlackRock, www.blackrock.com, accessed on June 6.
61. M. Hadani, M. Goranova, & R. Khan, 2011, Institutional investors, shareholder activism, and earnings management, *Journal of Business Research*, 64: 1352–1360; S. M. Jacoby, 2007, Principles and agents: CalPERS and corporate governance in Japan, *Corporate Governance*, 15: 5–15; L. Tihanyi, R. A. Johnson, R. E. Hoskisson, & M. A. Hitt, 2003, Institutional ownership differences and international diversification: The effects of boards of directors and technological opportunity, *Academy of Management Journal*, 46: 195–211.
62. S. Garg, 2013, Venture boards: Differences with public boards and implications for monitoring and firm performance, *Academy of Management Review*, in press; O. Faleye, R. Hoitash, & U. Hoitash, 2011, The costs of intense board monitoring, *Journal of Financial Economics*, 101: 160–181.
63. J. T. Campbell, T. C. Campbell, D. G. Sirmon, L. Bierman, & C. S. Tuggle, 2012, Shareholder influence over director nomination via proxy access: Implications for agency conflict and stakeholder value, *Strategic Management Journal*, 33: 1431–1451; C. M. Dalton & D. R. Dalton 2006, Corporate governance best practices: The proof is in the process, *Journal of Business Strategy*, 27(4): 5–7.
64. A. Tushke, W. G. Sanders, & E. Hernandez, 2013, Whose experience matters in the boardroom? The effects of experiential and vicarious learning on emerging market entry, *Strategic Management Journal*, in press; T. Dalziel, R. J. Gentry, & M. Bowerman, 2011, An integrated agency-resource dependence view of the influence of directors' human and relational capital on firms' R&D spending, *Journal of Management Studies*, 48: 1217–1242.
65. O. Faleye, 2011, CEO directors, executive incentives, and corporate strategic initiatives, *Journal of Financial Research*, 34: 241–277; C. S. Tuggle, D. G. Sirmon, C. R. Reutzel, & L. Bierman, 2010, Commanding board of director attention: Investigating how organizational performance and CEO duality affect board members' attention to monitoring, *Strategic Management Journal*, 31: 946–968.
66. S. Chahine, I. Filatotchev, & S. A. Zahra, 2011, Building perceived quality of founder-involved IPO firms: Founders' effects on board selection and stock market performance, *Entrepreneurship Theory and Practice*, 35: 319–335; Y. Ertimur, F. Ferri, & S. R. Stubben, 2010, Board of directors' responsiveness to shareholders: Evidence from shareholder proposals, *Journal of Corporate Finance*, 16: 53–72.
67. M. A. Valenti, R. Luce, & C. Mayfield, 2011, The effects of firm performance on corporate governance, *Management Research Review*, 34: 266–283; D. Reeb & A. Upadhyay, 2010, Subordinate board structures, *Journal of Corporate Finance*, 16: 469–486.
68. A. K. Gore, S. Matsunaga, & P. C Yeung, 2011, The role of technical expertise in firm governance structure: Evidence from chief financial officer contractual incentives, *Strategic Management Journal*, 32: 771–786; R. Duchin, J. G. Matsusaka, & O. Ozbas, 2010, *Journal of Financial Economics*, 96: 195–214.
69. A. Holehonnur & T. Pollock, 2013, Shoot for the stars? Predicting the recruitment of prestigious directors at newly public firms, *Academy of Management Journal*, in press; M. McDonald & J. Westphal, 2013, Not let in on the secret to success: How low levels of mentoring from incumbent directors negatively affect women and racial minority first-time director appointment to additional corporate boards, *Academy of Management Journal*, in press.
70. R. C. Anderson, D. M. Reeb, A. Upadhyay, & W. Zhao, 2011, The economics of director heterogeneity, *Financial Management*, 40: 5–38; S. K. Lee & L. R. Carlson, 2007, The changing board of directors: Board independence in S&P 500 firms, *Journal of Organizational Culture, Communication and Conflict*, 11(1): 31–41.
71. S. Crainer, 2011, Changing direction: One person can make a difference, *Business Strategy Review*, 22: 10–16; M. Z. Islam, 2011, Board-CEO-chair relationship, Working paper, http://ssrn.com/abstract=1861386; R. C. Pozen, 2006, Before you split that CEO/chair, *Harvard Business Review* 84(4): 26–28.
72. M. Huse, R. E. Hoskisson, A. Zattoni, & R. Vigano, 2011, New perspectives on board research: Changing the research agenda, *Journal of Management and Governance*, 15(1): 5–28; M. Kroll, B. A. Walters, & P. Wright, 2008, Board vigilance, director experience and corporate outcomes, *Strategic Management Journal*, 29: 363–382.
73. S. Boivie, S. D. Graffin, & T. G. Pollock, 2012, Time for me to fly: Predicting director exit at large firms, *Academy of Management Journal*, 55: 1334–1359; A. Agrawal & M. A. Chen, 2011, Boardroom brawls: An empirical analysis of disputes involving directors, http://ssrn.com/abstracts=1362143.
74. S. Muthusamy, P. A. Bobinski, & D. Jawahar, 2011, Toward a strategic role for employees in corporate governance, *Strategic Change*, 20: 127–138; Y. Zhang & N. Rajagopalan, 2010, Once an outsider, always an outsider? CEO origin, strategic change, and firm performance *Strategic Management Journal*, 31: 334–346.
75. B. Baysinger & R. E. Hoskisson, 1990, The composition of boards of directors and strategic control: Effects on corporate strategy, *Academy of Management Review*, 15: 72–87.
76. D. H. Zhu, 2013, Group polarization on corporate boards: Theory and evidence on board decisions about acquisition premiums, *Strategic Management Journal*, 800–822; G. A. Ballinger & J. J. Marcel, 2010, The use of an interim CEO during succession episodes and firm performance, *Strategic Management Journal*, 31: 262–283.
77. Boivie, Graffin, & Pollock, Time for me to fly; C. Shropshire, 2010, The role of the interlocking director and board receptivity in the diffusion of practices, *Academy of Management Review*, 35: 246–264.
78. D. Carey, J. J. Keller, & M. Patsalos-Fox, 2010, How to choose the right nonexecutive board leader, *McKinsey Quarterly*, May.
79. M. K. Bednar, 2012, Watchdog or lapdog? A behavioral role view of the media as a corporate governance mechanism, *Academy of Management Journal*, 55: 131–150; D. Northcott & J. Smith, 2011, Managing performance at the top: A balanced scorecard for boards of directors, *Journal of Accounting & Organizational Change*, 7: 33–56; L. Erakovic & J. Overall, 2010, Opening the 'black box': Challenging traditional governance theorems, *Journal of Management & Organization*, 16: 250–265.
80. I. Okhmatovskiy & R. J. David, 2011, Setting your own standards: Internal corporate governance codes as a response to institutional pressure, *Organization Science*, 1–22; J. L. Koors, 2006, Director pay: A work in progress, *The Corporate Governance Advisor*, 14(5): 14–31.
81. Y. Deutsch, T. Keil, & T. Laamanen, 2007, Decision making in acquisitions: The

effect of outside directors' compensation on acquisition patterns, *Journal of Management*, 33: 30–56.

82. F. A. Gul, B. Srinidhi, & A. C. Ng, 2011, Does board gender diversity improve the informativeness of stock prices? *Journal of Accounting and Economics*, 51: 314–338; D. A. Matsa & A. R. Miller, 2011, Chipping at the glass ceiling: Gender spillovers in corporate leadership, http://ssrn.com/abstract=1709462; A. J. Hillman, C. Shropshire, & A. A. Cannella, Jr., 2007, Organizational predictors of women on corporate boards, *Academy of Management Journal*, 50: 941–952.

83. M. van Essen, P. Heugens, J. Otten, & J. van Oosterhout, 2012, An institution-based view of executive compensation: A multilevel meta-analytic test, *Journal of International Business Studies*, 43: 396–423; M. J. Conyon, J. E. Core, & W. R. Guay, 2011, Are U.S. CEOs paid more than U.K. CEOs? Inferences from risk-adjusted pay, *Review of Financial Studies*, 24: 402–438.

84. C. Mangen & M. Magnan, 2012, "Say on pay": A wolf in sheep's clothing? *Academy of Management Perspectives*, 26 (1): 86–104; E. A. Fong, V. F. Misangyi, Jr., & H. L. Tosi, 2010, The effect of CEO pay deviations on CEO withdrawal, firm size, and firm profits, *Strategic Management Journal*, 31: 629–651; J. P. Walsh, 2009, Are U.S. CEOs overpaid? A partial response to Kaplan, *Academy of Management Perspectives*, 23(1): 73–75.

85. G. P. Martin, L. R. Gomez-Mejia, & R. M. Wiseman, 2013, Executive stock options as mixed gambles: Revisiting the behavioral agency model, *Academy of Management Journal*, 56: 451–472; K. Rehbein, 2007, Explaining CEO compensation: How do talent, governance, and markets fit in? *Academy of Management Perspectives*, 21(1): 75–77.

86. T. M. Alessandri, T. W. Tong, & J. J. Reuer, 2012, Firm heterogeneity in growth option value: The role of managerial incentives, *Strategic Management Journal*, 33: 1557–1566; D. H. M. Chng, M. S. Rodgers, E. Shih, & X.-B. Song, 2012, When does incentive compensation motivate managerial behaviors? An experimental investigation of the fit between compensation, executive core self-evaluation, and firm performance, *Strategic Management Journal*, 33: 1343–1362; D. Souder & J. M. Shaver, 2010, Constraints and incentives for making long horizon corporate investments, *Strategic Management Journal*, 31: 1316–1336.

87. E. A. Fong, 2010, Relative CEO underpayment and CEO behavior towards R&D spending, *Journal of Management Studies*, 47: 1095–1122; X. Zhang, K. M. Bartol, K. G. Smith, M. D. Pfarrer, & D. M. Khanin, 2008, CEOs on the edge: Earnings manipulations and stock-based incentive misalignment, *Academy of Management Journal*, 51: 241–258; J. P. O'Connor, R. L. Priem, J. E. Coombs, & K. M. Gilley, 2006, Do CEO stock options prevent or promote fraudulent financial reporting? *Academy of Management Journal*, 49: 483–500.

88. Y. Du, M. Deloof, & A. Jorissen, 2011, Active boards of directors in foreign subsidiaries, *Corporate Governance: An International Review*, 19: 153–168; J. J. Reuer, E. Klijn, F. A. J. van den Bosch, & H. W. Volberda, 2011, Bringing corporate governance to international joint ventures, *Global Strategy Journal*, 1: 54–66; K. Roth & S. O'Donnell, 1996, Foreign subsidiary compensation: An agency theory perspective, *Academy of Management Journal*, 39: 678–703.

89. B. Balasubramanian, B. S. Black, & V. Khanna, 2010, The relation between firm-level corporate governance and market value: A study of India, University of Michigan working paper series; A. Ghosh, 2006, Determination of executive compensation in an emerging economy: Evidence from India, *Emerging Markets, Finance & Trade*, 42(3): 66–90.

90. M. Ederhof, 2011, Incentive compensation and promotion-based incentives of mid-level managers: Evidence from a multinational corporation, *The Accounting Review*, 86: 131–154; C. L. Staples, 2007, Board globalization in the world's largest TNCs 1993–2005, *Corporate Governance*, 15: 311–332.

91. G. Pandher & R. Currie, 2013, CEO compensation: A resource advantage and stakeholder-bargaining perspective, *Strategic Management Journal*, 34: 22–41; Y. Deutsch, T. Keil, & T. Laamanen, 2011, A dual agency view of board compensation: The joint effects of outside director and CEO stock options on firm risk, *Strategic Management Journal*, 32: 212–227; P. Kalyta, 2009, Compensation transparency and managerial opportunism: A study of supplemental retirement plans, *Strategic Management Journal*, 30: 405–423.

92. R. Krause, K. Whitler, & M. Semadeni, 2013, Power to the principals! An experimental look at shareholder say-on-pay voting, *Academy of Management Journal*, in press; L. K. Meulbroek, 2001, The efficiency of equity-linked compensation: Understanding the full cost of awarding executive stock options, *Financial Management*, 30(2): 5–44.

93. 2013, The experts: Do companies spend too much on 'superstar' CEOs? *Wall Street Journal*, www.wsj.com, March 14.

94. Z. Dong, C. Wang, & F. Xie, 2010, Do executive stock options induce excessive risk taking? *Journal of Banking & Finance*, 34: 2518–2529; C. E. Devers, R. M. Wiseman, & R. M. Holmes, Jr., 2007, The effects of endowment and loss aversion in managerial stock option valuation, *Academy of Management Journal*, 50: 191–208.

95. D. Anginer, M. P. Narayanan, C. A. Schipani, & H. N. Seyhun, 2011, Should size matter when regulating firms? Implications from backdating of executive options, Ross School of Business working paper; T. G. Pollock, H. M. Fischer, & J. B. Wade, 2002, The role of politics in repricing executive options, *Academy of Management Journal*, 45: 1172–1182.

96. P. Berrone & L. R. Gomez-Mejia, 2009, Environmental performance and executive compensation: An integrated agency-institutional perspective, *Academy of Management Journal*, 52: 103–126.

97. V. V. Acharya, S. C. Myers, & R. G. Rajan, 2011, The internal governance of firms, *Journal of Finance*, 66: 689–720; R. Sinha, 2006, Regulation: The market for corporate control and corporate governance, *Global Finance Journal*, 16: 264–282.

98. T. Laamanen, M. Brauer, & O. Junna, 2013, Performance of divested assets: Evidence from the U.S. software industry, *Strategic Management Journal*, in press; T. Yoshikawa & A. A. Rasheed, 2010, Family control and ownership monitoring in family-controlled firms in Japan, *Journal of Management Studies*, 47: 274–295; R. W. Masulis, C. Wang, & F. Xie, 2007, Corporate governance and acquirer returns, *Journal of Finance*, 62: 1851–1889.

99. C. Devers, G. McNamara, J. Haleblian & M. Yoder, 2013, Do they walk the talk or just talk the talk? Gauging acquiring CEO and director confidence in the value-creation potential of announced acquisitions, *Academy of Management Journal*, in press; P.-X. Meschi & E. Métais, 2013, Do firms forget about their past acquisitions? Evidence from French acquisitions in the United States (1988–2006), *Journal of Management*, 39: 469–495; J. A. Krug & W. Shill, 2008, The big exit: Executive churn in the wake of M&As, *Journal of Business Strategy*, 29(4): 15–21.

100. 2013, Hedge fund 100 ranking, Institutional Investors Alpha, www.institutionalinvestorsalpha.com, accessed on June 7.

101. N. M. Boyson & R. M. Mooradian, 2011, Corporate governance and hedge fund activism, *Review of Derivatives Research*, 169–204; L. A. Bebchuk & M. S. Weisbach, 2010, The state of corporate governance research, *Review of Financial Studies*, 23: 939–961; T. W. Briggs, 2007, Corporate governance and a new hedge fund activism, *Empirical Analysis*, 32: 681–723.

102. S. Bainbridge, 2011, Hedge funds as activist investors, *ProfessorBainbridge.com*, www.professorbainbridge.com, March 21.

103. R. Greenwood, 2007, The hedge fund as activist, HBR Working knowledge, www.hbrworkingknowledge.com, August 22.

104. S. Saitto, 2013, Dell projects Icahn buyout has a $3.9 funding gap, *Bloomberg*, www.bloomberg.com, June 5; A. Ricadela, 2013, Dell trims CEO's pay by 14% as performance slips ahead of buyout, *Bloomberg*, www.bloomberg.com, June 4.

105. M. L. Humphery-Jenner & R. G. Powell, 2011, Firm size, takeover profitability, and the

effectiveness of the market for corporate control: Does the absence of anti-takeover provisions make a difference? *Journal of Corporate Finance*, 17: 418–437; K. Ruckman, 2009, Technology sourcing acquisitions: What they mean for innovation potential, *Journal of Strategy and Management*, 2: 56–75.

106. J. P. Walsh & R. Kosnik, 1993, Corporate raiders and their disciplinary role in the market for corporate control, *Academy of Management Journal*, 36: 671–700.

107. M. Schijven & M. A. Hitt, 2012, The vicarious wisdom of crowds: Toward a behavioral perspective on investor reactions to acquisition announcements, *Strategic Management Journal*, 33: 1247–1268; J. Haleblian, C. E. Devers, G. McNamara, M. A. Carpenter, & R. B. Davison, 2009, Taking stock of what we know about mergers and acquisitions: A review and research agenda, *Journal of Management*, 35: 469–502.

108. F. Bauer & K. Matzler, 2013, Antecedents of M&A success: The role of strategic complementarity, cultural fit and degree and speed of integration, *Strategic Management Journal*, in press; S. Mingo, 2013, The impact of acquisitions on the performance of existing organizational units In the acquiring firm: The case of the agribusiness company, *Management Science*, in press; A. Sleptsov, J. Anand, & G. Vasudeva, 2013, Relational configurations with information intermediaries: The effect of firm-investment bank ties on expected acquisition performance, *Strategic Management Journal*, in press.

109. 2013, Hostile takeover, *Investopedia*, www.investopedia.com, accessed on June 7.

110. P. Jiraporn & Y. Liu, 2011, Staggered boards, accounting discretion and firm value, *Applied Financial Economics*, 21: 271–285; O. Faleye, 2007, Classified boards, firm value, and managerial entrenchment, *Journal of Financial Economics*, 83: 501–529.

111. T. Sokoly, 2011, The effects of antitakeover provisions on acquisition targets, *Journal of Corporate Finance*, 17: 612–627; M. Martynova & L. Renneboog, 2010, A corporate governance index: Convergence and diversity of national corporate governance regulations, http://ssrn.com/abstract=1557627; 2007, Leaders: Pay slips; management in Europe, *Economist*, June 23, 14.

112. J. A. Pearce II & R. B. Robinson, Jr., 2004, Hostile takeover defenses that maximize shareholder wealth, *Business Horizons* 47(5): 15–24.

113. M. Humphery-Jenner, 2013, Takeover defenses, innovation and value creation: Evidence from acquisition decisions, *Strategic Management Journal*, in press; A. Kacperzyk, 2009, With greater power comes greater responsibility? Takeover protection and corporate attention to stakeholders, *Strategic Management Journal*, 30: 261–285.

114. P. Sieger, T. Zellweger, & K. Aquino, 2013, Turning agents into psychological principals: Aligning interests of non-owners through psychological ownership, *Journal of Management Studies*, 50: 361–388.

115. I. Haxhi & H. Ees, 2010, Explaining diversity in the worldwide diffusion of codes of good governance, *Journal of International Business Studies*, 41: 710–726; P. Witt, 2004, The competition of international corporate governance systems—a German perspective, *Management International Review*, 44: 309–333.

116. J. Block & F. Spiegel, 2011, Family firms and regional innovation activity: Evidence from the German Mittelstand, http://ssrn.com/abstract=1745362.

117. S. K. Bhaumik & A. Gregoriou, 2010, 'Family' ownership, tunneling and earnings management: A review of the literature, *Journal of Economic Surveys*, 24: 705–730; A. Tuschke & W. G. Sanders, 2003, Antecedents and consequences of corporate governance reform: The case of Germany, *Strategic Management Journal*, 24: 631–649; J. Edwards & M. Nibler, 2000, Corporate governance in Germany: The role of banks and ownership concentration, *Economic Policy*, 31: 237–268.

118. Tuschke, Sanders, & Hernandez, Whose experience matters in the boardroom?; D. Hillier, J. Pinadado, V. de Queiroz, & C. de la Torre, 2010, The impact of country-level corporate governance on research and development, *Journal of International Business Studies*, 42: 76–98.

119. Tuschke, Sanders, & Hernandez, Whose experience matters in the boardroom?

120. J. T. Addison & C. Schnabel, 2011, Worker directors: A German product that did not export? *Industrial Relations: A Journal of Economy and Society*, 50: 354–374; P. C. Fiss & E. J. Zajac, 2004, The diffusion of ideas over contested terrain: The (non)adoption of a shareholder value orientation among German firms, *Administrative Science Quarterly*, 49: 501–534.

121. A. Chizema, 2010, Early and late adoption of American-style executive pay in Germany: Governance and institutions, *Journal of World Business*, 45: 9–18; W. G. Sanders & A. C. Tuschke, 2007, The adoption of the institutionally contested organizational practices: The emergence of stock option pay in Germany, *Academy of Management Journal*, 50: 33–56.

122. F. Allen & M. Zhao, 2007, The corporate governance model of Japan: Shareholders are not rulers, working paper, University of Pennsylvania, www.finance.wharton.upenn.edu (a version also appears in *Peking University Business Review*, 2007).

123. 2010, Japan: Principles of corporate governance, *eStandards Forum*, www.estandardsforum.org, May.

124. D. R. Adhikari & K. Hirasawa, 2010, Emerging scenarios of Japanese corporate management, *Asia-Pacific Journal of Business Administration*, 2: 114–132; M. A. Hitt, H. Lee, & E. Yucel, 2002, The importance of social capital to the management of multinational enterprises: Relational networks among Asian and Western firms, *Asia Pacific Journal of Management*, 19: 353–372.

125. W. P. Wan, D. W. Yiu, R. E. Hoskisson, & H. Kim, 2008, The performance implications of relationship banking during macroeconomic expansion and contraction: A study of Japanese banks' social relationships and overseas expansion, *Journal of International Business Studies*, 39: 406–427.

126. P. M. Lee & H. M. O'Neill, 2003, Ownership structures and R&D investments of U.S. and Japanese firms: Agency and stewardship perspectives, *Academy of Management Journal*, 46: 212–225.

127. X. Wu & J. Yao, 2012, Understanding the rise and decline of the Japanese main bank system: The changing effects of bank rent extraction, *Journal of Banking & Finance*, 36: 36–50; I. S. Dinc, 2006, Monitoring the monitors: The corporate governance in Japanese banks and their real estate lending in the 1980s, *Journal of Business*, 79: 3057–3081.

128. K. Kubo & T. Saito, 2012, The effect of mergers on employment and wages: Evidence from Japan, *Journal of the Japanese and International Economics*, 26: 263–284; N. Isagawa, 2007, A theory of unwinding of cross-shareholding under managerial entrenchment, *Journal of Financial Research*, 30: 163–179.

129. B. Tricker, 2011, Tokyo Electric Power and the disaster at Fukushima Daiichi, Corporate Governance Blog, Oxford University Press, http://corporategovernanceoup.wordpress.com, April 20.

130. J. Yang, J. Chi, & M. Young, 2011, A review of corporate governance in China, *Asian-Pacific Economic Literature*, 25: 15–28.

131. H. Berkman, R. A. Cole, & L. J. Fu, 2010, Political connections and minority-shareholder protection: Evidence from securities-market regulation in China, *Journal of Financial and Quantitative Analysis*, 45: 1391–1417; S. R. Miller, D. Li, E. Eden, & M. A. Hitt, 2008, Insider trading and the valuation of international strategic alliances in emerging stock markets, *Journal of International Business Studies*, 39: 102–117.

132. W.A. Li & D.T. Yan, 2013, Transition from administrative to economic model of corporate governance, *Nankai Business Review International*, 4: 4–8.

133. J. Chi, Q. Sun, & M. Young, 2011, Performance and characteristics of acquiring firms in the Chinese stock markets, *Emerging Markets Review*, 12: 152–170; Y.-L. Cheung, P. Jiang, P. Limpaphayom, & T. Lu, 2010, Corporate governance in China: A step forward, *European Financial Management*, 16: 94–123; H. Zou & M. B. Adams, 2008, Corporate

ownership, equity risk and returns in the People's Republic in China, *Journal of International Business Studies*, 39: 1149–1168.

134. J. Li & C. Qian, 2013, Principal-principal conflicts under weak institutions: a study of corporate takeovers in China, *Strategic Management Journal*, 34: 498–508; S. Globerman, M. W. Peng, & D. M. Shapiro, 2011, Corporate governance and Asian companies, *Asia Pacific Journal of Management*, 28: 1–14.
135. P. Adithipyangkul, I. Alon, & T. Zhang, 2011, Executive perks: Compensation and corporate performance in China, *Asia Pacific Journal of Management*, 28: 401–425; T. Buck, X. Lui, & R. Skovoroda, 2008, Top executives' pay and firm performance in China, *Journal of International Business Studies*, 39: 833–850.
136. A. Cai, J.-H. Luo, & D.-F. Wan, 2012, Family CEOs: Do they benefit firm governance In China? *Asia Pacific Journal of Management*, 29: 923–947.
137. I. Oxelheim, A. Gregoric, T. Randoy, & S. Thomsen, 2013, On the internationalization of corporate boards: The case of Nordic firms, *Journal of International Business Studies*, 44: 173–194.
138. S. Muthusamy, P. A. Bobinski, & D. Jawahar, 2011, Toward a strategic role for employees in corporate governance, *Strategic Change*, 20: 127–138; T. Tse, 2011, Shareholder and stakeholder theory: After the financial crisis, *Qualitative Research in Financial Markets*, 3(1): 51–63; C. Shropshire & A. J. Hillman, 2007, A longitudinal study of significant change in stakeholder management, *Business & Society*, 46(1): 63–87.
139. J. M. Schaubroeck, S. T. Hannah, B. J. Avolio, S. W. J. Kozlowski, R. G. Lord, L. K. Trevino, N. Dimotakis, & A. C. Peng, 2012, Embedding ethical leadership within and across organizational levels, *Academy of Management Journal*, 55: 1053–1078; R. A. G. Monks & N. Minow, 2011, *Corporate governance*, 5th ed., New York: John Wiley & Sons.
140. J. S. Chun, Y. Shin, J. N. Choi, & M. S. Kim, 2013, How does corporate ethics contribute to firm financial performance? The mediating role of collective organizational commitment and organizational citizenship behavior, *Journal of Management*, 39: 853–877; S. P. Deshpande, J. Joseph, & X. Shu, 2011, Ethical climate and managerial success in China, *Journal of Business Ethics*, 99: 527–534.
141. A. P. Cowan & J. J. Marcel, 2011, Damaged goods: Board decisions to dismiss reputationally compromised directors, *Academy of Management Journal*, 54: 509–527; J. R. Knapp, T. Dalziel, & M. W. Lewis, 2011, Governing top managers: Board control, social categorization, and their unintended influence on discretionary behaviors, *Corporate Governance: An International Review* 19: 295–310.
142. Y. Jeong & R. J. Weiner, 2012, Who bribes? Evidence from the United Nations' oil-for-food program, *Strategic Management Journal*, 33: 1363–1383.
143. S.-H. Lee & D. H. Weng, 2013, Does bribery in the home country promote or dampen firm exports? *Strategic Management Journal*, in press; J. O. Zhou & M. W. Peng, 2012, Does bribery help or hurt firm growth around the world? *Asia Pacific Journal of Management*, 29: 907–921.
144. 2013, Corporate governance awards 2013, *World Finance*, www.worldfinance.com/awards, March 13.

# 11

# Organizational Structure and Controls

***Studying this chapter should provide you with the strategic management knowledge needed to:***

1. Define organizational structure and controls and discuss the difference between strategic and financial controls.
2. Describe the relationship between strategy and structure.
3. Discuss the functional structures used to implement business-level strategies.
4. Explain the use of three versions of the multidivisional (M-form) structure to implement different diversification strategies.
5. Discuss the organizational structures used to implement three international strategies.
6. Define strategic networks and discuss how strategic center firms implement such networks at the business, corporate, and international levels.

## BIG-BOX RETAILERS STRUGGLE TO CHANGE THEIR STRATEGIES AND STRUCTURES IN THE FACE OF ONLINE COMPETITION

A string of big-box retailers in consumer electronics and books have suffered bankruptcies due to the changing nature of competition in the retail sector. CompUSA closed through bankruptcy in 2008. This was followed by Circuit City's bankruptcy in November 2008, and its final door closings in March 2009. Borders, one of the original big-box booksellers, declared bankruptcy in 2011.

Early in its history, Borders had a well-developed inventory system and was popular, and the company began to take market share from independent book retailers. However, Borders began to make mistakes when Amazon.com's success at selling books on the Internet led it to diversification growth initiatives, such as its push into international markets. Borders seemed unable to structure its operations in a way that would allow different businesses in each country to market effectively. Borders seemed to have an insular and centralized management structure that was impervious to changes in the market. For example, when Barnes & Noble developed the capability to sell online, Borders signed an agreement with Amazon to handle its Internet sales. This was great for Amazon but a disaster for Borders because it sent customers and business to a major competitor. Not only does a company need to change its strategy appropriately, but it must also facilitate the management structure in a way that improves the implementation of the strategy. Although Barnes & Noble has done better than Borders, primarily because of its online strategy and through its NOOK reader and eBook store, its sales decreased in 2012, although its net income was still positive. Getting the strategy and structural emphases right between retail sales, NOOK sales, and Web site sales is a continuing challenge.

Getting the strategy and management structure emphases right is also a challenge for consumer electronics retailer Best Buy. Relative to Amazon, Best Buy has a number of disadvantages to which it is trying to adjust its management structure to get an appropriate mix. Amazon began as an online bookseller and had an earlier impact on Borders and Barnes & Noble because of its approach and its successful Kindle and Kindle Fire devices. Amazon eventually expanded its offerings into consumer electronics and many other department store products such as toys and furniture. Amazon played a large role in popularizing online shopping. Relative to big-box retailers, it has a number of advantages. Its virtual stores are much less costly than the brick and mortar buildings used by big-box retailers such as Best Buy. With no physical stores, Amazon incurs lower costs in leasing relative to long-term leases, labor costs, insurance, utilities, and other expenses associated with negotiating real estate and buildings for brick and mortar stores. It also has an efficient logistics network and distribution system with efficient warehousing. Interestingly, because Amazon does not operate physical stores with a location, it has traditionally been exempt from charging state sales taxes. As such, these cost differentials have allowed the company to offer lower prices and thus undercut sales available to brick and mortar stores such as Best Buy. Furthermore, Amazon has built its customer service to improve the shopping experience for its customers. It follows up to make sure that customers are satisfied with their purchases and offers hassle-free return policies. Best Buy, on the other hand, has frustrated customers through restocking fees if a return is sought. Amazon also has encouraged buyers to submit reviews on products purchased. This approach has been able to substitute somewhat for in-store customer sales representatives that provide advice to customers about which products to purchase.

Because consumer electronic products are visible in stores like Best Buy and Walmart, a new term has developed called "showrooming." This is where shoppers go to a brick and mortar store such as Best Buy and look at products and handle them, and then buy them online. In fact, there was a "price check mobile phone app" that appeared in 2011 which allowed in-store shoppers to scan and search a product and then immediately price-compare with Amazon.com or other online merchants. Best Buy and others responded with "price match guarantee" approaches. Also, brick and mortar stores are fighting back through customized technology and store-within-a-store concepts. Reebok, for instance, installed a build-your-own-sneakers kiosk in many brick and mortar shoe stores. Best Buy has recently signed a deal with Samsung to have a store-within-a-store approach to peddle Samsung consumer electronic products. Overall, the shopping public is turning to more digital experiences, especially for the age 40 and under shopper, and this approach may need to be developed by brick and mortar stores to update and improve in-store experiences.

Best Buy has tried an experiment internationally as well. In 2008, it formed a joint venture dubbed Best Buy Europe with Carphone Warehouse Europe, an independent mobile phone seller in Europe, where they initially planned to build American-style big-box electronic stores. However, this plan was aborted in 2011. As such, it has retreated from Europe, selling its 50 percent interest in this joint venture for $755 million and reporting a $200 million charge in 2013. This sale was spurred by its new CEO, Hubert Joly. However, Best Buy announced that it is not going to pull back from other international ventures such as those in Mexico, Canada, and China.

Best Buy is also seeking to increase revenue through better store space optimization and introducing a better Web-based platform to increase traffic and conversion rates through Internet sales. The change in strategy seems to be working, with the first quarter of 2013 showing the company's same-store U.S. sales increased for the first time in over a year. This change has also taken place because of a new leader, senior vice president Shawn Score, who has helped to improve the in-store shopping experience. This is very important because the retailer still drives more than 90 percent of its $50 billion in annual revenue from stores.

Although Best Buy wants to make changes through leadership and adjusting its strategy, it also needs to make structural changes as it implements this strategy through better control systems. It needs to monitor the number of sales it makes in each brick and mortar store, and those that it loses to online sales. Hopefully, its online sales will pick up after a customer comes to its online store. Best Buy estimates that roughly 20 percent of all consumer electronics are now bought online. As such, it needs to improve its online product descriptions and selections and reduce its high operating cost. Although its recent sales closure rate hasn't improved, customer satisfaction scores have ticked up. However, it confronts a high staff turnover rate. Staff turnover was around 60 percent in 2012, although it has eased a bit more recently. The historical average is 35 percent. As such, it needs to do a better job of structurally managing its human capital. Otherwise, consumers will go to online sources to get product information rather than from their sales staff. It remains to be seen whether Best Buy will be able to survive the online competition; however, recently it won a battle over legislation reducing the sales tax cost differential that Amazon has enjoyed versus brick and mortar stores. Best Buy's turnaround, so far, has been effective, but it remains to be seen whether it will make the right adjustments to survive and avoid bankruptcy such as those of CompUSA, Circuit City, and Borders.

Sources: G. Colvin, 2013, Your business model doesn't work anymore, *Fortune*, February 25, 42; S. Jakab, 2013, Best Buy's comeback story worth a read, *Wall Street Journal*, www.wsj.com, May 20; J. Lahart, 2013, You needn't be best to be a buy, *Wall Street Journal*, May 1, C16; J. Milliot, 2013, Barnes & Noble at the crossroads, *Publishers Weekly*, March 4, 6; C. O'Connor, 2013, Game on, Amazon! eBay rolls out one-hour delivery, targeting the Web and Wal-Mart, *Forbes*, May 7, 16; E. Savitz, 2013, Best Buy: Barclays, Stifel see turnaround, boost ratings, *Forbes*, www.forbes.com, February 19; D. Wolfe, 2013, Citi to buy $7 billion Best Buy card portfolio from Capital One, *American Banker*, February 20, 3; A. Zimmerman, 2013, Best Buy sells Europe business back to Carphone Warehouse, *Wall Street Journal*, www.wsj.com, April 30; A. Zimmerman, 2013, Can this former clerk save Best Buy? – Executive hopes to address 'pain points' that drive customers away, and reduce staff turnover, *Wall Street Journal*, April 26, B1; H. E. Combs, 2012, Best Buy's decline shows need to evaluate online strategies, *Furniture/Today*, September 19, 40.

Learn more about Barnes & Noble.
www.cengagebrain.com

As we explained in Chapter 4, all firms use one or more business-level strategies. In Chapters 6 through 9, we discuss other strategies firms may choose to use (corporate-level, international, and cooperative). After they are selected, strategies must be implemented effectively to make them work. Organizational structure and controls, this chapter's topic, provide the framework within which strategies are implemented and used in both for-profit organizations and not-for-profit agencies.[1] However, as we explain, separate structures and controls are required to successfully implement different strategies. In all organizations, top-level managers have the final responsibility for ensuring that the firm has matched each of its strategies with the appropriate organizational structure and that both change when necessary. Thus, the CEO of Best Buy, as illustrated in the Opening Case, is responsible for changing its organizational structure to effectively implement its business or corporate-level strategies to adjust to its competitive challenges. The match or degree of fit between strategy and structure influences the firm's attempts to earn above-average returns.[2] Thus, the ability to select an appropriate strategy and match it with the appropriate structure is an important characteristic of effective strategic leadership.[3]

Best Buy, eBay, and Staples have different challenges and have employed different strategies and different implementation approaches given the strategies selected. For example, eBay is in a different strategic position relative to Amazon. While Amazon competes directly with brick and mortar retail stores such as Best Buy, eBay has chosen to be an outlet of choice to support the Internet selling strategies of traditional brick and mortar retailers. Such stores can partner with eBay to develop an improved online strategy. This approach has helped eBay to improve its business model from its decline in consumer online auctions. Also, Staples has been protected somewhat from the retailing competition with Amazon because its main focus is on business customers rather than consumers. They are not as likely to use all the online information available the way consumers do and would rather have a high assortment of products and delivery convenience, which Staples provides for them. Also, Staples has been developing its online product base and has over 100,000 items available online as additional protection.[4]

Given their bankruptcies, it is clear that CompUSA, Circuit City, and Borders failed in their implementation approaches. As illustrated in the opening case, the jury is still out on Best Buy; in 2006 Best Buy was known as a well-run company, but now it is fighting for competitive parity with Amazon—if not survival. First, its decision to enter international markets likely failed because of poor implementation and management of international operations. Perhaps the fine tuning of its new leadership practices will help, but regional and even individual store adjustments will be needed. If it becomes overly centralized in its approach as did Borders, this may cause problems. If it is too decentralized, then the changes made may create disunity in the sales experience. Strategic management scholar Richard Rumelt sums up the problems challenging organizations such as Best Buy in his statement that "... weakly managed organizations tend to become less organized and focused."[5]

M. Stasy

Chip Somodevilla/Getty Images News/Getty Images

*General Electric's Chairman and CEO, Jeffrey Immelt, delivers opening remarks during the company's four-day event, "American Competitiveness: What Works." As part of its "Hire Our Heroes" program, GE says it will hire 5,000 veterans over the next five years and invest $580 million to expand its aviation business.*

This chapter opens with an introduction to organizational structure and controls. We then provide more details about the need for the firm's strategy and structure to be properly matched. Affecting firms' efforts to match strategy and structure is their influence on each other.[6] As we discuss, strategy has a more important influence on structure, although once in place, structure influences strategy.[7] Next, we describe the relationship between growth and structural change successful firms experience. We then discuss the different organizational structures firms use to implement separate business-level, corporate-level, international, and cooperative strategies. A series of figures highlights the different structures firms match with strategies. Across time and based on their experiences, organizations, especially large and complex ones, customize these general structures to meet their unique needs.[8] Typically, the firm tries to form a structure that is complex enough to facilitate use of its strategies but simple enough for all parties to understand and implement.[9] When strategies become more diversified, a firm must adjust its structure to deal with the increased complexity.

## 11-1 Organizational Structure and Controls

Research shows that organizational structure and the controls that are a part of the structure affect firm performance.[10] In particular, evidence suggests that performance declines when the firm's strategy is not matched with the most appropriate structure and controls.[11] Even though mismatches between strategy and structure do occur, research indicates that managers try to act rationally when forming or changing their firm's structure.[12] His record of success at General Electric (GE) suggests that CEO Jeffrey Immelt pays close attention to the need to make certain that strategy and structure remain matched, as evidenced by restructuring alignments in GE Capital, GE's financial services group, during the economic downturn. Since the downturn, GE Capital has shrunk by over a third; it previously accounted for 46 percent of GE's earnings. Immelt wants to reduce that to 30 percent while increasing the focus on the industrial businesses.[13]

### 11-1a Organizational Structure

**Organizational structure** specifies the firm's formal reporting relationships, procedures, controls, and authority and decision-making processes.[14] Developing an organizational structure that effectively supports the firm's strategy is difficult, especially because of the uncertainty (or unpredictable variation) about cause-effect relationships in the global economy's rapidly changing competitive environments.[15] When a structure's elements (e.g., reporting relationships, procedures, etc.) are properly aligned with one another, the structure facilitates effective use of the firm's strategies. Thus, organizational structure is a critical component of effective strategy implementation processes.[16]

**Organizational structure** specifies the firm's formal reporting relationships, procedures, controls, and authority and decision-making processes.

A firm's structure specifies the work to be done and how to do it, given the firm's strategy or strategies. Thus, organizational structure influences how managers work and the decisions resulting from that work. Supporting the implementation of strategies, structure is concerned with processes used to complete organizational tasks.[17] Having the right structure and process is important. For example, many product-oriented firms have been moving to develop service businesses associated with those products. As we learned in Chapter 6, GE is a successful diversified firm. The service extension strategy has been used by GE, for example, in financial services and oil and gas equipment services. However, research suggests that developing a separate division for such services in product-oriented companies, rather than managing the service business within the product divisions, leads to additional growth and profitability in the service business. GE developed a separate division for its financial services businesses. This helped facilitate GE's growth over the last two decades, although this business has been shrinking given the financial downturn.[18]

Effective structures provide the stability a firm needs to successfully implement its strategies and maintain its current competitive advantages while simultaneously providing the flexibility to develop advantages it will need in the future.[19] *Structural stability* provides the capacity the firm requires to consistently and predictably manage its daily work routines[20] while *structural flexibility* provides the opportunity to explore competitive possibilities and then allocate resources to activities that will shape the competitive advantages the firm will need to be successful in the future.[21] An effectively flexible organizational structure allows the firm to *exploit* current competitive advantages while *developing* new ones that can potentially be used in the future.[22] Alternatively, an ineffective structure that is inflexible may drive good employees away because of frustration and an inability to complete their work in the best way possible. As such, it can lead to a loss of knowledge by the firm, sometimes referred to as a knowledge spillover, which benefits competitors.[23]

Modifications to the firm's current strategy or selection of a new strategy call for changes to its organizational structure. However, research shows that once in place, organizational inertia often inhibits efforts to change structure, even when the firm's performance suggests that it is time to do so.[24] In his pioneering work, Alfred Chandler found that organizations change their structures when inefficiencies force them to.[25] Chandler's contributions to our understanding of organizational structure and its relationship to strategies and performance are quite significant. Indeed, some believe that Chandler's emphasis on "organizational structure so transformed the field of business history that some call the period before Chandler's work was published 'B.C.,' meaning 'before Chandler.'"[26]

Firms seem to prefer the structural status quo and its familiar working relationships until the firm's performance declines to the point where change is absolutely necessary.[27] For example, necessity is obviously the case for General Motors given that it went into bankruptcy to force the required restructuring.[28] As noted in the Opening Case, many firms are adjusting to a digital world, such as the competition between Best Buy and Amazon. It is unclear how Best Buy and other big-box retailers will survive given their cost structure relative to online competitors as they make the adjustment to have their own online approach to selling their products.

Top-level managers often hesitate to conclude that the firm's structure (or its strategy, for that matter) is the problem, because doing so suggests that their previous choices were not the best ones. Because of these inertial tendencies, structural change is often induced instead by actions from stakeholders (e.g., those from the capital market and customers—see Chapter 2 and Chapter 7) who are no longer willing to tolerate the firm's performance. For example, this happened at large department store operator J.C. Penney, as the former CEO, Myron Ullman, replaced a relatively new CEO, Ron Johnson, whose turnaround was not working.[29] Evidence shows that appropriate timing of structural change happens when top-level managers recognize that a current organizational structure no longer provides the coordination and direction needed for the firm to successfully implement its strategies.[30] Interestingly, many organizational changes take place in economic downturns because poor performance reveals organizational weaknesses. As we discuss next, effective organizational controls help managers recognize when it is time to adjust the firm's structure.

## 11-1b Organizational Controls

Organizational controls are an important aspect of structure.[31] **Organizational controls** guide the use of strategy, indicate how to compare actual results with expected results, and suggest corrective actions to take when the difference is unacceptable. It is difficult for the company to successfully exploit its competitive advantages without effective organizational controls. Properly designed organizational controls provide clear insights regarding behaviors that enhance firm performance.[32] Firms use both strategic controls and financial controls to support the implementation and use of their strategies.

**Strategic controls** are largely subjective criteria intended to verify that the firm is using appropriate strategies for the conditions in the external environment and the company's competitive advantages. Thus, strategic controls are concerned with examining the fit between what the firm *might do* (as suggested by opportunities in its external environment) and what it *can do* (as indicated by its competitive advantages). Effective strategic controls help the firm understand what it takes to be successful, especially where significant strategic change is needed.[33] Strategic controls demand rich communications between managers responsible for using them to judge the firm's performance and those with primary responsibility for implementing the firm's strategies (such as middle and first-level managers). These frequent exchanges are both formal and informal in nature.[34]

Strategic controls are also used to evaluate the degree to which the firm focuses on the requirements to implement its strategies. For a business-level strategy, for example, the strategic controls are used to study value chain activities and support functions (see Figures 3.3, 3.4, and 3.5, in Chapter 3) to verify that the critical value chain activities and support functions are being emphasized and properly executed. In fact, Nokia failed to employ effective strategic controls and is now fighting for survival due to its late response after the emergence of the smartphone.[35] With related corporate-level strategies, strategic controls are used by corporate strategic leaders to verify the sharing of appropriate strategic factors such as knowledge, markets, and technologies across businesses. To effectively use strategic controls when evaluating related diversification strategies, headquarter executives must have a deep understanding of each unit's business-level strategy.[36] As we described in the Opening Case, Borders' significant strategic problems likely stemmed at least partly from the ineffective use of strategic controls.

**Financial controls** are largely objective criteria used to measure the firm's performance against previously established quantitative standards. Accounting-based measures such as return on investment (ROI) and return on assets (ROA) as well as market-based measures such as economic value added are examples of financial controls. Partly because strategic controls are difficult to use with extensive diversification,[37] financial controls are emphasized to evaluate the performance of the firm using the unrelated diversification strategy. The unrelated diversification strategy's focus on financial outcomes (see Chapter 6) requires using standardized financial controls to compare performances between business units and associated managers.[38]

When using financial controls, firms evaluate their current performance against previous outcomes as well as against competitors' performance and industry averages. In the global economy, technological advances are being used to develop highly sophisticated financial controls, making it possible for firms to more thoroughly analyze their performance results and to assure compliance with regulations. Companies such as Oracle and SAP sell software tools that automate processes firms use to meet the financial reporting requirements specified by the Sarbanes-Oxley Act in the United States. As noted in Chapter 10, this act requires a firm's principal executive and financial officers to certify corporate financial and related information in quarterly and annual reports submitted to the Securities and Exchange Commission. These companies will likely develop software to help the financial services industry deal with the newest federal regulations on banking.

**Organizational controls** guide the use of strategy, indicate how to compare actual results with expected results, and suggest corrective actions to take when the difference is unacceptable.

**Strategic controls** are largely subjective criteria intended to verify that the firm is using appropriate strategies for the conditions in the external environment and the company's competitive advantages.

**Financial controls** are largely objective criteria used to measure the firm's performance against previously established quantitative standards.

Both strategic and financial controls are important aspects of each organizational structure, and as noted previously, any structure's effectiveness is determined using a combination of strategic and financial controls. However, the relative use of controls varies by type of strategy. For example, companies and business units of large diversified firms using the cost leadership strategy emphasize financial controls (such as quantitative cost goals), while companies and business units using the differentiation strategy emphasize strategic controls (such as subjective measures of the effectiveness of product development teams).[39] As previously explained, a corporation-wide emphasis on sharing among business units (as called for by related diversification strategies) results in an emphasis on strategic controls, while financial controls are emphasized for strategies in which activities or capabilities are not shared (e.g., in an unrelated diversification strategy).

As firms consider controls, it is important they properly balance the use of strategic and financial controls.[40] Indeed, overemphasizing one at the expense of the other can lead to performance declines. According to Michael Dell, an overemphasis on financial controls to produce attractive short-term results contributed to performance difficulties at Dell Inc. In addressing this issue, Dell said the following: "The company was too focused on the short term, and the balance of priorities was way too leaning toward things that deliver short-term results."[41] However, although there later was some improvement, there are continuing problems as Dell has not improved its competitive position and is now seeking a takeover by a private equity company to facilitate its restructuring effort.[42]

## 11-2 Relationships between Strategy and Structure

Strategy and structure have a reciprocal relationship, and if aligned properly, performance improves.[43] This relationship highlights the interconnectedness between strategy formulation (Chapters 4, 6–9) and strategy implementation (Chapters 10–13). In general, this reciprocal relationship finds structure flowing from or following selection of the firm's strategy. Once in place though, structure can influence current strategic actions as well as choices about future strategies. Consider, for example, the possible influences of Borders' structure and control system in influencing its strategy, as illustrated in the Opening Case. The overly centralized approach that it pursued led to a lack of adaptability in its businesses as it sought to meet the challenge of a change to digital books and online distribution. The centralized structure did not provide information from local stores that might have been useful in changing its technology strategy much sooner than it did. The general nature of the strategy/structure relationship means that changes to the firm's strategy create the need to change how the organization completes its work.

Alternatively, because structure likely influences strategy by constraining the potential alternatives considered, firms must be vigilant in their efforts to verify how their structure not only affects implementation of chosen strategies, but also the limits the structure places on possible future strategies. Research shows, however, that "strategy has a much more important influence on structure than the reverse."[44]

Regardless of the strength of the reciprocal relationships between strategy and structure, those choosing the firm's strategy and structure should be committed to matching each strategy with a structure that provides the stability needed to use current competitive advantages as well as the flexibility required to develop future advantages. Therefore, when changing strategies, the firm should simultaneously consider the structure that will be needed to support use of the new strategy; properly matching strategy and structure can create a competitive advantage. This process can be influenced by outside forces such as significant media attention, which may either hinder the change or foster it.[45]

## 11-3 Evolutionary Patterns of Strategy and Organizational Structure

Research suggests that most firms experience a certain pattern of relationships between strategy and structure. Chandler[46] found that firms tend to grow in somewhat predictable patterns: "first by volume, then by geography, then integration (vertical, horizontal), and finally through product/business diversification"[47] (see Figure 11.1). Chandler interpreted his findings as an indication that firms' growth patterns determine their structural form.

As shown in Figure 11.1, sales growth creates coordination and control problems the existing organizational structure cannot efficiently handle. Organizational growth creates the opportunity for the firm to change its strategy to try to become even more successful. However, the existing structure's formal reporting relationships, procedures, controls, and

**Figure 11.1** Strategy and Structure Growth Pattern

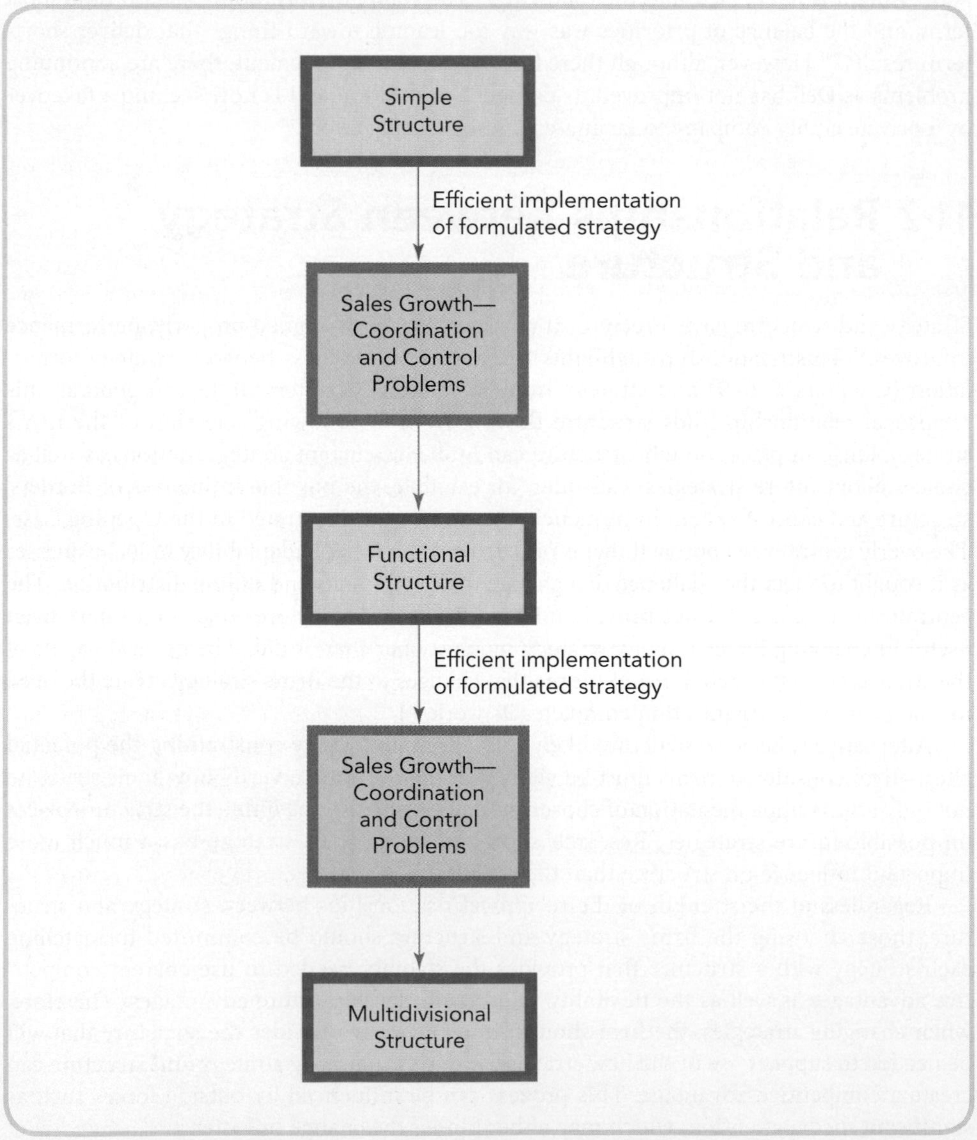

Simple Structure
↓ Efficient implementation of formulated strategy
Sales Growth—Coordination and Control Problems
↓
Functional Structure
↓ Efficient implementation of formulated strategy
Sales Growth—Coordination and Control Problems
↓
Multidivisional Structure

authority and decision-making processes lack the sophistication required to support using the new strategy.[48] A new structure is needed to help decision makers gain access to the knowledge and understanding required to effectively integrate and coordinate actions to implement the new strategy.[49]

Firms choose from among three major types of organizational structures—simple, functional, and multidivisional—to implement strategies. Across time, successful firms move from the simple to the functional to the multidivisional structure to support changes in their growth strategies.[50]

### 11-3a Simple Structure

The **simple structure** is a structure in which the owner-manager makes all major decisions and monitors all activities while the staff serves as an extension of the manager's supervisory authority.[51] Typically, the owner-manager actively works in the business on a daily basis. Informal relationships, few rules, limited task specialization, and unsophisticated information systems characterize this structure. Frequent and informal communications between the owner-manager and employees make coordinating the work to be done relatively easy. The simple structure is matched with focus strategies and business-level strategies, as firms implementing these strategies commonly compete by offering a single product line in a single geographic market. Local restaurants, repair businesses, and other specialized enterprises are examples of firms using the simple structure.

As the small firm grows larger and becomes more complex, managerial and structural challenges emerge. For example, the amount of competitively relevant information requiring analysis substantially increases, placing significant pressure on the owner-manager. Additional growth and success may cause the firm to change its strategy. Even if the strategy remains the same, the firm's larger size dictates the need for more sophisticated workflows and integrating mechanisms. At this evolutionary point, firms tend to move from the simple structure to a functional organizational structure.[52]

### 11-3b Functional Structure

The **functional structure** consists of a chief executive officer and a limited corporate staff, with functional line managers in dominant organizational areas such as production, accounting, marketing, R&D, engineering, and human resources.[53] This structure allows for functional specialization,[54] thereby facilitating active sharing of knowledge within each functional area. Knowledge sharing facilitates career paths as well as professional development of functional specialists. However, a functional orientation can negatively affect communication and coordination among those representing different organizational functions. For this reason, the CEO must verify that the decisions and actions of individual business functions promote the entire firm rather than a single function. The functional structure supports implementing business-level strategies and some corporate-level strategies (e.g., single or dominant business) with low levels of diversification. When changing from a simple to a functional structure, firms want to avoid introducing value-destroying bureaucratic procedures such as failing to promote innovation and creativity. As noted by Gary Hamel, "top-down control and bureaucracy are the fundamental principles of modern business management which are poisonous to innovation."[55]

### 11-3c Multidivisional Structure

With continuing growth and success, firms often consider greater levels of diversification. Successfully using a diversification strategy requires analyzing substantially greater amounts of data and information when the firm offers the same products in different markets (market or geographic diversification) or offers different products in several markets (product diversification). In addition, trying to manage high levels of diversification through functional

The **simple structure** is a structure in which the owner-manager makes all major decisions and monitors all activities while the staff serves as an extension of the manager's supervisory authority.

The **functional structure** consists of a chief executive officer and a limited corporate staff, with functional line managers in dominant organizational areas such as production, accounting, marketing, R&D, engineering, and human resources.

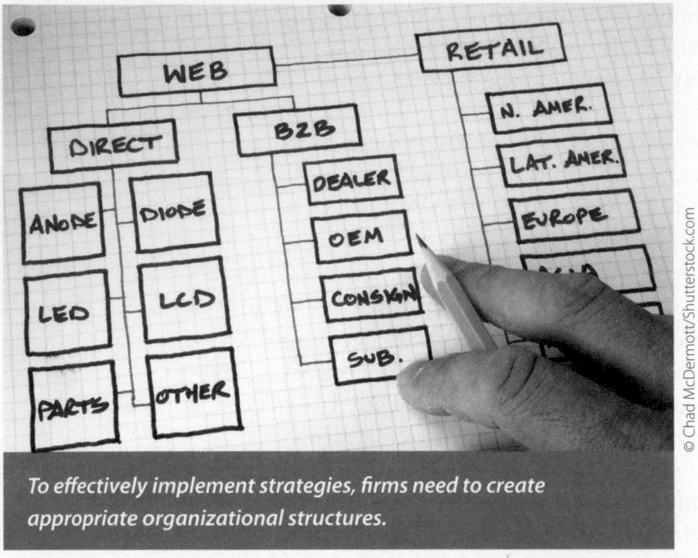


© Chad McDermott/Shutterstock.com

*To effectively implement strategies, firms need to create appropriate organizational structures.*

structures creates serious coordination and control problems,[56] a fact that commonly leads to a new structural form.[57]

The **multidivisional (M-form) structure** consists of a corporate office and operating divisions, each operating division representing a separate business or profit center in which the top corporate officer delegates responsibilities for day-to-day operations and business-unit strategy to division managers. Each division represents a distinct, self-contained business with its own functional hierarchy.[58] As initially designed, the M-form was thought to have three major benefits: "(1) it enabled corporate officers to more accurately monitor the performance of each business, which simplified the problem of control; (2) it facilitated comparisons between divisions, which improved the resource allocation process; and (3) it stimulated managers of poorly performing divisions to look for ways of improving performance."[59] Active monitoring of performance through the M-form increases the likelihood that decisions made by managers heading individual units will be in stakeholders' best interests. Because diversification is a dominant corporate-level strategy used in the global economy, the M-form is a widely adopted organizational structure.[60]

Used to support implementation of related and unrelated diversification strategies, the M-form helps firms successfully manage diversification's many demands.[61] Chandler viewed the M-form as an innovative response to coordination and control problems that surfaced during the 1920s in the functional structures then used by large firms such as DuPont and General Motors.[62] Research shows that the M-form is appropriate when the firm grows through diversification.[63] Partly because of its value to diversified corporations, some consider the multidivisional structure to be one of the twentieth century's most significant organizational innovations.[64]

No single organizational structure (simple, functional, or multidivisional) is inherently superior to the others.[65] Peter Drucker says the following about this matter: "There is no one right organization.... Rather the task ... is to select the organization for the particular task and mission at hand."[66] This statement suggests that the firm must select a structure that is "right" for successfully using the chosen strategy. Because no single structure is optimal in all instances, managers concentrate on developing proper matches between strategies and organizational structures rather than searching for an "optimal" structure. We now describe the strategy/structure matches that evidence shows positively contribute to firm performance.

The **multidivisional (M-form) structure** consists of a corporate office and operating divisions, each operating division representing a separate business or profit center in which the top corporate officer delegates responsibilities for day-to-day operations and business-unit strategy to division managers.

## 11-3d Matches between Business-Level Strategies and the Functional Structure

Firms use different forms of the functional organizational structure to support implementing the cost leadership, differentiation, and integrated cost leadership/differentiation strategies. The differences in these forms are accounted for primarily by different uses of three important structural characteristics: *specialization* (concerned with the type and number of jobs required to complete work[67]), *centralization* (the degree to which decision-making authority is retained at higher managerial levels[68]), and *formalization* (the degree to which formal rules and procedures govern work[69]).

## Using the Functional Structure to Implement the Cost Leadership Strategy

Firms using the cost leadership strategy sell large quantities of standardized products to an industry's typical customer. Firms using this strategy need a structure and capabilities that allow them to achieve efficiencies and produce their goods at costs lower than those of competitors.[70] Simple reporting relationships, a few layers in the decision-making and authority structure, a centralized corporate staff, and a strong focus on process improvements through the manufacturing function rather than the development of new products by emphasizing product R&D help to achieve the efficiencies and thus characterize the cost leadership form of the functional structure[71] (see Figure 11.2). This structure contributes to the emergence of a low-cost culture—a culture in which employees constantly try to find ways to reduce the costs incurred to complete their work.[72] They can do this through the development of a product design that is simple and easy to manufacture, as well as through the development of efficient processes to produce the goods.[73]

In terms of centralization, decision-making authority is centralized in a staff function to maintain a cost-reducing emphasis within each organizational function (engineering, marketing, etc.). While encouraging continuous cost reductions, the centralized staff also verifies that further cuts in costs in one function won't adversely affect the productivity levels of other functions.[74]

Jobs are highly specialized in the cost leadership functional structure; work is divided into homogeneous subgroups. Organizational functions are the most common subgroup, although work is sometimes batched on the basis of products produced or clients served.

**Figure 11.2** Functional Structure for Implementing a Cost Leadership Strategy

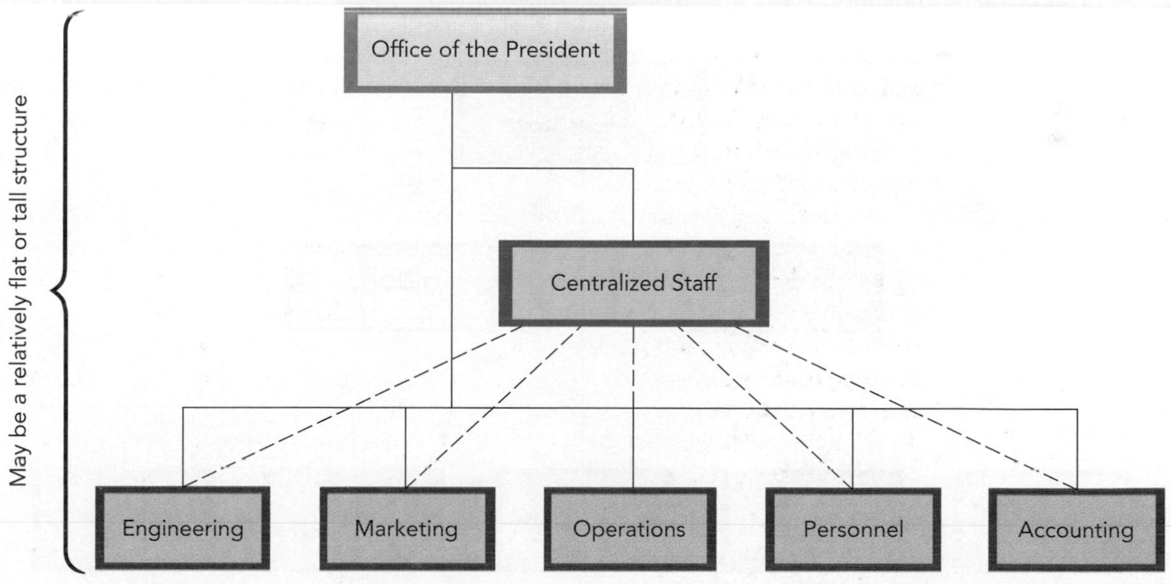

Notes:
- Operations is the main function
- Process engineering is emphasized rather than new product R&D
- Relatively large centralized staff coordinates functions
- Formalized procedures allow for emergence of a low-cost culture
- Overall structure is mechanistic; job roles are highly structured

Specializing in their work allows employees to increase their efficiency, resulting in reduced costs. Guiding individuals' work in this structure are highly formalized rules and procedures, which often emanate from the centralized staff.

Walmart Stores Inc. uses the functional structure to implement cost leadership strategies in each of its three segments (Walmart Stores, Sam's Clubs, and International Division). In the Walmart Stores segment (which generates the largest share of the firm's total sales), the cost leadership strategy is used in the firm's Supercenter, Discount, and Neighborhood Market retailing formats.[75] The stated purpose of Walmart from the beginning has been "saving people money to help them live better."[76] Although the slogan is relatively new, Walmart continues using the functional organizational structure in its divisions to drive costs lower. As discussed in Chapter 4, competitors' efforts to duplicate the success of Walmart's cost leadership strategies have generally failed, partly because of the effective strategy/structure matches in each of the firm's segments.

## Using the Functional Structure to Implement the Differentiation Strategy

Firms using the differentiation strategy produce products that customers hopefully perceive as being different in ways that create value for them. With this strategy, the firm wants to sell nonstandardized products to customers with unique needs. Relatively complex and flexible reporting relationships, frequent use of cross-functional product development teams, and a strong focus on marketing and product R&D rather than manufacturing and process R&D (as with the cost leadership form of the functional structure) characterize the differentiation form of the functional structure (see Figure 11.3). From this structure emerges a

**Figure 11.3** Functional Structure for Implementing a Differentiation Strategy

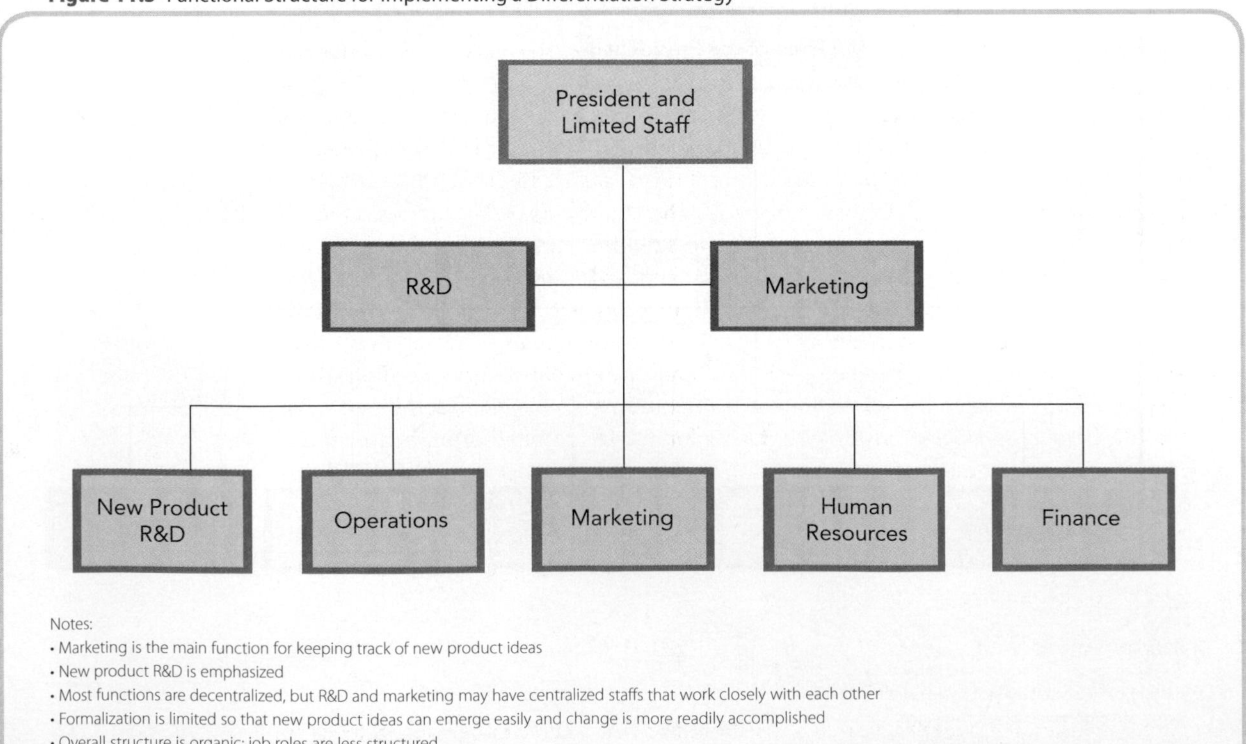

development-oriented culture in which employees try to find ways to further differentiate current products and to develop new, highly differentiated products.[77]

Continuous product innovation demands that people throughout the firm interpret and take action based on information that is often ambiguous, incomplete, and uncertain. Following a strong focus on the external environment to identify new opportunities, employees often gather this information from people outside the firm (e.g., customers and suppliers). Commonly, rapid responses to the possibilities indicated by the collected information are necessary, suggesting the need for decentralized decision-making responsibility and authority. It also requires building a strong technological capability and strategic flexibility, which allow the organization to take advantage of opportunities created by changes in the market.[78] To support the creativity needed and the continuous pursuit of new sources of differentiation and new products, jobs in this structure are not highly specialized. This lack of specialization means that workers have a relatively large number of tasks in their job descriptions. Few formal rules and procedures also characterize this structure. Low formalization, decentralization of decision-making authority and responsibility, and low specialization of work tasks combine to create a structure in which people interact frequently to exchange ideas about how to further differentiate current products while developing ideas for new products that can be crisply differentiated.

Under Armour has used a differentiation strategy and matching structure to create success in the sports apparel market. Under Armour's objective is to create improved athletic performance through innovative design, testing, and marketing, especially to professional athletes and teams, and translate that perception to the broader market. With a strong match between strategy and structure, it has successfully created innovative sports performance products and challenged Nike and other sports apparel competitors.[79]

### Using the Functional Structure to Implement the Integrated Cost Leadership/Differentiation Strategy

Firms using the integrated cost leadership/differentiation strategy sell products that create value because of their relatively low cost and reasonable sources of differentiation. The cost of these products is low "relative" to the cost leader's prices while their differentiation is "reasonable" when compared with the clearly unique features of the differentiator's products.

Although challenging to implement, the integrated cost leadership/differentiation strategy is used frequently in the global economy. The challenge of using this strategy is due largely to the fact that different value chain and support activities (see Chapter 3) are emphasized when using the cost leadership and differentiation strategies. To achieve the cost leadership position, production and process engineering need to be emphasized, with infrequent product changes. To achieve a differentiated position, marketing and new product R&D need to be emphasized while production and process engineering are not. Thus, effective use of the integrated strategy depends on the firm's successful combination of activities intended to reduce costs with activities intended to create additional differentiation features. As a result, the integrated form of the functional structure must have decision-making patterns that are partially centralized and partially decentralized. Additionally, jobs are semi-specialized, and rules and procedures call for some formal and some informal job behavior. All of this requires a measure of flexibility to emphasize one or the other set of functions at any given time.[80]

## 11-3e Matches between Corporate-Level Strategies and the Multidivisional Structure

As explained earlier, Chandler's research shows that the firm's continuing success leads to product or market diversification or both.[81] The firm's level of diversification is a function of decisions about the number and type of businesses in which it will compete as well as how it will manage the businesses (see Chapter 6). Geared to managing individual organizational functions, increasing diversification eventually creates information processing, coordination, and control problems that the functional structure cannot handle. Thus, using a diversification strategy requires the firm to change from the functional structure to the multidivisional structure to develop an appropriate strategy/structure match.

As defined in Figure 6.1, corporate-level strategies have different degrees of product and market diversification. The demands created by different levels of diversification highlight the need for a unique organizational structure to effectively implement each strategy (see Figure 11.4).

Cisco must use a differentiation strategy in order to compete in its several high technology product market segments. However, given the presence of major competitors in those markets, such as Hewlett-Packard and Huawei, and its loss of market share in its core market of routers, Cisco must also be sensitive to costs. Thus, cross-function cooperative structures and processes can be useful to integrate the two disparate dimensions of structure needed to implement Cisco's integrated cost leadership–differentiation strategy. In addition, Cisco needs to coordinate several related product units, and a parallel cooperative structure and processes should facilitate this cooperation at the corporate level. Therefore, Cisco's approach is similar to the cooperative M-form structure, discussed next.

## Using the Cooperative Form of the Multidivisional Structure to Implement the Related Constrained Strategy

The **cooperative form** is an M-form structure in which horizontal integration is used to bring about interdivisional cooperation. Divisions in a firm using the related constrained diversification strategy commonly are formed around products, markets, or both. In Figure 11.5, we use product divisions as part of the representation of the cooperative form of the multidivisional structure, although market divisions could be used instead of or in addition to product divisions to develop the figure.

Using this structure, News Corporation, as explained in the Strategic Focus, is moving to two separate businesses, one in print (News Corporation) and one in TV cable broadcast and movie production (21st Century Fox). Each of these separate businesses will be related constrained diversifiers implementing the cooperative structure. Cisco has implemented the related constrained strategy by acquiring a number of related businesses (see

The **cooperative form** is an M-form structure in which horizontal integration is used to bring about interdivisional cooperation.

**Figure 11.4** Three Variations of the Multidivisional Structure

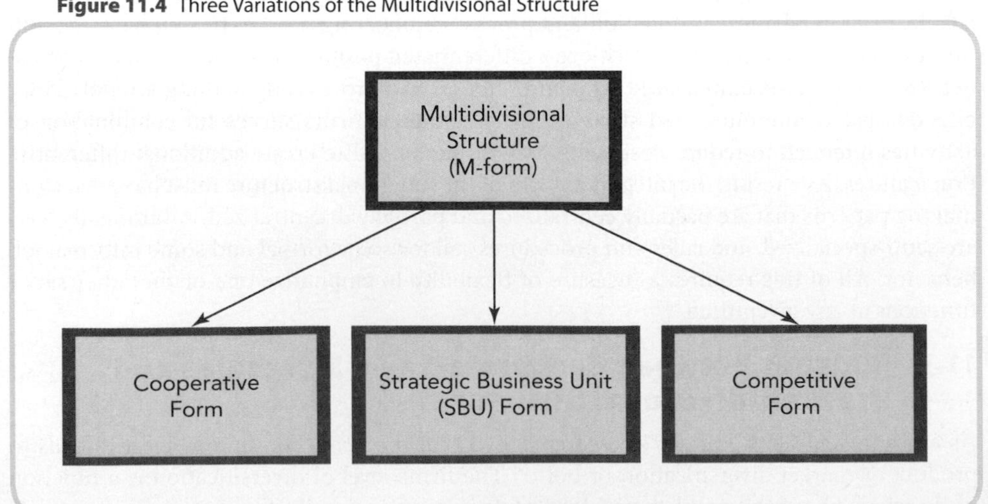

**Figure 11.5** Cooperative Form of the Multidivisional Structure for Implementing a Related Constrained Strategy

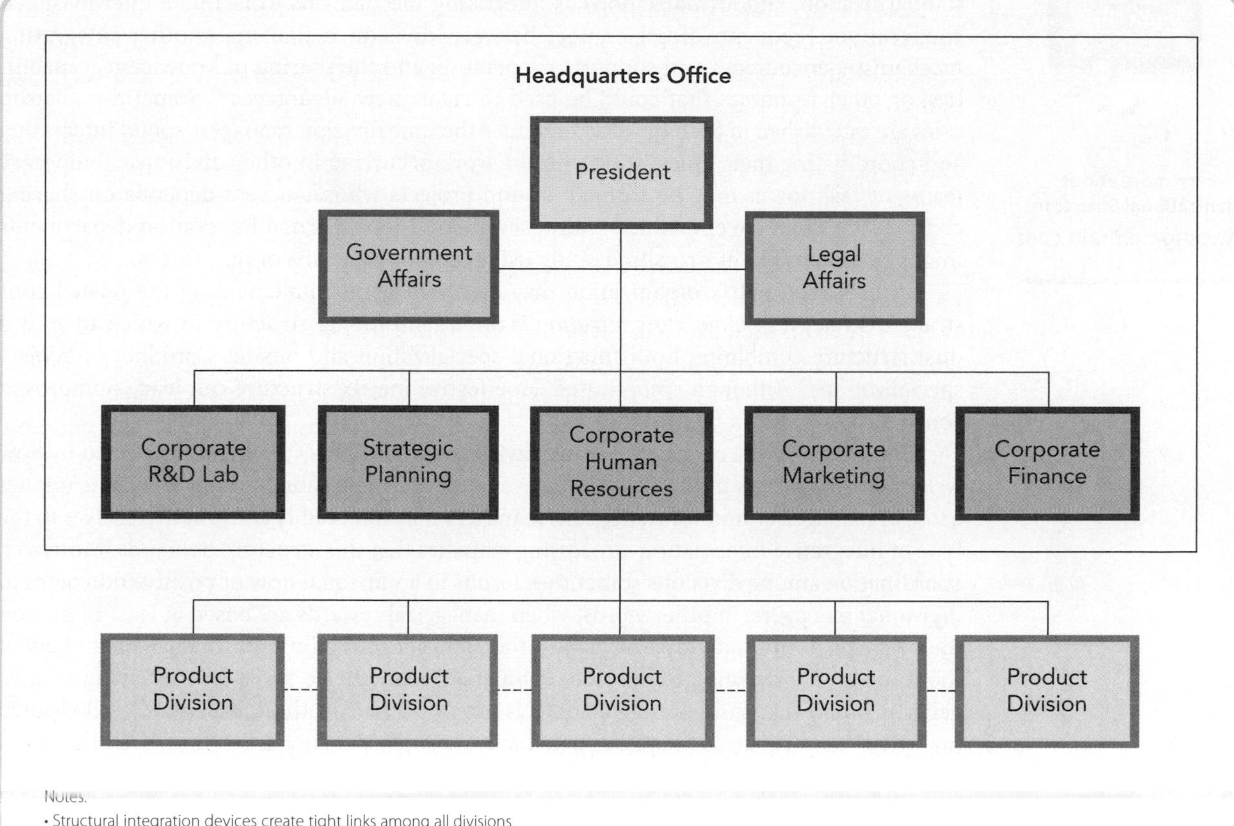


Notes:
- Structural integration devices create tight links among all divisions
- Corporate office emphasizes centralized strategic planning, human resources, and marketing to foster cooperation between divisions
- R&D is likely to be centralized
- Rewards are subjective and tend to emphasize overall corporate performance in addition to divisional performance
- Culture emphasizes cooperative sharing



the Opening Case in Chapter 7). Cisco tried to enter 30 consumer markets related to its core businesses in routers. This required implementation of the cooperative M-form, and Cisco tried to manage it with significant decentralization among the various business units to foster cooperation and synergy. However, there were too many markets, and the horizontal teams designed to foster collaboration and coordination across related businesses created significant challenges. In the end, there was not enough vertical structure to provide oversight and avoid the chaos created by the multiple cross-functional teams and management boards. Thus, Cisco has streamlined its set of businesses and balanced its vertical and horizontal structure to mirror the more common form of the cooperative structure. Interestingly, research suggests that informal ties may be even more important than formal coordination devices in achieving cooperation.[82]

Sharing divisional competencies facilitates the corporation's efforts to develop economies of scope. As explained in Chapter 6, economies of scope (cost savings resulting from the sharing of competencies developed in one division with another division) are linked with successful use of the related constrained strategy. Interdivisional sharing of competencies depends on cooperation, suggesting the use of the cooperative form of the multidivisional structure.[83] Cisco's new structure and processes hopefully will accomplish this.

Learn more about Organizational Structure.
www.cengagebrain.com

The cooperative structure uses different characteristics of structure (centralization, standardization, and formalization) as integrating mechanisms to facilitate interdivisional cooperation. Frequent, direct contact between division managers, another integrating mechanism, encourages and supports cooperation and the sharing of knowledge, capabilities, or other resources that could be used to create new advantages.[84] Sometimes, liaison roles are established in each division to reduce the time division managers spend integrating and coordinating their unit's work with the work occurring in other divisions. Temporary teams or task forces may be formed around projects whose success depends on sharing competencies that are embedded within several divisions. Formal integration departments might be established in firms frequently using temporary teams or task forces.

Ultimately, a matrix organization may evolve in firms implementing the related constrained strategy. A *matrix organization* is an organizational structure in which there is a dual structure combining both functional specialization and business product or project specialization.[85] Although complicated, an effective matrix structure can lead to improved coordination among a firm's divisions.[86]

The success of the cooperative multidivisional structure is significantly affected by how well divisions process information. However, because cooperation among divisions implies a loss of managerial autonomy, division managers may not readily commit themselves to the type of integrative information-processing activities that this structure demands. Moreover, coordination among divisions sometimes results in an unequal flow of positive outcomes to divisional managers. In other words, when managerial rewards are based at least in part on the performance of individual divisions, the manager of the division that is able to benefit the most by the sharing of corporate competencies might be viewed as receiving relative gains at others' expense. Strategic controls are important in these instances, as divisional managers' performance can be evaluated at least partly on the basis of how well they have facilitated interdivisional cooperative efforts. In addition, using reward systems that emphasize overall company performance, besides outcomes achieved by individual divisions, helps overcome problems associated with the cooperative form. Still, the costs of coordination and inertia in organizations limit the amount of related diversification attempted (i.e., they constrain the economies of scope that can be created).[87]

Learn more about Constellation Brands.
www.cengagebrain.com

### Using the Strategic Business Unit Form of the Multidivisional Structure to Implement the Related Linked Strategy

Firms with fewer links or less constrained links among their divisions use the related linked diversification strategy. The strategic business unit form of the multidivisional structure supports implementation of this strategy. The **strategic business unit (SBU) form** is an M-form structure consisting of three levels: corporate headquarters, SBUs, and SBU divisions (see Figure 11.6). The SBU structure is used by large firms and can be complex, given associated organization size and product and market diversity.

The divisions within each SBU are related in terms of shared products or markets or both, but the divisions of one SBU have little in common with the divisions of the other SBUs. Divisions within each SBU share product or market competencies to develop economies of scope and possibly economies of scale. The integrating mechanisms used by the divisions in this structure can be equally well used by the divisions within the individual strategic business units that are part of the SBU form of the multidivisional structure. In this structure, each SBU is a profit center that is controlled and evaluated by the headquarters office. Although both financial and strategic controls are important, on a relative basis, financial controls are vital to headquarters' evaluation of each SBU; strategic controls are critical when the heads of SBUs evaluate their divisions' performances. Strategic controls are also critical to the headquarters' efforts to determine whether the company has formed an effective portfolio of businesses and whether those businesses are being successfully

The **strategic business unit (SBU) form** is an M-form consisting of three levels: corporate headquarters, strategic business units (SBUs), and SBU divisions.

M. Stasy

## Strategic Focus — GLOBALIZATION

### A Change in Corporate Strategy Requires a Change in the Corporate Organizational Structure

*With the acquisition of Corona from Anheuser-Busch InBev, Constellation Brands became the third largest beer producer in the United States.*

In 2013, Constellation Brands Inc. became the third largest beer producer in the United States behind Anheuser-Busch InBev and MillerCoors. The opportunity appeared for Constellation through a merger between Anheuser-Busch InBev and Mexico's Grupo Modelo. The Justice Department would not allow the merger to take place unless Grupo Modelo's top import brand, Corona, was divested. This is the asset that Constellation acquired with the associated brewery over the Texas border in Mexico with distribution rights in the United States. Constellation had already signed a 50/50 joint venture with Modelo in 2007 to distribute the Mexican company's beer in the United States. As such, Constellation got to continue its distribution rights but also became a producer with the acquisition of the large brewery. Through this acquisition, Constellation will control nearly 50 percent of U.S. beer imports. Even though beer distribution is shrinking relative to other segments of overall alcohol sales, imported beers are a growing segment. In part, this is due to the growth of the Hispanic population in the United States.

Constellation started out as a small family wine producer in upstate New York. Through acquisitions, Constellation Brands has become the largest wine producer in the world. In particular, it has the largest share of premium wine distribution in the United States, the United Kingdom, Australia, and Canada, and the second largest in New Zealand. It also has a large set of brands in the spirits category. For instance, it owns Svedka Vodka and competes with Grey Goose, owned by Bacardi Limited, and Smirnoff owned by Diageo. It also owns other spirit brands including Black Velvet Canadian Whisky and Paul Masson Grande Amber Brandy.

Because it has three different types of producing technologies in wine, spirits, and beer, it must understand each of these processes and be able to have strategic control of these separate operations. Accordingly, the appropriate structure for these three types of operations requires the SBU structure such that you combine the wine, spirits, and beer operations into three different business groups with divisional structures for each brand within the group. As it has moved from being the producer of only wines to being a producer of spirits and beer, it has had to change its operating structure because it moved from being a related constrained diversifier to a related linked diversifier (mixed-related-unrelated). With this change, the better fit between strategy and structure would be the installation of the SBU structure and a move away from the cooperative structure. It may be possible to run the premium wine and spirits in the same group because they have similar distribution outlets. However, because there is not much production or operational relatedness in these business units, it may be better to keep them separate. Beer is both distributed differently (more of a consumer product) and produced differently than wine and spirits. Robert Sands, CEO of Constellation, acknowledges, "Constellation has a lot to learn about mixing barley and hops, but he notes the brewery is highly automated." He also sees some cost benefits across the whole corporation in being able to strike cheaper procurement deals for "glass bottles, cardboard, and freight, three big input costs, and improve its negotiation position with retailers by offering a full menu of alcohol." Although Constellation Brands has to change its structure due to its diversification strategy, News Corporation is reducing its diversification by splitting up its business into two separate firms.

In 2013, News Corporation approved a split of its media businesses. Over a number of years, it has acquired a number of media businesses both in television and print. It has been organized into an SBU-type of organization given its focus in different areas. In the split-up, the print media company will be called News Corp. and will have newspaper assets including the *Wall Street Journal*, *New York Post*, and *Times of London*. It will also have the book publisher HarperCollins. The other business will be called 21st Century Fox and will include the Fox broadcast and cable networks and 20th Century Fox studio, which produces movies and television programming. Rupert Murdock will continue as the CEO of 21st Century Fox and will remain the executive chairman of the board of News Corp.

The organization of these two businesses will likely have to change. The television and movie businesses will have more tightly related divisions and will likely move to the cooperative structure. Similarly, the print media business (News Corp.) will also have to move to the cooperative structure because it will be pursuing the related constrained strategy with all its business units interrelated. As such, it will likely change into two separate organizations using the cooperative structure where businesses are more related as a unitary firm that formerly used the SBU structure.

Sources: A. Collins, 2013, Strategic buyer AB InBev sells U.S. rights and other Modelo brands to Constellation, *Mergers & Acquisitions Report*, February 25, 5; A. Deckert, 2013, Constellation Brands gears up for changes, *Rochester Business Journal*, April 12, 3; M. Esterl, 2013, New U.S. brewing giant is crowned, *Wall Street Journal*, June 7, B6; B. Kindle, 2013, Constellation wants legal role in beer merger battle, *Wall Street Journal*, February 11, B5; A. Sharma, 2013, News Corp. shareholders approve split, *Wall Street Journal*, June 12, B5.

managed. Therefore, there is need for strategic structures that promote exploration to identify new products and markets, but also for actions that exploit the current product lines and markets.[88]

As illustrated in the Strategic Focus, Constellation Brands is likely to implement the SBU structure as it has different operational needs among its wine, spirits, and beer business

**Figure 11.6** SBU Form of the Multidivisional Structure for Implementing a Related Link Strategy

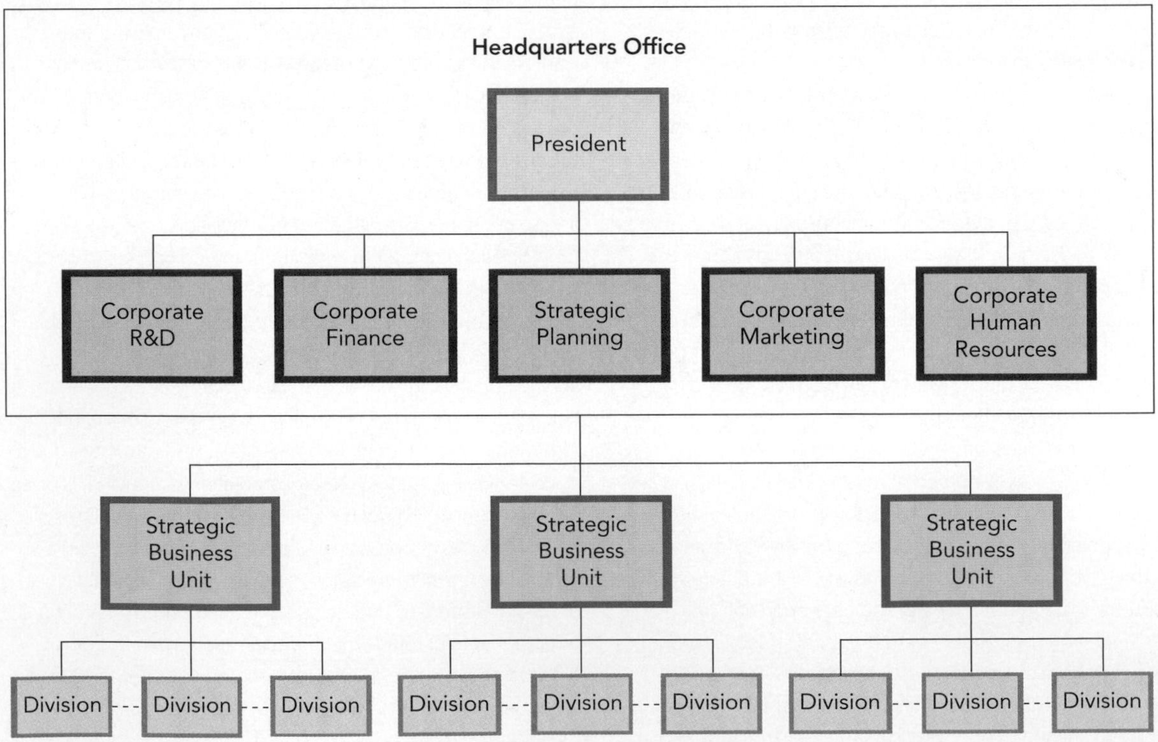

Notes:
- Structural integration among divisions within SBUs, but independence across SBUs
- Strategic planning may be the most prominent function in headquarters for managing the strategic planning approval process of SBUs for the president
- Each SBU may have its own budget for staff to foster integration
- Corporate headquarters staff members serve as consultants to SBUs and divisions, rather than having direct input to product strategy, as in the cooperative form

units. Sharing competencies among units within an SBU is an important characteristic of the SBU form of the multidivisional structure (see the notes to Figure 11.6). A drawback to the SBU structure is that multifaceted businesses often have difficulties in communicating this complex business model to stockholders.[89] Furthermore, if coordination between SBUs is needed, as is the case with Constellation Brands, problems can arise because the SBU structure, similar to the competitive form discussed next, does not readily foster cooperation across SBUs.

## Using the Competitive Form of the Multidivisional Structure to Implement the Unrelated Diversification Strategy

Firms using the unrelated diversification strategy want to create value through efficient internal capital allocations or by restructuring, buying, and selling businesses.[90] The competitive form of the multidivisional structure supports implementation of this strategy.

The **competitive form** is an M-form structure characterized by complete independence among the firm's divisions, which compete for corporate resources (see Figure 11.7). Unlike the divisions included in the cooperative structure, divisions that are part of the competitive structure do not share common corporate strengths. Because strengths are not shared, integrating devices are not developed for use by the divisions included in the competitive structure.

The **competitive form** is an M-form structure characterized by complete independence among the firm's divisions which compete for corporate resources.

The efficient internal capital market that is the foundation for using the unrelated diversification strategy requires organizational arrangements emphasizing divisional competition

**Figure 11.7** Competitive Form of the Multidivisional Structure for Implementing an Unrelated Strategy

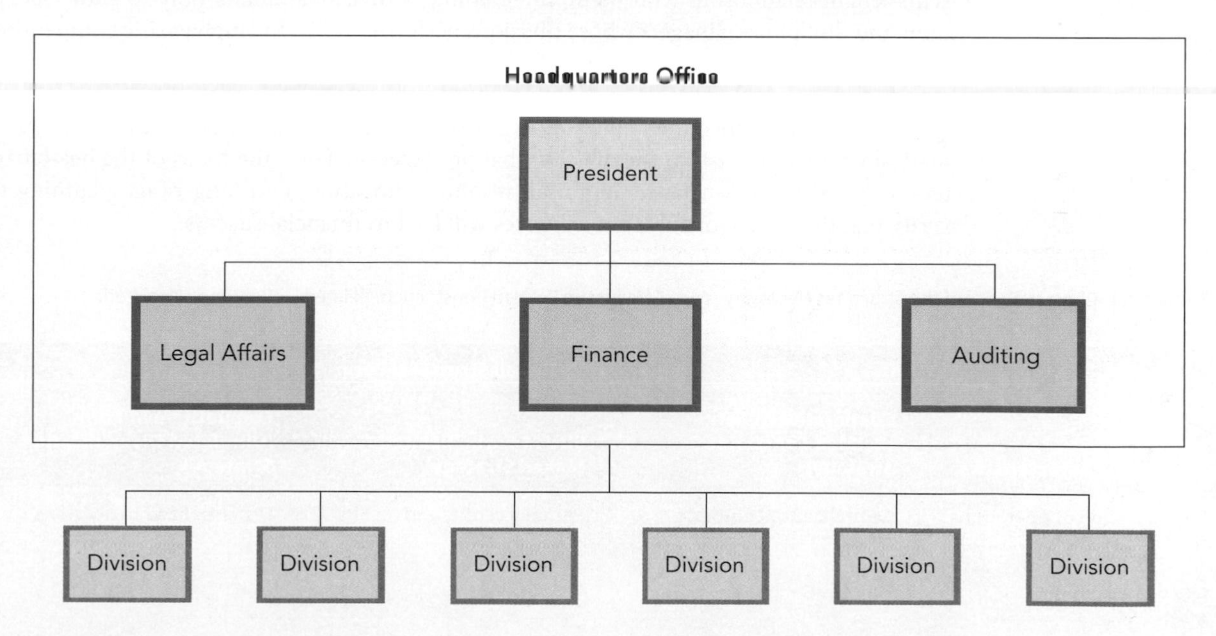

rather than cooperation.[91] Three benefits are expected from the internal competition. First, internal competition creates flexibility (e.g., corporate headquarters can have divisions working on different technologies and projects to identify those with the greatest potential). Resources can then be allocated to the division appearing to have the most potential to fuel the entire firm's success. Second, internal competition challenges the status quo and inertia, because division heads know that future resource allocations are a product of excellent current performance as well as superior positioning in terms of future performance. Last, internal competition motivates effort in that the challenge of competing against internal peers can be as great as the challenge of competing against external rivals.[92] In this structure, organizational controls (primarily financial controls) are used to emphasize and support internal competition among separate divisions and as the basis for allocating corporate capital based on divisions' performances.

Textron Inc., a large "multi-industry" company, seeks to identify, research, select, acquire, and integrate companies and has developed a set of rigorous criteria to guide decision making. Textron continuously looks to enhance and reshape its portfolio by divesting non-core assets and acquiring branded businesses in attractive industries with substantial long-term growth potential. Textron operates five independent businesses—Bell Helicopter, Cessna Aircraft, Textron Systems and Industrial (all manufacturing businesses), and Finance, "which are responsible for the day-to-day operation of their businesses." The "segment profit is an important measure used for evaluating performance and for decision-making purposes."[93] Many such firms use return on invested capital (ROIC) as a way to evaluate the contribution of its diversified set of businesses as they compete internally for resources.

To emphasize competitiveness among divisions, the headquarters office maintains an arm's-length relationship with them, intervening in divisional affairs only to audit operations and discipline managers whose divisions perform poorly. In emphasizing competition between divisions, the headquarters office relies on strategic controls to set rate-of-return targets and financial controls to monitor divisional performance relative to those targets. The headquarters office then allocates cash flow on a competitive basis, rather than automatically returning cash to the division that produced it. Thus, the focus of the headquarters' work is on performance appraisal, resource allocation, and long-range planning to verify that the firm's portfolio of businesses will lead to financial success.

**Table 11.1** Characteristics of the Structures Necessary to Implement the Related Constrained, Related Linked, and Unrelated Diversification Strategies

| | Overall Structural Form | | |
|---|---|---|---|
| **Structural Characteristics** | **Cooperative M-Form (Related Constrained Strategy)** | **SBU M-Form (Related Linked Strategy)** | **Competitive M-Form (Unrelated Diversification Strategy)** |
| Centralization of operations | Centralized at corporate office | Partially centralized (in SBUs) | Decentralized to divisions |
| Use of integration mechanisms | Extensive | Moderate | Nonexistent |
| Divisional performance evaluation | Emphasizes subjective (strategic) criteria | Uses a mixture of subjective (strategic) and objective (financial) criteria | Emphasizes objective (financial) criteria |
| Divisional incentive compensation | Linked to overall corporate performance | Mixed linkage to corporate, SBU, and divisional performance | Linked to divisional performance |

The three major forms of the multidivisional structure should each be paired with a particular corporate-level strategy. Table 11.1 shows these structures' characteristics. Differences exist in the degree of centralization, the focus of the performance evaluation, the horizontal structures (integrating mechanisms), and the incentive compensation schemes. The most centralized and most costly structural form is the cooperative structure. The least centralized, with the lowest bureaucratic costs, is the competitive structure. The SBU structure requires partial centralization and involves some of the mechanisms necessary to implement the relatedness between divisions. Also, the divisional incentive compensation awards are allocated according to both SBUs and corporate performance.

## 11-3f Matches between International Strategies and Worldwide Structure

As explained in Chapter 8, international strategies are becoming increasingly important for long-term competitive success in what continues to become an increasingly borderless global economy.[94] Among other benefits, international strategies allow the firm to search for new markets, resources, core competencies, and technologies as part of its efforts to outperform competitors.[95]

As with business-level and corporate-level strategies, unique organizational structures are necessary to successfully implement the different international strategies given the different cultural, institutional, and legal environments around the world.[96] Forming proper matches between international strategies and organizational structures facilitates the firm's efforts to effectively coordinate and control its global operations. More importantly, research findings confirm the validity of the international strategy/structure matches we discuss here.[97]

### Using the Worldwide Geographic Area Structure to Implement the Multidomestic Strategy

The *multidomestic strategy* decentralizes the firm's strategic and operating decisions to business units in each country so that product characteristics can be tailored to local preferences. Firms using this strategy try to isolate themselves from global competitive forces by establishing protected market positions or by competing in industry segments that are most affected by differences among local countries. The worldwide geographic area structure is used to implement this strategy. The **worldwide geographic area structure** emphasizes national interests and facilitates the firm's efforts to satisfy local differences (see Figure 11.8).

Since the 2008 economic crisis, the world has become more fragmented and there is more of a local or regional focus. For example, Caterpillar, a globally oriented company, is trying to localize better than in the past. One analyst noted the following: "Caterpillar thinks less about a single world market than many regional ones. The company is global, but where it can, it sources and produces locally, which is a natural hedge against everything from oil prices to currency risk to changing customer tastes."[98] Although Caterpillar is not necessarily a multidomestic firm per se, it is becoming more multidomestic in that it is emphasizing more localization. Many consumer product companies such as Procter and Gamble and Unilever have employed the multidomestic strategy because consumer products often need to be more locally responsive.[99] Using the multidomestic strategy requires little coordination between different country markets, meaning that integrating mechanisms among divisions around the world are not needed. Coordination among units in a firm's worldwide geographic area structure is often informal. As mentioned earlier, this may be the most effective form of cooperation.

The **worldwide geographic area structure** emphasizes national interests and facilitates the firm's efforts to satisfy local differences.

The multidomestic strategy/worldwide geographic area structure match evolved as a natural outgrowth of the multicultural European marketplace. Friends and family members of the main business who were sent as expatriates into foreign countries

**Figure 11.8** Worldwide Geographic Area Structure for Implementing a Multidomestic Strategy

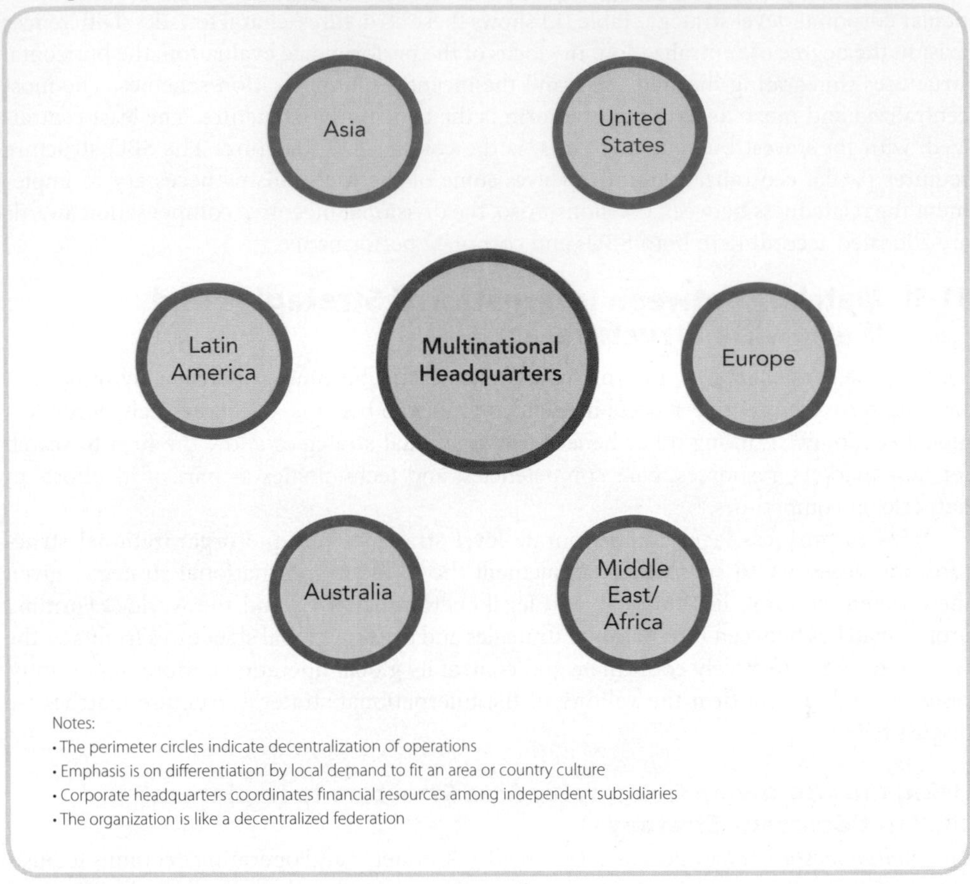


to develop the independent country subsidiary often used this structure for the main business. The relationship to corporate headquarters by divisions took place through informal communication.

A key disadvantage of the multidomestic strategy/worldwide geographic area structure match is the inability to create strong global efficiency. With an increasing emphasis on lower-cost products in international markets, the need to pursue worldwide economies of scale has also increased. These changes foster use of the global strategy and its structural match, the worldwide product divisional structure.

### Using the Worldwide Product Divisional Structure to Implement the Global Strategy

With the corporation's home office dictating competitive strategy, the *global strategy* is one through which the firm offers standardized products across country markets. The firm's success depends on its ability to develop economies of scope and economies of scale on a global level. Decisions to outsource or maintain integrated subsidiaries may in part depend on the country risk and institutional environment into which the firm is entering.[100]

In the **worldwide product divisional structure,** decision-making authority is centralized in the worldwide division headquarters to coordinate and integrate decisions and actions among divisional business units.

The worldwide product divisional structure supports use of the global strategy. In the **worldwide product divisional structure**, decision-making authority is centralized in the worldwide division headquarters to coordinate and integrate decisions and actions among divisional business units (see Figure 11.9). This structure is often used in rapidly growing firms that want to effectively manage their diversified product lines. Avon Products, Inc. is an example of a firm using the worldwide product divisional structure.

**Figure 11.9** Worldwide Product Divisional Structure for Implementing a Global Strategy

Worldwide Products Division

Worldwide Products Division

Worldwide Products Division

Global Corporate Headquarters

Worldwide Products Division

Worldwide Products Division

Worldwide Products Division

Notes:

- The "headquarters" circle indicates centralization to coordinate information flow among worldwide products
- Corporate headquarters uses many intercoordination devices to facilitate global economies of scale and scope
- Corporate headquarters also allocates financial resources in a cooperative way
- The organization is like a centralized federation



Avon is a global brand leader in products for women such as lipsticks, fragrances, and anti-aging skin care. Committed to "empowering women all over the world since 1886," Avon relies on product innovation to be a first mover in its markets. For years, Avon used the multidomestic strategy. However, the firm's growth came to a screeching halt in 2006. Contributing to this decline were simultaneous stumbles in sales revenues in emerging markets (e.g., Russia and Central Europe), the United States, and Mexico. To cope with its problems, the firm moved to implement aspects of the global strategy and to the worldwide product divisional structure to support its use. Today, Avon is organized around product divisions including Avon Color, the firm's "flagship global color cosmetics brand, which offers a variety of color cosmetics products, including foundations, powders, lip, eye, and nail products," Skincare, Bath & Body, Hair Care, Wellness, and Fragrance. The analysis of these product divisions' performances is conducted by individuals in the firm's New York headquarters. One of the purposes of changing strategy and structure is for Avon to control its costs and gain additional scale economies as paths to performance improvements. In 2012, a new CEO, Sheri McCoy, replaced Andrea Jung with the goal of continuing to foster integration and cost saving. She has signaled that Avon will exit Korea, Ireland, and Vietnam and continue to emphasize its brands. Direct selling online has become more important, but this can all be driven by Avon's 100,000 direct representatives, for example, through their Facebook contacts.[101]

Integrating mechanisms are important in the effective use of the worldwide product divisional structure. Direct contact between managers, liaison roles between departments, and both temporary task forces and permanent teams are examples of these mechanisms. The disadvantages of the global strategy/worldwide structure combination are the difficulty involved with coordinating decisions and actions across country borders and the inability to quickly respond to local needs and preferences. To deal with these types of disadvantages, Avon has approximately 6 million local salespeople in 100 countries who are committed to the organization and who help the company to become locally responsive. Another solution is to develop a regional approach in addition to the product focus, which might be similar to the combination structure discussed next.

## Using the Combination Structure to Implement the Transnational Strategy

The *transnational strategy* calls for the firm to combine the multidomestic strategy's local responsiveness with the global strategy's efficiency. Firms using this strategy are trying to gain the advantages of both local responsiveness and global efficiency.[102] The combination structure is used to implement the transnational strategy. The **combination structure** is a structure drawing characteristics and mechanisms from both the worldwide geographic area structure and the worldwide product divisional structure. The transnational strategy is often implemented through two possible combination structures: a global matrix structure and a hybrid global design.[103]

The global matrix design brings together both local market and product expertise into teams that develop and respond to the global marketplace. The global matrix design (the basic matrix structure was defined earlier) promotes flexibility in designing products and responding to customer needs. However, it has severe limitations in that it places employees in a position of being accountable to more than one manager. At any given time, an employee may be a member of several functional or product group teams. Relationships that evolve from multiple memberships can make it difficult for employees to be simultaneously loyal to all of them. Although the matrix places authority in the hands of the managers who are most able to use it, it creates problems in regard to corporate reporting relationships that are so complex and vague that it is difficult and time-consuming to receive approval for major decisions.

The **combination structure** is a structure drawing characteristics and mechanisms from both the worldwide geographic area structure and the worldwide product divisional structure.

We illustrate the hybrid structure in Figure 11.10. In this design, some divisions are oriented toward products while others are oriented toward market areas. Thus, in cases when

**Figure 11.10** Hybrid Form of the Combination Structure for Implementing a Transnational Strategy

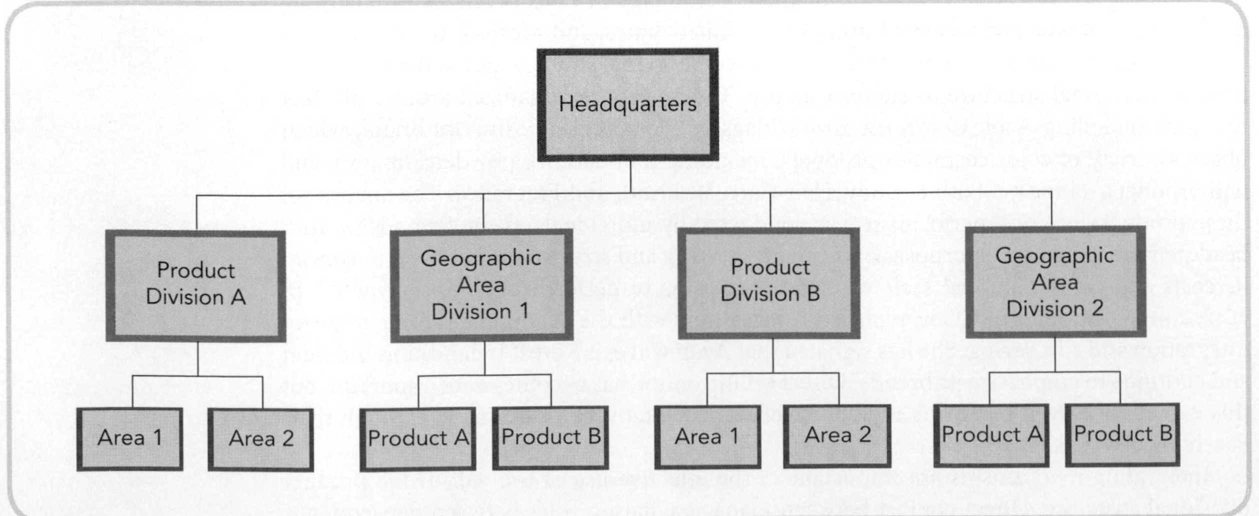

the geographic area is more important, the division managers are area-oriented. In other divisions where worldwide product coordination and efficiencies are more important, the division manager is more product-oriented.

The fit between the multidomestic strategy and the worldwide geographic area structure and between the global strategy and the worldwide product divisional structure is apparent. However, when a firm wants to implement the multidomestic and global strategies simultaneously through a combination structure, the appropriate integrating mechanisms are less obvious. The structure used to implement the transnational strategy must be simultaneously centralized and decentralized; integrated and nonintegrated; formalized and nonformalized. Sometimes the structure becomes too complex. P&G has been said to have a costly organization structure using the hybrid form: "P&G has a complex organizational structure that includes global business units that manage its brands and develop products in different categories, and geographical 'market development organizations' that work with retailers to sell products."[104]

When Panasonic Corporation (a Japanese company formally named Matsushita) started selling home appliances in the Chinese market several decades ago, its only attempt at localization was to offer less expensive versions of its developed market standard offerings. Japanese firms often sold standard products across the world, implementing the global strategy using the worldwide product divisional structure. However, they found that local competitors such as Haier were quickly outpacing their appliance sales in China, Haier's home market. Through this experience, Panasonic learned to engage more deeply within a country or regional market to adapt their appliances more closely to the demands of the local consumer. This led to Panasonic rethinking its company using the global strategy, and it has since sought to develop both the integrated global strategy as well as place emphasis on the local adaptations necessary to improve sales.[105]

IKEA has done a good job of balancing these organization aspects in implementing the transnational strategy.[106] IKEA is a global furniture retailer with more than 300 outlets in 39 countries and regions. IKEA focuses on lowering its costs and understanding its customers' needs, especially the needs of younger customers. It has been able to manage these seemingly opposite characteristics through its structure and management process. It has also been able to encourage its employees to understand the effects of cultural and geographic diversity on firm operations. The positive results from this are evident in the more than 600 million visitors to IKEA stores per year. It is also planning a large expansion in China and will need to adjust to the local market.[107] IKEA's system also has internal network attributes,[108] which are discussed next in regard to external interorganizational networks.

### 11-3g Matches between Cooperative Strategies and Network Structures

As discussed in Chapter 9, a network strategy exists when partners form several alliances in order to improve the performance of the alliance network itself through cooperative endeavors.[109] The greater levels of environmental complexity and uncertainty facing companies in today's competitive environment are causing more firms to use cooperative strategies such as strategic alliances and joint ventures.[110] The strategic focus on Unilever illustrates how it implements many cooperative strategies to accomplish both its growth objectives and environmental sustainability strategies (a topic introduced in Chapter 2 that relates to the physical environment).

As described in the Strategic Focus on Unilever, the breadth and scope of firms' operations in the global economy create many opportunities for them to cooperate.[111] In fact, a firm can develop cooperative relationships with many of its stakeholders, including customers, suppliers, and competitors, as well as NGOs. When a firm becomes involved with combinations of cooperative relationships, it is part of a strategic network, or what others call an alliance constellation or portfolio.[112]

Strategy Right NOW

Find out more about Jacobs Engineering Group.
www.cengagebrain.com

## Strategic Focus — SUCCESS

### Unilever Cooperates with Many Firms and Nonprofit Organizations to Implement Its Strategy While Creating a More Sustainable Environment

Unilever, a European-headquartered (in both the Netherlands and the United Kingdom) consumer products company focused on producing and distributing many food and beverage products, has sought to lead in making their products using a sustainable environment strategy. Historically consumer products companies, especially those from Europe, have pursued the multidomestic strategy, needing to adapt their products to each country or region market. Accordingly, most have implemented their strategy using the worldwide geographic area structure. Many consumer product companies, such as Avon, have begun to use aspects of the worldwide product structure to become more efficient. This is also the case with Unilever. However, Unilever has continued to emphasize the geographic areas but has done so using the transnational strategy while implementing the combination structure to meet local market responsiveness as well as better global efficiency objectives. Moreover, its CEO, Paul Pullman, who took the job in 2009, has also suggested, "Our purpose is to have a sustainable business model that is put at the service of the greater good."

Accordingly, it created a manifesto in 2010 called the Sustainable Living Plan where Unilever promised to double its sales at the same time as it cuts its environmental footprint in half by 2020. For example, one goal is to source all of its agricultural products in ways that "don't degrade the Earth." It also has a campaign promising to improve the well-being of one billion people by "persuading them to wash their hands or brush their teeth, or by selling them food with less salt or fat." It seeks to realize many of these goals through cooperative strategies with other profit-seeking organizations as well as nonprofit entities.

In 2011, for instance, Unilever signed a contract with Jacobs Engineering Group Inc. forming a global (overall corporate) alliance to facilitate the efficiency of Unilever's capital improvement projects around the world. Unilever has 250 manufacturing sites and is expanding aggressively, especially in developing and emerging economies, to support its ambitious growth goals. For example, it expects emerging economies to drive 75 percent of its growth in the long term. The alliance with Jacobs Engineering will be managed out of Singapore and will provide engineering services for Unilever's manufacturing facilities around the world. Both companies will "work as a team to insure their sustainable growth model," implement cost reductions, and "drive co-innovation and implement the harmonization and cross-category standardization of designs." The alliance will also work with supply chain team members to increase speed to market with designs that "reduce carbon, water, and waste footprints across its manufacturing sites."

*Unilever North America head Kees Kruythoff discusses how the global company sustainably sourced 100% of the palm oil it uses in products like shampoo, margarine, and soap by the end of 2012, achieving its goal three years ahead of schedule. This achievement is a direct result of its Sustainable Living Plan, launched in November 2010.*



In alignment with marketing growth goals, Unilever has initiated the Unilever Nutrition Network. This organization has divided the world into six regions focused on providing world-class nutrition and health innovation. Its goal is to generate ideas to facilitate sustainable product launches and improve existing products while strengthening their brand value. As part of this overall strategy, Unilever has used Salesforce's Chatter technology in the implementation of its new social marketing platform. This technology allows local markets and distributors of Unilever products to share insights and best practices with the marketing team from Unilever to help drive its "crafting brands for life" strategy.

The recent Unilever Sustainable Living Plan report (2012) described how the company is working with a number of non profit, nongovernment organizations (NGOs) to help address real issues, facilitate solutions for suppliers for improving sustainable living, and reach customers in society at large who need information to improve their sustainability approaches to life with better food security and poverty alleviation. Initiatives include partnering with the following NGOs: the Consumer Goods Forum; the World Business Council for Sustainable Development; the World Economic Forum; the Tropical Forest Alliance 2020; Refrigerants, Naturally; the Global Green Foundation Forum; and Zero Hunger Challenge and Scale-Up Nutrition initiatives supported by the United Nations.

Interestingly, Unilever no longer gives quarterly earnings guidance reports and suggests that this has allowed it to focus shareholders on its longer-term goals. Furthermore, since Pullman took over in 2009 it has sustained its positive growth trajectory with better income performance and associated stock market performance. As can be seen, it is accomplishing these things through better organizational design, lofty objectives, but also by using a number of cooperative strategies with many organizations outside the organization such as Jacobs Engineering and many NGOs.

Sources: 2013, In the green corner: How IBM, Unilever and P&G started winning again: Why big business is wising up to sustainability, *Strategic Direction*, 29(5): 19–22; 2013, Our nutrition network, www.unilever.com, accessed June 17; 2013, Unilever drives efficiency in capital investment program, www.unilever.com, accessed June 17; 2013, Unilever Sustainable Living Plan, www.unilever.com, accessed June 17; 2013, Unilever Annual Report 2012, www.unilever.com, accessed June 17; S. Anand & N. Gopalan, 2013, Consumers in India are an M&A target, *Wall Street Journal*, www.wsj.com, May 1; M. Gunther, 2013, Unilever's CEO has a green thumb, *Fortune*, June 10, 124–128; R. Shields, 2013, Unilever boosts international collaboration with social rollout, *Marketing Week*, www.marketingweek.com, May 2; A. Ignatius, 2012, Captain planet, *Harvard Business Review*, 90(6): 112–118.

A *strategic network* is a group of firms that has been formed to create value by participating in multiple cooperative arrangements. An effective strategic network facilitates discovering opportunities beyond those identified by individual network participants. A strategic network can be a source of competitive advantage for its members when its operations create value that is difficult for competitors to duplicate and that network members can't create by themselves.[113] Strategic networks are used to implement business-level, corporate-level, and international cooperative strategies.

Commonly, a strategic network is a loose federation of partners participating in the network's operations on a flexible basis. At the core or center of the strategic network, the *strategic center firm* is the one around which the network's cooperative relationships revolve (see Figure 11.11).

Because of its central position, the strategic center firm is the foundation for the strategic network's structure. Concerned with various aspects of organizational structure, such as formally reporting relationships and procedures, the strategic center firm manages what are often complex, cooperative interactions among network partners. To perform the tasks discussed next, the strategic center firm must make sure that incentives for participating in the network are aligned so that network firms continue to have a reason to remain connected.[114] The strategic center firm is engaged in four primary tasks as it manages the strategic network and controls its operations:[115]

*Strategic outsourcing.* The strategic center firm outsources and partners with more firms than other network members. At the same time, the strategic center firm requires network partners to be more than contractors. Members are expected to find opportunities for the network to create value through its cooperative work.[116]

*Competencies.* To increase network effectiveness, the strategic center firm seeks ways to support each member's efforts to develop core competencies with the potential of benefiting the network.

*Technology.* The strategic center firm is responsible for managing the development and sharing of technology-based ideas among network members. The structural requirement that members submit formal reports detailing the technology-oriented outcomes of their efforts to the strategic center firm facilitates this activity.[117]

*Race to learn.* The strategic center firm emphasizes that the principal dimensions of competition are between value chains and between networks of value chains. Because of

Figure 11.11 A Strategic Network

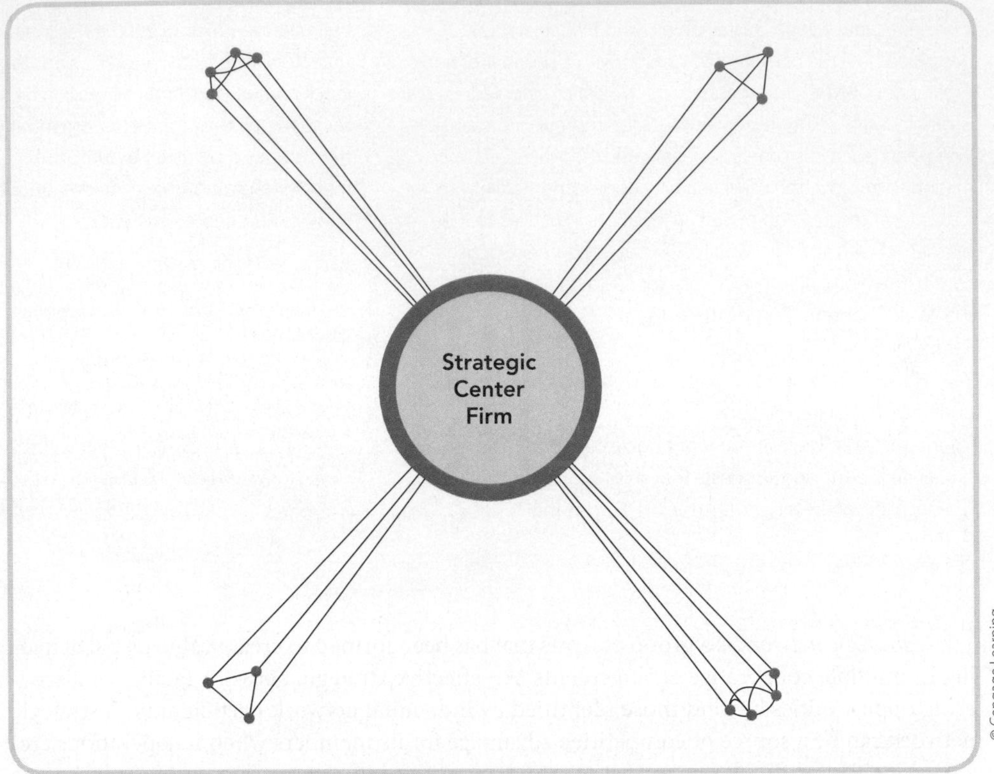


this interconnection, the strategic network is only as strong as its weakest value-chain link. With its centralized decision-making authority and responsibility, the strategic center firm guides participants in efforts to form network-specific competitive advantages. The need for each participant to have capabilities that can be the foundation for the network's competitive advantages encourages friendly rivalry among participants seeking to develop the skills needed to quickly form new capabilities that create value for the network.[118]

Interestingly, strategic networks are being used more frequently, partly because of the ability of a strategic center firm to execute a strategy that effectively and efficiently links partner firms. Improved information systems and communication capabilities (e.g., the Internet) make such networks possible.

## 11-4 Implementing Business-Level Cooperative Strategies

As noted in Chapter 9, the two types of business-level complementary alliances are vertical and horizontal. Firms with competencies in different stages of the value chain form a vertical alliance to cooperatively integrate their different, but complementary, skills. Firms combining their competencies to create value in the same stage of the value chain are using a horizontal alliance. Vertical complementary strategic alliances such as those developed by Toyota Motor Company are formed more frequently than horizontal alliances.[119]

A strategic network of vertical relationships such as the network in Japan between Toyota and its suppliers often involves a number of implementation issues.[120] First, the strategic center firm encourages subcontractors to modernize their facilities and provides them with technical and financial assistance to do so, if necessary. Second, the strategic center firm reduces its transaction costs by promoting longer-term contracts with subcontractors, so that supplier-partners increase their long-term productivity. This approach is diametrically opposed to that of continually negotiating short-term contracts based on unit pricing. Third, the strategic center firm enables engineers in upstream companies (suppliers) to have better communication with those companies with whom it has contracts for services. As a result, suppliers and the strategic center firm become more interdependent and less independent.

The lean production system (a vertical complementary strategic alliance) pioneered by Toyota and others has been diffused throughout many industries.[121] In vertical complementary strategic alliances, such as the one between Toyota and its suppliers, the strategic center firm is obvious, as is the structure that firm establishes. However, the same is not always true with horizontal complementary strategic alliances where firms try to create value in the same part of the value chain. For example, airline alliances are commonly formed to create value in the marketing and sales primary activity segment of the value chain (see Table 3.6). Because air carriers commonly participate in multiple horizontal complementary alliances such as the Star Alliance between Lufthansa, United (and originally Continental before its merger with United), US Airways, Thai, Air Canada, SAS, and others, it is difficult to determine the strategic center firm. Moreover, participating in several alliances can cause firms to question partners' true loyalties and intentions. Also, if rivals band together in too many collaborative activities, one or more governments may suspect the possibility of illegal collusive activities. For these reasons, horizontal complementary alliances are used less often and less successfully than their vertical counterpart, although there are examples of success, for instance, among auto and aircraft manufacturers.

Kai Pfaffenbach/Reuters

*Five jets form a star at Frankfurt Airport to mark the launch of the Star Alliance among Thai Airways, United Airlines, Lufthansa, Air Canada, and Scandinavian Airlines Systems. Horizontal complementary alliances are common in the airline industry.*

## 11-5 Implementing Corporate-Level Cooperative Strategies

Some corporate-level strategies are used to facilitate cost improvement. The Strategic Focus illustrates this through the global alliances between Unilever and Jacobs Engineering Group Inc. to facilitate the efficiency of Unilever's manufacturing sites around the world, while also emphasizing innovation to accomplish Unilever's sustainability objectives. Corporate-level cooperative strategies (such as franchising) are used to facilitate product and market diversification. As a cooperative strategy, franchising allows the firm to use its competencies to extend or diversify its product or market reach, but without completing a merger or acquisition.[122] Research suggests that knowledge embedded in corporate-level cooperative strategies facilitates synergy.[123] For example, McDonald's Corporation pursues a franchising strategy, emphasizing a limited value-priced menu in more than 100 countries. The McDonald's franchising system is a strategic network. McDonald's headquarters serves as the strategic center firm for the network's franchisees. The headquarters office uses strategic and financial controls to verify that the franchisees' operations create the greatest value for the entire network.

An important strategic control issue for McDonald's is the location of its franchisee units. Because it believes that its greatest expansion opportunities are outside the United States, the firm has decided to continue expanding in countries such as China and India, where it often needs to adjust its menu according to the local culture. For example, "McDonald's adapts its restaurants in India to local tastes; in a nation that is predominantly Hindu and reveres the cow, beef isn't on the menu, for instance, replaced by chicken burgers and vegetable patties."[124] As the strategic center firm around the globe for its restaurants, McDonald's is devoting the majority of its capital expenditures to develop units in non–U.S. markets.

## 11-6 Implementing International Cooperative Strategies

Strategic networks formed to implement international cooperative strategies result in firms competing in several countries.[125] Differences among countries' regulatory environments increase the challenge of managing international networks and verifying that, at a minimum, the network's operations comply with all legal requirements.[126]

*Distributed strategic networks* are the organizational structure used to manage international cooperative strategies. As shown in Figure 11.12, several regional strategic center firms are included in the distributed network to manage partner firms' multiple cooperative arrangements.[127] The structure used to implement the international cooperative strategy is complex and demands careful attention to be used successfully. This structure is illustrated in the Strategic Focus by the network of NGOs through which Unilever manages its various sustainability strategies as it seeks to realize its objective of improving the lives of one billion people around the world.

**Figure 11.12** A Distributed Strategic Network

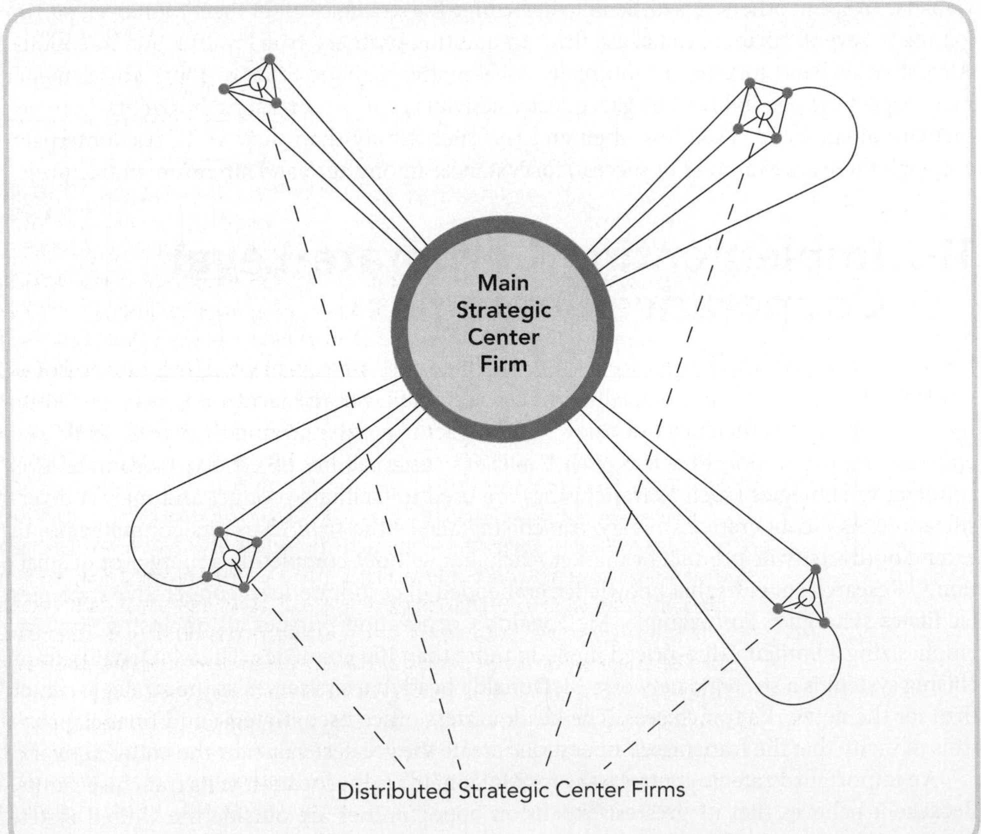

# SUMMARY

- Organizational structure specifies the firm's formal reporting relationships, procedures, controls, and authority and decision-making processes. Essentially, organizational structure details the work to be done in a firm and how that work is to be accomplished. Organizational controls guide the use of strategy, indicate how to compare actual and expected results, and suggest actions to take to improve performance when it falls below expectations. A proper match between strategy and structure can lead to a competitive advantage.
- Strategic controls (largely subjective criteria) and financial controls (largely objective criteria) are the two types of organizational controls used to implement a strategy. Both controls are critical, although their degree of emphasis varies based on individual matches between strategy and structure.
- Strategy and structure influence each other; overall though, strategy has a stronger influence on structure. Research indicates that firms tend to change structure when declining performance forces them to do so. Effective managers anticipate the need for structural change and quickly modify structure to better accommodate the firm's strategy when evidence calls for that action.
- The functional structure is used to implement business-level strategies. The cost leadership strategy requires a centralized functional structure—one in which manufacturing efficiency and process engineering are emphasized. The differentiation strategy's functional structure decentralizes implementation-related decisions, especially those concerned with marketing, to those involved with individual organizational functions. Focus strategies, often used in small firms, require a simple structure until such time that the firm diversifies in terms of products and/or markets.
- Unique combinations of different forms of the multidivisional structure are matched with different corporate-level diversification strategies to properly implement these strategies. The cooperative M-form, used to implement the related constrained corporate-level strategy, has a centralized corporate office and extensive integrating mechanisms. Divisional incentives are linked to overall corporate performance to foster cooperation among divisions. The related linked SBU M-form structure establishes separate profit centers within the diversified firm. Each profit center or SBU may have divisions offering similar products, but the SBUs are often unrelated to each other. The competitive M-form structure, used to implement the unrelated diversification strategy, is highly decentralized, lacks integrating mechanisms, and utilizes objective financial criteria to evaluate each unit's performance.
- The multidomestic strategy, implemented through the worldwide geographic area structure, emphasizes decentralization and locates all functional activities in the host country or geographic area. The worldwide product divisional structure is used to implement the global strategy. This structure is centralized in order to coordinate and integrate different functions' activities so as to gain global economies of scope and economies of scale. Decision-making authority is centralized in the firm's worldwide division headquarters.
- The transnational strategy—a strategy through which the firm seeks the local responsiveness of the multidomestic strategy and the global efficiency of the global strategy—is implemented through the combination structure. Because it must be simultaneously centralized and decentralized, integrated and nonintegrated, and formalized and nonformalized, the combination structure is difficult to organize and successfully manage. However, two structural designs are suggested: the matrix and the hybrid structure with both geographic and product-oriented divisions.
- Increasingly important to competitive success, cooperative strategies are implemented through organizational structures framed around strategic networks. Strategic center firms play a critical role in managing strategic networks. Business-level strategies are often employed in vertical and horizontal alliance networks. Corporate-level cooperative strategies are used to pursue product and market diversification. Franchising is one type of corporate strategy that uses a strategic network to implement this strategy. This is also true for international cooperative strategies, where distributed networks are often used.

# REVIEW QUESTIONS

1. What is organizational structure and what are organizational controls? What are the differences between strategic controls and financial controls? What is the importance of these differences?
2. What does it mean to say that strategy and structure have a reciprocal relationship?
3. What are the characteristics of the functional structures used to implement the cost leadership, differentiation, integrated cost leadership/differentiation, and focused business-level strategies?

4. What are the differences among the three versions of the multidivisional (M-form) organizational structures that are used to implement the related constrained, the related linked, and the unrelated corporate-level diversification strategies?

5. What organizational structures are used to implement the multidomestic, global, and transnational international strategies?

6. What is a strategic network? What is a strategic center firm? How is a strategic center used in business-level, corporate-level, and international cooperative strategies?

# EXPERIENTIAL EXERCISES

## EXERCISE 1: STRATEGY AND STRUCTURE RESPONSES TO "SHOWROOMING"

As highlighted in the opening case of this chapter, showrooming is the practice of shoppers examining merchandise in a traditional bricks and mortar store, then searching and buying online--often at a reduced price. A store in Australia went so far last year as to charge its customers $5 just to get inside the premises in an effort to forestall the practice. Further, a 2013 study by Anderson Robbins Research found that 67% of shoppers utilize their smartphones to see if there is a better price to be had elsewhere. Their work also found that a solid majority (62%) would leave the store and buy elsewhere for a 20% differential; 13 percent would buy elsewhere for any price differential. Companies can expect those numbers to climb unless steps are taken to mitigate the impact.

So what can organizations do to thwart the threat of this practice? Thanks to free shipping and easy returns (and, until recently, no taxes) the practice has flourished. It has been argued that Best Buy (some have dubbed them the Amazon showroom) and Walmart are the two stores most targeted by showrooming. However, the concept is not just aimed at large big box retailers as small businesses are at risk as well. So what is a company to do? The ability to select an appropriate strategy and match it with the appropriate structure is an important characteristic of effective strategic leadership,[128] according to your text. Your challenge in this assignment is to research the strategy and structure efforts underway at a firm level of analysis. Be prepared to identify in class how your firm is impacted negatively (do not pick a company favorably affected by showrooming for this assignment [i.e., Amazon]). In particular the assignment requires you to:

1. Identify a firm that you suspect is a target of showrooming. Get the instructor's approval ahead of time to avoid duplicates. You may identify a top retailer or other firm you think influential in this arena. You do not have to pick a large publicly held corporation; a small business you are familiar with that is impacted is a good choice as well.
2. Showrooming has really become influential in the last few years. Describe how your firm has changed during this time in terms of structure and strategy.
3. Summarize how these efforts are, or are not, paying off.

Complete this assignment using your teams.

## EXERCISE 2: IS STRUCTURE CONTAGIOUS?

Form two teams to analyze and recommend changes (if any) regarding pairs of competitors. Are these competitors, such as Walgreens and CVS, structured similarly or differently? How do their strategies and organization structures compare?

### PART ONE

Select a pair of competitors. You have wide latitude in this choice, such as large publicly held companies (i.e., Walgreens/CVS; Whole Foods/Kroger; American Airlines/Delta Airlines; Loews/Home Depot). Another option is to select two competitors that operate in your town that may be small to medium-sized firms. The important thing is that the firms should be competitors and roughly comparable in size.

### PART TWO

Research the firms and be prepared to address the following issues:

- Describe the strategies of the two firms—differences and similarities.
- Present the two firms' organizational structures and note differences and similarities.
- Does structure follow strategy as Chandler argues?
- Are the boards of directors structured similarly between the pair with regard to committees, meetings, and titles?
- Which one of these companies would you most likely desire to work for, all else being equal?

Be prepared to discuss your findings in a PowerPoint presentation to the class.

# VIDEO CASE

## A MATCH FOR ORGANIZATIONAL STRUCTURE AND CONTROL—GM BANKRUPTCY

Emerging from bankruptcy, GM's commitment to smaller, more fuel-efficient cars has resulted in a move from a GM corporation to a smaller GM company. Selling off and phasing out brands along with changing logos are steps toward a new GM. With the Obama administration's desire for a complete overhaul of GM's structure, the U.S. Treasury became the company's biggest stockholder while American taxpayers had greater than 60 percent ownership in the new company. New management teams representing stability and design appear to set the stage for a match point. On November 18, 2010, GM completed its initial public offering, emerging with a solid financial foundation that has enabled the company to produce great vehicles and build a bright future for employees, partners, and shareholders. A seasoned leadership team is committed to delivering vehicles with compelling designs, flawless quality and reliability, and leading safety, fuel economy and infotainment features.

Be prepared to discuss the following concepts and questions in class:

### Concepts

1. Organizational structure
2. Organizational controls
3. Strategic controls
4. Strategy and structure relationships

### Questions

1. Is GM's organizational structure aligned with its strategies? If so, why? If not, what is needed?
2. What organizational controls do you think were lacking in the old GM? What organizational controls are needed in the new GM?
3. What specific strategic controls do you believe are key to GM's future success? Should GM's value chain change?
4. Recognizing GM's current state, how do you see the new GM strategy and structure relationship? How do you see it evolving?

# NOTES

1. T. Felin, N. J. Foss, K. H. Heimeriks, & T. L. Madsen, 2012, Microfoundations of routines and capabilities: Individuals, processes, and structure, *Journal of Management Studies*, 49(8): 1351–1374; K. M. Eisenhardt, N. R. Furr, & C. B. Bingham, 2010, Microfoundations of performance: Balancing efficiency and flexibility in dynamic environments, *Organization Science*, 21: 1263–1273; P. Jarzabkowski, 2008, Shaping strategy as a structuration process, *Academy of Management Journal*, 51(4): 621–650.
2. R. Wilden, S. P. Gudergan, B. Nielsen, & I. Lings, 2013, Dynamic capabilities and performance: Strategy, structure and environment, *Long Range Planning*, 46(1/2): 72-96; R. Gulati & P. Puranam, 2009, Renewal through reorganization: The value of inconsistencies between formal and informal organization, *Organization Science*, 20(2): 422–440; R. E. Miles & C. C. Snow, 1978, *Organizational Strategy, Structure and Process*, New York: McGraw-Hill.
3. Y. Y. Kor & A. Mesko, 2013, Dynamic managerial capabilities: Configuration and orchestration of top executives' capabilities and the firm's dominant logic, *Strategic Management Journal*, 34(2): 233–244; S. T. Hannah & P. B. Lester, 2009, A multilevel approach to building and leading learning organizations, *Leadership Quarterly*, 20(1): 34–48; E. M. Olson, S. F. Slater, & G. T. M. Hult, 2007, The importance of structure and process to strategy implementation, *Business Horizons*, 48(1): 47–54; D. N. Sull & C. Spinosa, 2007, Promise-based management, *Harvard Business Review*, 85(4): 79–86.
4. J. P. Mangalindan, 2013, eBay is back!, *Fortune*, February 25, 58.
5. R. Rumelt, 2011, *Good Strategy/Bad Strategy: The Difference and Why It Matters*, New York: Crown Publishing Company.
6. P. Boumgarden, J. Nickerson, & T. R. Zenger, 2012, Sailing into the wind: Exploring the relationships among ambidexterity, vacillation, and organizational performance, *Strategic Management Journal*, 33(6): 587–610; R. D. Ireland, J. Covin, & D. Kuratko, 2009, Conceptualizing corporate entrepreneurship strategy, *Entrepreneurship Theory and Practice*, 33(1): 19–46; T. Amburgey & T. Dacin, 1994, As the left foot follows the right? The dynamics of strategic and structural change, *Academy of Management Journal*, 37: 1427–1452.
7. C. Gilbert, M. Eyring, & R. N. Foster, 2012, Two routes to resilience, *Harvard Business Review*, 90(12): 65–73; L. F. Monteiro, N. Arvidsson, & J. Birkinshaw, 2008, Knowledge flows within multinational corporations: Explaining subsidiary isolation and its performance implications, *Organization Science*, 19(1): 90–107; B. Keats & H. O'Neill, 2001, Organizational structure: Looking through a strategy lens, in M. A. Hitt, R. E. Freeman, & J. S. Harrison (eds.), *Handbook of Strategic Management*, Oxford, UK: Blackwell Publishers, 520–542.
8. R. E. Hoskisson, C. W. L. Hill, & H. Kim, 1993, The multidivisional structure: Organizational fossil or source of value? *Journal of Management*, 19: 269–298.
9. B. Grøgaard, 2012, Alignment of strategy and structure in international firms: An empirical examination, *International Business Review*, 21(3): 397–407; E. M. Olson, S. F. Slater, & G. T. M. Hult, 2005, The performance implications of fit among business strategy, marketing organization structure, and strategic behavior, *Journal of Marketing*, 69(3): 49–65.
10. F. A. Csaszar, 2012, Organizational structure as a determinant of performance: Evidence from mutual funds, *Strategic Management Journal*, 33(6): 611–632; T. Burns & G. M. Stalker, 1961, *The Management of Innovation*, London: Tavistok; P. R. Lawrence & J. W. Lorsch, 1967, *Organization and Environment*, Homewood, IL: Richard D. Irwin; J. Woodward, 1965, *Industrial Organization: Theory and Practice*, London: Oxford University Press.

11. A. Verbeke & L. Kano, 2012, An internalization theory rationale for MNE regional strategy, *Multinational Business Review*, 20(2): 135–152; A. M. Rugman & A. Verbeke, 2008, A regional solution to the strategy and structure of multinationals, *European Management Journal*, 26(5): 305–313; H. Kim, R. E. Hoskisson, L. Tihanyi, & J. Hong, 2004, Evolution and restructuring of diversified business groups in emerging markets: The lessons from chaebols in Korea, *Asia Pacific Journal of Management*, 21: 25–48.
12. M. Reilly, P. Scott, & V. Mangematin, 2012, Alignment or independence? Multinational subsidiaries and parent relations, *Journal of Business Strategy*, 33(2): 4–11; R. Kathuria, M. P. Joshi, & S. J. Porth, 2007, Organizational alignment and performance: Past, present and future, *Management Decision*, 45: 503–517.
13. K. Linebaugh, 2013, GE Capital chief expected to leave, *Wall Street Journal*, May 30, B1.
14. J. Qiu, L. Donaldson, & B. Luo, 2012, The benefits of persisting with paradigms in organizational research, *Academy of Management Perspectives*, 26(1): 93–104; R. Greenwood & D. Miller, 2010, Tackling design anew: Getting back to the heart of organization theory, *Academy of Management Perspectives*, 24(4): 78–88.
15. C. Cella, A. Ellul, & M. Giannetti, 2013, Investors' horizons and the amplification of market shocks, *Review of Financial Studies*, 26(7): 1607–1648; T. Yu, M. Sengul, & R. H. Lester, 2008, Misery loves company: The spread of negative impacts resulting from an organizational crisis, *Academy of Management Review*, 33(2): 452–472; R. L. Priem, L. G. Love, & M. A. Shaffer, 2002, Executives' perceptions of uncertainty sources: A numerical taxonomy and underlying dimensions, *Journal of Management*, 28: 725–746.
16. E. Claver-Cortés, E. M. Pertusa-Ortega, & J. F. Molina-Azorín, 2012, Characteristics of organizational structure relating to hybrid competitive strategy: Implications for performance, *Journal of Business Research*, 65(7): 993–1002; J. R. Maxwell, 2008, Work system design to improve the economic performance of the firm, *Business Process Management Journal*, 14(3): 432–446; Olson, Slater, & Hult, The importance of structure and process to strategy implementation.
17. B. Gong & R. A. Greenwood, 2012, Organizational memory, downsizing, and information technology: A theoretical inquiry, *International Journal of Management*, 29: 99–109; P. Legerer, T. Pfeiffer, G. Schneider, & J. Wagner, 2009, Organizational structure and managerial decisions, *International Journal of the Economics of Business*, 16(2): 147–159.
18. 2013, General Electric: The long game, *Financial Times*, www.ft.com, April 8; H. Gebauer & F. Putz, 2009, Organisational structures for the service business in product-oriented companies, *International Journal of Services Technology and Management*, 11(1): 64–81.
19. R. Kapoor & J. Lee, 2013, Coordinating and competing in ecosystems: How organizational forms shape new technology investments, *Strategic Management Journal*, 34(3): 274–296; R. D. Ireland & J. W. Webb, 2007, Strategic entrepreneurship: Creating competitive advantage through streams of innovation, *Business Horizons*, 50: 49–59; T. J. Andersen, 2004, Integrating decentralized strategy making and strategic planning processes in dynamic environments, *Journal of Management Studies*, 41: 1271–1299.
20. M. S. Feldman & W. J. Orlikowski, 2011, Theorizing practice and practicing theory, *Organization Science*, 22(5): 1240–1253; J. Rivkin & N. Siggelkow, 2003, Balancing search and stability: Interdependencies among elements of organizational design, *Management Science*, 49: 290–311; G. A. Bigley & K. H. Roberts, 2001, The incident command system: High-reliability organizing for complex and volatile task environments, *Academy of Management Journal*, 44: 1281–1299.
21. A. J. Bock, T. Opsahl, G. George, & D. M. Gann, 2012, The effects of culture and structure on strategic flexibility during business model innovation, *Journal of Management Studies*, 49(2): 279–305; S. Nadkarni & V. K. Narayanan, 2007, Strategic schemas, strategic flexibility, and firm performance: The moderating role of industry clockspeed, *Strategic Management Journal*, 28: 243–270; K. D. Miller & A. T. Arikan, 2004, Technology search investments: Evolutionary, option reasoning, and option pricing approaches, *Strategic Management Journal*, 25: 473–485.
22. S. A. Fernhaber & P. C. Patel, 2012, How do young firms manage product portfolio complexity? The role of absorptive capacity and ambidexterity, *Strategic Management Journal*, 33(13): 1516–1539; S. Raisch & J. Birkinshaw, 2008, Organizational ambidexterity: Antecedents, outcomes, and moderators, *Journal of Management*, 34: 375–409.
23. C. Camisón & A. Villar-López, 2012, On how firms located in an industrial district profit from knowledge spillovers: Adoption of an organic structure and innovation capabilities, *British Journal of Management*, 23(3): 361–382; R. Agarwal, D. Audretsch, & M. B. Sarkar, 2010, Knowledge spillovers and strategic entrepreneurship, *Strategic Entrepreneurship Journal*, 4: 271–283.
24. Rumelt, *Good Strategy/Bad Strategy*; B. W. Keats & M. A. Hitt, 1988, A causal model of linkages among environmental dimensions, macroorganizational characteristics, and performance, *Academy of Management Journal*, 31: 570–598.
25. A. Chandler, 1962, *Strategy and Structure*, Cambridge, MA: MIT Press.
26. D. Martin, 2007, Alfred D. Chandler, Jr., a business historian, dies at 88, *New York Times*, www.nytimes.com, May 12.
27. B. T. Pentland, M. S. Feldman, M. C. Becker, & P. Liu, 2012, Dynamics of organizational routines: A generative model, *Journal of Management Studies*, 49(8): 1484–1508; R. E. Hoskisson, R. A. Johnson, L. Tihanyi, & R. E. White, 2005, Diversified business groups and corporate refocusing in emerging economies, *Journal of Management*, 31: 941–965; J. D. Day, E. Lawson, & K. Leslie, 2003, When reorganization works, *The McKinsey Quarterly*, (2): 20–29.
28. B. Simon, 2009, Restructuring chief sees benefits in GM's maligned culture, *Financial Times*, July 4, 16.
29. D. Moin & E. Clark, 2013, Ullman returns as Johnson exits, *WWD: Women's Wear Daily*, April 9, 1.
30. S. Sonenshein, 2013, How organizations foster the creative use of resources, *Academy of Management Journal*, in press; S. K. Ethiraj, 2007, Allocation of inventive effort in complex product systems, *Strategic Management Journal*, 28: 563–584.
31. L. Marengo & C. Pasquali, 2012, How to get what you want when you do not know what you want: A model of incentives, organizational structure, and learning, *Organization Science*, 23(5): 1298–1310; A. M. Kleinbaum & M. L. Tushman, 2008, Managing corporate social networks, *Harvard Business Review*, 86(7/8): 26–27; P. K. Mills & G. R. Ungson, 2003, Reassessing the limits of structural empowerment: Organizational constitution and trust as controls, *Academy of Management Review*, 28: 143–153.
32. D. W. Lehman & J. Hahn, 2013, Momentum and organizational risk taking: Evidence from the National Football League, *Management Science*, 59(4): 852–868; M. A. Hitt, K. T. Haynes, & R. Serpa, 2010, Strategic leadership for the 21st century, *Business Horizons*, 53: 437–444; M. A. Desai, 2008, The finance function in a global corporation, *Harvard Business Review*, 86(7/8): 108–112.
33. R. MacKay & R. Chia, 2013, Choice, chance, and unintended consequences in strategic change: A process understanding of the rise and fall of Northco Automotive, *Academy of Management Journal*, 56(1): 208–230; I. Filatotchev, J. Stephan, & B. Jindra, 2008, Ownership structure, strategic controls and export intensity of foreign-invested firms in transition economies, *Journal of International Business Studies*, 39(7): 1133–1148; G. J. M. Braam & E. J. Nijssen, 2004, Performance effects of using the balanced scorecard: A note on the Dutch experience, *Long Range Planning*, 37: 335–349.
34. D. M. Cable, F. Gino, & B. R. Staats, 2013, Breaking them in or eliciting their best? Reframing socialization around newcomers' authentic self-expression, *Administrative*

*Science Quarterly*, 58(1): 1–36; J. Kratzer, H. G. Gemünden, & C. Lettl, 2008, Balancing creativity and time efficiency in multi-team R&D projects: The alignment of formal and informal networks, *R&D Management*, 38(5): 538–549; D. F. Kuratko, R. D. Ireland, & J. S. Hornsby, 2004, Corporate entrepreneurship behavior among managers: A review of theory, research, and practice, in J. A. Katz & D. A. Shepherd (eds.), *Advances in Entrepreneurship: Firm Emergence and Growth: Corporate Entrepreneurship*, Oxford, UK: Elsevier Publishing, 7–45.

35. M. Lev-Ram, 2013, Samsung's road to mobile domination, *Fortune*, February 04, 98–102; P. Burrows, 2011, Elop's fable, *Bloomberg Businessweek*, June 6, 56–61; Y. Doz & M. Kosonen, 2008, The dynamics of strategic agility: Nokia's rollercoaster experience, *California Management Review*, 50(3): 95–118.

36. K. Favaro, 2013, We're from corporate and we are here to help: Understanding the real value of corporate strategy and the head office, *Strategy+Business Online*, www.strategy+business.com, April 8; K. L. Turner & M. V. Makhija, 2006, The role of organizational controls in managing knowledge, *Academy of Management Review*, 31: 197–217; M. A. Hitt, R. E. Hoskisson, R. A. Johnson, & D. D. Moesel, 1996, The market for corporate control and firm innovation, *Academy of Management Journal*, 39: 1084–1119.

37. W. P. Wan, R. E. Hoskisson, J. C. Short, & D. W. Yiu, 2011, Resource-based theory and corporate diversification: Accomplishments and opportunities, *Journal of Management*, 37(5): 1335–1368; M. A. Hitt, L. Tihanyi, T. Miller, & B. Connelly, 2006, International diversification: Antecedents, outcomes, and moderators, *Journal of Management*, 32: 831–867; R. E. Hoskisson & M. A. Hitt, 1988, Strategic control and relative R&D investment in multiproduct firms, *Strategic Management Journal*, 9: 605–621.

38. I. Clark, 2013, Templates for financial control? Management and employees under the private equity business model, *Human Resource Management Journal*, 23(2): 144–159; S. Lee, K. Park, & H.-H. Shin, 2009, Disappearing internal capital markets: Evidence from diversified business groups in Korea, *Journal of Banking & Finance*, 33(2): 326–334; D. Collis, D. Young, & M. Goold, 2007, The size, structure, and performance of corporate headquarters, *Strategic Management Journal*, 28: 383–405.

39. S. S. Alsoboa & J. Aldehayyat, 2013, The impact of competitive business strategies on managerial accounting techniques: A study of Jordanian public industrial companies, *International Journal of Management*, 31(1): 545–555; X. S. Y. Spencer, T. A. Joiner, & S. Salmon, 2009, Differentiation strategy, performance measurement systems and organizational performance: Evidence from Australia, *International Journal of Business*, 14(1): 83–103; K. Chaharbaghi, 2007, The problematic of strategy: A way of seeing is also a way of not seeing, *Management Decision*, 45: 327–339.

40. S. K. Kim, J. D. Arthurs, A. Sahaym, & J. B. Cullen, 2013, Search behavior of the diversified firm: The impact of fit on innovation, *Strategic Management Journal*, 34(8): 999-1009.

41. S. Lohr, 2007, Can Michael Dell refocus his namesake? *New York Times*, www.nytimes.com, September 9.

42. S. Ovide, 2013, Dell: Icahn, Southeastern are $4 billion short, *Wall Street Journal*, www.wsj.com, June 3.

43. R. G. Eccles & G. Serafeim, 2013, The performance frontier, *Harvard Business Review*, 91(5): 50–60; Gebauer & Putz, Organisational structures for the service business in product-oriented companies; X. Yin & E. J. Zajac, 2004, The strategy/governance structure fit relationship: Theory and evidence in franchising arrangements, *Strategic Management Journal*, 25: 365–383.

44. Keats & O'Neill, Organizational structure, 531.

45. M. K. Bednar, S. Boivie, & N. R. Prince, 2013, Burr under the saddle: How media coverage influences strategic change, *Organization Science*, 24(3): 910–925; K. M. Green, J. G. Covin, & D. P. Slevin, 2008, Exploring the relationship between strategic reactiveness and entrepreneurial orientation: The role of structure-style fit, *Journal of Business Venturing*, 23(3): 356–383; Olson, Slater, & Hult, The importance of structure and process to strategy implementation; D. Miller & J. O. Whitney, 1999, Beyond strategy: Configuration as a pillar of competitive advantage, *Business Horizons*, 42(3): 5–17.

46. D. C. Mowery, 2010, Alfred Chandler and knowledge management within the firm, *Industrial & Corporate Change*, 19(2): 483–507; Chandler, *Strategy and Structure*.

47. Keats & O'Neill, Organizational structure, 524.

48. Wan, Hoskisson, Short & Yiu, 2011, Resource-based theory and corporate diversification: Accomplishments and opportunities; E. Rawley, 2010, Diversification, coordination costs and organizational rigidity: Evidence from microdata, *Strategic Management Journal*, 31: 873–891.

49. A. Campbell & H. Strikwerda, 2013, The power of one: Towards the new integrated organization, *Journal of Business Strategy*, 34(2): 4–12.

50. J. J. Strikwerda & J. W. Stoelhorst, 2009, The emergence and evolution of the multidimensional organization, *California Management Review*, 51(4): 11–31; I. Daizadeh, 2006, Using intellectual property to map the organisational evolution of firms: Tracing a biotechnology company from startup to bureaucracy to a multidivisional firm, *Journal of Commercial Biotechnology*, 13: 28–36.

51. C. Levicki, 1999, *The Interactive Strategy Workout*, 2nd ed., London: Prentice Hall.

52. P. L. Drnevich & D. C. Croson, 2013, Information technology and business-level strategy: Toward an integrated theoretical perspective, *MIS Quarterly*, 37(2): 483–509; E. E. Entin, F. J. Diedrich, & B. Rubineau, 2003, Adaptive communication patterns in different organizational structures, *Human Factors and Ergonomics Society Annual Meeting Proceedings*, 405–409; H. M. O'Neill, R. W. Pouder, & A. K. Buchholtz, 1998, Patterns in the diffusion of strategies across organizations: Insights from the innovation diffusion literature, *Academy of Management Review*, 23: 98–114.

53. 2013, Organizational structure, *Wikipedia*, en.wikipedia.org; Spencer, Joiner, & Salmon, Differentiation strategy, performance measurement systems and organizational performance.

54. P. Leinwand & C. Mainardi, 2013, Beyond functions, *Strategy+Business*, www.strategy-business.com, Spring, 1-5; Keats & O'Neill, Organizational structure, 539.

55. J. Cable, 2012, For innovation to flourish, "Bureaucracy must die", *Industry Week/IW*, 261(6): 54; C. M. Christensen, S. P. Kaufman, & W. C. Shih, 2008, Innovation killers, *Harvard Business Review*: Special HBS Centennial Issue, 86(1): 98–105; J. Welch & S. Welch, 2006, Growing up but staying young, *BusinessWeek*, December 11, 112.

56. O. E. Williamson, 1975, *Markets and Hierarchies: Analysis and Anti Trust Implications*, New York: The Free Press.

57. T. Hutzschenreuter & J. Horstkotte, 2013, Performance effects of top management team demographic faultlines in the process of product diversification, *Strategic Management Journal*, 34: 704–726; S. H. Mialon, 2008, Efficient horizontal mergers: The effects of internal capital reallocation and organizational form, *International Journal of Industrial Organization*, 26(4): 861–877; Chandler, *Strategy and Structure*.

58. J. Joseph & W. Ocasio, 2012, Architecture, attention, and adaptation in the multibusiness firm: General Electric from 1951 to 2001, *Strategic Management Journal*, 33(6): 633–660; R. Inderst, H. M. Müller, & K. Wärneryd, 2007, Distributional conflict in organizations, *European Economic Review*, 51: 385–402; J. Greco, 1999, Alfred P. Sloan, Jr. (1875–1966): The original "organization" man, *Journal of Business Strategy*, 20(5): 30–31.

59. Hoskisson, Hill, & Kim, The multidivisional structure, 269–298.

60. V. Binda, 2012, Strategy and structure in large Italian and Spanish firms, 1950–2002, *Business History Review*, 86(3): 503–525; W. G. Rowe & P. M. Wright, 1997, Related and unrelated diversification and their effect on human resource management controls, *Strategic Management Journal*, 18: 329–338.

61. C. E. Helfat & K. M. Eisenhardt, 2004, Inter-temporal economies of scope,

organizational modularity, and the dynamics of diversification, *Strategic Management Journal*, 25: 1217–1232; A. D. Chandler, 1994, The functions of the HQ unit in the multibusiness firm, in R. P. Rumelt, D. E. Schendel, & D. J. Teece (eds.), *Fundamental Issues in Strategy*, Cambridge, MA: Harvard Business School Press, 327.

62. O. E. Williamson, 1994, Strategizing, economizing, and economic organization, in R. P. Rumelt, D. E. Schendel, & D. J. Teece (eds.), *Fundamental Issues in Strategy*, Cambridge, MA: Harvard Business School Press, 361–401.
63. Hoskisson, Hill, & Kim, The multidivisional structure: Organizational fossil or source of value?
64. R. Duchin & D. Sosyura, 2013, Divisional managers and internal capital markets, *Journal of Finance*, 68(2): 387–429; O. E. Williamson, 1985, *The Economic Institutions of Capitalism: Firms, Markets, and Relational Contracting*, New York: Macmillan.
65. Keats & O'Neill, Organizational structure, 532.
66. M. F. Wolff, 1999, In the organization of the future, competitive advantage will lie with inspired employees, *Research Technology Management*, 42(4): 2–4.
67. E. Schulz, S. Chowdhury, & D. Van de Voort, 2013, Firm productivity moderated link between human capital and compensation: The significance of task-specific human capital, *Human Resource Management*, 52(3): 423–439; R. H. Hall, 1996, *Organizations: Structures, Processes, and Outcomes*, 6th ed., Englewood Cliffs, NJ: Prentice Hall, 13; S. Baiman, D. F. Larcker, & M. V. Rajan, 1995, Organizational design for business units, *Journal of Accounting Research*, 33: 205–229.
68. L. G. Love, R. L. Priem, & G. T. Lumpkin, 2002, Explicitly articulated strategy and firm performance under alternative levels of centralization, *Journal of Management*, 28: 611–627.
69. T. F. Gonzalez-Cruz, A. Huguet-Roig, & S. Cruz-Ros, 2012, Organizational technology as a mediating variable in centralization-formalization fit, *Management Decision*, 50(9): 1527–1548; Hall, *Organizations*, 64–75.
70. D. G. Sirmon, M. A. Hitt, R. D. Ireland, & B. A. Gilbert, 2011, Resource orchestration to create competitive advantage: Breadth, depth and life cycle effects, *Journal of Management*, 37(5): 1390–1412.
71. J. B. Barney, 2001, *Gaining and Sustaining Competitive Advantage*, 2nd ed., Upper Saddle River, NJ: Prentice Hall, 257.
72. H. Karandikar & S. Nidamarthi, 2007, Implementing a platform strategy for a systems business via standardization, *Journal of Manufacturing Technology Management*, 18: 267–280.
73. V. K. Garg, R. L. Priem, & A. A. Rasheed, 2013, A theoretical explanation of the cost advantages of multi-unit franchising, *Journal of Marketing Channels*, 20(1/2): 52–72; H. Wang & C. Kimble, 2010, Low-cost strategy through product architecture: Lessons from China, *Journal of Business Strategy*, 31(3): 12–20.
74. Olson, Slater, & Hult, The performance implications of fit.
75. M. Troy, 2012, Supplier expectations offer insight at Walmart, *Drug Store News*, November 19, 20–22; 2007, Wal-Mart Stores, Inc., *New York Times*, www.nytimes.com, July 21.
76. 2013, Our story, Walmart Corporate, www.walmartstores.com, June 14.
77. N. Takagoshi & N. Matsubayashi, 2013, Customization competition between branded firms: Continuous extension of product line from core product, *European Journal of Operational Research*, 225(2): 337–352; Sirmon, Hitt, Ireland, & Gilbert, Resource orchestration to create competitive advantage; Olson, Slater, & Hult, The performance implications of fit.
78. Bock, Opsahl, George, & Gann, The effects of culture and structure on strategic flexibility during business model innovation; K. Z. Zhou & F. Wu, 2010, Technological capability, strategic flexibility and product innovation, *Strategic Management Journal*, 31: 547–561.
79. 2013, Mission of Under Armour, www.underarmour.com, June 14; T. Heath, 2008, In pursuit of innovation at Under Armour: Founder Kevin Plank says Super Bowl commercial has generated "buzz," *Washington Post*, February 25, D03.
80. Claver-Cortés, Pertusa-Ortega, & Molina-Azorín, Characteristics of organizational structure relating to hybrid competitive strategy.
81. Chandler, *Strategy and Structure*.
82. L. Capron, 2013, Cisco's corporate development portfolio: A blend of building, borrowing and buying, *Strategy & Leadership*, 41(2): 27–30; R. M. Kanter, 2011, Cisco and a cautionary tale about teams, *Harvard Business Review*, blogs.hbr.org, May 9.
83. Y. M. Zhou, 2011, Synergy, coordination costs, and diversification choices, *Strategic Management Journal*, 32: 624–639; C. C. Markides & P. J. Williamson, 1996, Corporate diversification and organizational structure: A resource-based view, *Academy of Management Journal*, 39: 340–367; C. W. L. Hill, M. A. Hitt, & R. E. Hoskisson, 1992, Cooperative versus competitive structures in related and unrelated diversified firms, *Organization Science*, 3: 501–521.
84. Sirmon, Hitt, Ireland, & Gilbert, Resource orchestration to create competitive advantage; M. Makri, M. A. Hitt, & P. J. Lane, 2010, Complementary technologies, knowledge relatedness and invention outcomes in high technology mergers and acquisitions, *Strategic Management Journal*, 31: 602–628.
85. J. Wolf & W. G. Egelhoff, 2013, An empirical evaluation of conflict in MNC matrix structure firms, *International Business Review*, 22(3): 591–601; S. H. Appelbaum, D. Nadeau, & M. Cyr, 2008, Performance evaluation in a matrix organization: A case study (part two), *Industrial and Commercial Training*, 40(6): 295–299.
86. S. H. Appelbaum, D. Nadeau, & M. Cyr, 2009, Performance evaluation in a matrix organization: A case study (part three), *Industrial and Commercial Training*, 41(1): 9–14; M. Goold & A. Campbell, 2003, Structured networks: Towards the well-designed matrix, *Long Range Planning*, 36(5): 427–439.
87. O. Alexy, G. George, & A. J. Salter, 2013, Cui bono? The selective revealing of knowledge and its implications for innovative activity, *Academy of Management Review*, 38(2): 270–291; Rawley, Diversification, coordination costs, and organizational rigidity.
88. J. Huang & H. Kim, 2013, Conceptualizing structural ambidexterity into the innovation of human resource management architecture: The case of LG Electronics, *International Journal of Human Resource Management*, 24(5): 922–943; C. Fang, J. Lee, & M. A. Schilling, 2010, Balancing exploration and exploitation through structural design: The isolation of subgroups and organizational learning, *Organization Science*, 21: 625–642.
89. M. Kruehler, U. Pidun, & H. Rubner, 2012, How to assess the corporate parenting strategy? A conceptual answer, *Journal of Business Strategy*, 33(4): 4–17; M. M. Schmid & I. Walter, 2009, Do financial conglomerates create or destroy economic value? *Journal of Financial Intermediation*, 18(2): 193–216; P. A. Argenti, R. A. Howell, & K. A. Beck, 2005, The strategic communication imperative, *MIT Sloan Management Review*, 46(3): 84–89.
90. N. T. Dorata, 2012, Determinants of the strengths and weaknesses of acquiring firms in mergers and acquisitions: A stakeholder perspective, *International Journal of Management*, 29(2): 578–590; M. F. Wiersema & H. P. Bowen, 2008, Corporate diversification: The impact of foreign competition, industry globalization, and product diversification, *Strategic Management Journal*, 29: 115–132; R. E. Hoskisson & M. A. Hitt, 1990, Antecedents and performance outcomes of diversification: A review and critique of theoretical perspectives, *Journal of Management*, 16: 461–509.
91. A. Varmaz, A. Varwig, & T. Poddig, 2013, Centralized resource planning and yardstick competition, *Omega*, 41(1): 112–118; Hill, Hitt, & Hoskisson, Cooperative versus competitive structures, 512.
92. D. Holod, 2012, Agency and internal capital market inefficiency: Evidence from banking organizations, *Financial Management*, 41(1): 35–53; Lee, Park, & Shin, Disappearing internal capital markets: Evidence from diversified business groups in Korea; J. Birkinshaw, 2001, Strategies for

managing internal competition, *California Management Review*, 44(1): 21–38.

93. 2013, Our company, www.textron.com, June 14; Textron 2012 Annual Report.

94. R. M. Holmes, Jr., T. Miller, M. A. Hitt, & M. P. Salmador, 2013, The interrelationships among informal institutions, formal institutions and inward foreign direct investment, *Journal of Management*, in press; T. Yu & A. A. Cannella, Jr., 2007, Rivalry between multinational enterprises: An event history approach, *Academy of Management Journal*, 50: 665–686; S. E. Christophe & H. Lee, 2005, What matters about internationalization: A market-based assessment, *Journal of Business Research*, 58: 636–643.

95. A. H. Kirca, G. T. M. Hult, S. Deligonul, M. Z. Perryy, & S. T. Cavusgil, 2012, A multilevel examination of the drivers of firm multinationality: A meta-analysis, *Journal of Management*, 38: 502–530.

96. J.-L. Arregle, T. Miller, M. A. Hitt, & P. W. Beamish, 2013, Do regions matter? An integrated institutional and semiglobalization perspective on the internationalization of MNEs, *Strategic Management Journal*, 34(8): 910-934; T. M. Begley & D. P. Boyd, 2003, The need for a corporate global mind-set, *MIT Sloan Management Review*, 44(2): 25–32.

97. P. Almodóvar, 2012, The international performance of standardizing and customizing Spanish firms: The M curve relationships, *Multinational Business Review*, 20(4): 306–330; G. R. G. Benito, R. Lunnan, & S. Tomassen, 2011, Distant encounters of the third kind: Multinational companies locating divisional headquarters abroad, *Journal of Management Studies*, 48: 373–394; T. Kostova & K. Roth, 2003, Social capital in multinational corporations and a micro-macro model of its formation, *Academy of Management Review*, 28: 297–317.

98. R. Foroohar, 2012, The economy's new rules: Go glocal, *Time*, August 20, 26–32.

99. P. Punyatoya, 2013, Consumer evaluation of brand extension for global and local brands: The moderating role of product similarity, *Journal of International Consumer Marketing*, 25(3): 198–215; A. I. Mockaitis, L. Salciuviene, & P. N. Ghauri, 2013, On what do consumer product preferences depend? Determining domestic versus foreign product preferences in an emerging economy market, *Journal of International Consumer Marketing*, 25(3): 166–180.

100. J. H. Johnson, Jr., B. Arya, & D. A. Mirchandani, 2013, Global integration strategies of small and medium multinationals: Evidence from Taiwan, *Journal of World Business*, 48(1): 47–57; C. A. Bartlett & S. Ghoshal, 1989, *Managing Across Borders: The Transnational Solution*, Boston: Harvard Business School Press.

101. J. Goudreau, 2013, New Avon CEO vows to restore the 126-year-old beauty company to former glory, *Forbes*, www.forbes.com, February 27.

102. B. Brenner & B. Ambos, 2013, A question of legitimacy? A dynamic perspective on multinational firm control, *Organization Science*, 24(3): 773–795; M. P. Koza, S. Tallman, & A. Ataay, 2011, The strategic assembly of global firms: A microstructural analysis of local learning and global adaptation, *Global Strategy Journal*, 1: 27–46.

103. J. Qiu & L. Donaldson, 2012, Stopford and Wells were right! MNC matrix structures do fit a "high-high" strategy, *Management International Review*, 52(5): 671–689; B. Connelly, M. A. Hitt, A. DeNisi, & R. D. Ireland, 2007, Expatriates and corporate-level international strategy: Governing with the knowledge contract, *Management Decision*, 45: 564–581.

104. J. S. Lublin & S. Ng, 2013, P&G lines up executives in race for CEO Lafley's successor, *Wall Street Journal*, www.wsj.com, May 30.

105. T. Wakayama, J. Shintaku, & A. Tomofumi, 2012, What Panasonic learned in China, *Harvard Business Review*, 90(12): 109–113.

106. A. Ringstrom, 2013, One size doesn't fit all: IKEA goes local for India, China, www.reuters.com, March 7.

107. L. Lin, 2013, Ikea's Ohlsson targets fourfold increase in China stores by 2020, www.bloomberg.com, April 2.

108. J. Hultman, T. Johnsen, R. Johnsen, & S. Hertz, 2012, An interaction approach to global sourcing: A case study of IKEA, *Journal of Purchasing & Supply Management*, 10(1): 9–21.

109. I. Neyens & D. Faems, 2013, Exploring the impact of alliance portfolio management design on alliance portfolio performance, *Managerial & Decision Economics*, 34(3-5): 347–361.

110. J.-P. Roy, 2012, IJV partner trustworthy behaviour: The role of host country governance and partner selection criteria, *Journal of Management Studies*, 49: 332–355; V. A. Aggarwal, N. Siggelkow, & H. Singh, 2011, Governing collaborative activity: Interdependence and the impact of coordination and exploration, *Strategic Management Journal*, 32: 705–730; J. Li, C. Zhou, & E. J. Zajac, 2009, Control, collaboration, and productivity in international joint ventures: Theory and evidence, *Strategic Management Journal*, 30: 865–884.

111. L. Li, G. Qian, & Z. Qian, 2013, Do partners in international strategic alliances share resources, costs, and risks? *Journal of Business Research*, 66(4): 489–498; D. Li, L. E. Eden, M. A. Hitt, & R. D. Ireland, 2008, Friends, acquaintances, or strangers? Partner selection in R&D alliances, *Academy of Management Journal*, 51(2): 315–334.

112. R. Gulati, P. Puranam, & M. Tushman, 2012, Meta-organization design: Rethinking design in interorganizational and community context, *Strategic Management Journal*, 33: 571–586; J. Wincent, S. Anokhin, D. Örtqvist, & E. Autio, 2010, Quality meets structure: Generalized reciprocity and firm-level advantage in strategic networks, *Journal of Management Studies*, 47: 597–624.

113. V. Van de Vrande, 2013, Balancing your technology-sourcing portfolio: How sourcing mode diversity enhances innovative performance, *Strategic Management Journal*, 34(5): 610–621; T. P. Moliterno & D. M. Mahony, 2011, Network theory of organization: A multilevel approach, *Journal of Management*, 37: 443–467.

114. L. Dooley, D. Kirk, & K. Philpott, 2013, Nurturing life-science knowledge discovery: Managing multi-organisation networks, *Production Planning & Control*, 24(2/3): 195-207; A. T. Arikan & M. A. Schilling, 2011, Structure and governance of industrial districts: Implications for competitive advantage, *Journal of Management Studies*, 48: 772–803; R. D. Ireland & J. W. Webb, 2007, A multi-theoretic perspective on trust and power in strategic supply chains, *Journal of Operations Management*, 25: 482–497.

115. S. Albers, F. Wohlgezogen, & E. J. Zajac, 2013, Strategic alliance structures: An organization design perspective, *Journal of Management*, in press.

116. B. Baudry & V. Chassagnon, 2012, The vertical network organization as a specific governance structure: What are the challenges for incomplete contracts theories and what are the theoretical implications for the boundaries of the (hub-) firm? *Journal of Management & Governance*, 16(2): 285–303.

117. K. Zhou & D. Xu, 2012, How foreign firms curtail local supplier opportunism in China: Detailed contracts, centralized control, and relational governance, *Journal of International Business Studies*, 43(7): 677–692; J. Bae, F. C. Wezel, & J. Koo, 2011, Cross-cutting ties, organizational density and new firm formation in the U.S. biotech industry, 1994–98, *Academy of Management Journal*, 54: 295–311; J. Zhang & C. Baden-Fuller, 2010, The influence of technological knowledge base and organizational structure on technological collaboration, *Journal of Management Studies*, 47: 679–704.

118. R. Gulati, F. Wohlgezogen, & P. Zhelyazkov, 2012, The two facets of collaboration: Cooperation and coordination in strategic alliances, *Academy of Management Annals*, 6: 531–583; M. H. Hansen, R. E. Hoskisson, & J. B. Barney, 2008, Competitive advantage in alliance governance: Resolving the opportunism minimization-gain maximization paradox, *Managerial and Decision Economics*, 29: 191–208; G. Lorenzoni & C. Baden-Fuller, 1995, Creating a strategic center to manage a web of partners, *California Management Review*, 37(3): 146–163.

119. E. Revilla, M. Sáenz, & D. Knoppen, 2013, Towards an empirical typology of buyer–supplier relationships based on

absorptive capacity, *International Journal of Production Research*, 51(10): 2935–2951; A. C. Inkpen, 2008, Knowledge transfer and international joint ventures: The case of NUMMI and General Motors, *Strategic Management Journal*, 29(4): 447–453; J. H. Dyer & K. Nobeoka, 2000, Creating and managing a high-performance knowledge-sharing network: The Toyota case, *Strategic Management Journal*, 21: 345–367.

120. N. Lahiri & S. Narayanan, 2013, Vertical integration, innovation and alliance portfolio size: Implications for firm performance, *Strategic Management Journal*, 34(9): 1042–1064; L. F. Mesquita, J. Anand, & J. H. Brush, 2008, Comparing the resource-based and relational views: Knowledge transfer and spillover in vertical alliances, *Strategic Management Journal*, 29: 913–941; M. Kotabe, X. Martin, & H. Domoto, 2003, Gaining from vertical partnerships: Knowledge transfer, relationship duration and supplier performance improvement in the U.S. and Japanese automotive industries, *Strategic Management Journal*, 24: 293–316.

121. A. Alblas & H. Wortmann, 2012, Impact of product platforms on lean production systems: Evidence from industrial machinery manufacturing, *International Journal of Technology Management*, 57(1/2/3): 110–131; S. G. Lazzarini, D. P. Claro, & L. F. Mesquita, 2008, Buyer-supplier and supplier-supplier alliances: Do they reinforce or undermine one another? *Journal of Management Studies*, 45(3): 561–584; P. Dussauge, B. Garrette, & W. Mitchell, 2004, Asymmetric performance: The market share impact of scale and link alliances in the global auto industry, *Strategic Management Journal*, 25: 701–711.

122. Garg, Priem, & Rasheed, A theoretical explanation of the cost advantages of multi-unit franchising; A. M. Hayashi, 2008, How to replicate success, *MIT Sloan Management Review*, 49(3): 6–7; M. Tuunanen & F. Hoy, 2007, Franchising: Multifaceted form of entrepreneurship, *International Journal of Entrepreneurship and Small Business*, 4: 52–67.

123. W. Vanhaverbeke, V. Gilsing, & G. Duysters, 2012, Competence and governance in strategic collaboration: The differential effect of network structure on the creation of core and noncore technology, *Journal of Product Innovation Management*, 29(5): 784–802; A. Zaheer, R. Gözübüyük, & H. Milanov, 2010, It's the connections: The network perspective in interorganizational research, *Academy of Management Perspectives*, 24(1): 62–77.

124. J. DeTar, 2012, McDonald's shares rise amid India expansion move, *Investor's Business Daily*, www.news.investor.com, December 7; E. Bellman, 2009, Corporate news: McDonald's plans expansion in India, *Wall Street Journal*, June 30, B4.

125. Y. Lew & R. R. Sinkovics, 2013, Crossing borders and industry sectors: Behavioral governance in strategic alliances and product innovation for competitive advantage, *Long Range Planning*, 46(1/2): 13–38; T. W. Tong, J. J. Reuer, & M. W. Peng, 2008, International joint ventures and the value of growth options, *Academy of Management Journal*, 51: 1014–1029; C. Jones, W. S. Hesterly, & S. P. Borgatti, 1997, A general theory of network governance: Exchange conditions and social mechanisms, *Academy of Management Review*, 22: 911–945.

126. H. Liu, X. Jiang, J. Zhang, & X. Zhao, 2013, Strategic flexibility and international venturing by emerging market firms: The moderating effects of institutional and relational factors, *Journal of International Marketing*, 21(2): 79–98; M. W. Hansen, T. Pedersen, & B. Petersen, 2009, MNC strategies and linkage effects in developing countries, *Journal of World Business*, 44(2): 121–130; A. Goerzen, 2005, Managing alliance networks: Emerging practices of multinational corporations, *Academy of Management Executive*, 19(2): 94–107.

127. C. C. Phelps, 2010, A longitudinal study of the influence of alliance network structure and composition on firm exploratory innovation, *Academy of Management Journal*, 53: 890–913; L. H. Lin, 2009, Mergers and acquisitions, alliances and technology development: An empirical study of the global auto industry, *International Journal of Technology Management*, 48(3): 295–307.

128. Y. Y. Kor & A. Mesko, 2013, Dynamic managerial capabilities: Configuration and orchestration of top executives' capabilities and the firm's dominant logic,*Strategic Management Journal*,34(2): 233-244; S. T. Hannah & P. B. Lester, 2009, A multilevel approach to building and leading learning organizations, *Leadership Quarterly*, 20(1): 34–48; E. M. Olson, S. F. Slater, & G. T. M. Hult, 2007, The importance of structure and process to strategy implementation, *Business Horizons*, 48(1): 47–54; D. N. Sull & C. Spinosa, 2007, Promise-based management, *Harvard Business Review*, 85(4):79–86.

# 12

# Strategic Leadership

***Studying this chapter should provide you with the strategic management knowledge needed to:***

1. Define strategic leadership and describe top-level managers' importance.
2. Explain what top management teams are and how they affect firm performance.
3. Describe the managerial succession process using internal and external managerial labor markets.
4. Discuss the value of strategic leadership in determining the firm's strategic direction.
5. Describe the importance of strategic leaders in managing the firm's resources.
6. Explain what must be done for a firm to sustain an effective culture.
7. Describe what strategic leaders can do to establish and emphasize ethical practices.
8. Discuss the importance and use of organizational controls.

## A CHANGE AT THE TOP AT PROCTER & GAMBLE (P&G): AN INDICATION OF HOW MUCH THE CEO MATTERS?

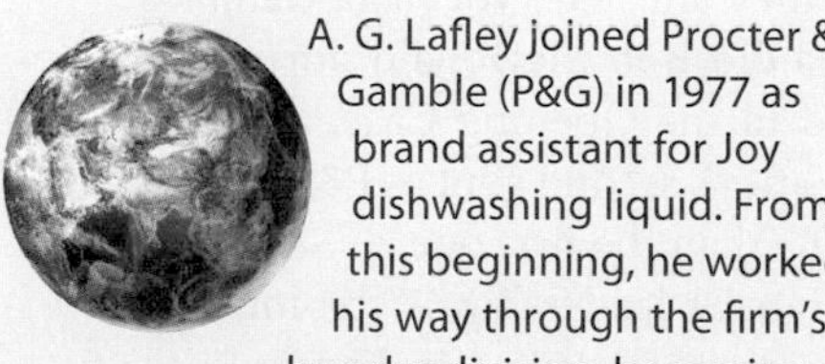

A. G. Lafley joined Procter & Gamble (P&G) in 1977 as brand assistant for Joy dishwashing liquid. From this beginning, he worked his way through the firm's laundry division, becoming highly visible as a result of number of successes including the launching of liquid Tide. A string of continuing accomplishments throughout the firm resulted in Lafley's appointment as P&G's CEO in June 2000, a post he held until retiring in mid-2009. Bob McDonald, who joined P&G in 1980, was Lafley's handpicked successor. McDonald took the top position at P&G in July 2009, but resigned under pressure in May 2013. Lafley, revered by many, was asked to come out of retirement and return to P&G as president, CEO and chairman of the board of directors. Lafley said that when contacted to return to P&G, he agreed immediately to do so, committing to remain "as long as needed to improve the company's performance." However, speculation is that Lafley likely would not remain beyond three years.

What went wrong for McDonald, a long-time P&G employee who seemed to know the firm well and who received Lafley's support? Not surprisingly, a number of possibilities have been mentioned in response to this question. Some concluded that under McDonald's leadership, P&G suffered from "poor execution globally," an outcome created in part by P&G's seemingly ineffective responses to aggressive competition in emerging markets. Other apparent problems were a failure to control the firm's costs and employees' loss of confidence in McDonald's leadership. Still others argued that McDonald did not fully understand the effects on U.S. consumers of the recession in place when he took over and that during that time period, P&G "was selling BMWs when cash-tight consumers were looking for Kias." The net result of these types of problems included P&G "losing a step to rivals like Unilever." In turn, this caused investors to become frustrated by "P&G's inability to consistently keep up with its rivals' sales growth and share price gains."

But why bring Lafley back? In a few words, because of his previous success. Among other achievements during his first stint as P&G's main strategic leader were building up the firm's beauty business, acquiring Gillette, expanding the firm's presence in emerging markets, and launching hit products such as Swiffer and Febreze. An overall measure of P&G's success during Lafley's initial tenure as CEO is the fact that the firm's shares increased 63 percent in value while the S&P fell 37 percent in value. Thus, multiple stakeholders including investors and employees may believe that Lafley can return the firm to the "glory days" it experienced from 2000 to 2009.

What are some actions Lafley is considering as he returns to P&G? Product innovations are a core concern and an area receiving a significant amount of attention. Analysts suggest that P&G needs to move beyond incremental innovations, seeking to again create entirely new product categories as it did with Swiffer and Febreze. This will be challenging at least in the short run given recent declines in allocations to the firm's research and development (R&D) programs. These reductions have resulted in a product pipeline focused mainly on "reformulating rather than inventing." Additionally, efforts are underway to continue McDonald's strong, recent commitments to reduce the firm's "bloated" cost structure and reenergize the competitive actions it will take in global markets.

Restructuring P&G's multiple brands and products into four sectors, each of which will be headed by a president, is a major change Lafley is initiating. Currently, the firm has two global business divisions—beauty and grooming and household care. Final decisions about the precise compositions of the four sectors were not announced by mid-2013. Speculation, though, was that each sector would be formed "to reflect synergies between various businesses." For example, one expectation was that paper-based products such as "Bounty paper towels, Charmin toilet paper, Pampers diapers and Always feminine care products" would be combined to form a sector. Moreover, Lafley's replacement was expected to be selected from among the four presidents who would be chosen to lead the new sectors.

Sources: D. Benoit, 2013, Critical P&G analysts still waiting on results, *Wall Street Journal*, www.wsj.com, May 24; D. Benoit, 2013, Procter & Gamble gets an upgrade, *Wall Street Journal*, www.wsj.com, May 24; J. Bogaisky, 2013, Congrats, Bill Ackman: Bob McDonald out at P&G; A. G. Lafley returning as CEO, *Forbes*, www.forbes.com, May 23; E. Byron & J. S. Lublin, 2013, Embattled P&G chief replaced by old boss, *Wall Street Journal*, www.wsj.com, May 23; L. Coleman-Lochner & C. Hymowitz, 2013, Lafley's CEO encore at P&G puts rock star legacy at risk: Retail, *Bloomberg*, www.bloomberg.com, May 28; J. S. Lublin & S. Ng, 2013, P&G lines up executives in race for CEO Lafley's successor, *Wall Street Journal*, www.wsj.com, May 30; J. Ritchie, 2013, P&G's hiring of Lafley may buy time for innovation, *Business Courier*, www.bizjournals.com, May 31.

Learn more about Procter & Gamble.
**www.cengagebrain.com**

As the Opening Case suggests, strategic leaders' work is demanding, challenging, and requires balancing short-term performance outcomes with long-term performance goals. Regardless of how long (or short) they remain in their positions, strategic leaders (and most prominently CEOs) affect a firm's performance.[1] A. G. Lafley affected Procter & Gamble's (P&G) performance during his initial service as CEO as did Bob McDonald during his slightly less than four-year term. Moreover, as described in the Opening Case, analysts, employees, and perhaps even customers are hopeful that Lafley's second stint as P&G's CEO will be as successful—and hopefully even more successful—than the first one.

A major message in this chapter is that effective strategic leadership is the foundation for successfully using the strategic management process. As implied in Figure 1.1 in Chapter 1 and through the Analysis-Strategy-Performance model, strategic leaders guide the firm in ways that result in forming a vision and mission. Often, this guidance finds leaders thinking of ways to create goals that stretch everyone in the organization as a foundation for enhancing firm performance. A positive outcome of stretch goals is their ability to provoke breakthrough thinking—thinking that often leads to innovation.[2] Additionally, strategic leaders work with others to verify that the analysis and strategy parts of the A-S-P model are completed in order to increase the likelihood the firm will achieve strategic competitiveness and earn above-average returns. We show how effective strategic leadership makes all of this possible in Figure 12.1.[3]

To begin this chapter, we define strategic leadership and discuss its importance and the possibility of strategic leaders being a source of competitive advantage for a firm. These introductory comments include a brief consideration of different styles strategic leaders may use. We then examine the role of top-level managers and top management teams and their effects on innovation, strategic change, and firm performance. Following this discussion is an analysis of managerial succession, particularly in the context of the internal and external managerial labor markets from which strategic leaders are selected. Closing the chapter are descriptions of five key leadership actions that contribute to effective strategic

M. Stasy

**Figure 12.1** Strategic Leadership and the Strategic Management Process

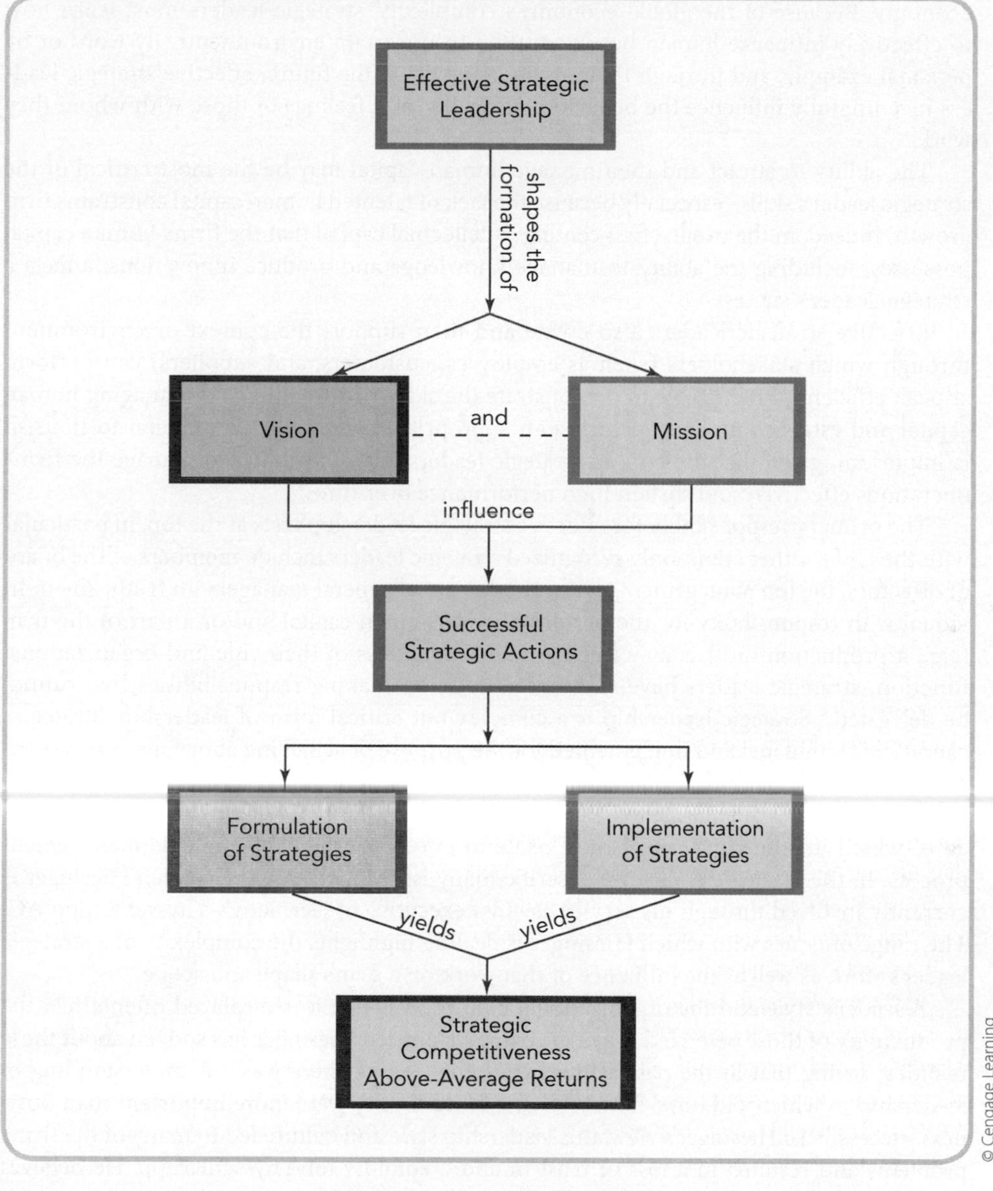


leadership—determining strategic direction, effectively managing the firm's resource portfolio, sustaining an effective organizational culture, emphasizing ethical practices, and establishing balanced organizational controls.

## 12-1 Strategic Leadership and Style

**Strategic leadership** is the ability to anticipate, envision, maintain flexibility, and empower others to create strategic change as necessary. **Strategic change** is change brought about as a result of selecting and implementing a firm's strategies. Multifunctional in nature, strategic leadership involves managing through others, managing an entire organization rather

**Strategic leadership** is the ability to anticipate, envision, maintain flexibility, and empower others to create strategic change as necessary.

**Strategic change** is change brought about as a result of selecting and implementing a firm's strategies.

than a functional subunit, and coping with change that continues to increase in the global economy. Because of the global economy's complexity, strategic leaders must learn how to effectively influence human behavior, often in uncertain environments. By word or by personal example, and through their ability to envision the future, effective strategic leaders meaningfully influence the behaviors, thoughts, and feelings of those with whom they work.[4]

The ability to attract and then manage human capital may be the most critical of the strategic leader's skills,[5] especially because the lack of talented human capital constrains firm growth. Indeed, in the twenty-first century, intellectual capital that the firm's human capital possesses, including the ability to manage knowledge and produce innovations, affects a strategic leader's success.[6]

Effective strategic leaders also create and then support the context or environment through which stakeholders (such as employees, customers, and suppliers) can perform at peak efficiency.[7] Being able to demonstrate the skills of attracting and managing human capital and establishing and nurturing an appropriate context for that capital to flourish is important, given that the crux of strategic leadership is the ability to manage the firm's operations effectively and sustain high performance over time.[8]

The primary responsibility for effective strategic leadership rests at the top, in particular with the CEO. Other commonly recognized strategic leaders include members of the board of directors, the top management team, and divisional general managers. In truth, any individual with responsibility for the performance of human capital and/or a part of the firm (e.g., a production unit) is a strategic leader. Regardless of their title and organizational function, strategic leaders have substantial decision-making responsibilities that cannot be delegated.[9] Strategic leadership is a complex but critical form of leadership. Strategies cannot be formulated and implemented for the purpose of achieving above-average returns without effective strategic leaders.

Learn more about Strategic Leadership.
www.cengagebrain.com

As a strategic leader, a firm's CEO is involved with a large number and variety of tasks, all of which in some form or fashion relate to effective use of the strategic management process. In the Strategic Focus, we describe many issues with which Heinrich Hiesinger is currently involved through his service as chief executive of Germany's ThyssenKrupp AG. The range of issues with which Hiesinger is dealing highlights the complexity of a strategic leader's work as well as the influence of that work on a firm's shape and scope.

A leader's style and the organizational culture in which it is displayed often affect the productivity of those being led. ThyssenKrupp's Heinrich Hiesinger has spoken about these realities, saying that in the past at the firm he is leading there was an "understanding of leadership in which 'old boys' networks' and blind loyalty were more important than business success."[10] In Hiesinger's view, this leadership style and culture led to many of the firm's problems and resulted in a loss of trust in and credibility for ThyssenKrupp. He believes the firm must now do everything possible to again earn both trust and credibility with stakeholders.

Learn more about Strategic Change.
www.cengagebrain.com

Transformational leadership is the most effective strategic leadership style. This style entails motivating followers to exceed the expectations others have of them, to continuously enrich their capabilities, and to place the interests of the organization above their own.[11] Transformational leaders develop and communicate a vision for the organization and formulate a strategy to achieve that vision. They make followers aware of the need to achieve valued organizational outcomes and encourage them to continuously strive for higher levels of achievement.

Transformational leaders have a high degree of integrity (Ray Kroc, founder of McDonald's, was a strategic leader valued for his high degree of integrity)[12] and character. Speaking about character, one CEO said the following: "Leaders are shaped and defined by character. Leaders inspire and enable others to do excellent work and realize their potential.

M. Stasy

# Strategic Focus FAILURE

## The Life of a CEO as a Firm's Primary Strategic Leader: Breadth, Depth, and Complexity

Based in Germany and known historically as a steel manufacturer, ThyssenKrupp AG is a diversified firm organized into six business areas—components technology, elevator technology, industrial solutions, materials services, steel Europe, and steel Americas (as of September 30, 2012, this business area is formally classified as a discontinued operation according to International Financial Reporting Standards). Globally, ThyssenKrupp has over 150,000 employees working in approximately 80 countries. The company, recognized today as a steel and engineering firm, is Germany's largest steelmaker by output.

*ThyssenKrupp AG's headquarters in Essen, Germany. A change in strategic leadership at the heavy industry giant has resulted in a change in strategy.*



The recent past has been unkind to ThyssenKrupp in terms of financial performance and relative to issues warranting attention. Accepting responsibility for reshaping the firm and handling the controversies facing it as a foundation for turning around its performance is Dr.-Ing. Heinrich Hiesinger. Formerly affiliated with another large German firm—Siemens—Hiesinger became chairman of the executive board of ThyssenKrupp in January 2011. To hopefully begin to ease stakeholders' concerns, Hiesinger has pledged a "fresh start" and indicated that he seeks to "put things right and implement a new corporate culture."

What are some of the issues Hiesinger is facing? One is financial in that the firm reported heavy losses during 2011 and 2012; the quality of 2013's financial performance was uncertain at mid-year. Contributing to these difficulties were ThyssenKrupp's steel operations in Brazil and the United States. With hindsight, deciding to expand into these markets was a mistake as indicated by the fact that both of them were unprofitable, largely because of "waning demand from the auto and construction industries and competition from China," conditions that weakened prices for the firm's products and negatively affected its profit margins. Brazil's third largest steelmaker, Cia. Siderurgica nacional SA (SID) was the leading bidder for ThyssenKrupp's plants in both Brazil and the United States.

The resignation in March 2013 of ThyssenKrupp's supervisory chairman and various scandals that emerged during the chairman's service were additional problems requiring Hiesinger's attention. Allegations of "price-fixing at the firm's railway-track-construction unit and charges of inappropriate business trips with union representatives and journalists" were issues that demanded Hiesinger's time and energy. As a result of the price-fixing charge, the firm was fined by the German competition authority. Another action taken to deal with the quality of ThyssenKrupp's corporate governance that the scandals suggest was the establishment of a whistleblower program for employees.

Hiesinger is also involved in reshaping the focus of ThyssenKrupp's competitive efforts. With a goal of converting the firm into an integrated technology provider, Hiesinger's decisions are causing the firm to concentrate on "making components for cars and heavy vehicles, building naval ships and submarines, and its elevator business." Once implemented, the firm's new emphases in terms of the business areas in which it competes will find it generating only about 30 percent of its revenue from steelmaking. Additionally, Hiesinger believes that China and Asia are growth markets for the firm, particularly for the elevator division. Accordingly, plans are underway for ThyssenKrupp to more than double its workforce in China by mid-2017.

Sources: T. Andresen, 2013, Thyssen woes tarnish 99-year-old steel baron's legacy, *Bloomberg*, www.bloomberg.com, May 21; J. Hromadko, 2013, Thyssen earnings: Loss widens on write-down of Brazil, U.S. plants, *Wall Street Journal*, www.wsj.com, May 15; J. Hromadko, 2013, ThyssenKrupp offers workers amnesty to resolve corruption case, *Wall Street Journal*, www.wsj.com, April 16; J. Hromadko, 2013, ThyssenKrupp chairman to step down, *Wall Street Journal*, www.wsj.com, March 8; A. Kirchfeld, J. P. Spinetto & C. Lucchesi, 2013, CSN said to be leading bidder for ThyssenKrupp Americas plants, *Bloomberg*, www.bloomberg.com, May 2; J. Ng, 2013, ThyssenKrupp looks to China, Asia for growth, *Wall Street Journal*, www.wsj.com, June 3.

As a result, they build successful, enduring organizations."[13] Additionally, transformational leaders have emotional intelligence. Emotionally intelligent leaders understand themselves well, have strong motivation, are empathetic with others, and have effective interpersonal skills.[14] As a result of these characteristics, transformational leaders are especially effective in promoting and nurturing innovation in firms.[15]

# 12-2 The Role of Top-Level Managers

As strategic leaders, top-level managers are critical to a firm's efforts to effectively use the strategic management process. To exercise the duties of this role, top-level managers make many decisions, such as the strategic actions and responses that are part of the competitive rivalry with which the firm is involved at a point in time (see Chapter 5). More broadly, they are involved with making many decisions associated with first selecting and then implementing the firm's strategies.

When making decisions related to using the strategic management process, managers (certainly top-level ones) often use their discretion (or latitude for action).[16] Managerial discretion differs significantly across industries. The primary factors that determine the amount of decision-making discretion held by a manager (especially a top-level manager) are (1) external environmental sources such as the industry structure, the rate of market growth in the firm's primary industry, and the degree to which products can be differentiated; (2) characteristics of the organization, including its size, age, resources, and culture; and (3) characteristics of the manager, including commitment to the firm and its strategic outcomes, tolerance for ambiguity, skills in working with different people, and aspiration levels (see Figure 12.2). Because strategic leaders' decisions are intended to help the firm outperform competitors, how managers exercise discretion when making decisions is critical to the firm's success[17] and affects or shapes the firm's culture.

Top-level managers' roles in verifying that their firm effectively uses the strategic management process are complex and challenging. Because of this, top management teams rather than a single top-level manager typically make the decisions relative to this important task.

## 12-2a Top Management Teams

The **top management team** is composed of the individuals who are responsible for making certain the firm uses the strategic management process, especially for the purpose of selecting and implementing strategies. Typically, the top management team includes the officers of the corporation, defined by the title of vice president and above or by service as a member of the board of directors.[18] Among other outcomes, the quality of a top management team's decisions affects the firm's ability to innovate and change in ways that contribute to its efforts to earn above-average returns.[19]

As previously noted, the complex challenges facing most organizations require the exercise of strategic leadership by a team of executives rather than by a single individual. Using a team to make decisions about how the firm will compete also helps to avoid another potential problem when these decisions are made by the CEO alone: managerial hubris. Research shows that when CEOs begin to believe glowing press accounts and to feel that they are unlikely to make errors, the quality of their decisions suffers.[20] Top-level managers need to have self-confidence but must guard against allowing it to become arrogance and a false belief in their own invincibility.[21] To guard against CEO overconfidence and the making of poor decisions, firms often use the top management team to make decisions required by the strategic management process.

The **top management team** is composed of the individuals who are responsible for making certain the firm uses the strategic management process, especially for the purpose of selecting and implementing strategies.

**Figure 12.2** Factors Affecting Managerial Discretion

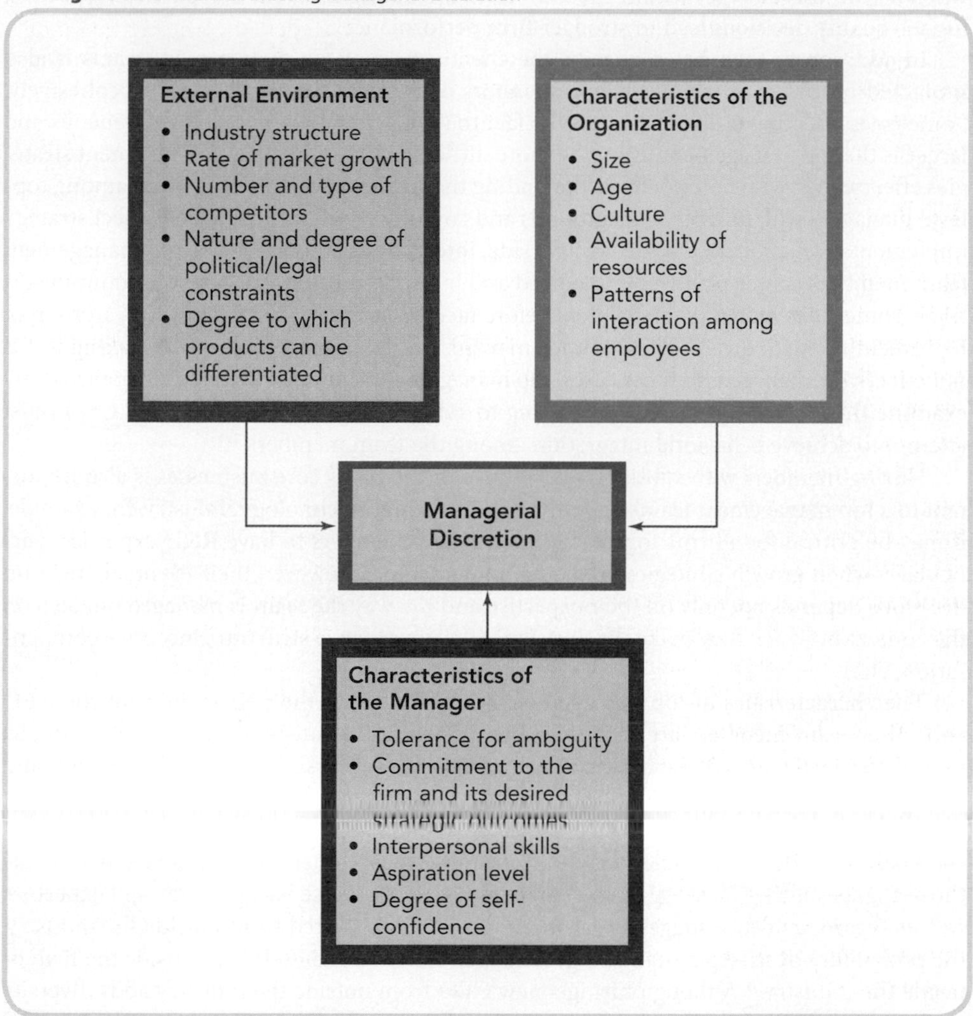


Source: Adapted from S. Finkelstein & D C. Hambrick, 1996, ***Strategic Leadership: Top Executives and Their Effects on Organizations,*** St. Paul, MN: West Publishing Company.

## Top Management Teams, Firm Performance, and Strategic Change

The job of top-level managers is complex and requires a broad knowledge of the firm's internal organization (see Chapter 3) as well as the three key parts of its external environment—the general, industry, and competitor environments (see Chapter 2). Therefore, firms try to form a top management team with knowledge and expertise needed to operate the internal organization, yet that also can deal with the firm's stakeholders as well as its competitors.[22] To have these characteristics normally requires a heterogeneous top management team. A **heterogeneous top management team** is composed of individuals with different functional backgrounds, experience, and education. Increasingly, having international experience is a critical aspect of the heterogeneity that is desirable in top management teams, given the globalized nature of the markets in which most firms now compete.

A **heterogeneous top management team** is composed of individuals with different functional backgrounds, experience, and education.

Research evidence indicates that members of a heterogeneous top management team benefit from discussing their different perspectives.[23] In many cases, these discussions and the debates they often engender increase the quality of the team's decisions, especially when a synthesis emerges within the team after evaluating different perspectives.[24] In turn, higher-quality decisions lead to stronger firm performance.[25]

In addition to their heterogeneity, the effectiveness of top management teams is also impacted by the value gained when members of these teams work together cohesively. Sometimes affecting team cohesion is the fact that, in general, the more heterogeneous and larger is the top management team, the more difficult it is for the team to implement strategies effectively.[26] Also noteworthy is the finding that communication difficulties among top-level managers with different backgrounds and cognitive skills can negatively affect strategy implementation efforts.[27] On the positive side, interactions among diverse top management team members can be positively supported and influenced through electronic communications, sometimes reducing the barriers before face-to-face meetings.[28] However, a group of top executives with diverse backgrounds may inhibit the process of decision making if it is not effectively managed. In these cases, top management teams may fail to comprehensively examine threats and opportunities, leading to suboptimal decisions. Thus, the CEO must attempt to achieve behavioral integration among the team members.[29]

Having members with substantive expertise in the firm's core businesses is also important to a top management team's effectiveness.[30] In a high-technology industry, for example, it may be critical for a firm's top management team members to have R&D expertise, particularly when growth strategies are being implemented. However, their eventual effect on decisions depends not only on their expertise and the way the team is managed but also on the context in which they make the decisions (the governance structure, incentive compensation, etc.).[31]

The characteristics of top management teams and even the personalities of the CEO and other team members are related to innovation and strategic change.[32] For example, more heterogeneous top management teams are positively associated with innovation and strategic change, perhaps in part because heterogeneity may influence the team or at least some of its members to think more creatively when making decisions and taking actions.[33]

Therefore, firms that could benefit by changing their strategies are more likely to make those changes if they have top management teams with diverse backgrounds and expertise. In this regard, evidence suggests that when a new CEO is hired from outside the industry, the probability of strategic change is greater than if the new CEO is from inside the firm or inside the industry.[34] Although hiring a new CEO from outside the industry adds diversity to the team, the top management team must be managed effectively to gain the benefits associated with that diversity. Consistent with earlier comments, we highlight here the value of transformational leadership to strategic change as the CEO helps the firm match environmental opportunities with its strengths, as indicated by its capabilities and core competencies, as a foundation for selecting and/or implementing new strategies.[35]

## The CEO and Top Management Team Power

We noted in Chapter 10 that the board of directors is an important governance mechanism for monitoring a firm's strategic direction and for representing stakeholders' interests, especially shareholders. In fact, higher performance normally is achieved when the board of directors is more directly involved in helping to shape the firm's strategic direction.[36]

Boards of directors, however, may find it difficult to direct the decisions and resulting actions of powerful CEOs and top management teams.[37] Often, a powerful CEO appoints a number of sympathetic outside members to the board or may have inside board members who are also on the top management team and report to her or him.[38] In either case, the CEO may significantly influence actions such as appointments to the board. Thus, the amount of discretion a CEO has in making decisions is related to the board of directors and the decision latitude it provides to the CEO and the remainder of the top management team.[39]

Tony Metaxas/Glow Images

*The power of the CEO and top management team relative to the board of directors is influenced by a number of factors.*

CEOs and top management team members can also achieve power in other ways. For example, a CEO who also holds the position of chairperson of the board usually has more power than the CEO who does not.[40] Some analysts and corporate "watchdogs" criticize the practice of *CEO duality* (which is when the CEO and the chairperson of the board are the same) because it can lead to poor performance and slow responses to change, partly because the tendency is for the board to reduce its efforts to monitor the CEO and other top management team members when CEO duality exists.[41]

Although it varies across industries, CEO duality occurs most commonly in larger firms. Increased shareholder activism has brought CEO duality under scrutiny and attack in both U.S. and European firms. In this regard, we noted in Chapter 10 that a number of analysts, regulators, and corporate directors believe that an independent board leadership structure without CEO duality has a net positive effect on the board's efforts to monitor top-level managers' decisions and actions, particularly with respect to financial performance. However, CEO duality's actual effects on firm performance (and particularly financial performance) remain inconclusive.[42] Moreover, recent evidence suggests that at least in a sample of firms in European countries, CEO duality positively affects performance when a firm encounters a crisis.[43] Thus, it seems that nuances or situational conditions must be considered when analyzing the outcomes of CEO duality on firm performance.

Top management team members and CEOs who have long tenure—on the team and in the organization—have a greater influence on board decisions. In general, long tenure may constrain the breadth of an executive's knowledge base. Some evidence suggests that with the limited perspectives associated with a restricted knowledge base, long-tenured top executives typically develop fewer alternatives to evaluate when making strategic decisions.[44] However, long-tenured managers also may be able to exercise more effective strategic control, thereby obviating the need for board members' involvement because effective strategic control generally leads to higher performance.[45] Intriguingly, it may be that "the liabilities of short tenure ... appear to exceed the advantages, while the advantages of long tenure—firm-specific human and social capital, knowledge, and power—seem to outweigh the disadvantages of rigidity and maintaining the status quo."[46] Overall then the relationship between CEO tenure and firm performance is complex and nuanced,[47] indicating that a board of directors should develop an effective working relationship with the top management team as part of its efforts to enhance firm performance.

Another nuance or situational condition to consider is the case in which a CEO acts as a *steward* of the firm's assets. In this instance, holding the dual roles of CEO and board chair facilitates the making of decisions and the taking of actions that benefit stakeholders. The logic here is that the CEO desiring to be the best possible steward of the firm's assets gains efficiency through CEO duality.[48] Additionally, because of this person's positive orientation and actions, extra governance and the coordination costs resulting from an independent board leadership structure become unnecessary.[49]

In summary, the relative degrees of power held by the board and top management team members should be examined in light of an individual firm's situation. For example, the abundance of resources in a firm's external environment and the volatility of that environment may affect the ideal balance of power between the board and the top management team. Moreover, a volatile and uncertain environment may create a situation where a powerful CEO is needed to move quickly. In such an instance, a diverse top management team may create less cohesion among team members, perhaps stalling or even preventing appropriate decisions from being made in a timely manner as a result. In the final analysis, an effective working relationship between the board and the CEO and other top management team members is the foundation through which decisions are made that have the highest probability of best serving stakeholders' interests.[50]

## 12-3 Managerial Succession

The choice of top-level managers—particularly CEOs—is a critical decision with important implications for the firm's performance.[51] As discussed in Chapter 10, selecting the CEO is one of the board of directors' most important responsibilities as it seeks to represent the best interests of a firm's stakeholders. Many companies use leadership screening systems to identify individuals with strategic leadership potential as well as to determine the criteria individuals should satisfy to be a candidate for the CEO position.

The most effective of these screening systems assesses people within the firm and gains valuable information about the capabilities of other companies' strategic leaders.[52] Based on the results of these assessments, training and development programs are provided to various individuals in an attempt to preselect and shape the skills of people with strategic leadership potential.

A number of firms have high-quality leadership programs in place, including Procter & Gamble (P&G), GE, IBM, and Dow Chemical. For example, P&G is thought to have talent throughout the organization that is trained to accept the next level of leadership responsibility when the time comes. Managing talent on a global basis, P&G seeks to consistently provide leaders at all levels in the firm with meaningful work and significant responsibilities as a means of simultaneously challenging and developing them. The value created by GE's leadership training programs is suggested by the fact that many companies recruit leadership talent from this firm.[53]

In spite of the value high-quality leadership training programs can create, there are many companies that have not established training and succession plans for their top-level managers or for others holding key leadership positions (e.g., department heads, sections heads). With respect to family-owned firms operating in the United States, a recent survey found that only 41 percent of those surveyed have established leadership contingency plans while 49 percent indicated that they "review succession plans (only) when a change in management requires it."[54] On a global scale, recent evidence suggests that "Only 45 percent of executives from 34 countries around the world say their companies have a process for conducting CEO succession planning."[55] Those leading firms throughout the world should recognize that the need for continuity in the use of their strategic management process is difficult to attain without an effective succession plan and process in place.

An **internal managerial labor market** consists of a firm's opportunities for managerial positions and the qualified employees within that firm.

An **external managerial labor market** is the collection of managerial career opportunities and the qualified people who are external to the organization in which the opportunities exist.

Organizations select managers and strategic leaders from two types of managerial labor markets—internal and external.[56] An **internal managerial labor market** consists of a firm's opportunities for managerial positions and the qualified employees within that firm. An **external managerial labor market** is the collection of managerial career opportunities and the qualified people who are external to the organization in which the opportunities exist.

Employees commonly prefer that the internal managerial labor market be used for selection purposes, particularly when the firm is choosing members for its top management team and a new CEO. Evidence suggests that these preferences are often fulfilled. For example, almost 70 percent of new CEOs selected in S&P 500 companies in the first quarter of 2013 were promoted from within.[57] In the same set of firms, roughly 75 percent of CEO appointments between 2007 and 2009 were from the internal managerial labor market, indicating that the primary source of CEO appointments in S&P 500 companies from 2007 until 2013 remained the same.[58] And in all probability, A. G. Lafley's replacement as CEO of Procter & Gamble (P&G), as discussed in the Opening Case, will be an internal candidate. Although some analysts anticipated that investors might champion the perceived need to hire from the external market to replace Lafley when he retires a second time, the general thinking was that such a hire was highly unlikely given the firm's "historically strong commitment to select new CEOs from within the company."[59]

With respect to the CEO position, several benefits are thought to accrue to a firm using the internal labor market to select a new CEO, one of which is the continuing commitment such a selection creates with respect to the existing vision, mission, and strategies. Also, because of their experience with the firm and the industry in which it competes, inside CEOs are familiar with company products, markets, technologies, and operating procedures. Another benefit is that choosing to hire a new CEO from within usually results in lower turnover among existing personnel, many of whom possess valuable firm-specific knowledge and skills. In summary, CEOs selected from inside the firm tend to benefit from their (1) clear understanding of the firm's personnel and their capabilities, (2) appreciation of the company's culture and its associated core values, (3) deep knowledge of the firm's core competencies as well as abilities to develop new ones as appropriate, and (4) "feel" for what will and will not "work" in the firm.[60]

In spite of the understandable and legitimate reasons to select CEOs from inside the firm, boards of directors sometimes prefer to choose a new CEO from the external managerial labor market. Conditions suggesting a potentially appropriate preference to hire from outside include (1) the firm's need to enhance its ability to innovate, (2) the firm's need to reverse its recent poor performance, and (3) the fact that the industry in which the firm competes is experiencing rapid growth.

Overall, the decision to use either the internal or the external managerial labor market to select a firm's new CEO is one that should be based on expectations; in other words, what does the board of directors want the new CEO and top management team to accomplish? We address this issue in Figure 12.3 by showing how the composition of the top management team and the CEO succession source (managerial labor market) interact to affect strategy. For example, when the top management team is homogeneous (its members have

**Figure 12.3** Effects of CEO Succession and Top Management Team Composition on Strategy

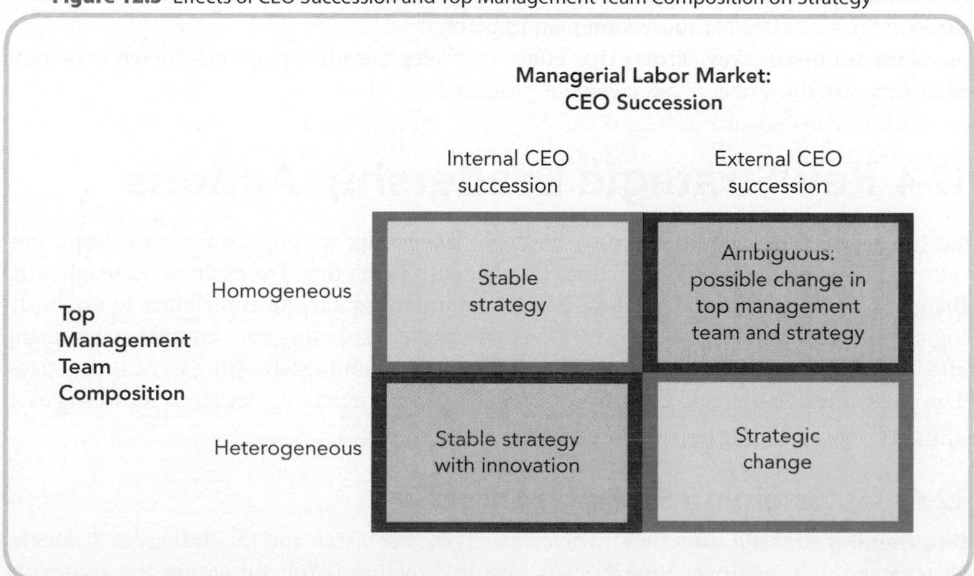

similar functional experiences and educational backgrounds) and a new CEO is selected from inside the firm, the firm's current strategy is unlikely to change. If the firm is performing well absolutely and relative to peers, continuing to implement the current strategy may be precisely what the board of directors wants to happen. Alternatively, when a new CEO is selected from outside the firm and the top management team is heterogeneous, the probability is high that strategy will change. This of course would be a board's preference when the firm's performance is declining, both in absolute terms and relative to rivals. When the new CEO is from inside the firm and a heterogeneous top management team is in place, the strategy may not change, but innovation is likely to continue. An external CEO succession with a homogeneous team creates a more ambiguous situation. Furthermore, outside CEOs who lead moderate change often achieve increases in performance, but high strategic change by outsiders frequently leads to declines in performance.[61] In summary, a firm's board of directors should use the insights shown in Figure 12.3 to inform its decision about which of the two managerial labor markets to use when selecting a new CEO.

An interim CEO is commonly appointed when a firm lacks a succession plan or when an emergency occurs requiring an immediate appointment of a new CEO. Companies throughout the world use this approach.[62] Interim CEOs are almost always from inside the firm; their familiarity with the company's operations supports their efforts to "maintain order" for a period of time. Indeed, a primary advantage of appointing an interim CEO is that doing so can generate the amount of time the board of directors requires to conduct a thorough search to find the best candidate from the external and internal markets. Legg Mason, one of the largest asset management firms in the world with eight affiliates serving individual and institutional clients on six continents, recently chose to promote its then-current interim CEO to the CEO position. This selection was made after the firm spent five months to evaluate over a dozen candidates in total from the external and internal managerial labor markets combined. Although supportive of the selected insider, an analyst also said that turnarounds of asset management firms (which is what many thought needed to happen at Legg Mason) are difficult, perhaps especially so for someone intimately familiar with the firm and its current structure.[63]

As we have discussed, managerial succession especially with respect to the CEO position is an important organizational event. In the Strategic Focus we further describe the importance of these plans and how some firms use them. Increasingly, because of their importance, all of a firm's stakeholders are expressing their strong desire that the board of directors has an effective succession plan in place.

Next, we discuss key actions that effective strategic leaders demonstrate while helping their firm use the strategic management process.

Find out more about Ford.
www.cengagebrain.com

## 12-4 Key Strategic Leadership Actions

Certain actions characterize effective strategic leadership; we present the most important ones in Figure 12.4. Many of the actions interact with each other. For example, managing the firm's resources effectively includes developing human capital and contributes to establishing a strategic direction, fostering an effective culture, exploiting core competencies, using effective and balanced organizational control systems, and establishing ethical practices. The most effective strategic leaders create viable options in making decisions regarding each of the key strategic leadership actions.[64]

**Determining strategic direction** involves specifying the vision and the strategy or strategies to achieve this vision over time

### 12-4a Determining Strategic Direction

**Determining strategic direction** involves specifying the vision and the strategy or strategies to achieve this vision over time.[65] The strategic direction is framed within the context of

M. Stasy

# Strategic Focus SUCCESS

## Keeping Quality People at the Top of The Firm's Leadership Structure: The Importance of Planning for Managerial Succession

As noted in Chapter 10 and as emphasized in this chapter as well, the board of directors is responsible for the firm having "an effective and sustainable CEO succession plan." Interestingly, surveys continue to reveal that boards note that succession planning is the top or second-most significant challenge they face in exercising their responsibilities. Moreover, only 16 percent of recently surveyed directors indicated that their board is effective at succession planning. This is potentially an issue in that the CEO succession process is being used more frequently in many nations and regions. In North America, for example, the average tenure for a CEO has declined from 10-plus years in the mid-1990s to under 5 years today.

Once in place, a CEO succession plan is the foundation for the CEO and the top management team to establish and operationalize effective succession plans for use throughout the organization regarding leadership positions and the management of the human capital that will fill those positions. Certainly with respect to the CEO, a fully developed and effective succession plan deals with actions to take for the purpose of selecting, developing, evaluating, and compensating the CEO. Obvious benefits from an effective CEO succession plan include those of supporting the firm's corporate governance procedures and increasing stakeholders' confidence that the board is acting in their best interests. In this regard, some analysts believe that "when a robust plan provides for a smooth CEO transition—whether a company is faced with a planned or an emergency succession—it will yield returns for stakeholders." Indeed, effective succession planning and execution are "absolutely vital to a company's sustainability."

In spite of the statistics reported here, a number of firms do have active succession plans in place. For example, Ford Motor Company's vice president of communications says that the firm "takes succession planning very seriously" and that the company has "succession plans in place for each of (its) key leadership positions." As is true with many companies though, Ford does not discuss its *specific* succession plans externally for competitive reasons. Many are interested to learn about Berkshire Hathaway's CEO succession plans. Warren Buffett, the firm's long-term CEO, has noted for several years in the firm's annual report that plans are in place and that in all likelihood, his job will be split into two (with one person becoming CEO of Berkshire's operating company and a second one assuming the leadership of Berkshire's investment portfolio).

In addition to selecting a new CEO from the formally defined internal and external managerial labor markets, a

*Gilt Groupe CEO Michelle Peluso assumed the position of CEO after previously serving on the firm's board of directors.*

trend of selecting a CEO from the firm's board of directors may be emerging. For example, board member Michelle Peluso was selected as Gilt Group's CEO to replace founder and then-current CEO Kevin Ryan. (Founded in 2007, Gilt Group offers "flash sales" opportunities to customers to buy luxury items at substantially reduced prices. Firms are willing to sell at steep discounts in order to reduce overstocked inventories.) As is the case with Peluso, a key advantage is that as a board member, an individual is deeply familiar with the firm's operations and the opportunities and threats facing it. Thus, "the director-turned-CEO succession model provides companies with a chief executive who is familiar with corporate strategy and key stakeholders, thereby reducing leadership transition risk."

Sometimes a firm "selects" a former CEO to return to the firm he or she previously led. This is the situation with A. G. Lafley at Procter & Gamble as described in this chapter's Opening Case. It is also the situation with India's Infosys Ltd., where founder and former CEO N. R. Narayana Murthy was brought back as the firm's CEO "in response to shareholder demands to revive the struggling technology company." Regardless of the approach used, the critical issue is for a firm's board of directors to intentionally form and then effectively use managerial succession plans that will best represent stakeholders' interests.

Sources: 2013, CEO succession planning and talent considerations, *Risk & Compliance Journal*, www.deloitte.wsj.com, May 28; 2013, CFO change at Time Warner Cable may underscore CEO succession, *CFO Journal*, www.blogs.wsj.com, May 1; 2013, Succession planning, *SpencerStuart*, www.stuartspencer.com, February; 2013, The experts: Do companies spend too much on 'superstar' CEOs? *Wall Street Journal*, www.wsj.com, March 14; 2013, More companies looking outside for their next CEO, *The Conference Board*, www.conference-board.org, May 1; V. Fuhrmans, 2013, GM names new Opel chief, *Wall Street Journal*, www.wsj.com, January 31; D. A. Thoppil, 2013, Infosys brings back founder, *Wall Street Journal*, www.wsj.com, June 1.

**Figure 12.4** Exercise of Effective Strategic Leadership

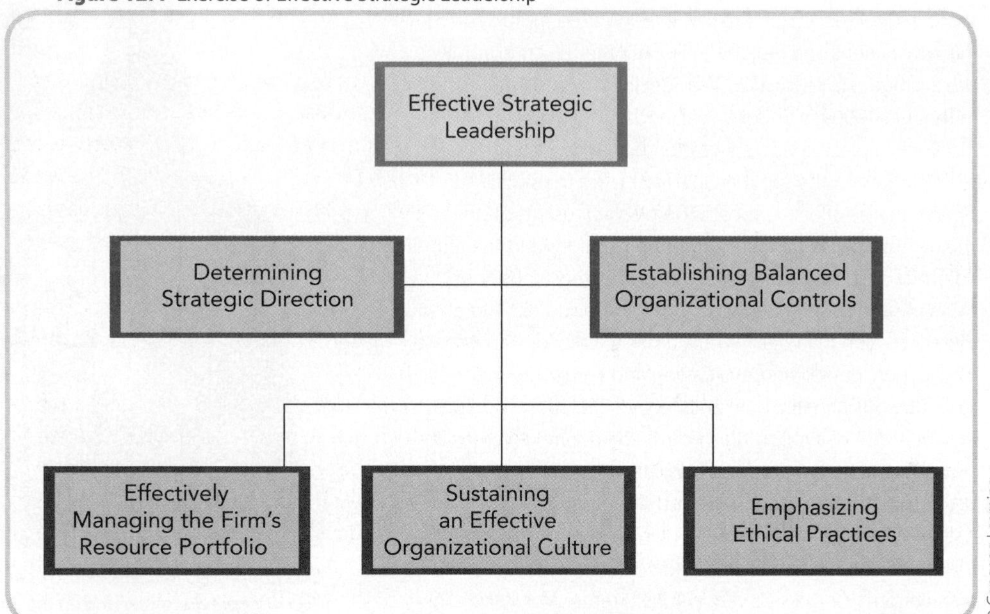


the conditions (i.e., opportunities and threats) strategic leaders expect their firm to face in roughly the next three to five years.

The ideal long-term strategic direction has two parts: a core ideology and an envisioned future. The core ideology motivates employees through the company's heritage while the envisioned future encourages them to stretch beyond their expectations of accomplishment and requires significant change and progress to be realized.[66] The envisioned future serves as a guide to many aspects of a firm's strategy implementation process, including motivation, leadership, employee empowerment, and organizational design. The strategic direction could include a host of actions such as entering new international markets and developing a set of new suppliers to add to the firm's value chain.[67]

Sometimes though, the work of strategic leaders does not result in selecting a strategy that helps a firm reach the vision that is part of its strategic direction. This can happen when top management team members and certainly the CEO are too committed to the status quo. While the firm's strategic direction remains rather stable across time, actions taken to implement strategies to reach that direction should be somewhat fluid, largely so the firm can deal with unexpected opportunities and threats that surface in the external environment.

An inability to adjust strategies as appropriate is often caused by an aversion to what decision makers conclude are risky actions. An aversion to perceived risk is common in firms that have performed well in the past and for CEOs who have been in their jobs for extended periods of time.[68] Research also suggests that some CEOs are erratic or even ambivalent in their choices of strategic direction, especially when their competitive environment is turbulent and it is difficult to identify the best strategy.[69] Of course, these behaviors are unlikely to produce high performance and may lead to CEO turnover. Interestingly, research has found that incentive compensation in the form of stock options encourages talented executives to select the best strategies and thus achieve the highest performance. However, the same incentives used with less talented executives produce lower performance.[70]

In contrast to risk-averse CEOs, charismatic ones may foster stakeholders' commitment to a new vision and strategic direction. Nonetheless, even when being guided by a charismatic CEO, it is important for the firm not to lose sight of its strengths and weaknesses when making changes required by a new strategic direction. The most effective charismatic CEO leads a firm in ways that are consistent with its culture and with the actions permitted by its capabilities and core competencies.[71]

Finally, being ambicultural can facilitate efforts to determine the firm's strategic direction and select and use strategies to reach it. Being ambicultural means that strategic leaders are committed to identifying the best organizational activities to take particularly when implementing strategies, regardless of their cultural origin.[72] Ambicultural actions help the firm succeed in the short term as a foundation for reaching its vision in the longer term.[73]

## 12-4b Effectively Managing the Firm's Resource Portfolio

Effectively managing the firm's portfolio of resources is another critical strategic leadership action. The firm's resources are categorized as financial capital, human capital, social capital, and organizational capital (including organizational culture).[74]

Clearly, financial capital is critical to organizational success; strategic leaders understand this reality.[75] However, the most effective strategic leaders recognize the equivalent importance of managing each remaining type of resource as well as managing the integration of resources (e.g., using financial capital to provide training opportunities to the firm's human capital). Most importantly, effective strategic leaders manage the firm's resource portfolio by organizing the resources into capabilities, structuring the firm to facilitate using those capabilities, and choosing strategies through which the capabilities can be successfully leveraged to create value for customers.[76] Exploiting and maintaining core competencies and developing and retaining the firm's human and social capital are actions taken to reach these important objectives.

### Exploiting and Maintaining Core Competencies

Examined in Chapters 1 and 3, *core competencies* are capabilities that serve as a source of competitive advantage for a firm over its rivals. Typically, core competencies relate to skills within organizational functions such as manufacturing, finance, marketing, and research and development. Strategic leaders must verify that the firm's core competencies are understood when selecting strategies and then emphasized when implementing those strategies. This suggests, for example, that with respect to their strategies, Apple understands and emphasizes its design competence while Netflix recognizes and concentrates on its competence of being able to deliver physical, digital, and original content.[77]

Core competencies are developed over time as firms learn from the results of the competitive actions and responses taken during the course of competing with rivals. On the basis of what they learn, firms continuously reshape their capabilities for the purpose of verifying that they are indeed the path through which core competencies are being developed and used to establish one or more competitive advantages.

Dan Akerson became CEO of GM in July, 2009, a time when the firm required a transformation in order to survive as the foundation for then being able to compete successfully against its global rivals. One of the first decisions Akerson made was to allocate resources for the purpose of building new capabilities in technology development and in marketing, especially in customer service. In turn, he wants the firm to find ways to develop these capabilities into core competencies.[78]

Efforts to reach these goals remain in place. With respect to customer service for example, GM now offers "two years of free oil changes, tire rotations and vehicle inspections on most new vehicle sales…"[79] The firm hopes that these services will increase customer loyalty and create "buzz" around its efforts to "upgrade" its Chevrolet portfolio. To further enhance its technological capabilities, GM hired 4,000 high technology workers who are to develop proprietary software for the firm's use and increased its total capital expenditures from $6.2 billion in 2011 to $8.1 billion in 2012.[80]

As we discuss next, human capital and social capital are critical to a firm's success. This is the case for GM as the firm strives to continuously improve its performance. One reason for human capital's importance is that it is the resource through which core competencies are developed and used.

## Developing Human Capital and Social Capital

**Human capital** refers to the knowledge and skills of a firm's entire workforce. From the perspective of human capital, employees are viewed as a capital resource requiring continuous investment.[81]

Bringing talented human capital into the firm and then developing that capital has the potential to yield positive outcomes. A key reason for this is that individuals' knowledge and skills are proving to be critical to the success of many global industries (e.g., automobile manufacturing) as well as industries within countries (e.g., leather and shoe manufacturing in Italy). This fact suggests that "as the dynamics of competition accelerate, people are perhaps the only truly sustainable source of competitive advantage."[82] In all types of organizations—large and small, new and established, and so forth—human capital's increasing importance suggests a significant role for the firm's human resource management function.[83] As one of a firm's support functions on which firms rely to create value (see Chapter 3), human resource management practices facilitate selecting and especially implementing the firm's strategies.[84]

**Human capital** refers to the knowledge and skills of a firm's entire workforce.

Effective training and development programs increase the probability that some of the firm's human capital will become effective strategic leaders. Increasingly, the link between effective programs and firm success is becoming stronger in that the knowledge gained by participating in these programs is integral to forming and then sustaining a firm's competitive advantage.[85] In addition to building human capital's knowledge and skills, these programs inculcate a common set of core values and present a systematic view of the organization, thus promoting its vision and helping form an effective organizational culture.

*A firm's human capital is critical to its success. One of strategic leaders most important responsibilities is developing human capital.*

© Goodluz/Shutterstock.com

Effective training and development programs also contribute positively to the firm's efforts to form core competencies.[86] Furthermore, the programs help strategic leaders improve skills that are critical to completing other tasks associated with effective strategic leadership, such as determining the firm's strategic direction, exploiting and maintaining the firm's core competencies, and developing an organizational culture that supports ethical practices. Thus, building human capital is vital to the effective execution of strategic leadership.

When investments in human capital (such as providing high-quality training and development programs) are successful, the outcome is a workforce capable of learning continuously. This is an important outcome in that continuous learning and leveraging the firm's expanding knowledge base are linked with strategic success.[87]

Learning also can preclude errors. Strategic leaders may learn more from failure than success because they sometimes make the wrong attributions for the successes.[88] For example, the effectiveness of certain approaches and knowledge can be context specific. Thus, some "best practices" may not work well in all situations. We know that using teams to make decisions can be effective, but sometimes it is better for leaders to make decisions alone, especially when the decisions must be made and implemented quickly (e.g., in crisis situations).[89] As such, effective strategic leaders recognize the importance of learning from success *and* from failure when helping their firm use the strategic management process.

When facing challenging conditions, firms may decide to lay off some of their human capital, a decision that can result in a significant loss of knowledge. Research shows that moderate-sized layoffs may improve firm performance primarily in the short run, but large layoffs produce stronger performance downturns in firms because of the loss of human capital.[90] Although it is also not uncommon for restructuring firms to reduce their investments in training and development programs, restructuring may actually be an important time to increase investments in these programs. The reason for this is that restructuring firms have less slack and cannot absorb as many errors; moreover, the employees who remain after layoffs may find themselves in positions without all the skills or knowledge they need to create value through their work.

Viewing employees as a resource to be maximized rather than as a cost to be minimized facilitates successful implementation of a firm's strategies, as does the strategic leader's ability to approach layoffs in a manner that employees believe is fair and equitable. A critical issue for employees is the fairness in the layoffs and how they are treated in their jobs, especially relative to their peers.[91]

**Social capital** involves relationships inside and outside the firm that help in efforts to accomplish tasks and create value for stakeholders.[92] Social capital is a critical asset given that employees must cooperate with one another and others, including suppliers and customers, in order to complete their work. In multinational organizations, employees often must cooperate across country boundaries on activities such as R&D to achieve performance objectives (e.g., developing new products).[93]

External social capital is increasingly critical to firm success in that few if any companies possess all of the resources needed to successfully compete against their rivals. Firms can use cooperative strategies such as strategic alliances (see Chapter 9) to develop social capital. Social capital can be built in strategic alliances as firms share complementary resources. Resource sharing must be effectively managed to ensure that the partner trusts the firm and is willing to share its resources.[94] Social capital created this way yields many benefits. For example, firms with strong social capital are able to be more ambidextrous; that is, they can develop or have access to multiple capabilities providing them with the flexibility to take advantage of opportunities and to respond to threats.[95]

Research evidence suggests that the success of many types of firms may partially depend on social capital. Large multinational firms often must establish alliances in order to enter new foreign markets; entrepreneurial firms often must establish alliances to gain access to resources, venture capital, or other types of resources (e.g., special expertise that the entrepreneurial firm cannot afford to maintain in-house).[96] However, a firm's culture affects its ability to retain quality human capital and maintain strong internal social capital.

**Social capital** involves relationships inside and outside the firm that help in efforts to accomplish tasks and create value for stakeholders.

## 12-4c Sustaining an Effective Organizational Culture

In Chapter 1, we defined *organizational culture* as the complex set of ideologies, symbols, and core values that are shared throughout the firm and influence how the firm conducts business. Because organizational culture influences how the firm conducts its business and helps regulate and control employees' behavior, it can be a source of competitive advantage.[97] Given that each firm's culture is unique, it is possible that a vibrant organizational culture is an increasingly important source of differentiation for firms to emphasize when pursuing strategic competitiveness and above-average returns. Thus, shaping the context within which the firm formulates and implements its strategies—that is, shaping the organizational culture—is another key strategic leadership action.[98]

### Entrepreneurial Mind-Set

Especially in large organizations, an organizational culture often encourages (or discourages) strategic leaders and those with whom they work from pursuing (or not pursuing) entrepreneurial opportunities. (We define and discuss entrepreneurial opportunities in some detail in Chapter 13.) This is the case in both for-profit and not-for-profit organizations.[99] This issue is important because entrepreneurial opportunities are a vital source of growth and innovation.[100] Therefore, a key action for strategic leaders to take is to encourage and promote innovation by pursuing entrepreneurial opportunities.[101]

One way to encourage innovation is to invest in opportunities as real options—that is, invest in an opportunity in order to provide the potential option of taking advantage of the opportunity at some point in the future.[102] For example, a firm might buy a piece of land to have the option to build on it at some time in the future should the company need more space and should that location increase in value to the company. Oil companies take out land leases with an option to drill for oil. Firms might enter strategic alliances for similar reasons. In this instance, a firm might form an alliance to have the option of acquiring the partner later or of building a stronger relationship with it (e.g., developing a new joint venture).[103]

*A firm's entrepreneurial mindset is composed of five dimensions: autonomy, innovativeness, risk taking, proactiveness, and competitive aggressiveness.*

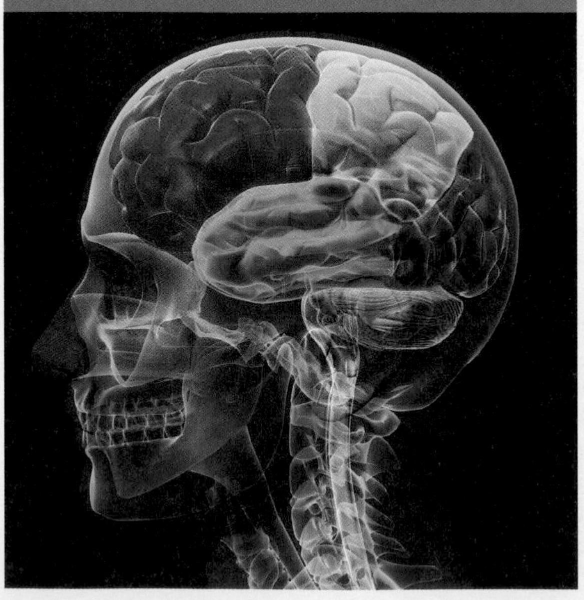



In Chapter 13, we describe how firms of all sizes use strategic entrepreneurship to pursue entrepreneurial opportunities as a means of earning above-average returns. Companies are more likely to achieve the success they desire by using strategic entrepreneurship when their employees have an entrepreneurial mind-set.[104]

Five dimensions characterize a firm's entrepreneurial mind-set: autonomy, innovativeness, risk taking, proactiveness, and competitive aggressiveness.[105] In combination, these dimensions influence the actions a firm takes to be innovative when using the strategic management process.

*Autonomy,* the first of an entrepreneurial orientation's five dimensions, allows employees to take actions that are free of organizational constraints and encourages them to do so. The second dimension, *innovativeness,* "reflects a firm's tendency to engage in and support new ideas, novelty, experimentation, and creative processes that may result in new products, services, or technological processes."[106] Cultures with a tendency toward innovativeness encourage employees to think beyond existing knowledge, technologies, and parameters to find creative ways to add value. *Risk taking* reflects a willingness by employees and their firm to accept measured levels of risks when pursuing entrepreneurial opportunities. The fourth dimension of an entrepreneurial orientation, *proactiveness,* describes a firm's ability to be a market leader rather than a follower. Proactive organizational cultures constantly use processes to anticipate future market needs and to satisfy them before competitors learn how to do so. Finally, *competitive aggressiveness* is a firm's propensity to take actions that allow it to consistently and substantially outperform its rivals.[107]

### Changing the Organizational Culture and Restructuring

Changing a firm's organizational culture is more difficult than maintaining it; however, effective strategic leaders recognize when change is needed. Incremental changes to the firm's culture typically are used to implement strategies.[108] More significant and sometimes even radical changes to organizational culture support selecting strategies that differ from those the firm has implemented historically. Regardless of the reasons for change, shaping and reinforcing a new culture requires effective communication and problem solving, along with selecting the right people (those who have the values desired for the organization), engaging in effective performance appraisals (establishing goals that support the new core values and measuring individuals' progress toward reaching them), and using appropriate reward systems (rewarding the desired behaviors that reflect the new core values).[109]

Evidence suggests that cultural changes succeed only when the firm's CEO, other key top management team members, and middle-level managers actively support them.[110] To effect change, middle-level managers in particular need to be highly disciplined to energize the culture and foster alignment with the firm's vision and mission.[111] In addition, managers must be sensitive to the effects of other changes on organizational culture. For example, downsizings can negatively affect an organization's culture, especially if they are not implemented in accordance with the dominant organizational values.[112]

## 12-4d Emphasizing Ethical Practices

The effectiveness of processes used to implement the firm's strategies increases when they are based on ethical practices. Ethical companies encourage and enable people at all levels to act ethically when doing what is necessary to implement strategies. In turn, ethical practices and the judgment on which they are based create "social capital" in the organization, increasing the "goodwill available to individuals and groups" in the organization.[113] Alternatively, when unethical practices evolve in an organization, they may become acceptable to many managers and employees.[114] Once deemed acceptable, individuals are more likely to engage in unethical practices to meet their goals when current efforts to meet them are insufficient.[115]

To properly influence employees' judgment and behavior, ethical practices must shape the firm's decision-making process and be an integral part of organizational culture. In fact, a values-based culture is the most effective means of ensuring that employees comply with the firm's ethical standards. However, developing such a culture requires constant nurturing and support in corporations located in countries throughout the world.[116]

As explained in Chapter 10, some strategic leaders and managers may occasionally act opportunistically, making decisions that are in their own best interests. This tends to happen when firms have lax expectations in place for individuals to follow regarding ethical behavior. In other words, individuals acting opportunistically take advantage of their positions, making decisions that benefit themselves to the detriment of the firm's stakeholders.[117] Strategic leaders as well as others in the organization are most likely to integrate ethical values into their decisions when the company has explicit ethics codes, the code is integrated into the business through extensive ethics training, and shareholders expect ethical behavior.[118] Thus, establishing and enforcing a meaningful code of ethics is an important action to take to encourage ethical decision making as a foundation for using the strategic management process.

Strategic leaders can take several actions to develop and support an ethical organizational culture. Examples of these actions include (1) establishing and communicating specific goals to describe the firm's ethical standards (e.g., developing and disseminating a code of conduct); (2) continuously revising and updating the code of conduct, based on inputs from people throughout the firm and from other stakeholders; (3) disseminating the code of conduct to all stakeholders to inform them of the firm's ethical standards and practices; (4) developing and implementing methods and procedures to use in achieving the firm's ethical standards (e.g., using internal auditing practices that are consistent with the standards); (5) creating and using explicit reward systems that recognize acts of courage (e.g., rewarding those who use proper channels and procedures to report observed wrongdoings); and (6) creating a work environment in which all people are treated with dignity.[119] The effectiveness of these actions increases when they are taken simultaneously and thereby are mutually supportive. When strategic leaders and others throughout the firm fail to take actions such as these—perhaps because an ethical culture has not been created—problems are likely to occur.

## 12-4e Establishing Balanced Organizational Controls

Organizational controls (discussed in Chapter 11) have long been viewed as an important part of the strategic management process particularly the parts related to implementation (see Figure 1.1). Controls are necessary to help ensure that firms achieve their desired outcomes. Defined as the "formal, information-based … procedures used by managers to maintain or alter patterns in organizational activities," controls help strategic leaders build credibility, demonstrate the value of strategies to the firm's stakeholders, and promote and support strategic change.[120] Most critically, controls provide the parameters for implementing strategies as well as the corrective actions to be taken when implementation-related adjustments are required. For example, in light of an insider-trading scandal, KPMG LLP recently announced that it intends to consider the possibility of enhancing its training and monitoring programs. The firm's existing safeguards "include training for employees, a whistleblower system and monitoring of the personal investments of partners and managers."[121]

In this chapter, we focus on two organizational controls—strategic and financial—that were introduced in Chapter 11. Strategic leaders are responsible for helping the firm develop and properly use these two types of controls.

As we explained in Chapter 11, financial control focuses on short-term financial outcomes. In contrast, strategic control focuses on the *content* of strategic actions rather than their *outcomes*. Some strategic actions can be correct but still result in poor financial outcomes because of external conditions such as an economic recession, unexpected domestic or foreign government actions, or natural disasters. Therefore, emphasizing financial controls often produces more short-term and risk-averse decisions, because financial outcomes may be caused by events beyond leaders and managers' direct control. Alternatively, strategic control encourages lower-level managers to make decisions that incorporate moderate and acceptable levels of risk because leaders and managers throughout the firm share the responsibility for the outcomes of those decisions and actions resulting from them.

The challenge for strategic leaders is to balance the use of strategic and financial controls for the purpose of supporting efforts to improve the firm's performance. The Balanced Scorecard is a tool strategic leaders use to achieve the sought after balance.

### The Balanced Scorecard

The **balanced scorecard** is a tool firms use to determine if they are achieving an appropriate balance when using strategic and financial controls as a means of positively influencing performance.[122] This tool is most appropriate to use when evaluating business-level strategies; however, it can also be used with the other strategies firms implement (e.g., corporate, international, and cooperative).

The **balanced scorecard** is a tool firms use to determine if they are achieving an appropriate balance when using strategic and financial controls as a means of positively influencing performance.

The underlying premise of the balanced scorecard is that firms jeopardize their future performance when financial controls are emphasized at the expense of strategic controls.[123]

This occurs because financial controls provide feedback about outcomes achieved from past actions but do not communicate the drivers of future performance. Thus, an overemphasis on financial controls may promote behavior that sacrifices the firm's long-term, value-creating potential for short-term performance gains.[124] An appropriate balance of strategic controls and financial controls, rather than an overemphasis on either, allows firms to achieve higher levels of performance.

Four perspectives are integrated to form the balanced scorecard: *financial* (concerned with growth, profitability, and risk from the shareholders' perspective), *customer* (concerned with the amount of value customers perceive was created by the firm's products), *internal business processes* (with a focus on the priorities for various business processes that create customer and shareholder satisfaction), and *learning and growth* (concerned with the firm's effort to create a climate that supports change, innovation, and growth). Thus, using the balanced scorecard finds the firm seeking to understand how it responds to shareholders (financial perspective), how customers view it (customer perspective), the processes to emphasize to successfully use its competitive advantage (internal perspective), and what it can do to improve its performance in order to grow (learning and growth perspective).[125] Generally speaking, firms tend to emphasize strategic controls when assessing their performance relative to the learning and growth perspective, whereas the tendency is to emphasize financial controls when assessing performance in terms of the financial perspective.

Firms use different criteria to measure their standing relative to the scorecard's four perspectives. We show sample criteria in Figure 12.5. The firm should select the number of

**Figure 12.5** Strategic Controls and Financial Controls in a Balanced Scorecard Framework

| Perspectives | Criteria |
|---|---|
| Financial | • Cash flow<br>• Return on equity<br>• Return on assets |
| Customer | • Assessment of ability to anticipate customers' needs<br>• Effectiveness of customer service practices<br>• Percentage of repeat business<br>• Quality of communications with customers |
| Internal Business Processes | • Asset utilization improvements<br>• Improvements in employee morale<br>• Changes in turnover rates |
| Learning and Growth | • Improvements in innovation ability<br>• Number of new products compared to competitors<br>• Increases in employees' skills |

criteria that will allow it to have both a strategic and financial understanding of its performance without becoming immersed in too many details.[126]

Strategic leaders play an important role in determining a proper balance between strategic and financial controls, whether they are in single-business firms or large diversified firms. A proper balance between controls is important, in that "wealth creation for organizations where strategic leadership is exercised is possible because these leaders make appropriate investments for future viability [through strategic control], while maintaining an appropriate level of financial stability in the present [through financial control]."[127] In fact, most corporate restructuring is designed to refocus the firm on its core businesses, thereby allowing top executives to reestablish strategic control of their separate business units.[128]

Successfully using strategic control frequently is integrated with appropriate autonomy for the various subunits so that they can gain a competitive advantage in their respective markets.[129] Strategic control can be used to promote the sharing of both tangible and intangible resources among interdependent businesses within a firm's portfolio. In addition, the autonomy provided allows the flexibility necessary to take advantage of specific marketplace opportunities. As a result, strategic leadership promotes simultaneous use of strategic control and autonomy.

As we have explained in this chapter, strategic leaders are critical to a firm's ability to successfully use all parts of the strategic management process, including strategic entrepreneurship, which is the final topic included in the "strategy" part of this book's Analysis-Strategy-Performance model. We turn our attention to this topic in the final chapter.

## SUMMARY

- Effective strategic leadership is a prerequisite to successfully using the strategic management process. Strategic leadership entails the ability to anticipate events, envision possibilities, maintain flexibility, and empower others to create strategic change.
- Top-level managers are an important resource for firms to develop and exploit competitive advantages. In addition, when they and their work are valuable, rare, imperfectly imitable, and nonsubstitutable, strategic leaders are also a source of competitive advantage.
- The top management team is composed of key managers who play a critical role in selecting and implementing the firm's strategies. Generally, they are officers of the corporation and/or members of the board of directors.
- The top management team's characteristics, a firm's strategies, and its performance are all interrelated. For example, a top management team with significant marketing and research and development (R&D) knowledge positively contributes to the firm's use of a growth strategy. Overall, having diverse skills increases the effectiveness of most top management teams.
- Typically, performance improves when the board of directors and the CEO are involved in shaping a firm's strategic direction. However, when the CEO has a great deal of power, the board may be less involved in decisions about strategy formulation and implementation. By appointing people to the board and simultaneously serving as CEO and chair of the board, CEOs increase their power.
- In managerial succession, strategic leaders are selected from either the internal or the external managerial labor market. Because of their effect on firm performance, the selection of strategic leaders has implications for a firm's effectiveness. There are a variety of reasons that companies select the firm's strategic leaders from either internal or external sources. In most instances, the internal market is used to select the CEO, but the number of outsiders chosen is increasing. Outsiders often are selected to initiate major changes in strategy.
- Effective strategic leadership has five key leadership actions: determining the firm's strategic direction, effectively managing the firm's resource portfolio (including exploiting and maintaining core competencies and managing human capital and social capital), sustaining an effective organizational culture, emphasizing ethical practices, and establishing balanced organizational controls.
- Strategic leaders must develop the firm's strategic direction, typically working with the board of directors to do so. The strategic direction specifies the image and character the firm wants to develop over time. To form the strategic direction, strategic leaders evaluate the conditions (e.g., opportunities and threats in the external environment) they expect their firm to face over the next three to five years.

- Strategic leaders must ensure that their firm exploits its core competencies, which are used to produce and deliver products that create value for customers, when implementing its strategies. In related diversified and large firms in particular, core competencies are exploited by sharing them across units and products.
- The ability to manage the firm's resource portfolio and the processes used to effectively implement its strategy are critical elements of strategic leadership. Managing the resource portfolio includes integrating resources to create capabilities and leveraging those capabilities through strategies to build competitive advantages. Human capital and social capital are perhaps the most important resources.
- As a part of managing resources, strategic leaders must develop a firm's human capital. Effective strategic leaders view human capital as a resource to be maximized—not as a cost to be minimized. Such leaders develop and use programs designed to train current and future strategic leaders to build the skills needed to nurture the rest of the firm's human capital.
- Effective strategic leaders build and maintain internal and external social capital. Internal social capital promotes cooperation and coordination within and across units in the firm. External social capital provides access to resources the firm needs to compete effectively.
- Shaping the firm's culture is a central task of effective strategic leadership. An appropriate organizational culture encourages the development of an entrepreneurial mind-set among employees and an ability to change the culture as necessary.
- In ethical organizations, employees are encouraged to exercise ethical judgment and to always act ethically. Improved ethical practices foster social capital. Setting specific goals to meet the firm's ethical standards, using a code of conduct, rewarding ethical behaviors, and creating a work environment where all people are treated with dignity are actions that facilitate and support ethical behavior.
- Developing and using balanced organizational controls is the final key leadership action associated with effective strategic leadership. The balanced scorecard is a tool that measures the effectiveness of the firm's strategic and financial controls. An effective balance between these two controls allows for flexible use of core competencies, but within the parameters of the firm's financial position.

## REVIEW QUESTIONS

1. What is strategic leadership? Why are top-level managers considered to be important resources for an organization?
2. What is a top management team, and how does it affect a firm's performance and its abilities to innovate and design and bring about effective strategic change?
3. What is the managerial succession process? How important are the internal and external managerial labor markets to this process?
4. What is the effect of strategic leadership on determining the firm's strategic direction?
5. How do strategic leaders effectively manage their firm's resource portfolio to exploit its core competencies and leverage the human capital and social capital to achieve a competitive advantage?
6. What must strategic leaders do to develop and sustain an effective organizational culture?
7. As a strategic leader, what actions could you take to establish and emphasize ethical practices in your firm?
8. Why are strategic controls and financial controls important aspects of strategic leadership and the firm's strategic management process?

## EXPERIENTIAL EXERCISES

### EXERCISE 1: THE CEO AND THE TOP MANAGEMENT TEAM

Corporate governance and the fiduciary role the board of directors plays as it oversees the company's operations were examined in Chapter 10. The composition of the top management team is critical in assessing the strategic direction of a firm. It is not uncommon for a powerful CEO and top management team to thwart the desires of the board. There are various ways in which a CEO may become powerful; it may be the result of equity ownership, tenure, expertise, or by appointing sympathetic board members. This exercise will allow you to assess the power of a CEO and his or her team and develop your thoughts regarding their relationship to the board.

### Part One

Identify with your team the firm you would like to study. Pick a company that is publicly traded so that you have adequate information about the executives.

### Part Two

Explore the power relationship between the CEO and his/her top management team (TMT) and the board. You should at a minimum be able to address the following points:

1. CEO tenure
2. TMT tenure
3. TMT relationships to the CEO (i.e., were they hired during the tenure of the current CEO or his/her predecessor?)
4. Board member tenure and structure (i.e., does the board structure possess a lead independent director? Is CEO duality present?)
5. Describe the CEO and his/her TMT in terms of experience and networks. For example, do members of the TMT sit on other firms' boards of directors? Are there any overlaps with their employer's board?
6. What conclusions do you reach regarding the power relationship between the CEO and the board?

Be prepared to discuss this utilizing a PowerPoint presentation of your findings and conclusions.

## EXERCISE 2: HOW COME THEY HIRED THAT PERSON?

According to a study by Booz & Co., 15% of CEOs left their large public corporations in 2012, the second highest turnover percentage since the consulting firm started keeping records over a decade ago. There is some thinking that this 15% or so is the new normal and that firms' boards are becoming less willing to allow an incumbent CEO to remain when performance or other issues arise. Of course many of these turnover events are scheduled as a result of the board undertaking its fiduciary role in planning for the succession of an incumbent.

ABC News ran a report on the most recent top 7 CEO disasters. They named, in no particular order:

- Ron Johnson, J.C. Penney
- John Riccitiello, Electronic Arts Inc
- Andrew Mason, Groupon
- Brian Dunn, Best Buy
- Andrea Jung, Avon
- Leo Apotheker, HP
- Christopher Kubasik, Lockheed Martin

In your teams, analyze one of the above CEO dismissals with the approval of your instructor. During your analysis, answer at a minimum the following questions:

1. Characterize the dismissal. Why was the CEO fired?
2. Examine the replacement in terms of either the external or internal labor market. Why did the company choose one over the other?
3. Does it appear that a succession plan was in place?
4. Describe the impact of the CEO dismissal upon the top management team.

Be prepared to present your results in class.

# VIDEO CASE ▶

## AN EXAMPLE OF STRATEGIC LEADERSHIP: MEG WHITMAN, FORMER CEO OF EBAY

Meg Whitman, former CEO of eBay and current CEO of Hewlett-Packard (HP), is a pioneer at creating a global marketplace and contributing to the development of an e-commerce revolution. However, Whitman has encountered challenges and difficulties while achieving the significant levels of success she has recorded. The long hours she has worked sacrifices time with her family, a reality for which she occasionally feels somewhat guilty. To some degree though, Whitman's love of working with others within corporations and helping individuals reach their potential as they contribute to their firm's success allows her to feel that she is facilitating the growth and development of an entire corporation such as eBay. Despite having trade-offs between home and work, Whitman contends that she would do it all over again. Whitman resigned as CEO of eBay in November 2007, but remained on the board and served as an advisor to the current CEO, John Donahoe, until late 2008. Whitman left a very positive legacy as a result of her effectiveness as eBay's CEO. Of course, she seeks to make positive, value-creating contributions during her current work as HP's CEO.

After watching the video, be prepared to discuss the following concepts and questions in class:

### Concepts

- Strategic leadership
- Top management team
- Human capital
- Social capital
- Organizational culture

## Questions

1. In what ways did Meg Whitman's characteristics and the orientations resulting from them contribute to her effectiveness as CEO at eBay?
2. How is Meg Whitman appropriate for a top management team?
3. What do you think would be Whitman's approach to human capital?
4. How important is social capital to eBay's success?
5. What was the organizational culture like at eBay during Whitman's time as the firm's CEO? Is there evidence that an entrepreneurial mind-set was a part of that culture? If so, what is that evidence?

## NOTES


1. C.-N. Chung & X. R. Luo, 2013, Leadership succession and firm performance in an emerging economy: Successor origin, relational embeddedness, and legitimacy, *Strategic Management Journal*, 34: 338–357; A. Mackey, 2008, The effect of CEOs on firm performance, *Strategic Management Journal*, 29: 1357–1367.
2. V. Govindarajan, 2012, The timeless strategic value of unrealistic goals, *HBR Blog Network*, www.hbr.org, October 22.
3. B.-J. Moon, 2013, Antecedents and outcomes of strategic thinking, *Journal of Business Research*, 66: 1698–1708; M. A. Hitt, K. T. Haynes, & R. Serpa, 2010, Strategic leadership for the 21st century, *Business Horizons*, 53: 437–444; R. D. Ireland & M. A. Hitt, 2005, Achieving and maintaining strategic competitiveness in the 21st century: The role of strategic leadership, *Academy of Management Executive*, 19: 63–77.
4. M. T. Hansen, H. Ibarra, & U. Peyer, 2013, The best-performing CEOs in the world, *Harvard Business Review*, 91(1): 81–95; M. D. Watkins, 2012, How managers become leaders, *Harvard Business Review*, 90(6): 65–72.
5. B. A. Campbell, R. Coff, & D. Kryscynski, 2012, Rethinking sustained competitive advantage from human capital, *Academy of Management Review*, 37: 376–395; M. A. Hitt, C. Miller, & A. Colella, 2011, *Organizational Behavior*, 3rd ed., Hoboken, NJ: John Wiley & Sons.
6. M. A. Axtle-Ortiz, 2013, Perceiving the value of intangible assets in context, *Journal of Business Research*, 56: 417–424.
7. P. J. H. Schoemaker, S. Krupp, & S. Howland, 2013, Strategic leadership: The essential skills, *Harvard Business Review*, 91(1/2): 131–134.
8. J. J. Sosik, W. A. Gentry, & J. U. Chun, 2012, The value of virtue in the upper echelons: A multisource examination of executive character strengths and performance, *Leadership Quarterly*, 23: 367–382.
9. D. M. Cable, F. Gino, & B. R. Staats, 2013, Breaking them in or eliciting their best? Reframing socialization and newcomers' authentic self-expression, *Administrative Science Quarterly*, 58: 1–36; T. Hulzschenreuter, I. Kleindienst, & C. Greger, 2012, How new leaders affect strategic change following a succession event: A critical review of the literature, *The Leadership Quarterly*, 23: 729–755.
10. J. Ewing, 2012, Embattled German steel maker reports a huge loss, *New York Times*, www.nytimes.com, December 11.
11. J. C. Ryan & S. A. A. Tipu, 2013, Leadership effects on innovation propensity: A two-factor full range of leadership model, *Journal of Business Research*, 66: 2116–2129; A. E. Colbert, A. L. Kristof-Brown, B. H. Bradley, & M. R. Barrick, 2008, CEO transformational leadership: The role of goal importance congruence in top management teams, *Academy of Management Journal*, 51: 81–96.
12. T. G. Buchholz, 2007, The Kroc legacy at McDonald's, *The Conference Review Board*, July/August, 14–15.
13. H. S. Givray, 2007, When CEOs aren't leaders, *BusinessWeek*, September 3, 102.
14. Y. Dong, M.-G. Seo, & K. Bartol, 2013, No pain, no gain: An affect-based model of developmental job experience and the buffering effects of emotional intelligence, *Academy of Management Journal*, in press; D. Goleman, 2004, What makes a leader? *Harvard Business Review*, 82(1): 82–91.
15. C. M. Leitch, C. McMullan, & R. T. Harrison, 2013, The development of entrepreneurial leadership: The role of human, social and institutional capital, *British Journal of Management*, 24: 347–366; Y. Ling, Z. Simsek, M. H. Lubatkin, & J. F. Veiga, 2008, Transformational leadership's role in promoting corporate entrepreneurship: Examining the CEO-TMT interface, *Academy of Management Journal*, 51: 557–576.
16. T. Hutzschenreuter & I. Kleindienst, 2013, (How) does discretion change over time? A contribution toward a dynamic view of managerial discretion, *Scandinavian Journal of Management*, in press; T. L. Waldron, S. D. Graffin, J. F. Porac, & J. B. Wade, 2013, Third-party endorsements of CEO quality, managerial discretion, and stakeholder reactions, *Journal of Business Research*, in press.
17. R. Klingebiel, 2012, Options in the implementation plan of entrepreneurial initiatives: Examining firms' attainment of flexibility benefit, *Strategic Entrepreneurship Journal*, 6: 307–334; D. G. Sirmon, J.-L. Arregle, M. A. Hitt, & J. W. Webb, 2008, The role of family influence in firms' strategic responses to threat of imitation, *Entrepreneurship Theory and Practice*, 32: 979–998.
18. M. Menz, 2012, Functional top management team members: A review, synthesis, and research agenda, *Journal of Management*, 38: 45–80; A. M. L. Raes, U. Glunk, M. G. Heijitjes, & R. A. Roe, 2007, Top management team and middle managers, *Small Group Research*, 38: 360–386.
19. A. Ganter & A. Hecker, 2013, Configurational paths to organizational innovation: Qualitative comparative analyses of antecedents and contingencies, *Journal of Business Research*, in press; O. R. Mihalach, J. J. P. Jansen, F. A. J. Van Den Bosch, & H. W. Volberda, 2012, Offshoring and firm innovation: The moderating role of top management team attributes, *Strategic Management Journal*, 33: 1480–1498.
20. J. Li & Y. Tang, 2010, CEO hubris and firm risk taking in China: The moderating role of managerial discretion, *Academy of Management Journal*, 53: 45–68; M. L. A. Hayward, V. P. Rindova, & T. G. Pollock, 2004, Believing one's own press: The causes and consequences of CEO celebrity, *Strategic Management Journal*, 25: 637–653.
21. J. J. Reuer, T. W. Tong, & C.-W. Wu, 2012, A signaling theory of acquisition premiums: Evidence from IPO targets, *Academy of Management Journal*, 55: 667–683.
22. A. Carmeli, A. Tishler, & A. C. Edmondson, 2012, CEO relational leadership and strategic decision quality in top management teams: The role of team trust and learning from failure, *Strategic Organization*, 10: 31–54; V. Souitaris & B. M. M. Maestro, 2010, Polychronicity in top management teams: The impact on strategic decision processes and performance in new technology ventures, *Strategic Management Journal*, 31: 652–678.
23. R. Olie, A. van Iteraon, & Z. Simsek, 2012–13, When do CEOs versus top management

teams matter in explaining strategic decision-making processes? Toward an institutional view of strategic leadership effects, *International Studies of Management and Organization*, 42(4): 86–105; Y. Ling & F. W. Kellermans, 2010, The effects of family firm specific sources of TMT diversity: The moderating role of information exchange frequency, *Journal of Management Studies*, 47: 322–344.

24. R. Klingebiel & A. De Meyer, 2013, Becoming aware of the unknown: Decision making during the implementation of a strategic initiative, *Organization Science*, 24: 133–153; A. Srivastava, K. M. Bartol, & E. A. Locke, 2006, Empowering leadership in management teams: Effects on knowledge sharing, efficacy, and performance, *Academy of Management Journal*, 49: 1239–1251; D. Knight, C. L. Pearce, K. G. Smith, J. D. Olian, H. P. Sims, K. A. Smith, & P. Flood, 1999, Top management team diversity, group process, and strategic consensus, *Strategic Management Journal*, 20: 446–465.

25. T. Buyl, C. Boone, W. Hendricks, & P. Matthyssens, 2011, Top management team functional diversity and firm performance: The moderating role of CEO characteristics, *Journal of Management Studies*, 48: 151–177; B. J. Olson, S. Parayitam, & Y. Bao, 2007, Strategic decision making: The effects of cognitive diversity, conflict, and trust on decision outcomes, *Journal of Management*, 33: 196–222.

26. S. Finkelstein, D. C. Hambrick, & A. A. Cannella, Jr., 2008, *Strategic Leadership: Top Executives and Their Effects on Organizations*, New York: Oxford University Press.

27. A. Minichilli, G. Corbetta, & I. C. Macmillan, 2010, Top management teams in family-controlled companies: 'Familiness', 'faultlines', and their impact on financial performance, *Journal of Management Studies*, 47: 205–222; J. J. Marcel, 2009, Why top management team characteristics matter when employing a chief operating officer: A strategic contingency perspective, *Strategic Management Journal*, 30: 647–658.

28. J. I. Canales, 2013, Constructing interlocking rationales in top-driven strategic renewal, *British Journal of Management*, in press; B. J. Avolio & S. S. Kahai, 2002, Adding the "e" to e-leadership: How it may impact your leadership, *Organizational Dynamics*, 31: 325–338.

29. T. Buyl, C. Boone, & W. Hendriks, 2013, Top management team members' decision influence and cooperative behavior: An empirical study in the information technology industry, *British Journal of Management*, in press; Z. Simsek, J. F. Veiga, M. L. Lubatkin, & R. H. Dino, 2005, Modeling the multilevel determinants of top management team behavioral integration, *Academy of Management Journal*, 48: 69–84.

30. A. A. Cannella, J. H. Park, & H. U. Lee, 2008, Top management team functional background diversity and firm performance: Examining the roles of team member collocation and environmental uncertainty, *Academy of Management Journal*, 51: 768–784.

31. A. S. Cui, R. J. Calantone, & D. A. Griffith, 2011, Strategic change and termination of interfirm partnerships, *Strategic Management Journal*, 32: 402–423; M. Jensen & E. J. Zajac, 2004, Corporate elites and corporate strategy: How demographic preferences and structural position shape the scope of the firm, *Strategic Management Journal*, 25: 507–524.

32. A. E. Colbert, M. R. Barrick, & B. H. Bradley, 2013, Personality and leadership composition in top management teams: Implications for organizational effectiveness, *Personnel Psychology*, in press; S. Nadkarni & P. Hermann, 2010, CEO personality, strategic flexibility and firm performance: The case of the Indian business process outsourcing industry, *Academy of Management Journal*, 53: 1050–1073.

33. K. Liu, J. Li, W. Hesterly, & A. A. Cannella, Jr., 2012, Top management team tenure and technological inventions at post-IPO biotechnology firms, *Journal of Business Research*, 65: 1349–1356; H. Li & J. Li, 2009, Top management team conflict and entrepreneurial strategy making in China, *Asia Pacific Journal of Management*, 26: 263–283; S. C. Parker, 2009, Can cognitive biases explain venture team homophily? *Strategic Entrepreneurship Journal*, 3: 67–83.

34. J. Tian, J. Haleblian, & N. Rajagopalan, 2011, The effects of board human and social capital on investor reactions to new CEO selection, *Strategic Management Journal*, 32: 731–747; Y. Zhang & N. Rajagopalan, 2003, Explaining the new CEO origin: Firm versus industry antecedents, *Academy of Management Journal*, 46: 327–338.

35. P. Y. T. Sun & M. H. Anderson, 2012, Civic capacity: Building on transformational leadership to explain successful integrative public leadership, *The Leadership Quarterly*, 23: 309–323; I. Barreto, 2010, Dynamic capabilities: A review of the past research and an agenda for the future, *Journal of Management*, 36: 256–280.

36. M. L. McDonald & J. D. Westphal, 2010, A little help here? Board control, CEO identification with the corporate elite, and strategic help provided to CEOs at other firms, *Academy of Management Journal*, 53: 343–370; L. Tihanyi, R. A. Johnson, R. E. Hoskisson, & M. A. Hitt, 2003, Institutional ownership and international diversification: The effects of boards of directors and technological opportunity, *Academy of Management Journal*, 46: 195–211.

37. K. B. Lewellyn & M. I. Muller-Kahle, 2012, CEO power and risk taking: Evidence from the subprime lending industry, *Corporate Governance: An International Review*, 20: 289–307; S. Wu, X. Quan, & L. Xu, 2011, CEO power, disclosure quality and the variability in firm performance, *Nankai Business Review International*, 2: 79–97; B. R. Golden & E. J. Zajac, 2001, When will boards influence strategy? Inclination times power equals strategic change, *Strategic Management Journal*, 22: 1087–1111.

38. S. Kaczmarek, S. Kimino, & A. Pye, 2012, Antecedents of board composition: The role of nomination committees, *Corporate Governance: An International Review*, 20: 474–489; M. Carpenter & J. Westphal, 2001, Strategic context of external network ties: Examining the impact of director appointments on board involvement in strategic decision making, *Academy of Management Journal*, 44: 639–660.

39. M. van Essen, P.-J. Engelen, & M. Carney, 2013, Does 'good' corporate governance help in a crisis? The impact of country- and firm-level governance mechanisms in the European financial crisis, *Corporate Governance: An International Review*, 21: 201–224; M. A. Abebe, A. Angriawan, & Y. Lui, 2011, CEO power and organizational turnaround in declining firms: Does environment play a role? *Journal of Leadership and Organizational Studies*, 18: 260–273.

40. C.-H. Liao & A. W.-H. Hsu, 2013, Common membership and effective corporate governance: Evidence from audit and compensation committees, *Corporate Governance: An International Review*, 21: 79-92.

41. C. P. Cullinan, P. B. Roush, & X. Zheng, 2012, CEO/Chair duality in the Sarbanes-Oxley era; board independence versus unity of command, *Research on Professional Responsibility and Ethics in Accounting*, 16: 167–183; C. S. Tuggle, D. G. Sirmon, C. R. Reutzel, & L. Bierman, 2010, Commanding board of director attention: Investigating how organizational performance and CEO duality affect board members' attention to monitoring, *Strategic Management Journal*, 32: 640–657; J. Coles & W. Hesterly, 2000, Independence of the chairman and board composition: Firm choices and shareholder value, *Journal of Management*, 26: 195–214.

42. R. Krause & M. Semadeni, 2013, Apprentice, departure, and demotion: An examination of the three types of CEO-board chair separation, *Academy of Management Journal*, 56: 805–826.

43. M. van Essen, P.-J. Engelen, & M. Carney, 2013, Does "good" corporate governance help in a crisis? The impact of country- and firm-level governance mechanisms in the European financial crisis, *Corporate Governance: An International Review*, 21: 201–224.

44. E. Matta & P. W. Beamish, 2008, The accentuated CEO career horizon problem: Evidence from international acquisitions, *Strategic Management Journal*, 29: 683–700; N. Rajagopalan & D. Datta, 1996, CEO characteristics: Does industry matter? *Academy of Management Journal*, 39: 197–215.

45. B. W. Lewis, J. L. Walls, & G. W. S. Dowell, 2013, Difference in degrees: CEO

characteristics and firm environmental disclosure, *Strategic Management Journal*, 34: in press; R. A. Johnson, R. E. Hoskisson, & M. A. Hitt, 1993, Board involvement in restructuring: The effect of board versus managerial controls and characteristics, *Strategic Management Journal*, 14 (Special Issue): 33–50.

46. Z. Simsek, 2007, CEO tenure and organizational performance: An intervening model, *Strategic Management Journal*, 28: 653–662.

47. X. Luo, V. K. Kanuri, & M. Andrews, 2013, How does CEO tenure matter? The mediating role of firm-employee and firm-customer relationships, *Strategic Management Journal*, 34: in press.

48. M. Hernandez, 2012, Toward an understanding of the psychology of stewardship, *Academy of Management Review*, 37: 172–193.

49. B. K. Boyd, M. F. Santos, & W. Shen, 2012, International developments in executive compensation, *Corporate Governance: An International Review*, 20: 511–518; D. Miller, I. LeBreton-Miller, & B. Scholnick, 2008, Stewardship vs. stagnation: An empirical comparison of small family and non-family businesses, *Journal of Management Studies*, 51: 51–78; J. H. Davis, F. D. Schoorman, & L. Donaldson, 1997, Toward a stewardship theory of management, *Academy of Management Review*, 22: 20–47.

50. A. Holehonnur & T. Pollock, 2013, Shoot for the stars? Predicting the recruitment of prestigious directors at newly public firms, *Academy of Management Journal*, in press; B. Espedal, O. Kvitastein, & K. Gronhaug, 2012, When cooperation is the norm of appropriateness: How does CEO cooperative behavior affect organizational performance? *British Journal of Management*, 23: 257–271.

51. X. Zhang, N. Li, J. Ullrich, & R. van Dick, 2013, Getting everyone on board: The effect of differentiated transformational leadership by CEOs on top management team effectiveness and leader-related firm performance, *Journal of Management*, in press.

52. S. D. Graffin, S. Boivie, & M. A. Carpenter, 2013, Examining CEO succession and the role of heuristics in early-stage CEO evaluation, *Strategic Management Journal*, 34: 383–403; W. Shen & A. A. Cannella, 2002, Revisiting the performance consequences of CEO succession: The impacts of successor type, postsuccession senior executive turnover, and departing CEO tenure, *Academy of Management Journal*, 45: 717–734.

53. J. P. Donlon, 2013, 40 best companies for leaders 2013, *Chief Executive*, www.chiefexecutive.net, January 12.

54. 2013, Deloitte, Perspectives on family-owned businesses: Governance and succession planning, www.deloitte.com, January.

55. 2013, Intersearch survey reveals status of CEO succession plans in companies around the world, Intersearch, www.pendlpiswanger.at/images/content/file/Artikel/CEO succession, February.

56. S. Mobbs & C. G. Raheja, 2012, Internal managerial promotions: Insider incentives and CEO succession, *Journal of Corporate Finance*, 18: 1337–1353; S. Rajgopal, D. Taylor, & M. Venkatachalam, 2012, Frictions in the CEO labor market: The role of talent agents in CEO compensation, *Contemporary Accounting Research*, 29: 119–151.

57. 2013, 2013 Q1 S&P CEO transitions, SpencerStuart, www.spencerstuart.com, May.

58. A. Guarino & D. X. Martin, 2013, The $40 trillion succession risk: Most boards think it's hedged, but it isn't, Korn/Ferry Institute, www.kornferry.com, March.

59. B. Jopson, 2013, P&G reshuffle to help line up Lafley successor, *Financial Times*, www.ft.com, May 31.

60. C. M. Elson & C. K. Ferrere, 2012, When searching for a CEO, there's no place like home, *Wall Street Journal*, www.wsj.com, October 29.

61. Y. Zhang & N. Rajagopalan, 2010, Once an outsider, always an outsider? CEO origin, strategic change and firm performance, *Strategic Management Journal*, 31: 334–346.

62. V. Mehrotra, R. Morck, J. Shim, & Y. Wiwattanakantang, 2013, Adoptive expectations: Rising sons in Japanese family firms, *Journal of Financial Economics*, 108: 840–854; G. A. Ballinger & J. J. Marcel, 2010, The use of an interim CEO during succession episodes and firm performance, *Strategic Management Journal*, 31: 262–283.

63. K. Grind, J. S. Lublin, & M. Lamar, 2013, Daunting challenges at Legg Mason, *Wall Street Journal*, www.wsj.com, February 13.

64. T. Hutzschenreuter, I. Kleindienst, & C. Greger, 2012, How new leaders affect strategic change following a succession event: A critical review of the literature, *The Leadership Quarterly*, 23: 729–755; J. Kotter, 2012, Accelerate! *Harvard Business Review*, 90(11): 45–58.

65. L. Mirabeau & S. Maguire, 2013, From autonomous strategic behavior to emergent strategy, *Strategic Management Journal*, 34: in press; G. A. Shinkle, A. P. Kriauciunas, & G. Hundley, 2013, Why pure strategies may be wrong for transition economy firms, *Strategic Management Journal*, 34: in press.

66. P. Herrmann & S. Nadkarni, 2013, Managing strategic change: The duality of CEO personality, *Strategic Management Journal*, 34: in press; T. Barnett, R. G. Long, & L. E. Marler, 2012, Vision and exchange in intra-family succession: Effects on procedural justice climate among nonfamily managers, *Entrepreneurship Theory and Practice*, 36: 1207–1225.

67. S. Mantere, H. A. Schildt, & J. A. A. Sillince, 2012, Reversal of strategic change, *Academy of Management Journal*, 55: 172–196; S. Sonenshein, 2012, Explaining employee engagement with strategic change implementation: A meaning-making approach, *Organization Science*, 23: 1–23.

68. P. Chaigneau, 2013, Explaining the structure of CEO incentive pay with decreasing relative risk aversion, *Journal of Economics and Business*, 67(May/June): 4–23; G. Chen & D. C. Hambrick, 2012, CEO replacement in turnaround situations: Executive (mis) fit and its performance implications, *Organization Science*, 23: 225–243; P. L. McClelland, X. Ling, & V. L. Barker, 2010, CEO commitment to the status quo: Replication and extension using content analysis, *Journal of Management*, 36: 1251–1277.

69. J. R. Mitchell, D. A. Shepherd, & M. P. Sharfman, 2011, Erratic strategic decisions: When and why managers are inconsistent in strategic decision making, *Strategic Management Journal*, 32: 683–704; N. Plambeck & K. Weber, 2010, When the glass is half full and half empty: CEOs' ambivalent interpretations of strategic issues, *Strategic Management Journal*, 31: 689–710.

70. A. J. Wowak & D. C. Hambrick, 2010, A model of person-pay interaction: How executives vary in their response to compensation arrangements, *Strategic Management Journal*, 31: 803–821.

71. C. P. M. Wilderom, P. T. van den Berg, & U. J. Wiersma, 2012, A longitudinal study of the effects of charismatic leadership and organizational culture on objective and perceived corporate performance, *The Leadership Quarterly*, 23: 835–848.

72. M.-J. Chen & D. Miller, 2012, West meets east: Toward an ambicultural approach to management, *Academy of Management Perspectives*, 24: 17–24; M.-J. Chen & D. Miller, 2011, The relational perspective as a business mindset: Managerial implications for East and West, *Academy of Management Perspectives*, 25: 6–18.

73. M. Y. C. Chen, C. Y. Y. Lin, H.-E. Lin, & E. F. McDonough, III, 2012, Does transformational leadership facilitate technological innovation? The moderating roles of innovative culture and incentive compensation, *Asia Pacific Journal of Management*, 29: 239–264.

74. M. D. Huesch, 2013, Are there always synergies between productive resources and resource deployment capabilities? *Strategic Management Journal*, 34: in press; J. Kraaijenbrink, J.-C. Spender, & A. J. Groen, 2010, The resource-based view: A review and assessment of its critiques, *Journal of Management*, 36: 349–372; J. Barney & A. M. Arikan, 2001, The resource-based view: Origins and implications, in M. A. Hitt, R. E. Freeman, & J. S. Harrison (eds.), *Handbook of Strategic Management*, Oxford, UK: Blackwell Publishers, 124–188.

75. S. D. Julian & J. C. Ofori-dankwa, 2013, Financial resource availability and corporate social responsibility expenditures in a sub-Saharan economy: The institutional difference hypothesis, *Strategic Management Journal*, 34: in press;

T. Vanacker, V. Collewaert, & I. Pacleman, 2013, The relationship between slack resources and the performance of entrepreneurial firms: The role of venture capital and angel investors, *Journal of Management Studies*, in press.

76. E. A. Clinton, S. Sciascia, R. Yadav, & F. Roche, 2013, Resource acquisition in family firms: The role of family-influenced human and social capital, *Entrepreneurship Research Journal*, 3: 44–61; H. A. Ndofor, D. G. Sirmon & X. He, 2011, Firm resources, competitive actions and performance: Investigating a mediated model with evidence from the in-vitro diagnostics industry, *Strategic Management Journal*, 32: 640–657.
77. A. Carr, 2013, Death to core competency: Lessons from Nike, Apple, Netflix, *Fast Company*, www.fastcompany.com, February 14.
78. B. Simon, 2011, GM's new chief executive in reshuffle, *Financial Times*, www..ft.com, January 20.
79. J. Bennett, 2013, GM offers free car-care to bolster U.S. sales, *Wall Street Journal*, www.wsj.com, June 6.
80. M. Wayland, 2013, GM CEO and chairman Dan Akerson's remarks at 2013 annual shareholders meeting, *MLive*, http://blog.mlive.com, June 6.
81. A. J. Nyberg & R. E. Ployhart, 2013, Context-emergent turnover (CET) theory: A theory of collective turnover, *Academy of Management Review*, 38: 109–131; R. E. Ployhart, C. H. Van Idderkinge, & W. J. MacKenzie, 2011, Acquiring and developing human capital in service contexts: The interconnectedness of human capital resources, *Academy of Management Journal*, 54: 353–368; N. W. Hatch & J. H. Dyer, 2004, Human capital and learning as a source of sustainable competitive advantage, *Strategic Management Journal*, 25: 1155–1178.
82. M. A. Hitt, L. Bierman, K. Uhlenbruck, & K. Shimizu, 2006, The importance of resources in the internationalization of professional service firms: The good, the bad and the ugly, *Academy of Management Journal*, 49: 1137–1157; M. A. Hitt, L. Bierman, K. Shimizu, & R. Kochhar, 2001, Direct and moderating effects of human capital on strategy and performance in professional service firms: A resource-based perspective, *Academy of Management Journal*, 44: 13–28.
83. H. Aquinis, H. Joo, & R. K. Gottfredson, 2013, What monetary rewards can and cannot do: How to show employees the money, *Business Horizons*, 56: 241–249; M. F. Correia, R. Campose Cunha, & M. Scholten, 2013, Impact of M&A on organizational performance: The moderating role of HRM centrality, *European Management Journal*, 31: 323–332.
84. R. R. Kehoe & P. M. Wright, 2013, The impact of high-performance human resource practices on employees' attitudes and behaviors, *Journal of Management*, 39: 366–391.
85. Z. J. Zhao & J. Anand, 2013, Beyond boundary spanners: The 'collective bridge' as an efficient interunit structure for transferring collective knowledge, *Strategic Management Journal*, 34: in press; J. Pfeffer, 2010, Building sustainable organizations: The human factor, *Academy of Management Perspectives*, 24(1): 34–45.
86. K. Z. Zhou & C. B. Li, 2012, How knowledge affects radical innovation: Knowledge base, market knowledge acquisition, and internal knowledge sharing, *Strategic Management Journal*, 33: 1090–1102.
87. J. R. Lecuona & M. Reitzig, 2013, Knowledge worth having in 'excess': The value of tacit and firm-specific human resource slack, *Strategic Management Journal*, 34: in press; T. R. Holcomb, R. D. Ireland, R. M. Holmes, & M. A. Hitt, 2009, Architecture of entrepreneurial learning: Exploring the link among heuristics, knowledge, and action, *Entrepreneurship, Theory & Practice*, 33: 173–198.
88. Y. Zheng, A. S. Miner, & G. George, 2013, Does the learning value of individual failure experience depend on group-level success? Insights from a university technology transfer office, *Industrial and Corporate Change*, in press; R. Hirak, A. C. Peng, A. Carneli, & J. M. Schaubroeck, 2012, Linking leader inclusiveness to work unit performance: The importance of psychological safety and learning from failure, *The Leadership Quarterly*, 23: 107–117.
89. Hitt, Miller, & Colella, *Organizational Behavior*.
90. R. Hoskisson, W. Shi, H. Yi, & J. Jin, 2013, The evolution and strategic positioning of private equity firms, *Academy of Management Perspectives*, 27: 22–38; P. M. Norman, F. C. Butler, & A. L. Ranft, 2013, Resources matter: Examining the effects of resources on the state of firms following downsizing, *Journal of Management*, in press; R. D. Nixon, M. A. Hitt, H. Lee, & E. Jeong, 2004, Market reactions to corporate announcements of downsizing actions and implementation strategies, *Strategic Management Journal*, 25: 1121–1129.
91. R. J. Bies, 2013, The delivery of bad news in organizations: A framework for analysis, *Journal of Management*, 39: 136–162; B. C. Holtz, 2013, Trust primacy: A model of the reciprocal relations between trust and perceived justice, *Journal of Management*, 37: in press.
92. C. Galunic, G. Krtug, & M. Gargiulo, 2012, The positive externalities of social capital: Benefiting from senior brokers, *Academy of Management Journal*, 55: 1213–1231; P. S. Adler & S. W. Kwon, 2002, Social capital: Prospects for a new concept, *Academy of Management Review*, 27: 17–40.
93. Y.-Y. Chang, Y. Gong, & M. W. Peng, 2012, Expatriate knowledge transfer, subsidiary absorptive capacity, and subsidiary performance, *Academy of Management Journal*, 55: 927–948; S. Gao, K. Xu, & J. Yang, 2008, Managerial ties, Absorptive capacity & innovation, *Asia Pacific Journal of Management*, 25: 395–412.
94. K. H. Heimeriks, M. Schijven, & S. Gates, 2012, Manifestations of higher-order routines: The underlying mechanisms of deliberate learning in the context of postacquisition integration, *Academy of Management Journal*, 55: 703–726; P. Ozcan & K. M. Eisenhardt, 2009, Origin of alliance portfolios: Entrepreneurs, network strategies, and firm performance, *Academy of Management Journal*, 52: 246–279; W. H. Hoffmann, 2007, Strategies for managing a portfolio of alliances, *Strategic Management Journal*, 28: 827–856.
95. Q. Cao, Z. Simsek, & H. Zhang, 2010, Modelling the joint impact of the CEO and the TMT on organizational ambidexterity, *Journal of Management Studies*, 47: 1272–1296; A. S. Alexiev, J. J. P. Jansen, F. A. J. Van den Bosch. & H. W. Volberda, 2010, Top management team advice seeking and exploratory innovation: The moderating role of TMT heterogeneity, *Journal of Management Studies*, 47: 1343–1364.
96. G. Cuevas-Rodriguez, C. Cabello-Medina, & A. Carmona-Lavado, 2013, Internal and external social capital for radical product innovation: Do they always work well together? *British Journal of Management*, in press; B. J. Hallen & K. M. Eisenhardt, 2012, Catalyzing strategies and efficient tie formation: How entrepreneurial firms obtain investment ties, *Academy of Management Journal*, 55: 35–70.
97. A. Klein, 2011, Corporate culture: Its value as a resource for competitive advantage, *Journal of Business Strategy*, 32(2): 21–28; J. B. Barney, 1986, Organizational culture: Can it be a source of sustained competitive advantage? *Academy of Management Review*, 11: 656–665.
98. B. Schneider, M. G. Ehrhart, & W. H. Macey, 2013, Organizational climate and culture, *Annual Review of Psychology*, 64: 361–388; E. F. Goldman & A. Casey, 2010, Building a culture that encourages strategic thinking, *Journal of Leadership and Organizational Studies*, 17: 119–128.
99. P. G. Klein, J. T. Mahoney, A. M. McGahan, & C. N. Pitelis, 2013, Capabilities and strategic entrepreneurship in public organizations, *Strategic Entrepreneurship Journal*, 7: 70–91; R. D. Ireland, J. G. Covin, & D. F. Kuratko, 2009, Conceptualizing corporate entrepreneurship strategy, *Entrepreneurship Theory and Practice*, 33(1): 19–46.
100. M. S. Wood, A. McKelvie, & J. M. Haynie, 2013, Making it personal: Opportunity individuation and the shaping of opportunity beliefs, *Journal of Business Venturing*, in press; R. D. Ireland & J. W. Webb, 2007, Strategic entrepreneurship: Creating competitive advantage through streams of innovation, *Business Horizons*, 50: 49–59.
101. P. L. Schultz, A. Marin, & K. B. Boal, 2013, The impact of media on the legitimacy

of new market categories: The case of broadband internet, *Journal of Business Venturing*, in press; S. A. Alvarez & J. B. Barney, 2008, Opportunities, organizations and entrepreneurship, *Strategic Entrepreneurship Journal*, 2: 171–174.

102. R. E. Hoskisson, M. A. Hitt, R. D. Ireland, & J. S. Harrison, 2013, *Competing for Advantage*, 3rd ed., Thomson Publishing, Mason, OH. Y. Li & T. Chi, 2013, Venture capitalists' decision to withdraw: The role of portfolio configuration from a real options lens, *Strategic Management Journal*, 34: in press.

103. T. W. Tong & S. Li, 2013, The assignment of call option rights between partners in international joint ventures, *Strategic Management Journal*, 34: in press.

104. C. Bjornskov & N. Foss, 2013, How strategic entrepreneurship and the institutional context drive economic growth, *Strategic Entrepreneurship Journal*, 7: 50–69; M. A. Hitt, R. D. Ireland, D. G. Sirmon, & C. A. Trahms, 2011, Strategic entrepreneurship: Creating value for individuals, organizations and society, *Academy of Management Perspectives*, 25(2): 57–75; P. G. Kein, 2008, Opportunity discovery, entrepreneurial action and economic organization, *Strategic Entrepreneurship Journal*, 2: 175–190.

105. G. T. Lumpkin & G. G. Dess, 1996, Clarifying the entrepreneurial orientation construct and linking it to performance, *Academy of Management Review*, 21: 135–172.

106. Lumpkin & Dess, Clarifying the entrepreneurial orientation construct, 142.

107. Ibid., 137.

108. C. L. Wang & M. Rafiq, 2013, Ambidextrous organizational culture, contextual ambidexterity and new product innovation: A comparative study of UK and Chinese high-tech firms, *British Journal of Management*, in press; P. Pyoria, 2007, Informal organizational culture: The foundation of knowledge workers' performance, *Journal of Knowledge Management*, 11(3): 16–30.

109. A. W. Langvardt, 2012, Ethical leadership and the dual roles of examples, *Business Horizons*, 55: 373–384; M. Kuenzi & M. Schminke, 2009, Assembling fragments into a lens: A review, critique, and proposed research agenda for the organizational work climate literature, *Journal of Management*, 35: 634–717.

110. M. N. Kastanakis & B. G. Voyer, 2013, The effect of culture on perception and cognition: A conceptual framework, *Journal of Business Research*, in press; J. Kotter, 2011, Corporate culture: Whose job is it? *Forbes*, http://blog.forbes.com/johnkotter, February 17.

111. M. I. Garces & P. Morcillo, 2012, The role of organizational culture in the resource-based view: An empirical study of the Spanish nuclear industry, *International Journal of Strategic Change Management*, 4: 356–378; E. Mollick, 2012, People and process, suits and innovators: the role of individuals in firm performance, *Strategic Management Journal*, 33: 1001–1015.

112. W. McKinley, S. Latham, & M. Braun, 2013, Organizational decline and innovation: Turnarounds and downward spirals, *Academy of Management Review*, in press; R. Fehr & M. J. Gelfand, 2012, The forgiving organization: A multilevel model of forgiveness at work, *Academy of Management Review*, 37: 664–688; E. G. Love & M. Kraatz, 2009, Character, conformity, or the bottom line? How and why downsizing affected corporate reputation, *Academy of Management Journal*, 52: 314–335.

113. Adler & Kwon, Social capital.

114. J. L. Campbell & A. S. Goritz, 2013, Culture corrupts! A qualitative study of organizational culture in corrupt organizations, *Journal of Business Ethics*, in press; J. Pinto, C. R. Leana, & F. K. Pil, 2008, Corrupt organizations or organizations of corrupt individuals? Two types of organization-level corruption, *Academy of Management Review*, 33: 685–709.

115. A. Arnaud & M. Schminke, 2012, The ethical climate and context of organizations: A comprehensive model, *Organization Science*, 23: 1767–1780; M. E. Scheitzer, L. Ordonez, & M. Hoegl, 2004, Goal setting as a motivator of unethical behavior, *Academy of Management Journal*, 47: 422–432.

116. J. A. Pearce, 2013, Using social identity theory to predict managers' emphases on ethical and legal values in judging business issues, *Journal of Business Ethics*, 112: 497–514; M. Zhao, 2013, Beyond cops and robbers: The contextual challenge driving the multinational corporation public crisis in China and Russia, *Business Horizons*, 56: 491–501.

117. I. Okhmaztovksiy & R. J. David, 2012, Setting your own standards: Internal corporate governance codes as a response to institutional pressure, *Organization Science*, 23: 155–176; X. Zhang, K. M. Bartol, K. G. Smith, M. D. Pfaffer, & D. M. Khanin, 2008, CEOs on the edge: Earnings manipulation and stock-based incentive misalignment, *Academy of Management Journal*, 51: 241–258; M. A. Hitt & J. D. Collins, 2007, Business ethics, strategic decision making, and firm performance, *Business Horizons*, 50: 353–357.

118. M. S. Schwartz, 2013, Developing and sustaining an ethical corporate culture: The core elements, *Business Horizons*, 56: 39–50; J. M. Stevens, H. K. Steensma, D. A. Harrison, & P. L. Cochran, 2005, Symbolic or substantive document? Influence of ethics codes on financial executives' decisions, *Strategic Management Journal*, 26: 181–195.

119. W. H. Bishop, 2013, The role of ethics in 21st century organizations, *Journal of Business Ethics*, in press; B. E. Ashforth, D. A. Gioia, S. L. Robinson, & L. K. Trevino, 2008, Re-viewing organizational corruption, *Academy of Management Review*, 33: 670–684.

120. Control (management), 2013, *Wikipedia*, http://en.wikipedia.org/wiki/control, June 6; M. D. Shields, F. J. Deng, & Y. Kato, 2000, The design and effects of control systems: Tests of direct- and indirect-effects models, *Accounting, Organizations and Society*, 25: 185–202.

121. M. Rapoport, 2013, KPMG finds its safeguards 'sound and effective,' *Wall Street Journal*, www.wsj.com, June 4.

122. M. Friesl & R. Silberzahn, 2012, Challenges in establishing global collaboration: Temporal, strategic and operational decoupling, *Long Range Planning*, 45: 160–181; R. S. Kaplan & D. P. Norton, 2009, The balanced scorecard: Measures that drive performance (HBR OnPoint Enhanced Edition), *Harvard Business Review*, Boston, MA, March; R. S. Kaplan & D. P. Norton, 2001, The strategy-focused organization, *Strategy & Leadership*, 29(3): 41–42.

123. B. E. Becker, M. A. Huselid, & D. Ulrich, 2001, *The HR Scorecard: Linking People, Strategy, and Performance*, Boston: Harvard Business School Press, 21.

124. R. S. Kaplan & D. P. Norton, 2001, Transforming the balanced scorecard from performance measurement to strategic management: Part I, *Accounting Horizons*, 15(1): 87–104.

125. R. S. Kaplan, 2012, The balanced scorecard: Comments on balanced scorecard commentaries, *Journal of Accounting and Organizational Change*, 8: 539–545; R. S. Kaplan & D. P. Norton, 1992, The balanced scorecard—measures that drive performance, *Harvard Business Review*, 70(1): 71–79.

126. A. Danaei & A. Hosseini, 2013, Performance measurement using balanced scorecard: A case study of pipe industry, *Management Science Letters*, 3: 1433–1438; M. A. Mische, 2001, *Strategic Renewal: Becoming a High-Performance Organization*, Upper Saddle River, NJ: Prentice Hall, 181.

127. G. Rowe, 2001, Creating wealth in organizations: The role of strategic leadership, *Academy of Management Executive*, 15(1): 81–94.

128. J. Xia & S. Li, 2013, The divestiture of acquired subunits: A resource dependence approach, *Strategic Management Journal*, 34: 131–148; R. E. Hoskisson, R. A. Johnson, D. Yiu, & W. P. Wan, 2001, Restructuring strategies of diversified business groups: Differences associated with country institutional environments, in M. A. Hitt, R. E. Freeman, & J. S. Harrison (eds.), *Handbook of Strategic Management*, Oxford, UK: Blackwell Publishers, 433–463.

129. J. Wincent, S. Thorgren, & S. Anokhin, 2013, Managing maturing government-supported networks: The shift from monitoring to embeddedness controls, *British Journal of Management*, in press.

# 13

# Strategic Entrepreneurship

***Studying this chapter should provide you with the strategic management knowledge needed to:***

**1** Define strategic entrepreneurship and corporate entrepreneurship.

**2** Define entrepreneurship and entrepreneurial opportunities and explain their importance.

**3** Define invention, innovation, and imitation, and describe the relationship among them.

**4** Describe entrepreneurs and the entrepreneurial mind-set.

**5** Explain international entrepreneurship and its importance.

**6** Describe how firms internally develop innovations.

**7** Explain how firms use cooperative strategies to innovate.

**8** Describe how firms use acquisitions as a means of innovation.

**9** Explain how strategic entrepreneurship helps firms create value.

## INNOVATION'S IMPORTANCE TO COMPETITIVE SUCCESS

In survey after survey, chief executive officers (CEOs) say that innovation (defined in this chapter as a process firms use to create a commercial product from an invention) is critically important to their firm's success, and there is evidence supporting this assessment. For example, research results show that particularly for firms competing in turbulent global business environments and with respect to their efforts to develop innovations internally, "innovation is an important driver of the organic growth necessary to generate sustained, above-average returns." Simultaneously though, a large percentage of CEOs say that they are relatively dissatisfied with the number of innovations their firm is producing. Thus, while CEOs place high value on innovation, they are dissatisfied with the output flowing from their firm's efforts to innovate. In this chapter, we suggest that engaging in strategic entrepreneurship (defined later) is an approach firms can use to deal with this issue in that through strategic entrepreneurship firms learn how to produce a larger quantity of successful innovations.

Successful innovations satisfy needs that are important to customers. For this reason, innovative companies develop and nurture strong ties or relationships with current and potential customers. Identifying product functionalities or features for which companies are willing to pay is a key outcome firms seek when interacting with customers. Increasingly, firms are discovering that a larger number of customers are interested in understanding "a product's sustainability credentials and (are) willing to pay a premium for environmentally sound products and services." Knowing this, firms are then able to pursue innovations that will satisfy customers' needs or interests.

Thus, with a focus on customers, the number of ways companies can innovate is virtually unlimited. For example, some argue that a number of Chinese companies are targeting "middle-market" consumers, defined as individuals who desire to purchase "good enough" products. Broadly speaking, these are products "that emphasize price competitiveness and sufficient functionalities, rather than customization and the most advanced technologies." By focusing on cost innovation, these firms demonstrate their belief that for middle-market customers, firms should orient their innovation efforts to learning how to be highly competitive on price while delivering value with which customers are satisfied in light of the price they pay for a product. Several factors facilitate the efforts of Chinese cost innovators, including a relentless focus on finding "unconventional ways to economize through product design, production processes, or choice of materials" and the intention of producing products with a balance among price, quality, and functions that appeal to middle-market consumers. The important point here is that firms should seek to innovate within the context of a customer's group's needs.

In terms of competitive rivalry (see Chapter 5), successful innovations have competitive implications. This is the case with respect to premeasured pod detergents, a recent innovation in the laundry-soap business. A number of firms now produce this product but Procter & Gamble (P&G) is dominant, with roughly 75 percent of total pod sales. A competitive issue is that some in the industry argue that "Pod is killing the laundry detergent category." How is this possible? At issue here is the fact that an attribute of the innovative pod is that it "ushered in the area of 'unit dose' products." In this sense, consumers use the exact amount of detergent needed each time clothes are washed. The disadvantage for laundry-soap manufacturers is that historically, they could count on extra sales from customers who used too much detergent virtually every time they used a washing machine. With pods, product waste is eliminated, resulting in a reduction in the overall laundry detergent market. The situation with pods highlights the complexity that can be associated with successful innovations!

Sources: D. Boyd & J. Goldenberg, 2013, Think inside the box, *Wall Street Journal*, www.wsj.com, June 14; D. Kiron, N. Kruschwitz, K. Haanaes, M. Reeves, & E. Goh, 2013, The innovation bottom line, *bcg.perspectives*, www.bcgperspectives.com, February 5; M. Krigsman, 2013, The new CIO: Chief innovation officer, *Wall Street Journal*, www.wsj.com, June 10; M. Reeves, K. Haanaes, J. Hollingsworth, & F. L. S. Pasini, Ambidexterity: The art of thriving in complex environments, *bcg.perspectives*, www.bcgperspectives.com, February 19; H. Zablit & B. Chui, 2013, The next wave of Chinese cost innovators, *bcg.perspectives*, bcgperspectives.com, January 23.

Learn more about strategic entrepreneurship.
www.cengagebrain.com

In previous chapters, we noted that *organizational culture* refers to the complex set of ideologies, symbols, and core values that are shared throughout the firm and that influence how the firm conducts business. Thus, as the social energy that drives or fails to drive an organization's actions, culture influences firms' efforts to innovate.[1]

As noted in the Opening Case, establishing effective relationships with various stakeholders and particularly with customers is critical to firms' efforts to innovate. One reason for this is that through these relationships, firms gain access to knowledge that typically has the potential to meaningfully inform the innovations they seek to produce.[2] This association between networks of relationships and innovation exists as firms compete both domestically and internationally.[3] Moreover, this set of relationships helps firms identify opportunities to pursue and strategies to implement to exploit today's opportunities while simultaneously trying to find opportunities to exploit in the future.

The focus of this chapter is on strategic entrepreneurship, which is a framework firms use to effectively integrate their entrepreneurial and strategic actions. More formally, **strategic entrepreneurship** is the taking of entrepreneurial actions using a strategic perspective. In this process, the firm tries to find opportunities in its external environment that it can exploit through innovations. Identifying opportunities to exploit through innovations is the *entrepreneurship* dimension of strategic entrepreneurship; determining the best way to competitively manage the firm's innovation efforts is the *strategic* dimension.[4] Thus, firms using strategic entrepreneurship integrate their actions to find opportunities, innovate, and then implement strategies for the purpose of appropriating value from the innovations they have developed to pursue identified opportunities.[5]

We consider several topics to explain strategic entrepreneurship. First, we examine entrepreneurship and innovation in a strategic context. Definitions of entrepreneurship, entrepreneurial opportunities, and entrepreneurs as those who engage in entrepreneurship to pursue entrepreneurial opportunities are presented. We then describe international entrepreneurship, a process through which firms take entrepreneurial actions outside of their home market. After this discussion, the chapter shifts to descriptions of the three ways firms innovate—internally, through cooperative strategies, and by acquiring other companies.[6] We discuss these methods separately. Not surprisingly, most large firms use all three methods to innovate. The chapter closes with summary comments about how firms use strategic entrepreneurship to create value.

**Strategic entrepreneurship** is the taking of entrepreneurial actions using a strategic perspective.

Before turning to the chapter's topics, we note that a major portion of the material in this chapter deals with entrepreneurship and innovation that takes place in established organizations. This phenomenon is called **corporate entrepreneurship**, which is the use or application of entrepreneurship within an established firm.[7] Corporate entrepreneurship is critical to the survival and success of for-profit organizations[8] as well as public agencies.[9] Of course, innovation and entrepreneurship play a critical role in the degree of success achieved by startup entrepreneurial ventures as well. Because of this, a significant portion of the content examined in this chapter is equally important in both entrepreneurial ventures and established organizations.

## 13-1 Entrepreneurship and Entrepreneurial Opportunities

**Entrepreneurship** is the process by which individuals, teams, or organizations identify and pursue entrepreneurial opportunities without being immediately constrained by the resources they currently control.[10] **Entrepreneurial opportunities** are conditions in which new goods or services can satisfy a need in the market. These opportunities exist because of competitive imperfections in markets and among the factors of production used to produce them or because they were independently developed by entrepreneurs.[11] Entrepreneurial opportunities come in many forms, such as the chance to develop and sell a new product and the chance to sell an existing product in a new market.[12] Firms should be receptive to pursuing entrepreneurial opportunities whenever and wherever they may surface.

As these two definitions suggest, the essence of entrepreneurship is to identify and exploit entrepreneurial opportunities—that is, opportunities others do not see or for which they do not recognize the commercial potential—and manage risks appropriately as they arise.[13] As a process, entrepreneurship results in the "creative destruction" of existing products (goods or services) or methods of producing them and replaces them with new products and production methods.[14] Thus, firms committed to entrepreneurship place high value on individual innovations as well as the ability to continuously innovate across time.[15]

We study entrepreneurship at the level of the individual firm. However, evidence suggests that entrepreneurship is the economic engine driving many nations' economies in the global competitive landscape.[16] Thus, entrepreneurship and the innovation it spawns are important for companies competing in the global economy and for countries seeking to stimulate economic climates with the potential to enhance the living standard of their citizens.

## 13-2 Innovation

In his classic work, Schumpeter argued that firms engage in three types of innovative activities.[17] **Invention** is the act of creating or developing a new product or process. **Innovation** is a process used to create a commercial product from an invention. Thus, innovation follows invention[18] in that invention brings something new into being while innovation brings something new into use. Accordingly, technical criteria are used to determine the success of an invention whereas commercial criteria are used to determine the success of an innovation.[19] Finally, **imitation** is the adoption of a similar innovation by different firms. Imitation usually leads to product standardization, and imitative products often are offered at lower prices but without as many features. Entrepreneurship is critical to innovative activity in that it acts as the linchpin between invention and innovation.[20]

For most companies, innovation is the most critical of the three types of innovative activities. The reason for this is that while many companies are able to create ideas that lead

**Corporate entrepreneurship** is the use or application of entrepreneurship within an established firm.

**Entrepreneurship** is the process by which individuals, teams, or organizations identify and pursue entrepreneurial opportunities without being immediately constrained by the resources they currently control.

**Entrepreneurial opportunities** are conditions in which new goods or services can satisfy a need in the market.

**Invention** is the act of creating or developing a new product or process.

**Innovation** is a process used to create a commercial product from an invention.

**Imitation** is the adoption of a similar innovation by different firms.

Learn more about innovation.
www.cengagebrain.com

to inventions, commercializing those inventions sometimes proves to be difficult.[21] Patents are a strategic asset and the ability to regularly produce them can be an important source of competitive advantage, especially when a firm intends to commercialize an invention and when it competes in a knowledge-intensive industry (e.g., pharmaceuticals).[22] In a competitive sense, patents create entry barriers for a firm's potential competitors.[23]

Peter Drucker argued that "innovation is the specific function of entrepreneurship, whether in an existing business, a public service institution, or a new venture started by a lone individual."[24] Moreover, Drucker suggested that innovation is "the means by which the entrepreneur either creates new wealth-producing resources or endows existing resources with enhanced potential for creating wealth."[25] Thus, entrepreneurship and the innovation resulting from it are critically important for all firms seeking strategic competitiveness and above-average returns.

The realities of global competition suggest that to be market leaders, companies must regularly innovate. This means that innovation should be an intrinsic part of virtually all of a firm's activities.[26] Moreover, firms should recognize the importance of their human capital to efforts to innovate.[27] Thus, as this discussion suggests, innovation is a key outcome firms seek through entrepreneurship and is often the source of competitive success, especially for companies competing in highly competitive and turbulent environments.[28]

**Entrepreneurs** are individuals, acting independently or as part of an organization, who perceive an entrepreneurial opportunity and then take risks to develop an innovation to exploit it.

The person with an **entrepreneurial mind-set** values uncertainty in markets and seeks to continuously identify opportunities in those markets that can be pursued through innovation.

## 13-3 Entrepreneurs

**Entrepreneurs** are individuals, acting independently or as part of an organization, who perceive an entrepreneurial opportunity and then take risks to develop an innovation to exploit it. Entrepreneurs can be found throughout different parts of organizations—from top-level managers to those working to produce a firm's products.

Entrepreneurs tend to demonstrate several characteristics: they are highly motivated, willing to take responsibility for their projects, self-confident, and often optimistic.[29] In addition, entrepreneurs tend to be passionate and emotional about the value and importance of their innovation-based ideas.[30] They are able to deal with uncertainty and are more alert to opportunities than others.[31] To be successful, entrepreneurs often need to have good social skills and to plan exceptionally well (e.g., to obtain venture capital).[32] Entrepreneurship entails much hard work if it is to be successful, but it can also be highly satisfying—particularly when entrepreneurs recognize and follow their passions. According to Jeff Bezos, Amazon.com's founder: "One of the huge mistakes people make is that they try to force an interest on themselves. You don't choose your passions; your passions choose you."[33]

*Jeff Bezos, CEO of Amazon.com, at the Kindle launch in Santa Monica, California. Bezos has demonstrated an entrepreneurial mind-set throughout his tenure at Amazon.com.*

Ted Soqui/Ted Soqui Photography/Corbis

Evidence suggests that successful entrepreneurs have an entrepreneurial mind-set that includes recognition of the importance of competing internationally as well as domestically.[34] The person with an **entrepreneurial mind-set** values uncertainty in markets and seeks to continuously identify opportunities in those markets that can be pursued through innovation.[35] Those without an entrepreneurial mind-set tend to view opportunities to innovate as threats.[36]

Because it has the potential to lead to continuous innovations, an individual's entrepreneurial mind-set can be a source of competitive

M. Stasy

advantage for a firm. Entrepreneurial mind-sets are fostered and supported when knowledge is readily available throughout a firm. Indeed, research shows that units within firms are more innovative when people have access to new knowledge.[37] Transferring knowledge, however, can be difficult, often because the receiving party must have adequate absorptive capacity (or the ability) to understand the knowledge and how to productively use it.[38] Learning requires that the new knowledge be linked to the existing knowledge. Thus, managers need to develop the capabilities of their human capital to build on their current knowledge base while incrementally expanding it.

Some companies are known to be highly committed to entrepreneurship, suggesting that many working within them have an entrepreneurial mind-set. In 2012, *Fast Company* identified Nike as the most innovative company with Amazon.com, Square, Splunk, Fab, Uber, Sprovil, Pinterest, Safaricom, and Target also among the top 10 most innovative firms.[39] Nike was chosen as the most innovative company for 2012 largely because the firm launched two successful innovations—FuelBand and Flyknit Racer—during that year. FuelBand is an electronic bracelet that measures an individual's movement throughout the day whether playing tennis, jogging, or simply walking. The Flyknit Racer is a featherlight shoe that to the person wearing it, feels like a sock sitting on top of a sole. The shoe is thought to be more environmentally friendly and, over the long term, is expected to be less expensive to manufacture.

## 13-4 International Entrepreneurship

**International entrepreneurship** is a process in which firms creatively discover and exploit opportunities that are outside their domestic markets.[40] Thus, entrepreneurship is a process that many firms exercise at both the domestic and international levels.[41] This is true for entrepreneurial ventures as suggested by the fact that approximately one-third of them move into international markets early in their life cycle. Large, established companies commonly have significant foreign operations and often start new ventures in international markets, too. For example, Microsoft and Huawei recently formed a partnership to launch "a new full-functionality Windows Phone specifically designed for Africa—Huawei 4Afrika."[42]

A key reason that firms choose to engage in international entrepreneurship is that in general, doing so enhances their performance.[43] Nonetheless, those leading firms should also understand that taking entrepreneurial actions in markets outside the firm's home setting is challenging and not without risks, including those of unstable foreign currencies, problems with market efficiencies, insufficient infrastructures to support businesses, and limitations on market size.[44] Thus, the decision to engage in international entrepreneurship should be a product of careful analysis.

Even though entrepreneurship is a global phenomenon, meaning that it is practiced across the world, its rate of use differs within individual countries. For example, the results of a well-known study that is completed annually (called the Global Entrepreneurship Monitor) showed that the 10 most entrepreneurial countries in 2012 were (from the most to the least entrepreneurial): the United States, Sweden, Australia, Iceland, Denmark, Canada, Switzerland, Belgium, Norway, Netherlands, and Taiwan (the Netherlands and Taiwan tied for the tenth position).[45] The 2012 analysis of entrepreneurship throughout the world also showed that for the first time in the report's 13-year history, "the rate of business formation among women eclipsed the rate among men in three nations (Ghana, Nigeria, and Thailand)" and was nearly equal in four other nations.[46] As usual, the report also found a strong positive relationship between the rate of entrepreneurship and economic development within a country.

**International entrepreneurship** is a process in which firms creatively discover and exploit opportunities that are outside their domestic markets.

Culture is one reason for the different rates of entrepreneurship among countries across the globe. Research suggests that a balance between individual initiative and a spirit of cooperation and group ownership of innovation is needed to encourage entrepreneurial behavior. This means that for firms to be entrepreneurial, they must provide appropriate autonomy and incentives for individual initiative to surface while simultaneously promoting cooperation and group ownership of an innovation as a foundation for successfully exploiting it. Thus, international entrepreneurship often requires teams of people with unique skills and resources, especially in cultures that place high value on either individualism or collectivism. In addition to a balance of values for individual initiative and cooperative behaviors, firms engaging in international entrepreneurship must concentrate more so than companies engaging in domestic entrepreneurship only on building the capabilities needed to innovate and on acquiring the resources needed to make strategic decisions through which innovations can be successfully exploited.[47]

The level of investment outside of the home country made by young ventures is also an important dimension of international entrepreneurship. In fact, with increasing globalization, a larger number of new ventures have been "born global."[48] One reason for this is likely related to the fact that new ventures that enter international markets increase their learning of new technological knowledge and thereby enhance their performance.[49]

The probability of entering and successfully competing in international markets increases when the firm's strategic leaders, and especially its top-level managers, have international experience.[50] Because of the learning and economies of scale and scope afforded by operating in international markets, both young and established internationally diversified firms often are stronger competitors in their domestic market as well. Additionally, as research has shown, internationally diversified firms are generally more innovative.[51]

The ability of a firm to develop and sustain a competitive advantage may be based partly or largely on its ability to innovate. This is true for firms engaging in international entrepreneurship as well as those that have yet to do so. As we discuss next, firms can follow different paths to innovate internally. Internal innovation is the first of three approaches firms use to innovate.

## 13-5 Internal Innovation

Efforts in firms' research and development (R&D) function are the source of internal innovations. Through effective R&D, firms are able to generate patentable processes and goods that are innovative in nature. Increasingly, successful R&D results from integrating the skills available in the global workforce. Thus, the ability to have a competitive advantage based on innovation is more likely to accrue to firms capable of integrating the talent of human capital from countries around the world.[52]

R&D and the new products and processes it can spawn affect a firm's efforts to earn above-average returns while competing in today's global environment. Because of this, firms try to use their R&D labs to create disruptive technologies and products. This is the case for China's Huawei Technologies Co. a firm that is increasing its allocations to R&D. Currently, the amount Huawei allocates to R&D is second among firms competing in the telecom equipment industry. Huawei is increasing its emphasis on R&D to become more innovative as a foundation for surviving in a highly competitive and rapidly consolidating industry structure.[53] Being able to continuously and successfully innovate such as Huawei is trying to do can create a competitive advantage for firms in many industries.[54] Although critical to long-term competitive success, the outcomes of R&D investments are uncertain and often not achieved in the short term, meaning that patience is required as firms evaluate the outcomes of their R&D efforts.[55]

## 13-5a Incremental and Radical Innovation

Firms invest in R&D to produce two types of innovations—incremental and radical. Most innovations are *incremental*—that is, they build on existing knowledge bases and provide small improvements in current products. Incremental innovations are evolutionary and linear in nature.[56] In general, incremental innovations tend to be introduced into established markets where customers understand and accept a product's characteristics. From the firm's perspective, incremental innovations tend to yield lower profit margins compared to those associated with the outcomes of radical innovations, largely because competition among firms offering products to customers that have incremental innovations is primarily on the price variable.[57] Adding a different kind of whitening agent to a soap detergent is an example of an incremental innovation, as are minor improvements in the functionality in televisions (e.g., slightly better picture quality). Companies introduce more incremental than radical innovations to markets, largely because they are cheaper, easier, and faster to produce, and involve less risk. However, incremental innovation can be risky for firms if its frequency of introduction creates more change than can be appropriately absorbed.[58]

In contrast to incremental innovations, *radical innovations* usually provide significant technological breakthroughs and create new knowledge. Revolutionary and nonlinear in nature, radical innovations typically use new technologies to serve newly created markets. The development of the original personal computer was a radical innovation.

Second Sight Medical Products has requested approval from the U.S. Food and Drug Administration (FDA) for its bionic eye, called Argus II. Technically, this product is "a retinal prosthesis, which appears to help some blind or nearly blind individuals see again."[59] The Argus II is a radical innovation, as would be the development of painkilling drugs that are difficult to abuse. With encouragement from the FDA, more than a dozen pharmaceutical companies from Pfizer Inc. to startups are trying to develop these products. The FDA's interest is for companies to find ways to manufacture legitimate drugs in ways that would make it very difficult for abusers to tamper with them to obtain benefits the federal agency deems undesirable and counterproductive—both for individuals and society.[60]

Because they establish new functionalities for users, radical innovations have strong potential to lead to significant growth in revenue and profits. For example, Toyota's innovation, embodied in the Prius, "the first mass-produced hybrid-electric car," changed this segment of the automobile industry.[61] Developing new processes is a critical part of producing radical innovations. Both types of innovations can create value, meaning that firms should determine when it is appropriate to emphasize either incremental or radical innovation. However, radical innovations have the potential to contribute more significantly to a firm's efforts to earn above-average returns, although they may be more risky.

Radical innovations are rare because of the difficulty and risk involved in their development. The value of the technology and the market opportunities are highly uncertain.[62] Because radical innovation creates new knowledge and uses only some or little of a firm's current product or technological knowledge, creativity is required; and creativity is as important to efforts to innovate in not-for-profit organizations as it is in for-profit

*Second Sight Medical Products' implantable device takes the place of damaged cells inside the eye. The device may help patients to perform daily tasks by allowing them to detect light and dark in the environment.*

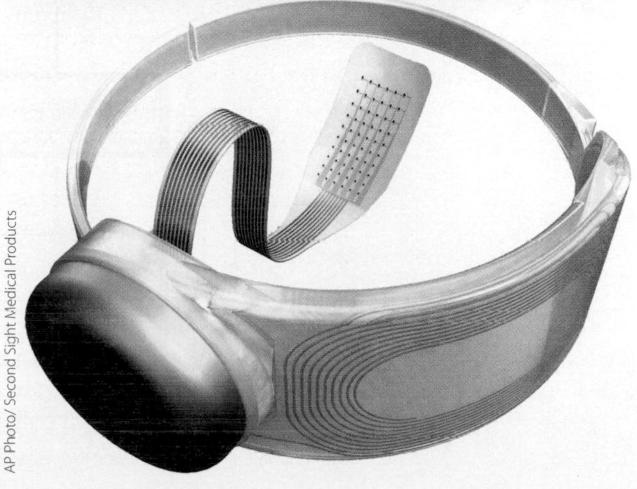

AP Photo/ Second Sight Medical Products

firms.[63] Creativity is an outcome of using one's imagination. In the words of Jay Walker, founder of Priceline.com, "Imagination is the fuel. You're not going to get innovation if you don't have imagination." Imagination finds firms thinking about what customers will want in a changing world. For example, Walker says, those seeking to innovate within a firm could try to imagine "what the customer is going to want in a world where for instance, their cellphone is in their glasses."[64] Imagination is more critical to radical than incremental innovations.

Creativity itself does not directly lead to innovation. Rather, creativity as generated through imagination discovers, combines, or synthesizes current knowledge, often from diverse areas.[65] Increasingly, when trying to innovate, firms seek knowledge from current users to understand their perspective about what could be beneficial innovations to the firm's products.[66] Collectively, the gathered knowledge is then applied to develop new products that can be used in an entrepreneurial manner to move into new markets, capture new customers, and gain access to new resources.[67] Such innovations are often developed in separate business units that start internal ventures.[68]

Strong, supportive leadership is required for the type of creativity and imagination needed to develop radical innovations. The fact that creativity is "messy, chaotic, sometimes even disgusting, and reeks of failure, experimentation and disorganization"[69] is one set of reasons leadership is so critical to its success.

This discussion highlights the fact that internally developed incremental and radical innovations result from deliberate efforts. These deliberate efforts are called *internal corporate venturing*, which is the set of activities firms use to develop internal inventions and especially innovations.[70]

As shown in Figure 13.1, autonomous and induced strategic behaviors are the two types of internal corporate venturing. Each venturing type facilitates development of both incremental and radical innovations. However, a larger number of radical innovations spring from autonomous strategic behavior while a larger number of incremental innovations come from induced strategic behavior.

In essence, autonomous strategic behavior results in influences to change aspects of the firm's strategy and the structure in place to support its implementation. In contrast, induced strategic behavior results from the influences of the strategy and structure the firm currently

**Figure 13.1** Model of Internal Corporate Venturing

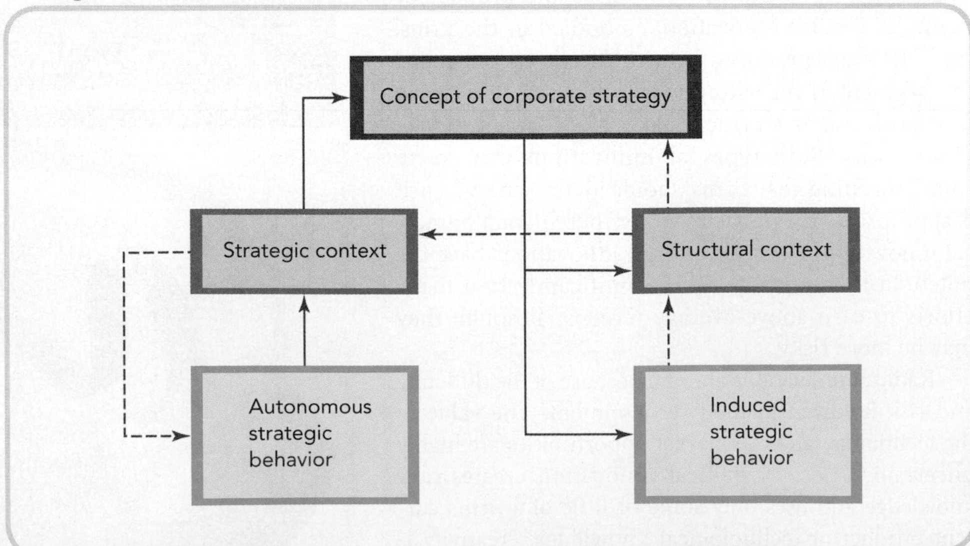


Source: Adapted from R. A. Burgelman, 1983, A model of the interactions of strategic behavior, corporate context, and the concept of strategy, *Academy of Management Review*, 8:65.

has in place to support efforts to innovate (see Figure 13.1). These points are emphasized in the discussions below of the two types of internal corporate venturing.

## 13-5b Autonomous Strategic Behavior

*Autonomous strategic behavior* is a bottom-up process in which product champions pursue new ideas, often through a political process, by means of which they develop and coordinate the actions required to innovate and to bring the innovation to the market.[71] A *product champion* is an individual with an entrepreneurial mind-set who seeks to create support for developing an innovation. Product champions play critical roles in moving innovations forward.[72] Commonly, product champions use their social capital to develop informal networks within the firm. As progress is made, these networks become more formal as a means of pushing an innovation to marketplace success.[73] Internal innovations springing from autonomous strategic behavior differ from the firm's current strategy and structure, taking it into new markets and perhaps new ways of creating value.

As a means of innovating, autonomous strategic behavior is more effective when new knowledge, especially tacit knowledge, is diffused continuously throughout the firm.[74] Interestingly, some of the processes important to promote innovation through autonomous strategic behavior vary by the environment and country in which a firm operates. For example, the Japanese culture is high on uncertainty avoidance. As such, research has found that Japanese firms are more likely to engage in autonomous strategic behavior under conditions of low uncertainty because they prefer stability.[75]

## 13-5c Induced Strategic Behavior

Induced strategic behavior, the second form of corporate venturing through which innovations are developed internally, is a top-down process whereby the firm's current strategy and structure foster innovations that are closely associated with that strategy and structure.[76] In this form of venturing, the strategy in place is filtered through a matching structural hierarchy. In essence, induced strategic behavior results in internal innovations that are consistent with the firm's current strategy. Thus, the firm's CEO and its top management team play an active and key role in induced strategic behavior.[77] This is the case at IBM, where CEO Virginia Rometty recently challenged the firm's employees "to move faster and respond more quickly to customers" as a foundation for developing innovations that will facilitate the firm's efforts to "shift to new computing models."[78]

Other companies are also interested in stimulating induced strategic behavior. Playing catch-up to Amazon.com in the e-commerce space, Walmart is relying on its existing strategy and structure to develop "a vast new logistics system that includes building new warehouses for Web orders, but also uses workers in stores to pack and mail items to customers." In describing these enhancements to the firm's strategy, CEO Mike Duke said that after a rough start, the firm is beginning to gain traction in its efforts to innovatively find ways to successfully compete against Amazon.com.[79] Given its interest in expanding its hardware offerings, Microsoft is using its current strategy and structure to innovate for the purpose of developing new products such as "a smaller, 7-inch version of a tablet to compete with popular gadgets like Apple's iPad Mini."[80]

*Apple's iPad Mini is another in a long line of successful internal innovations.*

Max Herman/Alamy

# 13-6 Implementing Internal Innovations

An entrepreneurial mind-set is critical to firms' efforts to innovate internally, partly because such a mind-set helps them deal with the environmental and market uncertainty that are associated with efforts taken to commercialize inventions. When facing uncertainty, firms try to continuously identify the most attractive opportunities to pursue strategically. This means that using an entrepreneurial mind-set finds firms being simultaneously oriented to identifying opportunities, developing innovations that are appropriate to those opportunities, and to executing strategies to successfully exploit opportunities in the marketplace. Often, firms provide incentives to individuals to be more entrepreneurial as a foundation for successfully developing internal innovations, sometimes encouraging work teams to specify what they believe are the most appropriate incentives for the firm to use.[81]

Having processes and structures in place through which a firm can successfully exploit developed innovations is critical. In the context of internal corporate ventures, managers must allocate resources, coordinate activities, communicate with many different parties in the organization, and make a series of decisions to convert the innovations resulting from either autonomous or induced strategic behaviors into successful market entries.[82] As we describe in Chapter 11, organizational structures are the sets of formal relationships that support processes managers use to exploit the firm's innovations.

Effective integration of the functions involved in internal innovation efforts—from engineering to manufacturing and distribution—is required to implement the incremental and radical innovations resulting from internal corporate ventures.[83] Increasingly, product development teams are being used to achieve the desired integration across organizational functions. Such integration involves coordinating and applying the knowledge and skills of different functional areas to maximize innovation.[84] Teams must help to make decisions as to the projects to continue supporting as well as those to terminate. Emotional commitments sometimes increase the difficulty of deciding to terminate an innovation-based project.

## 13-6a Cross-Functional Product Development Teams

Cross-functional product development teams facilitate efforts to integrate activities associated with different organizational functions, such as design, manufacturing, and marketing. These teams may also include people from major suppliers because they have knowledge that can meaningfully inform a firm's innovation processes.[85] In addition, new product development processes can be completed more quickly and the products more easily commercialized when cross-functional teams work collaboratively.[86] Using cross-functional teams, product development stages are grouped into parallel processes so the firm can tailor its product development efforts to its unique core competencies and to the needs of the market.

Horizontal organizational structures support cross-functional teams in their efforts to integrate innovation-based activities across organizational functions.[87] Therefore, instead of being designed around vertical hierarchical functions or departments, the organization is built around core horizontal processes that are used to produce and manage innovations. Some of the horizontal processes that are critical to innovation efforts are formal and are defined and documented as procedures and practices. More commonly, however, these important processes are informal and are supported properly through horizontal organizational structures—structures that typically find individuals communicating frequently on a face-to-face basis.

Team members' independent frames of reference and organizational politics are two barriers with the potential to prevent effective use of cross-functional teams to integrate the activities of different organizational functions.[88] Team members working within a distinct specialization (e.g., a particular organizational function) may have an independent frame of reference typically based on common backgrounds and experiences. They are likely to use the same decision criteria to evaluate issues such as product development efforts when making decisions within their functional units.

Research suggests that functional departments vary along four dimensions: time orientation, interpersonal orientation, goal orientation, and formality of structure.[89] Thus, individuals from different functional departments having different orientations in terms of these dimensions can be expected to perceive innovation-related activities differently. For example, a design engineer may consider the characteristics that make a product functional and workable to be the most important of its characteristics. Alternatively, a person from the marketing function may judge characteristics that satisfy customer needs to be most important. These different orientations can create barriers to effective communication across functions and may even generate intra-team conflict as different parts of the firm try to work together to innovate.[90]

Some organizations experience a considerable amount of political activity (called organizational politics). How resources will be allocated to different functions is a key source of such activity. This means that inter-unit conflict may result from aggressive competition for resources among those representing different organizational functions. This type of conflict between functions creates a barrier to cross-functional integration efforts. Those trying to form effective cross-functional product development teams seek ways to mitigate the damaging effects of organizational politics. Emphasizing the critical role each function plays in the firm's overall efforts to innovate is a method used in many firms to help individuals see the value of inter-unit collaborations.

## 13-6b Facilitating Integration and Innovation

Shared values and effective leadership are important for achieving cross-functional integration and implementing internal innovations.[91] As part of culture, shared values are framed around the firm's vision and mission and become the glue that promotes integration between functional units.

Strategic leadership is also important to efforts to achieve cross-functional integration and promote internal innovation. Working with others, leaders are responsible for setting goals and allocating resources needed to achieve them. The goals include integrated development and commercialization of new products. Effective strategic leaders also ensure a high-quality communication system to facilitate cross-functional integration. A critical benefit of effective communication is the sharing of knowledge among team members who in turn are then able to communicate an innovation's existence and importance to others in the organization. Shared values and leadership practices shape the communication routines that make it possible to share innovation-related knowledge throughout the firm.[92]

## 13-6c Creating Value from Internal Innovation

The model in Figure 13.2 shows how firms seek to create value through internal innovation processes (autonomous strategic behavior and induced strategic behavior). As shown, an entrepreneurial mind-set is foundational to the firm's efforts to consistently identify entrepreneurial opportunities that it can pursue strategically with and through innovations. Cross-functional teams are important for promoting integrated new product design ideas and commitment to their subsequent implementation. Effective leadership and shared values promote integration and vision for innovation and commitment to it. The end result of successful innovations is the creation of value for stakeholders such as customers and shareholders.[93] However, competitive rivalry (see Chapter 5) affects the degree of success a firm achieves through its innovations. Thus, firms must carefully study competitors' responses to their innovations to have the knowledge required to know how to adjust their innovation-based efforts and even when to abandon them if market conditions indicate the need to do so.[94]

**Figure 13.2** Creating Value through Internal Innovation Processes

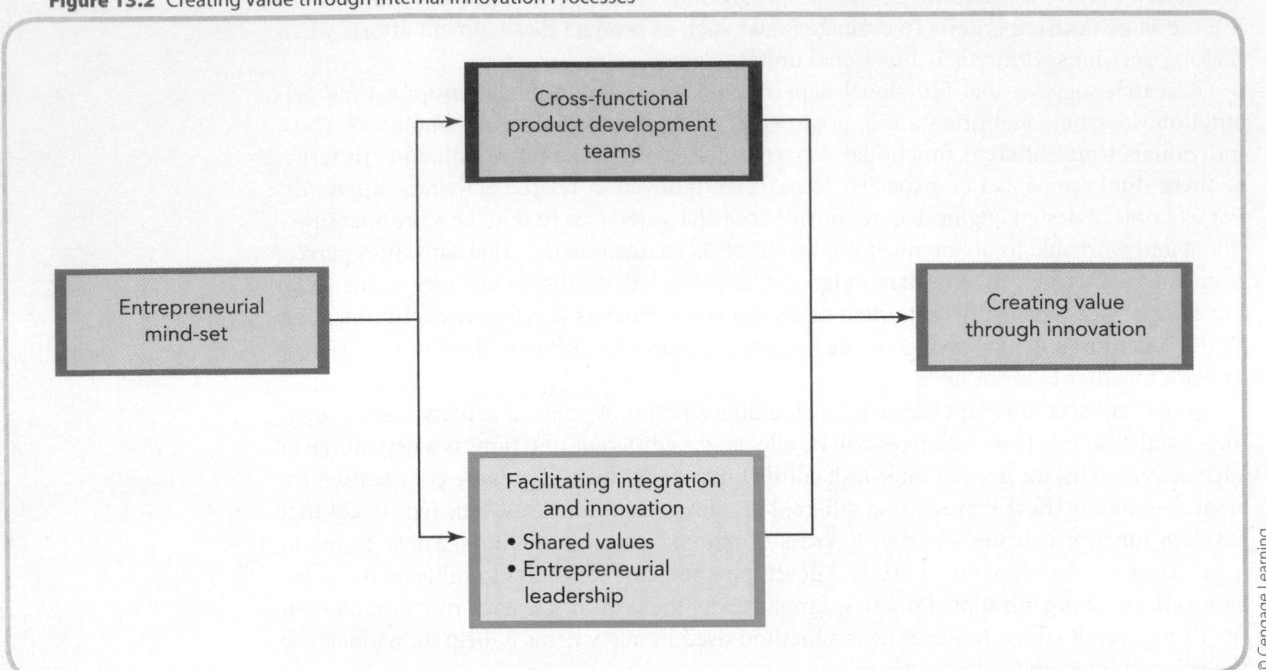


But as we discuss in the Strategic Focus, some efforts to create value through internal innovation fail. This appears to be J.C. Penney's experience during Ron Johnson's short tenure as the firm's CEO. We discussed some of Johnson's innovations and the strategy through which they were to be exploited in Chapter 4's Opening Case. Overall, the innovations Johnson developed were more radical than incremental. However, it seems that these internal innovations did not create value for JCP's stakeholders because the efforts undertaken to implement the strategy through which these innovations were to be exploited resulted in significant declines in sales revenue and the price of the firm's stock, as well as Johnson's ouster as CEO.

In the next two sections, we discuss the other approaches firms use to innovate—cooperative strategies and acquisitions.

Learn more about Disney.
www.cengagebrain.com

## 13-7 Innovation through Cooperative Strategies

Alliances with other firms can contribute to innovations in several ways. First, they provide information on new business opportunities and the innovations that might be developed to exploit them.[95] In other instances, firms use cooperative strategies to align what they believe are complementary assets with the potential to lead to future innovations. Compared to other approaches to innovation, combining complementary assets through alliances has the potential to more frequently result in "breakthrough" innovations.[96]

Rapidly changing technologies, globalization, and the need to innovate at world-class levels are primary influences on firms' decisions to innovate by cooperating with other companies. Indeed, some believe that because of these conditions, firms are becoming increasingly dependent on cooperative strategies as a path to innovation and, ultimately, to competitive success in the global economy.[97]

M. Stasy

## Strategic Focus — FAILURE

### An Innovation Failure at JC Penney: Its Causes and Consequences

In Chapter 4's Opening Case, we described the strategy that now former CEO Ron Johnson designed and tried to implement at JC Penney (JCP). As it turns out, part of the trouble was that the firm's target "middle market" customers did not respond well to the new strategy and the innovations associated with it. In fact, some say that Johnson's innovations and strategy alienated what had historically been the firm's target customers.

Johnson came to JCP after successful stints at Target and Apple. At Apple, he was admired for the major role he played in developing that firm's wildly successful Apple Stores, which a number of analysts say brought about "a new world order in retailing." It was Johnson's ability to establish what some viewed as path-breaking visions and to develop innovations to reach them that appealed to JCP's board when he was hired.

Likening JCP to the Titanic, Johnson came to the CEO position believing that innovation was the key to shaking up the firm. Moreover, he reminded analysts, employees, and the like that he came to JCP to "transform" the firm, not to marginally improve its performance. Describing what he intended to do at JCP, Johnson said that "In the U.S., the department store has a chance to regain its status as the leader in style, the leader in excitement. It will be a period of true innovation for this company."

The essence of Johnson's vision for JCP was twofold. First, he eliminated the firm's practice of marking up prices on goods and then offering discounts, heavy promotions, and coupons to entice its bargain-hunting target customers. Instead, Johnson introduced a three-tiered pricing structure that focused on what were labelled "everyday low prices." To customers though, the pricing structure was confusing and failed to convince them that the "everyday low prices" were actually "low enough" compared to competitors' prices.

Innovation was at the core of the second part of the new CEO's vision, with one objective being to give JCP a younger, hipper image. The innovations Johnson put into place to create this image included establishing branded boutiques within JCP's stores. To do this, JCP set up branded boutiques "along a wide aisle, or 'street' dotted with places to sit, grab a cup of coffee or play with Lego blocks." With an initial intention of having 100 branded shops within JCP stores by 2015, Johnson asked people "to envision an entire store of shops with a street and square in the middle representing a new way to interface with the customer." Disney was one of the brands to be included as a shopping destination, as were Caribou Coffee, Dallas-based Paciugo Gelato & Café, and Giggle, a store dedicated to making "it a whole lot easier to become a parent" by offering innovative and stylish "must-have baby items." In addition, and as noted in Chapter 4's Opening Case, Levi's, IZOD, Liz Claiborne, and Martha

*Merchandise by Jonathan Adler is on display in a remodeled portion of JC Penney at Citrus Park Mall in Tampa, Florida.*

Stewart branded items were to be included as part of the boutiques.

But as noted, these innovations and the strategy used to exploit them did not work. So what went wrong? Considering the components of the model shown in Figure 13.2 yields a framework to answer this question. While it is true that Johnson had an entrepreneurial mind-set, cross-functional teams were not used to facilitate implementation of the desired innovations such as the boutique stores. In essence, it seems that Johnson himself, without the involvement of others throughout the firm, was instrumental in deciding that the boutiques were to be used as well as how they were to be established and operated within selected JCP's stores. In addition, the values associated with efforts to change JCP from its historic roots of being a general merchant in the space between department stores and discounters to becoming a firm with a young, hip image were not shared among the firm's stakeholders. Finally, Johnson's work as an entrepreneurial leader was seemingly not as effective as should have been the case. Among mistakes made in this regard were trying to implement too many changes too quickly without adequately testing customers' reactions to those changes, and more broadly, a failure to fully understand customers and their needs. Because of mistakes such as these, the level of success desired at JCP through internally developed innovations was not attained.

Sources: 2013, J.C. Penney ousts CEO Ron Johnson, *Wall Street Journal*, www.wsj.com, April 8; D. Benoit, 2013, J.C. Penney asks customers for second chance, *Wall Street Journal*, www.wsj.com, May 1; D. Benoit, 2013, Ackman thought Johnson could turn around 'titanic' JCPenney, *Wall Street Journal*, www.wsj.com, April 8; S. Gerfield, 2013, J.C. Penney rehires Myron Ullman to clean up Ron Johnson's mess, *Bloomberg Businessweek*, www.businessweek.com, April 11; S. Clifford, 2013, J.C. Penney's new plan is to reuse its old plans, *New York Times*, www.nytimes.com, May 16; S. Denning, 2013, J.C. Penney: Was Ron Johnson's strategy wrong? *Forbes*, www.forbes.com, April 9; M. Halkias, 2012, J.C. Penney's Ron Johnson shows off his vision of future to 300 analysts, *Dallas News*, www.dallasnews.com, September 19.

Both entrepreneurial ventures and established firms use cooperative strategies to innovate. An entrepreneurial venture, for example, may seek investment capital as well as established firms' distribution capabilities to successfully introduce one of its innovative products to the market.[98] Alternatively, more-established companies may need new technological knowledge and can gain access to it by forming a cooperative strategy with entrepreneurial ventures.[99] Alliances between large pharmaceutical firms and biotechnology companies increasingly have been formed to integrate the knowledge and resources of both to develop new products and bring them to market.

In some instances, large established firms form an alliance to innovate. This is the case for Inter IKEA Group, the parent company of the IKEA furniture brand, and Marriott International Inc. These firms have formed an alliance to develop Moxy, a new hotel brand that the companies believe is innovative in its design and the value it will create for customers. Novel construction techniques that will keep manufacturing costs down is IKEA's innovation for the alliance while unique design for the "value-oriented" segment is Marriott's innovation. Thus, the Moxy brand is being developed to innovatively combine value with style. In the words of Marriott's CEO: "This is a fresh new take on the economy segment. I think it will benefit from being new and combining value with style. Too much of the value product you see in Europe is devoid of style." Initially, 50 units of the budget hotels with style will open in Europe.[100]

However, alliances formed to foster innovation are not without risks. In addition to conflict that is natural when firms try to work together to reach a mutual goal, the members of an alliance also take a risk that a partner will appropriate their technology or knowledge and use it for its own benefit.[101] Carefully selecting partner firms mitigates this risk. The ideal partnership is one in which the firms have complementary skills as well as compatible strategic goals.[102] When this is the case, firms encounter fewer challenges and risks as they try to effectively manage the partnership they formed to develop innovations. Companies also want to constrain the number of cooperative arrangements they form to innovate in that becoming involved in too many alliances puts them at risk of losing the ability to successfully manage each of them.[103]

## 13-8 Innovation through Acquisitions

Firms sometimes acquire companies to gain access to their innovations and to their innovative capabilities.[104] One reason companies do this is that capital markets value growth; acquisitions provide a means to rapidly extend one or more product lines and increase the firm's revenues.[105] In spite of this fact, a firm should have a strategic rationale for a decision to acquire a company. Typically, the rationale is to gain ownership of an acquired company's innovations and access to its innovative capabilities. A number of large pharmaceutical companies have acquired firms, largely for these purposes. For example, Pfizer Inc. recently acquired NextWave Pharmaceuticals, Inc., a company with a focus on developing and commercializing products to treat attention deficit hyperactivity disorder (ADHD). Through this acquisition, Pfizer gained ownership of NextWave's innovative Quillivant XR drug that treats ADHD as well as access to the firm's efforts to develop an extended-release chewable tablet version of the drug.[106]

Similar to internal corporate venturing and strategic alliances, acquisitions are not a risk free approach to innovation. A key risk of acquisitions is that a firm may substitute an ability to buy innovations for an ability to develop them internally. This may result when a firm concentrates on financial controls to identify, evaluate, and then manage acquisitions. Of course, strategic controls are the ones through which a firm identifies a strategic rationale to acquire another company as a means of developing innovations. Thus, the likelihood a firm will be successful in its efforts to innovate increases by developing an appropriate balance between financial and strategic controls. In spite of the risks though, choosing to acquire companies with complementary capabilities and knowledge sets can support a firm's efforts to innovate successfully when the acquisitions are made for strategic purposes and are then properly integrated into the acquired firm's strategies.[107]

The ability to learn new capabilities that can facilitate innovation-related activities from acquired companies is an important benefit that can accrue to an acquiring firm. Additionally, firms that emphasize innovation and carefully select companies to acquire that also emphasize innovation and the technological capabilities on which innovations are often based are likely to remain innovative.[108] To gain this benefit though, the operations of the companies with this emphasis must be effectively integrated.[109]

To close this chapter, we describe how strategic entrepreneurship helps firms create value for stakeholders.

## 13-9 Creating Value through Strategic Entrepreneurship

Entrepreneurial ventures and younger firms often are more effective at identifying opportunities than are larger established companies.[110] As a consequence, entrepreneurial ventures often produce more radical innovations than do larger, more established organizations. Entrepreneurial ventures' strategic flexibility and willingness to take risks at least partially account for their ability to identify opportunities and then develop radical innovations as a foundation for exploiting them. Alternatively, larger, well-established firms often have more resources and capabilities to manage their resources for the purpose of exploiting identified opportunities, but these efforts by large firms generally result in more incremental than radical innovations.

Thus, younger, entrepreneurial ventures generally excel in the *taking of entrepreneurial actions* part of strategic entrepreneurship while larger, more established firms generally excel at the *using a strategic perspective* part of strategic entrepreneurship. Another way of thinking about this is to say that entrepreneurial ventures excel at opportunity-seeking (that is, entrepreneurial) behavior while larger firms excel at advantage-seeking (that is, strategic) behavior. However, competitive success and superior performance relative to competitors accrues to firms that are able to identify and exploit opportunities and establish a competitive advantage as a result of doing so.[111] On a relative basis then, entrepreneurial ventures are challenged to become more strategic while older, more established firms are challenged to become more entrepreneurial.

Firms trying to learn how to simultaneously be more entrepreneurial and strategic (that is, firms trying to use strategic entrepreneurship) recognize that after identifying opportunities, entrepreneurs within entrepreneurial ventures and established organizations must develop capabilities that will become the basis of their firm's core competencies and competitive advantages. The process of identifying opportunities is entrepreneurial, but this activity alone is not sufficient to create maximum wealth or even to survive over time. As we learned in Chapter 3, to successfully exploit opportunities, a firm must develop capabilities that are valuable, rare, difficult to imitate, and nonsubstitutable. When capabilities satisfy these four criteria, the firm has one or more competitive advantages to use in efforts to exploit the identified opportunities. Without a competitive advantage, the firm's success will be only temporary (as explained in Chapter 1). An innovation may be valuable and rare early in its life, if a market perspective is used in its development. However, competitive actions must be taken to introduce the new product to the market and protect its position in the market against competitors to gain a competitive advantage.[112] In combination, these actions constitute strategic entrepreneurship.

## Strategic Focus

SUCCESS

### Pursuing Competitive Success by Using Strategic Entrepreneurship

Over the years, both Boeing and Airbus have shown an ability to identify and pursue entrepreneurial opportunities. For these firms, this means that they are able to produce innovative airplanes that satisfy a need in the markets they serve.

Fuel to operate airplanes is a major cost borne by airline companies, Boeing and Airbus's customers. For some time, these two firms have recognized that an opportunity exists to manufacture highly fuel-efficient products as a way of helping customers reduce their costs. The two companies also knew that innovation and a strategic perspective would be critical to their efforts to profitably produce, sell, and maintain highly fuel-efficient medium- and long-range jets. Indeed, with respect to the long-range market, some analysts suggest for example, that a "war of the wide-bodies" now exists between Boeing and Airbus. Given the expenses incurred to produce these innovative products, "investors are focusing more on how profitably the companies produce planes than on how many more contracts they land."

These firms have developed similar innovations as the foundation for producing their new fuel-efficient products. The 350 is the core new product for Airbus while the 787 Dreamliner serves this role for Boeing. Initially, Boeing committed to innovations with respect to a number of dimensions (cabin pressure, a smoother ride, less maintenance, larger windows, changes to pilot training to enhance the efficiency and effectiveness of these efforts, and engine swapping—an innovation that makes it possible to easily convert from one manufacturer's engine to another's if a plane is sold to another customer) when producing the 787.

Demonstrating the competitive rivalry between these companies (firms that have resource similarity and market commonality—see Chapter 5) is the opinion among some analysts that "The A350 has the same innovations more or less as the Dreamliner, the 787." In this regard, the belief is that the A350 "is pretty equivalent, the same amount or proportion of carbon for the lightness of the material, just as many electrical devices" and so forth. Thus, both firms are using carbon-fiber composites for the skin of the planes. Additionally, the underneath of the 787 includes "highly engineered" titanium as well as an assortment of cutting-edge aluminum alloys. Overall, the A350 "is 53% composites by weight compared to 50% for the Dreamliner."

For the most part, Airbus and Boeing have pursued radical innovations to develop the A350 and 787, respectively. As discussed in this chapter, radical innovation can lead to significant increases in sales and profitability for firms. These outcomes are achieved when innovation and the entrepreneurial actions associated with it are taken through a strategic perspective. Boeing's decision to offer three versions of the 787 to serve different customer groups is an example of a strategic action the firm is taking to gain maximum benefit from the 787. Not surprisingly, Airbus has developed or is developing products that compete against these versions of the 787. Thus, the two firms are using a strategic perspective as a foundation to the entrepreneurial actions they are taking.

*A New Boeing 787 Dreamliner rolls out of the hangar. The 787 incorporates several radical innovations designed to help Boeing capture a larger share of the airliner market and improve its profitability.*

Risk is another issue associated with radical innovations. In the words of an airline company official: "You can't introduce an airplane so radically different without there being issues." Boeing has indeed encountered issues with its radically innovative 787 such as those concerning the use of lithium-ion batteries (see the discussion of this issue in Chapter 5). This is not unexpected though. In fact, some believe that "Boeing's experience (with the 787) offers a reminder that innovation—for all its value—doesn't come as easily as a catchphrase. It can get messy." In this regard, a key challenge both Airbus and Boeing face going forward is to execute strategies that will allow them to benefit fully from their innovative products.

Sources: M. Cauchi, 2013, Carriers buy more fuel-efficient jets, *Wall Street Journal*, www.wsj.com, April 22; M. Dunlop, 2013, Innovations that make the 787 different, *HeraldNet*, www.heraldnet.com, January 24; D. Michaels, 2103, Airbus A350 completes maiden flight, *Wall Street Journal*, www.wsj.com, June 14; D. Michaels, 2013, Innovation is messy business, *Wall Street Journal*, www.wsj.com, January 24; D. Michaels, 2013, Their new materials, *Wall Street Journal*, www.wsj.com, June 16; D. Terdiman, 2013, It's Airbus' A350 vs. Boeing's Dreamliner in the 'war of the wide-bodies', *CNET*, www.cnet.com, March 20.

Some large organizations are trying to become more capable of effectively using strategic entrepreneurship. For example, an increasing number of large, widely known firms, including Wendy's International, Gucci Group, Starbucks, and Perry Ellis International have established a top-level managerial position commonly called president or executive vice president of emerging brands. Other companies such as Coca-Cola, GE, Whirlpool, and Humana have established a position within their top management teams to focus on innovation.[113] These individuals are often known as chief innovation officers.

The essential responsibility of top-level managers focusing on emerging brands or innovation is to verify that their firm is consistently finding entrepreneurial opportunities. Those holding these positions work collaboratively with the firm's chief strategy officer. In this sense, those responsible for identifying opportunities the firm might want to pursue and those responsible for selecting and implementing the strategies the company would use to pursue those opportunities share responsibility for verifying that the firm is taking entrepreneurial actions using a strategic perspective. Through their work, these individuals also help the firm determine the innovations necessary to pursue an opportunity and if those innovations should be developed internally, through a cooperative strategy, or by completing an acquisition. In the final analysis, the objective of these top-level managers is to help firms identify opportunities and then develop successful incremental and radical innovations and strategies to exploit them.

In the Strategic Focus, we describe how Boeing and Airbus (a part of European Aeronautic Defence & Space Co.) have both pursued opportunities to create innovative new airplanes (the A350 for Airbus and the 787 for Boeing). As you will see by reading the Strategic Focus, the firms are using strategic entrepreneurship as a foundation for efforts to achieve success with their new products.

Find out more about Airbus.
www.cengagebrain.com

# SUMMARY

- Strategic entrepreneurship is the taking of entrepreneurial actions using a strategic perspective. Firms using strategic entrepreneurship simultaneously engage in opportunity-seeking and advantage-seeking behaviors. The purpose is to continuously find new opportunities and quickly develop innovations to exploit them.
- Entrepreneurship is a process used by individuals, teams, and organizations to identify entrepreneurial opportunities without being immediately constrained by the resources they control. Corporate entrepreneurship is the application of entrepreneurship (including the identification of entrepreneurial opportunities) within ongoing, established organizations. Entrepreneurial opportunities are conditions in which new goods or services can satisfy a need in the market. Increasingly, entrepreneurship positively contributes to individual firms' performance and stimulates growth in countries' economies.
- Firms engage in three types of innovative activities: (1) invention, which is the act of creating a new good or process, (2) innovation, or the process of creating a commercial product from an invention, and (3) imitation, which is the adoption of similar innovations by different firms. Invention brings something new into being while innovation brings something new into use.
- Entrepreneurs see or envision entrepreneurial opportunities and then take actions to develop innovations to exploit them. The most successful entrepreneurs (whether they are establishing their own venture or are working in an ongoing organization) have an entrepreneurial mind-set, which is an orientation that values the potential opportunities available because of marketplace uncertainties.
- International entrepreneurship, or the process of identifying and exploiting entrepreneurial opportunities outside the firm's domestic markets, is important to firms around the globe. Evidence suggests that firms capable of effectively engaging in international entrepreneurship outperform those competing only in their domestic markets.
- Three basic approaches are used to produce innovation: (1) internal innovation, which involves R&D and forming internal corporate ventures, (2) cooperative strategies such as strategic alliances, and (3) acquisitions. Autonomous strategic behavior and induced strategic behavior are the two forms of internal

corporate venturing. Autonomous strategic behavior is a bottom-up process through which a product champion facilitates the commercialization of an innovation. Induced strategic behavior is a top-down process in which a firm's current strategy and structure facilitate the development and implementation of product or process innovations. Thus, induced strategic behavior is driven by the organization's current corporate strategy and structure while autonomous strategic behavior can result in a change to the firm's current strategy and structure arrangements.

- Firms create two types of innovations—incremental and radical—through internal innovation that takes place in the form of autonomous strategic behavior or induced strategic behavior. Overall, firms produce more incremental innovations, but radical innovations have a higher probability of significantly increasing sales revenue and profits. Cross-functional integration is often vital to a firm's efforts to develop and implement internal corporate venturing activities and to commercialize the resulting innovation. Cross-functional teams now commonly include representatives from external organizations such as suppliers. Additionally, integration and innovation can be facilitated by developing shared values and effectively using strategic leadership.
- To gain access to the specialized knowledge required to innovate in the global economy, firms may form a cooperative relationship such as a strategic alliance with other companies, some of which may be competitors.
- Acquisitions are another means firms use to obtain innovation. Innovation can be acquired through direct acquisition, or firms can learn new capabilities from an acquisition, thereby enriching their internal innovation abilities.
- The practice of strategic entrepreneurship by all types of firms, large and small, new and more established, creates value for all stakeholders, especially for shareholders and customers. Strategic entrepreneurship also contributes to the economic development of countries.

# REVIEW QUESTIONS

1. What is strategic entrepreneurship? What is corporate entrepreneurship?
2. What is entrepreneurship and what are entrepreneurial opportunities? Why are they important aspects of the strategic management process?
3. What are invention, innovation, and imitation? How are these concepts interrelated?
4. What is an entrepreneur and what is an entrepreneurial mind-set?
5. What is international entrepreneurship? Why is it important?
6. How do firms develop innovations internally?
7. How do firms use cooperative strategies to innovate and to have access to innovative capabilities?
8. How does a firm acquire other companies to increase the number of innovations it produces and improve its capability to innovate?
9. How does strategic entrepreneurship help firms create value?

# EXPERIENTIAL EXERCISES

## EXERCISE 1: CAN CORPORATIONS REALLY INNOVATE?

According to an article in the Harvard Business Review titled "The New Corporate Garage" by Scott Anthony (2012), big companies are unshackling innovation in ways that resemble their more nimble and smaller counterparts. Anthony suggests there are three trends behind this shift. "First, the increasing ease and decreasing cost of innovation mean that start-ups now face the same short-term pressures that have constrained innovation at large companies; as soon as a young company gets a whiff of success, it has to race against dozens of copycats. Second, large companies, taking a page from start-up strategy, are embracing open innovation and less hierarchical management and are integrating entrepreneurial behaviors with their existing capabilities. And third, although innovation has historically been product- and service-oriented, it increasingly involves creating business models that tap big companies' unique strengths."

While the press is replete with innovation stories for startups, many large corporations are taking significant steps to instill an entrepreneurial culture within their bureaucracy. Your challenge in this exercise is to identify some ways that corporations are igniting innovation capabilities at their organizations. You can complete this assignment in one of two ways. First, you may choose a particular company and research it for the purpose of identifying steps the firm is taking to improve its innovation capabilities. A second approach is to utilize any one of a number of websites that are designed to assist companies help to foster and improve their innovative capabilities. These sites can be studied to identify a number of activities firms complete to enhance their innovation skills. A few websites that can be examined for this purpose are listed below, but you should feel free to uncover and use a site that you find.

- Rocket Space (http://rocket-space.com/)
- Corporate Innovation Lab (http://corporateinnovationlab.com/)
- Nine Sigma (http://www.ninesigma.com/)
- InnoCentive (http://www.innocentive.com/)
- YourEncore (http://www.yourencore.com/)
- Yet2.com (http://www.yet2.com/)

Working in teams, your assignment is to research a company or a web enabler for companies interested in improving their innovation or entrepreneurial capabilities. You should be prepared to describe:

1. The mission of your web or company.
2. What you find interesting or unusual about the approach to innovation specified by the web provider or the company you selected.
3. How the organization goes about improving innovative capabilities.
4. Your overall impression of the approach and its usefulness.

## EXERCISE 2: THE SOCIAL NATURE OF ENTREPRENEURSHIP

Entrepreneurship is said to be as much about social connections and networks as it is about the fundamentals of running a new venture. The relationships that an entrepreneur can count on are also key resources of financial capital, human capital, mentoring, and legal advice.

Various popular blogs covering social media and Web 2.0 identify some of the top social networks for entrepreneurs. Some of the more popular ones are:

- LinkedIn
- The Funded
- PartnerUp
- Young Entrepreneur
- Startup Nation
- Go BIG Network
- Biznik
- Perfect Business
- Cofounder
- Entrepreneur Connection

In teams, pick one social network from the list or another you might favor (your instructor will ensure that there is a unique choice for each team). Spend some time on the selected network's website reading the posts to get a feel for the types of information presented. Prepare a 10-minute presentation to the class on your network site and be sure to address the following, at a minimum:

1. Provide an overview of the site—what it is used for, how popular it is, features, types of conversations, etc.
2. What is unique about this site and why does it attract followers? What technologies are enabled here—RSS, Twitter, etc.?
3. Describe the target audience for this website. Who would use it and what types of information are available to entrepreneurs?
4. How do you think this site maintains its presence? Does it support itself with ad revenue, corporate sponsors, not-for-profit sponsors, or by some other means?
5. Would this site be useful for corporate entrepreneurs as well as startup entrepreneurs? If so, how?

# VIDEO CASE

## A NEW ENTREPRENEUR ON THE BLOCK: SARA BLAKELY, FOUNDER AND ENTREPRENEUR/SPANX

SPANX, creating a slimming/invisible underlayer garment, surfaced about 10 years ago. Sara Blakely, founder and entrepreneur, confronted with the male-dominated manufacturing of women's shapewear, was able to offer a female-oriented solution. With shapewear an expanding segment in a newly competitive market, Blakely designs a wide range of SPANX products by placing herself in the position of a customer. Currently, SPANX generates around $250 million in annual sales.

Be prepared to discuss the following concepts and questions in class as they apply to SPANX and Sara Blakely:

### Concepts

- Strategic entrepreneurship
- Corporate entrepreneurship
- Entrepreneurial opportunities
- Innovation
- Entrepreneurial mind-set
- International entrepreneurship

## Questions

1. Is there evidence of strategic entrepreneurship in the account of Sara Blakely?
2. Does Sara Blakely set the stage for corporate entrepreneurship?
3. What entrepreneurial opportunities do you see ahead for Sara Blakely?
4. How would you classify the SPANX innovation? What advantages and risks are associated with the SPANX innovation?
5. Does Sara Blakely have an entrepreneurial mind-set?
6. Should Sara Blakely pursue international entrepreneurship? Why or why not? What concerns might she have?

## NOTES


1. T. Buschgens, A. Bausch, & D. B. Balkin, 2013, Organizational culture and innovation: A meta-analytic review, *Journal of Product Innovation Management*, 30: 763–781.
2. A. Lipparini, G. Lorenzoni, & S. Ferriani, 2013, From core to periphery and back: A study on the deliberate shaping of knowledge flows in interfirm dyads and networks, *Strategic Management Journal*, in press.
3. P. C. Patel, S. A. Fernhaber, P. P. McDougall-Covin, & R. P. van der Have, 2013, Beating competitors to international markets: The value of geographically balanced networks for innovation, *Strategic Management Journal*, in press.
4. M. Wright, B. Clarysse, & S. Mosey, 2012, Strategic entrepreneurship, resource orchestration and growing spin-offs from universities, *Technology Analysis & Strategic Management*, 24: 911–927.
5. P. G. Klein, J. T. Mahoney, A. M. McGahan, & C. N. Pitelis, 2013, Capabilities and strategic entrepreneurship in public organizations, *Strategic Entrepreneurship Journal*, 7: 70–91; M. A. Hitt, R. D. Ireland, D. G. Sirmon, & C. A. Trahms, 2011, Strategic entrepreneurship: Creating value for individuals, organizations, and society. *Academy of Management Perspectives*, 25: 57–75.
6. H. Yang, Y. Zheng, & X. Zhao, 2013, Exploration or exploitation? Small firms' alliance strategies with large firms, *Strategic Management Journal*, in press; J. Q. Barden, 2012, The influences of being acquired on subsidiary innovation adoption, *Strategic Management Journal*, 33: 1269–1285.
7. D. F. Kuratko & D. B. Audretsch, 2013, Clarifying the domains of corporate entrepreneurship, *International Entrepreneurship and Management Journal*, in press; K. Shimizu, 2012, Risks of corporate entrepreneurship: Autonomy and agency issues, *Organization Science*, 23: 194–206.
8. D. Urbano & A. Turro, 2013, Conditioning factors for corporate entrepreneurship: An in(ex)ternal approach, *International Entrepreneurship and Management Journal*, in press; A. J. Kacperczyk, 2012, Opportunity structures in established firms: Entrepreneurship versus intrapreneurship in mutual funds, *Administrative Science Quarterly*, 57: 484–521.
9. V. Hinz & S. Ingerfurth, 2013, Does ownership matter under challenging conditions? *Public Management Review*, in press.
10. M. Griffiths, J. Kickul, S. Bacq, & S. Terjesen, 2012, A dialogue with William J. Baumol: Insights on entrepreneurship theory and education, *Entrepreneurship Theory and Practice*, 36: 611–625; P. M. Moroz & K. Hindle, 2012, Entrepreneurship as a process: Toward harmonizing multiple perspectives, *Entrepreneurship Theory and Practice*, 36: 781–818.
11. J. T. Perry, G. N. Chandler, & G. Markova, 2012, Entrepreneurial effectuation: A review and suggestions for future research, *Entrepreneurship Theory and Practice*, 36: 837–861; S. A. Alvarez & J. B. Barney, 2008, Opportunities, organizations and entrepreneurship, *Strategic Entrepreneurship Journal*, 2: 265–267.
12. N. J. Foss, J. Lyngsie, & S. A. Zahra, 2013, The role of external knowledge sources and organizational design in the process of opportunity exploitation, *Strategic Management Journal*, in press; P. G. Klein, 2008, Opportunity discovery, entrepreneurial action and economic organization, *Strategic Entrepreneurship Journal*, 2: 175–190.
13. J. Tang, K. M. Kacmar, & L. Busenitz, 2012, Entrepreneurial alertness in the pursuit of new opportunities, *Journal of Business Venturing*, 27: 77–94; S. A. Zahra, 2008, The virtuous cycle of discovery and creation of entrepreneurial opportunities, *Strategic Entrepreneurship Journal*, 2: 243–257.
14. J. Schumpeter, 1934, *The Theory of Economic Development*, Cambridge, MA: Harvard University Press.
15. C. A. Siren, M. Kohtamaki, & A. Kuckertz, 2012, Exploration and exploitation strategies, profit performance, and the mediating role of strategic learning: Escaping the exploitation trap, *Strategic Entrepreneurship Journal*, 6: 18–41; M. Hughes, S. Martin, R. Morgan, & M. Robson, 2010, Realizing product-market advantage in high-technology international new ventures: The mediating role of ambidextrous innovation, *Journal of International Marketing*, 18: 1–21; J. H. Dyer, H. B. Gregersen, & C. Christensen, 2008, Entrepreneur behaviors and the origins of innovative ventures, *Strategic Entrepreneurship Journal*, 2: 317–338.
16. C. Bjornskov & N. Foss, 2013, How strategic entrepreneurship and the institutional context drive economic growth, *Strategic Entrepreneurship Journal*, 7: 50–69; W. J. Baumol, R. E. Litan, & C. J. Schramm, 2007, *Good Capitalism, Bad Capitalism, and the Economics of Growth and Prosperity*, New Haven: Yale University Press.
17. Schumpeter, *The Theory of Economic Development*.
18. L. Aarikka-Stenroos & B. Sandberg, 2012, From new-product development to commercialization through networks, *Journal of Business Research*, 65: 198–206.
19. M. I. Leone & T. Reichstein, 2012, Licensing-in fosters rapid invention! The effect of the grant-back clause and technological unfamiliarity, *Strategic Management Journal*, 33: 965–985; R. A. Burgelman & L. R. Sayles, 1986, *Inside Corporate Innovation: Strategy, Structure, and Managerial Skills*, New York: Free Press.
20. K. R. Fabrizio & L. G. Thomas, 2012, The impact of local demand on innovation in a global industry, *Strategic Management Journal*, 33: 42–64; M. W. Johnson, 2011, Making innovation matter. *Bloomberg Businessweek*, www.businessweek.com, March 3.
21. H. Scarbrough, J. Swan, K. Amaeshi, & T. Briggs, 2013, Exploring the role of trust in the deal-making process for early-stage technology ventures, *Entrepreneurship Theory and Practice*, in press; S. F. Latham & M. Braun, 2009, Managerial risk, innovation and organizational decline, *Journal of Management*, 35: 258–281.
22. L. Marengo, C. Pasquali, M. Valente, & G. Dosi, 2012, Appropriability, patents, and rates of innovation in complex products industries, *Economics of Innovation and New Technology*, 21: 753–773; S. Moon, 2011, How does the management of research impact

the disclosure of knowledge? Evidence from scientific publications and patenting behavior, *Economics of Innovation & New Technology*, 20: 1–32.

23. M. Ridley, 2013, A welcome turn away from patents, *Wall Street Journal*, www.wsj.com, June 21.
24. P. F. Drucker, 1998, The discipline of innovation, *Harvard Business Review*, 76(6): 149–157.
25. Ibid.
26. B. R. Bhardwaj, Sushil, & K. Momaya, 2011, Drivers and enablers of corporate entrepreneurship: Case of a software giant from India, *Journal of Management Development*, 30: 187–205.
27. Y. Yanadori & V. Cui, 2013, Creating incentives for innovation? The relationship between pay dispersion in R&D groups and firm innovation performance, *Strategic Management Journal*, in press.
28. J. Lampel, P. P. Jha, & A. Bhalla, 2012, Test-driving the future: How design competitions are changing innovation, *Academy of Management Perspectives*, 26: 71–85; G. F. Alberti, S. Sciascia, C. Tripodi, & F. Visconti, 2011, The entrepreneurial growth of firms located in clusters: A cross-case study, *International Journal of Technology Management*, 54: 53–79.
29. C. J. Sutter, J. W. Webb, G. M. Kistruck, & A. V. G. Bailey, 2013, Entrepreneurs' responses to semi-formal illegitimate institutional arrangements, *Journal of Business Venturing*, in press; D. Ucbasaran, P. Westhead, M. Wright, & M. Flores, 2010, The nature of entrepreneurial experience, business failure and comparative optimism, *Journal of Business Venturing*, 25: 541–555; K. M. Hmielski & R. A. Baron, 2009, Entrepreneurs' optimism and new venture performance: A social cognitive perspective, *Academy of Management Journal*, 52: 473–488.
30. J.-L. Arregle, B. Batjargal, M. A. Hitt, J. W. Webb, T. Miller, & A. S. Tsui, 2013, Family ties in entrepreneurs' social networks and new venture growth, *Entrepreneurship Theory and Practice*, in press; M.-D. Foo, 2011, Emotions and entrepreneurial opportunity evaluation, *Entrepreneurship: Theory & Practice*, 35: 375–393; M. S. Cardon, J. Wincent, J. Singh, & M. Drovsek, 2009, The nature and experience of entrepreneurial passion, *Academy of Management Review*, 34: 511–532.
31. M. McCaffrey, 2013, On the theory of entrepreneurial incentives and alertness, *Entrepreneurship Theory and Practice*, in press; M. S. Wood, A. McKelvie, & J. M. Haynie, 2013, Making it personal: Opportunity individuation and the shaping of opportunity beliefs, *Journal of Business Venturing*, in press.
32. S. W. Smith & S. K. Shah, 2013, Do innovative users generate more useful insights? An analysis of corporate venture capital investments in the medical device industry, *Strategic Entrepreneurship Journal*, 7: 151–167; W. Stam, S. Arzlanian, & T. Elfring, 2013, Social capital of entrepreneurs and small firm performance: A meta-analysis of contextual and methodological moderators, *Journal of Business Venturing*, in press.
33. T. Prive, 2013, Top 32 quotes every entrepreneur should live by, *Forbes*, www.forbes.com, May 2.
34. J. G. Covin & D. Miller, 2013, International entrepreneurial orientation: Conceptual considerations, research themes, measurement issues, and future research directions, *Entrepreneurship Theory and Practice*, in press.
35. J. York, S. Sarasvathy, & A. Wicks, 2013, An entrepreneurial perspective on value creation in public-private ventures, *Academy of Management Review*, 28: 307–309; A. Chwolka & M. G. Raith, 2012, The value of business planning before start-up—A decision-theoretical perspective, *Journal of Business Venturing*, 27: 385–399.
36. P. C. Ross, 2013, Encouraging innovation in the corporate environment, *Wall Street Journal*, www.wsj.com, May 30.
37. W. Drechsler & M. Natter, 2012, Understanding a firm's openness decisions in innovation, *Journal of Business Research*, 65: 438–445; W. Tsai, 2001, Knowledge transfer in intraorganizational networks: Effects of network position and absorptive capacity on business unit innovation and performance, *Academy of Management Journal*, 44: 996–1004.
38. M. Spraggon & V. Bodolica, 2012, A multidimensional taxonomy of intra-firm knowledge transfer processes, *Journal of Business Research*, 65: 1273–1282; S. A. Zahra & G. George, 2002, Absorptive capacity: A review, reconceptualization, and extension, *Academy of Management Review*, 27:185–203.
39. A. Carr, 2013, Nike: The No. 1 most innovative company of 2013, *Fast Company*, www.fastcompany.com, February 11.
40. S. Terjesen, J. Hessels, & D. Li, 2013, Comparative international entrepreneurship: A review and research agenda, *Journal of Management*, in press; P. Ellis, 2011, Social ties and international entrepreneurship: Opportunities and constraints affecting firm internationalization, *Journal of International Business Studies*, 42: 99–127.
41. A. N. Kiss, W. M. Davis, & S. T. Cavusgil, 2012, International entrepreneurship research in emerging economies: A critical review and research agenda, *Journal of Business Venturing*, 27: 266–290; C. Williams & S. H. Lee, 2011, Political heterarchy and dispersed entrepreneurship in the MNC, *Journal of Management Studies*, 48: 1243–1268.
42. 2013, Microsoft, Huawei partner to launch affordable Windows smartphones for Africa, *Ventures*, www.ventures-africa.com, February 5.
43. P. Almodovar & A. M. Rugman, 2013, The M curve and the performance of Spanish international new ventures, *British Journal of Management*, in press; S. A. Fernhaber, B. A. Gilbert, & P. P. McDougal, 2008, International entrepreneurship and geographic location: An empirical examination of new venture internationalization, *Journal of International Business Studies*, 39: 267–290.
44. P. Stenholm, Z. J. Acs, & R. Wuebker, 2013, Exploring country-level institutional arrangements on the rate and type of entrepreneurial activity, *Journal of Business Venturing*, 28: 176–193; H. Ren, B. Gray, & K. Kim, 2009, Performance of international joint ventures: What factors really make a difference and how? *Journal of Management*, 35: 805–832.
45. 2013, Switzerland ranks in the top ten most entrepreneurial countries, *Startupticker.ch*, http://startupticker.ch, May 6.
46. J. D. Harrison, 2013, New rankings: The world's top nations for female entrepreneurs, *On Small Business*, www.washingtonpost.com, June 17.
47. E. Autio, S. Pathak, & K. Wennberg, 2013, Consequences of cultural practices for entrepreneurial behaviors, *Journal of International Business Studies*, 44: 334–362; U. Stephan & L. M. Uhlaner, 2010, Performance-based vs. socially supportive culture: A cross-cultural study of descriptive norms and entrepreneurship, *Journal of International Business Studies*, 41: 1347–1364; R. A. Baron & J. Tang, 2009, Entrepreneurs' social skills and new venture performance: Mediating mechanisms and cultural generality, *Journal of Management*, 35: 282–306.
48. T. K. Madsen, 2013, Early and rapidly internationalizing ventures: Similarities and differences between classifications based on the original international new venture and born global literatures, *Journal of International Entrepreneurship*, 11: 65–79; D. Kim, C. Basu, G. M. Naidu, & E. Cavusgil, 2011, The innovativeness of born-globals and customer orientation: Learning from Indian Born-Globals, *Journal of Business Research*, 64: 879–886.
49. S. A. Fernhaber & D. Li, 2013, International exposure through network relationships: Implications for new venture internationalization, *Journal of Business Venturing*, 28: 316–334; L. Sleuwaegen & J. Onkelinx, 2013, International commitment, post-entry growth and survival of international new ventures, *Journal of Business Venturing*, 28: in press; S. A. Zahra, R. D. Ireland, & M. A. Hitt, 2000, International expansion by new venture firms: International diversity, mode of market entry, technological learning and performance, *Academy of Management Journal*, 43: 925–950.
50. D. J. McCarthy, S. M. Puffer, & S. V. Darda, 2010, Convergence in entrepreneurial leadership style: Evidence from Russia, *California Management Review*, 52(4): 48–72; H. U. Lee & J. H. Park, 2008, The influence

of top management team international exposure on international alliance formation, *Journal of Management Studies*, 45: 961–981; H. G. Barkema & O. Chvyrkov, 2007, Does top management team diversity promote or hamper foreign expansion? *Strategic Management Journal*, 28: 663–680.

51. C. B. Bingham & J. P. Davis, 2012, Learning sequences: Their existence, effect, and evolution, *Academy of Management Journal*, 55: 611–641; M. Mors, 2010, Innovation in a global consulting firm: When the problem is too much diversity, *Strategic Management Journal*, 31: 841–872.
52. A. Pe'er & T. Keil, 2013, Are all startups affected similarly by clusters? Agglomeration, competition, firm heterogeneity, and survival, *Journal of Business Venturing*, 28: 354–372; A. Teixeira & N. Fortuna, 2010, Human capital, R&D, trade, and long-run productivity: Testing the technological absorption hypothesis for the Portuguese economy, 1960–2001, *Research Policy*, 39: 335–350.
53. S. Schechner, S. E. Ante, & S. Grundberg, 2013, Huawei builds clout through R&D, *Wall Street Journal*, www.wsj.com, February 24.
54. R. Kapoor & R. Adner, 2012, What firms make vs. what they know: How firms' production and knowledge boundaries affect competitive advantage in the face of technological change, *Organization Science*, 23: 1227–1248; R. Reed, S. Storrud-Barnes, & L. Jessup, 2012, How open innovation affects the drivers of competitive advantage: Trading the benefits of IP creation and ownership for free invention, *Management Decision*, 50: 58–73.
55. R. J. Genry & W. Shen, 2013, The impacts of performance relative to analyst forecasts and analyst coverage on firm R&D intensity, *Strategic Management Journal*, 34: 121–130; L. A. Bettencourt & S. L. Bettencourt, 2011, Innovating on the cheap, *Harvard Business Review*, 89(6): 88–94.
56. P. Ritala & P. Hurmelinna-Laukkanen, 2013, Incremental and radical innovation in coopetition—The role of absorptive capacity and appropriability, *Journal of Product Innovation Management*, 30: 154–169; C. B. Bingham & J. P. Davis, 2012, Learning sequences: Their existence, effect, and evolution, *Academy of Management Journal*, 55: 611–641.
57. S. Roy & K. Sivakumar, 2012, Global outsourcing relationships and innovation: A conceptual framework and research propositions, *Journal of Product and Innovation Management*, 29: 513–530.
58. D. McKendrick & J. Wade, 2010, Frequent incremental change, organizational size, and mortality in high-technology competition, *Industrial and Corporate Change*, 19(3): 613–639.
59. S. Wang, 2013, Why a startup, not big pharma, leads development of a bionic eye, *Wall Street Journal*, www.wsj.com, January 30.
60. T. W. Martin & J. D. Rockoff, 2013, Unmeltable, uncrushable: The holy grail in painkillers, *Wall Street Journal*, www.wsj.com, May 5.
61. T. Magnusson & C. Berggren, 2011, Entering an era of ferment—radical vs incrementalist strategies in automotive power train development, *Technology Analysis & Strategic Management*, 23: 313–330; 2005, Getting an edge on innovation, *BusinessWeek*, March 21, 124.
62. B. Buisson & P. Silberzahn, 2010, Blue Ocean or fast-second innovation? A four-breakthrough model to explain successful market domination, *International Journal of Innovation Management*, 14: 359–378; A. J. Chatterji, 2009, Spawned with a silver spoon? Entrepreneurial performance and innovation in the medical device industry, *Strategic Management Journal*, 30: 185–206.
63. Z. Lindgardt & B. Shaffer, 2012, Business model innovation in social-sector organizations, *bcg.perspectives*, bcgperspectives.com, November 7.
64. 2013, The power of imagination, *Wall Street Journal*, www.wsj.com, February 25.
65. D. Lavie & I. Drori, 2012, Collaborating for knowledge creation and application: The case of nanotechnology research programs, *Organization Science*, 23: 704–724.
66. A. K. Chatterji & K. Fabrizio, 2012, How do product users influence corporate invention? *Organization Science*, 23: 971–987.
67. N. R. Furr, F. Cavarretta, & S. Garg, 2012, Who changes course? The role of domain knowledge and novel framing in making technology changes, *Strategic Entrepreneurship Journal*, 6: 236–256; J. M. Oldroyd & R. Gulati, 2010, A learning perspective on intraorganizational knowledge spill-ins, *Strategic Entrepreneurship Journal*, 4: 356–372.
68. M. L. Sosa, 2013, Decoupling market incumbency from organizational prehistory: Locating the real sources of competitive advantage in R&D for radical innovation, *Strategic Management Journal*, 34: 245–255; S. A. Hill, M. V. J. Maula, J. M. Birkinshaw, & G. C. Murray, 2009, Transferability of the venture capital model to the corporate context: Implications for the performance of corporate venture units, *Strategic Entrepreneurship Journal*, 3: 3–27.
69. J. Brady, 2013, Some companies foster creativity, others fake it, *Wall Street Journal*, www.wsj.com, May 21.
70. A. Sahaym, H. K. Steensma, & J. Q. Barden, 2010, The influence of R&D investment on the use of corporate venture capital: An industry-level analysis, *Journal of Business Venturing*, 25(4): 376–388; R. A. Burgelman, 1995, *Strategic Management of Technology and Innovation*, Boston: Irwin.
71. D. Kandemir & N. Acur, 2012, Examining proactive strategic decision-making flexibility in new product development, *Journal of Product Innovation Management*, 29: 608–622.
72. K. B. Kahn, G. Barczak, J. Nicholas, A. Ledwith, & H. Perks, 2012, An examination of new product development best practice, *Journal of Product Innovation Management*, 29: 180–192.
73. S. S. Durmusoglu, 2013, Merits of task advice during new product development: Network centrality antecedents and new product outcomes of knowledge richness and knowledge quality, *Journal of Product Innovation Management*, 30: 487–499; D. Kelley & H. Lee, 2010, Managing innovation champions: The impact of project characteristics on the direct manager role, *Journal of Product Innovation Management*, 27: 1007–1019.
74. N. Kim, S. Im, & S. F. Slater, 2013, Impact of knowledge type and strategic orientation on new product creativity and advantage in high-technology firms, *Journal of Product Innovation Management*, 30: 136–153; U. de Brentani & S. E. Reid, 2012, The fuzzy front-end of discontinuous innovation: Insights for research and management, *Journal of Product Innovation Management*, 29: 70–87.
75. C. Webster & A. White, 2010, Exploring the national and organizational cultural mix in service firms, *Journal of the Academy of Marketing Science*, 38: 691–703; M. Song & M. M. Montoya-Weiss, 2001, The effect of perceived technological uncertainty on Japanese new product development, *Academy of Management Journal*, 44: 61–80.
76. L. Mirabeau & S. Maguire, 2013, From autonomous strategic behavior to emergent strategy, *Strategic Management Journal*, in press.
77. S. Im, M. M. Montoya, & J. P. Workman, Jr., 2013, Antecedents and consequences of creativity in product innovation teams, *Journal of Product Innovation Management*, 30: 170–185; S. Borjesson & M. Elmquist, 2012, Aiming at innovation: A case study of innovation capabilities in the Swedish defence industry, *International Journal of Business Innovation and Research*, 6: 188–201.
78. S. E. Ante, 2013, IBM's chief to employees: Think fast, move faster, *Wall Street Journal*, www.wsj.com, April 24.
79. S. Banjo, 2013, Wal-Mart's e-stumble, *Wall Street Journal*, www.wsj.com, June 18.
80. L. Luk & S. Ovide, 2013, Microsoft working with suppliers on designs for touch-enabled watch device, *Wall Street Journal*, www.wsj.com, April 15.
81. P. Patanakul, J. Chen, & G. S. Lynn, 2012, Autonomous teams and new product development, *Journal of Product Innovation Management*, 29: 734–750.
82. S. Kuester, C. Homburg, & S. C. Hess, 2012, Externally directed and internally directed market launch management: The role of organizational factors in influencing new product success, *Journal of Product Innovation Management*, 29: 38–52.

83. G. Barcjak & K. B. Kah, 2012, Identifying new product development best practice, *Business Horizons*, 56: 291–305; C. Nakata & S. Im, 2010, Spurring cross-functional integration for higher new product performance: A group effectiveness perspective, *Journal of Product Innovation Management*, 27: 554–571.

84. J. P. Eggers, 2012, All experience is not created equal: Learning, adapting, and focusing in product portfolio management, *Strategic Management Journal*, 33: 315-335; R. Slotegraaf & K. Atuahene-Gima, 2011, Product development team stability and new product advantage: The role of decision-making processes, *Journal of Marketing*, 75: 96–108; R. Cowan & N. Jonard, 2009, Knowledge portfolios and the organization of innovation networks, *Academy of Management Review*, 34: 320–342.

85. M. Brettel, F. Heinemann, A. Engelen, & S. Neubauer, 2011, Cross-functional integration of R&D, marketing, and manufacturing in radical and incremental product innovations and its effects on project effectiveness and efficiency, *Journal of Product Innovation Management*, 28: 251–269.

86. D. De Clercq, N. Thongpapanl, & d. Dimov, 2013, Getting more from cross-functional fairness and product innovativeness: Contingency effects of internal resource and conflict management, *Journal of Product Innovation Management*, 30: 56–69; G. Gemser & M. M. Leenders, 2011, Managing cross-functional cooperation for new product development success, *Long Range Planning*, 44: 26–41.

87. F. Aime, S. Humphrey, D. DeRue, & J. Paul, 2013, The riddle of heterarchy: Power transitions in cross-functional teams, *Academy of Management Journal*, 56: in press.

88. E. L. Anthony, S. G. Green, & S. A. McComb, 2013, Crossing functions above the cross-functional project team: The value of lateral coordination among functional department heads, *Journal of Engineering and Technology Management*, in press; V. V. Baunsgaard & S. Clegg, 2013, 'Walls or boxes': The effects of professional identity, power and rationality on strategies for cross-functional integration, *Organization Studies*, in press.

89. M. Baer, K. T. Dirks, & J. A. Nickerson, 2013, Microfoundations of strategic problem formulation, *Strategic Management Journal*, 34: 197–214; R. Oliva & N. Watson, 2011, Cross-functional alignment in supply chain planning: A case study of sales and operations planning, *Journal of Operations Management*, 29: 434–448; A. C. Amason, 1996, Distinguishing the effects of functional and dysfunctional conflict on strategic decision making: Resolving a paradox for top management teams, *Academy of Management Journal*, 39: 123–148.

90. H. K. Gardner, 2012, Performance pressure as a double-edged sword: Enhancing team motivation while undermining the use of team knowledge, *Administrative Science Quarterly*, 57: 1–46; D. Clercq, B. Menguc, & S. Auh, 2009, Unpacking the relationship between an innovation strategy and firm performance: The role of task conflict and political activity, *Journal of Business Research*, 62: 1046–1053; M. A. Cronin & L. R. Weingart, 2007, Representational gaps, information processing, and conflict in functionally heterogeneous teams, *Academy of Management Review*, 32: 761–773.

91. Y. Chung & S. E. Jackson, 2013, The internal and external networks of knowledge-intensive teams: The role of task routineness, *Journal of Management*, 39: 442–468; J. Daspit, C. J. Tillman, N. G. Boyd, & V. McKee, 2013, Cross-functional team effectiveness: An examination of internal team environment, shared leadership, and cohesion influences, *Team Performance Management*, 19: 34–56.

92. H. K. Gardner, F. Gino, & B. R. Staats, 2012, Dynamically integrating knowledge in teams: Transforming resources into performance, *Academy of Management Journal*, 55: 998–1022; A. Grant, 2012, Leading with meaning: Beneficiary contact, prosocial impact, and the performance effects of transformational leadership, *Academy of Management Journal*, 55: 150–176.

93. Q. Li, P. Maggitti, K. Smith, P. Tesluk, & R. Katila, 2013, Top management attention to innovation: The role of search selection and intensity in new product introductions, *Academy of Management Journal*, 55: in press; N. Stieglitz & L. Heine, 2007, Innovations and the role of complementarities in a strategic theory of the firm, *Strategic Management Journal*, 28: 1–15.

94. V. Gaba & S. Bhattacharya, 2012, Aspirations, innovation, and corporate venture capital: A behavioral perspective, *Strategic Entrepreneurship Journal*, 6: 178–199; K. Wennberg, J. Wiklund, D. R. DeTienne, & M. S. Cardon, 2010, Reconceptualizing entrepreneurial exit: Divergent exit routes and their drivers, *Journal of Business Venturing*, 25: 361–375.

95. H. Milanov & S. A. Fernhaber, 2013, When do domestic alliances help ventures abroad? Direct and moderating effects from a learning experience, *Journal of Business Venturing*, in press; S. Terjesen, P. C. Patel, & J. G. Covin, 2011, Alliance diversity, environmental context and the value of manufacturing capabilities among new high technology ventures, *Journal of Operations Management*, 29: 105–115; P. Ozcan & K. M. Eisenhardt, 2009, Origin of alliance portfolios: Entrepreneurs, network strategies, and firm performance, *Academy of Management Journal*, 52: 246–279.

96. S. Zu, F. Wu, & E. Cavusgil, 2013, Complements or substitutes? Internal technological strength, competitors alliance participation, and innovation development, *Journal of Product Innovation Management*, 30: 750–762; D. Dunlap-Hinkler, M. Kotabe, & R. Mudambi, 2010, A story of breakthrough versus incremental innovation: Corporate entrepreneurship in the global pharmaceutical industry, *Strategic Entrepreneurship Journal*, 4: 106–127.

97. J. West & M. Bogers, 2013, Leveraging external sources of innovation: A review of research on open innovation, *Journal of Product Innovation Management*, in press; D. Li, L. Eden, M. A. Hitt, & R. D. Ireland, 2008, Friends, acquaintances, or strangers? Partner selection in R&D alliances, *Academy of Management Journal*, 51: 315–334.

98. C. Beckman, K. Eisenhardt, S. Kotha, A. Meyer, & N. Rajagopalan, 2012, Technology entrepreneurship, *Strategic Entrepreneurship Journal*, 6: 89-93; J. T. Eckhardt & S. A. Shane, 2011, Industry changes in technology and complementary assets and the creation of high-growth firms, *Journal of Business Venturing*, 26: 412–430.

99. D. Li, 2013, Multilateral R&D alliances by new ventures, *Journal of Business Venturing*, 28: 241–260; G. Dushnitsky & D. Lavie, 2010, How alliance formation shapes corporate venture capital investment in the software industry: A resource-based perspective, *Strategic Entrepreneurship Journal*, 4: 33–48; S. A. Alvarez & J. B. Barney, 2001, How entrepreneurial firms can benefit from alliances with large partners, *Academy of Management Executive*, 15(1): 139–148.

100. A. Berzon & K. Hudson, 2013, IKEA's parent plans a hotel brand, *Wall Street Journal*, www.wsj.com, March 5.

101. X. Jiang, M. Li, S. Gao, Y. Bao, & F. Jiang, 2013, Managing knowledge leakage in strategic alliances: The effects of trust and formal contracts, *Industrial Marketing Management*, in press; A. Kaul, 2013, Entrepreneurial action, unique assets, and appropriation risk: Firms as a means of appropriating profit from capability creation, *Organization Science*, in press; B. Lokshin, J. Hagedoorn, & W. Letterie, 2011, The bumpy road of technology partnerships: Understanding causes and consequences of partnership and mal-functioning, *Research Policy*, 40: 297–308.

102. G. Cuevas-Rodriguez, C. Cabello-Medina, & A. Carmona-Lavado, 2013, Internal and external social capital for radical product innovation: Do they always work well together? *British Journal of Management*, in press; M. A. Hitt, M. T. Dacin, E. Levitas, J. L. Arregle, & A. Borza, 2000, Partner selection in emerging and developed market contexts: Resource-based and organizational learning perspectives, *Academy of Management Journal*, 43: 449–467.

103. R. Vandaie & A. Zaheer, 2013, Surviving bear hugs: Firm capability, large partner alliances, and growth, *Strategic Management Journal*, in press; G. Duysters & B. Lokshin, 2011, Determinants of alliance portfolio complexity and its effect on innovative performance of companies, *Journal of Product Innovation Management*, 28: 570–585.
104. A. Madhok & M. Keyhani, 2012, Acquisitions as entrepreneurship: Asymmetries, opportunities, and the internationalization of multinationals from emerging economies, *Global Strategy Journal*, 2: 26–40;
105. M. A. Hitt, D. King, H. Krishnan, M. Makri, M. Schijven, K. Shimizu, & H. Zhu, 2009, Mergers and acquisitions: Overcoming pitfalls, building synergy and creating value, *Business Horizons,* 52: 523–529; H. G. Barkema & M. Schijven, 2008, Toward unlocking the full potential of acquisitions: The role of organizational restructuring, *Academy of Management Journal,* 51: 696–722.
106. 2012, Pfizer acquires NextWave Pharmaceuticals, Inc., *Pfizer News & Media*, www.pfizer.com, November 28.
107. M. Humphrey-Jenner, 2013, Takeover defenses, innovation, and value creation: Evidence from acquisition decisions, *Strategic Management Journal*, 34: in press; M. Makri, M. A. Hitt, & P. J. Lane, 2010, Complementary technologies, knowledge relatedness, and invention outcomes in high technology M&As, *Strategic Management Journal*, 31: 602–628.
108. M. Wagner, 2013, Determinants of acquisition value: The role of target and acquirer characteristics, *International Journal of Technology Management*, 62: 56–74; M. E. Graebner, K. M. Eisenhardt, & P. T. Roundy, 2010, Success and failure in technology acquisitions: Lessons for buyers and sellers, *Academy of Management Perspectives*, 24: 73–92; M. A. Hitt, J. S. Harrison, & R. D. Ireland, 2001, *Mergers and Acquisitions: A Guide to Creating Value for Stakeholders*, New York: Oxford University Press.
109. F. Bauer & K. Matzler, 2013, Antecedents of M&A success: The role of strategic complementarity, cultural fit, and degree and speed of integration, *Strategic Management Journal*, in press; S. Mingo, 2013, The impact of acquisitions on the performance of existing organizational units in the acquiring firm: The case of an agribusiness company, *Management Science*, in press.
110. R. Fini, R. Grimaldi, G. L. Marzocchi, & M. Sobrero, 2012, The determinants of corporate entrepreneurial intention within small and newly established firms, *Entrepreneurship Theory and Practice*, 36: 387–414; D. Elfenbein & B. Hamilton, 2010, The small firm effect and the entrepreneurial spawning of scientists and engineers, *Management Science,* 56: 659–681.
111. B. Larraneta, S. A. Zahra, & J. L. G. Gonzalez, 2012, Enriching strategic variety in new ventures through external knowledge, *Journal of Business Venturing*, 27: 401–413; H. Greve, 2011, Positional rigidity: Low performance and resource acquisition in large and small firms, *Strategic Management Journal*, 32: 103–114.
112. S. M. Lee, D. L. Olson, & S. Trimi, 2012, Co-innovation: Convergenomics, collaboration, and co-creation for organizational values, *Management Decision*, 50: 817–831;G. Wu, 2012, The effect of going public on innovative productivity and exploratory search, *Organization Science*, 23: 928–950; D. G. Sirmon & M. A. Hitt, 2009, Contingencies within dynamic managerial capabilities: Interdependent effects of resource investment and deployment on firm performance, *Strategic Management Journal,* 30: 1375–1394.
113. R. B. Tucker, 2013, Are chief innovation officers delivering results? *Innovation Excellence*, www.innovationexcellence.com, March 22.

# Name Index

## A



## B

# C

## H

## I



## J

## M

## S

## T

## U



## V



## W

# Company Index

## T



## U



## V



## W



## X



## Y



## Z

# Subject Index

## D



## E

## J



## K



## L



## M

## N



## O



## P